Texts, Scribes and Transmission

Manuscript Cultures of the Ismaili Communities and Beyond

Edited by
Wafi A. Momin

I.B.TAURIS
LONDON • NEW YORK • OXFORD • NEW DELHI • SYDNEY
in association with
THE INSTITUTE OF ISMAILI STUDIES
LONDON, 2022

I.B. TAURIS
Bloomsbury Publishing Plc
50 Bedford Square, London, WC1B 3DP, UK
1385 Broadway, New York, NY 10018, USA
29 Earlsfort Terrace, Dublin 2, Ireland

In association with
The Institute of Ismaili Studies
Aga Khan Centre, 10 Handyside Street, London N1C 4DN
www.iis.ac.uk

First published in Great Britain 2022

A catalogue record for this book is available from the British Library.

A catalog record for this book is available from the Library of Congress.

ISBN: HB: 978-0-7556-4537-4
PB: 978-0-7556-4538-1
ePDF: 978-0-7556-4539-8
eBook: 978-0-7556-4540-4

Typeset by RefineCatch Limited, Bungay, Suffolk

The Institute of Ismaili Studies

The Institute of Ismaili Studies was established in 1977 with the object of promoting scholarship and learning on Islam, in the historical as well as contemporary contexts, and a better understanding of its relationship with other societies and faiths.

The Institute's programmes encourage a perspective which is not confined to the theological and religious heritage of Islam, but which seeks to explore the relationship of religious ideas to broader dimensions of society and culture. The programmes thus encourage an interdisciplinary approach to the materials of Islamic history and thought. Particular attention is also given to issues of modernity that arise as Muslims seek to relate their heritage to the contemporary situation.

Within the Islamic tradition, the Institute's programmes promote research on those areas which have, to date, received relatively little attention from scholars. These include the intellectual and literary expressions of Shiʿism in general, and Ismailism in particular.

In the context of Islamic societies, the Institute's programmes are informed by the full range and diversity of cultures in which Islam is practised today, from the Middle East, South and Central Asia, and Africa to the industrialized societies of the West, thus taking into consideration the variety of contexts which shape the ideals, beliefs and practices of the faith.

These objectives are realised through concrete programmes and activities organized and implemented by various departments of the Institute. The Institute also collaborates periodically, on a programme-specific basis, with other institutions of learning in the United Kingdom and abroad.

The Institute's academic publications fall into a number of inter-related categories:

1. Occasional papers or essays addressing broad themes of the relationship between religion and society, with special reference to Islam.
2. Monographs exploring specific aspects of Islamic faith and culture, or the contributions of individual Muslim thinkers or writers.
3. Editions or translations of significant primary or secondary texts.
4. Translations of poetic or literary texts which illustrate the rich heritage of spiritual, devotional and symbolic expressions in Muslim history.
5. Works on Ismaili history and thought, and the relationship of the Ismailis to other traditions, communities and schools of thought in Islam.
6. Proceedings of conferences and seminars sponsored by the Institute.
7. Bibliographical works and catalogues which document manuscripts, printed texts and other source materials.

This book falls into category six listed above.

In facilitating these and other publications, the Institute's sole aim is to encourage original research and analysis of relevant issues. While every effort is made to ensure that the publications are of a high academic standard, there is naturally bound to be a diversity of views, ideas and interpretations. As such, the opinions expressed in these publications must be understood as belonging to their authors alone.

Contents

Acknowledgements xi
Note on Contributors xiii
Transliteration, Dates, and Abbreviations xv

Introduction 1
Wafi A. Momin

SECTION I: THE SHAPING OF A NEW FIELD

1. Ismaili Manuscripts and Modern Scholarship in Ismaili Studies 23
Farhad Daftary
2. Husain Hamdani, Paul Kraus, and a Suitcase Full of Manuscripts 47
François de Blois

SECTION II: *RASĀʾIL IKHWĀN AL-ṢAFĀʾ*, *KITĀB AL-ZĪNA*, AND THEIR MANUSCRIPT TRADITION

3. The *Ikhwān al-Ṣafā*'s Epistles on Logic in Some Manuscripts of the IIS Arabic Collection 57
Carmela Baffioni
4. The Missing Link? MS 1040: An Important Copy of the *Rasāʾil Ikhwān al-Ṣafāʾ* in the Collection of The Institute of Ismaili Studies 81
Omar Alí-de-Unzaga
5. The Manuscript Copies of Abū Ḥātim al-Rāzī's *Kitāb al-Zīna* at The Institute of Ismaili Studies 137
Cornelius Berthold

SECTION III: EXPLORING TWO EARLY ṬAYYIBĪ WORKS AND THEIR TRANSMISSION

6. The *Majmūʿ al-tarbiya* between Text and Paratext: Exploring the Social History of a Community's Reading Culture 163
Delia Cortese

7. Textual, Orthographic Variations and Scribes' Annotations: A Possible Tool for the Transmission Analysis of the Text? 183
Monica Scotti

SECTION IV: REVISITING NIZĀRĪ HISTORY OF ALAMŪT TIMES

8. Alamūt and Badakhshān: Newly Identified *Sargudhasht-i Sayyidnā* Manuscripts and their Background 207
Miklós Sárközy

9. *ʿAhd-i Sayyidnā*, a Newly Discovered Treatise on the Consolidation of the Nizārī *Daʿwa* in Alamūt 237
Karim Javan

10. The Discovery, Description and Publication of the Manuscripts of Two Major Nizārī Ismaili Texts from the Alamūt Period: The *Haft Bāb* and the *Dīwān-i Qāʾimiyyāt* of Ḥasan-i Maḥmūd-i Kātib 257
S. J. Badakhchani

SECTION V: COMMUNAL SCRIPT, SCRIBAL ELITE, AND SATPANTH MANUSCRIPT CULTURE

11. Khwājah Sindhi (Khojki): Its Name, Manuscripts and Origin 275
Shafique N. Virani

12. A Forgotten Voice: The Agency of the Scribal and Literate Elite and the Satpanth Manuscript Culture 303
Wafi A. Momin

SECTION VI: IDENTITY, CULTURAL INTERACTIONS, AND ESOTERIC INTERPRETATION AMONG CENTRAL ASIAN ISMAILI COMMUNITIES

13. Ismaili-Sufi Relationships in the Light of the Niʿmat Allāhī Manuscripts in the Holdings of The Institute of Ismaili Studies 331
Orkhan Mir-Kasimov
14. Poems of Allegiance: Shāh Ḍiyāʾī-i Shughnānī's *Salām-nāma* 347
Nourmamadcho Nourmamadchoev
15. The *Ṣaḥīfat al-nāẓirīn*: Reflections on Authorship and Confessional Identity in a 15th-Century Central Asian Text 369
Daniel Beben
16. *The Seven Pillars of the Sharīʿa* and the Question of Authority in Central Asian Ismaili Manuscripts: An Ismaili Esoteric Discourse 389
Yahia Baiza

SECTION VII: APPROACHING TEXTUAL TRANSMISSION THROUGH QURʾĀNIC MANUSCRIPTS AND HOLOGRAPH/AUTOGRAPH COPIES

17. Writing the Qurʾān between the Lines: Preliminary Remarks on Marginalia in the Qurʾān Manuscripts held by The Institute of Ismaili Studies 415
Asma Hilali
18. The Making of Holographs/Autographs: Case Studies from the Special Collections of The Institute of Ismaili Studies 431
Walid Ghali

List of Illustrations 451
Index 455

Acknowledgements

This book has long been in the making and many individuals have contributed towards its production. Its genesis goes back to the symposium *Before the Printed Word: Texts, Scribes and Transmission*, convened by the Ismaili Special Collections Unit (ISCU) of The Institute of Ismaili Studies on 12–13 October 2017 in London. The symposium was, in many ways, the first of its kind that the Institute had organised. Bringing together 21 scholars from diverse fields, it provided a platform for younger researchers and specialists to share their perspectives on different aspects of the manuscript cultures of Ismaili communities, and through them to discuss relevant facets of textual practices prevalent in the milieus where these communities flourished. I would like to thank Farhad Daftary, Omar Alí-de-Unzaga, Gurdofarid Miskinzoda and Zauhar Meghji for sharing their ideas and extending support during the conceptualisation stage of the symposium.

For the past many years, I have shared the fascination of studying and working with the special collections at the Institute with my colleagues at ISCU and other departments. Conversations with them have made my task of conceptualising research and educational activities pertaining to these collections both an intellectually stimulating and personally satisfying one—to all of them, I express my gratitude. I would especially like to thank Nourmamadcho Nourmamadchoev and Naureen Ali for taking a big share of responsibility in the planning and organisation of the symposium. Nourmamadcho went out of his way to prepare high-resolution images from a number of manuscripts that accompany this book. It also gives me pleasure to recall the assistance of those who most generously gave of their time in taking care of the logistical aspects of the symposium; they include Naushin Shariff, Semina Halani, Aly Jafferani, Tanaz Koradia, Tareq Razzouk, Zehra Shallwani and Nadir Wazir.

To all the presenters, panel chairs and participants of the symposium, I am most grateful for their stimulating discussions and probing questions. This volume would not have been possible without the contributors who adapted their ideas and talks for this volume, for their timely responses to my queries and reminders, and for their patience throughout the book's editing and publishing stages.

Others have contributed in important ways during the publishing stage of the book. Farhad Daftary and Tara Woolnough offered invaluable support and eased many an administrative hurdle. Patricia Salazar put this volume through a meticulous copyediting and identified a suitable cover image. Shohzodamamad Mamadsherzodshoev and his team in Khorog responded to my queries promptly in connection with some manuscripts from Central Asia. And the comments and suggestions of two anonymous reviewers greatly benefitted the contributors in the revision of their chapters. To all of them, I offer my thanks.

Lastly, I would like to express gratitude to my family which has been a great source of support. My mother, (late) father, brother and sister have always stood by me in my decisions, with their unconditional love and care. During the course of this project, Qudsia and Murtaza cheered me up with their humour and smiles and sustained me with their love; their understanding allowed me to devote the time that this project demanded during the challenging times of the pandemic. In Qudsia, I have a friend and an intellectual partner with whom I have discussed every idea that has occurred to me, including the ones that informed this project. I dedicate this book to her.

Wafi Momin

Note on Contributors

Omar Alí-de-Unzaga is a Research Associate and Head of the Qur'ānic Studies Unit in the Department of Academic Research and Publications at The Institute of Ismaili Studies.

S. Jalal Badakhchani is a former Senior Research Associate in the Department of Academic Research and Publications at The Institute of Ismaili Studies.

Carmela Baffioni is former Professor of History of Islamic philosophy at the University of Naples "L'Orientale" and is now a Senior Research Fellow at The Institute of Ismaili Studies.

Yahia Baiza is a Research Associate in the Central Asian Studies Unit, Department of Academic Research and Publications at The Institute of Ismaili Studies.

Daniel Beben is Assistant Professor of History and Religious Studies at Nazarbayev University in Kazakhstan.

Cornelius Berthold is a Research Associate at Hamburg University's Cluster of Excellency 'Understanding Written Artefacts'.

François de Blois has taught at SOAS and at Hamburg University and held research positions at University College London, Cambridge University and the Institute for Advanced Study (Princeton).

Delia Cortese is Senior Lecturer in Religious Studies, Middlesex University, London.

Farhad Daftary is Co-Director of The Institute of Ismaili Studies and the Head of its Department of Academic Research and Publications.

Walid Ghali is Associate Professor of Islamic and Arabic studies at the Institute for the Study of Muslim Civilizations, Aga Khan University and Head of the Aga Khan Library in the United Kingdom.

Asma Hilali is Associate Professor at the University of Lille, France.

Karim Javan is a Research Associate in the Ismaili Special Collections Unit at The Institute of Ismaili Studies.

Orkhan Mir-Kasimov is a Senior Research Fellow in the Shiʿi Studies Unit, Department of Academic Research and Publications at The Institute of Ismaili Studies.

Wafi Momin is Head of the Ismaili Special Collections Unit at The Institute of Ismaili Studies.

Nourmamadcho Nourmamadchoev is a Research Associate and Projects Coordinator in the Ismaili Special Collections Unit at The Institute of Ismaili Studies.

Miklós Sárközy is Associate Professor at Károli Gáspár University of the Hungarian Reformed Church in Budapest.

Monica Scotti is an independent scholar, formerly a Fellow in the Department of Asia, Africa and Mediterranean Studies, University of Naples "L'Orientale".

Shafique N. Virani is Distinguished Professor of Islamic Studies at the University of Toronto and founder of its Centre for South Asian Civilizations.

Transliteration, Dates, and Abbreviations

The book draws upon a host of languages with their own scholarly conventions; therefore, no effort has been made to impose a strict transliteration system that may be applicable to all. This is also fitting for a volume that deals with issues pertaining to manuscript cultures where fluidity rules more than standardisation. However, some basic streamlining of conventions has been adopted here. Transliteration of Arabic and Persian terms is based on a modified standard of the *International Journal of Middle East Studies*. For other languages, standard transliteration conventions of those languages have been observed in the respective chapters. In general, diacritics have been avoided for well-known dynasties, toponyms and languages.

Dates before the 19th century are mostly indicated in both *hijrī* and Common Era forms. Where only one date is given, it is invariably in Common Era form. In bibliographic references, some works published from Iran indicate dates in the modern solar *hijrī* calendar (marked as 'Sh.') and Common Era forms. Some dates in Chapters 11 and 12 are indicated in the Indian Vikram Samvat calendar (marked as 'VS') followed by the corresponding Common Era dates.

Abbreviations

EI2 *Encyclopaedia of Islam*, 2nd edition, ed. H. A. R. Gibb et al. Leiden–London, 1960–2004.

EI3 *Encyclopaedia of Islam Three Online*, ed. Kate Fleet et al. Leiden, 2010–.

Introduction

Wafi A. Momin

On a visit to Lucknow, perhaps sometime in the late 1920s, the Russian Orientalist Wladimir Ivanow (1886–1970) chanced upon what he described as 'a bundle of disjointed leaves belonging to a quite modern manuscript copy of an Arabic book, torn and worm-eaten'.[1] By then Ivanow was a seasoned book-buyer with extensive experience of acquiring thousands of manuscripts in Central Asia, Iran and India for institutions like the Asiatic Museum of the Russian Academy of Sciences (St. Petersburg) and the Asiatic Society of Bengal (Calcutta), as well as for himself. He does not reveal how he found this particular bundle of leaves. From the reminiscences of one of his book-buying ventures in Lucknow in 1927, we gather that it was an exhausting process demanding immense patience, but one that amply rewarded in the end. Ventures of this kind required familiarity with the functioning of dispersed book markets and invariably involved delicate dealings with brokers and, through them, with potential book owners and sellers. They further demanded an encyclopaedic knowledge on a range of subjects in multiple languages, along with skills in negotiating the right price for desired books. By the time Ivanow settled in India towards the end of 1920, he could confidently claim a fair grasp of the intricacies of book trade, a breadth of exposure to Persian and Arabic literature, and access to a network of learned circles interested in the subjects that were close to his heart.[2]

In the world of book markets scattered throughout prominent centres of Muslim learning, such as Lucknow, an experienced and knowledgeable buyer like Ivanow was bound to come across many unexpected treasures, some readily apparent, others less so. The bundle of leaves that he found on that particular visit was a chance find.[3] Its 'discovery' in Lucknow was in itself something of an enigma, if not totally out of order, for the contents of the bundle belonged to a tightly guarded body of religious literature. They were destined to make, some years later, a poignant mark in laying the foundations of what is now widely acknowledged as the distinct field of Ismaili studies. Ivanow could not immediately make much of the contents which seemed to him to have dealt with 'some philosophical matters'. He nonetheless bought the bundle though it remained unexamined in his boxes for a while. When he finally got a chance to study it, he was able to ascertain with the help of his 'learned Ismaili friends' that the leaves in fact contained the text of a bibliographic work, *Fahrasat al-kutub wa'l-rasā'il*, compiled by the Ṭayyibī writer, Ismāʿīl b. ʿAbd al-Rasūl al-Majdūʿ (d. *ca*. 1183/1769).[4]

In hindsight, this incidental discovery of the *Fihrist al-Majdūʿ* (as it is commonly known) by Ivanow proved to be a momentous event. It was not the first occasion when religious texts produced within one or another branch of (what is now generally regarded as) the larger 'Ismaili'[5] dispensation had come to the attention of the Orientalists. Ivanow himself had earlier worked, while associated with the Asiatic Museum, with a relatively smaller collection of manuscripts housed there containing texts of this nature; his knowledge of such works only expanded in the subsequent years. By that time, many other scholars in the western world too had accumulated information about some fragments of this body of literature, access to which was made possible through the sporadic interactions of a handful of Orientalists and diplomats with the scattered pockets of Ismaili communities over the last century or so. Utilising by and large what was known around this time (barring some omissions), Louis Massignon could attempt in 1922 the first sketch of the textual sources relating to the Ismaili movement.[6] But against this state of knowledge, the finding of the *Fihrist* was nothing short of a game-changer. Being a bibliographic record of scores of works meant for the religious edification of the Dā'ūdī Bohras at different stages of progression, the *Fihrist* revealed perhaps for the first time to the outside world the staggering wealth this literary heritage represented, even if it primarily dealt with textual materials studied by a particular branch within the larger Ismaili tradition. Realising its importance, Ivanow was quick to transform the contents of the 'bundle of disjointed leaves' into *A Guide to Ismaili*

Literature (published in 1933), adding a great deal of what he knew of the textual works produced by other branches of the Ismailis.

As one might expect, the *Guide* sparked much enthusiasm among scholarly circles which barely had access to the kind of materials described in it, the bulk of which was held in private libraries in India, Central Asia, Iran and elsewhere.[7] Ivanow's reach to the treasures of these libraries was gradual—his decades of experience and engagement with the learned circles of the Ismaili communities was paramount in winning their trust, and in ensuring his way to these treasures. We thus find him expressing time and again an immense gratitude to what he characterised in the *Guide* as the 'enlightened' and 'broad-minded Ismaili friends', alluding to how by sharing information and books pertaining to their religious heritage many of them had departed from a time-honoured practice of safeguarding these materials from outsiders. From this time onwards, we also see the burgeoning of a collaborative nexus between western enthusiasts and Ismaili scholars, a collaboration that was further nurtured by the establishment of some key institutions with the support of the leaders and literati of the concerned communities. At the heart of this new scholarly enterprise was a commitment to revisit the history of the Ismailis in light of what many of them were open to share from their own private libraries.

A similar and noteworthy collaboration transpired around this time, further away in Berlin and London, through the intellectual exchange and friendship between two renowned scholars, Paul Kraus and Ḥusayn al-Hamdānī. Their writings brought to the fore many of the previously little-known works from al-Hamdānī's family library, representing centuries of Fatimid-Ṭayyibī intellectual and literary riches. It was also through the manuscripts shared by al-Hamdānī that Kraus found a vital impetus to his own investigations on the doctrinal developments in early Ismaili tradition and their wider scholastic ramifications. Describing Kraus's passionate dedication to his work in the early 1930s when he had made acquaintance of al-Hamdānī, his friend Hans Lewy recalled how Kraus once told him 'with sparkling eyes' that he had managed to receive a manuscript from al-Hamdānī for one night which ostensibly linked the alchemist Jābir b. Ḥayyān's corpus with Ismaili writings, a connection that he was rigorously working to establish. Lewy observed, '[a]fter a long vigil, Kraus returned triumphant at dawn to the institute, his work done'.[8] As we learn from the letters exchanged between Kraus and al-Hamdānī—forming the subject-matter of Chapter 2 in this book—there also developed between them the idea of a bibliographic project similar to what Ivanow had brought out, a plan that was aborted after the *Guide*'s publication.

Indeed, ever since the appearance of Ivanow's *Guide* the identification and publication of textual sources transmitted via privately circulating manuscripts, and the production of bibliographic surveys expanding upon an ever growing repository of 'Ismaili literature', have remained a hallmark of scholarship in Ismaili studies. This preoccupation is understandable when viewed against the backdrop of the treatment long afforded to the heritage of the Ismaili communities based largely on materials ill-disposed towards them (as reminded by quite a few chapters in this volume). Connected with this preoccupation, in some ways, are also the scholarly assessments that continue to lament the destruction of the Ismaili religious corpus, notably in the form of the tragic fate of the libraries established under the Fatimids and the Nizārīs of Alamūt times.[9] An incessant search for what might have survived in the face of such real or perceived atrocities has therefore claimed a greater share of attention from those who have dedicated themselves to studying the history of these communities over the last eight or so decades.

Leaving aside the somewhat contested question of the extent and nature of disintegration these libraries and their collections might have witnessed, a number of reports confirm their periodic plundering and even large-scale destruction amidst economic and political calamities encountered by the Fatimid empire and the Nizārī state of Alamūt.[10] Beyond these comparatively well-documented cases, manuscript and book collections in possession of dispersed Ismaili communities have reportedly been subjected to intermittent confiscation or suppression right through to the modern times.[11] Compounding this, we can be sure of disasters, environmental factors or simple negligence contributing to the loss of many valuable manuscripts, especially in those parts of the world long inhabited by these communities.[12] It is, of course, difficult to estimate what might have been permanently lost in the wake of such unfortunate episodes, much less the full range of materials housed in the said repositories. But the surviving manuscripts, originating from a cross-section of the

Ismaili circles, point to a staggering wealth of textual contents produced or cultivated by them, and bear witness to their rich intellectual, literary and scientific pursuits, whether during periods of political efflorescence or otherwise.

A number of chapters in this volume thus reflect the approaches of textual scholarship, but their discussion of specific texts especially consider the questions surrounding their transmission, drawing particularly upon the insights offered and challenges posed by the manuscripts that served as a vital conduit in this process. Quite a few chapters bring forward hitherto unknown or little-known works, and ponder over their implications for specific episodes or broader trends in the history of the Ismaili tradition (see Chapters 9, 10, 14 and 16). Still others engage with previously less examined or unexplored manuscripts and shed light on how they inform or revise our understandings of better acquainted texts, including those circulated beyond the Ismaili communities (see Chapters 3, 4, 5, 6, 7, 8, 13, 15, 17 and 18). Taken together, all the chapters dwell on a number of features in the manuscripts at their disposal—from paratextual elements like marginalia, annotations and colophons to orthographic/textual variations, scribal practices and codicological aspects—and bring them into relationship with the larger questions of textual transmission. Beyond engaging with the manuscripts, they probe into a host of other aspects, such as circulation of texts, reading culture, social history, issues of authorship, communal script, religious identity, interactions of ideas across ideological denominations and more. Moreover, as many contributors worked with digital versions of the manuscripts, their discussions (indirectly) bear the imprint of how scholars confront the challenges and opportunities offered by the proliferation of digital texts.

A large number of the surviving manuscripts, representing the Ismaili literary heritage, are housed at The Institute of Ismaili Studies (IIS) founded in London in 1977. In addition, relatively smaller manuscript collections form part of a few libraries in Asia, Africa, Europe and North America, while a substantial number still exists in private holdings within different branches of the Ismailis.[13] The origins of the manuscript collections at the IIS go back to the decades following the publication of Ivanow's *Guide*. With his initial base in Bombay, when Ivanow embarked in 1931 on a formal and long-term association with the Ismailis as an employed researcher, his tasks included the acquisition of source materials that could facilitate a research and publications programme focused on the history, literature and doctrines of the Ismailis, as well as those of other associated groups. From roughly the mid 19th until at least the early decades of the 20th century, Bombay functioned as the headquarters and (in some ways) an intellectual powerhouse of the Nizārīs when their imams (known as the Aga Khans) adopted this flourishing commercial capital as their residence. In this period, followers of the Aga Khans from other parts of India and beyond frequented Bombay, and among them were many learned individuals often in possession of valuable handwritten books passed down in their families for generations. Earlier in the 20th century, the head of the Dāʾūdī Bohras, Ṭāhir Sayf al-Dīn (d. 1965), moved his administrative headquarters to Bombay where roots of the community lay at least to the first half of the 19th century. This made Bombay a cultural hub where a large number of Ismailis gravitated around this time, and it could hardly have been more fortuitous for Ivanow and others invested in the aforementioned programme.

A major impetus to their efforts came with the founding of two institutions in Bombay, first Islamic Research Association in 1933, and subsequently the Ismaili Society in 1946, the latter dedicated to 'the promotion of independent and critical study of all matters connected with Ismailism'.[14] In time, from a handful of Persian manuscripts and others in Indic languages belonging to the holdings of the Nizārī community's headquarters in Bombay, such materials began to grow exponentially. Ivanow's decades of experience in book-buying and his invaluable contacts with learned circles doubtlessly paved the way in accessing and acquiring manuscripts from the Nizārī and Bohra literati then visiting Bombay.[15] Furthermore, his periodic (at times 'official') visits to Ismaili settlements additionally brought to his knowledge otherwise inaccessible private libraries. Beyond the sources that were of direct relevance to the stated objectives of the aforementioned institutions, namely those focusing on 'Ismailism', their acquisition efforts also spanned into a wide array of connected themes, notably the traditions of mystics and other Shiʿi groups in Islam. It was more than evident to the concerned stakeholders that in order to better understand the evolution of the Ismaili tradition, a comparative perspective was indispensable. Hence, the manuscripts acquired through such institutional efforts came to represent a hybrid mix of other works from a cross-section of Muslim heritage. It was the manuscripts brought together since the early 1930s, containing materials directly related to Ismaili heritage and those shared by other traditions in Islam, that became the nucleus of the manuscript repository at the IIS during its earlier years.

The names of the many learned individuals and the circumstances of their lives, whose collections helped build this manuscript repository during those foundational decades, have not been systematically documented in the sources at our disposal. Occasionally, the publications of the Islamic Research Association and the Ismaili Society make a passing reference to some of them, acknowledging their generous sharing of manuscript(s) for the edition of a given text, or their support in other ways. Aside from this, on rare occasions in the very manuscripts brought together at that time, the names of certain individuals who facilitated the research activities of the likes of Ivanow by supplying source materials are inscribed. These learned individuals formed part of a literary network that stretched across the length and breadth of the Muslim world wherever the Ismaili communities had lived. Through this network, they travelled to cosmopolitan centres like Bombay and participated in intellectual and educational activities, not just by sharing knowledge and materials at their disposal but by copying texts that they came to know about and deemed important enough to take back home. Discussions of certain manuscripts and texts in this volume bring to light such transregional literary networks which were instrumental in supporting the said scholarly enterprise. Among the individuals who belonged to this network in the first half of the last century (upon whom Ivanow drew in various ways) are Mūsā Khān Khurāsānī, Sayyid Munīr Badakhshānī, Alimahomed J. Chunara, V. N. Hooda, and Ḥājī Qudratullāh Baig among others.[16]

The nucleus of the manuscript collections from the initial years of the IIS was augmented through subsequent acquisitions and donations over the decades. Their growth mirrored, moreover, the varied arenas in the study of Islam with which the IIS has been engaged since its inception. Among some noteworthy scholarly collections which have since become part of the Institute's manuscript holdings are those belonging to the Ṭayyibī scholars Zāhid ʿAlī (d. 1958) and Abbas

Hamdani (d. 2019) (the latter representing a large portion of the Hamdani family's library), and those of Chottu Lakhani (of Mumbai) and the Syrian Muṣṭafā Ghālib (d. 1981), the last two hailing from the Nizārī community. From these manuscripts, especially those originating from the Hamdani library, one sees not only the textual items pertaining to Ismaili heritage but many Zaydī, Twelver Shiʿi and Sunni works and others on a host of subjects from Arabic language and literature to mathematics, astronomy and medicine. This rich mix of textual contents therefore also points to the wide-ranging scholastic pursuits of generations of scholars involved in the transmission of knowledge.

In short, the diverse body of textual wealth nurtured among the Ismaili communities for centuries and preserved for a long time in private libraries in different regions of the Near East, Central and South Asia bears witness to their religious, intellectual and scientific legacy. In the cultivation and dissemination of this legacy, a network of literary associations was active throughout these regions which connected their respective communities across geographical and cultural boundaries, as is evident from the circulation of people, ideas and texts between Yemen and Egypt, Egypt and Syria, Yemen and India, Iran and Central Asia, India and Iran and so forth. Many facets of the workings of these literary associations are embedded in the discussions offered by different chapters in this volume.

While a large portion of the manuscripts at the IIS concentrates on 'Ismaili' materials, upon which several chapters in this volume draw, a substantial number of these manuscripts also embody a rich taxonomy ranging from texts concentrating on the Qur'ān, religious sciences, philosophy, logic and mysticism, on one hand, to those dealing with poetry, lexicography, grammar, rhetoric, astronomy, optics, mathematics and alchemy, on the other. The discussions of manuscript cultures from different regions in this volume are enriched by some contributions which deal with aspects of textual transmission and literary networks using the lens of materials and practices shared by Muslim communities at large and beyond (see, for example, Chapters 3, 4, 5, 12, 13, 17 and 18).

A noteworthy feature of the manuscripts originating from Ismaili circles, particularly those produced among the Ṭayyibīs of India and the Nizārīs of Badakhshān, is the fairly late date when many of them were copied. In fact, a number of manuscripts in this category continued to be transcribed and remained in circulation well into the 20th century. In an age dominated by *printed* books, the incessant production and relevance of these *handwritten* books require some comments. Among the Ṭayyibī communities, as noted, a bulk of religious and doctrinal texts have remained closely guarded until recent times owing to their perceived status as repositories of esoteric wisdom and therefore only accessible to the 'initiated' ones. Hence, limiting the printing of these materials was one way of ensuring their reduced or controlled dissemination.[17] What seems to have also reinforced this process is a culture of learning centred on manuscripts right through to the present times. So, as part of Bohra education conducted at their seminary in Surat, Jāmiʿa Sayfiyya, students are required to study and copy from manuscripts; their own copies are then kept in the Jāmiʿa library.[18]

On the other hand, the strict Soviet-era policies together with limited availability of printing facilities, especially in remote mountainous regions of Badakhshān, might explain the continuous dissemination of knowledge through handwritten books among the Nizārī communities of the region until the second half of the 20th century.[19] These exigencies perhaps resulted in how printed texts were seemingly deemed authoritative or rare artefacts in some cases, as they became 'source' copies for the ongoing transcribing of texts (a practice noted by some chapters in this volume dealing with Badakhshān manuscripts). Moreover, the implications of the overlap between the production and circulation of handwritten and printed texts become evident in how the features and devices generally associated with the technologies of manuscript and print came to mutually inform each other.[20]

A combination of cost considerations and technical hurdles also dictated scholarly reliance on hand-copied texts well into the 20th century, and thereby led to the continuous proliferation of manuscripts with 'Ismaili' texts during the age of print. For instance, from the letters exchanged between Henry Corbin and Ivanow towards the end of the 1940s and early 1950s, we learn of Corbin's repeated requests for two Ṭayyibī texts, *Kanz al-Walad* and *al-Shumūs al-Zāhira*, of which Ivanow had corrupt copies available in Bombay. However, the exorbitant price of photostats and microfilming prevented their easy reproduction, which may partly be attributed to the challenges of the post-war era. Ivanow therefore arranged for their copying through the assistance of some scribes by using better manuscript copies accessible to them. The identity of these scribes is not revealed, but they clearly belonged to Bohra circles with access to Ṭayyibī libraries. So, the availability of scribal skills among the Bohras passed down for centuries remained relevant well into the 20th century to counter the challenges of the reproduction of certain texts.[21]

These scribes formed an integral segment of the literary networks, and aspects of their craft and social circumstances shed a great deal of light on our understanding of the larger questions surrounding the transmission of texts and circulation of ideas. Discussions in some chapters of this volume focus on issues dealing with the practices and social and intellectual roles of scribes, as well as their ideological proclivities in their respective societies.

It is hoped that this book[22] would contribute to the ongoing scholarly debates about Ismaili history and its rich intellectual and literary trends from the perspective of the dynamic manuscript cultures nurtured by the Ismailis. In addition, the discussions, ideas and arguments in the chapters aspire to offer insights into our understanding of the textual heritage of the wider Muslim and other societies from which the Ismaili communities originated.

The book consists of eighteen chapters divided into seven sections. In the first section, two chapters shed light on the factors and forces that led to the shaping of (what is now widely recognised as) a new subset within the broader Islamic studies focused on the Ismaili tradition. The first chapter by Farhad Daftary gives a panoramic view of the key stages, from roughly the beginning of the 19th century to the present, which paved the way first for the emergence and then the solidification of this new field. In the unfolding of these stages, he shows how the gradual accessibility to manuscript sources on the part of the Orientalists of the 19th and the early 20th century planted the initial seeds. But what played the role of a catalyst and accelerated this process was a large-scale 'discovery' and study of these sources from roughly the early 1930s onwards. These developments are contextualised by Daftary against the backdrop of doctrinal, philosophical and legal works produced among the Fatimids, Ṭayyibīs and Nizārīs, the knowledge of which was itself the consequence of the transformations brought about by the discovery of the manuscript materials. The chapter brings home the point (as argued by Daftary in his previous works) that the inaccessibility of the materials preserved in Ismaili libraries, until the early decades of the 20th century, caused misconceptions and misinformation to have prevailed for a long time in popular and scholarly circles.

In the next chapter, François de Blois contextualises a collection of 55 letters, penned by Paul Kraus (1904–1944) and addressed to Ḥusayn al-Hamdānī (1901–1962), sharing observations on their importance. Gifted by Ḥusayn's son Abbas Hamdani to The Institute of Ismaili Studies, the letters shed valuable light on the personal and intellectual life of these two scholars. They offer a rare glimpse into the close friendship and collaboration that developed between them who, from the 1930s onwards, made some seminal contributions to this burgeoning field. The letters particularly reveal how through al-Hamdānī's generous and unprecedented sharing of his family's collection of manuscripts, Kraus carried out pioneering research in this arena, and thus became one of the first European scholars to lay hands on and utilise parts of a closely guarded manuscript treasures long preserved among the Ṭayyibī communities of the Yemen and India.

Section II focuses on the manuscript tradition of two widely transmitted textual productions, the encyclopaedic compendium *Rasā'il Ikhwān al-Ṣafā'* (compiled *ca.* 4th/10th century), and the lexicographical and heresiographical work *Kitāb al-Zīna* of Abū Ḥātim al-Rāzī (d. 322/934–935). An important feature of these two texts is their transmission in numerous manuscripts originating from Ismaili circles and beyond. The first chapter by Carmela Baffioni offers a rigorous analysis of three of the Institute's *Rasā'il Ikhwān al-Ṣafā'* manuscripts, focusing particularly on the five logical epistles with which the first part of the encyclopaedia is concluded. Analysis of these manuscripts is compared by Baffioni with previous editions of the epistles, including her own critical edition published in 2010. Her painstaking analysis and observations remind one of the fluid world of manuscripts constantly calling into question our approaches to 'critical' editions, and the challenges that textual scholars time and again encounter in reconciling the findings of new materials with existing knowledge.

In the next chapter, Omar Alí-de-Unzaga analyses IIS manuscript MS 1040 of the *Rasā'il Ikhwān al-Ṣafā'*. He places it among the oldest, complete and dated manuscripts of the epistles he has identified. Despite its age and importance, MS 1040 was not included in the list of manuscripts used for a new edition of the epistles currently being undertaken by The Institute of Ismaili Studies and Oxford University Press. After discussing miscellaneous features of MS 1040, such as date, scribe, provenance and other paratextual elements, Alí-de-Unzaga offers a detailed assessment of various epistles copied in the manuscript, comparing them with other editions and manuscripts where relevant to bring out important textual variations previously little noticed. In particular, his analysis shows (through the case of some specific epistles) that part of this encyclopaedic corpus was being actively engaged with by scribes during the process of its transmission, with new material constantly being introduced or previous material rearranged in the process. He thus questions many of the conclusions previously arrived at by researchers in the scholarship on *Rasā'il Ikhwān al-Ṣafā'*. His assessment, it is hoped, will draw more attention to this and other manuscripts of the epistles housed at the IIS in future discussions of the transmission of the text.

The final chapter in this section by Cornelius Berthold devotes attention to the *Kitāb al-Zīna*. Though compiled by an important intellectual from early Ismaili movement, its popularity outside of Ismaili circles is borne out by its many older manuscripts found in the libraries of Yemen, Baghdad and elsewhere; the book was also known to the famous bibliographer Ibn al-Nadīm (d. 385/995) who described it as a 'large book' of nearly 'four hundred leaves'. The chapter examines the arrangement and structure of *Kitāb al-Zīna* in light of the existing editions (partial or complete), and compares them to its known and accessible manuscripts. Through an assessment of fifteen manuscripts of the text offered in the chapter, Berthold shows the complex history of its transmission, alongside its wider popularity in different milieus right up to the first half of the 20th century. An important aspect of the chapter is its closer examination of the *Kitab al-Zīna* manuscripts housed at the IIS, shedding light on such aspects as their date and provenance, codicological features, textual variances and other stylistic peculiarities. In light of this analysis he revisits the previously articulated notion that the IIS manuscripts of the text bear close similarities and constitute 'siblings', as compared to other manuscript copies, and argues for a more nuanced approach to this issue backed by an extensive collation of the manuscripts.

The two chapters in Section III concentrate on issues of textual transmission, scribal practices and reading culture in the Ṭayyibī tradition. Delia Cortese's chapter examines the IIS manuscripts of the 12th-century compilation, *Majmūʿ al-tarbiya*, traditionally ascribed to Muḥammad b. Ṭāhir b. Ibrāhīm al-Ḥārithī (d. 584/1188). Arranged in two volumes, *Majmūʿ al-tarbiya* is an anthology of both complete texts or extracts (from longer works) on a range of instructional topics, many of which were composed during Fatimid and early Ṭayyibī times. Cortese grapples with a range of problems encountered in approaching a complex textual production like the *Majmūʿ al-tarbiya* which served as a model for later compilations in the Ṭayyibī tradition. She looks at the shifting relationship of 'paratextual' features found in different manuscript copies—ranging from marginal annotations and glosses to colophons and ownership seals—with the 'main' body of the text. In light of this relationship, she raises a number of important questions about different roles of the compiler, and how he might have negotiated those roles within the Ṭayyibī religious hierarchy with which he was closely associated. Based on the paratextual readings and other aspects of the text, Cortese argues that al-Ḥārithī's association with the text as its compiler is not straightforward and self-evident as it is generally believed. She also assesses the status *Majmūʿ al-tarbiya* enjoyed as an educational and learning text by different readers in the Ṭayyibī circle where access to knowledge was closely guarded, as well as its eventual fate (and that of its manuscripts) after the outburst of the reformist reaction among the Bohras in modern times.

Next, Monica Scotti looks at varied features of the IIS manuscripts of *Mukhtaṣar al-uṣūl* by the Ṭayyibī scholar ʿAlī b. Muḥammad b. al-Walīd (d. 612/1215) and raises questions about its transmission. ʿAlī b. Muḥammad served as the chief head (*dāʿī muṭlaq*) of the Ṭayyibīs and was a prolific writer who penned numerous treatises on a range of doctrinal matters; a *Dīwān* is also to his credit. *Mukhtaṣar al-uṣūl* deals with different themes, integrated in the treatise's main objective of refuting the position of certain groups of Muslims viewed by ʿAlī b. Muḥammad as his adversaries. Drawing our attention to a range of textual variations and orthographic idiosyncrasies, she attempts to contextualise them in light of the scribal interventions evident from the manuscripts of the text. Scotti raises the potential relevance of the resulting record of variances and other peculiarities found in the manuscripts and points to their possible usefulness in understanding the transmission of the text.

The history and doctrines of the Nizārīs of Alamūt times, as viewed through the lens of certain texts, form the focus of the three chapters in Section IV. The first chapter by Miklós Sárközy revisits the biographical account of Ḥasan-i Ṣabbāḥ, *Sargudhasht-i Sayyidnā*, in light of its hitherto little examined manuscripts from the Badakhshān region. It first touches upon the importance of the text by placing it in the historiography of Alamūt and the surviving sources concerning the Nizārī tradition from this era. The major discussion points of the chapter are enriched by the author's contextualisation of the previously well-known versions of the *Sargudhasht*, transmitted either as quotations in Persian chronicles, or as an independent text in previously known and better-studied manuscripts. In offering an assessment of the manuscripts from Badakhshān, Sárközy subjects them to a rigorous analysis by considering a number of aspects, including their provenance, background of the copyists, different titles used for the text and the content; these factors are brought to bear on the question of the vicissitudes of the *Sargudhasht* in the milieu of Badakhshān and beyond. Sárközy argues that in the Badakhshān versions of the text, one sees an effort to forge ideological linkages with Alamūt by creating association between Ḥasan-i Ṣabbāḥ and Nāṣir-i Khusraw, the latter being widely revered in Central Asia. This is particularly witnessed in the manner the biographical component of the text is encrusted with doctrinal and legendary elements reflecting the ethos of Central Asian Ismaili communities during a critical juncture of Qāsim Shāhī rejuvenation in the region.

Karim Javan, in the next chapter, introduces what he considers a 'newly discovered' treatise dealing notably with the internal circumstances in the early history of the Nizārī community in Alamūt. While the treatise itself is not named in the manuscripts at Javan's disposal, he designates it as *'Ahd-i Sayyidnā*, following the central theme of the administration of an oath (*'ahd*) by Ḥasan-i Ṣabbāḥ to the residents of Alamūt. Taking cue from the reference to Nāṣir al-Dīn Muḥtasham (d. 655/1257) as the 'King of the East' (*shahanshāh-i mashriqī*) in the text, Javan places its composition during the time of his governorship. The text's narrative covers the early decades of Nizārī rule and its political struggle against the Saljuqs. It is particularly rich in furnishing details about the hardships the residents of Alamūt endured at that time and the manner in which they sought to cope with them. The identification of this text, as well as Javan's assessment of the circumstances of its composition and its potential author, will no doubt generate further scholarly interest and discussion.

In the final chapter of this section, Jalal Badakhchani reflects on the identification of certain manuscripts that led to the recasting of Alamūt history and Nizārī doctrines in new light. These manuscripts relate to two texts, namely *Dīwān-i Qā'imiyyāt* and the *Haft Bāb*, both from the pen of (until recently) a little known figure, Ḥasan-i Maḥmūd-i Kātib. The texts are contextualised in light of an intellectual collaboration between Ḥasan-i Maḥmūd-i Kātib and two other luminaries from later Alamūt times—Naṣīr al-Dīn Ṭūsī and Nāṣir al-Dīn Muḥtasham—at a crucial moment when the doctrine of *qiyāmat* in Nizārī preaching was undergoing modifications under different lords of Alamūt. Such modifications in the doctrine, Badakhchani argues, required wider consultation with the best minds who were serving different territories. The chapter also offers insights on how the discovery of *Dīwān-i Qā'imiyyāt* and that of the better manuscript copies of *Haft Bāb* offer a counter narrative to the widely circulated distortions about the doctrines of the Nizārīs and the genealogy of their imams.

The two chapters in Section V devote attention to aspects of a little explored manuscript tradition cultivated among the Ismaili and some other communities from South Asia. These communities often bear the designation 'Satpanthī' owing to the teachings of Satpanth (lit., the 'true path') propagated to them through the medium of *Ginān* literature. Shafique Virani, in the first chapter, examines some key questions pertaining to the name and origins of the communal script in which the bulk of the manuscripts (cultivated among these communities) has been copied. He explores the transition of the name of the script, from Sindhi to Khojkī, by bringing an extensive body of evidence to bear on this question. Making a case for this manuscript tradition to have gone back much earlier than what the surviving manuscript evidence might suggest, he offers new reflections on the possible origins of the script beyond what has hitherto been widely accepted.

The next chapter by Wafi Momin focuses on a largely forgotten group of scribes and literate gentry who were at the forefront of cultivating Satpanth manuscripts, and disseminating the literary, religious and didactic genres transcribed therein. The chapter first foregrounds how the Khojas—who form a major group among the Satpanthī communities—have long been viewed predominantly as a community of merchants and traders which has had major implications for how their religious identity has hitherto been construed. The factors behind this imagining have been traced by him through an examination of the reports by colonial officials and other observers, as well as the nature of Satpanth historiography which has largely focused on a group of charismatic saints in assessing the formation of the tradition. Moving beyond this paradigm, Momin explores different features from the Satpanth manuscripts which point to literary, social and ideological aspects of the role of scribes and literati among whom were those who hailed from the Khoja circles. The chapter thus makes the case for revisiting the popular images associated with the Khojas in light of the evidence borne by the manuscripts.

The four chapters in Section VI examine issues pertaining to the emergence and growth of the Ismaili communities in Central Asia and their relationship with other socio-religious groups. First, Orkhan Mir-Kasimov engages with the much debated topic of the Ismaili-Sufi relationship, assessing it from the viewpoint of the works attributed to Shāh Niʿmatullāh Walī (d. 834/1430–1431) that are found in the manuscripts originating from Ismaili circles in Badakhshān. The chapter begins by contextualising the relationship between Shiʿi and Sufi traditions, especially in the post-Mongol Persianate world, and offers some broad propositions for the possibility of mutual attractions in Niʿmatullāh's teachings and Ismaili doctrines. This is followed by a discussion of both poetical and prose works, ascribed to Shāh Niʿmatullāh Walī and transmitted in the Badakhshān manuscripts. Mir-Kasimov draws our attention to several ideas expressed in Niʿmatullāh's corpus and their possible convergence and alignment with Ismaili teachings; these include shared notions of divinely sanctioned leadership, religious authority, messianic deliverance, and praises to Imam ʿAlī. The chapter is thus an important intervention demonstrating the intellectual and doctrinal underpinnings of the relationship between the Ismailis and the Niʿmatullāhīs, the historical affinity of which has long been acknowledged by scholars.

The next chapter by Nourmamadcho Nourmamadchoev introduces a little-known figure from Badakhshān, Shāh Ḍiyāʾī-i Shughnānī, and his poetical work *Salām-nāma*. In this ode, the poet expresses devotion to Imam ʿAlī and other imams in his progeny, couching this central theme within the Qurʾānic paradigm and some episodes from the Prophet's life. The chapter situates the life and works of Shāh Ḍiyāʾī in the political climate of Badakhshān and the power struggle between Timurids, Shaybānīds and local rulers in the region during the 15th and 16th centuries. It was from the local rulers of Shughnān, his native place, that Shāh Ḍiyāʾī traced his descent. Piecing together the clues available on his life from various sources, including his poetic repertoire, Nourmamadchoev places him between the first half of the 16th and first quarter of the 17th century. The chapter foregrounds the issues of religious identity and the fluid nature of what constituted the legitimate line of imams in the context of Badakhshān, while opening up discussion on approaching the interaction of ideas across ideological denominations.

Next, Daniel Beben re-examines the authorship of *Ṣaḥīfat al-Nāẓirīn* (also known as *Sī ū shish ṣaḥīfa*), a doctrinal text commonly attributed to Sayyid Suhrāb Walī Badakhshānī. The figure of Sayyid Suhrāb has held a prominent place among the Ismailis of Central Asia, as evident from a rich body of hagiographical accounts connecting him with Nāṣir-i Khusraw. Beben examines a number of available manuscripts of the text, housed at the IIS and other repositories, and argues for the possibility of its two redactions, one attributed to Sayyid Suhrāb and the other to one Ghiyāth al-Dīn Iṣfahānī, who served the Timurid governors in Badakhshān during the second half of the 15th century. By bringing together evidence from manuscripts, hagiographical tradition and genealogical records, Beben puts forward some propositions explaining the transmission of the text in two redactions, including that Ghiyāth al-Dīn was probably the original author of the text, being possibly an Ismaili *dāʿī* (but subsequently forgotten), and with the further likelihood that he and Sayyid Suhrāb might have been one and the same individual.

Yahia Baiza, in the final chapter of this section, offers textual analysis of a widely copied doctrinal work in Central Asian manuscripts of

Ismaili provenance, known as *Haft Arkān-i Sharīʿa* ('Seven Pillars of the *Sharīʿa*'). He first provides a codicological assessment of the manuscripts at his disposal, and the problems they pose in approaching the issues of the text's transmission. The examination of *Haft Arkān-i Sharīʿa* is contextualised by Baiza against the discourse of *tāʾwīl* as developed among Ismaili intellectuals of different eras, which is then brought to bear on relevant facets of the text.

The two chapters in the last section use the examples of IIS manuscripts to discuss the problems encountered in approaching the transmission of Qurʾānic text, as well as the nature and compilation of holograph/autograph manuscripts. In the first chapter, Asma Hilali approaches the transmission of the Qurʾānic text by moving away from a general focus on a supposed 'original' version believed to be at its core, based on which available fragments of the Qurʾān manuscripts are then assessed. Rather, she shifts the focus to often overlooked aspects of the marginalia and interlinear annotations and other glosses encountered in these manuscripts. She also suggests looking at the Qurʾānic text in light of the particular contexts as reflected in these manuscripts. Her chapter focuses on a selection of Qurʾān manuscripts and fragments from the IIS collection and discusses their distinct features, based on which it shows connections between the variants encountered in these manuscript copies and the larger cultural and educational practices prevalent in Muslim societies.

The final chapter by Walid Ghali offers insights into the nature of autograph and holograph manuscripts in the Arabic manuscript tradition by considering a host of paratextual features in a select group of IIS manuscripts. His discussion looks at the nuances of terminology in Arabic language pertaining to these categories and how they relate to corresponding categories established in western scholarship.

NOTES

1 Wladimir Ivanow, *A Guide to Ismaili Literature* (London, 1933), p. v.

2 Ivanow first visited Lucknow in the summer of 1914. After he took residence in India, he visited the city multiple times and many other places within and outside India to acquire manuscripts for the Asiatic Society of Bengal where he was employed between 1921 and 1930 to catalogue the Society's Oriental manuscripts. In his memoirs, Ivanow provides insights into some of his excursions for the acquisition of manuscripts; see Farhad Daftary, ed., *Fifty Years in the East: The Memoirs of Wladimir Ivanow* (London, 2015), pp. 59–60, 114–117 (for his 1915 journey to Bukhara where he managed to purchase

1,047 manuscripts for the Asiatic Museum), and pp. 155–158 (for his visits to Lucknow in 1915 and 1927). Over time, Ivanow himself came to own a large number of manuscripts; on his first visit to the Royal Asiatic Society of Bombay in 1914, he could boast that the Society 'possessed only 30 quite uninteresting Persian manuscripts, fewer than I myself owned' (Daftary, ed., *Fifty Years in the East*, p. 58). Drawing on his personal experiences, he even published guidelines for those seeking to purchase manuscripts from Iran, providing practical advice to circumvent the problems involved in the process; see his 'Exportation of Manuscripts from Persia', *Journal of the Royal Asiatic Society* (1929), pp. 441–443.

3 W. Ivanow, *Ismaili Literature: A Bibliographical Survey* (2nd ed., Tehran, 1963), p. xii.

4 Ivanow, *A Guide to Ismaili Literature*, pp. v–vii.

5 The term 'Ismaili' and other collocations based on it are employed here as umbrella designations for many a religio-political current united by a shared history and heritage, including those represented by the Fatimids, Ṭayyibīs and Nizārīs.

6 See Chapter 1 in this volume for a discussion of these developments.

7 See Paul Kraus, 'La bibliographie Ismaëlienne de W. Ivanow', *Revue des Études Islamiques*, 6 (1932), pp. 483–490; and reviews of the *Guide* in *Rivista degli studi orientali*, 15 (1934), pp. 114–116, *Acta Orientalia*, 13 (1935), pp. 241–242, and *Journal of the Royal Asiatic Society* (1935), p. 206.

8 Joel Kraemer, 'The Death of an Orientalist: Paul Kraus from Prague to Cairo', in Martin Kramer, ed., *The Jewish Discovery of Islam: Studies in Honor of Bernard Lewis* (Tel Aviv, 1999), p. 186.

9 See, for example, W. Ivanow, ed. and tr., *Kalami Pir: A Treatise on Ismaili Doctrine* (Bombay, 1935), p. v; Delia Cortese, *Ismaili and Other Arabic Manuscripts: A Descriptive Catalogue of Manuscripts in the Library of The Institute of Ismaili Studies* (London, 2000), p. xii; Farhad Daftary, *The Ismāʿīlīs: Their History and Doctrines* (2nd ed., Cambridge, 2007), pp. 5, 193–194, 253, 396; and Shafique Virani, *The Ismailis in the Middle Ages: A History of Survival, A Search for Salvation* (Oxford, 2007), pp. 8, 22, 92ff. For a revisionist take on the supposed destruction of the Fatimid book collections by Ṣalāḥ al-Dīn, see Fozia Bora, 'Did Ṣalāḥ al-Dīn Destroy the Fatimids' Books? An Historiographical Enquiry', *Journal of the Royal Asiatic Society*, Series 3, 25 (2015), pp. 21–39.

10 On the plundering and destruction of book collections developed under the Fatimids and the Nizārīs of Alamūt, see the reports cited in Paul Walker, 'Libraries, Book Collection and the Production of Texts by the Fatimids', *Intellectual History of the Islamicate World*, 4 (2016), pp. 12–13, and the eye-witness account of ʿAṭā-Malik Juwaynī (in his *Ta'rīkh-i Jahān-gushā*) in John Boyle, tr., *The History of the World Conqueror* (Manchester, 1958), vol. 2, p. 719.

11 For the harshness faced by the Ismailis of Badakhshān under Soviet rule and the suppression of their religious books, see Frank Bliss, *Social and Economic Change in the Pamirs (Gorno-Badakhshān, Tajikistan)*, tr. Nicola Pacult et al. (London, 2006), pp. xv, 79–80, 227–229. For a recent episode of the confiscation of religious books of Sulaymānīs in Najran by Saudi authorities, see Tahera Qutbuddin, 'A Brief Note on Other Tayyibi Communities: Sulaymanis and 'Alavis', in Farhad Daftary, ed., *A Modern History of the Ismailis: Continuity and Change in a Muslim Community* (London, 2011), p. 356.

12 A large number of manuscripts in the Dā'ūdī Bohra centre in Surat were destroyed in the fire that devastated the city in 1837; see Saifiyah Qutbuddin, 'History of the Da'udi Bohra Tayyibis in Modern Times: The *Daʿis*, the *Daʿwat* and the Community', in Daftary, ed., *A Modern History of the Ismailis*, p. 300.

13 It includes a large collection of Fatimid and Ṭayyibī manuscripts in Dā'ūdī Bohra libraries in India; as per Tahera Qutbuddin they represent 'approximately 524 titles, 10,000 manuscripts, in Mumbai [Bombay] and several thousand more in Surat'; see Tahera Qutbuddin, 'The Da'udi Bohra Tayyibis: Ideology, Literature, Learning and Social Practice', in Daftary, ed., *A Modern History of the Ismailis*, p. 343.

14 W. Ivanow, ed., *The Ismaili Society of Bombay: The Tenth Anniversary (16-2-1946—16-2-1956)* (Bombay, 1956), pp. 1–2; the circumstances that led to the foundation of both the institutions are described by Ivanow in his autobiography; see Daftary, ed., *Fifty Years in the East*, esp. pp. 89–95.

15 Daftary, ed., *Fifty Years in the East*, pp. 84, 89–90ff.

16 On Mūsā Khān Khurāsānī, see ibid., pp. 89–90. On Sayyid Munīr Badakhshānī, see Ivanow, *A Guide to Ismaili Literature*, pp. 99–100ff., and Muzaffar Zoolshoev, 'Forgotten Figures of Badakhshān: Sayyid Munir al-Din Badakhshani and Sayyid Haydar Shah Mubarakshahzada', in Dagikhudo Dagiev and Carole Faucher, ed., *Identity, History and Trans-Nationality in Central Asia: The Mountain Communities of Pamir* (London, 2019), pp. 143–155. The contribution of A. J. Chunara and V. N. Hooda is acknowledged in quite a few of Ivanow's publications. Ḥājī Qudratullāh Baig supplied manuscript copies of some Persian texts to Ivanow, including those of *Rawḍa-i Taslīm*, *Pandiyāt-i Jawānmardī*, *Umm al-Kitāb*, and *Haft Bāb-i Abū Isḥāq* which Ivanow used for the edition of these texts; see Ḥājī Qudratullāh Baig, *Ta'rīkh Tā'mīr-i Sinṭiral Jamā'at Khāna Gilgit* (Baltit, Hunza, 1967), p. 9. I was able to confirm the identity of two manuscripts in the IIS holdings which were prepared by Ḥājī Qudratullāh Baig on Ivanow's request in 1935 and bear notes to this effect; see *Pandiyāt-i Jawānmardī*, MS Per 35 (MS 154), p. 84; and *Rawḍa-i Taslīm*, MS Per 44 (MS 171), p. 129. The names of the Bohra literati are not provided by Ivanow but we know that he relied on many of them too (see below).

17 See François de Blois, *Arabic, Persian and Gujarati Manuscripts: The Hamdani Collection in the Library of The Institute of Ismaili Studies* (London, 2011), pp. xiii–xiv; Qutbuddin, 'The Da'udi Bohra Tayyibis', p. 344; and Chapter 6 in this volume. To maintain secrecy, the Ṭayyibī scribes also resorted to using the so-called 'secret' scripts to conceal information in their manuscripts; see de Blois, *Arabic, Persian and Gujarati Manuscripts*, pp. xxii–xxiii, 108.

18 Qutbuddin, 'The Da'udi Bohra Tayyibis', p. 343.

19 Sayyid Munīr Badakhshānī, for example, who spent a great deal of time in India published many Persian texts in Bombay (see Ivanow, *A Guide to Ismaili Literature*, pp. 91, 99–100ff.). In 1933, Ivanow lamented how until thirty years ago there were several publishing firms in Bombay printing books in Arabic and Persian which included a large number of Shi'i texts; their disappearance 'completely killed this important auxiliary to Shi'ite research' (Ivanow, *A Guide to Ismaili Literature*, p. 5, n. 1).

20 See Chapter 6 for a discussion of some aspects of this interface. It is also particularly evident in the technology of lithography (extensively used by some Ismaili communities) where scribal practices continued to be mechanically reproduced in the lithographically printed texts.

21 See Sabine Schmidtke, ed., *Correspondence Corbin—Ivanow: Lettres échangées entre Henry Corbin et Vladimir Ivanow de 1947 à 1966* (Paris, 1999), esp. pp. 33, 35, 40–41, 46, 48–49, 53–60, 62–63, 67–71, 76, 78–80, 82, 91, 93–94, 97, 99, 102–103, 105.

22 The chapters in this book were originally presented in the Symposium *Before the Printed Word: Texts, Scribes and Transmission*, organised by the Ismaili Special Collections Unit of The Institute of Ismaili Studies on 12–13 October 2017.

SECTION I

THE SHAPING OF A NEW FIELD

1

Ismaili Manuscripts and Modern Scholarship in Ismaili Studies

Farhad Daftary

The Ismailis represent the second most important community of Shiʿi Muslims, after the Ithnāʿasharī or Twelver Shiʿis. In the course of their long and complex history dating back to the formative era of Islam, they elaborated a variety of intellectual and literary traditions and made significant contributions to Islamic thought and culture. Ismaili thought and literature attained their summit under the Fatimid Imam-caliphs who ruled over a flourishing empire for more than two centuries from 297/909. It was indeed during the Fatimid phase of their history that the Ismailis produced a vast literature dealing with a range of topics, from exoteric (*ẓāhirī*) works to the esoteric (*bāṭinī*) ones and the allegorical exegesis or *ta'wīl* of the sacred scriptures. Major institutions of learning, such as the Dar al-ʿIlm or House of Knowledge, as well as libraries were also established by the Fatimid Imam-caliphs, who as the Ismaili imams of the time ruled over the Fatimid caliphate, the first major Shiʿi caliphate challenging the legitimacy of the Sunni caliphate of the Abbasids. It was under such circumstances that Cairo, the capital city founded by the Fatimids themselves, rivalled the Abbasid capital at Baghdad as a centre of learning and the sciences as well as international trade and commerce, not only with India but also with the occident.

However, the literary heritage of the Ismailis was not generally accessible to outsiders, who were not themselves generally interested in acquiring reliable information on the Ismailis and their intellectual achievements. This was because from early on when the Ismaili *dāʿīs* or missionaries disseminated the message of the revolutionary *daʿwa* of the Ismailis, this community of Imami Shiʿi Muslims had been designated by their Sunni adversaries, including the Abbasid caliphs themselves, as the *malāḥida* or 'heretics'. The Ismailis had indeed challenged the Sunni-Abbasid establishment with the religio-political message of their *daʿwa* which called for the demise of the Abbasids who, in the eyes of all Shiʿi Muslims, had usurped the right of ʿAlī b. Abī Ṭālib and his Ḥusaynid ʿAlid descendants, from amongst the Prophet Muḥammad's family (*ahl al-bayt*), to rule over the Muslim community (*umma*).

It was under such circumstances that the Sunni-Abbasid establishment launched an anti-Ismaili literary campaign soon after the establishment of the Fatimid caliphate in North Africa. This campaign aimed to defame and refute the Ismailis, who were now represented in the polemical tradition as the arch enemies of Islam, because they strove to destroy Islam from within. In this polemical tradition, initiated by Abū ʿAbd Allāh Muḥammad b. ʿAlī b. Rizām al-Kūfī, better known as Ibn Rizām, who lived in Baghdad during the first half of the 4th/10th century, the ʿAlid genealogy of the Fatimid Imam-caliphs was also refuted.[1] Indeed through the concerted efforts of the Abbasids and their Sunni *ʿulamāʾ*, a 'black legend' was soon put into circulation regarding Ismaili motives, teachings and practices. In these fictitious accounts, a host of shocking doctrines and secret practices were attributed to the Ismailis, items that would be abundantly sufficient to qualify them for being considered as heretics or deviators from the 'right path' in Islam. These maliciously fabricated accounts circulated widely and in due course became accepted as accurate descriptions of Ismaili doctrines and practices. In particular, they provided a main source of information for Sunni heresiographers, such as al-Baghdādī (d. 429/1037),[2] who generated another important category of writings against the Ismailis.

Meanwhile, after the Nizārī-Mustaʿlian schism of 487/1094 in the Ismaili *daʿwa* and community, the Nizārī Ismailis founded their own state under the initial leadership of Ḥasan-i Ṣabbāḥ (d. 518/1124).[3] This state with scattered territories in Persia and Syria and a vast network of mountain fortresses survived for some 166 years until it was destroyed by the Mongols in 654/1256. A second wave of anti-Ismaili polemics started soon after Ḥasan-i Ṣabbāḥ had established himself at the fortress of Alamūt in 483/1090. This new literary campaign was launched by the foremost contemporary Sunni scholar, al-Ghazālī (d.

505/1111), who was commissioned by the reigning Abbasid caliph al-Mustaẓhir (r. 487–512/1094–1118) to write a major treatise in refutation of the Ismailis. In this polemical work, known as *al-Mustaẓhirī* after the Abbasid caliph, al-Ghazālī while focussing on attacking the doctrine of *taʿlīm* or the necessity of authoritative teaching by the Ismaili imam of the time, as reformulated afresh by Ḥasan, reiterated the 'black legend' of the earlier Sunni polemicists.[4] Meanwhile, the all-powerful Saljūq vizier, Niẓām al-Mulk (d. 485/1092), had cited the Ismailis amongst the foremost enemies of Islam and the Saljūq sultan in his own 'mirror for princes' type of book addressed to Sultan Malikshāh (r. 465–485/1073–1092).[5] This new anti-Ismaili campaign was accompanied by major military expeditions dispatched from early on by the Saljūqs against Alamūt and other Ismaili strongholds in Persia.

Subsequently, the Ismailis found a new adversary in the Christian Crusaders who had allegedly arrived in the Middle East to liberate their own co-religionists. The Crusaders seized Jerusalem, their primary objective, in 492/1099 and then engaged in extensive military, commercial and diplomatic encounters with the Fatimids in Egypt and the Nizārī Ismailis in Syria, with lasting consequences in terms of the distorted image of the Nizārī Ismailis in Europe. The Nizārī Ismailis of Syria attained the peak of their power and fame under the leadership of Rāshid al-Dīn Sinān, who was their chief *dāʿī* for some three decades until his death in 589/1193. It was in the time of Sinān, the original 'Old Man of the Mountain' of the Crusader sources, that European chroniclers of the Crusades and a number of European travellers and diplomatic emissaries began to write about the Nizārī Ismailis, who were now designated in the occidental sources as the 'Assassins'.

The Crusader circles and their occidental historians, who were not interested in collecting accurate information about Islam as a religion and its internal divisions despite their proximity to Muslims, remained completely ignorant of Muslims in general and the Ismailis in particular. In fact, the Syrian Nizārī Ismailis were the first Shiʿi Muslim community with whom the Crusaders had come into contact. However, the Crusaders remained unaware of the religious identity of the Ismailis and had only vague and generally erroneous ideas regarding the Sunni-Shiʿi division in Islam. It was under such circumstances that the Frankish circles themselves began to fabricate and put into circulation both in the Latin Orient and in Europe a number of tales about the secret practices of the Ismailis. It should be noted that none of the variants of these sensational tales are to be found in contemporary Muslim sources, including the most hostile ones written by the Sunni historians during the 6th/12th and 7th/13th centuries.

The Crusaders were particularly impressed by the highly exaggerated reports and rumours of the assassinations attributed to the Ismailis and the daring behaviour of their *fidāʾī*s, self-sacrificing devotees who carried out targeted missions in public places and normally lost their own lives in the process. It may be recalled that in the 6th/12th century, almost any assassination of any religio-political significance committed in the central Islamic lands was readily attributed to the daggers of the Ismaili *fidāʾī*s. This explains why these imaginative tales revolved around the recruitment and training of the would-be *fidāʾī*s, because they were meant to provide satisfactory explanations for behaviour that would otherwise seem irrational or strange to the medieval European mind.

The so-called Assassin legends consisted of a number of interconnected tales, including the '*ḥashīsh* legend' and the 'paradise legend'.[6] The tales developed in stages and finally culminated in a synthesis popularised by Marco Polo (d. 1324).[7] The Venetian traveller, and/or his ghost writer Rustichello of Pisa, added their own contribution in the form of a 'secret garden of paradise', where bodily pleasures were supposedly procured for the *fidāʾī*s with the aid of *ḥashīsh* by their mischievous chief, the Old Man, as part of their indoctrination and training. By the 8th/14th century, the Assassin legends had acquired wide currency and were generally accepted as reliable descriptions of secret Ismaili practices, in much the same way as the earlier 'black legend' of the Muslim authors. Henceforth, the Nizārī Ismailis were portrayed in medieval European sources as a sinister order of drugged 'assassins' bent on indiscriminate murder and mayhem. In sum, by the beginning of the 13th/19th century, Europeans still perceived the Ismailis in utterly confused and fanciful manners. Indeed, until the recovery and study of Ismaili manuscript sources, the Ismailis were studied and evaluated almost exclusively on the basis of the evidence collected or often fabricated by their adversaries. As a result, all types of erroneous attributions or myths continued to circulate about the Ismailis who were, thus, totally misrepresented in both Islamic and European sources.

In the meantime, the Ismailis themselves had produced a very rich and diversified literature. In particular, as noted, it was during the Fatimid period of their history that the Ismaili *dāʿī*s, who were at the same time the scholars and writers of their community, composed what were to become known as the classical texts of Ismaili literature dealing with a multitude of exoteric (*ẓāhirī*) and esoteric (*bāṭinī*) subjects, ranging from autobiographies, histories and legal compendia, to works on the *ḥaqāʾiq* covering cosmology, eschatology and soteriology, as well as *taʾwīl* or esoteric exegesis which became the hallmark of Ismaili thought. The Ismaili *dāʿī*s elaborated distinctive literary and intellectual traditions. In particular, certain *dāʿī*s of the Iranian lands, such as Abū Yaʿqūb al-Sijistānī (d. after 361/971) and Ḥamīd al-Dīn al-Kirmānī (d. after 411/1020), amalgamated Ismaili theology with Neoplatonism and other philosophical traditions into complex metaphysical systems of thought as expressed in numerous treatises written in Arabic. Only Nāṣir-i Khusraw (d. after 462/1070), the last major proponent of this Iranian school of philosophical theology, composed all of his works in Persian.

With the establishment of the Fatimid state, the need had also arisen for promulgating a legal code, even though Ismailism was never imposed on all subjects of the Fatimid state as their official religion. Ismaili law was codified during the early Fatimid period mainly as a result of the efforts of al-Qāḍī al-Nuʿmān (d. 363/974), the foremost jurist of the Fatimids. It was indeed during the Fatimid period that Ismailis made their contributions to Islamic theology and philosophy in general and to Shiʿi thought in particular. Modern recovery of Ismaili literature clearly attests to the richness and diversity of the literary and intellectual heritage of the Ismailis of Fatimid times.

The Ṭayyibī Ismailis of Yemen and South Asia have preserved a good portion of the literary heritage of the Ismailis, including the classical texts of the Fatimid period and the works written by the Ṭayyibīs themselves. These manuscript sources, collectively designated as '*al-khizāna al-maknūna*', or the 'guarded treasure', were mostly transferred after the 10th/16th century from Yemen to India, where they continued to be copied by better-educated Bohras of Gujarat and elsewhere. This literature was classified and described for the first time by al-Majdūʿ, a Dāʾūdī Ṭayyibī Bohra scholar who died in 1183/1769.[8]

The Nizārī Ismailis of the Alamūt period, too, maintained a sophisticated intellectual outlook and a literary tradition, despite their preoccupation with their survival in an extremely hostile environment. Ḥasan-i Ṣabbāḥ himself was a learned theologian and is credited with establishing an impressive library at the castle of Alamūt. Later, other major Ismaili fortresses in Persia and Syria were equipped with significant collections of books, documents and scientific instruments. In the doctrinal field, however, only a handful of Ismaili texts have survived directly from that period. These include Ḥasan-i Maḥmūd-i Kātib's *Haft bāb*, or Seven Chapters, and also the corpus of Ismaili works written during the final decades of the Alamūt period by, or attributed to, Naṣīr al-Dīn al-Ṭūsī (d. 672/1274), one of the most learned Shiʿi scholars of all time who spent three decades in the Ismaili fortress communities of Persia. It was during his stay with the Ismailis that al-Ṭūsī, as explained in his spiritual autobiography *Sayr va sulūk*, willingly converted to Ismailism. It should be noted that from early on in the history of the Nizārī Ismailis, Ḥasan-i Ṣabbāḥ had chosen Persian in preference to Arabic as the literary language of the Persian-speaking Nizārīs. As a result, the literature produced by al-Ṭūsī and generally by the Nizārī Ismailis of Persia, Afghanistan and Central Asia during the Alamūt period and subsequent times, is entirely written in Persian.

The Ismaili manuscript sources, written in Arabic, Persian and later in Indic languages, have been preserved secretly in numerous collections in Yemen, Syria, Persia, Afghanistan, Central Asia and South Asia. The Arabic literature has been preserved almost exclusively by the Ṭayyibī Ismailis, who are better known in South Asia as Bohras, while the Persian literature has been preserved mainly by the Nizārī Ismailis of Persia and those of the Central Asian region of Badakhshān, now divided between Tajikistan and Afghanistan. At present, there are also major libraries of Arabic Ismaili manuscripts in Surat, Bombay and Baroda, seats of the Dāʾūdī and ʿAlawī Ṭayyibīs in India, and in some private collections in Yemen and Saudi Arabia within the Sulaymānī Ṭayyibī communities in those regions. The Persian Ismaili manuscripts, reflecting the Nizārī Ismaili traditions except for the works of Nāṣir-i Khusraw, have survived in numerous private collections held by the Nizārī Ismailis of the Persian-speaking countries and regions. The Syrian Nizārī Ismailis, who retained Arabic as their religious language, developed their own limited literature in Arabic. They also preserved some of the Ismaili works of the Fatimid period.

The largest collection of Arabic and Persian Ismaili manuscripts in the West is located at The Institute of Ismaili Studies in London. The latter institution also holds a large number of devotional works of the South Asian Nizārī Ismailis, who are more generally designated as Khojas. These works, known as *gināns*, are composed in Gujarati and other Indic languages, and written mostly in the Khojkī script developed by the Khojas of Sind. The *gināns*, representing the religious tradition of the Khojas known as Satpanth, or the 'true path', contain a diversity of mystical, mythological, didactic, cosmological and eschatological themes. Many *gināns* contain ethical and moral instructions.

Modern progress in Ismaili studies awaited the recovery and study of the literary heritage of the Ismailis—a heritage that had remained hidden for centuries. The process started gradually, but gained momentum exponentially, ushering in nothing short of a revolution in Ismaili studies. Indeed, no other branch of Islamic studies has experienced parallel progress through access to manuscript sources. In fact, an entirely new field of modern Ismaili studies was established in the 20th century as a result of recovering the Ismaili manuscript sources on a large scale. Four separate phases may be distinguished in the development of scholarship on the Ismailis.

Phase I: Orientalist Perspectives, 1810–1930

A new phase in the study of Islam in general, and to some extent of the Ismailis, occurred in the early 19th century with increased access of the orientalists to the textual sources of the Muslims, including especially the Arabic and Persian manuscripts that were variously acquired by the Bibliothèque Nationale, Paris, and other major European libraries. Scientific orientalism had been initiated a while earlier with the establishment in 1795 of the École des Langues Orientales Vivantes in Paris. Baron A. I. Silvestre de Sacy (1758–1838), the most eminent orientalist of his time, was the first professor of Arabic in that newly founded institution of oriental languages. In 1806, he was also appointed to the new chair of Persian at the Collège de France. Subsequently, with an increasing number of students and a wide circle of correspondents and disciples, de Sacy acquired the distinction of being the teacher of the most prominent orientalists of the first half of the 19th century. Be that as it may, the orientalists now began their more scholarly study of Islam on the basis of the manuscript sources which were written mostly in Arabic and by Sunni authors. Consequently, they too studied Islam according to Sunni perspectives and treated Shiʿi Islam as the 'heterodox' interpretation of Islam in contrast to Sunnism which was taken to represent Islamic 'orthodoxy'. Needless to add that Western scholarship on Islam has continued to be mainly shaped by its Arabo-Sunni perspectives. At any rate, it was mainly on this basis, as well as the continued appeal of the seminal Assassin legends, that the orientalists launched their own studies of the Ismailis.

De Sacy, with his lifelong interest in the Druze religion, became a pioneer in this emerging area of investigation. Meanwhile, the Nizārī Ismailis of the Middle East and Persia had begun to attract the attention of a few European diplomats and travellers. Jean Baptiste L. J. Rousseau (1780–1831), the French consul-general in Aleppo from 1809 to 1816, who was also interested in Oriental Studies and maintained a close professional relationship with de Sacy, was the first person to draw the attention of European orientalists to the existence of contemporary Ismailis as well as some of their local traditions and texts. In 1810, he prepared a memoir on the Syrian Ismailis of his time, which contained a range of interesting historical, social and religious details obtained through his contacts with Ismailis themselves.[9] This memoir received much publicity in Europe, mainly because of de Sacy's association with it. Rousseau also supplied some information to Europeans about the Persian Ismailis. He had visited that country in 1807–1808 as part of an official French delegation sent to the court of the contemporary Qājār monarch, Fatḥ ʿAlī Shāh (r. 1797–1834). Rousseau was surprised to find out that there were still many Ismailis in Persia and that they had their Imam, Shāh Khalīl Allāh, a descendant of Ismāʿīl b. Jaʿfar. This imam, he was told, resided in the village of Kahak, near Maḥallāt, and was highly revered by his followers, including those who came regularly from India to receive his blessings.

The first few Ismaili manuscripts to become known to the orientalists also came from Syria, the first region of European interest in the

Ismailis. Here, too, Rousseau played another pioneering role. This diplomat, who was an avid collector of oriental manuscripts, obtained an anonymous Ismaili work from Maṣyāf, one of the major Ismaili centres in Syria. This Arabic manuscript, containing a number of fragments on religious doctrines of the Ismailis, had been procured for Rousseau in 1809. In 1812, as the first instance of its kind, some extracts from this manuscript, as translated by Rousseau himself and communicated to de Sacy, were published in Paris.[10] Subsequently Rousseau sent this Ismaili source to the Société Asiatique in Paris, and its full Arabic text was later published, together with its French translation, by Stanislas Guyard (1846–1884).[11] A few years later, Guyard published the text and translation of yet another Ismaili work, the first such source containing historical information.[12] This Arabic manuscript on the life and the miraculous deeds of Rāshid al-Dīn Sinān, composed around 1324, had been recovered in Syria in 1848 by the dragoman of the Prussian consulate Joseph Catafago and then sent to Paris. Meanwhile, a few other Ismaili texts of Syrian provenance had been acquired by a Protestant missionary in Syria, and sent to distant America.[13] These early discoveries of the Ismaili sources were, however, few and far between.

Meanwhile, de Sacy himself had written an important memoir on the so-called Assassins, which he read before the Institut de France in May 1809.[14] In this memoir, de Sacy also solved the mystery of the name 'Assassins', explaining its connection to the Arabic word *ḥashīsh*. He was able to cite Arabic texts in which the Nizārī Ismailis were called *ḥashīshī* (plural, *ḥashīshiyya*). This name had been applied to the Nizārī Ismailis as a term of abuse, designating people of lax morality. It was the pejorative name that gave rise to imaginative tales fabricated by the Crusader circles. De Sacy and other orientalists also correctly identified the so-called Assassins as the Ismailis representing a Shiʿi Muslim community. However, the orientalists, too, were still obliged to study the Ismailis on the basis of the hostile Sunni sources and the fictitious occidental accounts of the Crusader circles. As a result, de Sacy and other orientalists endorsed unwittingly, and to various degrees, the anti-Ismaili 'black legend' of the medieval Sunni polemicists and the Assassin legends of the Crusaders.

As a background to the story of the Druzes, de Sacy also concerned himself with the early history of the Ismailis, without having had access to any Ismaili writings. In his major work on the Druzes, which was his final work, he devoted a long introduction to the origins and early history of the Ismailis.[15] There, de Sacy based himself exclusively on the Sunni polemical accounts of Ibn Rizām and Akhū Muḥsin, as preserved by al-Nuwayrī. He, therefore, echoed their malicious views and presented the controversial ʿAbd Allāh b. Maymūn al-Qaddāḥ as the real founder of Ismailism,[16] amongst other baseless accusations.

De Sacy's treatment of early Ismailism, and the Nizārī Ismailis of the Alamūt times, set the general frame within which other orientalists of the 19th century studied the medieval history of the Ismailis. It was under such circumstances that misrepresentation and plain fiction came to permeate the first European book devoted exclusively to the history of the Persian Nizārī Ismailis of the Alamūt period. The Austrian orientalist-diplomat author of this book, Joseph von Hammer-Purgstall (1774–1856), endorsed Marco Polo's narrative in its entirety as well as the medieval defamations levelled against the Ismailis by their Sunni detractors. Published in German in 1818, this book achieved great success in Europe and was soon translated into French and English.[17] This book continued to serve as the standard history of the Nizārī Ismailis at least until the 1930s.

With a few exceptions, European scholarship made little further progress in the study of the Ismailis during the second half of the 19th century, while Ismaili sources still remained generally inaccessible to orientalists. The outstanding exception was provided by the historical studies of the French orientalist Charles François Defrémery (1822–1883), who collected a large number of references from various Muslim chronicles on the Ismailis of Persia and Syria, and published the results in two long articles.[18]

The Ismailis continued to be misrepresented to various degrees by orientalists such as Michael J. de Goeje (1836–1909), who nevertheless made valuable contributions to the study of the Qarmaṭīs of Bahrayn, but whose erroneous interpretation of Fatimid-Qarmaṭī relations was generally adopted.[19] There had also appeared for the first time a history of the Fatimids by Ferdinand Wüstenfeld (1808–1899), which was a compilation from a range of Arabic chronicles without any extracts from Ismaili sources. The unsatisfactory state of the field is clearly attested to by the fact that the next Western book on the Fatimids, written some four decades later by De Lacy Evans O'Leary (1872–1957) of Bristol University, still did not cite any Ismaili sources.[20]

Meanwhile, Paul Casanova (1861–1926), who had already published some numismatic notes on the Nizārī Ismailis of the Alamūt period,[21] and later produced some important studies on the Fatimids, announced in 1898 his discovery of a manuscript at the Bibliothèque Nationale, Paris, containing the last section of the *Rasā'il Ikhwān al-Ṣafā'* (The Epistles of the Brethren of Purity).[22] This French orientalist was the first European scholar to recognise the Ismaili affiliation of this famous encyclopaedic work. Earlier, the German orientalist Friedrich Dieterici (1821–1903) had published many parts of the *Rasā'il*, with a German translation, without realising their Ismaili connection.[23]

Other types of information on the Ismailis had now started to appear. In 1895, whilst travelling in Syria, the Swiss orientalist Max van Berchem (1863–1921) read and studied almost all of the epigraphic evidence of the Ismaili fortresses in Syria.[24] As noted above, P. Casanova was the first orientalist to produce a study on the Ismaili coins minted at Alamūt. Much information on the Ismaili Khojas of South Asia and the forty-sixth Ismaili Imam, Ḥasan ʿAlī Shāh Aga Khan I (1817–1881), also became available in the course of a complicated legal case investigated by the High Court of Bombay, known as the Aga Khan Case, which culminated in the famous judgement of 1866.[25] All these developments, together with general progress in the publication of new Muslim sources and new interpretations of the old ones, were continuously preparing the ground, in broad terms, for a revaluation of the Ismailis as well.

In the opening decades of the 20th century, more Ismaili manuscripts preserved in Yemen and Central Asia began to be recovered, though still on a limited basis. In 1903, Giuseppe Caprotti (1869–1919), an Italian merchant who had spent some three decades in Yemen, brought a collection of Arabic manuscripts from Yemen to Italy and sold it to the Ambrosiana Library in Milan. The Ambrosiana's Caprotti Collection of codices was later found, by its cataloguer Eugenio Griffini (1878–1925), to contain several Ismaili texts.[26] Meanwhile, some Russian scholars and officials had become aware of the existence of Ismaili groups within the Central Asian regions of the Russian empire, and they now made attempts to establish contacts with them and study their teachings. These Central Asian Ismailis, who lived mainly in the mountainous region of Badakhshān, belonged exclusively to the Nizārī branch of Ismailism. The Ismailis of Badakhshān, now divided by the Oxus River (Āmū Daryā) between Tajikistan and Afghanistan, have preserved the literary heritage of the Nizārīs produced during the Alamūt period and subsequent centuries, all written in the Persian language.

Since 1895, the area lying north and east of the Panj River (a major headwater of the Oxus) had come under the effective control of Russian military officials, although according to the determination of the Anglo-Russian boundary commission of the same year, the region situated on the right bank of the Panj had been formally handed over to the Khanate of Bukhārā, while designating the left-bank region as Afghan territory. At any rate, Russians now travelled freely in the Upper Oxus region. Count Aleksey A. Bobrinskiy (1861–1938), a Russian scholar who studied the inhabitants of the Wakhān and Ishkāshim districts of Badakhshān in 1898, published the first account of the Ismailis of those parts.[27] Subsequently, in 1914, Ivan I. Zarubin (1887–1964), the eminent Russian ethnologist and expert in Tajik dialects, acquired a small collection of Persian Ismaili manuscripts from the western Pamir districts of Shughnān and Rūshān, which was presented two years later to the Asiatic Museum of the Imperial Russian Academy of Sciences in St. Petersburg. This collection was later catalogued by Wladimir Ivanow (1886–1970), a leading pioneer of modern Ismaili studies who was then Assistant Keeper of the oriental manuscripts at the Asiatic Museum.[28] In 1918, the Asiatic Museum received a second collection of Persian Ismaili manuscripts. These texts had been acquired a few years earlier, from the Upper Oxus region, by Aleksandr A. Semenov (1873–1958),[29] a Russian pioneer in Ismaili studies from Tashkent. He had already studied certain beliefs of the Shughnānī Ismailis whom he had first visited in 1898.[30] These Ismaili manuscripts of Central Asian provenance, comprising less than twenty genuine items, then constituted the largest holding of Ismaili manuscripts in any European library; both collections are currently housed at the Russian Institute of Oriental Manuscripts in St. Petersburg, which has absorbed the collections of the Asiatic Museum and other oriental institutions of the former Academy of Sciences of the USSR (Akademiia Nauk SSSR).[31]

By the 1920s, the knowledge of the orientalists on Ismaili literature was still very limited as reflected in the first Western bibliography of Ismaili works compiled by Louis Massignon (1883–1962), the foremost French pioneer in Shiʿi studies.[32] Little further progress was made in the study of the Ismailis during the 1920s, aside from the publication of some of the works of the Persian Ismaili *dāʿī*, poet and philosopher Nāṣir-i Khusraw (d. after 462/1070), including his *Wajh-i dīn* based on the manuscript in the Zarubin Collection of the Asiatic Museum,[33] and a few studies by Semenov and Ivanow.[34] Indeed, by 1927, when the entry 'Ismāʿīlīya' by Clément Huart (1854–1926), appeared in the second volume of *The Encyclopaedia of Islam*, European orientalist studies on the subject still essentially displayed the misrepresentations of the Crusaders and the defamations of the medieval Sunni polemicists. Even an eminent orientalist of the stature of Edward G. Browne (1862–1926), who covered the Ismailis only in a tangential manner in his magisterial four-volume survey of Persian literature, merely reiterated the standard orientalist tales of his predecessors on the Nizārī Ismailis, who had also continued to be referred to as the Assassins, a medieval and pejorative misnomer.[35] Be that as it may, by the end of the 1920s, the ground had been broadly prepared for the initiation of a totally new phase in the study of the Ismailis.

Phase II: Commencement of Modern Scholarship, 1931–1945

This phase marked the initial stage of modern scholarship in Ismaili studies, founded on the recovery and study of genuine Ismaili sources on an unprecedented scale. This phase was initiated in the early 1930s in Bombay, where significant collections of Ismaili manuscripts have been preserved. Wladimir Ivanow was the driving force behind this breakthrough. It is no exaggeration to claim that perhaps in no other area of Islamic studies has the contribution of a single individual been so consequential as that of Ivanow in the context of modern Ismaili studies.[36]

Ivanow had come into contact with Ismaili manuscripts while working in the Asiatic Museum. He had also met some Persian Ismailis in 1912, when he was conducting fieldwork in Khurāsān on Persian dialects, his original field of study. At any rate, he left Russia in 1918 following the Russian Revolution, and eventually settled down in India. In 1930 he established contact with members of the Ismaili Khoja community in Bombay, offering his scholarly services to them. In due course, he was introduced to the forty-eighth and then current Ismaili Imam, Sultan Muhammad Shah, Aga Khan III (1885–1957), who approved of Ivanow's research proposal. In January 1931, the Ismaili Imam formally commissioned Ivanow to start investigating the history and teachings of the Ismailis on the basis of their literary heritage. Henceforth, systematic recovery of the hidden literary treasures of the Ismailis became the prime concern of Ivanow, who was to spend the next three decades in Bombay, where members of both branches of the Ismaili community, the Nizārīs known as Khojas and the Ṭayyibī Mustaʿlians known as Bohras, lived and possessed collections of manuscripts. Ivanow's formal association with the Nizārī Ismaili community also enabled him to gain access to the Persian texts of that community, preserved mainly in Central Asia, Afghanistan and Persia. However, his friendship with a number of Ismaili Bohra scholars, who had rich collections of manuscripts, also put him in touch with the Arabic Ismaili literature of the Fatimid period and later Ṭayyibī times. These Bohra scholars also played key roles in ushering in the modern phase of Ismaili studies. In this context, three Bohra scholars who were educated in England, should be mentioned: Asaf A. A. Fyzee (1899–1981), Ḥusayn F. al-Hamdānī (1901–1962) and Zāhid ʿAlī (1888–1958).

Professor Fyzee, who belonged to the most learned Sulaymānī Ṭayyibī family of Bohras in India and had studied law at the University of Cambridge, possessed a valuable collection of Ismaili manuscripts, which he later donated to the Bombay University Library.[37] Fyzee made these texts readily available to Ivanow and other scholars. He also made modern scholars aware of the existence of an independent Ismaili school of jurisprudence (*madhhab*) through his own research and numerous publications,[38] including the critical edition of al-Qāḍī al-Nuʿmān's *Daʿāʾim al-Islām*, the legal code of the Fatimid state which is still used by the Ṭayyibī Ismailis.

Ḥusayn al-Hamdānī, belonging to a prominent Dāʾūdī Ṭayyibī family of scholars with Yemeni origins, had received his doctorate in 1931 from the School of Oriental (and African) Studies in London, where he studied under Professor Hamilton A. R. Gibb (1895–1971). In addition to a number of studies of his own, he made his vast collection of manuscripts, originally preserved in Yemen and then relocated to Gujarat, available to Ivanow and numerous other scholars, such as Paul Kraus (1904–1944) and Louis Massignon, who were then becoming interested in Ismaili studies. In fact, he played a key role in opening up this emerging field to Western scholarship.[39] Ḥusayn al-Hamdānī's collection of manuscripts was distributed amongst some of his descendants, and a major portion came into the possession of his son, Professor Abbas Hamdani (1926–2019), who recently donated these manuscripts to The Institute of Ismaili Studies in London.[40]

Zāhid ʿAlī, who hailed from another learned Dāʾūdī Ṭayyibī Bohra family in India, received his doctorate from the University of Oxford, where he prepared a critical edition of the *Dīwān* of poetry of Ibn Hāniʾ (d. 362/973), the foremost Ismaili poet of North Africa, for his thesis under the supervision of Professor David S. Margoliouth (1858–1940). He was also the first author in modern times to have written, in Urdu, a scholarly history of the Fatimids as well as a work on Ismaili doctrines on the basis of a variety of Ismaili sources.[41] The Zāhid ʿAlī Collection of some 226 Arabic Ismaili manuscripts, was also donated in 1997 by his family to The Institute of Ismaili Studies,[42] where these texts are now made available to scholars worldwide.

It was under such circumstances that Ivanow published in 1933 the first detailed catalogue of Ismaili works, citing some 700 separate titles.[43] These sources, written by a multitude of Ismaili authors, such as Abū Ḥātim al-Rāzī (d. 322/934), Jaʿfar b. Manṣūr al-Yaman (d. *ca.* 346/957), Abū Yaʿqūb al-Sijistānī (d. after 361/971), al-Qāḍī al-Nuʿmān (d. 363/974), Ḥamīd al-Dīn al-Kirmānī (d. after 411/1020), al-Muʾayyad fi'l-Dīn al-Shīrāzī (d. 470/1078), and Nāṣir-i Khusraw (d. after 462/1070), and many later authors who lived in Yemen, Syria, Persia and other regions, attested to the hitherto unknown richness and diversity of Ismaili literary and intellectual traditions. The initiation of modern scholarship in Ismaili studies may indeed be traced to the publication of this very catalogue, which provided for the first time a scientific framework for research in this new field of Islamic studies.

Recognising the importance of institutional support for Ismaili studies and publications, in the same year (1933) Ivanow founded in Bombay the Islamic Research Association, with the collaboration of Asaf Fyzee and a few other Ismaili friends. The Ismaili Imam, Aga

Khan III, acted as the patron of this institution. Four of Ivanow's own earliest editions of Persian Nizārī Ismaili texts appeared in 1933, in lithograph form, in this institution's series of publications. Subsequently, Ivanow focused for a while on the early history of the Ismailis, while editing several more Arabic and Persian texts, including the enigmatic *Umm al-kitāb*, which has been preserved in an archaic form of Persian by the Ismailis of Badakhshān.[44] Ivanow's early Ismaili studies culminated in a substantial work on the early Ismailis and the Fatimids, published in 1942 in the series of the Islamic Research Association.[45] This publication also contained a number of extracts from Arabic Ismaili texts edited and translated for the first time here.

In his research, Ivanow supplemented literary sources with archaeological and epigraphic evidence. In this context, in 1937 he discovered the tombs of several Nizārī Ismaili Imams in the villages of Anjudān and Kahak, in central Persia, enabling him to fill certain gaps in the post-Alamūt history of that community.[46] In fact, it was Ivanow himself who identified what he termed the 'Anjudān revival' in the religious and literary activities of the Nizārī Ismailis—a period stretching from the middle of the 9th/15th century to the late 11th/17th century. Ivanow also embarked on several archaeological surveys of Alamūt and other Ismaili fortresses of Persia.[47] By the time Ivanow's article 'Ismāʿīlīya' was published in 1936 in the supplementary volume to the first edition of *The Encyclopaedia of Islam*, the Ismailis were already treated with much greater accuracy by contemporary scholars; the modern scholarship in Ismailis studies had now clearly commenced.

Phase III: Consolidation of Modern Scholarship, 1946–1977

This was the phase of consolidation and further progress in modern Ismaili studies, building on the foundations created in Phase II. This phase started with the establishment of the Ismaili Society in 1946 in Bombay, which provided further institutional impetus to this field. This institution, too, was created through the efforts of W. Ivanow and under the patronage of Aga Khan III. By contrast to the mandate of the Islamic Research Association, the Ismaili Society would exclusively promote research on all aspects of Ismaili history, thought and literature.[48] The Ismaili Society's various series of publications, under the editorship of Ivanow, were devoted mostly to his own monographs as well as editions and translations of mainly Persian Nizārī Ismaili texts. In addition to publishing the Ismaili works of Naṣīr al-Dīn al-Ṭūsī (d. 672/1274), dating to the late Alamūt period, Ivanow now recovered and published several significant texts of the Anjudān period in Ismaili history, including the *Pandiyāt-i javānmardī*, containing the sermons of Imam Mustanṣir bi'llāh (d. 885/1480), as well as works of Abū Isḥāq Quhistānī (d. after 904/1498) and Khayrkhwāh-i Harātī (d. after 960/1553). It was also Ivanow who, for the first time, classified Ismaili history in terms of several main phases in a brief historical survey published in 1952, representing the first scholarly work of its kind.[49]

During this phase, Ivanow also acquired a large number of Arabic and Persian Ismaili manuscripts for the Ismaili Society's Library. These resources were transferred, in the 1980s, to The Institute of Ismaili Studies Library in London. Meanwhile, numerous Ismaili texts had begun to be critically edited and studied, preparing the ground for continued scholarship in the field.

Ivanow generously shared his knowledge as well as the manuscript resources of the Ismaili Society with other scholars. In particular, he established a close working relationship with Henry Corbin (1903–1978), the French philosopher and Islamicist who commuted regularly between Paris and Tehran, where he had founded the Iranology Department of the Institut Franco-Iranien. As attested in the correspondence exchanged between these two scholars, during 1947–1966,[50] Ivanow readily prepared (handwritten) copies of the Ismaili manuscripts at his disposal in Bombay and sent them to Corbin, who launched his own 'Bibliothèque Iranienne' series of publications, in which several Arabic and Persian Ismaili works appeared simultaneously in Tehran and Paris.[51] Corbin represented a new generation of scholars with interests in Ismaili studies. Another early member of this group was Muḥammad Kāmil Ḥusayn (1901–1961), the Egyptian scholar who edited several Arabic Ismaili texts of the Fatimid period in his 'Silsilat Makhṭūṭāt al-Fāṭimiyyīn' series, published in Cairo. He also co-edited the *dāʿī* Ḥamīd al-Dīn al-Kirmānī's chief work, *Rāḥat al-ʿaql*, written in the tradition of 'philosophical theology' of the Iranian school, for the Ismaili Society.[52] It was due to Ivanow's foundational work on the Nizārī Ismailis that Marshall Hodgson

(1922–1968) was enabled to write the first scholarly history of the Nizārī Ismailis of the Alamūt period. This book, published in 1955, finally replaced von Hammer's legendary account written in 1818.[53] Indeed, Ivanow himself may doubtless be considered as the founder of modern Nizārī Ismaili studies.

Ivanow indefatigably recovered, studied and published a good portion of the extant Persian literature of the Nizārī Ismailis, as well as maintaining systematic efforts to recover other types of Ismaili manuscripts. At the same time, Ivanow continued to promote research in the field. By 1963, when he published an expanded edition of his Ismaili catalogue, Ivanow had identified a few hundred more Ismaili titles,[54] while the field of Ismaili studies as a whole had witnessed incredible progress. Meanwhile, others representing yet another generation of scholars, such as Bernard Lewis (1916–2018), Samuel M. Stern (1920–1964), Abbas Hamdani (1926–2019) and Wilferd Madelung, were entering the field with their own original studies,[55] especially on the early Ismailis and their relations with the dissident Qarmaṭīs.[56]

Meanwhile, a number of Russian scholars, such as Lyudmila V. Stroeva (1910–1993) and Andrey E. Bertel's (1926–1995), had maintained the earlier interests of their compatriots in Ismaili studies, though conducting their investigations within narrow Marxist frameworks. Some of these scholars were also involved in acquiring large collections of Persian manuscripts from the Badakhshān region of Central Asia.[57] At the same time, ʿĀrif Tāmir (1921–1998), belonging to the small Muḥammad-Shāhī Nizārī community of Syria, was making a number of Ismaili texts of Syrian provenance available to scholars, albeit often in faulty editions, similarly to his compatriot Muṣṭafā Ghālib (1923–1981), who hailed from the Qāsim-Shāhī branch of the Nizārī Ismaili community. Meanwhile, several Egyptian scholars, who were interested in the medieval history of their country, notably Ḥasan Ibrāhīm Ḥasan (1892–1968), Jamāl al-Dīn al-Shayyāl (1911–1967), Muḥammad J. Surūr (1911–1992), ʿAbd al-Munʿim Mājid (1920–1999), and more recently Ayman F. Sayyid, made further contributions to Fatimid studies, complementing Ismaili studies in general. After the pioneering efforts of Gaston Wiet (1887–1971) and a few other Westerners, the Fatimid period of Islamic history was now studied also by a number of European scholars, such as Marius Canard (1888–1982)[58] and Claude Cahen (1909–1991), drawing on Ismaili-Fatimid sources. W. Madelung summed up the state of the field in his seminal article 'Ismāʿīliyya', published in 1973 in the new (second) edition of *The Encyclopaedia of Islam*. The progress in the recovery of Ismaili texts during 1933–1977, which had made the astonishing breakthrough in the field possible, is well reflected in Professor Ismail K. Poonawala's monumental catalogue published in 1977, which identifies more than 1,300 titles written by some 200 authors.[59]

Phase IV: Continuing Progress, 1977–Present

Progress in Ismaili studies has proceeded at an unprecedented rate during the last four decades, as more Ismaili sources are recovered from Central Asia, and other regions, and an increasing number of them are systematically edited and studied by more newcomers to the field, such as Ismail K. Poonawala, Heinz Halm, Paul E. Walker and Daniel de Smet, as well as the established scholars. Building on the cumulative results of modern scholarship in the field, the present writer was able to compile the first comprehensive history of the Ismailis, covering all branches of the community and all regions where they live.[60] In this phase, a key role is currently performed by The Institute of Ismaili Studies, founded in 1977 in London by the forty-ninth and present Ismaili Imam, H. H. Prince Karim Aga Khan IV.[61] This institution also holds nearly 3,000 manuscripts in Arabic, Persian and Indic languages, representing the largest collection of its kind at least in the West. The Institute also continues to acquire, in a structured fashion, more manuscripts from Tajik and Afghan regions of Badakhshān, while its holdings of manuscripts have been augmented significantly by several donations, including the Zāhid ʿAlī and Hamdani collections. The Institute makes these manuscript resources, now kept in its Ismaili Special Collections Unit, readily available to scholars worldwide, contributing to further progress in the field.

The Institute of Ismaili Studies is already serving as the central point of reference for Ismaili scholarship, making its own contributions through various programmes of research and publications. Amongst these, particular mention should be made of the 'Ismaili Texts and Translations Series', in which critical editions of Arabic and Persian texts are published together with English translations and contextualising introductions. The Institute has also embarked on producing a complete critical edition and annotated English translation of the *Rasā'il Ikhwān al-Ṣafā'* (Epistles of the Brethren of Purity), launched in 2008. More than twenty scholars participate in this 20-volume project. Earlier, Professor Yves Marquet (1911–2008) had produced a vast corpus of studies on this enigmatic work, whose authorship and date of composition are still subjects for debate. Building on his work, as well as the contributions of her own teacher Alessandro Bausani (1921–1988), Professor Carmela Baffioni is a key member of the Institute's team of scholars currently engaged in this project. Amongst the various regional Ismaili traditions that have received scholarly attention in recent decades, particular mention may be made of the Satpanth tradition of the Ismaili Khojas of South Asian origins, as reflected in their *ginān* devotional literature. Here Professors Azim Nanji and Ali Asani have made major contributions.

Many Ismaili texts have now been published in critical editions, while an increasing number of secondary studies on various aspects of Ismaili history and thought have been produced by at least three successive generations of scholars, as documented in this author's bibliography of the Ismaili sources and studies.[62] With these developments, based on the increased accessibility of Ismaili textual materials to a growing number of scholars, the sustained scholarly study of the Ismailis, which by the final decade of W. Ivanow's life in the 1960s had already greatly deconstructed the anti-Ismaili tales of medieval times, promises to dissipate the remaining misrepresentations of the Ismailis rooted in either the 'hostility' or the 'imaginative ignorance' of the earlier generations.

NOTES

1 Ibn Rizām's anti-Ismaili treatise has not survived, but it was used extensively a few decades later by another polemicist, Sharīf Abu'l-Ḥusayn Muḥammad b. ʿAlī, better known as Akhū Muḥsin. The latter's own anti-Ismaili work, written around 372/982, has not survived either. These early anti-Ismaili accounts have been preserved fragmentarily by several later authors, notably al-Nuwayrī (d. 733/1333), Ibn al-Dawādārī (d. after 736/1335) and al-Maqrīzī (d. 845/1442). See, for instance, Taqī al-Dīn Aḥmad b. ʿAlī al Maqrīzī, *Ittiʿāẓ al-ḥunafā'*, ed. Ayman F. Sayyid (Damascus, 2010), vol. 1, pp. 20–27, 173–237; partial English translation, *Towards a Shiʿi Mediterranean Empire: Fatimid Egypt and the Founding of Cairo*, tr. Shainool Jiwa (London, 2009), pp. 122–187.

2 Abū Manṣūr ʿAbd al-Qāhir b. Ṭāhir al-Baghdādī, *al-Farq bayn al-firaq*, ed. M. Badr (Cairo, 1328/1910), pp. 265–299.

3 See F. Daftary, 'Ḥasan-i Ṣabbāḥ and the Origins of the Nizārī Isma'ili Movement', in F. Daftary, ed., *Mediaeval Isma'ili History and Thought* (Cambridge, 1996), pp. 181–204; reprinted in his *Ismailis in Medieval Muslim Societies* (London, 2005), pp. 124–148.

4 Abū Ḥāmid Muḥammad al-Ghazālī, *Faḍā'iḥ al-bāṭiniyya*, ed. 'Abd al-Raḥmān Badawī (Cairo, 1964), especially pp. 21–36; English translation, Richard J. McCarthy in his *Freedom and Fulfillment* (Boston, 1980), pp. 175–286; see also F. Daftary, *Ismaili Literature: A Bibliography of Sources and Studies* (London, 2004), p. 177.

5 Niẓām al-Mulk, Abū 'Alī Ḥasan b. 'Alī, *Siyar al-mulūk (Siyāsat-nāma)*, ed. H. Darke (2nd ed., Tehran, 1347 Sh./1968), pp. 282–311; English translation, H. Darke, *The Book of Government; or, Rules for Kings* (2nd ed., London, 1978), pp. 208–231.

6 For a survey of these tales, see F. Daftary, *The Assassin Legends: Myths of the Isma'ilis* (London, 1994), pp. 88–127.

7 Marco Polo, *The Book of Ser Marco Polo, The Venetian, Concerning the Kingdoms and Marvels of the East*, ed. and tr. H. Yule, 3rd revised ed. by H. Cordier (London, 1929), vol. 1, pp. 139–146.

8 Ismā'īl b. 'Abd al-Rasūl al-Majdū', *Fahrasat al-kutub wa'l-rasā'il*, ed. 'Alī Naqī Munzavī (Tehran, 1344 Sh./1966).

9 J. B. L. J. Rousseau, 'Mémoire sur les Ismaélis et les Nosaïris de Syrie, adressé à M. Silvestre de Sacy', *Annales des Voyages*, 14 (1811), pp. 271–303. This memoir was later incorporated into Rousseau's expanded work entitled *Mémoire sur les trois plus fameuses sectes du Musulmanisme: les Wahabis, les Nosaïris et les Ismaélis* (Paris, 1818), pp. 51 ff.

10 J. B. L. J. Rousseau, 'Extraits d'un livre qui contient la doctrine des Ismaélis', *Annales des Voyages*, 18 (1812), pp. 222–249.

11 *Fragments relatifs à la doctrine des Ismaélis*, ed. and French tr. S. Guyard, in *Notices et extraits des mansucrits de la Bibliothèque Nationale*, 22 (1874), pp. 177–428; also published separately in 1874 in Paris.

12 S. Guyard, 'Un grand maître des Assassins au temps de Saladin', *Journal Asiatique*, 7 série, 9 (1877), pp. 324–489. The hagiographical text here, entitled *Faṣl min al-lafẓ al-sharīf*, and attributed to Sinān, may have been compiled by the Syrian Nizārī Ismaili *da'ī* Abū Firās Shihāb al-Dīn al-Maynaqī (d. 937/1530 or a decade later), or possibly another Abū Firās who lived earlier. See also J. Catafago, 'Lettre de M. Catafago à M. Mohl', *Journal Asiatique*, 4 série, 12 (1848), pp. 72–78, 485–493.

13 Edward S. Salisbury, 'Translation of Two Unpublished Arabic Documents, Relating to the Doctrines of the Ismâ'ilis and other Bâṭinian sects', *Journal of the American Oriental Society*, 2 (1851), pp. 257–324.

14 A. I. Silvestre de Sacy, 'Mémoire sur la dynastie des Assassins, et sur l'étymologie de leur nom', *Mémoires de l'Institut Royal de France*, 4 (1818), pp. 1–84; reprinted in Bryan S. Turner, ed., *Orientalism: Early Sources*, volume I, *Readings in Orientalism* (London, 2000), pp. 118–169. Shorter versions of this memoir were published earlier in the *Moniteur*, 210 (1809), pp. 828–830, and in *Annales des Voyages*, 8 (1809), pp. 325–343. There is a complete English translation of the 1818 version, 'Memoir on the Dynasty of the Assassins, and on the Etymology of their Name', in F. Daftary, *The Assassin Legends*, pp. 129–188.

15 A. I. Silvestre de Sacy, *Exposé de la religion des Druzes* (Paris, 1838), vol. 1, introduction, pp. 20–246. See also de Sacy's 'Recherches sur l'initiation à la secte des Ismaéliens', *Journal Asiatique*, 1 série, 4 (1824), pp. 298–311, 321–331; reprinted in Jean-Claude Frère, *L'ordre des Assassins: Hasan Sabbah, le Vieux de la Montagne et l'Ismaélisme* (Paris, 1973), pp. 261–274.

16 See W. Ivanow, *The Alleged Founder of Ismailism* (Bombay, 1946), and F. Daftary, "Abd Allāh b. Maymūn al-Qaddāḥ', *Encyclopaedia Islamica*, ed. W. Madelung and F. Daftary (Leiden, 2008–), vol. 1, pp. 167–169.

17 J. von Hammer-Purgstall, *Die Geschichte der Assassinen aus Morgenländischen Quellen* (Stuttgart and Tübingen, 1818); English tr. *The History of the Assassins, derived from*

Oriental Sources, tr. O. C. Wood (London, 1835; reprinted, New York, 1968); French translation, *Histoire de l'ordre des Assassins*, tr. J. J. Hellert and P. A. de la Nourais (Paris, 1833; reprinted Paris, 1961). See also F. Daftary, 'Order of the Assassins: J. von Hammer and the Orientalist Misrepresentation of the Nizari Ismailis', *Iranian Studies*, 39 (2006), pp. 71–81; reprinted in F. Daftary, *Ismaili History and Intellectual Traditions* (London and New York, 2018), pp. 212–222.

18 C. F. Defrémery, 'Nouvelles recherches sur les Ismaéliens ou Bathiniens de Syrie, plus connus sous le nom d'Assassins', *Journal Asiatique*, 5 série, 3 (1854), pp. 373–421, and 5 (1855), pp. 5–76, and his 'Essai sur l'histoire des Ismaéliens ou Batiniens de la Perse, plus connus sous le nom d'Assassins', *Journal Asiatique*, 5 série, 8 (1856), pp. 353–387, and 15 (1860), pp. 130–210; this article remained unfinished.

19 M. J. de Goeje, *Mémoire sur les Carmathes du Bahraïn et les Fatimides* (Leiden, 1862; 2nd ed., Leiden, 1886), and his 'La fin de l'empire des Carmathes du Bahraïn', *Journal Asiatique*, 9 série, 5 (1895), pp. 5–30; reprinted in Turner, *Orientalism*, vol. 1, pp. 263–278.

20 De Lacy E. O'Leary, *A Short History of the Fatimid Khalifate* (London, 1923; reprinted, Delhi, 1987).

21 P. Casanova, 'Monnaie des Assassins de Perse', *Revue Numismatique*, 3 series, 11 (1893), pp. 343–352.

22 P. Casanova, 'Notice sur un manuscrit de la secte des Assassins', *Journal Asiatique*, 9 série, 11 (1898), pp. 151–159.

23 See F. Daftary, *Ismaili Literature*, pp. 168, 170–171.

24 M. van Berchem, 'Épigraphie des Assassins de Syrie', *Journal Asiatique*, 9 série, 9 (1897), pp. 453–501; reprinted in his *Opera Minora* (Geneva, 1978), vol. 1, pp. 453–501; also reprinted in Turner, *Orientalism*, vol. 1, pp. 279–309.

25 See Asaf A. A. Fyzee, *Cases in the Muhammadan Law of India and Pakistan* (Oxford, 1965), pp. 504–549; also A. Shodan, *A Question of Community: Religious Groups and Colonial Law* (Calcutta, 1999), pp. 82–116, and T. Purohit, *The Aga Khan Case: Religion and Identity in Colonial India* (Cambridge, MA, 2012), containing controversial views as well as questionable interpretations.

26 E. Griffini, 'Die jüngste ambrosianische Sammlung arabischer Handschriften', *Zeitschrift der Deutschen Morgenländischen Gesellschaft*, 69 (1915), especially pp. 80–88.

27 A. A. Bobrinskiy, 'Sekta Ismailiya v Russkikh i Bukharskikh predelakh Sredney Azii', *Étnograficheskoe Obozrenie*, 2 (1902), pp. 1–20.

28 V. A. Ivanov, 'Ismailitskie rukopisi Aziatskago Muzeya. Sobranie I. Zarubina, 1916 g.', *Bulletin de l'Académie Impériale des Sciences de Russie*, 6 series, 11 (1917), pp. 359–386. See also W. Ivanow, *Fifty Years in the East: The Memoirs of Wladimir Ivanow*, ed. F. Daftary (London, 2015), pp. 47–54.

29 A. A. Semenov, 'Opisanie ismailitskikh rukopisey, sobranni̇̈kh A. A. Semyonovïm', *Bulletin de l'Académie des Sciences de Russie*, 6 series, 12 (1918), pp. 2171–2202.

30 See F. Daftary, *Ismaili Literature*, pp. 381–382.

31 See O. F. Akimushkin et al., *Persidskie i Tadzhiskie rukopisi, Instituta Narodov Azii an SSSR*, ed. N. D. Muklukho-Maklai (Moscow, 1964), vol. 1, pp. 54–55, 208, 259, 313, 356, 530, 541, 600, 608.

32 L. Massignon, 'Esquisse d'une bibliographie Qarmaṭe', in R. A. Nicholson and T. W. Arnold, ed., *A Volume of Oriental Studies Presented to Edward G. Browne on his 60th birthday* (Cambridge, 1922), pp. 329–338; reprinted in L. Massignon, *Opera Minora*, ed. Y. Moubarac (Paris, 1969), vol. 1, pp. 627–639. This bibliography does not include the then recently acquired Ismaili manuscripts of the Asiatic Museum, St. Petersburg.

33 Nāṣir-i Khusraw, *Wajh-i dīn*, ed. M. Ghanīzāda and M. Qazvīnī (Berlin, 1343/1924).

34 See Asaf A. A. Fyzee, 'Materials for an Ismaili Bibliography: 1920–1934', *Journal of the Bombay Branch of the Royal Asiatic Society*, New Series, 11 (1935), pp. 59–65. See also Ivanow, *Fifty Years*, pp. 185–187, and F. Daftary, *Ismaili Literature*, pp. 137, 138, 139, 140.

35 E. G. Browne, *A Literary History of Persia* (London and Cambridge, 1902–1928), vol. 1, pp. 391–415, and vol. 2, pp. 190–211, 453–460.
36 See F. Daftary, 'Bibliography of the Publications of the Late W. Ivanow', *Islamic Culture*, 45 (1971), pp. 55–67; revised and annotated in Ivanow, *Fifty Years*, pp. 185–207; F. Daftary, 'Modern Ismaili Studies and W. Ivanow's Contributions', in Ivanow, *Fifty Years*, pp. 9–36; see also F. Daftary, 'Ivanow, Vladimir', *Encyclopaedia Iranica*, vol. 14, pp. 298–300.
37 See M. Goriawala, *A Descriptive Catalogue of the Fyzee Collection of Ismaili Manuscripts* (Bombay, 1965), describing some 200 manuscripts. See also A. A. A. Fyzee, 'A Collection of Fatimid Manuscripts', in N. N. Gidwani, ed., *Comparative Librarianship: Essays in Honour of Professor D. N. Marshall* (Delhi, 1973), pp. 209–220.
38 See F. Daftary, 'The Bibliography of Asaf A. A. Fyzee', *Indo-Iranica*, 37 (1984), pp. 49–63.
39 See Ḥ. F. al-Hamdānī, 'Some Unknown Ismāʿīlī Authors and their Works', *Journal of the Royal Asiatic Society* (1933), pp. 359–378.
40 F. de Blois, *Arabic, Persian and Gujarati Manuscripts: The Hamdani Collection in the Library of The Institute of Ismaili Studies* (London, 2011). A portion of Ḥusayn al-Hamdānī's collection, which still remains uncatalogued, was donated to the Bombay University Library.
41 See F. Daftary, *Ismaili Literature*, p. 422.
42 D. Cortese, *Arabic Ismaili Manuscripts: The Zāhid ʿAlī Collection in the Library of The Institute of Ismaili Studies* (London, 2003).
43 W. Ivanow, *A Guide to Ismaili Literature* (London, 1933). See also P. Kraus, 'La bibliographie Ismaëlienne de W. Ivanow', *Revue des Études Islamiques*, 6 (1932), pp. 483–490, and Ivanow, *Fifty Years*, pp. 80–96.
44 *Ummu'l-kitāb*, ed. W. Ivanow, in *Der Islam*, 23 (1936), pp. 1–132. Ivanow's edition was translated into Italian by Pio Filippani-Ronconi (Naples, 1966; reprinted, Rome and San Demetrico Corone, 2016).
45 W. Ivanow, *Ismaili Tradition Concerning the Rise of the Fatimids* (London, etc., 1942).
46 W. Ivanow, 'Tombs of Some Persian Ismaili Imams', *Journal of the Bombay Branch of the Royal Asiatic Society*, New Series, 14 (1938), pp. 49–62.
47 For the earliest results of these efforts, see W. Ivanow, 'Alamut', *The Geographical Journal*, 77 (1931), pp. 38–45, and his 'Some Ismaili Strongholds in Persia', *Islamic Culture*, 12 (1938), pp. 383–396.
48 F. Daftary, 'Anǰojman-e Esmāʿīlī', *Encyclopaedia Iranica*, vol. 2, p. 84.
49 W. Ivanow, *Brief Survey of the Evolution of Ismailism* (Leiden, 1952).
50 Sabine Schmidtke, ed., *Correspondance Corbin—Ivanow: Lettres échangées entre Henry Corbin et Vladimir Ivanow de 1947 à 1966* (Paris, 1999).
51 See Daniel de Smet, 'Henry Corbin et études Ismaéliennes', in M. A. Amir-Moezzi et al., ed., *Henry Corbin, Philosophe et sagesses des religions du livre* (Turnhout, 2005), pp. 105–118, and D. Shayegan, 'Corbin, Henry', *Encyclopaedia Iranica*, vol. 6, pp. 268–272.
52 Ḥamīd al-Dīn Aḥmad b. ʿAbd Allāh al-Kirmānī, *Rāḥat al-ʿaql*, ed. M. K. Ḥusayn and M. M. Ḥilmī (Cairo, 1953).
53 Marshall G. S. Hodgson, *The Order of Assassins: The Struggle of the Early Nizārī Ismāʿīlīs against the Islamic World* (The Hague, 1955; repr. New York, 1980; repr. Philadelphia, 2005). This book, mislabelled as admitted subsequently by the author himself, was based partially on Hodgson's doctoral thesis submitted to the University of Chicago in 1951. See also M. Hodgson, 'The Ismāʿīlī State', in *The Cambridge History of Iran*: Volume 5, *The Saljuq and Mongol Periods*, ed. John A. Boyle (Cambridge, 1968), pp. 422–482.
54 W. Ivanow, *Ismaili Literature: A Bibliographical Survey* (Tehran, 1963).
55 See Daftary, *Ismaili Literature*, pp. 285–287, 326–329, 332–334 and 394–398. See also J. D. Latham and H. W. Mitchell, 'The Bibliography of S. M. Stern', *Journal of Semitic Studies*, 15 (1970), pp. 226–238; reprinted with additions in S. M. Stern, *Hispano-Arabic*

Strophic Poetry: Studies by Samuel Miklos Stern, ed. L. P. Harvey (Oxford, 1974), pp. 231–245, and F. Daftary, 'Bibliography of the Works of Wilferd Madelung', in F. Daftary and J. W. Meri, ed., *Culture and Memory in Medieval Islam: Essays in Honour of Wilferd Madelung* (London, 2003), pp. 5–40.

56 In particular, see S. M. Stern, 'Ismāʿīlīs and Qarmaṭians', in *L'élaboration de l'Islam* (Paris, 1961), pp. 99–108; reprinted with several other relevant works in his *Studies in Early Ismāʿīlism* (Jerusalem and Leiden, 1983); W. Madelung, 'Fatimiden und Baḥrainqarmaṭen', *Der Islam*, 34 (1959), pp. 34–88; English translation (slightly revised), 'The Fatimids and the Qarmaṭīs of Baḥrayn', in F. Daftary, ed., *Mediaeval Ismaʿili History and Thought* (Cambridge, 1996), pp. 21–73; his 'Das Imamat in der frühen ismailitischen Lehre', *Der Islam*, 37 (1961), pp. 43–135; reprinted in W. Madelung, *Studies in Medieval Shiʿism*, ed. S. Schmidtke (Farnham, Surrey, 2012), article VII; English translation by Patricia Crone, 'The Imamate in Early Ismaili Doctrine', *Shii Studies Review*, 2 (2018), pp. 62–155. The two long articles by Madelung cited here were based on his doctoral thesis, written under the supervision of Professor Bertold Spuler (1911–1990) at the University of Hamburg, from which he received his doctorate in 1957. See also F. Daftary, 'Samuel Stern and Early Ismāʿīlism', *Journal of Modern Jewish Studies*, 20 (2021), pp. 469–481.

57 See, for instance, Andrey E. Bertel's and M. Bakoev, *Alfavitnïy katalog rukopisey obnaruzhennïkh v Gorno-Badakhshanskoy Avtonomnoy Oblasti ékspeditsiey 1959–1963 gg. / Alphabetic Catalogue of Manuscripts found by 1959–1963 Expedition in Gorno-Badakhshān Autonomous Region*, ed. B. G. Gafurov and A. M. Mirzoev (Moscow, 1967).

58 F. Daftary, 'Marius Canard (1888–1982): A Bio-bibliographical Notice', *Arabica*, 33 (1986), pp. 251–262.

59 I. K. Poonawala, *Biobibliography of Ismāʿīlī Literature* (Malibu, CA, 1977). Since then, Professor Poonawala has identified many additional titles in the course of his ongoing efforts to produce a second edition of this standard work of reference.

60 F. Daftary, *The Ismāʿīlīs: Their History and Doctrines* (Cambridge, 1990; 2nd ed., Cambridge, 2007).

61 See Paul E. Walker, 'Institute of Ismaili Studies', *Encyclopaedia Iranica*, vol. 12, pp. 164–166.

62 F. Daftary, *Ismaili Literature: A Bibliography of Sources and Studies* (London, 2004).

2

Husain Hamdani, Paul Kraus, and a Suitcase Full of Manuscripts

François de Blois

The purpose of this chapter is to give a brief overview of my work on an edition of the correspondence between Paul Kraus and Husain Hamdani. I will first introduce these two famous scholars, and then share some preliminary observations on the letters exchanged between them.

Husain Hamdani[1] belonged to an eminent scholarly family of the Dāʾūdī Bohra community in Western India. The family's Indian presence can be traced back to ʿAlī b. Saʿīd al-Yaʿburī al-Hamdānī, who was born in the Ḥarāz region of the Yemen, an old Ismaili stronghold, in about 1718. At the invitation of the 39th *dāʿī*, Ibrāhīm Wajīh al-Dīn, ʿAlī b. Saʿīd emigrated to India around the middle of the 18th century. His son Ibrāhīm, his grandson Fayḍ Allāh, and especially his great-grandson Muḥammad ʿAlī were all prominent religious scholars and educators within the small and secretive Dāʾūdī community.

In the middle of the 19th century the Hamdani family got caught up in a controversy within the community. The 46th *dāʿī*, Muḥammad Badr al-Dīn died in 1840 without apparently naming a successor. The leadership of the community was assumed by ʿAbd al-Qādir Najm al-Dīn, but some of the *ʿulamāʾ* questioned his legitimacy. The division was kept under wraps for nearly half a century, only to come out in public at the time of Ṭāhir Sayf al-Dīn, who was declared *dāʿī* in 1915, and who bolstered his claim to be leader of the Dāʾūdī community in a court case that went as far as the Privy Council in London. Fayḍ Allāh b. Muḥammad ʿAlī al-Hamdānī testified against him, and as a result he and his entire family were ejected from the Dāʾūdī community and ostracised. Together with a few other families they regrouped as the Reformist denomination.

Fayḍ Allāh's elder son, ʿAbd al-Ḥusayn, or, as he preferred to call himself, plain Husain Hamdani, was born in Surat in 1901, and experienced the bitter split in the community as a young man. He received a traditional religious education from his father, but then went on to complete a Master's degree at Bombay University, one of the first Bohras to receive a modern secular education. After finishing his MA he decided to acquire a doctorate in Arabic and Islamic studies in England. He set off from Bombay by sea, passed through the Suez Canal, stopped off for a while in Egypt, and arrived in England in October 1928. His original plan had been to study in Oxford, but for some reason this did not materialise, so he inscribed in the School of Oriental (now Oriental and African) Studies, London, where H. A. R. Gibb agreed to be his supervisor. He finished his degree in 1931 with an edition and study of an important Ismaili esoteric treatise, the *Zahr al-maʿānī* by the 15th-century Yemeni author and *dāʿī* ʿImād al-Dīn Idrīs; unfortunately this edition was never published.

As material for his thesis, Husain Hamdani brought with him from India not only at least one manuscript of the *Zahr al-maʿānī*, but what must have been a very large number of Ismaili manuscripts of works from the pre-Fatimid, Fatimid, Yemeni and Indian periods. It is important to realise that up until then all of these works were totally unknown to international scholarship and were treated as top-secret esoteric writings both by the Reformists and by the followers of the contested *dāʿī*.

Husain Hamdani returned to India in 1931. He came under severe attack from members of his own community for having violated the secrecy of the sectarian writings by showing them to foreign scholars, and even his father showed disapproval and for a while prevented him from consulting the family's collection of manuscripts. Eventually he reconciled with his father and was able to resume his work. He took a number of teaching positions in India before emigrating to Pakistan after the partition of India in 1947. After some unsatisfactory attempts to find a footing in the university system he entered the Pakistan civil service and found a position as an attaché at the Pakistan Embassy in Cairo. Then, in 1950 he took up a teaching position at Cairo's Kulliyāt Dār al-ʿUlūm. He died in Cairo in 1962 at the age of 61.

After his father's death, Abbas Hamdani reassembled a significant portion of the family's collection of manuscripts and generously put them at the disposal of scholars working on Ismaili matters—one thinks in particular of Professor Madelung. Now he has donated the entire collection to The Institute of Ismaili Studies.[2]

During his stay in England Husain Hamdani made several trips to Berlin, then arguably the hub of scholarly and scientific activity in the world, and it was there that he made the acquaintance of another young scholar, the great Arabist Paul Kraus, an acquaintance which quickly blossomed into a very fruitful scholarly collaboration and a deep personal friendship.

Paul Kraus[3] was born in 1904 in Prague, then the capital of the Kingdom of Bohemia within the Austro-Hungarian Empire, in a secular German-speaking Jewish family. After the First World War he became a citizen of the now independent Republic of Czechoslovakia. Kraus studied Oriental languages (in the broadest sense of the word) at the German University of Prague. After two years he set off to the Near East to perfect his knowledge of languages, visited Egypt and Syria, lived for a while in Mandatory Palestine, attending lectures at the recently-founded Hebrew University in Jerusalem. In 1927 he returned to Europe and completed a doctorate on Old Babylonian letters at the University of Berlin.

Kraus settled in Berlin, was a Dozent at the University, and had a research position at the Institute for the History of the Natural Sciences (*Forschungsinstitut für Geschichte der Naturwissenschaften*) under Julius Ruska (1867–1949), and he quickly won the admiration of the famous Hans-Heinrich Schaeder (1896–1957), professor of Oriental languages in Berlin, the high priest of Arabic and Iranian studies in Germany.

In 1933 the Nazis came to power and Kraus, like all university employees of Jewish origin, was immediately relieved of his position. At this fateful turning in his life he received an invitation from Louis Massignon to continue his work in Paris. Kraus lived in Paris under very strained circumstances from 1933 to 1936, when he accepted a teaching position at King Fuad I University in Cairo. He enjoyed the support of the Egyptian minister of education, the famous blind scholar Ṭāhā Ḥusayn (1889–1973), but became increasingly disappointed with the situation at the university and in the country. On 12 October 1944 he received a visit from Ṭāhā Ḥusayn informing him that, following a change of government in Egypt and the fall from royal favour of the Wafd party, both he and Kraus were now out of a job. Later the same day Paul Kraus ended his own life. He was only 40.

Husain Hamdani visited Berlin for the first time in 1930, and met Paul Kraus there. Kraus immediately recognised the importance of the Hamdani manuscripts for the history of Islam and began to study them. The first fruit of this study was his article on Hebrew and Syriac quotations in Ismaili manuscripts, published in January 1931.[4] After expressing, in the first sentence of the article, his gratitude to Husain Hamdani for putting the manuscripts at his disposal, Kraus proceeded to publish and discuss passages from three books by Ḥamīd al-Dīn al-Kirmānī, plus a passage from another one of Kirmānī's books quoted in the *ʿUyūn al-akhbār* by ʿImād al-Dīn Idrīs. At that time none of these books were known, even by title, outside of the Ṭayyibī Ismaili community. What is astonishing is the very short time (just a few months) between the first meeting of these two scholars and the completion and publication of Kraus's article, showing the profound knowledge of the whole scope of Arabic and Islamic literature on the part of the 26-year-old author.

In the following six years Kraus published further epoch-making studies based on Ismaili manuscripts from the Hamdani collection: notably his reconstruction of the lost *Kitāb al-zumurrud* by Ibn al-Rawandī on the basis of the refutation of the same in the *Majālis* of al-Mu'ayyad fi'l-Dīn, and then his recovery of the lost philosophical works of Abū Bakr al-Rāzī, in particular his notorious book 'The Destruction of the Religions', on the basis of its refutation by the Ismaili author Abū Ḥātim al-Rāzī.

The upshot of this was that thanks to the collaboration of Husain Hamdani, Paul Kraus was actually the first scholar outside of the Ismaili communities who was able to write about Ismailism on the basis of genuine Ismaili material from the Fatimid and Ṭayyibī traditions. Everything that had earlier been written about Ismailism, even by leading scholars like Michael J. de Goeje (1836–1909) or Ignác Goldziher (1850–1921), was based on external and on the whole polemical material. The opening up of the Ismaili libraries put the understanding of Ismailism on a completely new footing.

Included in the Hamdani donation to The Institute of Ismaili Studies is a folder containing 55 letters from Paul Kraus to Husain Hamdani, as well as two short messages from Kraus's wife, Hadasa Mednitzki, and one from Kraus's one-time mentor, Julius Ruska, the head of the Institute for the History of the Natural Sciences; these likewise are addressed to Husain Hamdani, so 58 letters all together. I am preparing an edition of these letters, which are from the period from 1930 to 1939, though the largest number of them are from the three years from the first meeting between the two scholars in 1930 until Kraus's emigration to Paris in 1933. Most of the letters are typewritten, though some are written by hand. Most are in German, a language that Husain Hamdani obviously knew, but some of the later letters are in English or a mixture of English and German. They cover, of course, only one side of the dialogue between the two scholars. I have tried very hard to locate Husain Hamdani's letters to Paul Kraus, but have had no success.

In the letters at my disposal Paul Kraus discusses at considerable length and with great fervour a large number of fundamental issues involving Ismaili religious literature. Many of these issues are addressed in Kraus's published papers, but a considerable number are not. These will doubtless prove of value to researchers in the field. At the same time, these letters provide us with a fascinating insight into the deep personal friendship between two scholars from totally different backgrounds.

The first letter is dated Berlin, 1st August 1930. Husain Hamdani has departed from his first visit to Germany and is in Paris, en route to London. The tone of the letter is friendly, but a bit distant. It begins with '*Lieber Herr Hamdani*' and uses the polite forms of the personal pronouns. The second letter is from the 24th of the same month, begins with '*Lieber Husain Hamdani*' and is very long. Shortly after this Kraus paid a visit to Husain Hamdani in London and after his return to Berlin he penned letter no. 5, dated 30th November 1930, addressed now to '*Lieber Husain*' and using the pronouns of the second person singular. It is evident that the trip to London was a turning point in their friendship.

The letters from the following months and years discuss the content of the Ismaili texts, the usual academic chit-chat about jobs and salaries, complaints about slow publishers and badly printed proofs, friends and rivals in their professional life, but also very personal matters.

At the time Paul Kraus was married to the first of his eventually three spouses, Hadasa Mednitzki, whom he had met in Palestine, and who, in these letters, is always called 'Leila'—she is the Laylā to Kraus's Majnūn—and who signs her letters to Hamdani with the same name. In 1932 she gave birth to a daughter, Helene, about whom Kraus writes at some length. According to those in the know the baby was in fact not Kraus's child, but that of his colleague and so-called friend, Shlomo Pines (1908–1990).[5] Leila accompanied Kraus to Paris, but soon afterwards they divorced, and in 1936 Kraus married Bettina Strauss, a Berlin Arabist like himself, and sister of the political scientist Leo Strauss (1899–1973). In his letters from Cairo Kraus refers to her simply as '*meine Frau*'. Bettina died in 1942 in childbirth. Her daughter Jenny survived and was brought up by her uncle Leo, eventually becoming Distinguished Professor of Classics at the University of Virginia, Jenny Strauss Clay. In June 1944, just months before his suicide, Kraus married his third wife Dorothee Metlitzky, who lived until 2001.

Husain Hamdani, before his departure for London, married Zaynab Bā'ī, a descendant in the seventh generation of the 40th *dāʿī*, Hibat Allāh al-Mu'ayyad fi'l-Dīn. She gave birth to their son Abbas in 1926. While in Berlin, Husain Hamdani embarked on an affair of the heart with the secretary at the Institute for the History of the Natural Sciences, a certain Liselotte Schwaebsch, whom Husain calls Lilo, and who also uses this name in her handwritten additions to several of the letters in this collection. So we have Kraus's Leila and Hamdani's Lilo. In one of his letters, Paul Kraus expresses with a candour that is only possible between extremely close friends his belief in the sincerity of Lilo's feelings and his hope that his friend would not let her down. But of course, things worked out differently. Husain Hamdani returned to India, and Lilo eventually married a man by the name of Stockinger, who appears to have died after 1949. For his part, Husain Hamdani, after he had settled in Egypt, took an Egyptian lady, Sayyida Aḥsan from Samannūd, as his second wife, which of course was his right as a Muslim, in about 1950. Abbas Hamdani informed me that in 1969, fulfilling an instruction of his deceased father, he visited Liselotte Stockinger in Munich and paid his compliments to her. She died not long afterwards.

What is strikingly absent in Kraus's letters is any reference to the deteriorating political situation in Germany. Only as late as letter 46, dated 22 March 1933, one day before the *Ermächtigungsgesetz* which brought Hitler to power, does Kraus conclude a learned letter to his Indian friend with the words: 'Otherwise things are going well. You have doubtless heard from the newspapers and from Lilo about the political upheaval. Germany has changed a lot.' In the next letter, dated 11th April, Kraus announces his imminent departure for Paris.

Once in Paris, Kraus becomes more outspoken. In letter 51, from 22 September 1933, Kraus complains about how bad the libraries in Paris are. 'The Staatsbibliothek in Berlin was splendid. But that is also the only thing that I find splendid in Germany (and unfortunately it was set up by the Jew Weil), otherwise nothing takes me back there and even if someone paid me a lot of money I would not go back to that hell. I do not know if news from Germany gets through to you, but what one hears here from private sources and from the newspapers of the emigres that are published here and in Prague is simply horrible. Of course I am still in contact with old Ruska, and I correspond still with Schaeder and a very few others. But otherwise I want to have nothing to do with "*Deutschland über Alles*", nor with "*Deutsche Wissenschaft*" and its representatives, who during the last events have behaved in so disgracefully cowardly a fashion (*so schmählich feige*).'

During his very short life Paul Kraus made plans for many studies which he was not able to complete. One of these was for a comprehensive bibliography of the surviving Ismaili literature, with a detailed account of the contents of each work, which he planned to write together with Husain Hamdani. This plan was pre-empted to a considerable degree by W. Ivanow's (1886–1970) *A Guide to Ismaili literature*, published in 1933. Ivanow's book is essentially a concise summary of the 18th-century *Fihrist* by al-Majdūʿ, giving (in Ivanow's case) the title and author of each work and a very short account of its content based on the much more detailed description by al-Majdūʿ. Kraus had a low opinion of Ivanow's book, which he describes in one of the letters as 'simplistic and superficial (*summarisch und oberflächlich*)', adding that 'it is a pity that we were not quicker'.

And in another letter Kraus refers to his famous review of Ivanow's book[6] for Louis Massignon's (1883–1962) *Revue des Études islamiques*. 'I have not said too much, but after a few introductory "appreciating" remarks I have given a long list of improvements in the style of his own notices. I think there is no point in criticising the old man sharply. He has done his best as far as his intellectual capacities go (*Er hat seinen geistigen Kapazitäten entsprechend das beste getan*). And to say that he has only listed numbers and names instead of detailed descriptions of the works has no point unless one does it better oneself.'

The letters from the last years in Paris and in Cairo become increasingly pessimistic and indeed bitter. He lives with his wife and her baby in a one-room slum in Paris. Somebody steals his typewriter and he has to write his letters by hand. His students in Cairo are stupid and arrogant. It is not easy reading. We see the career of a brilliant scholar cut short by a cruel avalanche of events. We can only take comfort from the magnificent body of work that he has left behind for us.

NOTES

1 See the sketch of his life by his son, Abbas Hamdani, in my *Arabic, Persian and Gujarati Manuscripts: The Hamdani Collection in the Library of The Institute of Ismaili Studies* (London, 2011), pp. xxxii–xxxiv. I have supplemented this with the help of oral information supplied by Abbas Hamdani and of some diaries and letters of Husain Hamdani himself.

2 I had the privilege of being asked to catalogue them. My catalogue of the first part of the Hamdani donation was published in 2011, and a second volume, describing the remainder of the donation, is in preparation.

3 For biographical details, see Charles Kuentz, 'Paul Kraus (1904–1944)', *Bulletin de l'Institut d'Égypte*, 37 (1944–1945), pp. 431–441 (with a comprehensive bibliography of Kraus's publications on pp. 438–441). See also Joel L. Kraemer, 'The Death of an Orientalist: Paul Kraus from Prague to Cairo', in Martin Kramer, ed., *The Jewish Discovery of Islam: Studies in Honor of Bernard Lewis* (Tel Aviv, 1999), pp. 181–223, and Rémy Brague's introduction to his edition of Paul Kraus, *Alchemie, Ketzerei, Apokryphen im frühen Islam* (Hildesheim, 1994). I am grateful to Paul Kraus's daughter Jenny Strauss Clay for further information and help.

4 'Hebräische und Syrische Zitate in Ismāʿīlitischen Schriften', *Der Islam*, 19 (1931), pp. 243–263.

5 See Kramer, 'The Death of an Orientalist', p. 215, n. 38.

6 P. Kraus, 'La bibliographie Ismaëlienne de W. Ivanow', *Revue des Études Islamiques*, 6 (1932), pp. 483–490.

SECTION II

RASĀʾIL IKHWĀN AL-ṢAFĀʾ, *KITĀB AL-ZĪNA*, AND THEIR MANUSCRIPT TRADITION

3

The *Ikhwān al-Ṣafā'*'s Epistles on Logic in Some Manuscripts of the IIS Arabic Collection

Carmela Baffioni

Introduction

In this chapter I will report the results of the examination of three manuscripts from the Arabic collection of The Institute of Ismaili Studies (MS 1040, MS 576, and MS 927), all of which contain versions of the *Rasā'il Ikhwān al-Ṣafā'*. I have considered the parts reporting the logical epistles—the five treatises that conclude the first section of the encyclopaedia.

The logical epistles deal with Porphyry's *Isagoge*, and the *Categories*, *On Interpretation*, *Prior* and *Posterior Analytics* by Aristotle.

In 2010 I established a new edition of the logical epistles based on the beautiful but often corrupt MS Atif Efendi 1681, dated 1182 CE, Istanbul Collection (labelled as [ع])[1] that often differs, sometimes in a significant way, from Buṭrus al-Bustānī's edition, Beirut, Dār al-Ṣādir 1957[2] (henceforth: Ṣ) and the other printed versions.[3] Two of the manuscripts I consulted—the Laud Or. 260, dated 1560 CE, Oxford, Bodleian Library ([خ]) and the Marsh 189, n.d.,[4] Oxford, Bodleian Library ([غ])[5]—provide a very different version of Epistle 'On the *Isagoge*'.[6]

In this chapter I describe the versions of MS 1040, MS 576 and MS 927 and compare them with Ṣ and my edition. For the sake of space, readings and omissions are simply listed. The relevance of many of them from the theoretical standpoint will be addressed on another occasion.

MS 1040, MS 576, and MS 927 in the Catalogues

MS 1040, MS 576, and MS 927 are all listed in the catalogues of Arabic manuscripts of the IIS.

MS 1040 is said to contain the first half and part of the second half of the encyclopaedia. The copyist is indicated as al-Ḥasan b. al-Nuʿmānī al-Ismāʿīlī. The manuscript was probably copied in Persia. After the indication of the date (Shaʿbān 953/October 1546), we read:

> 3 fly-leaves, 746 leaves (753 numbered); 21 lines per page; 300 × 190/195 × 100 mm.; elegant black *naskhī*; occasional words and diagrams in red; illuminated double-page opening with polychrome head-piece and text within gold 'clouds'; headings in white on illuminated panels; text within gold, red and blue frame;[7] numerous diagrams and grids; some annotations and corrections in the margins (occasionally in red); old paper restorations, worm-eaten, hole with loss of text on f. 162; 18th-century Persian purple morocco binding with blind-stamped medallions and cartouches on both covers; defective in the middle and incomplete at the end.[8]

As for MS 576, after the mention of the *incipit*, number of pages (861), dimensions (25.5 × 15 cm) and number of lines (21), we read:

> Fine Oriental wove paper. Clear *naskhī* hand. Illuminated headpiece, chapter headings and borders; rubrics. Leather washable cloth binding (without flap). *Qism* 1-2. No date (late 11/17th century).[9]

MS 927 is said to contain selections and extracts from the *Rasāʾil*. The copyist (Isḥāq b. al-Shaykh al-Fāḍil Sulaymānjī), place (Shāhjahānpūr), and date (Friday 18 Shaʿbān 1311/23 February 1894) are indicated. Then we read:

> 145 pp.; 16 lines per page; 218 × 135/150 × 75 mm.; clear black *naskhī*; punctuation and some of the marginal corrections and additions in red; 19th-century western-style morocco binding, gilt.[10]

To these descriptions I add what follows (referred to the logical epistles only).[11]

MS 1040

Double numeration on the *recto*, at the upper left margin, in Western and Arabic figures, the Arabic figures exceeding the Western by twelve units.[12] Back flyleaves almost completely covered by scripts.[13] Patches on the external margins, sometimes in the internal or upper margins. At p. 105/117r, patch in the central lower margin, with some letters written upside down.[14] Consumed cover, especially at the corners. Back cover very damaged. The page that follows the logical epistles torn at the centre.

Clear, generally unvocalised writing. The eulogy that opens the propaedeutical section continues after the *basmala* with *rabb yassir wa-tammim bi'l-khayr*. Afterwards, the section is said to include thirteen epistles, but the epistles are presently fourteen, all of them being regularly numbered. Perhaps, the copyist based himself on the tradition of thirteen epistles, testified by [ع], where Epistles 'On the *On Interpretation*' and 'On the *Prior Analytics*' are considered to be one epistle only, so that Epistle 'On the *Posterior Analytics*' is the 13th[15]—though afterwards the copyist went on by numbering the treatises as he found them in his model.

The first epistle 'On Number' is said to belong to the *jumla al-iḥdā wa-khamsīn risāla fī tahdhīb al-nafs wa-iṣlāḥ al-akhlāq*—it is introduced by exactly the same words as epistles in [ع]. Then the text goes on with a long eulogy that extends for more than four lines:

> *Al-ḥamd li'llāh alladhī lā taḥsunu al-ashyā' illā an yakūna bad'ahā ḥamduhu, wa-kull nāṭiq wa-sākit fa-huwa ʿabduhu alladhī tāhat al-albāb fī ʿiẓmatihi wa-dhallat lahu ʿuqūl ahl maʿrifatihi ʿinda mā shahadat min ʿazz* [word added in the margin] *jabarūtihi wa-ṣalawātihi wa-taḥyātihi ʿalā khayr khilqihi* [ح instead of خ in the MS PDF] *wa-tartībihi Muḥammad al-nabī wa-ālihi wa-ʿatratihi wa'l-muntajiyyīn min aṣḥābihi wa-ʿashīratihi wa'l-ṣāliḥīn min ʿibādihi wa-ummatihi.*

The first epistles are given in the traditional *quadrivium* succession: 1. 'On Arithmetics', 2. 'On Geometry', 3. 'On Astronomy', 4. 'On Music', 5. 'On Geography'.[16] The others follow in the current succession.

The words *faṣl* and *iʿlam*, relevant phrases, geometrical figures and other relevant elements are generally written in red ink. In other cases, relevant words or phrases are emphasised by lines above the words, also in red ink.

Peculiar orthography: Missing or mistaken diacritical dots (in case of verbs, this makes it difficult to establish concordances). *Alif maqṣūra* instead of long *alif*. Double *yā'* instead of single *yā'*. Final *hamza* not written. *Hamza* instead of *hamza*ed *wāw*. Long *alif* instead of *alif madda*. Prosthetic *alif* at the third sing. person of the verb. *Wa-* at the end of a line. *Yā'* instead of *hamza*.

There are frequent additions (marginal, interlinear, between the words), often indicated by *signes-de-renvoi* (*iḥāla*) in the text and sometimes framed by square or rectangular cases. Words often completed between the lines.[17]

MS 576[18]

Script on front flyleaves. Index of epistles on the *recto* of the second page. In the upper *recto* of the third page, at the centre, the title: *Rasā'il Ikhwān al-Ṣafā' wa-Khullān al-Wafā'*. Pagination in Arabic figures, at the centre in the upper margin of each page, starting by "1" at the beginning of Epistle 'On Arithmetics'. Page-numbers not always clearly visible. Script contoured by rectangular frames that are constituted by two external lines, one blue and one red, and a frame filled with gold (sometimes the gold fades into yellow), also contoured by two close, dark lines. The titles of the epistles are inserted in frames, constituted by an external border filled with blue ink, contoured by two silver limits, and ornated inside by white stylised flowers. The internal frame is blue on the right and left sides, with two rosettes in red and white on each side. The titles of the epistles are inserted in a golden background that terminates, on the right and the left, with arabesqued triangular extremities finished in red. The words of the titles appear in white and are not always perfectly visible. The titles of the various chapters inserted in the text without emphasis.

The original manuscript reveals a much clearer calligraphy than the hasty, unvocalised writing appearing in the PDF. However, the position of diacritical dots is not always clear, and concordances are difficult to establish in the case of verbs. No use of *masṭara*.

Also in this manuscript the succession is Arithmetics—Geometry—Astronomy—Music—Geography, etc. After Epistle 'On Morals', at p. 239.17 there is a new title, *al-Risāla fī ikhtilāf al-akhlāq ahl al-'ālam*, apparently referring to the same treatise. Afterwards, the logical epistles follow.

The word *iʿlam* is sometimes emphasised by a stroke above. Catchwords are written upside down and in very small letters.

Peculiar orthography: *Alif madda* instead of long *alif*. *Alif maqṣūra* instead of long *alif*. Double *yā'* instead of single *yā'*. Final *hamza* not written. Long *alif* instead of *alif madda*. No prosthetic *alif* at the end of the third pl. person. Prosthetic *alif* at the third sing. person of the verb. *Thalāth* and derivative forms with small *alif*. *Wa-* at the end of a line. *Yā'* instead of *alif maqṣūra*. *Yā'* instead of *hamza*.

Spare marginal additions and repetitions; sometimes, mistaken words closed between two small apical “v”.

The eulogy that ends the section is written in form of a triangle with vertex downward; the vertex is constituted by a *hā'* (abbreviation of *nihāya*, or *intahā*).

MSS 1040 and 576 share almost all their peculiar readings as well as eulogies and endings, with small additions in MS 576. In the opening *basmalas*, MS 576 adds *wa-bihi nastaʿīn* (‘from Him we seek help’).

MS 927[19]

Numeration in Western figures at the upper left angle of each *recto*, beginning from ‘2’ at the start of the text when there is an Index (the content of f. 1v is still to be identified). 16 lines until f. 138v; 17 lines from f. 139r, perhaps with a change of hand. The epistles follow each other with no emphasising of titles, but the content of the text calls for careful identification. Catchwords.

Peculiar orthography: Long *alif* instead of *alif madda*. *Thalāth* and derivative terms written with small *alif*.

Very numerous marginal additions (in all the margins). Besides additions, the titles or the content of the various sections are written in the margins, apparently in ink of a different colour.

Epistles ‘On the *Categories*’ and ‘On the *On Interpretation*’ are missing; the others are incomplete.

Epistle ‘On the *Isagoge*’

MS 1040

The text extends from f. 138/150v13 to f. 140/152r6.

MS 576

The text extends from p. 332.5 to p. 334.16.

Single readings: *Al-anwāʿ mawjūda* instead of *al-nawʿ* (397.20).

Common Features in MS 1040 and MS 576

Omissions: 390.5–395.3 (*lammā kāna al-insān afḍal al-mawjūdāt ... mutaʿallaqa bi'l-mawṣūf*); instead, the manuscripts continue with a text that is the same as the first chapter of the version provided in [خ] and [غ]. 395.5–397.20 (*wa-iʿlam anna al-alfāẓ allatī tustaʿmiluhā al-falāsifa ... li-jamīʿ jinsihi*); the manuscripts elaborate the chapter 'On the six words (*alfāẓ*)' so as to reproduce the same text as chapter 2 of [خ] and [غ]. 398.1–403.9 (*Faṣl fī anna al-ashyā' kulluhā ... jannāt*); the manuscripts elaborate the final part of the treatise (*wa-iʿlam bi-annahu ... fī Qāṭīghūrīās*, 403.11–21) reproducing the rest of chapter 2 of [خ] and [غ].

Titles and endings are different from [خ] and [غ]. Their ending[20] (*yatlū hādhā'l-kitāb wa'l-ḥamdu li'llāh wa-ṣallā'llāh ʿalā sayyidinā Muḥammad al-nabī wa-ālihi al-a'imma al-ṭāhirīn wa-sallama taslīman ʿalayhim ajmaʿīn wa-ḥasbunā'llāh wa-niʿam al-wakīl*) is identical, except for the addition of a *hā'* (= *nihāya*, or *intahā*) after *ajmaʿīn*, and of *tammat* after *al-wakīl* in MS 576.

MS 927

The text provided covers two *folios* only (101r12–102r2).

The title is: *Min*—'from', perhaps to indicate it to be a selection—*risāla Īsāghūjī al-ʿāshira*, supplemented by the following addition in the margin: *Fī'l-alfāẓ al-sitta allatī tastaʿmiluhā al-ḥukamā' fī'l-manṭiq wa-hiya al-jins wa'l-nawʿ wa'l-shakhṣ al-dālla hādhihi'l-thalātha ʿalā'l-aʿyān allatī hiya al-mawṣūfāt, wa-thalātha minhā dāllāt ʿalā'l-maʿānī allatī hiya al-ṣifāt wa-hiya al-faṣl wa'l-khaṭṭ* [sic, instead of *al-khāṣṣ*] *wa'l-ʿaraḍ*. In the text, *min al-qism al-awwal* follows.

Omissions: Due to *homoioteleuton*: 392.1–6 (*wa-dhālika anna'l-nuṭq al-lafẓī ... alladhī huwa amr rūḥānī maʿqūl*). Other omissions: After the title, from the opening eulogy to *al-manṭiq mushtaqq min naṭaqa yanṭuq nuṭqan* (391.20). Addition of *ilā qawlihi* after 392.8 (*mā'it*); the text begins again at *fa-naqūlu inna al-ḥurūf thalātha anwāʿ* (392.20). 392.21–393.2 (*fa'l-fikriyya . . . bi-ṭarīq al-ʿaynayn*). After *dalīlan* (393.6), unreadable word and, afterwards, *ilā qawlihi* with omission of 393.7–16 (*sanubayyina . . . mukhāṭabāt wa-muḥāwarāt*). After *huwa mīzān al-ḥaqq* (394.4), *ilā qawlihi* with omission of 394.5–397.7 (*wa-lammā kāna ikhtilāf al-nās . . . al-nibāḥ li'l-kilāb*). After *ʿalima dhālika aw lam yaʿlam*, addition of *ilā qawlihi fī'l-risāla al-thāniya ʿashar*. One addition between the words. Some auto-corrections (interlinear addition of dropped letters of some words).

At f. 102r2 the epistle ends. The manuscript continues with Epistle ‘On the *Prior Analytics*’, also partially reported.

Epistle ‘On the *Categories*’

MS 1040

The text, unvocalised, extends from f. 140/152r7 to f. 144/156v12.

Peculiar orthography: Final *hamza* not written. Long *alif* instead of *alif madda*. No prosthetic *alif* at the end of the third pl. person. *Yā'* instead of *alif maqṣūra*. *Yā'* instead of *hamza*. In correspondence to 408.9 and 12, contrary to the general use, the word *iʿlam* is not written in red ink. *In*, *fa-in* attached to the various forms of *kāna*. Some words split between two lines, such as *ka'l-wāḥid* (405.8); *al-asbāgh* (406.16); *k-al-zarʿ* (408.24, written as: كا الذرع); *k-al-ashkāl* (409.6: كا الأشكال; splitting found also in MS 576); *fa'l-mulāzama* (409.20: فا الملازمة); *k-al-āb* (410.4: كا الاب); *ka'l-kitāba* (410.24: كا الكتابة); *k-al-raqṣ* (411.1: كا الرقص; the second part of the word begins at the new page); *bi'l-ṭabʿ* (412.8: با لطبع). In the final eulogy, the *tā'* in *takwīn* is written with the two dots one above the other.

Omissions: 406.24–407.1 (*fa'l-insān nawʿ al-anwāʿ . . . min jins al-muḍāf*). 410.6 (*Fa-ammā dhuwātuhā*; in MS 576: *fa-inna*).

Single readings: *Al-fiʿl wa'l-infiʿāl* (emended) instead of *yafʿal wa-yanfaʿil* (405.14). *Khāṣṣiya* substituted by *khāṣṣa* (410.2).

Mistakes: Cacographies: أدررع instead of *adhruʿ* (407.6); in *al-ʿudhūba* (411.15), addition of الولو between the letters. Mistaken diacritical dots: *k-al-dhabīb* instead of *k-al-dabīb* (409.3); *khāna* instead of *ḥāna* (412.4 twice; but the second time the dot seems to have been deleted). Mistaken omissions: *ghayr maʿānī* in the phrase *maʿānīhā ghayr maʿānī* (407.19); *ghayrihā* in the phrase *wa-ghayrihā min al-ṭuʿūm* (411.15–16). Other mistakes: In the phrase *al-qābil li'l-aʿrāḍ* (407.4), *al-qābil* is written with a *hamza* above the *bā'*. In the phrase *mā yuqālu lahu* (407.6), *ammā* instead of *mā*. *Aqsāmihā* instead of *inqisāmihā* (411.4). Autocorrections: In the phrase *al-mawjudāt k-al-wāḥid ... baʿd al-wāḥid* (405.8–9), there is الموعودات instead of *al-mawjūdāt*, with emendation لمعدو (for المعدودات) above the word; the final words *baʿd al-wāḥid* are deleted (with addition above them of لتي) and repeated at the beginning of the new line. In the phrase *laysat bi'l-jawhar* (407.8), با is written above *laysat*, and deleted; in the new line there is بالجوهر. Above *wa'l-aʿmāl* (410.1), there is حوال instead of *al-aḥwāl*. When we read *irādatihi*—as in MS 576—instead of *idāratihi* (410.9), the copyist set a stroke above it and emended in the margin to *ilā dhātihi*. يروذان instead of *yadūrāni* (410.13), emended above to ىد (undotted). After *al-ʿadam* (411.24), the words *la yajtamiʿāni ka-mā an al-ḍiddayni* are deleted by a series of little oblique dashes, then the text goes on. In the expression *ṣāḥib dhālika* (413.5), *dhāl* added above the *bā'* of *ṣāḥib*. Four additions between the words; four in the margin, signalled by *signes-de-renvoi* above the words in the text; and two between the lines (in one case, only a part of a word is added).

MS 576

The text extends from p. 334.17 to p. 343.22. The copyist tends to complete words writing the last letter between the lines. After *al-mutaḍādda* (407.5), the phrase is ended by a sort of circle with a *hā'* in the middle. After *al-basīṭa* (410.14), the line is completed with a sort of heart upside down.

Peculiar orthography: قاطوغورياس instead of قاطيغورياس. *Khāṣṣiya* instead of *khāṣṣa* (409.15, as in my edition). *Arā'* with two long *alifs* instead of آراء. مياون instead of مئون (409.14).

Omissions: Due to *homoioteleuton*: 406.19–20 (*al-nāmī ... li-mā taḥtahu min*); 411.17 (*yakūnu fī'l-jism ... fa'l-ākhar ayḍan*). Other omissions: 404.5–6 (*wa-bayyannā ... wāḥidan wāḥidan*); 411.15–16 (*wa-ghayrihā min al-ṭuʿūm ... wa-min khāṣṣiya*).

Single readings: *Al-jāliya* instead of *al-jalīla* (404.11, as in my edition); *sammū* instead of *laqabū* (405.1).

Mistakes: Cacographies: أسنامه instead of *asnānihi* (412.5). Other mistakes: After *nawʿāni* instead of *nawʿayni* (409.7, as in MS 1040), repetition of *mufāraqa ka'l-nafs wa'l-ʿaql, wa* [at the end of the line] *ghayr mufāraqa*. *Qīla* instead of *qābala* (411.6). Repetition of *ḥusn* ... *nawʿāni* [with a sign above] *ka-mā yuqālu lahu* (410.22). Some corrections.

Common Features in MSS 1040 and 576

Mistakes: Cases of *lectio facilior*: *adraka* instead of *adrada* (412.4). Confusion of letters: الأسباغ instead of غابصلأا (413.5).[21] Autocorrections: In the expression *jins al-matā* (407.22), after *jins* the copyist writes *al-matā* with a ductus similar to *allatī*, deletes the word, and then—as in MS 576—writes *matā* (cf. f. 141/153v19). قسطة الأفسط instead of *f.ṭsa al-afṭas* (409.21), emended above to فطوسة الأفطس; MS 576 has الأفسط فسطة.

Ending: In the final eulogy, the words *rabb al-ʿālamīn* ... *ajmaʿīn* are substituted by: *ḥamd al-shākirin wa-sallā'llāh ʿalā sayyidinā Muḥammad wa-ālihi al-a'imma al-akramīn al-abrār al-ṭayyibīn wa-sallama ʿalayhi wa-ʿalayhim ajmaʿīn salāman muttaṣilan ilā yawm al-dīn ḥasbunā'llāh wa-niʿam al-wakīl*. MS 576 adds *al-ṭāhirīn* after *al-ṭayyibın*, and *tammat* after *al-wakıl*.

Epistle 'On the *On Interpretation*'

MS 1040

The text extends from f. 144/156v13 to f. 147/159r19.

Peculiar orthography: *Sukūn* written above the *ʿayn* of *maʿlūma* (417.2). *Taʿālā* written as *taʿā* with the long *alif* above the word. *In* attached to the following *kānat*.

Omissions: Due to *homoioteleuton*: 416.6 (*mā kāna* ... *al-aqāwīl*); 416.17–18 (*bi-Zayd al-fulānī* ... *aradtu*). Other omissions: 416.2 (*lam yatabayyinu* ... *bāna*).

Readings: *Bi-simāt* instead of *bi-ṣifāt* (417.2). *Wa-idhā katharat al-mawṣūfāt wa'l-ṣifa wāḥida* instead of *wa-idhā katharat al-ṣifāt wa'l-mawṣūf wāḥid* (418.15–16). After *Zayd kātib* (418.17), addition of *wa-Khālid kātib wa-ʿUmar kātib wa-idhā katharat al-ṣifāt wa'l-mawṣūf wāḥid fa'l-qaḍāyā takūnu* [undotted] *kathīra mithla qawlika*.

Mistakes: Casual use of verbal concordances. Four marginal additions (one of which perpendicular to the script, and one unclear and partly deleted), and two additions between the lines (even of dropped parts of words; in two cases, dropped letters are added under the word).

MS 576

The text extends from p. 344.1 to p. 349.3. Sometimes, *iʿlam* is emphasised by a line above.

Peculiar orthography: *In* attached to the following *kalām*.

Omissions: Due to *homoioteleuton*: 417.2 (*muḥaṣṣalan bi-ṣifāt maʿlūma maʿrūfa, wa-dhālika anna'l-mawṣūf*); 418.5 (*wa-sālibatuhā . . . ḥārra*); 418.15–16 (*wa-idhā katharat . . . Zayd kātib*); 418.21–22 (*wa'l-kammiya . . . bi'l-kayfiyya*). Other omissions: 415.21–22 (*mithlu qawlika . . . ḥukm al-salb*); 419.2–3 (*wa-law lam yakun al-mumkin limā ʿurifa al-mumtaniʿ*).

Readings:

415.15–17 Ṣ	[ع]	MS 576
Idhā qulta: al-nār ḥārra fa-ṣidq, wa-idhā qulta: bārida, fa-kadhib; wa-idhā qulta: al-nār laysat bi-bārida fa-ṣidq, wa-idhā qulta: laysat bi-ḥārra fa-kadhib.	*Idhā qulta: al-nār ḥārra fa-hiya ṣidq, wa-idhā qulta: al-nār laysat bi-ḥārra fa-hiya kadhib. Wa-idhā qulta: hiya bārida fa-kadhib, wa-idhā qulta: laysat bi-bārida fa-ṣidq.*	*Idhā qulta: al-nār ḥārra fa-ṣidq, wa-idhā qulta: bārida, fa-kadhib; wa-idhā qulta: al-nār ḥārra fa-ṣidq, laysat bi-bārida fa-ṣadaqat, wa-idhā qulta: laysat bi-ḥārra fa-kadhabat.*

Mistakes: Mistaken omissions: 415.1 (*al-ḥurūf*). Other mistakes: *al-ḥikma* instead of *al-ḥukm* (416.1). Autocorrections: سوار instead of *sūran* (سوراً, 416.11) with deleted *alif*. Addition of *hā'* to *yumkin* (416.16) to obtain the correct *yumkinuhu*, with *hā'* not linked to the word.

Common Features in MSS 1040 and 576

Peculiar orthography: In the title, بارميناس instead of بارامانياس (in my edition: ارمينياس باري).

Readings: Instead of *wa'l-kalb laysa yataḥarraku* (417.18), MS 1040 has *wa'l-kalb yataḥarraku wa'l-kalb laysa yataḥarraku*, and MS 576 *wa'l-kalb yataḥarraku, al-kalb laysa yataḥarraku.*

416.2–4 Ṣ	[ع]	MS 576	MS 1040
. . . *matā kāna qawl al-qā'il muḥtamilan li'l-ta'wīl, lam yatabayyanu fīhi al-ṣidq wa'l-kadhib, wa-matā kāna ghayr muḥtamil li'l-ta'wīl, bāna fīhi al-ṣidq wa'l-kadhib.*	. . . *matā kāna qawl al-qā'il muḥtamilan li'l-ta'wīl, fa-lā yatabayyanu fīhi al-ṣidq wa'l-kadhib, wa-matā kāna ghayr muḥtamil li'l-ta'wīl, bāna fīhi al-ṣidq wa'l-kadhib.*	. . . *matā kāna qawl al-qā'il yaḥtamilu al-ta'wīl, thumma yatabayyanu fīhi al-ṣidq wa'l-kadhib*	. . . *matā kāna qawl al-qā'il yaḥtamilu al-ta'wīl, fīhi al-ṣidq wa'l-kadhib.*

Mistakes: Confusion of letters: *dufiʿa* instead of *rufiʿa* (417.9). Mistaken omissions: *lā* from *lā yumkin* (416.14); *maʿānī* (418.4). Other mistakes: *fī fīhi* instead of *fīhi* (415.10). Addition of *wāḥid* to *kull* (418.24: *laysa kull wāḥid min al-nās bi-kātib*). After *mithla qawlika* (419.11), as in my edition, the words *kull nār ḥārra wa-kull ḥārra nār wa-rubbamā takūnu qabl al-ʿaks kādhiba wa-baʿdahu ṣādiqa mithla qawlika* are added. MS 576 has, however, *kull ḥarāra* instead of *kull ḥārra* and, mistakenly, *baʿdahā* instead of *baʿdahu*). This addition may have fallen in the other manuscripts consulted due to *homoioteleuton*.

Ending: Instead of 419.15–16 Ṣ, both manuscripts (and my edition) have: *Tammat al-risāla wa'l-ḥamd li'llāh rabb al-ʿālamīn wa-sallā'llāh ʿalā rasūlihi sayyidinā Muḥammad al-nabī wa-ālihi al-a'imma al-ṭāhirīn wa-sallama taslīman ḥasbunā'llāh wa-niʿam al-wakīl.* MS 576 adds: *wa-niʿam al-mawlā wa-niʿam al-naṣīr.*

Epistle 'On the *Prior Analytics*'

MS 1040

The text extends from f. 147/159r19 to f. 151/163r16. More or less at the beginning, at f. 147/159v, there are two marginal additions (the first extended for some lines), perhaps of a different hand, hinting at the late introduction of the fourth figure of the syllogism.[22]

Peculiar orthography: *Fa-innahu* (422.10) written at the end of a line, between the lines as فانا, then deleted and re-written at the beginning of the new line as ھناف. قاطوغورياس instead of قاطيغورياس (425.18). *Hamza* + *yā'* instead of double *yā'* in *maqāyīs*. *In* attached to the words that follow—*kāna* and other forms of the verb, and *kull*.

Omissions: 424.1 (the title *Faṣl fī bayān . . . al-manṭiqiyya*).

Readings: *Kull insān ḥajar* instead of *kull insān ḥayawān* (423.10; consequently, *mūjiba kādhiba* instead of *mūjiba ṣādiqa*; afterwards, addition of *wa-kull ḥajar ḥayawān mūjiba kādhiba natījatuhā wa-kull insān ḥayawān*).[23]

Mistakes: Cacographies: المتوحف instead of *al-munzaḥif* (424.6). Mistaken omissions: 420.15 (*mawḍūʿan fī'l-ukhrā . . . jamīʿan*; these words should explain the second figure of the syllogism). Other mistakes: *Khāṣima* instead of *khāṣṣiya* (423.20, which demonstrates the copyist's ignorance). *Lā anna* instead of *li-anna* (426.5 and 427.3). Autocorrections: There is an *alif* before *mīzān* (425.8), deleted by a dash. In *al-ashyā' al-mustawiya* (425.9), after *al-ashyā'* there are the words *lahā abʿād wa-hiya*, deleted by dashes. At *illā min ashyā'* (425.13), there is *al-* for *al-ashyā'*, deleted. After *fa-dhakarū* (425.17), there is *fī ittikhādh al-mīzān*, deleted by dashes. After *min al-tanāquḍ* (426.11), there is لا إلى مج, deleted in red ink. One repetition. Two emended words. One word completed in the margin. Four additions in the margins and three between the lines; additions sometimes marked by *signes-de-renvoi*.

MS 576

The text extends from p. 349.5 to p. 356.12. Sometimes, there is a line above *wa-iʿlam*.

Peculiar orthography: بارانانياس (sic) instead of بارامانياس (in my edition: ارمينياس باري) (425.18). *Arā'* with two long *alif*s instead of آراء (the same writing in MS 1040 in correspondence to 425.5). In some cases, *in* attached to *kānat*. Single *yā'* instead of double *yā'* in *maqāyīs*.

Omissions: Due to *homoioteleuton*:[24] 421.17–19 (*al-thānī . . . li-annahā min al-shakl*); 422.1 (*yuntajāni . . . ṣādiqa*); 422.5–7 (*natījatuhumā . . . juz'iyya sāliba ṣādiqa*); 423.7–8 (*mūjiba kādhiba wa-kull ṭā'ir*); 423.8–9 (*natījatuhumā . . . mūjiba kādhiba*);[25] 427.14–15 (*wa-qad qīla . . . al-falsafa*). Other omissions: 421.22–23 (*kulliya kānat . . . idhā qīla kull*); 423.14 (*min ayna . . . wa-lā yadrī*); 425.1–2 (*baynahum . . . quḍiya*). Two words are emended.

Readings: *Kull ḥajar ḥayawān* instead of *kull insān ḥayawān* (423.10, as in my edition). After *fa-in kāna mawḍū'an fī iḥdāhumā maḥmūlan fī'l-ukhrā* (420.12), addition of *wa-yakūnu maḥmūlan fī kullayhimā li'l-ukhrā. Shay'* instead of *natīja* (421.17). *Al-kutub* instead of *al-qiyāsāt* (424.1; in my edition: *al-ṭuruq*).

Mistakes: Cacographies: امنه instead of *minhu* (427.6); فعلك instead of *fa-la'allaka* (428.1). Confusion of letters: *dāmū* instead of *rāmū* (422.16), and *dāma* instead of *rāma* (427.11): a sign of the copyist's ignorance, in the second case common to MS 1040. Other mistakes: Repetition of *yataḥarrūna al-ṣawāb* (426.9–10). Two emended words.

Common Features in MSS 1040 and 576

Peculiar orthography: Aristotle's work is indicated in the titles as *Anālūṭīqā al-ūlā* instead of *Anālūṭīqā*. سلوجموس instead of سلوجيموس (سلوجسموس in my edition). منهاتين instead of من هاتين. الشري instead of *al-shirā'* (424.11). *Hamza + yā'* instead of double *yā'* in *makāyīl*.

Omissions: Due to *homoioteleuton*: 422.7–8 (*natījatuhumā . . . sāliba ṣādiqa*). Other omissions: 422.14 (*al-muqaddimāt wa'l-natīja kādhiba kullahā aw ṣādiqa kullahā*, as in my edition; there is instead: *kādhibatan kullahā*); and—as in my edition—the titles at pp. 425.5, 426.1–2, 427.8 (in MS 927[26] as well) Ṣ.

Readings: *Wa-kull ṭā'ir ḥayawān, kull insān ḥayawān, wa-kull ḥayawān ṭā'ir* instead of *kull insān ḥayawān* (421.15). *Matā tubayyinu imkān an* instead of *mīzān* (422.18).

Mistakes: Cacographies: الغي (?) instead of *tughāfilū* (423.21; in my edition: *allafū* ألفَوا). *Al-zarrā'* instead of *al-dhirā'* (424.10 and 425.8; the second time MS 576 writes, mistakenly, الزاراع). الوفات instead of *al-wifāq* (427.6). Metathesis of letters (*taḥrīf*): *yataṣaffaḥa* instead of *yatafaḥḥaṣa* (422.15, as in my edition). *Al-ḥirz* instead of *al-ḥazr* (424.15 and 18; perhaps the copyists were copying from a mistaken model). Other mistakes: curiously, نز و instead of *tazwīj* (تزويج, 421.10 and 14;

probably, they copied from a model with cacography and could not detect the correct word). *Yatabayyinu* instead of *yabqī* (426.19).

Ending: *tammat al-risāla bi-ʿawn Allāh subḥānahu wa'l-ḥamd li'llāh waḥdahu wa-ṣallā 'llāh ʿalā rasūlihi sayyidinā Muḥammad al-nabī wa-ālihi al-a'imma al-ṭāhirīn wa-sallama taslīman ḥasbunā'llāh wa-niʿam al-wakīl*, to which MS 576 adds *wa-niʿam al-mawlā wa-niʿam al-naṣīr*.[27]

MS 927

The text extends from f. 102r3 (beginning at *al-insān qādir ʿalā*, 426.3) to f. 102v12–13 (*ilā qawlihi* [with a line above] *fi'l-risāla al-rābiʿa ʿashara*).

Peculiar orthography: *Arā'* with two long *alif* instead of آراء.

Omissions: 426.9–10 (*yatajannabūna . . . yajtahidūna fī dhālika*); 426.16–22 (*aw mithlu man yaʿtaqidu . . . wa'l-burhān al-ḥaqīqī*); 427.6–7 (the end of the chapter, *wa-kayfa . . . fī maʿlūmātihi*).

Readings: *Yaḥsubu* instead of *yaḥussu* (427.4).

Three marginal additions, two of which perpendicular to the script. One addition between the words, one between the lines, and two repetitions of a word (once the repetition has been deleted).

Epistle 'On the *Posterior Analytics*'

MS 1040

The text extends from f. 151/163r16 to f. 161/173v18. The word *faṣl* (at 430.4) marked and larger, retraced in red ink, as if it were a title. Some words emphasised by a line above, in red ink. Nine marginal additions, even long ones, seven of which signalled by a *signe-de-renvoi* in the text. One of them at f. 158/170r (*mimmā fī bidāya . . . ma'khūdha*, 444.11–12), perpendicular to the script, in three lines, and framed by three lines constituting a rectangle around the addition. Ink-spot at *fa-laʿallaka* (451.20).

Peculiar orthography: قاطوغورياس instead of قاطيغورياس. *In* is attached to the following word—in general, *kāna* and other forms of the verb, and *kull*. One word is split in two lines. *Mā dhā* instead of *mādhā*. تعه instead of *taʿālā*. الحيوة instead of *al-ḥayāh*. السيؤل instead of *al-suyūl* (441.8 and 9).

Omissions: Due to *homoioteleuton*: 432.7 (*fa-in qīla: mā al-ṣifāt al-mutaḍadda?*); 439.1–2 (*wa-sabab . . . funūn al-maqāyīs*).

Readings: *Mutazayyifa* instead of *muttazina* (431.18). التجبين instead of *al-tamyīz* (432.14). *Al-qiyās* instead of *al-miqyās* (433.12). *Baynahā* instead of *jinsihi* (434.6, perhaps for *baytihā*; this may be a sign of the existence of a different version of the text).

Mistakes: Cacographies: الجد instead of *al-jald* (431.6). *Al-muqawwima* (432.10) written as المقيومة. *Al-murakkab* (431.11) written as: الركب. كا instead of *kānū* (435.8). *Al-insān* (436.9) written as: الا نسان. ينتتج instead of *yantiju* (436.16). *Tarkībihi* (437.12) written as: ركيبه. المقاملة instead of *al-maqāla* (438.6). السالة instead of *al-sayyāla* (440.5). انصنات instead of *insibāb* (441.8). *Bilā* (442.17) written as: بل ا. لأنهار instead of *li-annahā* (445.11). المتالمين instead of *al-muta'ammilīn*, and مثالا منها instead of *mithālātihā* (445.12). مقتدمتين instead of *muqaddimatayn* (445.15). الا نسانية (two words) instead of *al-insāniyya* (448.13). *Yumkinaka* (449.8) written as: يمنك. صولا instead of *uṣūlan* (449.21). *Ayyuhā* (451.14) written as: عيها (sic). Mistaken diacritical dots: تسنج instead of تسنح (436.10). المجاورات instead of *al-muḥāwarāt* (436.17). Other mistakes: *Li-ʿaql* instead of *al-ʿaql* (437.22). *ʿĀlam* instead of *ʿilm* in the locution *ʿilm al-ṭabīʿiyyāt* (441.4). *Al-ruṭūba* instead of *li-ruṭūba* (442.8). *Al-manṭiqa* instead of *al-manṭiqiyya* (444.17). *Illā* instead of *lā* (449.6). *Al-akhlāq al-malā'ika* instead of *al-akhlāq al-malakiyya* (451.16). *Aʿmāl al-zakiyya* instead of *al-aʿmāl al-zakiyya* (451.17). Autocorrections: *Kathīran* instead of *kathīr* (436.5), with *alif* deleted. *Aw iʿwijājihi* instead of *wa-* (437.3), with *alif* deleted. *Baʿd mā . . . ʿallama bi'l-fiʿl* (438.1–2) deleted with small dashes in red ink. After *kutub al-handasa* (440.17), there is فا between the lines, deleted with a stroke. At 447.10, فا written at the end of a line, deleted and re-written as: *fa-ammā* at the beginning of the new line. *Akhlāqan wa-ʿādāt* (449.5) deleted with a stroke. At 449.20, *fa-ammā* written at the end of a line, deleted and re-written at the beginning of the new line, with an emphasis of a line in red ink above. *Ḥāṣṣatāni* (450.10) emended by adding تا between the lines; *ḥawāṣṣ* was added as well, but it was deleted. Eleven emended words, two of which perhaps erased; one word repeated at the beginning of the new line. Two additions under the line, one of which between two words; two between the words; three between the lines; one between the lines at the beginning of a line.

MS 576

The text extends from p. 356.13 to p. 376.6. Note that the second and the third page of the text are both numbered '357' so that, afterwards, the right-page bears odd paginations. Words often unclear at the end of a line. A *hā'* fills the line at p. 359.11. In the title at 437.4 the word *faṣl* is not visible and followed by a sort of *hā'* (or two small circles, p. 362.12). At 437.5, after *min jiha iʿwijājihi*, addition of *al-qiyās wa-kayfa'l-taḥarruz*—, these words are part of the title given at line 4, which had been dropped). Some words emphasised by a line above. Some *hā'* fill the end of lines.

Peculiar orthography: الحيوة insted of *al-ḥayāh*. السوآل instead of *al-su'āl*. تعا instead of *taʿālā*. *Subḥānahu* with small *alif*. *In* attached to the following *kull*.

Omissions: Due to *homoioteleuton*: 432.4–5 (*al-jism . . . mā ḥadd*); 434.3–6 (*al-ʿilla . . . ʿalā ithbāt*); 437.4–5 (the title *Faṣl fī kayfiyya . . . al-taḥarruz minhu*, plus *wa-*);[28] 438.10–12 after *al-bāqiya* (*mutasāwiya . . . kānat al-bāqiya*); 440.10–11 (*illā bi-tilka'l-ḥāssa. . . min al-maḥsūsāt*); 449.10 (*sabaqūka . . . maʿa alladhīna*). Other omissions: 430.1 (*min al-anwāʿ . . . ḥaqīqat al-ashkhāṣ*); 433.7 (*lā* from *lā yumkinuhu*); 437.14 (*wa-mā huwa*—the second question).

Readings: *Al-rasā'il al-ilāhiyya* instead of *al-risāla al-ilāhiyya* (436.8, as in my edition). *Nūr* instead of *lawn* (440.5).

Mistakes: Cacographies: *Aʿnī* (430.2) written as: اعين. شا instead of *shākil* (430.18). منزنغة instead of *muttazina* (431.18). كميته instead of *kammiya* (432.1). *ʿInda* in the phrase *ʿinda al-su'āl* (432.2) written as: عن, but as the *nūn* appears in the 'linked' form, this may be a case of illegible end of line. حكمه instead of *ḥukmahu* (432.18). *Huwiyyāt* (437.18) written as: هولات. *Māhiyyatuhā* (437.21) written as: ماهيها. ابعض instead of *baʿḍ* (441.5). ان صاب instead of *wa-insibāb* (441.8). الممدود instead of *al-mudūd* (441.7 and 9). أويلها instead of *awā'iluhā* (444.12; cf. اويل instead of *awā'il* at 446.15). يحلف instead of *yakhlu* (446.9). الخفو (undotted) instead of *al-khafīf* (446.10). المحازيا instead of *al-muḥādhayāt* (447.14). الكبر instead of *al-kubrā* (448.6). بل instead of *bilā* (448.7). *Al-insān* (448.12) written as: للانسان. *Musabbaʿ* instead of *muttasaʿ* (450.8). Cases of *lectio facilior*: *Al-ajnās* instead of *al-iḥsās* (429.9). *Majhūl* instead of *majbūl* (449.13). Confusion of letters: *Jāhidan* instead of *jāhilan* (433.13). Metathesis of letters: *Bi'l-ḥirz* instead of *bi'l-ḥazr*

(432.9). Other mistakes: *Al-maʿnā qawlinā* instead of *maʿnā qawlinā* (430.12). تميزه instead of متميزة (430.13). *Al-ḥawāss tudriku al-ḥawāss* instead of *al-ḥawāss tudriku an* (433.2). After *bi-anna* (450.13), addition of *min al-ḥayawān mā lahu ḥāssa wāḥida, wa-minhā mā lahu*—a repetition of line 10. Autocorrections: the words *waʾl-arkān min* deleted by a diagonal dash at the beginning of the line (431.16). موالفة instead of *muʾallafa* (431.19), with *alif* deleted by a stroke. After *anā* (437.6), there is an *alif* deleted by two strokes. *Laysa* instead of *laysat* (441.23, with *tāʾ* added above the circle of the *sīn*). After *al-ṣūra* (443.13), there is *lahu fa-ammā*, deleted by a stroke.[29] After *wa-mithlu qawlihi* (445.6), mistaken addition of *inna kull jawhar*, closed between two apical "v" to indicate the mistake. Three words repeated: *al-khams* (436.13) on the first line of the new page, *kull* (446.5) and *ʿalayhi* (450.1).

Common Features in MSS 1040 and 576

Peculiar orthography: *Arāʾ* with two long *alif*s instead of آراء. *Qiyāma* with small *alif*. *Alladhīnahum* instead of *alladhīna hum* (434.15). *ʿIllatahumā* written as: علة هما (442.6). All three manuscripts have *jalla thanāʾuhu* instead of *jalla jalāluhu* (445.1; eulogy omitted in my edition; in MSS 1040 and 576 only at 451.14).

Omissions: Due to *homoioteleuton*: 437.16–17 (*thumma yuqāsu . . . awāʾil al-ʿuqūl*); 447.18–19 (*ka-mā bayyannā . . . bi-qaṣd qāṣid*); 447.19–20 (*wa-innamā . . . abadī al-wujūd*). Other omissions: 435.17–19 (*fa-idhā kāna . . . dalālatihi*); 443.2–3 (*fa-idhā ʿakastahu . . . dhū lawn*); 445.18–19 (*wa-ʿalā hādhāʾl-mithāl . . . ilā barāhina ukhar*, as in my edition); and—as in my edition—the titles at pp. 430.11, 432.16,[30] 435.1–2, 436.12, 438.4, 438.18, 441.15, 442.10–11,[31] 443.9, 444.10 (in MS 927 as well), 448.11, 450.9, 451.1 Ṣ.

Readings: After *ṭuruq* (429.9), addition of *maʿlūmāt wa-*, but MS 576 has, mistakenly, *maʿlūmāt* only. Addition of *wa-limaiyyatuhā* to *wa-kayfiyyatuhā* (433.4, as in my edition). *Al-maṣnūʿa* instead of *al-mawḍūʿa* (433.5, as in my edition; unclear in MS 576). *Subḥānahu* instead of *ʿazza wa-jalla* (436.3, written with small *alif* in MS 576; *taʿālā* in my edition). To indicate the line in the geometrical examples, MS 1040 has اب in red ink (as in my edition) instead of "= ا" (as the line is indicated in 440.14 and 440.17 Ṣ), while MS 576 has أ only in the first case, and nothing is visible after the *alif* in the second case. After *min ajl annahumā min jins al-muḍāf* (441.18), MS 1040 adds: *wa'l-ashyā' allatī hiya jins al-muḍāf wa-*; MS 576 adds: *wa'l-ashyā' allatī hiya min jins al-muḍāf*.[32] *Lā al-ʿaql* instead of *bi'l-ʿaql* (441.18; MS 1040 adds the *alif* between the lines; my edition has *bi'l-fiʿl*). Instead of *qawluhu an lā yustaʿmalu fī'l-burhān al-aʿrāḍ al-mulāzima innamā huwa li-anna* (442.12), MS 1040 has *fa-innamā qāla min ajl anna* only; MS 576 has *lā yustaʿmalu fī'l-burhān al-aʿrāḍ al-mulāzima fa-innamā qāla hādhā min ajl anna*. *Al-asmā'* instead of *al-ashyā'* (442.13). *Lā budda* instead of *fāʿila lahu* (442.15). *Wa'lladhī yabqī yubrahina bi-annahā jawhar wa-ʿaraḍ fa-yuḍāfu ilā hādhihi'l-muqaddimāt ... hādhihi'l-ukhrā* instead of *wa'lladhī yanbaghī li-yubrahina bi-annahā jawhar lā ʿaraḍ an yuḍāfu ilā hādhihi'l-muqaddimāt ... hādhihi'l-ukhrā* (446.7–8). *Khārij al-ʿālam* instead of *fī'l-ʿālam* (447.1, as in my edition). After *li-man zaʿama annahu minhum* (451.13), addition of *wa-laysa minhum* (as in my edition).

Mistakes: Cacographies: *Al-ḥajb* instead *of al-ḥajar* (430.15). يخصها (431.9) written as: يخصيها. *Al-awwalāni* (431.10) written as: الاولات. دوار instead of دور (434.19). *Istabāna* (435.8) written in MS 1040 as: اسبان, in MS 576 as: ابان. خال instead of *khalā'* (436.1). يسبح (436.14) instead of *yantiju*. مابين instead of منتي (436.21, omitted in my edition). ارسطاطا ليس 437.12)) as if it were two words. نهار instead of *anhār* (440.1). *Fawq* instead of *firq* (440.8; perhaps as a result of a cacography in the model). قبلة instead of قبل (441.17; MS 576 has قبله that makes no sense here). معين (undotted in MS 1040) instead of *maʿnā* (446.17). فرغ instead of *furiḍa* (448.6; cacography in the model?). Confusion of letters: *Muḥrikan* instead of the correct *muḥriqan* (439.14).[33] *Mujassadan* (or, as is clear in MS 576, *mujassaran*) instead of *mujarraban* (448.20). Metathesis of letters: *Taṣaffaḥa* instead of *tafaḥḥaṣa* (434.19). *Al-thalātha* instead of *al-thālitha* (446.5). Mistaken diacritical dots: تزعزع instead of *taraʿraʿa* (439.11). *Al-sharāb* instead of the rare *al-sarāb*, and عدران instead of *ghudrān* (440.1). كا الجثة instead of *al-janna* (452.1). Mistaken omissions: 438.9 (*ashyā' mutasāwiya* after *wa-in zīda ʿalā ashyā' mutasāwiya*, evidently considered to be a *homoioteleuton*); 440.3 (*illā*); 446.22 (*mawjūdan* in the phrase *idhā laysa mawjūdan*). Other mistakes: *Hādhā'l-khashaba* instead of *hādhihi'l-khashaba* (430.15). *Al-jins al-ʿilla* instead of *jins al-ʿilla* (434.9). *Li-anna* instead of *anna* (435.15). *Nafs al-insāniyya* instead of *al-nafs al-insāniyya* (438.1). Instead of *yubnā* (438.5), MS 1040 has نبينا,

and MS 576 has بينا. *Ḥajr* instead of *juzʾ* (439.14, probably by attraction of the following *aḥjār*). *Liʾl-ʿilla dhātiyya* instead of *al-ʿilla dhātiyya* (443.1). *Al-qiyās al-burhān* instead of *al-qiyās al-burhānī* (443.14; the same mistake occurs at 444.4, in MS 1040 only). *Al-kullī* instead of *al-kurī* (447.16, referred to *al-shakl*, perhaps because of ignorance of the matter). *Abadī al-wijūd* instead of *abadiyya al-wujūd* (447.19). *Faʾl-ʿilla* instead of *mā ʿilla* (448.9; perhaps because of a cacography in the model).

Ending: *Wa-hadāka wa-iyyānā* instead of *wa-hadāna wa-iyyāka* (452.1–2); omission of *innahu ruʾūf biʾl-ʿibād*. At line 4, *Muḥammad al-nabī wa-ālihi al-aʾimma* instead of *Muḥammad wa-ālihi*. At lines 4–7, omission of *wa-bihā . . . al-hayūlā waʾl-ṣūra* (451.4–7); at the end, MS 576 alone gives: *kathīran*.

MS 927

The text begins at f. 102v14 with *fa-qad ʿarafta wa-stabāna* (444.3). In correspondence to *bālighan mā buligha* (445.16), there is in the margin: *Fī anwāʿ al-madhāhib*, after which the epistle seems to be ended. At f. 103v7–8 the text continues with *Min risālat al-ḥayawānāt*, and a passage of this treatise is quoted. Afterwards, various passages titled in the margins follow.[34]

Omissions: 444.12–16 (*ka-mā bayyannā . . . fī awāʾil al-maqāmāt*), with addition of *ilā qawlihi*; 445.12–13 (*wa-in kānat . . . al-mutaʿallimīn*).

Readings: *Mudraka* instead of *marʾiyya* (445.12).

Mistakes: *ʿIlla aw maʿlūla munfaʿila* instead of *ʿilla fāʿila aw maʿlūl munfaʿil* (445.5).

A Special Omission

In Epistle 'On the *Posterior Analytics*', MSS 1040 and 576 and my edition omit the words *wa-yusammā hādhāʾl-shakl bi-shakl al-ʿurūs* ('this figure is called "the figure of the bride"', 445.20–21), referring to the Pythagorean theorem described in the passage. The French mathematician and historian Paul Tannery (1843–1904) claimed this definition to have appeared for the first time in the Byzantine writer Georgios Pachymeres (1242–1310), an important author in the history of the struggle for primacy between Arabs and Byzantines.

Tannery did not realise, however, that hints at the definition were already found in Plato's *Republic* (546). The word νύμφη indicates not only the bride, but an insect—the name would derive from a similarity between the well-known geometrical figure and that of a winged insect.

Many years ago, I found the definition in the Muslim theologian and philosopher Fakhr al-Dīn al-Rāzī (1149–1210). This way, the definition became at least one century older, and its origin (contradicting Tannery) seemed to be Arabic rather than Byzantine.

Afterwards, I found the same definition in the Ikhwanian treatise. At that time, I was not yet aware of the complexity of the manuscript tradition of the *Rasāʾil*. Thus, I assumed it to be older than the 12th century. The discussion is now reopened by the omission of the definition in [ع] (considered to be the oldest manuscript available of the *Rasāʾil*), and in the IIS manuscripts that I have examined and seem closely related to [ع]. Does such an omission suggest the definition to be later—for instance, contemporary with Fakhr al-Dīn al-Rāzī? From a personal communication of the late Abbas Hamdani, the manuscript at the basis of the Ṣādir edition and the other printed editions of the *Rasāʾil* is older than [ع]. So, the issue has not yet found a solution.

Conclusion

Though no clear conclusion can be stated until the whole manuscripts have been explored and compared with the other available versions of all the epistles, we can propose some provisional considerations.

1) The presence of the short alternative version of Epistle 'On the *Isagoge*' (with small differences from [خ] and/or [غ]) demonstrates that its tradition has lasted for centuries. Note, however, that the special version of Epistle 'On the Kinds of Proper Attitude' provided by [غ] has no correspondence in any of the manuscripts examined.

2) Apart from the cases highlighted above, MSS 1040 and 576 share almost all their peculiar readings and their ending—though with further small additions in MS 576. MS 927 has numerous independent readings, but it often resembles my edition. We can summarise the readings common to my edition as follows:

	MS 1040 alone	MS 576 alone	The 2 MSS	MS 927	The 3 MSS
Ep. on *Categories*	8[35]	12	59		
Ep. on the *On int.*	1	2	23		
Ep. on *Pr. An.*	4	6	49	7	7[36]
Ep. on *Post. An.*	17[37]	16	168	4	8[38]

3) The presence of so many readings common to my edition confirms the importance of [ع]—and of the manuscripts linked to it—in the history of the manuscript tradition of the *Rasā'il*, hence, the usefulness of the new edition based on [ع]. If the manuscripts examined are Ismaili, we might even wander whether [ع], to which they are so close, is also Ismaili.

4) The high number of single readings in the MSS examined confirms the massive commixtures in the manuscript tradition already noted in my editions of the *Rasā'il*, and hence the impossibility of tracing any sort of *stemma codicum*. MSS 1040 and 576 may have a common origin/model. MS 1040, however, is corrupt in several places and the best copy is often provided by MS 576. Compare, for instance, 403.15–19:

[. . .] واحد[1] يستعمله[2] صاحب الفلسفة في أقاويله . . . . فالذي يستعمله صاحب اللغة . . . أحدها جنس البلدي، والآخر جنس الصناعي،[3] والآخر جنس النسبي. فالجنس . . . الصناعي كقولك لجماعة تشير[4] إليهم فتقول:[5] نجارون[6] حدادون[7] خبازون[8] وما شاكله.

[1] 576: وحد.

[2] 1040: يستعملها.

[3] 1040: الضاعي.

[4] 1040: سقط: تشير إليهم فتقول: نجارون حدادون خبازون وما شاكله؛ والنسبي كقولك لجماعة (homoioteleuton).

[5–8] 576: فيقولها نجاريين حداديين خبازين.

5) Some cases confirming the chronology attributed to MSS 1040 and 576 are found in our epistles. For instance, the cacography وقة instead of *waqt* in correspondence to 412.4 in MS 1040, while MS 576 has وقيه that seems an emendation of the MS 1040 writing; or the cacography for *al-qaḍāyā* (418.21) in MS 1040 that—perhaps because of its unintelligibility—has been dropped in MS 576; or, in MS 1040,

ان عموا instead of *anʿamū* (438.20, with two dots above the *mīm*) in consequence of which MS 576 wrote, without understanding, ان عمق.

In other cases, however, MS 1040 provides emendations or additions that are the same as in MS 576. For instance, in the text provided after the common omission of 397.12–17 (*allatī hiya aʿrāḍ . . . yataʿāqibuhā ḍidduhā*), after *wa-biʾl-khawāṣṣ taṣīru al-anwāʿ*, MS 1040 mistakenly adds *ammāʾl-jins fa-huwa kull lafẓa dālla ʿalā jamāʿa mukhtalifa ṣuwarahā* between apical "v", then the text continues (with small differences and some "v" emphasising, I assume, these differences), as in MS 576. MS 1040 emends *nawʿayni* (409.7) to *nawʿāni*, as in MS 576. MS 1040 emends *dhikr* to *dhikrihā* (428.4), as in MS 576, by adding *-hā* in the margin.[39] In the phrase *wa-an takūnu al-muqaddima kulliya* (443.5), MS 1040 (that has *yakūnu*) adds between the lines حد and, afterwards, اي; MS 576 adds, more correctly, احدي. In MS 1040, *fa-idh* instead of *fa-idhan* (443.8) with the second *alif* erased; *fa-idh* in MS 576. After *al-dawarān* (448.4), addition of *in* (sic, as in MS 576) in MS 1040 that wrote the *alif* and added the *nūn* between the letters.

The copyist of MS 1040 made mistakes he emended during revision, sometimes differently from MS 576. For instance, in the phrase *innaʾl-khams aqdam min al-sitta* (412.10), MS 1040 has *fī* instead of *min*, deleted by the copyist who wrote *min* between *aqdam* and *fī*; MS 576 has *fī*. After *al-sitta*, MS 1040 adds in the margin *al-ʿadad*, deleted; MS 576 has *al-ʿadad*. MS 1040 has *fīhā* instead of *fīhi* (416.2, with *alif* deleted); MS 576 has *fīhā*. MS 1040 adds *ghayr* between the lines in the phrase *ghayr al-insān ḥayawān* (417.4; in my edition: *lā*), omitted in MS 576. MS 1040 adds *hiya* to *humā* (418.10), deleted; MS 576 has *hiya*. The copyist must have compared various copies.

All the above-mentioned cases allow us to hypothesise a common model. This is also demonstrated by recurring writings such as the surprising ارسطاطا ليس (437.12) as if they were two words), منهاتين as a single word, or the attachment of *in* to words beginning by *kaf*—in MS 576 alone we find *in-kalām*—, or the indication in titles of Aristotle's *Prior Analytics* as *Anālūṭīqā al-ūlā* and not *Anālūṭīqā*.

NOTES

1 C. Baffioni, ed. and tr., *On Logic: An Arabic Critical Edition and English Translation of Epistles 10–14* (New York and London, 2010).

2 In my presentation, I refer to the pages and lines of this edition.

3 Ed. Wilāyat Ḥusayn, Bombay 1887–1889; ed. Khayr al-Dīn al-Ziriklī, Cairo 1928; ed. ʿĀrif Tāmir, Beirut 1995. On the older editions of the *Rasāʾil* see Omar Alí-de-Unzaga's contribution in this book, *infra*, pp. 82–84.

4 Since only the PDFs of individual epistles have been provided for the preparation of the new edition of the epistles of the *Ikhwān al-Ṣafāʾ* sponsored by the IIS, it is impossible for me at the moment to know whether the complete manuscripts Atif Efendi 1681, خ, and غ indicate the place of copy. As for the Ṣādir edition, it is not known which manuscripts it was prepared on.

5 The manuscript has been indicated as undated in the list given by the editors-in-chief, but Alí-de-Unzaga indicates the year 1574 (see *infra*, p. 86).

6 Baffioni, *On Logic*, pp. 167–179 and Alí-de-Unzaga, *infra*, p. 100.

7 A more detailed description of such frames is given in Alí-de-Unzaga, *infra*, p. 89.

8 D. Cortese, *Ismaili and Other Arabic Manuscripts: A Descriptive Catalogue of Manuscripts in the Library of The Institute of Ismaili Studies* (London and New York, 2000), pp. 28–29. On the incompleteness of this manuscript see Alí-de-Unzaga, *infra*, p. 81.

9 A. Gaçek, *Catalogue of Arabic Manuscripts in the Library of The Institute of Ismaili Studies*, vol. 1 (London, 1984), p. 91.

10 Cortese, *Ismaili and Other Arabic Manuscripts*, p. 29 (the whole description at pp. 29–30).

11 I had prepared my descriptions on the basis of the PDFs provided by the IIS. I am extremely grateful to Wafi Momin, Head of Ismaili Special Collections Unit of the IIS, for having granted me the rare privilege of a double-check on the original manuscripts, which allowed me to add further details to my former descriptions. I also thank Dr Nourmamadcho Nourmamadchoev and Naureen Ali for their assistance during the inspection of the manuscripts.

12 The blank page at the beginning (p. 1 in pencil, in Western figure) has an unclear number written in Arabic figure (probably '12'), around which there is an ink blot that seems to have spotted the folios below, preventing from reading the numeration of the first three folios.

13 Some of these scripts are described by Alí-de-Unzaga *infra*, p. 88.

14 The paper layer on the top hides the letters of the first line. I see:

1st line: [. . .] فر (ور؟) س ء (د؟) ى سح

2nd line: [. . .] لبعواباخلا

3rd line: [ت؟] ناكثرا

Before the first *alif*, there is a dotted letter. As it does not appear to be linked to the *alif*, it might be the second part of a dotted *tāʾ marbūṭa* that completes the first, unreadable word (perhaps, one can detect ورق) rather than a *nūn*.

15 The most recent hypothesis regarding the number of the epistles is Wilferd Madelung's who speaks of the splitting of Epistle 12 into two as the responsibility of Maslama al-Qurṭubī. 'Maslama al-Qurṭubī's Contribution to the Shaping of the Encyclopedia of the Ikhwān al-Ṣafāʾ', in *Labor Limae. Atti in onore di Carmela Baffioni*, ed. Straface Antonella, Carlo De Angelo and Andrea Manzo, *Studi Maġrebini*, 12–13 (2014–2015), vol. 1, pp. 403–417, at pp. 413–414. See also Alí-de-Unzaga, *infra*, p. 100.

16 According to Madelung, 'The replacement of music by geography as the fourth science probably occurred in the east not long after Maslama's death. It is confirmed in the table of contents of some manuscripts containing a revised version of Abū Sulaymān's table of contents'; 'Maslama al-Qurṭubī's Contribution', p. 415. See also Alí-de-Unzaga, *infra*, pp. 97 and 126–127.

17 Alí-de-Unzaga emphasises that the mistakes in this otherwise beautiful and precious manuscript are due to the fact that the scribe was neither an Arab nor learned. See *infra*, p. 90.

18 This description is based on a PDF in black and white that does not show any cover. Many words are unclear because of unequal pressure of the ink and the appearance in

transparency of the script of the rear page. The direct inspection of the manuscript revealed a coral red fabric cover in ramages (perhaps of silk), torn at the corners, which was added when the manuscript was restored.

19 This description is based on a PDF in black and white that does not show any cover. Direct inspection of the manuscript reveals a brown leather cover with gold decorations and a kind of amandine at the centre. The same amandine is repeated on the spine five times, between double lines. The gold in the back cover is partially faded. The binding is later than the manuscript. In the inside, the spine is in red cloth and above, there is red and blue marbled paper. In the text, some words have been emphasised by a red line above, and some marginal notes are also in red ink.

20 Neither Ṣ nor my edition has any ending.

21 Possibly due to bad pronunciation of the one who dictated the text. By speaking of 'dictation', I do not mean the practice in use in some *milieux*—but not, as Ismail K. Poonawala remarked during discussion, in Ismaili *milieux*. I only mean occasional help to the writer by someone who dictated to him the text to be copied.

22 I have to postpone the discussion on these additions to another occasion.

23 The manuscript tradition of the whole passage (*kull insān ṭāʾir . . . wa-kull insān ṭāʾir, mūjiba kādhiba*, 423.7–9 Ṣ) seems especially corrupt: MS 1040 adds in the inner margin: *mūjiba kādhiba, wa-kull ṭāʾir nāṭiq*; and in my edition the words *nāṭiq, mūjiba kādhiba . . . mūjiba kādhiba, wa-kull ṭāʾir* are missing.

24 These omissions lead to incomplete descriptions of the various syllogisms.

25 See above, n. 23.

26 MS 927 adds *faṣl* (as in my edition) after *al-ḥaqīqī* (426.22).

27 This conclusion is different from that of my edition.

28 The title is partially added at line 5 after *iʿwijājihi*.

29 These words reappear later, after *al-muqawwima*.

30 MS 576 adds this title after *fa-naqūlu* (432.19).

31 Different words of the title are omitted in the three manuscripts.

32 My edition adds: *waʾl-ashyāʾ allatī min jins al-muḍāf*.

33 See above, n. 21.

34 Their identification has to be postponed to another occasion.

35 One of which is dubious because of diacritics.

36 Note that the three manuscripts resemble each other (but not my edition) in 2 cases.

37 This is the only case in which MS 1040 has more similarities than MS 576.

38 The three manuscripts resemble each other (but not my edition) in 4 cases.

39 Instead of the following word, *mā*, at the beginning of the following line there is an *alif* only (probably substituted by the marginal addition of *-hā*), missing in MS 576.

4

The Missing Link? MS 1040: An Important Copy of the *Rasāʾil Ikhwān al-Ṣafāʾ* in the Collection of The Institute of Ismaili Studies*

Omar Alí-de-Unzaga

In this chapter I describe and analyse an important 10th-/16th-century manuscript of the *Epistles of the Pure Brethren* (*Rasāʾil Ikhwān al-Ṣafāʾ*) from the collection of The Institute of Ismaili Studies (IIS), London: MS 1040.[1] This manuscript is important not only because it has remained unexplored until now, but also mainly because it is the copy of the *Epistles* that bears the closest resemblance to the edition published in Bombay by Nūr al-Dīn b. Jīwā Khān at the end of the 1880s, an edition that was the basis of all subsequent prints and reprints of the 20th century, as I shall explain.[2]

Perhaps the most important reason why MS 1040 has been ignored lies in the way it has been characterised. The published catalogue that describes it states that the manuscript is 'defective in the middle and incomplete at the end' and that it only contains *'al-niṣf al-awwal* [i.e. the first half] and part of the second half'.[3] The catalogue does not elaborate on this, but this assessment is likely to have resulted from a superficial comparison of the manuscript with a printed edition of the *Rasāʾil*. If that is the case, then this is an example of what François de Blois has termed a 'pitfall': judging a manuscript against a particular printed edition of the text and not *vis-à-vis* other manuscripts of the same work,[4] which can throw light on the different versions or transmission strands of that given work. In reality, MS 1040 contains the whole corpus, i.e. fifty-two epistles, and is fairly complete (see the section 'Size, Style and Numeration' below).

Furthermore, despite being available in the central London location of the IIS and in spite of its relative early dating, the manuscript has not been employed by any of the contributors to the new critical edition of the *Epistles* published by Oxford University Press in association with the IIS itself.[5]

The unfairness of the assessment of MS 1040 is exacerbated by the fact that the most commonly available print is the text published in 1376/1957 in Beirut, at the Dār Bayrūt and Dār Ṣādir publishing houses, by Buṭrus b. Sulaymān al-Bustānī (d. 1969). This was a reproduction, with very minor cosmetic touches and slight modifications, of a print published in Cairo twenty-nine years earlier by the Syrian journalist Khayr al-Dīn al-Ziriklī (d. 1976) in 1347/1928 at the al-Maṭbaʿa al-ʿArabiyya publishing house. In a brief afterword (vol. 4, p. 479) Ziriklī recognises that he was too busy to prepare the text by himself as he had originally intended, which was meant to consist of 'emendations' (*taṣḥīḥ*) and the collation (*muqābala*) of the text with manuscripts (*uṣūl*), including, as he says, a copy held at the 'Royal Library' (Dār al-Kutub al-Malakiyya) in Cairo. He does not give details, but we may infer that he had most probably intended to consult MS 9509.[6] Instead, Ziriklī acknowledges that the work was actually carried out by a group of three scholars: Amīn Efendi Saʿīd, Shaykh Aḥmad Muṣṭafā and Shaykh Aḥmad Yūsuf, although we are told nothing on whether they did or did not consult the Cairo manuscript.

As it turns out, upon close and careful examination we can observe that Ziriklī's text actually shamelessly plagiarised and collated two of the editions available at that time, both produced in the final years of the 19th century.[7] The two editions plagiarised by Ziriklī are:

a) the above-mentioned edition published by Nūr al-Dīn b. Jīwā Khān, a prolific Bombay-based Ismaili Ṭayyibī Bohra publisher. This edition, produced in 1305–1306 (1887–1889) at Jīwā Khān's printing press, called Nukhbat al-Akhbār, is the only complete edition so far, and is based on an otherwise unidentified manuscript. All Jīwā Khān tells us in the initial 'notice' (*iʿlān*, p. 1) is that it was a 'sound (or, authenticated) ancient copy' (*nuskha qadīma ṣaḥīḥa*), without further elaboration as to the condition or details of the manuscript. The title page of the edition refers to the author: 'The Book of the Pure Brethren and Sincere Friends by the noble imam, the master of masters, our

Lord Aḥmad b. ʿAbd Allāh (*Kitāb Ikhwān al-Ṣafāʾ wa Khullān al-Wafāʾ li'l-imām al-humām, quṭb al-aqṭāb mawlānā Aḥmad b. ʿAbd Allāh*), thus indicating the Ṭayyibī ascription of the work to one of the Ismaili imams from the 3rd/9th century 'period of concealment' (*dawr al-satr*). Although we are not told much about the origin of the manuscript, circumstantial evidence points to a provenance from a senior Ismaili Bohra collection, given that Jīwā Khān states that he sought permission to publish it 'from one of the author's descendants' (*min baʿḍi sulālati'l-muʾallif*). Since Ṭayyibī *dāʿī*s trace their ancestry to the Ismaili imams,[8] and since such permission could only have been granted by the Bohra leader, or *Dāʿī Muṭlaq*, this may be read as a subtle allusion to the Dāʿī Muṭlaq of the time, ʿAbd al-Ḥusayn Ḥusām al-Dīn (d. 1891). As to the geographical provenance, many of the Bohra manuscripts were produced in Yemen, but we do not know either whether this copy came from Yemen or from India itself. Its date is also unknown, so we have to content ourselves with the term *qadīm*. The zealous reservedness of some Bohra libraries in India has kept their manuscripts away from public view, but perhaps future research will succeed in the enterprise of trying to identify the manuscript used by Jīwā Khān in their valuable collections. It is to Jīwā Khān's text that MS 1040 is closely related.

b) The second edition used by Ziriklī was published some forty years earlier by the Egyptian journalist and political activist ʿAlī Yūsuf (d. 1913). A former graduate of al-Azhar, he published it in Cairo, at the Maṭbaʿat al-Ādāb, in 1306/1888–1889. Again, ʿAlī Yūsuf's text was most likely based on the Cairo manuscript. His edition was doubly prey to misfortune: on the one hand, only Part One of the *Epistles* was published—it is not inconceivable that this was due to pressure from al-Azhar, whose *shaykh*s were against the promotion of certain works.[9] Furthermore, ʿAlī Yūsuf's edition has, most regrettably, fallen into oblivion and still remains off the radar of scholarship.

Ziriklī and his team simply lifted Jīwā Khān's text, but they also used ʿAlī Yūsuf for alternative readings, especially for the chapter headings and even for diagrams in Part One. Ziriklī removed the Bombay edition's attribution to the Ismaili imam from the title page. He also added substantial introductions by prestigious scholars such as Aḥmad

Zakī (d. 1934) and Ṭāhā Ḥusayn (d. 1973). As for the text itself, Ziriklī's team broke it up into paragraphs and introduced punctuation. By doing this, they in effect repackaged the Bombay text but with the attributes of a modern book. A meagre number of notes explaining difficult words were added and some 'corrections' were implemented (for Ṭibāwī's critique of this, see my Conclusion below). If it is wrong to speak about a 'Cairo edition', it is even more misleading to use the term 'Beirut edition'. At most, we can use the term 'print' for those texts. Scholarship's attention should focus on Jīwā Khān's original edition, especially when working with manuscripts, as I shall demonstrate.

In what follows, I will provide a description of MS 1040 with a view to situating it in relation to the copies which have been used for the IIS/OUP critical edition, in relation to other manuscripts I have accessed and consulted, and in relation to Jīwā Khān's edition, given its affinity with MS 1040.

Description of IIS MS 1040

Date

The manuscript contains a colophon at the end of Part Two, or 'the first half' (*al-niṣf al-awwal*), on f. Ar417v/W405v, at the end of Epistle 31. The colophon dates the manuscript on the last day of Shaʿbān of the year 953AH, which corresponds to 4 November 1546. This means that, of the twenty-four complete and dated manuscripts of the *Epistles* that I have managed to identify so far, of which I have had access to seventeen, MS 1040 is the eleventh oldest, being older than five of the manuscripts used in the IIS/OUP critical edition (see Table 4.1 for details of all manuscripts).[10] It is the second oldest complete dated copy currently held in a European repository, after MS 6647-8 from the Bibliothéque nationale de France (henceforth BnF) in Paris, which is about 250 years older. I consulted other manuscripts of the *Rasāʾil* from the IIS collections only sporadically.[11]

Background, Location and Scribe

It is possible that more than one scribe were employed on this manuscript. However, on the colophon page, a note in red ink tells us

Table 4.1 The place of IIS MS 1040 among the complete dated manuscripts of the *Rasā'il Ikhwān al-Ṣafā'*.(i)

	AH dating	AD equivalent	folios	City/ Copist	MS no. (Collection)	Library	City
1	578 (13 Ṣafar)	1182 (25 June)	581	Shammākhiyya / ✓	MS 1681 [ع]	Atif Efendi	Istanbul
2	667(ii)	1268	492	— / —	MS 41 [سج]	Salar Jung Museum	Hyderabad
3w	675 (22 Shaʿbān)(iii)	1275 (5 Feb.)	409	[Yazd] / —	MS 6647-8 [د]	BnF	Paris
4*	686 (5 Ramaḍān)	1287 (21 Oct.)	412	Baghdad / —	MS 4708	Majlis-i Shūra-yi Millī	Tehran
5	686 (Shawwāl)	1287 (Nov.-Dec.)	323	Baghdad / ✓	MS 3638 (Esad Efendi) [أ]	Süleymaniye mosque	Istanbul
6	704 (11 Rabīʿ II)	1304 (19 Nov.)	370	— / ✓	MS 2130-1 (Feyzullah Efendi) [ف، ق]	Millet Yazma Eser Kütüphanesi	Istanbul
7	820 (22 Jumādā I)(iv)	1417 (15 July)	531	— / —	MS 871 [ل]	Köprülü	Istanbul
8	[bet. 857-886](v)	[bet. 1453-81]	338	— / —	MS 870 [ك]	Köprülü	Istanbul
9*	887	1482	?	? / —	MS 1199 (Yeni Cami)	Süleymaniye mosque	Istanbul
10	**953 (*ākhir* Shaʿbān)**	**1546 (4 Nov.)**	**737**	**— / ✓**	**MS 1040 [ي]**	**Institute of Ismaili Studies**(vi)	**London**
11	968 (13 Ṣafar)(vii)	1560 (13 Nov.)	367	— / ✓	MS 260 (Laud Or.) [خ]	Bodleian	Oxford

(continued)

Table 4.1 *(continued)*

	AH dating	AD equivalent	folios	City/ Copist	MS no. (Collection)	Library	City
12*	968 (18 Shaʿbān)	1561 (14 May)	?	Cairo/ ✓	MS 1555	University Central Lib.	Tehran
13	981 (25 Ramaḍān)	1574 (28 Jan.)	395	— / —	MS 189 (Marsh) [غ]	Bodleian	Oxford
14w	1020 (*awāsiṭ* Ramadān)	1611 (mid Nov.)	529	— / —	MS 2303 [ر]	BnF	Paris
15*	1055	1645	631	— / —	MS 8 (*Falsafa*)	State Central Library(viii)	Hyderabad
16	1061 (25 Jumādā I)	1651 (16 May)	475	— / ✓	MS 2863	Nuruosmaniye	Istanbul
17w	1065 (1 Muḥarram)	1654 (11 Nov.)	488	— / ✓	MS 2304 [ز]	BnF	Paris
18*	1088 (27 Ṣafar)	1677 (1 May)	597	— / —	MS 2358-9	British Library	London
19*	1096 (26 Rajab)	1683 (21 July)	402	— / ✓	MS 4518(ix)	British Library	London
20w	1153 (2 Ṣafar)	1740 (29 April)	414	— / ✓	MS 2305	BnF	Paris
21*	1190	1776-7	489	— / —	MS 2222	Khuda Bakhsh	Patna
22w	1200	1785-6	294	— / —	MS arab. 652	Staatsbibliothek	Munich
23	1208	1793-4	688	— / —	MS 1278	Majlis-i Shūra-yi Millī	Tehran
24	1228	1813	389	— / —	MS 2341-4	BnF	Paris

KEY

*: MSS that I have been unable to consult; ✓: given;—: not given; w: available online; BnF: Bibliothèque national de France; bet.: between; ?: unknown to me.

(i) The table does not include undated copies, or manuscripts of the Persian translations of the *Epistles;* the Arabic letters after a manuscript are the letters assigned to them in the OUP/IIS critical edition.

(ii) This is given on f. 295b as the date of transcript ('probably of the prototype' according to the cataloguer).

(iii) The date given in the Foreword of the IIS/OUP critical editions ('AH 695') is incorrect; the manuscript was collated in Yazd 30 years later (beginning of Rajab 709=mid December 1309).

(iv) This is the date in the colophon. It applies to Epistles 43-52. Epistles 1-42 may be much older, judging by the writing. The cataloguer assumes a date *ca*. the end of 6th/12th century but no reasons are given.

(v) Although undated, this copy refers to the Ottoman Sultan Muḥammad al-Fātiḥ (Mehmed the Conqueror, r. 855-886 /1451-1481) with his epithet, which he gained at the conquest of Constantinople in 857/1453.

(vi) Now housed at the Aga Khan Centre, London. See above, note 2.

(vii) Not 967 as stated in some of the IIS/OUP edition volumes (Ep.4, p. 1; Ep. 32-36, p. 68; Ep. 39-41, p. 248; Ep. 48 p. 48 (gives 969), and Ep. 49-51, p. 27). The scribe is a certain Aḥmad b. ʿAlī al-Suʿūd.

(viii) Formerly known as Āṣafiyya Library. Catalogue no. 93 ('Uthmān ʿAlī Khān Bahādur Mīr, *Fihrist-i mashrūḥ-i baʿḍ-i kutub-i nafisa-i qalamiyya makhzūna-i kutubkhāna-i Āṣafiyya Sarkār-i ʿĀlī* (Hyderabad, 1338-1347/1928-1937), vol. 2, pp. 273-274.

(ix) Has a lacuna by which it lacks epistle 33 (and a few folios before and after).

that it was copied by the otherwise unknown al-Ḥasan b. ʿAlī al-Nuʿmānī al-Ismāʿīlī. This scribe does not appear in the other catalogues of the IIS manuscripts. The name 'al-Ismāʿīlī' could be simply a family name and is not necessarily a religious *nisba* indicating that the scribe was an Ismaili Shiʿi; however, this possibility cannot be discarded either. Although there are no indications of an explicitly and unequivocally Ismaili affiliation in the paratextual elements of the manuscript (i.e. there is no dedication to or mention of any specific imam or *dāʿī* by name), the eulogies found after the mention of the Prophet and his family have a very marked Shiʿi undertone, much more so than in other manuscripts. (See below on the closing formulas.)

No place of copy is mentioned in the text but we have enough evidence to infer that the manuscript was—if not copied—at least used in the region of Greater Khorasan. Delia Cortese is of the opinion that it was 'probably copied in Persia' without further elaboration. The flyleaves at the end, which contain numerous owner notes including debts, medicine recipes and even mystical poems (one is by the celebrated 6th/12th-century Sufi poet Sanāʾī Ghaznawī), do certainly give the general impression that the manuscript was owned and used (and maybe produced too) by Persian speakers up until the 20th century. The most readable writing is a debt note for the purchase of medicines, with the name of a certain Fatḥ Muḥammad Khān. The year given is 1330 (i.e. 1912) and the place of copy is named as 'Darrah-i Yūsuf', which can be identified with the valley also known as Darrah-i Ṣūf in modern day Afghanistan. The area is located between 120–170 km south of Balkh, and used to be on the caravan route that went from Balkh and Mazār-i Sharīf towards the southwest all the way to Bāmyān.[12] If we assume that the copy was produced in that region, we can place it within the southern part of the dominion of the Khānate of Bukhārā, which at that time was under the Shībānid (or Shaybānid) dynasty, and more particularly during the rule of ʿAbd al-Laṭīf b. Kūchkūnjī (r. 947–959/1540–1552), who had his capital in Samarqand further up north.[13] It is worth noting that the Shaybānids were promoters of Sunnī Islam, unlike their major rivals, the Shiʿi Safavids.

Size, Style and Numeration

MS 1040 has 737 folios, although it seems it may have originally had at least 752 (see below). This is quite an unusual number for the *Rasā'il* manuscripts, as the average length of the complete copies is around 450 folios, and the second largest is a long way away (MS 1681 from the Atif Efendi Library in Istanbul with 581 folios, which incidentally is the oldest dated manuscript and the copy used as the basis of many of the volumes in the IIS/OUP critical editions). This shows that the IIS manuscript was lavishly produced, possibly for an important person or purpose, and with aesthetic considerations (see Figure 4.1). The size of the folios is quite large (30 × 19 cm, almost like a modern A4). However, an elaborate quadruple frame, with blue, red and black lines and gold filling, leaves a stylised tall and narrow text-box of only 19.5 × 10 cm, with 21 lines per page. There are only about 12–14 words per line. The text itself is written with extreme care and elegance, most probably by a professional artist. The beginning of each part, which always falls on the verso (*ẓahr*) side of the folio (Part One: f. Ar14/W1v, Part Two: f. Ar174/W162v; Part Three: f. Ar406/W418v; Part Four: f. 508/W491v) is decorated with an ornate head-piece which uses the space up to the top of the folio. The head-pieces are polychrome but gold and blue predominate. The first head-piece is different from the other three, as it marks the beginning of the work. Each epistle is headed by a rectangular cartouche with a multi-coloured frame made up of several lines. The cartouche background is painted in blue, with various flowery decorations. In the centre, the epistle title is written in white ink, in the middle of a cloud-like shape which lined with gold paper. The title cartouches of the first epistle of each part (as well as epistles 2 and 3 of Part One) are the most elaborate, while a simpler style is used for the rest. The text on the first two pages is particularly ornate, as it is surrounded by gold-paper filled clouds in between the lines.[14] Such decorations are unique among all other available manuscripts of the *Rasā'il*. Although it would be speculative to argue for an Ismaili ownership or production context, the ornamentation clearly shows that this copy was considered special for whoever produced it. As far as I am aware, only three other manuscripts have title decorated cartouches for each epistle: MSS Köprülü 870, Ragip Pasha 840 and IIS 576.[15]

Figure 4.1 Title page of the first treatise (*On Arithmetic*) from the Epistles of the Pure Brethren (*Rasāʾil Ikhwān al-Ṣafāʾ*), MS 1040 of the Collection of The Institute of Ismaili Studies, London (f. Ar14/W1v). The manuscript is dated 953/1543.

Paradoxically, however, the innumerable mistakes at the lexical, punctuation and vocalisation level tell us that the scribe was definitely not an Arabic speaker, and certainly not trained as a scholar. The copy was not put through a collation or checking process, so it lacks the soundness of other copies that display a scholarly input.

The folios are numbered on the top-left corner of the recto (*wajh*) side of the folios with Arabic-Indic numbers (... ٣ ،٢ ،١) in black ink and also with Arabic-Western numbers (1, 2, 3 ...) in pencil. I shall henceforth refer to them as Ar/W, respectively. As we have it, the manuscript begins with f. Ar14/W1 (see the '*Fihrist*' section below). The pencil numeration was obviously inserted later.

Only two folios are missing in the middle of the text.[16] The last folio is Ar753/W746. It appears to end abruptly, without a final colophon. The sign ٥ for, '*intahā*,' is placed at the end (f. Ar753/W746v, corresponding to Jīwā Khān's edition, vol. 4, p. 396.2–4 (= Bustānī's 1957 print, vol. 4, p. 445.9–11). (See further comments on Epistle 52 below). At the bottom of the last existing folio a paper note was stuck on to the last line of the text box, with a different, later and more careless hand, which includes the number of folios and a reference saying there are no missing leaves: *'awrāqu ikhwāni'l-ṣafā' thalāthatu wa khamsūna wa sab'umi'a 753, lā yadhhabu waraq.'* If we add the 737 current folios, plus the *Fihrist* (see below) and the two missing leaves, we have a total of 752 original leaves.

Closing formulas

As with many other manuscripts of the *Epistles,* the formulas that close each epistle are not consistent across the corpus in MS 1040. Blessings on the Prophet and his family are usual, in a multitude of variations, in all the manuscripts. What is less common in the manuscripts is the explicit mention of the imams in that formula. In MS 1040 we do find the imams mentioned in closing formulas, albeit only in ten epistles – all in Part One (Epistles 1–4, 7 and 10–14). There is nothing in the contents of these epistles to justify this. This could be explained by the likelihood that the *Rasā'il* corpus was transmitted in parts. An alternative explanation is a possible change of scribe after the completion of Part One. A closer look at specific words (such as the *basmala*, or common conjunctions) seems to support the thesis that two hands are at work. For example, in most of Part One words like *fī*, *'alā, alladhī* and so on are written in a more rounded style, with the final *yā'* curving into a straight line under the word, while in most of the rest they tend to be written with more defined angles. These observations are only tentative as they are based on random naked eye samples. A more detailed codicological analysis would be required for more definite conclusions.

The typical formula here is *ṣallā'llāhu 'alā sayyidnā Muḥammadini'l-nabī wa ālihi'l-a'imma [al-ṭayyibīn] al-ṭāhirīn wa sallama taslīman 'alayhim ajma'īn* (May God bless our lord Muhammad the Prophet and his family, the righteous and pure imams, may He shower immense peace over them all). Epistle 4 is even more explicit, as it mentions Ali: *ṣallā'llāhu 'alā sayyidnā Muḥammadin khātimi'l-nabiyyīn wa 'alā waṣiyyihi 'Aliyyin afḍali'l-waṣiyyīn wa 'alā 'itratihimā'l-ṭāhirīna'l-a'immati'l-hādīn wa sallama taslīmā* (May God bless our lord Muhammad, the seal of the prophets, and upon his legatee Ali, the best of legatees, and their pure descendants, the right-guided imams, and may He shower [them] with immense peace). It is remarkable that the mention of the imams completely disappears after Part One and only two other epistles, both in Part Two (Epistles 17 and 27) include *ālihi* (his family), after the mention of the Prophet, in their closing formulas. As mentioned above, this could be explained by a change of scribe, or a change of patron, or changing political circumstances in which dissimulation was called for. Another strong possibility is that the transmission of the *Epistles* manuscripts was not necessarily copying from complete copies, but from different copies of each of the four Parts, or perhaps from incomplete manuscripts.

The Individual Epistles in MS 1040

I now proceed to describe the individual epistles in MS 1040. The reader will notice that of the fifty-two epistles, only forty are mentioned. This is because my analysis focuses on those epistles where I have identified significant similarities or variations between MS 1040 and other manuscripts or editions, as well as those epistles where the scholars working in the new critical edition have found relevant differences.[17] I have paid particular attention to the relationship of this manuscript with Jīwā Khān's edition, which is a very close relationship indeed, and with ʿAlī Yūsuf's edition for Part One only. The length of my discussion will vary from epistle to epistle depending on the extent of the variations. In the manuscript tradition of the *Rasā'il*, as we shall see, there are numerous cases where individual manuscripts (and groups of manuscripts) contain epistles in shorter versions while others display longer versions, and I shall point that out when relevant.

Fihrist

The vast majority of manuscripts that I have consulted do contain a contents section, or *fihrist,* that describes the contents and aim of the four Parts of the *Rasā'il* as well as of each individual epistle.[18] In the case of MS 1040 this content section is not extant but it must have originally been part of the manuscript. We can infer this from the folio numeration, which, as mentioned above, begins with f. 14 in the

Arabic-Indic numeration. This was later numbered as f. 1 in Arabic-Western numbers. Once the *fihrist* had been lost, the older numeration did not make sense. This explains why the Arabic-Indic numbers of the first three existing folios (ff. Ar14, 15 and 16) were rubbed and now appear smudged, although they can still be discerned.

Part One

Epistle 1: On Arithmetic

The decorative aspects in this epistle have been discussed above. The Arabic-Indic numeration has skipped one folio towards the end of the epistle, so we find the sequence f. Ar25/W12 – Ar [unnumbered]/W13 – Ar26/W14. As for the text, the majority of the variants attributed to 'the Dār Ṣādir edition' (i.e. Bustānī's print), in Nader El-Bizri's recent critical edition[19] using the siglum [Ṣ], can be traced to MS 1040. The text of this epistle is identical, or nearly so, to Jīwā Khān's Bombay edition, with the exception of the initial laudatory formula, which is missing altogether in that edition. MS 1040 gives:

القسم الأولى [كذا] في الرياضية التعليمية

الرسالة الأول [كذا]

بِسْمِ اللهِ الرَّحْمٰنِ الرَّحِيمِ. رَبِّ يَسِّرْ وَتَمِّمْ بِالْخَيْرِ.

القِسمُ الأوَّل من الأقسام الأربعة في الرياضيات يشتمل على ثَلْثَة عشر الأولى منها في العدد وهو الأرثماطيقى من جملة الإحدى وخمسين رِسَالة في تهذيب النفس وإصلاح الأخلاق. الحمد لله الذي لا تحسن الأشيَاءَ إلاّ أن يكون بدؤها حمده وكل ناطق وَساكت فَهو عبده الذي تاهت الألباب في عظمته و ذلت له عقول أهل معرفته عندمَا شهدت من [عزّ°] جبروته وصلواته وتحياته على خير خلقه [كذا] وبريّته مُحمَّد النَّبِيّ وآله وعترته وَلمنتجيين [كذا] من أصحَابه وعشيرته والصَّالحين من عباده وأمّته. اعلم، أَيّدَك الله وإيَّانا بروح منه، بأنه لمّا كان من مذاهب إخوانِنا الكرام، أيدهم الله، النظر في جميع علوم الموجودات . . .

> Part One on the Mathematical and Educational [epistles].
>
> Epistle 1.
>
> In the Name of God, the Merciful, the Compassionate. Lord, make things easy and perfect us with goodness!
>
> Part One of Four, on the mathematical [epistles], containing thirteen [epistles], the first of them being on numbers or 'Arithmetic', from a total of fifty-one epistles on the refinement of the soul and the improvement of character.
>
> Praise be to God, for things are not good that do not begin with His praise. Every speaking and silent one is his servant. Minds get lost in His greatness. The intellects of the people who possess cognisance of Him (*ahl maʿrifatihi*) point to Him when they witness the might of His omnipotence. May His blessings and greetings be on His best creation and creature, the Prophet Muhammad, on his family and offspring, on his chosen companions, on his kinsfolk, on His righteous servants, and on his community.
>
> Know, may God assist you and us *with a spirit from Himself* [Q.58:22] that since the teachings of our noble brethren, may God assist them, consist of reflection on the sciences of the existing beings . . .

It is worth remarking that the exact same laudatory formula is found only in two other manuscripts, one of them being the oldest surviving copy, MS Atif 1681 (f. 5v),[21] the other being BnF MS 2305 (f. 6r). Modified versions of the laudatory formula are given in most other manuscripts, which are less explicit in the praise of the Prophet's family. In Table 4.2 I give the variants of the mention of the Prophet Muhammad and the words that follow:

Table 4.2 Mention of the Prophet Muhammad and the words that follow.

His Messenger Muhammad and all his family (*rasūlihi Muḥammad wa ālihi ajmaʿīn*)	MSS Mahdavi 7437, f. 7v Köprülü 871, f. 5v Köprülü 870, f. 4r BnF 2304, f. 4v
Muhammad and his offspring (*Muḥammad wa ʿitratihi*)	MSS Esad 3638, f. 3v Feyzullah 2130, f. 2v

the Prophet Muhammad and his offspring (*Muḥammad al-nabī wa ʿitratihi*)	MSS Laud Or. 255, f. 5 Munich arab. 652, f. 1v BnF 2341, f. 1v
the Prophet Muhammad, his offspring and the righteous of his community (*Muḥammad al-nabī wa ʿitratihi wa'l-ṣāliḥīna min ummatihi*)	SOAS MS Or. 45812, f. 3v
His Messenger Muhammad, his family and all his companions (*rasūlihi Muḥammad wa ālihi wa saḥbihi ajmaʿīn*)	Nuruosmaniye MS 2863, f. 5v ʿAlī Yūsuf's ed. p. 12
the Prophet Muhammad and the righteous of his community (*Muḥammad al-nabī wa'l-ṣāliḥīna min ummatihi*)	MSS BnF 2303 f. 5v Majlis 1278 p. 7
(No introductory text at all and therefore no laudatory formula is given in some manuscripts)	MSS Sālār Jung 41, Esad 3637 (has a different beginning), Hunt 296, Escorial 923, Laud Or. 260, Marsh 189, IIS 576, Garrett 4263, and the editions of Dieterici and Jīwā Khān.

The Shiʿi character of the laudatory formulas in MS 1040 is clear. Three remarks are in order. The first regards the phrase 'every speaking and silent one (*kullu nāṭiq wa sākit*) is His servant.' This could be regarded as a veiled reference to the Ismaili idea that each of the prophets that pronounce the outer aspects of the revealed law, and are therefore called 'speakers' (*nāṭiq*, pl. *nuṭaqā'*), are followed by the 'silent ones' (*ṣāmit*, pl. *ṣawāmit*) who explain the inner or esoteric aspects.[22] However, the word *sākit* and not *ṣāmit* is used here; further, the *nāṭiq/sāmit* concept does not appear in the *Epistles*. Thus, any connection to it is only speculative. Secondly, MS 1040 is the only copy (together with the other two mentioned above) that give here several expressions for the members of the Prophet's blood relations: his family (*ālihi*), his offspring (*ʿitratihi*) and his kinsfolk (*ʿashīratihi*). These may be mere synonyms, but could also be seen as an effort to emphasise the importance and status of different relations to the Prophet, i.e. the members of his household, his direct descendants (that is, the imams) and his closest relatives. The third point that indicates a Shiʿi background is the selective blessing request for 'his chosen companions' (*al-muntajabīn min aṣḥābihi*).[23] The expression may be read as a restrictive version of the common Sunni inclusion of blessings for 'all his companions' (*aṣḥābuhu ajmaʿīn*).

Epistle 2: On Geometry

The epistle 'On Geometry' appears in two versions in the manuscripts: the short version and the long version, the latter being an expansion of the former. MS 1040 contains the shorter version, as does also IIS MS 576 (pp. 61–77). This is the same version as given in Jīwā Khān's edition (vol. 1, pp. 43–55), as well as the following five other manuscripts, the first two of which are older than MS 1040: MS Sālār Jung 41 (f. 22 r/p. 43) – the second oldest known complete manuscript in the world[24] and the direct antecedent of the undated MS Esad 3637[25] – and Escorial 923 (ff. 19v-20r), which has a slightly different ending;[26] the other are: MSS Marsh 189 (pp. 28-9), which is only 28 years older than MS 1040; BnF 2341 (f. 12v), which omits the sentence that refers to the *Ikhwān al-Ṣafā*''s *madhhab*; and Esad 3637 (ff. 17v-18r). The longer version, which has extra chapters full of diagrams, was given in ʿAlī Yūsuf's edition (pp. 34–55).[27] In this case the latter was chosen by Ziriklī over the Bombay version (and was later reproduced by Bustānī). El-Bizri's critical edition is based on some of the manuscripts containing the longer version.[28]

Can MS 1040's shorter version reflect an older text that was later expanded? Some evidence does point to this, since at least two manuscripts, namely the oldest extant manuscript, MS Atif 1681 (f. 21v) and a near contemporary of MS 1040, MS Garrett 4263 (f. 15r), place a conclusion note ('*tammat al-risāla*') at the end of the shorter version (El-Bizri's edition, p. 128, tr. 145), and then go on to add the extra chapters (which are six in the critical edition).

Epistle 3: On Astronomy

As compared with other manuscripts, the title on this epistle in MS 1040 has the same wording as in MS Sālār Jung 41 and MS2130 of the Feyzullah Efendi collection at the National Public Manuscripts Library (Millet Yazma Eser Kütüphanesi) in Istanbul, which add the words 'and the course of the planets' (*wa masīr al-kawākib*). The text of the three poetry fragments (one in Arabic and two in Persian) on f. W30r is similar to the Jīwā Khān's edition (vol. 1, p. 70). In MS 1040 the Persian poems are followed by an Arabic paraphrase, which appear also in IIS MS 576 (p. 96) and in Jīwā Khān's edition (though not in ʿAlī Yūsuf's edition, as consequently not in Ziriklī's or Bustānī's prints, which reproduced ʿAlī Yūsuf's text in this case). MS 1040 does not set the poetic lines with a caesura, but red dots are used as punctuation to separate hemistiches and verses.

Epistles 4 and 5: On Music and *On Geography*

In MS 1040, Epistle 4 is 'On Music' and Epistle 5 'On Geography'. The same order occurs in the two oldest complete manuscripts (MSS Atif 1681 and Sālār Jung 41) as well as in other copies: Feyzullah 2130, Escorial 923, Esad 3637 and IIS 576 (only the latter is more recent than MS 1040), as opposed to other manuscripts that follow the reverse order. The reversed order was followed in Jīwā Khān's edition (and the subsequent prints), as well as in the new critical edition.[29] The ending of *On Music* in MS 1040 (f. Ar 75/W 62v) states that with this epistle concludes the 'first section' (*tamma bi-tamāmihā'l-juz'u'l-awwal*). Wright's critical edition[30] reproduces the endings in various manuscripts, but none of them contain the same remark.

Epistle 6: On Proportion

MS 1040 does not have the appendix identified by El-Bizri[31] as appearing in MS Atif 1681 and other manuscripts.[32] In this MS 1040 again coincides with Jīwā Khān's edition. Other copies that do not include the appendix either are MSS Sālār Jung 41, Nuruosmaniye 2863 and Munich arab. 652.

Epistle 7: On the Theoretical Crafts

Godefroid de Callataÿ's critical edition[33] has identified some extra paragraphs in a number of manuscripts.[34] He pointed out that MS Atif 1681 (and only a few other copies) does not contain the extra text. I may add that MS 1040 is to be grouped with MS Atif 1681, as it does not include those extra lines; the same is true of MSS Sālār Jung 41, Majlis 1278, SOAS Or. 45812, Munich arab. 652, BnF 2341 and IIS 576.[35] Here again, Jīwā Khān's edition is aligned with MS 1040.

Epistle 8: On the Practical Crafts

El-Bizri[36] identified a short passage that repeats itself in MS Atif 1681 and found that it occurs also in another copy, MS Esad 3638. I have identified the passage in five further manuscripts which reproduce the same repetition, one of them being MS 1040 (f. Ar100/92v). The others are MSS IIS 576 (p. 230), Munich arab. 652 (f. Ar37/W36v), BnF 2341 (f. 47v) and Garrett 4263 (f. 74v).[37] Some lines further down, El-Bizri (p. 8) noted a piece of text missing in MS Atif 1681, but found in other copies. The said passage appears in MS 1040 (Ar106/W94v) almost verbatim when compared to the Jīwā Khān edition (vol. 1, p. 33–34). Mistakes aside, the only real difference between the two is the word *khawwāṣṣ/khāliṣ*, and the use of *faṣl* (chapter) where Jīwā Khān gives *iʿlam* (know).

Epistle 9: On Character Traits

During my work to prepare the critical edition of this epistle I paid special attention to how Jīwā Khān's edition compares with the manuscripts. My study yields very clear results. The comparison shows that among all copies, one manuscript, MS 1040, is considerably and undoubtedly the closest to that edition. As I used MS Atif 1681 as the basis of the edition, I focused on the variants of other manuscripts and editions with regard to that copy. We can see that Jīwā Khān's text presents unique readings, i.e. different to all the other texts (including MS Atif 1681) in 449 variants and MS 1040 differs from all in 555 variants. Those numbers are inconclusive; however, the startling result comes when we focus on the variants where Jīwā Khān's text does coincide with copies other than MS Atif 1681: it coincides with MS 1040 in over two thousand variants (out of which 665 are variants in which Jīwā Khān and MS 1040 both differ from all the other texts considered in the edition). On the other hand, Jīwā Khan's coincidence with other texts is appreciably and considerably much lower (see Table 4.3).

Table 4.3 Number of variants with regard to MS Atif 1681 in which Jīwā Khān's edition coincides with these MSS/editions.

IIS 1040	2,067
Feyzullah 2130	303
ʿAlī Yūsuf's ed.	273
Esad 3638	267
Sālār Jung 41	206
BnF 6647	185
Mahdavi 7437	146

The closeness between Jīwā Khān's and MS 1040 is reinforced when we consider the times they coincide with other copies, but not with each other. Thus Jīwā Khān's edition coincides with other texts and not MS 1040 a total of 219 times, and MS 1040 coincides with other text and not Jīwā Khān's edition 235 times. Given the thousands of variations found, these are very low numbers, which reinforces the affinity between the two texts (see Table 4.4).

Table 4.4 No. of times that MS 1040 coincides with these copies but not with Jīwā Khān's ed.; and that Jīwā Khān's ed. coincides with these copies but not with MS 1040.

	Times that MS 1040 coincides with these copies but not with Jīwā Khān's ed.	Times that Jīwā Khān's ed. coincides with these copies but not with MS 1040
Mahdavi 7437	4	10
BnF 6647	21	18
Sālār Jung 41	27	27
Esad 3638	47	52
Feyzullah 2130	80	106
ʿAlī Yūsufs ed.	56	6
TOTAL	235	219

Epistle 10: On the Isagoge

MS 1040 presents this epistle in its shorter version, which seems to have been a feature in some of the 10th/16th-century manuscripts of the *Epistles*. It shares this characteristic with only three other manuscripts: the undated MS IIS 576, and two manuscripts that are almost contemporaries of MS 1040: MSS Laud Or. 260 and Marsh 189, which were copied 14 and 28 years after MS 1040 respectively. Whether the shorter version represents an older matrix of the text or a later curtailed version is a matter for further speculation.

Epistle 12: On Peri Hermeneias

MS 1040, like the vast majority of manuscripts, does not include the extra text found in MS Esad 3638, as identified by Baffioni.[38]

Epistles 13 and 14: On the Prior Analytics and the Posterior Analytics

In MS 1040 Epistles 13 and 14 are 'On the Prior Analytics' and the 'Posterior Analytics' respectively, so Part One consists of fourteen epistles in this copy. In that, MS 1040 seems to follow Koprülü MS 871, which was copied more than a century earlier. Jiwā Khān's edition follows the same line (vol. 1, pp. 125–130 and 131–146). Most other manuscripts only count thirteen epistles in Part One (as does 'Alī Yūsuf's edition, which counts thirteen epistles, although in reality it contains fourteen, with an unnumbered epistle (on *Anūlūtiqā al-ūlā*, pp. 298–304) between epistles 12 and 13 called 'the fourth logical' epistle (*al-rābiʿa min al-manṭiqiyyāt*), and with epistle no. 13 entitled *fī'l-Burhān* (pp. 305–324).[39] For his 'edition' of these two epistles, Ziriklī chose to reproduce Jīwā Khān's text.

Part Two

Epistle 15 = II.1 On Matter and Form[40]

The appendix identified by Carmela Baffioni[41] in some of the manuscripts is not found in MS 1040. The text in our copy roughly corresponds to MS Atif 1681. In Epistle 15 Jīwā Khān's edition basically corresponds with MS 1040 except that the latter does not have the first and last lines included in the Bombay edition (and in most other MSS, judging by Baffioni's work).

Epistle 16 = II.2 On the Heavens

As Baffioni has noted, some manuscripts (in fact, most of them) display a diagram of the spheres of the cosmos in the fourth chapter, 'On the composition of the spheres. . .', of this epistle.[42] Unfortunately, the critical edition did not reproduce the diagram, which consists of a number of concentric circles, so future research could explore this aspect of the textual transmission of the work (since there are variations among the manuscripts in how this diagram is depicted). Other manuscripts[43] left a blank for the chart but it was never drawn: this was the case of Jīwā Khān's edition (vol. 2, p. 18), although interestingly Ziriklī (vol. 2, p. 23) did include the diagram.[44] Yet a small minority of copies have no chart at all and do not even leave a space for it. This is the case of MS 1040 (f. Ar182/W170v) and IIS MS 576 (p. 395).[45] As with the previous epistle, the appendixes found by Carmela Baffioni[46] in some of the manuscripts are not found in MS 1040 either. Also, f. Ar186/W174r[47] has a marginal note next to the mention of the Persian year, which says 'The Persian year has 365 days' (*al-sanatu'l-fārisiyyatu thalāthumi'atu yawmin wa khamsatu wa sittūna yawman*).[48]

Epistle 19 = II.5 On Minerals

This is the first epistle in MS 1040 that adds, after the initial *basmala*, the Qur'ānic verse 27:59 (*Praise belongs to God, and peace be on His servants whom He has chosen. What, is God better, or that they associate? – al-ḥamdu li'llāhi wa salāmun 'alā 'ibādihi'llādhī'ṣṭafā a-Allāhu khayrun ammā yushrikūn*). This feature is repeated only in five other epistles of Part Two (epistles 23 and 27–30). The same formula presumably appeared in the manuscript used by Jīwā Khān since in his edition it introduces all the epistles, except in the logic epistles (nos. 10-14)[49] and epistles 45 and 46 ('On Companionship', and 'On Faith' respectively).

Epistles 19, 20 and 21 = II.5, 6 and 7

As seen in the manuscripts used in Carmela Baffioni's critical edition, the introduction of each of these epistles in those copies refers to the previous epistles – respectively – as the Epistle 'On Doctrines' (no. 42), the Epistle 'On the Theoretical Crafts' (7), and the Epistle 'On Minerals'

(19).[50] All the other extra manuscripts that I have consulted (including IIS MS 85) follow the same referencing style. Jīwā Khān's edition follows this order too. However, in MS 1040 the introductions of these epistles refer to the immediately previous epistles in the sequential order of the corpus as we have it. This is also the case in IIS MS 576. In this, both manuscripts are unique.

Epistle 22 = II.8 On Animals

The bulk of this epistle is formed by the famous allegorical fable that narrates the debate between humans and animals before the king of the jinn. The fable comes to a close when the king consults a wise cosmopolitan man described as combining the best traits of all cultures. The wise man then praises the 'friends of God' (*awliyā' Allāh*) as the best of all creation, and mentions how their qualities are innumerable. Lenn Goodman states that after the phrase *wa lam yablaghū kunha maʿrifatihā* ('although nobody has managed to grasp the ultimate essence of those qualities'—my translation) 'the modern printed editions', which he calls 'the Ziriklī, Tāmir and Bustānī editions,' 'fill out the story here, as if to compensate for the seeming abruptness and surprising turn of the last few pages'.[51] In reality—as I have shown—the passage alluded to comes from Jīwā Khān's edition (vol. 2, p. 345). However, a close inspection into the diversity of the manuscript tradition of the *Rasā'il* reveals a more nuanced picture. With regard to the ending of this Epistle, manuscripts fall under three groupings:

a) in one group of manuscripts, the wise man's speech on the qualities of friends of God is followed by the king's final verdict – that animals are to be subject to humans until 'a [new] cycle begins' (*ḥattā yasta'nifu'l-dawr*). At this point the text exhorts the reader not to take the fable as 'children's play' (*mulāʿibat al-ṣibyān*), as the authors use expressions and allusions to express deeper truths. The epistle is concluded with a closing formula. That the mention of the cycle is a more Ismaili-sounding ending is made evident by the fact that four Ismaili manuscripts use this text: three are now in the IIS collection and the fourth was the manuscript used by Jīwā Khān. The oldest manuscript in this group is MS 1040. The other two copies at the

IIS are MS 576 (p. 690) and MS 84 (pp. *326–329),[52] a 19th-century manuscript that contains only this epistle.[53] The final lines in these four manuscripts do have differences, but the passage is basically the same. The Ismaili character of the fable was highlighted by Yves Marquet, who interpreted the symbolism of the animals and the bee as referring to the Ismaili initiates and the imam. Marquet also found parallels between the seven animal kingdoms and the prophetic cycles, the last of which is the cycle of the Qā'im, the rightful imam who is awaited to restore justice.[54] If this interpretation is correct, the final passage in this group, with its mention of a new cycle, would be perfectly in line with the allegorical intention of the fable.

A subgroup of manuscripts also incorporate some phrases as in group a), to the effect that animals are to be subject to humans, although they notably miss the mention of the new cycle. These include MSS BnF 2303 (f. 236r), SOAS Or. 45812 (ff. 124v-125r) and BnF 2305 (f. 209r). The same ending is found in the 1812 Calcutta edition of the Debate by the Shiʿi Yemeni author and poet Aḥmad b. Muḥammad b. ʿAlī al-Anṣārī al-Yamanī al-Shirwānī (d. 1840).[55]

b) In the largest group, which includes many of the oldest manuscripts,[56] the wise man's speech is simply followed by a final sentence saying that the authors have laid out the qualities of the friends of God in their fifty-one epistles, to which a brief closing formula is added. Goodmann's critical edition follows the text of this group.

c) Yet other manuscripts present further variations, which were not considered in Goodman's edition. For instance, Köprülü MS 871 (f. 256v–258r) adds a whole two-and-a-half page chapter on self-knowledge, and MS Marsh 189 (f. 193r) adds an extra passage of about 20 lines where the king of the jinn continues to speak. Editing these extras remains a desideratum. An extra chapter is also found at the end of Friedrich Dieterici's 1879 edition of the fable.[57] This chapter is the allegorical tale of the two islands[58] which is part of Epistle 44, 'On the Belief of the Pure Brethren', in all known manuscripts. Dieterici used BnF MS 2303 and Shirwānī's edition (neither of which has this extraneous addition), as well as MS 5039 from the Staatsbibliothek in Berlin (Sprenger collection no. 1946), so the latter manuscript needs to be examined.

Epistles 29 and 30 = II.15 and 16

The title and number of these two epistles are transposed in MS 1040 (although the numbers were corrected later in the margin in red ink). In his critical edition of Epistle 29, 'On Life and Death', Eric Ormsby notes an additional short passage at the beginning of the text from the so-called 'Beirut edition'.[59] This was of course a reproduction of the text in Jīwā Khān's edition (vol. 2, p. 332), via Ziriklī's print. I have examined all other manuscripts available to me that were not used by Ormsby and MS 1040 is the sole copy where the extra text is found (f. Ar 383/W371r), highlighting once more its closeness to Jīwā Khān's edition.

Epistle 30 = II.16 On Pleasure

Two groups of manuscripts can be identified, depending on whether a chapter (Chapter 1 in Ormsby's critical edition)[60] is positioned at the beginning or at the end of the epistle. MS 1040 (f. Ar407/W395v.9-Ar408/W396r.15), belongs to the latter group, together with the four manuscripts identified by Ormsby.[61] To these we can also add another five manuscripts, including IIS MS 576, f. 154v–159r.[62] Unlike MS 1040, in Jīwā Khān's edition the passage is found in the middle (vol. 2, pp. 345.ult–346.13). Even though Ormsby has attempted to note the variations in the 'Beirut edition', he has left out some notable passages, which again can be seen in MS 1040.[63]

Some further differences between MS 1040 and Jīwā Khān's text can be detected in this epistle. For instance, in chapter 8 (as numbered in Ormsby's translation) there are two quotes of poetry. While MS 1040 (f. Ar399/W387r = Ormsby p. 33, tr. p. 87) follows the text as found in the vast majority of manuscripts,[64] Jīwā Khān's edition (vol. 2, pp. 353, copied by Ziriklī, vol. 2, p. 81 = Bustānī, vol. 3, pp. 66, 67) cites them in the reversed order and with slightly different surrounding text. In this detail, the Bombay edition stands apart from the known manuscript tradition. In a third line of poetry given further down, Jīwā Khan (vol. 2, p. 357.1) does coincide with MS 1040 (f. 389v.8-9, marked '*shi'r*' in red ink) and the other manuscripts (= Ormsby, p. 37, tr. p. 92).

Epistle 31 = II.17 On Languages

Here, as in the previous epistle, MS 1040 is markedly different from Jīwā Khān's edition. This epistle is found in two versions in the manuscript tradition; accordingly, we can group the various copies, with regard to this epistle, into what may be termed the *ʿayn* family, after MS Atif (عاطف) Efendi 1681, and the *alif* family, after MS Esad (أسعد) Efendi 3638, taking the two oldest representatives as the eponyms of each 'group'.[65]

a) MS 1040 is part of the *ʿayn* family, which also includes IIS MS 576 and ten other manuscripts.[66] The text of the epistle is short (with an average across manuscripts of 13 pages) and has no internal chapters. MS 1040 has red overlining on the word *iʿlam* or similar words that introduce new ideas. The most striking feature in this family is the mention, in the final section, of a number of personalities from the Greek tradition such as Asclepius, Galen and Aristotle (and his *Categories*), and from the Arabic-Islamic tradition such as Ibn ʿAbbās (and his *tafsīr*) and Abū Ḥātim al-Sijistānī, the Basran linguist (d. 255/869).

b) The *alif* family presents a much longer version with an average of 44 pages, which is more than three times larger than the shorter version. It has numerous chapters (17 in MS Esad 3638). This version was also found in the manuscript used by Jīwā Khān (and therefore in the printed editions).[67] There are some touching points between the two versions where they share some text, but by and large they are two separate textual traditions. The longer version contains a specialist (one could say 'professional') treatment of sound, speech and writing. It remains a desideratum to publish the shorter version and ascertain whether it is the original text or a summary of the longer version.

c) One manuscript (MS Feyzullah 2130) combines both versions, and places one (the *alif* long version) after the other (the shorter *ʿayn* version), although the part corresponding to the shorter version is half the size of that found in the other manuscripts.[68]

At the end of this epistle MS 1040 states that it is followed by 'the thirty-first epistle'—obviously a mistake as it should have said 'thirty-second'. Following this, as mentioned earlier, there is a colophon concluding Part Two, that includes the date and the scribe's name in large red ink. Interestingly, it calls the work 'The Book of the Epistles of the Pure Brethren' (*Kitāb Rasāʾil Ikhwān al-ṣafāʾ*), a term that occurs in another manuscripts too.

Part Three

Epistles 32 and 33:

These two epistles are the first and the second of Part Three. They represent one of the best loci to understand the complexities of the textual transmission of the *Rasāʾil*. Paul Walker has already offered valuable comments in his critical edition;[69] here I will supplement them by bringing MS 1040 as a new player in the discussions on the textual history of the *Epistles*. I would argue that MS 1040 (at least in these two epistles) may represent an older text that was not yet touched by later additions, especially the addition of the extra version of Epistle 32 (called '32b' by Walker).

From the available manuscripts we can differentiate three 'blocks' of text: 'A', 'B', and 'C' (which correspond to Walker's edition's Epistles 32, 33 and 32b respectively),[70] and we can distinguish four groups of manuscripts (I-IV) by the way they employ, omit, select, mix and entitle these blocks. Even within each group, epistles are ordered differently and start and end at varying points. See Table 4.5 for a synoptic diagram:

1) Group I manuscripts contain only 'A' and 'B', but not 'C'. The most ancient copy in this group is MS 6647-8 [ك], which combines 'A' and 'B' into one epistle. A subgroup of manuscripts (I.2), share extra characteristics. MS 1040 is the oldest manuscript of this subgroup, which also includes MSS BnF 2303 [ر] and 2305, Majlis 1278 and SOAS Or. 45812. They all call 'B' 'On the Intellectual Principles according to the Pure Brethren' (*Fī'l-mabādi'i'l-ʿaqliyyati ʿalā raʾy ikhwāni'l-ṣafāʾ*). There are only four other manuscripts known so far to have used the term '*Ikhwān al-Ṣafāʾ*" in the title of 'B': MSS Sālār Jung 41 (f. 300v), which is the second oldest complete manuscript of the *Epistles*; its 'relative' Esad 3637 [ن] (f. 335r—see group IV for both); Laud Or. 255 [ح],[71] and the undated IIS 83, f. 7v (which also uses the name in 'C', f. 15r).[72] Jīwā Khān's edition is related to both IIS manuscripts. Another feature of MS 1040 and subgroup I.2 is that 'A' is quite short (MS 1040, f. 406v–408r = Walker's edition, pp. 5-10.12), that and 'B' (f. 408v–415v = Walker, pp. 10.14–33) starts in what is the middle of 'A' in other manuscripts (see Table 4.5). Finally, MS 1040 is also interesting in that it is the second oldest dated copy to contain a

Table 4.5 Epistles 32 and 33 in IIS MSS 1040 and 83 compared to other manuscripts.(i)

	I (A&B)									II (A&B&C)						III (A&C)			IV (B&C)				
	I.1				I.2																		
	د	ق	ل	خ	**IIS MS 1040**	ر	BnF 2305	MAJ	SOAS	ع	أ	ح	ج	**IIS MS 83**	JK	ك	NUR	ز (ii)	سج	ن	غ	MUN	BnF 2341-4
AH	675	704	820	967	**953**	1020	1153	1208	nd	578	686	1046	1094	**nd**		ca 857	1016	1065	667	nd	981	1200	1228
A	1	2	1	1	**1**	1	1	1	1	1	2	2	1	**1**	1	1	1(2nd)	1	—	—	—	—	—
					2*	2*	2*	2*	2*							2	2	2	—	nn			
B		1	2	2						2	1		2	**2***		—	—	—	2*	2*	2	2	2
C	—	—	—	—	—	—	—	—	—	1b	nn	1	(1)	**2***	2*	(1)	1 (1st)	(1)	1	1	1	1	1

(i) For the Arabic letters seee Table 4.1. Abbreviations: IIS = The Institute of Ismaili Studies; BnF = Bibliothèque nationale de France; MAJ = Majlis MS 1278; SOAS = MS Or. 45812; JK: Jīwā Khān's ed. (vol 3, pp. 2–15 and 16–24); MUN = Munich MS arab. 652; NUR = Nuruosmaniye MS 2863; AH: *hijrī* date; nd: not dated; nn: not numbered.

(ii) This is the text followed in Dieterici's edition, vol. 1 (1883), pp. 1–14.

*: Tittle includes '"according to the Pure Brethren"'; the number (1-2) indicates the order; NB: In [أ] the order is: C-B-A; in [ن] C—with part of '"A"' inserted in the middle-B.

poem in 'B' (f. Ar422/W410v.2–5), something that only happens in three other manuscripts: two from Group III (MSS Köprülü 871 [ك] (last lines of the second epistle), which is older, and BnF 2304 [ز] (f. 286r), and one in group IV, MS Esad 3637 [ن] (f. 335/W334v.33-35). The poem does appear in Jīwā Khān's edition (vol. 3, p. 7 = Bustānī vol. 3, p. 187). Unfortunately, the poem does not seem to have caught Walker's attention in his edition.[73] The author of the poem remains unidentified.

2) Group II manuscripts add an extra epistle ('C'), in various order combinations (see Table 4.5). The oldest dated manuscript (MS Atif 1681 [ع]) belongs to this group, although, as Walker has rightly pointed out, the scribe adds notes showing awareness that this was a variant found in other manuscripts, e.g. 'I found this epistle . . . in some of the copies [as I have given it] up to this point, but in another copy I found it as follows . . .' (*ilā hādhā'l mawḍiʿi wajadtu hādhihi'l risālati . . . fī baʿḍi'l-nusakhi, wa wajadtuhā fī nuskhatin ukhrā hakadhā wa hiya. . .*, f. 325v.7–9). This scribal comment is also found in MS Hunt 296 [ج] (f. 263v.6–7). In addition, three manuscripts in this group (MSS Atif 1681 [ع], and the Bodleian MSS Hunt 296 [ج] and Laud Or. 255 [ح]) juxtapose the titles of the two epistles as being 'according to Pythagoras' and 'according to the moderns (*aḥdāth*)', respectively. The latter title is given to 'B' in the first two manuscripts and to an epistle that combines 'A' and 'B' in others.[74] Another IIS copy, MS 83 can be considered as part of this group. Jīwā Khān's Epistle 31 (*Fī mabādi'i'l-mawjūdāti'l-ʿaqliyyati ʿalā ra'y al-fīthāgūriyyīn*), which merges 'A' and 'B' into one, coincides with MS 1040 almost in the entirety of the text, including the chapters (though not in the divisions and titles of the epistles); and his Epistle 32 (*Fī'l-mabādi'i'l-ʿaqliyyati ʿalā ra'y ikhwāni'l-ṣafā'*) includes a text corresponding to 'C' in MS 83. Jīwā Khān's edition's base manuscript was clearly much closer to the IIS manuscripts than to other copies; it appears to be a combination of the textual traditions found in MSS IIS 1040 and 83.

3) Group III misses 'B' and includes a large part of 'C' into 'A'.

4) Group IV contains 'C' and 'B' (in that order) and misses 'A'. In MS Esad 3637 [ن] a whole folio containing part of 'A' text was later inserted

just before the end of 'C' (f. 334r–v), violating even the continuity of the catchwords; that folio is written by a different, more cursive, hand, with tighter text and more lines per page than usual (36 instead of 29). This untitled 'epistle', which only has a *basmala* as a heading, begins by referring to it thus: 'Now, in his second epistle, we should like to mention the ranks of the intellectual principles according to the opinion of our brethren, may God assist them' (*wa nurīdu'l-ān an nadhkura fī hādhihi'l-risālati'l-thāniyati marātibal-mabādi'i'l-'aqliyyati 'alā ra'y ikhwāninā, ayyadahumu'llāh*).

Epistle 34 = III.3: On the Macrocosm

MS 1040 contains the version found in all manuscripts bar one.[75] As Ismail Poonawala has mentioned, a few manuscripts add a long extra passage at the end of the epistle. Among these, current research has only identified MS Marsh 189 but it should not be discarded that it may be found in other copies yet to be explored. The base manuscript of Jīwā Khān's edition also included an addition at the normal end of the epistle (vol. 3, p. 31= Bustānī, vol. 3, p. 221), where the scribe added: 'After this there is an addition which is not found in other manuscripts; maybe it was added from previous epistles' (*wa ba'da hādhihi ziyādatun lam tūjad fī sā'iri'l-nusakh; la'allahā zuyyidat min rasā'ili mutaqaddima*). Poonawala has rightly pointed out the similarities between parts of this addition and passages from various other epistles.[76] However, the Jiwā Khān 'addition' as a whole is nothing else than the majority of Epistle 51 'On the Order of the Universe' as found in his very same edition (vol. 4, pp. 281–286 = Bustānī, vol. 4, pp. 273–281).

Epistle 35 = III.4: On Intellect and the Intelligible

MS 1040 begins this epistle (titled 'The Fourth Epistle on the Intellect and the Intelligible') by referring to the Epistle 'On the Macrocosm' (34), then 'On the Intellectual Principles' and then the Epistle 'On Sense and the Sensible' (24). The same is the case in IIS MS 83 (f. 54r).[77] All other manuscripts only refer to the latter, including all the extra copies, complete or otherwise, that I have consulted. This had been identified by Paul Walker[78] as a unique variation occurring only in Jīwā Khān's edition (vol. 3, p. 37) (or what he calls 'BCB' after Bombay–Cairo–Beirut) as well as in another copy, MS Feyzullah 2131, which is 200 years older than MS 1040. We can now establish that Jīwā Khān's edition reproduces the beginning of this epistle in MS 1040 verbatim, except one word (it gives *tashbīhāt* instead of *tanbīhāt*). Once again, we find a link between MS 1040 and Jīwā Khān's editions (as well as with MS Feyzullah 2130-1, in this case too). As for another extra addition identified by Walker in the Feyzullah manuscript and another two copies, namely the mention of the aim of the epistle, we may also add MSS Munich arab. 652 and BnF 2341; however, it is not present in MS 1040.

Epistle 36 = III.5: On Periods and Cycles

This epistle provides different astronomical values. De Callataÿ's critical edition has shown the differences among the various manuscripts. Focusing on the numbers corresponding to each type of astral conjunctions, i.e. the first eight figures given at the start of the epistle,[79] we can see that MS 1040 (f. 428r) contains several mistakes, which makes the manuscript scientifically inaccurate and unreliable. However, when contrasted with other variants, the figures in his manuscript show a close affinity with Jiwā Khān's edition as well as with IIS MS 83.[80]

Epistle 39 = III.8: On Movement

No great variations are observed in MS 1040. However, I will simply point to two notes where Baffioni's critical edition makes observations on the 'Ṣādir edition', which led me to check this manuscript. In this case, we can see some of the changes made by Ziriklī and Bustānī. In the first and second chapters of our manuscript (f. Ar472/W452v.3, 13), a kind of intermediate movement is described as *mu'arrab/mu'arraban* (or *muwararrab/muwarraban*, as the *hamza* is not written) *bayna dhālika*.[81] The same was given in Jīwā Khān's edition (vol. 3, p. 100. 1, 13). However, the first instance was removed by Ziriklī (vol. 3, p. 306.15), which gives only *bayna dhālika*, and this omission was reproduced by Bustānī (vol. 3, p. 322.18); the second instance was left as it was by Ziriklī (p. 307.3) but 'corrected' by Bustānī (p. 323.8) to *muwāribatan*, with an explanatory note. This change is clearly an editorial intervention as the word is not found in the manuscript tradition.

In the second chapter,[82] a kind of wind that blows upwards is called [الروابع] *al-rawabiʿ* in MS 1040 (f. Ar473/W453r.14). Two other manuscripts give the same form, although most manuscripts, including the oldest ones, give [الزوابع] *al-zawābiʿ*.[83] Jīwā Khān's edition (p. 101.10–11) gives [الزوائغ] *al-zawāʾigh*, which is only found in one manuscript – IIS MS 83 (f. 81r.5).[84] This was reproduced in Ziriklī's print (p. 308.5), which adds a footnote saying 'perhaps it is more correct [to say] *al-zawābiʿ*'. Bustānī (p. 324.16–17) reproduced the text and even the footnote verbatim.

Next, the name of a wind that blows downwards is provided in Arabic (*zamharīr*) as well as in Persian. The latter is given in MS 1040 (ibid., line 15) as *bādh-i damah* (although the *kasra* of the *iḍāfa* is not written, so it is possible to read *bādh damah*), which is the reading in most manuscripts, including the oldest – MS Atif 1681.[85] Jīwā Khān's edition (ibid., line 11) gives *bād-i damah* (the variation *dāl*/*dhāl*, being negligible).[86] However, Ziriklī's print (ibid., p. 6) introduced an *alif*, either by mistake or as a misguided correction and gave *abād-damah*, all as one word; this error was reproduced in Bustānī's print.

This shows that while Jīwā Khān's edition followed the manuscript tradition, and is in line with the manuscripts coming from Ismaili collections, the Cairo and Beirut prints introduced changes quite uncritically (again, see the Conclusion).

Epistle 40 = III.9: On Cause and Effect

This epistle includes a list of the Pure Brethren's philosophical questions, which roughly correspond to Aristotles's ten categories.[87] Baffioni has analysed the differences within this list across the thirteen manuscripts used in her critical edition.[88] I have consulted twenty-three manuscripts: the ones used in the critical edition and the other eight copies, plus MS 1040 and MS 83 from the IIS. The results again, reveal a close connection between the Ismaili manuscripts and Jīwā Khān's edition. The list of the philosophical questions is found twice in this epistle, first in the definition of philosophy (*falsafa*/*ḥikma*), and secondly, again only a few lines later. In the first instance only the IIS Ismaili manuscripts (MS 1040, f. 468r/v and MS 83, f. 89f/p. 176) include the question *hal hiya*, giving a list of nine questions, instead of eight, as is the case with all other manuscripts (bar the occasional omission). Thus, the first list is given in these two mansucripts as: *...al-ḥikma.... hiya maʿrifat ḥaqāʾiq al-ashiyāʾ ... hal hiya wa mā hiya wa kam hiya wa ay shayʾ hiya wa kayfa/ hiya wa ayna hiya wa matā hiya wa lima kānat wa man hiya* ('...philosophy ... consists of cognisance of the true nature of things ... [namely] whether they are, what they are, how many they are, which things they are, how they are, where they are, when they are, why they are, and who they are'). Jīwā Khān's edition (vol. 3, p. 114.22–23) follows the same text as the Ismaili manuscripts (and this was naturally repeated by Ziriklī and later Bustānī).

In the second instance, all copies start the list with *hal huwa* and give nine questions (again, bar the occasional omission, as noted by Baffioni);[89] however, while all other manuscripts only number the first question (*awwaluhā hal huwa ...* – 'the first [question] is "is it?"...'), the two Ismaili manuscripts are the only ones, together with the copy used in Jīwā Khān's edition (p. 115.3–5), to number each of the questions. Thus they give: *awwaluhā hal huwa wa'l-thānī mā huwa wa'l-thālith lima huwa wa'l-rābiʿ kam huwa wa'l-khāmis ay shayʾ huwa* [MS 1040 omits *huwa* here] *wa'l-sādis kayfa huwa wa'l-sābiʿ ayna huwa wa'l-thāmin matā huwa wa'l-tāsiʿ man huwa* ('the first [question is], is it? the second, what is it? the third, why is it? the fourth, how many is it? the fifth, which thing? the sixth, how is it? the seventh, where is it? the eighth, when is it? and the ninth, who is it?'). Ziriklī reproduces this text verbatim (and Bustānī later on as well).

Epistle 41 = III.10: On Definitions

Following Poonawala's critical edition,[90] I give here the division of this epistle in MS 1040: 1. Preamble; 2. Definitions; 3. Chapter (on shape, although the space for the word *faṣl* has been left empty); 4. Chapter (on numbers, ratio and geometry); 5. Chapter (more definitions); 6. Chapter on colours and flavours; 7. Conclusion. Judging by Poonawala's descriptions, the text follows Atif MS 1681.[91] In turn,

Jīwā Khān's edition follows the text of MS 1040 almost to the letter, which provides further evidence for the interconnectedness of both texts. It is noticeable that the catchword at the bottom of f. 491v is unrequited, which means that the final folio of Part Three was lost and as a result the last sentence and the end formula (possibly 4–5 lines) are missing. Although f. Ar508/W492r is blank, the numeration (which must be later) has not been affected and Part Four starts naturally on the verso side.

Part Four

Epistle 42 = IV.1: On Doctrines

This epistle, one of the longest in the whole corpus, has not been critically edited yet. Upon a cursory perusal it appears to coincide with the text in Jīwā Khān's edition.

Epistle 45 = IV.4: On Companionship

There seems to be three versions of this epistle. Samer Traboulsi's critical edition has identified an irregularity that alters the order of the text of this epistle in certain manuscripts whereby a large portion in the middle[92] is skipped over but is then added at the end; the correct order, as per Traboulsi's description, is preserved in MS Atif 1681 (and other copies).[93] MS 1040 also concurs with this version and therefore does not belong to the line of 'corrupted' manuscripts.[94] This is another case in which MS 1040 belongs to the *ʿayn* family, at least for this epistle. A third version, completely different to all other manuscripts (albeit with some touching points), is found in MS Laud Or. 260, which seems to have escaped Traboulsi's attention. An edition of the third version of this epistle is now in order.

Epistle 46 = IV.5: On Belief

This epistle displays signs that the prototype had a hole in the middle, as f. Ar599/W592 presents, on both recto and verso, staggered blanks in five consecutive lines. This also shows that MS 1040 was not compared or collated with another copy.

Epistle 48 = IV.7: On the Call to God[95]

This is one of the most important epistles in the whole corpus, as it contains passages that appear to have been written by an ʿAlid imam in hiding. He refers to the various types or groups of Shiʿas, which are classified according to their relation to him. Some scholars like Yves Marquet have argued that this may have been a letter sent to the followers of the imam which later became the prime, core text to which many more epistles were added to make up the corpus as we know it.[96]

In the manuscript tradition we can distinguish three distinct groups of manuscripts (which I will refer to as A, B and C) according to the different ways of arranging the contents and their length, depending on the chapters they include or omit. Of the twenty-one copies I was able to consult, roughly half fall under group A. MS 1040 is among the longest in this group. In group A Epistle 48 has the following four-parts structure (I use here the chapter divisions, with my own numbering, as found in MS 1040 and also in Jīwā Khān's edition, which is extremely close to the IIS copy): i) the imam's taxonomy of the Shiʿa (introduction and chapter 1, roughly corresponding to Hamdani edition's chapters 17-18); ii) a very extensive story of an Indian king and his vizier (chapters 2 –5= Hamdani 22-25) narrated within the dialogue between an Indian prince and a sage. As Shadha Almutawa has described, the story derives from *Kitāb Bilawhar wa Budhāsaf* (or Yudhāsaf), an Arabic version of the biography of Buddha, which is known to have been transmitted in Ismaili milieus, and indeed was first published as a lithograph by Jīwā Khān himself straight after he published the *Epistles*;[97] iii) a typology of the ranks and kinds of the imam's followers, the brethren (*ikhwān*) (chapters 6 –11 = Hamdani 1-7); and iv) advice on how to conduct the 'summons' or 'call' (*daʿwa*) to accept the authority of the imam among people in various classes (philosophers who are skeptical about revelation, those who are skeptical about the soul, courtiers and civil servants, rulers, scholars who neglect the soul and finally the Shiʿis) (chapters 12–22 = Hamdani 8-15). One noteworthy point in MS 1040 is that it has a correction within a triangle in the margin (f. 622v). Some *faṣl* headings are left blank.

Group A also includes three IIS manuscripts (MS 1040, MS 87 and Hamdani MS 1482) and the base manuscript used in Jīwā Khān's edition, as well as other manuscripts (see Table 4.6). The extent of the manuscripts varies between 20 and 22 chapters. MS 1040 has 21. An extra chapter (no. 22) is found in the two other IIS manuscripts, as well as in Jīwā Khān's edition, and in two further copies. See Table 4.6 for a synoptic view.

Group B copies present a completely different arrangement. Most manuscripts in this group begin with the typology of the brethren (chapter 6), continue with the *daʿwa* to various groups and then move on to the taxonomy of the Shiʿa (chapters 20-21). The story (chapters 2–5) is placed at the very end. Manuscripts in group B vary in length from 13 to 21 chapters.[98]

In group C the epistle starts with instructions on addressing the skeptical philosophers, continues with the typologies of the pure brethren, and later moves to the description of the Shiʿa, ending with the story of the Indian king.

Regarding the question whether it is possible to ascertain if one of the three arrangements is earlier than the others, no definitive answer can be given. Group A includes the third oldest manuscript of the Epistles (BnF MS 6647-8). The IIS MSS 87 (f. 117r) and Hamdani 1482 (f. 196r) present evidence of having antecedents from Group B, as they have the typical epistle-closing formula at the end of the story (chapter 5: *waffaqaka'llāh, ayyuhā'l-akhu'l-bārru'l-raḥīm, wa jamīʿa ikhwānanā'l-fuḍalā'al-kurrāma ḥaythu kānū fī'l-bilād, innahu Ra'ūfun bi'l-ʿibād*), followed by what looks like the end formula of Epistle 7 of Part Three (i.e. Epistle 48), which it calls 'On the address to those inclined to philosophy who doubt the revealed path and ignore/neglect the mysteries of the prophetic books' *(tammat al-risālatu'l-sābiʿatu mina'l-qismi'l-rābiʿ, al-mawsūmatu fī khiṭābi'l-mutafalsafīna'l-shākkīna fī amri'l-sharīʿa, al-ghāfilīna ʿan asrāri'l-kutubi'l-nabawiyyati min Rasā'ili ikhwāni'l-ṣafā'i wa khillāni'l-wafā'i min kalāmi'l-ṣūfiyya)*, which is the title of chapter 14.

Group B includes the two oldest complete manuscripts: MSS Atif 1681, used by Hamdani as the basis for his edition, and Sālār Jung 41. However, there is scribal evidence that some copies of this group were aware that some previous rearrangement had taken place. Thus, in the middle of MSS Sālār Jung 41 (f. 459v/918), Esad 3637 (f. W531r), Köprülü 871 (f. 496r) and Laud Or. 255 (f. W355v), after chapter 21 and before the introduction and chapter 1, we find the following note, with slight variants across the manuscripts: 'End [of the chapter]. He [i.e. presumably the imam] addressed him [i.e. the 'brother'] first in the previously mentioned chapter at the beginning of this Epistle, as follows : 'Know, may God assist you, that we have brethren and friends who are among the noblest and most virtuous of people scattered in the land' up to His [God's] words : "Indeed the party of God is victorious"'. Then he concluded it with this chapter' ('*Tamma; awwalan khāṭabahu bi'l-faṣli'l-muqaddam dhikruhu fī awwali hādhihi'l-risāla, wa huwa: "[w]aʿlam, ayyuhā'l-akh [or ayyadaka Allāh] bi-anna lanā ikhwān[an] wa aṣdiqā' min kurrām al-nās wa fuḍalā'ihim mutafarriqīn [fī al-bilād]" ilā qawluhu "fa inna ḥizb Allāh hum al-ghālibūn". Thumma tammamahu [*or *tamma tatimmat] bi-hādhā al-faṣl.*[99] What follows corresponds to a shorter repetition of chapter 6 (=Hamdani 17).

Group C consists of the 4th and 5th oldest complete manuscripts, dating to the end of the 7th and beginning of the 8th century AH (13th–14th century).

As we can see, this epistle presents us with a vibrant history of additions, subtractions and rearrangements. I personally find it futile to try and see which one is more original. What is important for us is that these three groups represent three alternative ways of reading the material, perhaps with different emphasis depending on what was placed where (especially at the outset). In this regard, one is reminded of so called experimental or aleatory novels that can be read in any order), such as Marc Saporta"s *Composition no. 1*,[100] which can be started on any page, or Julio Cortázar's *Royuela*,[101] whose author himself proposes various reading orders and possibilities. As with these *romans permutationnels*, what is important for us is not so much who wrote the work or how it was written, but how and by whom it was read.

Table 4.6 Synoptic view of Epistle 48. (numbers of chapters and blocks are given).

GROUP A

MSS	Chapters	total
BnF 6647-8	1-20	20
IIS 1040	**1-21**	**21**
IIS 87 and Hamdani 1482	**1-16** **20-21** **17-19** **22**	**22**
SOAS Or. 45812 and Majlis 1278[(i)]	1-8 9 10 12-22	21
BnF 2303 and 2304; Nuruosmaniye 2863,[(ii)] and Jīwā Khān	1-22	22

GROUP B

Chapters	total
6-16 20-21[(iii)] 1[(iv)] 17-19 2-5 Atif 1681,[(v)] Sālār Jung 41,[(vi)] Esad 3637, BnF 2341-4,[(vii)] Köprülü 871,[(viii)] Laud Or. 255, and Munich arab. 652. (the introduction is missing; the latter two have a *faṣl* heading between chapters 4 and 5)	**21**
6-9 12-13 18 14-16 1-5 Laud Or. 260 (no introduction; ch 9 is in a short version; 14 is only one paragraph)	**15**
6-8 12-16 19 2-5 Marsh 189 (no introduction or ch. 1; ch. 14 is only one paragraph; ch. 4 is short)	**13**

GROUP C

Chapters	total
12-16 20-21 6-9 Intro + ch. 1 17-19 2-5 Esad 3638 (ch. 9 is the short version; avoids ch. 10-11)	**19**
12-16 20-21+ Intro + ch. 1 17-19 2-5 Feyzullah 2131	**15**

[i] Both the SOAS and the Majlis copies have some significant lacunae. In the latter, chapters 9 and 10 are only a few lines long. It lacks the whole of chapter 11. It also lacks the final lines of chapter 22 (at p. 609) and is missing the first few folios of Epistle 49.
[ii] In both MSS BnF 2304 (from f. 427r) and Nuruosmaniye 2863 (from f. 418v), chapters 18–22 are placed in a different epistle titled *fī mukhāṭabat al-ʿummāl wa'l-kuttāb*, which is the title of chapter 18 in other manuscripts.
[iii] In MSS Atif 1681 and Feyzullah 2130-1, after chapter 21, there is a mixed text without a *faṣl* heading that includes the beginning of chapter ١٨, then jumps to 2 lines from chapter 7 again; then jumps to two lines from Epistle 44; and then adds lines of text not found elsewhere; it finishes with Q. 38:22, like chapter 17.
[iv] Introduction before chapter 1 only in MSS Sālār Jung 41 and Esad 3637.
[v] Does not have the introduction; *faṣl* headings not present in chapters 1, 6–7, 9, 10–13.
[vi] Ends chapter 7 (f. 452v/p.904) with a markedly Shiʿi formula: *al-ḥamdu li'llāhi rabbi'l-ʿālamīn wa ṣallā'llāhu ʿalā'l-nabiyyi'l-muṣṭafā Muḥammad wa ālihi'l-ṭāhirīna'l-ṭayyibīna ajmaʿīn*. It calls chapter 8 *al-faṣl al-thānī*.
[vii] Shorter introduction, chapters 6–16, 20–21, Introduction, chapter 1 (incomplete), 17 (with no beginning), 18–19, 2–5. The incompleteness of chapters 1 and 17 is due to a homeoteleuton between the words *al-salām* and *sallam*.
[viii] Chapter 2 in Koprülü MS 871 lacks the opening line.

Philosophical and Sufi elements are present in this epistle as in many others. Outward Shiʿi elements, too, can be detected in this epistle in many of the manuscripts. For instance, while some copies from groups B and C introduce chapter 8 with a formula (*tawakkaltu. . .*) of praise for God and blessings on the Prophet, MSS Atif 1681, Laud Or 255 [ح], and Munich arab. 652, add, 'and on Ali, the best legatee' (*wa ʿalā ʿAliyyin khayri'l-waṣiyyīn. . .*).[102] Yet, MS 1040 and group A are more explicitly Ismaili as they lay the emphasis on the imam's description of the different groups of the Shiʿa and how they relate to him, by placing those passages at the very start of the Epistle. There is no doubt that this group is more likely to have circulated in Ismaili circles, judging by the provenance of the IIS manuscripts and the Jīwā Khān edition.

Epistle 49 = IV.8: On Spiritual Beings

As Wilferd Madelung has shown in his critical edition (pp. 272–278), Epistle 49 exists in a shorter and a longer version (which he calls 49a and 49b). Madelung argues that the shorter version is the original.[103] Apart from the three manuscripts used by Madelung for the edition of the shorter version,[104] I have identified this version in MS 1040, but also in three other copies: MSS Sālār Jung 41 (ff. 467v-475r/pp. 934-

949) – which in general is the antecedent of MS Esad 3627 – Munich arab. 652 (f. W278r–282r), and BnF 2341 (f. 370r–374v). The text is basically the same in all seven manuscripts, with differences only in the ending. All these manuscripts finish the epistle with Qurʾānic citations but they differ in how many they include. Both MSS Munich arab. 652 and BnF 2341 have only five Qurʾānic citations, ending with Q. 2:268, and without a closing formula; Laud Or. 255 has the previous five and seven more verses, ending with Q. 6:130; further to that, MS 1040, together with MSS Esad 3637 and Köprülü 871 add another 38 verses (with a total of 50), ending with Q. 104:6. The closing formula is one sentence longer in MS Esad 3637, and even one more sentence in MS 1040 and MS Sālār Jung 41. The last two are, if only marginally, the longest of all and their end coincides almost verbatim with the end of the base manuscript of Jīwā Khān's edition.

As for the longer version, in addition to the manuscripts identified by Madelung, I have seen it in six other manuscripts, one of them in the IIS collections. These are MSS 1) Garrett 4263 (ff. 127r-139r),[105] 2) IIS 87 (ff. *146r–181v), 3) SOAS Or. 45812 (ff. 246r–252v), 4) BnF 2303 (ff. 468r–480r), which ends in the same way as MS Atif 1681 (used by Madelung as the basis for the edition), 5) Majlis 1278,[106] and 6) Nuruosmaniye 2863 (ff. 421r–436r).[107] Critical editions do not need a large number of copies, but researchers should access a larger pool of manuscripts before venturing into definitive and cut-and-dry conclusions, as the discovery of another copy may cause any hasty diagnosis to crumble. The above manuscripts should be compared closely with the edited text; especially interesting would be a comparison between IIS MS 87 and Jīwā Khān's text, as they both come from a Bohra Ismaili, presumably Indian, background.

As I will show also in the discussion on Epistle 52, it would not be correct to attribute to Jīwā Khān's Bombay edition (let alone the 'Ṣādir edition'!) any responsibility for merging shorter and longer versions of various epistles, as the manuscript tradition provides examples that the 'merging' happened during the scriptorial transmission. Madelung and Uy, building on a previous conclusion by de Callataÿ and Hafflans in their critical edition of the short version of Epistle 52 ('52a'), state that 'the Sadir [sic] edition merges material from both the long and the shorter versions of Epistle 49, presenting the hybrid as a single unit' (p. 27). With regard to Epistle 49, one IIS copy, Hamdani MS

1482 (dated 1126/1714), contains evidence that the merging of versions may go back centuries: originally, it contained the long version (f. 134r-); later two small folios (later numbered 170–171) were added after f. 169v. and bound together with the rest of the text in a clumsy pastiche, but one that preserves an alternative expanded version, or at least vestiges of it. In these small folios the ending of the long version was written again, but this time merged with a part from the shorter version as we know it (see Table 4.7). The long version is ended (f. 170r.12), as in the other manuscripts, with Q. 21:104 (*kamā bada'nā awwala khalqin nuʿīduhu waʿdan ʿalaynā innā kunnā fāʿilīn*), and without any indication or formula the text continues with the end of verse Q. 2:52 (. . . *āyātuhu wa'llāhu ʿalīmun ḥakīm*).[108] It then adds the final twenty Qur'ānic citations from the shorter version, finishing with Q. 114:6 (*mina'l-jinnati wa'l-nās*). The final line of the shorter version is written on top of the original ending of the long version (f. 172r), whose last lines have been crossed.

Here, again, further research must be conducted including additional manuscripts from collections India, but also Iran, Turkey and elsewhere, to establish the origins of the textual tradition present in Jīwā Khān's manuscript.

A further point that has not been identified by previous research is that the same passage, from the quotation of Q. 91:7-10 (starting *wa nafsin wa mā sawwāhā*) up to the words '*al-ajal wa'l-fawt*', is found both in the middle of the shorter version of Epistle 49 (MS 1040, ff. 652v.17–653v.3) and at the beginning of Epistle 38 'On Resurrection' (MS 1040 ff. 443v.14– 445r.ult.). This is also the case in the other manuscripts. In the Jīwā Khān's Bombay edition the passage is located near the point when the long version ends and the text joins the shorter version (vol. 4, p. 259.ult–261.1 = vol. 3. 77.ult.–79.1).[109]

Epistle 50 = IV.9: On Governance

This epistle, with its complexities, variations and different versions, has been edited in a masterly way by Carmela Baffioni.[110] Baffioni has shown how the text in MS Atif 1681 provides a different reading than that of the 'Ṣādir edition' (which should now be corrected to 'Jīwā Khān's edition'). The text of this epistle in MS 1040 is followed closely by Jīwā Khān's text, but also by two manuscripts in the IIS collections

Table 4.7 Synoptic view of Epistle 49.*

MSS IIS 1040, Sālār Jung 41, Munich arab. 652, BnF 2341		Shorter →		version
MSS Garrett 4263, **IIS 87**, SOAS 45812, BnF 2303, Majlis 1278, Nuruosmaniye 2863	Longer →	version		
MS Hamdani 1482	Longer →	version	→	shorter v.
	Longer →	version		shorter v.
Jīwā Khān's ed.	pp. 230-ca242	ca242-247	248-259	259-264
Bustānī	pp. 198-ca215	ca215-224	224-242	242-249

*: The manuscripts given here are copies not used in Madelung's edition

(MS 87 and Hamdani MS 1482). Compared to other manuscripts, the text of this epistle in MS 1040 is extremely close to MS Sālār Jung 41, the direct antecedent of MS Esad 3637, a copy used by Baffioni. Therefore the similarities pointed out by Baffioni between the 'Ṣādir edition' and MS Esad 3637 should be seen in the context of the connection between MS 1040 and MS Sālār Jung 41. A more detailed analysis of these two copies may throw more light on the Ismaili provenance of some of the variations.

Epistle 51 = IV.10: On the Order of the Universe

Nuha Alshaar has been the only scholar so far to use an IIS manuscript (MS 87) for the critical edition, although other copies in the IIS collection could also have been consulted.[111] In her analysis of Epistle 51, Alshaar identified three variant versions in the manuscripts.

Building on her work, we can say that IIS MSS 1040 and Hamdani 1482 also contain version 'B'.[112]

As with Epistle 50 there is a confluence of MS 1040, MSS Sālār Jung 41 (and its descendant MS Esad 3638) and Köprülü 871. I have compared the three IIS manuscripts and Jīwā Khān's edition,[113] from which it can be it can be concluded that a) MS 1040 stands alone (possibly due to its numerous errors at word level, but also for its omissions); b) MS 87 is followed very closely by Hamdani MS 1482; and c) Jiwa Khān's edition follows mostly MS 87 and secondarily also MS 1040. A thorough comparison between Jīwā Khān's edition and other manuscripts from the Ismaili collections at the IIS must be conducted in future, as more possible lines of contact could be found.

Epistle 52 = IV.11: On Magic

We have reached the final epistle of the corpus. The epistle 'On Magic' can also be found in a shorter and a longer version. In this case, these are two different texts. The longer version is roughly five times larger. Here again, MS 1040 proves to be an important witness to the history of the *Epistles'* textual transmission and in particular of the affinity that exists between this copy and the base manuscript used by Jīwā Khān for his Bombay edition, since both texts combine the shorter and the longer versions into one, as I shall discuss. De Callataÿ and Halflants have published the critical edition of the short version (which they call Epistle 52a).[114] In addition to the manuscripts used by them, I have been able to identify the long version in five other manuscripts[115] and the shorter version in three further copies.[116](See Table 4.8) Of special interest here is MS Sālār Jung 41, whose text is identical to MS Esad 3637, with the same title ('Epistle Fifty-One', *al-risālatu'l-ḥādiyatu wa'l-khamsūn*), and even with the same textual characteristics identified by de Callataÿ and Halflants as 'lacunae'. Since the text in these lacunae does not detract from the logic of the flow, it could be hypothesised that they may not mean that text is missing; rather the Sālār Jung MS may represent an earlier text which was later emended in other copies. More research is required on this front.

The study of de Callataÿ and Halflants provides an excellent and meticulous scholarly analysis of the complexities of Epistle 52.

However, it makes a number of assumptions which must now be revised in light of MS 1040 (and other manuscripts I shall discuss below). Halflants's technical introduction states, 'Whereas the manuscripts at my disposal seem to agree in providing a single version of the text for the rest of the *Rasā'il*, that is, from Epistle 1 to Epistle 50, I observe that this is not the case for these two epistles' (p. 70). Clearly the subsequent edition of the various epistles (as well as my analysis of IIS MS 1040 in the present chapter) have rendered this statement obsolete. Among other things, de Callataÿ's introduction says that 'al-Bustānī is completely silent about his source(s)' (p. 2). As I have demonstrated, al-Bustānī reprinted Ziriklī's text with minor corrections, and Ziriklī plagiarised Jīwā Khān's edition (and also ʿAlī Yūsuf's edition of Part One) – see my discussion above. With regard to the shorter and longer versions of Epistle 52, de Callataÿ says that "we are also to infer that the three editions of Bombay, Cairo, and Beirut were solely responsible for having merely juxtaposed these versions with one another under the same generic title [. . .] That Beirut [sic] would have followed a manuscript where the shorter and the long versions were already side-by-side seems to me unlikely' (p. 3). These assertions, which do not in any sense tarnish the quality of the serious work done by de Callataÿ and Halflants, need revision. In what follows I offer my contribution to the discussion, by bringing the IIS manuscripts into the conversation.

MS 1040 is one of at least three manuscripts that attach the shorter and longer versions together (although it is the only one I have been able to consult). It starts with the shorter version (ff. W663r–683r). As with all the other epistles it is headed with a decorated cartouche including the title (*al-risālatu'l-ḥādiya ʿashara* [sic] *fī māhiyyati'l-siḥri wa'l-ʿazā'imi wa'l-ʿayn*). The epistle commences with the full *basmala* and the phrase '*wa bihi nastaʿīn*', common at the beginning of many epistles in this manuscript. A gap was left where the word '*iʿlam*' should have been written. The text ends with the phrase '*kamā huwa ahluhu wa mustaḥiqquhu wa huwa ḥasbunā wa niʿam al-wakīl*'.[117] This shows that the ending of the shorter version in MS 1040 is exactly the same as in Koprülü MS 871 and in Jīwā Khān's edition. Immediately after the end of the short version, a new gold ornamental cartouche (the only one in the whole manuscript not introducing an epistle) opens the longer version (ff. W683r–746v), bearing the title *Bayān ḥaqīqat al-siḥr wa ghayrihi*, without any scribal indication to explain the reason for a new title (see Figure 4.2). Notably, Jīwā Khān's edition uses the same title, but simply places it in the same brackets used for chapter headings. The text of the longer version in MS 1040 opens with the *basmala* and a blank space (for the word *iʿlam*, 'know', which was not written), followed by '*ayyuhā al-akh, ayyadaka wa iyyānā bi-rūḥin minhu anna'l-siḥra yataṣarrafu fi'l-lughati'l-ʿarabiyyati/ ʿalā maʿānin kathīra. . .*,' (f. 683r-v). For the ending of the epistle and the whole manuscripts see section '*Size, Style and Numeration*' above. The text closes with, '*waffaqaka wa iyyānā wa jamīʿa ikhwānanā al-muʾminīna bi-raḥmatika yā arḥama'l-rāḥimīn*' (f. Ar753/W746v, corresponding to Jīwā Khān's edition, vol. 4, p. 396.4 = Bustānī, vol. 4, p. 445.11). This is several pages before Jīwā Khan's ending but MS 1040 is not unique in this, as the ending is very close to the ones in other copies, such as MSS BnF MS 6648, Feyzullah 2131 and Ragip Pasha 840. It seems that, among the copies that have the longer version, these three have a

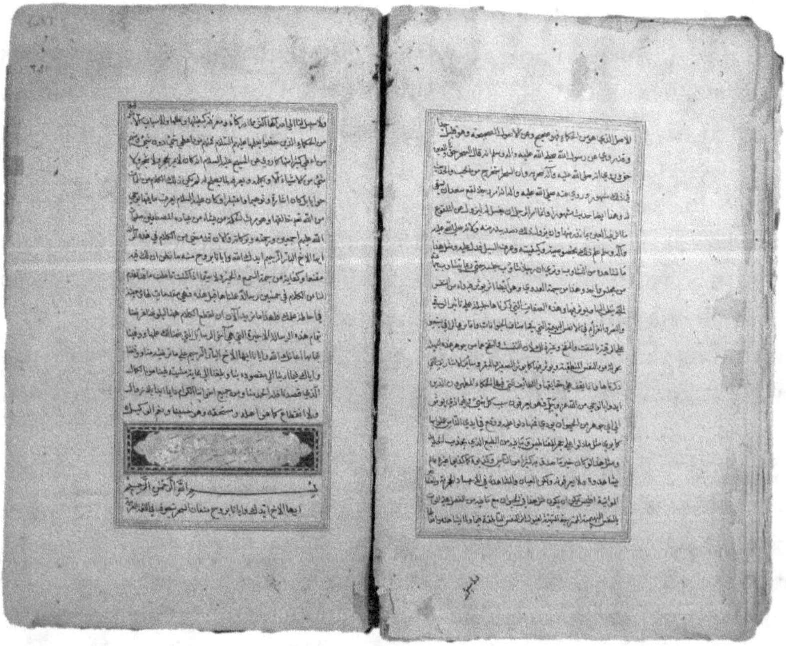

Figure 4.2 Pages from IIS MS 1040 showing the end of the shorter version of Epistle 52 *On Magic* followed by the longer version, which is headed by a decorative title (f. Ar690/W683r).

Table 4.8 Synoptic view of Epistle 52.

Ep. 52a [i]	Shorter v.		
Ep. 52b [ii]		Longer version	
Ep. 52 a + b [iii]	Shorter v.	Longer version	
Ep. 52 b + a [iv]		Longer version	Shorter v.

[i] MSS Sālār Jung 41, Esad 3637, Köprülü 871, Munich arab. 652, and BnF 2341.
[ii] MSS Atif 1681, BnF 6647-8, Esad 3638, Feyzullah 2130, Köprülü 870, Laud Or. 260, Marsh 189, BnF 2303, BnF 2304, Nuruosmaniye 2863, BnF 2305, IIS 87, Hamdani 1482, and Majlis 1278.
[iii] **MSS IIS 1040**, British Library Or. 2359, and Jīwā Khān's ed.
[iv] MS Ragip Pasha 840.

shorter text while others add material that amounts to more than 10 published pages. Once again, further research is required.

Now, MS 1040 is not alone in combining the two versions in the same manuscript even if in a different order (see Table 4.8). A manuscript which I have not consulted yet, MS. Or. 2359 (copied in 1088/1677) of the British Library (formerly at the British Museum), is likely to contain both versions, judging by Charles Rieu's description in his 1894 catalogue, which speaks of 'an additional treatise, called the 53rd, on the art of divination, and on judicial astronomy (ff. 262b-307)', which clearly points to the long version, as shown by the number of leaves and the initial lines provided by Rieu. Further research is required on this.[118] A third copy has been identified by de Callataÿ: [119] the undated MS 840 (new numeration MS 1085) of the Ragip Pasha Library in Istanbul (ff. 453v–496r) starts with the long version and follows it with the shorter version, which the scribe, in red ink, refers to as 'another copy', as it is headed '*al-nuskhatu'l-ukhrā fī risālati māhiyyati'l-siḥri wa'l-'āzā'im*'. The text is shorter than in other manuscripts (about two pages shorter than MS Esaf Efendi 3637). The end of the shorter version corresponds to Jiwā Khān's edition, vol. 4, pp. 306.25.[120]

Conclusion

In 1929, the young Palestinian scholar 'Abd al-Laṭīf al-Ṭībāwī (d. 1981), who later published numerous articles on the *Rasā'il* both in Arabic and English, especially on the topic of education, published a furious, scathing attack on Ziriklī's plagiarism of Jīwā Khān's Bombay edition of the Epistles, publicly exposing some of the speculative 'corrections' exerted on the text, and denouncing the lack of recourse to manuscripts. Among other things, he wrote:

> 'We truly do not need the aforementioned Bombay edition of the Epistles reprinted on satin paper instead of old yellow paper, and broken down and divided into paragraphs instead of running lines and pages without a break. No, we do not need that before other things. We first need a sound text that gathers the largest possible number of variants.'[121]

And yet, despite Ṭibāwī's warnings, scholars have continued to use Ziriklī's travesty, and, worse, Bustānī's pirated reprint of it, naming it 'the Beirut edition' or the 'Ṣādir edition', without paying attention to Jīwā Khan's pioneering edition. The latter was not free from errors—quite the contrary—, and it was not a critical edition either, but it was genuinely based on a manuscript. True, the manuscript was not described in detail. We do not know to what extent Jīwā Khān reproduced his manuscript to the letter or whether he carried out interventions. We ignore whether the manuscript still exists or has been lost. We also do not know whether Jīwā Khān used other manuscripts (although he only mentions one). For these reasons, until now, scholars have found it difficult to relate the edition (in whichever appellation) to the manuscripts as they have been coming to light. In this chapter, I have presented irrefutable evidence that MS 1040, from the IIS's collections, is by far the closest relative to the copy used by Jīwā Khān. This has been done by analysing this manuscript *vis-à-vis* the copies facilitated by Nader El-Bizri's commendable efforts of obtaining the best possible manuscripts for the OUP–IIS critical edition, as well as many other copies, some of which were previously unknown or unexplored.

Many more manuscripts await to be explored, but the results of the present analysis are clear. I suggest that the text in the tradition represented by MS 1040 has a close relationship with the manuscript used by Jīwā Khān and should be considered an important part of its genealogy. My claim is not that MS 1040 is identical to Jiwā Khān's edition, far from that. For instance, the order of the epistles on Music and Geography are different, and the versions of some epistles (notably epistles 10, 31, 32, 33, 49 and 51) are very different. One of the main discoveries of the OUP—IIS critical editions is that it has been practically impossible to find a copy which is more 'original' than others. The *Epistles* corpus seems to have been alive during the process of transmission, with scribes adding and taking, mixing and matching available texts, and possibly also adding to them. The work was, perhaps even from its inception, in constant flux and expansion. My contention is that the *Epistles* belonged not only to the authors, but also to its readers; that the *ikhwān al-ṣafā'* were not only those who composed the work, but also those who transmitted it, who appropriated it, often expanding and enlarging it, be it with extra paragraphs (sometimes dismissed as 'interpolations'), be it with amplified versions of whole individual epistles. Another major discovery is that the similarities found between manuscripts have enabled us to group them into 'families'. Nevertheless, it is not possible to apply these groupings to the complete corpus of epistles in one copy and the complete corpus in another. At most, we can find affinities and affiliations between manuscripts at the level of individual epistles. My working inference from this is that scribes may not have always had the whole corpus to work with, but they may have worked with different copies of different epistles, or sometimes copies of one part, but not another. Some evidence of this is found in MS 1040 when we see one type of formulas in most of Part One including the mention of the imams, a mention which disappears in the other three parts. We find texts changing and expanding (and contracting!) up until at least the 10th/16th century (the period to which MS 1040 belongs). Sufis, Ismailis and many others laid claim to the *Rasā'il*. The fact that MS 1040 is extremely close to Jīwā Khān's edition, as well as to other copies from Ismaili private collections now housed at the IIS, seems to indicate that they belong to the family of texts that were appropriated and transmitted by and in Ismaili circles. The closeness between MS 1040 and Jīwā Khān's edition is best seen at the microcosmic level of the word-by-word comparison throughout the corpus. Yet, especially relevant is the remarkable closeness between both in epistles 2, 35, 40, 45, 48, 50 and 52. The ending of Epistle 22 (with the mention of a new historical cycle) is also evidence of a group of manuscripts that seem to share some, albeit subtle, Ismaili flavour. To conclude, this chapter has contributed to expanding the pool of manuscripts considered for the establishment of the text of the *Rasāʾil*. Even though MS 1040's text is not very reliable at the lexical level, and therefore the manuscript is not among the strongest candidates to establish the text, this copy is an important witness in the history of the transmission of the *Epistles*. Only future research will be able to reinforce (or otherwise) this conclusion. As with the story of the elephant in the dark, scholars must be very careful when drawing conclusions based on a handful of manuscripts. MS 1040 is a new piece in the puzzle of the *Epistles* and one which must be reckoned with from now on.

NOTES

* The present study is an abridged version of a larger analysis of the manuscripts of the *Rasāʾil* at The Institute of Ismaili Studies, which I intend to publish in the near future.

1 The manuscript is housed at the Ismaili Special Collections Unit, which is a research and preservation unit of the IIS. As of mid 2018, the IIS moved to the newly-built Aga Khan Centre in London. The merged library of the IIS and the Institute for the Study of Muslim Civilisations is now known as the Aga Khan Library in the same Centre. While the Ismaili Special Collection Unit is physically located on the same floor as the library, it is a separate entity and does not operate under the library management.

2 My thanks to Wafi Momin for comments that allowed me to improve this piece. My gratitude goes also to Wafi Momin and Nourmamadcho Nourmamadchoev for providing physical access to the manuscript, especially since it is quite fragile. While I have accessed other manuscripts independently, the large majority of digital copies I have used for this research were obtained by Nader El-Bizri, to whom all those interested in *Ikhwān al-Ṣafāʾ* studies are deeply indebted. Thanks also to Tara Woolnough for making those copies available so generously.

3 Delia Cortese, *Ismaili and Other Arabic Manuscripts: A Descriptive Catalogue of Manuscripts in the Library of The Institute of Ismaili Studies* (London, 2000), p. 28, seq. no. 44.

4 François de Blois, *Arabic, Persian and Gujarati Manuscripts: The Hamdani Collection in the Library of The Institute of Ismaili Studies* (London, 2001), p. 85.

5 Thirty-nine epistles in fifteen volumes (i.e., three quarters of the corpus) have been published so far (early 2022) in the Epistles of the Brethren of Purity Series, general editor, Nader El-Bizri (Oxford, Oxford University Press in association with The Institute of Ismaili Studies, 2008–). Henceforth 'IIS/OUP edition'. In what follows I will only give the year of publication for each volume.

6 Dated 18 Rabīʿ al-awwal 1279 = 13 September 1862; see *Fihrist al-kutub al-ʿarabiyya al-mahfūẓa biʾl-kutubkhana al-khidiwiyya al-miṣriyya*, vol. 6 (Cairo, 1308/1890–1891), pp. 94–95. I had planned to check this manuscript but the Covid-19 pandemic restrictions forced me to postpone it for the future.

7 An earlier edition, containing selections from forty epistles, was published by Friedrich Dieterici, *Die Abhandlungen der Ichwân es-safâ in Auswahl* (Leipzig, 1883–1886), in three tomes. He mainly used MSS BnF 2304, Munich arab. 652 and Marsh 189. See Table 4.1 below for details. Whether or not ʿAlī Yūsuf knew of, or used, Dieterici's edition, is a question for future research.

8 I have been unable to find written documentation to corroborate these ancestry claims. I am grateful to Husain Jasani for confirming that the three Ṭayyibī lines of *dāʿīs* (Dāʾūdī, Sulaymānī and ʿAlawī) do regard themselves as descending from the Ismaili imams. Whether this refers to spiritual or physical descendence is a matter for further research.

9 See Indira Falk Gesink, *Islamic Reform and Conservatism: Al-Azhar and the Evolution of Modern Sunni Islam* (London, 2014), p. 118ff.

10 In addition, I have also consulted fifteen other manuscripts. One of them is complete but undated, i.e. (1) MS 3637 [ن] from the Esad Efendi collection at the Suleymaniyye Mosque Library in Istanbul) and the others are incomplete. These are two manuscripts that are older than MS 1040: 2-3) MS 5255 (dated 11 Rajab 607/5 January 1211) and MS 1831 (dated 621/1224), both from the Library of the National Consultative Assembly (Majlis-i Shūrā-yi Millī) in Tehran (available online); 4) MS 7437 [ط] (dated 640/1242-3) from the private collection of Aṣghar Mahdawī (d. 2004) now at Tehran University Library; 5) MS 923/Casiri (or 928/Derembourg) [ش] (dated Dhū'l-Ḥijja 862/October–November 1458) from the Library of the El Escorial Monastery, near Madrid; four that are more recent: 6) MS 4263 (dated 1 Jumāda II 956/16 June 1551) from the Yehuda section of the Garrett Collection at the Princeton University Library (https://catalog.princeton.edu/catalog/4941772); 7) MS 1482 (dated 18 Jumāda I 1126/31 May 1714) from the collection donated by Abbas Hamdani (d. 2019) to the IIS; 8) MS 87 (dated Rajab 1114/1702) of the IIS collections; and 9) IIS MS 84 (dated Rabīʿ al-ākhir 1239/December 1823); and six undated copies: 10) MS 5038 [ب] from the Staatsbibliothek in Berlin (Wetsztein collection no. 1153); 11) MS Or. 255 [ح] from the Laud collection at the Bodleian Library in Oxford (produced before 1636); 12) MS 296 [ج] from the Hunt collection at the Bodleian Library (produced before 1774); 13) IIS MS 576; 14) MS Or. 45812 from the Library of School of Oriental and African Studies, London (SOAS); and 15) MS 83 from the IIS. Naturally, there are yet other copies (both complete and incomplete), mostly in India, Iran and Turkey, but I do not yet have enough details on all of them, nor I have been able to peruse all of them either digitally or in person.

11 See previous note. Their catalogue details are found in Adam Gacek, *Catalogue of Arabic Manuscripts in the Library of The Institute of Ismaili Studies*, vol. 1 (London, 1984), pp. 91–93, seq. no. 110, and de Blois, *Arabic, Persian and Gujarati Manuscripts*, p. 84ff.

12 With special thanks to Karim Javan for reading the content of the notes more closely than I could. On *Darrahi-Ṣūf/Darrah-i Yūsuf*, see Muḥammad-Amīn Zawārī, 'Darrah-i Ṣūf', *Dānishnāmah-i Jahān-i Islām*, vol. 17 (accessed online: http://rch.ac.ir/article/Details/9201) and Daniel Balland, 'Darra-ye Ṣūf', *Encyclopaedia Iranica*, vol 7, fascicle 1, pp. 62–63.

13 On the dynasty see Robert Duncan McChesney, 'Shībānids', *EI2*, vol. 9, pp. 428–431.

14 Other details provided in Delia Cortese's catalogue (p. 29): 'The binding is 18th-century Persian purple morocco with blind-stamped medallions and cartouches on both covers; illuminated double-page opening with polychrome head-piece and text within gold 'clouds'; old paper restorations, worm-eaten; (. . .) occasional words and diagrams in red; headings in white on illuminated panels; numerous diagrams and grids; some annotations and corrections in the margins (occasionally in red).'

15 Other *Rasāʾil* manuscripts with significant decorations are: MS Esad 3638, which contains the famous miniature of the authors of the Epistles. The painting is based on the discussion on the authors of the Epistles by Abū'l-Ḥasan ʿAlī al-Bayhaqī, *Taʾrīkh Ḥukamāʾ al-Islām*, ed. Muḥammad Kurd ʿAlī (Damascus, 1946), pp. 35–36 (no. 18); and MS Laud Or. 255, with ninety-six miniatures (ff. 114–156) illustrating the debate between humans and animals in Epistle 22 'On Animals'. BnF MS 2304 has a frontispiece and an ornate initial head-piece; MS Feyzullah 2130 has a frontispiece but little else. Other manuscripts have one initial head-piece: MSS Sālār Jung 41, Laud Or. 260 (which also gives beautiful charts and diagrams in the Epistle on Astronomy) and Ragip Pasha 840 (see my discussion on Epistle 52 below).

16 One in Epistle 2 (f. Ar27/W15) and one in Epistle 41 (f. Ar507), which is the last folio of the epistle and of Part Three.

17 As a result, my present analysis excludes epistles 11, 17–18, 23–28, 37 and 43–44.

18 The *Fihrist* is missing also from MSS Escorial 923, Garrett 4263, BnF 2341 and Munich arab. 652.

19 *On Arithmetic & Geometry* (Epistles 1–2), ed. and tr. Nader El-Bizri (2013).

20 The word '*izz*' has been added in the margin, with the sign 'صـ' (for *ṣaḥīḥ*, or 'correct').

21 With the only differences that MS Atif 1681 omits '*wa taḥiyyātihi*' and gives '*ahl al-maʿrifa*' instead of '*ahl maʿrifatihi*'. The laudation formula from MS Atif 1681 has been reproduced by El-Bizri (Arabic p. 8 n. 4) although it was removed from the main text of his critical edition and relegated to a footnote. Three corrections should be made to El-Bizri's transcription: i) '*tāhat al-albābu*' instead of '*nāhat al-albābu*'; ii) the word after '*wa ālihi*' is '*wa ʿitratihi*', which is perfectly clear in the manuscript (while El-Bizri notes the word has been erased (*al-kalima maṭmūsa*); iii) '*khalqihi wa bariyyatihi*' instead of '*khalqihi wa bazīnatihi*'; iv) '*muntajabīn*' [chosen] instead of '*muntajīn*' [saved]. In addition, another emendation must be made to El-Bizri's translation (p. 65, see note), as the 'Ṣādir' text does not reproduce the formula at all.

22 See Farhad Datfary, *The Ismāʿīlīs*, 2nd ed. (Cambridge, 2007), pp. 83, 86, 132, 222.

23 MS 1040 gives 'منتجيين', with two '*yā'*s'. I propose to follow the reading of MS Atif 1681 ('*muntajabīn*') as the blessing '*[wa ʿalā] aṣḥābihi'l-muntajabīn*' is common in Shiʿi sources; see e.g. *al-Ṣaḥīfa al-Sajjādiyya al-Kāmila*, attributed to the Shiʿi imam ʿAlī b. Ḥusayn 'Zayn al-ʿĀbidīn' (with introduction by Muḥammad Bāqir al-Ṣadr, Beirut, n.d.; the phrase appears in the 'Tuesday Supplication', p. 283). Note that MS BnF 2305 gives '*muntakhabīn*' (selected). I am indebted to Carmela Baffioni for alerting me to my previous misreading of this phrase and to Feras Hamza and Maha Yaziji for their help with different readings of this word.

24 See Table 1 for details. I would like to thank the Director and staff of the Salar Jung Museum for sharing a digital copy with me for my research.

25 It has been assumed that MS 3637 is from the 7th/13th century; however, no codicological or palaeographic arguments have been adduced or proposed for such speculation. See Nader El-Bizri's foreword to each of the volumes in the OUP-IIS Epistles of the Brethren of Purity Series. All the evidence that I have seen points to a much later dating, as the text of that particular copy is often similar to 9th/15th-century manuscripts, such as Koprülü MS 871, or 10th/16th century ones, like MS 1040.

26 Michael Casiri, *Bibliotheca Arabico-Hispana Escurialensis (sive librorum omnium Mss. Quos Arabice ab auctoribus magnam partem Arabo-Hispanis compositur Bibliotheca Coenobii Escurial complectitur)* (Madrid, 1760), vol. 1, p. 364. This manuscript was later given the number 928; see *Les manuscrits arabes de l'Escurial déecrits d'après les notes de Hartwig Derenbourg revues et complétées* par H.P.J. Renaud (Paris, 1941), vol. 2, fascicle 3, p. 37. The wrong details for this manuscript are given in El-Bizri's critical edition (p. 55), which confuses it with MS 900 of the same collection.

27 Note that the pages are in the wrong order in this edition (at least for this epistle). The text of the shorter version ends on p. 49 in ʿAlī Yūsuf's edition (reproduced in Ziriklī's print, p. 66, and Bustānī's copy, p. 104).

28 *On Arithmetic & Geometry*, ed. El-Bizri, pp. 53–57. The text of the shorter version ends on p. 128 (tr. p. 145). El- Bizri does note the end of the shorter version (although he does not refer to it as such) in MS Esad 3637 [ن].

29 See *On Geography* (*Epistle* 4), ed. and tr. Ignacio Sánchez and James Montgomery (2014), and *On Music* (*Epistle* 5), ed. and tr. Owen Wright (2011).

30 Ibid. pp. 190–191.

31 *On Composition and the Arts* (*Epistles 6-8*), ed. and tr. Nader El-Bizri and Godefroid de Callataÿ (2018), pp. 7, 44–45, tr. pp. 68–69.

32 I have identified three further copies that contain the appendix: MSS Majlis 1278 (p. 102), SOAS Or. 45812 (f. 43v), and Garrett 4263 (f. 66v, given after the closure of the epistle).
33 *On Composition and the Arts*, p. 86 and Appendix A (pp. 167–172).
34 To the manuscripts identified by de Callataÿ as containing the extra text we should add MSS Nuruosmaniye 2863 (f. 59r; where the variants are similar to Köprülü MS 870) and Garrett 4263 (f. 72r; similar to MS Esad 3637).
35 It is worth noting that the order in MS Sālār Jung 41 is Epistle 7 'On 'On the Practical Crafts' followed by Epistle 8 'On the Theoretical Crafts'; in both MSS Munich arab. 652 and BnF 2341 the titles for Epistles 7 and 8 are 'On the Theoretical Crafts' and 'On the Practical Crafts', respectively, but the contents are transposed.
36 *On Composition and the Arts*, p. 7.
37 I have checked five other MSS (Sālār Jung 41, Nuruosmaniye MS 2863, BnF 2305, Majlis 1278, and SOAS Or. 45812) and the repetition does not occur in them.
38 *On Logic (Epistles 10–14)*, ed. Carmela Baffioni (2010), pp. 181–187. I have checked a further six manuscripts and none of them have Esad 3638's addition. They all include the Prior Analytics part as a chapter of Epistle 12, although they introduce it differently: '*faṣl fī'l-qiyās*' (MSS Sālār Jung 41, BnF 2341 and Munich arab. 652); '*faṣl*' (SOAS MS Or. 45812); '*Anūlūṭīqā*' (MSS BnF 2305 and Majlis 1278).
39 This is similar to British Library MS Or. 4518, where the Prior and Posterior Analytics are counted as one epistle (no. 13). See Charles Rieu, *Supplement to the Catalogue of Arabic Manuscripts in the British Museum* (London, 1894). pp. 480–483, catalogue no. 708.
40 From here on I refer to each epistle with its number within its part (e.g. II.1, II.2, etc).
41 *On the Natural Sciences (Epistles 15–21)*, ed. and tr. Carmela Baffioni (2013), pp. 360–369.
42 *On the Natural Sciences*, pp. 66ff. Twelve manuscripts include the diagram. To the eight copies mentioned by Baffioni (MSS Atif 1681, Mahdavi 7437, BnF 6647, Esad 3638, Feyzullah 2130, Köprülü 871, Köprülü 870 and Esad 3637) we may add the following four: MSS Nuruosmaniye 2863 (f. 113v), BnF 2305 (f. 132r: chart with 13 spheres, including the four elements too), BnF 2341 (f. 154v – ditto) and IIS MS 85 (f. 19v – this has the circles but omits the words).
43 To the four mentioned by Baffioni (MSS Laud Or. 260, BnF 2304, Escorial 923, and Marsh 189), we may also add the following four: MSS Sālār Jung MS 41 (f. Ar 122v/p. 264), Munich arab. 652 (f. Ar74/73r), Majlis 1278 (p. 184) and SOAS Or. 45812 (f. 76r).
44 As ʿAlī Yūsuf's edition did not cover Part Two, Ziriklīs's diagram was, arguably, taken from the Cairene MS 9509 mentioned above, although this needs to be corroborated.
45 These two copies are to be added to the four already mentioned by Baffioni that do not have a diagram or a blank space: MSS Berlin 5038, Hunt 296, Laud Or. 255, and BnF 2303. Of these, only the Berlin manuscript is older than MS 1040. Dieterici's edition did not include the chart either.
46 *On the Natural Sciences*, pp. 385–392.
47 Equivalent to Baffioni's critical edition, p. 108, tr., p. 151 (Chapter 17, 'On the rotation of the stars. . .').
48 One additional unique feature at the end of Jīwā Khān's edition of this epistle is the addition of a table of astronomical dimensions (vol. 2, p. 34), which has no precedent in any of the manuscripts I have consulted. This leads me to the working hypothesis that Jīwā Khān may have added the table himself as an editor. As always, this table was reproduced by Ziriklī (vol. 2, p. 44).
49 See Carmela Baffioni's critical edition, pp. 247, p. 355 (where she notes that this reference is absent from MS Laud 260) and p. 409 respectively. Baffioni does not provide any further comments on this apparent anomaly.
50 The only two manuscripts that do not refer to the previous epistles in Ep. 19–21 are Munich arab. 652 and BnF 2341.

51 *The Case of the Animals versus Man Before the King of the Jinn* (*Epistle* 22), ed. and tr. Lenn E. Goodman and Richard McGregor (2010), p. 279.5, tr. p. 315.6 n. 566.

52 I use asterisk for manuscripts pages or folios that do not have a number written on them.

53 Adam Gacek, *Catalogue*, vol. 1, pp. 91–93, seq. no. 110 (B). A detailed analysis of IIS MSS 576 and 84, and a comparison with Jīwā Khān's text will show their dependency on the text first established by MS 1040.

54 Yves Marquet, *La philosophie des Ihwān al-Ṣafā'*, new edition, Paris-Milan, 1999, pp. 196–199.

55 His name is spelt on the cover as 'Schuekh Ahmud-bin Moohummud Schurwan-ool-Yummunee', *Tuḥfat Ikhwān al-Ṣafā'—Ichwan-oos-Suffa, in the original Arabic* (Calcutta, 1812) (see pp. 435–438). Unfortunately Shirwānī does not provide information on the manuscript he used.

56 Some manuscripts in this group are earlier than MS 1040: Atif MS 1681; Sālār Jung 41 (Ar 230r/p. 459—not used by Goodmann), BnF MS 6647; MS Esad 3638; MS Feyzullah 2130; Köprülü MS 870; Escorial MS 923 and MS 895; and some later: MS Laud 260; Nuruosmaniye 2863 (f. 212r); Munich arab. 652 (f. Ar135/W134r); Majlis 1278 (p. 305 – the last three MSS were not consulted by Goodmann) and BnF MS 2304; the ending in BnF MS 2341 is close to this group but slightly different. The short ending is also found in some undated MSS: Hunt 296; Esad 3637 (f. 253r) and Laud Or. 255 (end at the phrase *ṭūl azmānihim wa duhūrihim*).

57 *Thier und Mensch vor dem König der Genien* (Leipzig, 1879), see pp. 135–138; second edition, 1881.

58 See G. de Callataÿ, 'The Two Islands Allegory in the Rasā'il Ikhwān al-Ṣafā': A Walk Through Philosophical Metaphors Literary Motifs', *Ishraq* 4 (2013), pp. 71–81.'

59 *On Life, Death, and Languages*, ed. and tr. Eric Ormsby (2021), p. 6; tr. p. 48, n. 1.

60 Ibid., pp. 46–47, tr. pp. 70–71.

61 MSS Feyzullah 2130 (unnumbered folios); Köprülü 871 (f. 320v); Esad 3637 (f. 321r-v), and Laud Or. 255 (f. Ar220/W224r-v).

62 The other copies in this group are: MSS SOAS Or. 45812 (f. 151r-v), Munich arab. 652 (f. 166v) and BnF 2341 (f. 236v) and 2305 (f. 255 r-v). For the dates of these manuscripts see Table 4.1.

63 For example, 1) MS 1040 Ar394r/W382.14-next page.13 = Jīwā Khān, vol. 2, pp. 347.22-348.14 = Ormsby p. 27.14; 2) Ar397r/W385.7-11 = Jīwā Khān, vol. 2, pp.350.26-351.2 = Ormsby, p. 30.10 (this text should have been included in the critical edition, as it is left out in some manuscripts because of an omission caused by homeoteleuton, from *al-kufr* to *al-kafra* and 3) Ar398/W386.13-15 = Jīwā Khān 353.4-5 = Ormsby, p. 32.15.

64 I have checked all the manuscripts not included in Ormsby's critical edition and the only irregularities are found in MSS Marsh 189 (f. 229v/p. 447), which lacks the second poetry line; and BnF 2305 (f. 253r), which omits the whole passage with the first two poetry lines.

65 I conducted my study of this epistle before the publication of Ormsby's critical edition, which is based on MS Esad 3638; see *On Life, Death, and Languages*, p. 11.

66 The *'ayn* family includes: MSS Atif 1681 [ع] (ff. 316r– 322r); Sālār Jung 41 (ff. 289v–295v/pp. 578–590); BnF 6647–8 (ff. 214r–219r); Köprülü 871 (ff. 321r–325v); Esad 3637 (ff. 321v–329r); Laud Or. 255 (ff. 224v–229r), Hunt 296 (ff. 255v–261r). To these we may now add: MSS IIS 576 (pp. 848–862); Munich arab. 652 (ff. Ar167/W166v–Ar171/W170r); and BnF 2341 (ff. 236v– 240v).

67 The *alif* family includes ten manuscripts and two editions: MSS Esad 3638 [أ] (ff. 159v–175v), Köprülü 870 [ك] (ff. 191r–211r), Marsh 189 (ff. 233r–253r), BnF 2303 [ر] (ff. 289v–314v) and BnF 2304 [ز] (ff. 252v–278v). The latter is the basis for Dieterici's translation: *Die Anthropologie der Araber im zehnten Jahrhundert n. Chr.* (Leipzig, 1871); repr. (Hildesheim, 1969), pp. 159–221; see Jīwā Khān's edition, vol. 2, pp. 365–429.

Further copies I have explored include: MSS Nuruosmaniye 2863 (ff. 251v–277r); BnF 2305 (ff. 255v–276r); Majlis 1278 (pp. 372–409); SOAS Or. 45812 (ff. 151v–166r), and IIS 86 (ff. 159r–219v).

68 The part corresponding to the shorter version in the Feyzullah copy (ff. 174v–176v) stops at MS 1040 f. 400v.3 and misses the last 10 folios of MS 1040. This is followed by the long version (ff. 176v– 202?v). The numeration in this manuscript is unstable.

69 *Sciences of the Soul and Intellect, Part I* (*Epistles 32–36*), ed. and tr. Paul E. Walker, David Simonowitz, Ismail K. Poonawala, and Godefroid de Callataÿ (2016).

70 For convenience of reference, I give here the volume and page numbers in Jīwā Khān's (JK) edition and in Ziriklī's (Z) and Bustānī's (B) prints, as well as in Walker's (W) edition and translation: 'A': JK 3:2-7 = Z 3:182-8 = B 3:179-86 = W 5-15 (tr. 17–23); 'B': JK 3:7-15 = Z 3:189-99 = B 3:187–98 = W 35–50 (tr. 41–52); 'C': JK 3:16–24 = Z 3: 200–210 = B 3:199–211 = W 16–33 (tr. 27–38).

71 In this MS, 'B' is not an epistle, but a '*faṣl*' on Epistle 32 titled '*Fī-mabādi' al-ʿālam al-jismānī ʿalā ra'y al-ḥukamā' min ikhwān al-ṣafā*" (f. 234r).

72 For IIS MS 83 see Gacek, Catalogue, vol. 1, pp. 91–93, seq. no. 110 (E).

73 I have further consulted the following MSS: IIS 1040 and 83, Sālār Jung 41, SOAS Or. 45812, BnF 2305 and 2341, Nuruosmaniye 2863, Munich arab. 652 and Majlis 1278, but the poem is not found in them. Note that the letters attributed to the BnF manuscripts are wrong in the volume *Sciences of the Soul and Intellect, Part I*, p. 1.

74 As in BnF MS 6647-8 [د], this copy adds 'B' as a '*faṣl*' of 'A' (starting at f. 234r).

75 Other manuscripts I consulted, in addition to the ones used in Poonawala's critical edition, include MSS Sālār Jung 41, SOAS Or. 45812, BnF 2305 and 2341, Nuruosmaniye 2863, Munich arab. 652, Majlis 1278 and IIS 83.

76 *Sciences of the Soul and Intellect, Part I*, p. 72, and note 55.

77 The main text refers to the Epistle 'On the Macrocosm' only. The reference to 'On the Intellectual Principles' and 'On Sense and the Sensible' is added in the margin.

78 *Sciences of the Soul and Intellect, Part I*, pp. 110–111.

79 *Sciences of the Soul and Intellect, Part I*, p. 124, tr., p. 196 (table on p. 169).

80 These are the numbers as given in IIS MSS 1040 and 83, and Jīwā Khān's Khān's edition: (I give an asterisk for the numbers that are wrong; I underline the errors which are unique to all three and not other manuscripts). MS 1040: 21, 30*, 35, 21, 21*, 1, 110* and 42,200*; IIS MS 83 (f. 39v): 21, 30*, 35, 21, 31*, 1, 110* and 93,600*. Jīwā Khān (vol. 4, p. 49): 21, 30*, 35, 21, 31*, 1, 120 and 43,200.

81 *Sciences of the Soul and Intellect, Part III* (*Epistles 39–41*), ed. and tr. Carmela Baffioni and Ismail K. Poonawala (2017), p. 8.12, tr., p. 136, n. 7 and p. 10.6, tr., p. 138. Note that Baffioni's Baffioni's n. 7 is misplaced – it should be located on p. 138, which is the point where Bustānī added the footnote.

82 At Baffioni's point [7.], p. 10, tr., p. 141, n. 32.

83 MSS Köprülü 871 and Hunt 296 give *al-rawābiʿ*, like MS 1040. To the manuscripts mentioned by Baffioni as giving *al-zawābiʿ* we may now add MSS Nuruosmaniye 2863, BnF 2305, BnF 2341, Munich arab. 652, SOAS Or. 45812, Majlis 1278 and Majlis 5255.

84 The closest form is found in MS Sālār Jung 41 (f. 338v/p. 676): [الزوايع] *al-zawā'iʿ*, or perhaps [الذوايع] *al-dhawā'iʿ*.

85 To the manuscripts consulted by Baffioni we can add the following: *Bādh-i damah* is found in MSS BnF 2341 and Munich arab. 652; *Bād-i damah* is found in MSS Sālār Jung 41 and IIS 83, f. 81r.5- note that the latter gives '*damah*' with *tā marbūṭa* at the end).

86 Baffioni (*Sciences of the Soul and Intellect* p. 14, tr., p. 141, n. 33) gives 'bādhadama'.

87 *Ousía, posón, poión, prós ti, poû, póte, keîsthai, échein, poieîn and páschein (substance, how much/quantity, what kind/quality, relative relation, where/place, when/time, position, being/state, doing/action and affection).* See Aristotle, *Categories, 1b.25–2a.4* in *Aristotle, Categories; On Interpretation; Prior Analytics*, tr. H. P. Cooke and Hugh Tredennick (Cambridge, MA, 1938), pp. 16–19.

88 *Sciences of the Soul and Intellect, Part III*, pp. 50–51. Baffioni (p. 92, n. 28) highlights the importance of the *man hiya/huwa* (who are they/is it?) question as an original contribution of the *Ikhwān al-Ṣafā'*, but unfortunately it has been omitted from her edition and translation (pp. 65 and 66, tr. 179 and 180).

89 Further to the copies studied by Baffioni we may add the following observations: 1) like Atif MS 1681, a tree-like diagram containing the nine questions is also given in MSS Munich arab. 652 and BnF 2341 (although none refer to the image in the text). Both give *kam* instead of *lima*, like MS BnF 2303.

90 *Sciences of the Soul and Intellect, Part III*, pp. 269–273.

91 And others, including British Library MS Or 6692 (dated 646/1248–1249), the sixth oldest manuscript in the world if we count partial copies too.

92 This text corresponds to pp. 100 (at the *faṣl* heading)–121.3 of Traboulsi's edition. See Ian Netton's translation in the same volume, pp. 122 (If one of our brothers. . .)–129 (. . .they are a contemptuous people).

93 *On Companionship and Belief* (*Epistles 43–45*), ed. Samer F. Traboulsi, tr. Toby Mayer and Ian R. Netton (2017), p. 3. There is obviously a misprint, as the text says Epistle '43' instead of '45'. The 'sound' copies of Epistle 45, as identified by Traboulsi, are also found in MSS BnF 6647-8, Koprülü 871 and Koprülü 870. To these we may now include, apart from MS 1040, MSS Nuruosmaniye 2863, BnF 2305, BnF 2341 and Majlis 1831.

94 Traboulsi's 'corrupted' copies include: MSS Esad 3638, Fezyullah 2131, BnF 2303, Laud Or. 255, Esad 3637, Marsh 189 and BnF 2304. To these we may now add: MSS Sālār Jung 41, SOAS Or. 45812, Munich arab. 652, Majlis 1278, Majlis 5255 and IIS 87.

95 After I submitted this chapter, Abbas Hamdani published his critical edition and translation of this epistle with Abdallah Soufan: *The Call to God* (*Epistle 48*) (2019). I could only inspect it superficially, but enough to ascertain that their findings are not dissimilar from mine.

96 Yves Marquet, 'Ikhwān al-Ṣafā'', *EI3*, pp. 1071–1072. For a partial French translation of this epistle and an attempt at identifying those groups, see idem, 'Les Épîtres des Ikhwân as-Safâ', oeuvre ismaïlienne,' *Studia Islamica*, 61 (1985), pp. 57–79, esp. pp. 63–66.

97 Bombay, 1306/1888–1889. On this story see Shadha Almuwata, *Imaginative Cultures and Historic Transformations: Narrative in Rasā'il Ikhwān al-Ṣafā'* (PhD Dissertation, University of Chicago, 2013), pp. 80–133. Almuwata provides a complete translation of the story (pp. 81-100). While icharacters in the story in Epistle 48 characters are anonymous, Bilawhar the sage is mentioned by name in the same Epistle (chapter 9), and also elsewhere: Epistle 22 'On Animals' and Epistle 45 'On Companionship' (see indexes of the IIS/OUP edition volumes).

98 One manuscript (BnF MS 2305) has a shorter version with only five chapters, in this order: 1, 6–8, 9 (shorter version), and the final four lines of chapter 22.

99 My thanks to Nuha Alshaar for helping me with this note.

100 Paris, Seuil, 1962, originally published as 150 unbound pages.

101 Buenos Aires, 1963. It has 155 chapters. Cortázar suggests that the novel can be read up to chapter 56 and that the rest can be ignored. Alternatively, he provides a table at the beginning of the book with an alternative order of reading: chapters 73 – 1 – 2 – 116 – 3 – 84 – etc.

102 However, other copies (Sālār Jung 41, Esad 3637) do not include the reference to ʿAlī.

103 Wilferd Madelung has put forward the claim that the longer version is the work of Maslama al-Qurṭubī in 'Maslama al-Qurṭubī's Contribution to the Shaping of the Encyclopedia of the *Ikhwān al-Ṣafā*'' in Antonella Straface, et al., eds., *Studi Maġrebini*, 12-13 (2014-2015), 'Labor Limae. Atti in onore di Carmela Baffioni', vol. 1, pp. 403–417.

104 MSS Köprülü MS 871, MSS Esad 3637 and Laud Or. 255.

105 Note the change of hand half way through f. 127v, when the text becomes much more dense and there are more lines per page.

106 In this manuscript, the text of Epistle 49 is organised in a different way as compared to other copies. Some of the text (pp. 609.21–620) is part of the previous epistle. The title of Epistle 49 is on pp. 620 and ends on p. 627. Perhaps a more detailed analysis is needed to see whether this copy is a witness to the development of Epistle 49 into two different versions.

107 In addition, MS BnF 2305 contains selected passages from the long version (corresponding to the following pages in the Beirut edition: 198.7–11; 199.5–7; 200.3–7; 202.11–203.12; 206.1–17; 212.8–213.21; 214.5–216.16; 216.20–217.4; 217.16–224.5; 225.3– (with gaps); 240.1–5; 240.13–15; 240.19–241.1). I have not seen a similar 'abridgement' in any other manuscript or epistle.

108 Jīwā Khān edition, vol. 4, p. 263.13 = Bustānī, vol. 4, p. 247.19 = Madelung's critical edition of epistle Epistle '49a', p. 50.14 (tr. p. 69.11).

109 Bustānī's 1957 print: vol. 4, pp. 243.1–244.9 = vol. 3, pp. 289.ult.–291.9.

110 *On God and the World* (*Epistles* 49–51), ed. and tr. Wilferd Madelung, Cyril Uy, Carmela Baffioni and Nuha Alshaar (2019), pp. 237–291 (Arabic).

111 I would like to thank Nuha Alshaar for generously sharing with me a copy of her critical edition and translation even before its publication.

112 Incidentally, Alshaar (pp. 384, 387) proposes the possibility that Atif MS 1681 may be a palimpsest; however a closer looks demonstrates that it is simply a case of ink being seen through the paper on the other side.

113 I hope to publish a more in-depth comparison.

114 *On Magic I (Epistle 52, version a),* ed. and tr. Godefroid de Callataÿ and Bruno Halflants (2011).

115 The long version is found in the following MSS: 1) Nuruosmaniye 2863 (ff. 428r–473v), whose ending corresponds to Jīwā Khan, vol. 4, p. 396.4 – Bustānī, vol. 4:445.11 (like MS 1040) with a closing formula, but then attaches a 2 ½-page text (ff. 473v–475r) headed by '*kalāmun bi-ba'ḍi'l-muḥaqqiqīn*', beginning with the *basmala* and after this comes the colophon; 2) BnF 2305 (ff. 398r–414r), although it has a large lacuna at f. 398v. of around 18 pages (corresponding to Jīwā Khān's Khān's ed., vol. 4, p. 309.20 = Bustānī, vol. 4:313.9, then 311.3–7 = 315.4–9 and then 323.19 = 333.1). The last identifiable passage is near the end of the manuscript (f. 413r.30), corresponding to Jīwā Khān, vol. 4:400.15 = Bustānī, vol. 4:451.16; 3) IIS 87 (ff. 209v–330v), 4) Hamdani 1482 (the folios are out of order; the correct sequence should be ff. 18a–32b (of the extra leaves), then 1r–99v, and then 215r–228r, and 5) Majlis 1278 (pp. 636–687).

116 The shorter version is found in the following MSS: 1) Sālār Jung 41 (ff. 486r-492v/pp. 971–984); it lacks the colophon page and so it is also missing about the last ten lines of the epistle, if compared with MS Esad 3637 (ends at Jīwā Khān, vol. 4, p. 306.19 = Bustānī, vol. 4, p. 308.23 = de Callataÿ and Halflants's critical edition, p. 93.6, tr., p. 151. ult.); 2–3) Munich arab. 652 (ff. W288v–294v) and BnF 2341 (ff. 382v–389r) starting at Jīwā Khān, vol. 4, p. 288.5 = Bustānī, vol. 4:284.8 and ending at Jīwā Khān, p. 309.2 = Bustānī, p. 312.9 (like MS 1040 but with a different closing formula).

117 = Jīwā Khān vol. 4, p. 309.8 = Bustānī, vol. 4, p. 352.14-15 = De Callataÿ and Halflants, p. 105, tr. 158.

118 Charles Rieu, *Supplement*, pp. 483–484; catalogue nos. 709–710). I have also identified two further manuscripts where different texts are added to the long version of Epistle 52: 1) SOAS MS Or. 45812 has the long version (ff. 259r–272r) but ends halfway through the text present in other manuscripts; the last identifiable passage is on f. 271r (= Jīwā Khān, vol. 4, p. 362.17 = Bustānī, vol. 4:394.2), but it adds two more pages (which are different). The text is the followed by a red-ink title: *tammat al-risāla [sic] al-riyāḍiyya tatlūhā al-rasā'ilu'l-nāmūsiyyatu wa hiya aḥada 'ashara* [sic] *risālatan,*

al-ūlā minhā. The text that follows is a long passage (ff. 272r–276v) that calls itself *al-risāla al-jāmiʿa*, which reaches the end of the manuscript. The passage is a summary/explanation of epistles 43–52; a detailed comparative analysis is needed to ascertain the exact identity of this text. 2) Ragip Pasha MS 839 (f. 597v = Bust 449.7): the scribe adds additional materials that he/she found in other manuscripts (in ff. 598v–602). The images of the last pages have been published in Maḥmūd al-Sayyid al-Dughaym's catalogue (vol. 6, pp. 560–562); see next note.

119 I would like to thank Godefroid de Callataÿ for kindly sharing with me his finding that this MS contained both versions, one after the other; in a mutual exchange, I also informed him about MS 1040 and British Library MS 2358-9. The new 10-volume catalogue of the Ragip Paşa Library by Maḥmūd al-Sayyid al-Dughaym contains reproductions of the beginning, ending and significant pages of manuscripts: *Fihris al-Makhṭūṭāt al-ʿArabiyya waʾl-Turkiyya waʾl-Fārisiyya fī Maktabat Rāghib Pāshā* (Jeddah, 2016). For MS 840 see vol. 6, pp. 563–564 + images.

120 = Bustānī, vol. 4, p. 309.7 = de Callataÿ's critical edition, p. 94.6, tr. 152.13.

121 ʿAbd al-Laṭīf al-Ṭībāwī, 'Ḥawla Rasāʾil Ikhwān al-Ṣafa", *al-Kashshāf*, vol. 3, part 8, Jumāda I 1348/ October 1929, pp. 562–581, quote pp. 573–574. I would like to thank my colleague Prof. Bilal Orfali, and MS Fatme Chehouri, of the American University in Beirut for kindly providing with me a copy of this article.

5

The Manuscript Copies of Abū Ḥātim al-Rāzī's *Kitāb al-Zīna* at The Institute of Ismaili Studies*

Cornelius Berthold

Introduction

The lexicographic encyclopaedia *Kitāb al-Zīna* is probably the most well known and also the largest extant work by the Ismaili *dāʿī* Abū Ḥātim al-Rāzī (d. 322/934–935). We know of three surviving copies which were written around the 5th–7th/11th–13th centuries. However, despite their importance as some of the oldest Ismaili text witnesses in existence, all are fragmentary and at least two of them, kept in Baghdad and Sanaa, have not been easily accessible to Western scholars over the last years. Seven more recent and largely undamaged manuscript copies exist in the Ismaili Special Collections Unit at The Institute of Ismaili Studies in London. We know of 15 codices worldwide but since many contain only either the first or second half of the book, not counting fragments, a total number is difficult to give. This chapter will briefly introduce the content and structure of the *Kitāb al-Zīna* and present the text witnesses known today, focusing especially on the manuscript copies preserved at the IIS in London. In his complete edition of the book, published in 2015, Saʿīd al-Ghānimī has implied that the London copies form 'siblings' (*akhawāt*) of witnesses, united by the same variant readings. This assumption will be discussed after describing and comparing the manuscripts from the IIS in terms of their codicological characteristics.

Abū Ḥātim al-Rāzī and his *Kitāb al-Zīna*

The biography of Abū Ḥātim Aḥmad ibn Ḥamdān al-Rāzī, as we know him today, was largely pieced together from various sources by Samuel

Miklos Stern in his 1960 article 'The Early Ismā'īlī Missionaries in North-West Persia and in Khurāsān and Transoxania'. While not completely unproblematic,[1] his conclusions will be considered valid for the present chapter. According to them, Abū Ḥātim al-Rāzī (who is not to be confused with the *ḥadīth* scholar Abū Ḥātim Muḥammad ibn Idrīs al-Rāzī, d. 277/890)[2] hailed from Warsanān in Northwestern Iran.[3] He must have studied in Baghdad under the grammarians Tha'lab (d. 291/904)[4] and al-Mubarrad (d. 286/900)[5] because he claims in the *Kitāb al-Zīna* to have listened to their teachings.[6] Soon after, he rose to power within the Ismaili *da'wa* in the area of Rayy, eventually exerting his influence as far as Ṭabaristān, Isfahan and Azerbaijan in the early 4th/10th century. He supposedly converted a few of the quickly-changing local rulers and debated in public with the philosopher Abū Bakr al-Rāzī (called Rhazes in Europe) before falling out of favour and being forced to flee to Azerbaijan. Either on the way or shortly after his arrival he died; the year 322/934–935 is only reported by Ibn Ḥajar al-'Asqalānī (d. 852/1449).[7]

Abū Ḥātim al-Rāzī is known today for his philosophical thinking, as attested by his two extant books *Kitāb al-Iṣlāḥ* and *A'lām al-Nubūwa*. The former was a response to his fellow Ismaili *dā'ī* Muḥammad ibn Aḥmad al-Nasafī (d. 332/943) and his Neoplatonic speculations. Since al-Nasafī's *Kitāb al-Maḥṣūl* is not preserved,[8] Abū Ḥātim al-Rāzī's 'correction' remains the oldest extant Ismaili Neoplatonic work. The *A'lām al-Nubūwa* is a rendition of his debates with Rhazes—who is simply called 'the apostate' (*al-mulḥid*)[9]—which were most likely re-worked in his favour. Two of Abū Ḥātim al-Rāzī's books appear to be lost: one entitled *Kitāb al-Jāmi'* which is mentioned by Ibn al-Nadīm who states that it dealt with '*fiqh* and other things'.[10] The second is a book refuting those who believe in resurrection (*raj'a*). Abū Ḥātim al-Rāzī claims in a section of his *Kitāb al-Zīna* that he wrote it for those who wish to inform themselves further.[11]

The *Kitāb al-Zīna* seems to be his largest extant work. One of the earliest descriptions, again to be found in Ibn al-Nadīm's *Fihrist*, succinctly calls it a 'big [work] on grammar on 400 leaves'.[12] Indeed, the focus on language, specifically a lexicographical approach, is the most noticeable quality of the book. In his foreword, Abū Ḥātim al-Rāzī states that he sets out to explain terms and names with the help of Qur'ānic verses and the poetry of famous poets. Scholars, jurists and other learned and gallant men should be well informed about the meaning of these words—so that they can use this knowledge as a great ornament *(zīna ʿaẓīma)* to themselves.[13] After an introduction in praise of the Arabic language and its poetry, the terms or lemmas discussed mostly come from the field of religion, with words related to God and his creation followed by chapters dealing with the hereafter, created beings in the world, faith and disbelief, religions and Islamic sects, religious duties, etc. The topics thus merge into one another, coming from the divine and reaching worldly spheres, and it has been argued that this order might have a model in Neoplatonic thought.[14] I will repeat here a structure of the book based on Jamal Ali's proposal but with a few modifications. I will refer to these sections throughout this chapter.

I Virtues of the Arabic language and poetry
II God's names and attributes
III Terms related to creation and God
IV Supernatural creatures (e.g. angels)
V Terms related to the afterlife, reward and punishment
VI Terms related to nature, astronomy, geography
VII Theological terms related to faith and disbelief
VIII Non-Islamic religions
IX Introduction to sectarianism, Islamic sects
X Terms related to prophethood and religious officials (prophets, priests etc.)
XI Terms related to revelation (Qurʾān, Bible)
XII Religious duties
XIII Terms related to Qurʾān and *fiqh*
XIV Linguistic terms
XV Family members
XVI Miscellaneous[15]

The only historically-attested grouping of the chapters can be found in the margins of a fragmentary manuscript from Yemen (Sanaa, Great Mosque, Eastern Library (?), 46 lugha, no. 3 in my list below), where e.g. the chapters on sectarianism and Islamic sects are introduced as the 'sixth part'; the section starting with *al-farīḍa* is even labelled 'the tenth of the parts of Abū Ḥātim al-Rāzī, may God be pleased with him'.[16] This marginal hand is different from that of the main text, as are at least some of the other hands which made additions, such as corrections and explanations of the terms used in the text. It is therefore not clear how old or authoritative this structure is, given that even in the manuscript it is a later addition and not an element introduced by the original scribe. While the Ismaili scholar Ḥusayn al-Hamdānī suspected that it might have been transmitted from the author's original (*bi-aṣl al-mu'allif aw bi-nuskha mansūkha minhu*),[17] the lack of evidence in other manuscript copies makes this unlikely in my opinion. I would rather expect this to be a singular later addition that was supposed to make the book easier to read, or a sign of a certain recension of the *Kitāb al-Zīna* at the most. Much more relevant for the present chapter, however, is the division of the book into two halves. It takes place in the middle of the section about faith and disbelief (VII), between the chapters *al-shirk* and *al-ilḥād*, which clearly does not correspond to a transition in the content. However, as it is roughly in the middle of the whole text, it seems clear that it must be related to writing space.[18] This two-part division is attested already in the oldest manuscript copies of the text. The Yemeni manuscript just mentioned, for example, contains only the second half of the book. This is unfortunate in as far as we do not have the aforementioned marginal notes marking the book's structure for the first half. The copy from Leipzig University Library, Ms.or.377 (no. 1 in my list below), also refers to a 'second part' on f. 10r, but in a different way which I will present further down.

There are two manuscript copies, one from 1364/1945 (no. 15 in my list below) and the other certainly not much older (no. 13), which contain footnotes. They thus appear to be drafts for edition projects. The earliest published editions, however, do not seem to have relied on them. Ḥusayn al-Hamdānī had intended to release a complete edition of the text, the first two fascicles of which were published in 1956 (containing section I from my list above) and 1958 (sections II–V). Unfortunately, he died in 1962 after having suffered a stroke which left his work unfinished.[19] For reasons not entirely known, Ḥusayn al-Hamdānī added the secondary title *fī l-Kalimāt al-Islāmiyya al-ʿArabiyya*, which was subsequently understood by many to be the true and complete title of the book.[20] As early as 1972, it was repeated by ʿAbdallāh Sallūm al-Sāmarrāʾī when he published an edition of section IX as an appendix to his book *al-Ghulūw wa'l-Firaq al-Ghāliya fi'l-Ḥaḍāra al-Islāmiyya*. He furthermore created confusion by calling the edited section 'the third part' (*al-qism al-thālith*) of the book, which can neither be right with regard to the original structure of the *Kitāb al-Zīna*, nor with regard to the fascicles published by al-Hamdānī, to which it does not connect: several sections with almost 40 chapters are missing in between. In 2011, as part of my PhD project, I started working on a new edition of sections VIII and IX, based on the newly discovered Leipzig manuscript. In 2015, one year before defending my thesis, Saʿīd al-Ghānimī published his edition of the whole book in two volumes. While I disagree on some conclusions in the preface and have noticed several occurrences in the edited text where the relevant witnesses were not documented precisely (or at all), this edition still helps in grasping the encyclopaedia as a whole and I have used it extensively for the present paper.

Extant Manuscript Copies of the *Kitāb al-Zīna*

The present chapter gives me the chance to revisit the list of text witnesses of the *Kitāb al-Zīna* that I had given in 2014[21] and correct a few errors that have become apparent since. The list is not extensive with regards to codicological details as I intend to focus on some of them later. Not all manuscripts can be safely dated but I will still order them roughly chronologically, beginning with the presumably oldest.

1. Leipzig, Universitätsbibliothek, Ms.or.377 (*ca.* 5th/11th century): This manuscript was discovered by Verena Klemm almost a decade after it had been acquired by the library in 1996. On 171 folios we find three different hands (ff. 1–9; 10–165; 166–171) on various sorts of Middle Eastern paper. It has thus to be considered a composite manuscript, bound together from different codicological units. Only the first two parts contain material from the *Kitāb al-Zīna*, specifically starting with chapters on earthly creations (islands, settlements, animals; from section VI of the book).[22] The second hand starts a few chapters before the complex on faith and disbelief (VII), even though its title page (f. 10r) claims that it was 'from the second part' of the book (*min al-juz' al-thānī min kitāb al-zīna*), as if referring to the usual two-part

division which takes places somewhat later within VII. It breaks off in the section about religious officials (X). The third part contains an as-yet unidentified philosophical text with an intriguing colophon (f. 167r) attesting to an origin in the district of Rayy in 544/1149. However, since the handwriting is clearly from a different scribe, it cannot be used to date the *Kitāb al-Zīna* portions of the codex.[23] For this reason, I arranged for a 14C analysis of the second hand's paper to be made in 2015.[24] The results indicated that the manuscript was then probably written in the early 5th/11th century.[25] My own studies are mainly based on this fragmentary copy of the *Kitāb al-Zīna*.

2. Baghdad, Iraqi National Museum, no. 1306 (*ca.* 6th/12th century): This 243 folios manuscript[26] appears to contain the whole book but a closer look reveals several defects such as missing text, dittographies (at least one case where half of a page had been written twice by the scribe) or serious transpositions. A major mechanical lacuna occurs immediately after the start of the chapter *al-ṭayf wa'l-ṭā'if* (section IV); the next page contains the end of *al-amṣār* (section VI), thus almost 30 chapters in between are missing. This had prompted me earlier to assume that there were different recensions of the text, distinguishable by different chapter orders.[27] As it turned out, however, it was mainly this manuscript's poor condition which had misled me. Three of these 'missing' chapters, starting with *al-thawwāb*, are attached at the end of the codex. Beginning in the chapter on *al-ʿaql* (section VII), material on Islam, faith and disbelief is interspersed, even though it occurs again at its proper place slightly later in the same section. Saʿīd al-Ghānimī has noted these defects in his footnotes[28] but has not given a concise overview about the lacunae and transpositions of the codex. Considering the questionable quality of the manuscript, it has to be called into question why both ʿAbdallāh Sallūm al-Sāmarrāʾī[29] and al-Ghānimī[30] claim to have used it as their main text witness. However, I have to add that during my own work on section IX of the book, I have on a few occasions (which I, regrettably, have not noted down) seen text in al-Sāmarrāʾī's edition that could not possibly have come from the Baghdad manuscript which he cites as his only witness of the text, after all. The manuscript does not have a colophon; the hypothetical

dating above is by Ḥusayn al-Hamdānī and based on the style of handwriting.[31]

3. Sanaa, Great Mosque, Eastern Library, 46 lugha (*ca.* 7th/13th century): The third of the three oldest known manuscripts is (or at least was) stored in the Great Mosque in Sanaa. The so-called Eastern Library is administered by the Ministry of Endowments, the Maktabat al-Awqāf wa'l-Irshād.[32] There is a microfilm copy in Cairo's Dār al-Kutub al-Miṣriyya with the shelf-mark 4337 jīm. This manuscript contains the second half of the *Kitāb al-Zīna* on 220 folios (which are foliated as 84–304). The dating by al-Hamdānī is again based on cautious palaeographic evaluation; the only tangible dating we have is a collation remark from 924/1518 (f. 304).[33] What makes the content of this manuscript unique are the already mentioned marginal notes about the book's grouping of chapters. Ff. 303v–304r contain several secondary entries worth investigating (as do the flyleaves in the front), which mention military encounters and casualties in the late 10th/16th century.
4. Sanaa, Great Mosque, Eastern Library, 45 lugha (*ca.* 9th–10th/15th–16th century):[34] This Yemeni manuscript is probably one of the most fragmentary. On only 76 folios (but approx. 30 lines per page) there is material ranging from shortly after the beginning of the book to somewhere in section X. However, several folios are transposed and large lacunae are to be expected.[35] The manuscript contains many marginalia. Its microfilm copy in the Dār al-Kutub al-Miṣriyya has the shelf-mark 4336 jīm.
5. Sanaa, Great Mosque, Western Library/Dār al-Makhṭūṭāt,[36] no. 2119, formerly lugha 4 and, before that, no. 63 adab in the library of the imam Yaḥyā al-Mutawakkil ʿala llāh (*ca.* 11th/17th century):[37] On 115 folios it contains almost the complete first half of the book, breaking off only one chapter earlier than usual. It was written by several hands from a Yemeni model, according to al-Hamdānī.[38] For the microfilm copies (Dār al-Kutub al-Miṣriyya and the collection of the Hamdānī family) no shelf-marks are given.
6. Mumbai, collection of Asghar Ali Engineer (12th/18th century): This manuscript was described by Ismail K. Poonawala who also had a microfilm copy made which is now at the Research Library

at the University of California, Los Angeles (shelf-mark: Microfilm PJ 6617, A28, 1800a). The complete book is preserved on 366 folios, including a six-page index with page numbers in the beginning. Variant readings and corrections can be found in the margins, as is the case with emphases of the chapter headings and other important terms mentioned in the text. The colophon does not indicate a date but Poonawala estimates that it must be more than two centuries old.[39]

7. India, collection of Shaykh ʿAbd al-Qayyūm ʿIsābhāʾī (sic) (1309/1891): This manuscript is described by Poonawala and Jamal Ali. It is slightly incomplete as it does not go beyond the last but one chapter, on *al-jibt waʾl-ṭāghūt*.[40]
8. IIS London, Hamdani Collection,[41] MS 1410 (1306/1888) (see Figure 5.1): Ḥusayn al-Hamdānī used this manuscript as his main text witness and considered it a sister of MS 1411 (no. 9), not least because both were relatively recent and copied from a common Yemeni exemplar, according to his judgement.[42] In fact, at least five different hands worked on this 198 folio copy; they can be distinguished not least by their different usage of eulogies, as I can attest to from my own work on the heresiographical section of the *Kitāb al-Zīna*.[43] The number of lines per page varies between 21 and 34. The margins are frequently used for corrections and for highlighting chapter headings as well as keywords from the text like *ḥadīth, qirāʾa* or *qawl*.
9. IIS London, Hamdani Collection, MS 1411 (late 13th/19th century?) (see Figure 5.2): Aside from MS 1410, this is the second 'modern' manuscript which Ḥusayn al-Hamdānī used in his edition. It contains the complete book on no less than 680 folios, the number being so high due to only 15 lines per page being used. Marginal additions can be found occasionally and a list of chapters is inserted before the main text. Not all of these chapter headings appear as such in the main text. The first one, the 'explanation of pronouncing the letters' (*bayān makhārij al-ḥurūf*), is later repeated in the margins in the manuscript (p. 19), but in the main text, the transition is fluent. In contrast to MS 1410 with its many traces of usage, MS 1411 is a very neat and orderly copy.

Each of the manuscripts from the Zahid Ali Collection contains only one half of the book. However, the only matched set among them appears to be MS 1269 and MS 1271. MSS 1317 and 1290 are distinguished by their footnotes; they appear to be made in preparation for at least one edition project.

10. IIS London, Zahid Ali Collection,[44] MS 1270 (1314/1897): This copy, written by a certain Yūsuf ʿAlī ibn Myānṣāḥib ʿAbd al-ʿAzīz ibn al-Mājid ibn Mullā Khānbhāʾī Islāmpūrī, features the first half of the book on 267 folios (533 pages). The manuscript is written regularly with only few marginalia. In contrast, on its first page—the back of which contains the beginning of the main text—the title of the book and Abū Ḥātim al-Rāzī's name are repeated several times, along with two presumed years of his passing, 322 (which is the year given by Ibn Ḥajar al-ʿAsqalānī in his *Lisān al-Mīzān,*[45] in fact the only specific date we have) and 362, which is given a question mark on its two occurrences. In the lower half, the section dealing with Abū Ḥātim al-Rāzī's books from Ibn al-Nadīm's *Fihrist* is quoted twice, apparently based on an Egyptian edition. In the list of chapters that is part of the introduction, a later hand has added the respective page numbers as numerals. There are also secondary entries numerating the chapters added, e.g. on p. 8 (*al-bāb al-thānī*) or p. 10, where the note 'the third chapter' has been crossed out again.
11. IIS London, Zahid Ali Collection, MS 1269 (late 19th or early 20th century): This copy is written on 241 folios with a few pages remaining blank (ff. 103–106 and 109–112), probably inserted later for text to fill the lacunae which exist in these two places: the catchwords at the bottom of ff. 102v and 108v do not correspond to the first words written ff. 107r and 113r, respectively. The Eastern Arabic foliation continues across these slightly smaller leaves, so it was likely added after the loss of the original folios. Otherwise, the manuscript is cleanly produced and written in a regular *naskh* hand. The text contains the first half of the *Kitāb al-Zīna*.
12. IIS London, Zahid Ali Collection, MS 1271 (late 19th or early 20th century): This is a neatly-written copy of the second half[46] of the book on 270 folios. What distinguishes this text witness from the

others is a four-page *fihrist*, a list of at least all major chapter headings of this second half of the encyclopaedia (ff. 1v–3r).[47] As mentioned above, it shares a few common features with MS 1269. With both, the overall format is roughly 24–26 × 13 cm, the written area 16.5 × 9 cm. There are 17 lines per page and both the handwriting and the placement of catchwords at the bottom of the pages seems identical.

13. IIS London, Zahid Ali Collection, MS 1317 (late 13th–early 14th/early 20th century): This copy of the second half of the book is written on 296 folios/592 pages. Delia Cortese reports 37 loose gatherings and a lost ending. In fact, the text on the last page is still in the middle of the chapter on idols (section XVI according to my list above), which means that some ten chapters would have come afterwards. The manuscript contains extensive annotations by a second hand. They sometimes extend from footnotes into the margins or onto specifically inserted pages. These annotations reference Qurʾānic verses, elaborate on persons or terms mentioned in the text and sometimes refer to printed editions.
14. Unknown location (1338/1919): This manuscript is mentioned by Zāhid ʿAlī in MS 1290 (p. 29ff., see also no. 15 in this list) where he records the copyist: Aḥsan (or Iḥsān, as al-Ghānimī reads it)[48] Ismāʿīl Muḥammad al-Ḥājj al-Yaʿbarī al-Kharrāzī who finished the manuscript in Karachi. According to my knowledge, it is the only copy of the *Kitāb al-Zīna* which features a frame around the text block, at least on the first pages, executed in simple double red lines. There is a microfilm copy of this manuscript in Tehran's Central Library.[49] When I only knew about this microfilm and not its manuscript original back in 2014, I had suggested IIS London, MS 1411, as one possible candidate,[50] which I can now rectify.
15. IIS London, Zahid Ali Collection, MS 1290 (1364–1365/1945–1946) (see Figure 5.3): This 508 folios/1016 pages[51] manuscript contains the first part of the *Kitāb al-Zīna* with an extensive introduction (pp. 1–46) and discussion of the book, its author and the sources he used. Footnotes are used frequently for comments and additional information. Zāhid ʿAlī himself finished the main text on the 17th of Shaʿbān, 1364/July 27th, 1945 and the introduction

on the 10th of Shawwāl 1365/September 6th, 1946.[52] He states that he based his text on six manuscripts of which, however, only four are mentioned:[53]

a. an otherwise unknown manuscript copy from Berlin which I unfortunately could not locate in the records of the Berlin State Library,
b. IIS London MS 1270 (no. 10 in this list),
c. a (probably Indian?) copy from an unknown scribe, and
d. a somewhat difficult case: He describes a manuscript *(nuskha)* in the possession of his friend A[saf]. A[li]. A[sghar]. Fyzee of the Faculty of Law in Mumbai. He then says '(photo?) copied (*muṣawwara*) from a manuscript. . .' and gives a short description of the Karachi copy (no. 14 in this list), which suggests that this is some kind of photographic reproduction, otherwise the given codicological details would be difficult to explain.

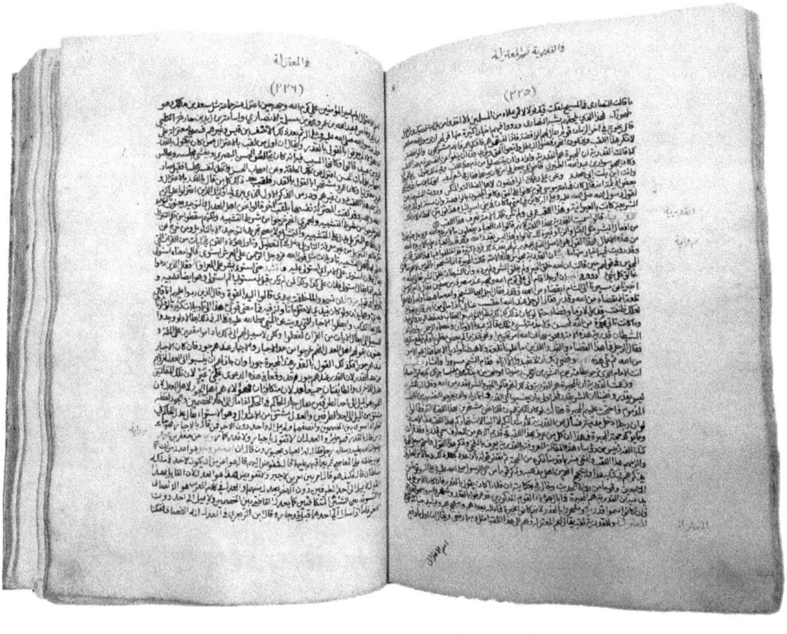

Figure 5.1 Double page from IIS London, Hamdani Collection, MS 1410, pp. 225–226, showing two chapters on the Muʿtazila and a change of scribal hands (and pen) at the end of p. 226.

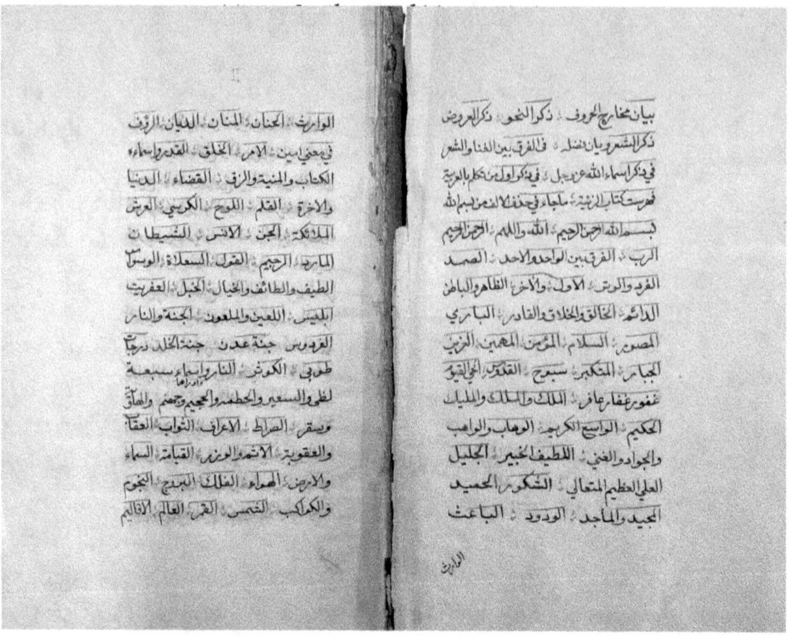

Figure 5.2 Beginning of IIS London, Hamdani Collection, MS 1411, showing the start of a list of chapter headings.

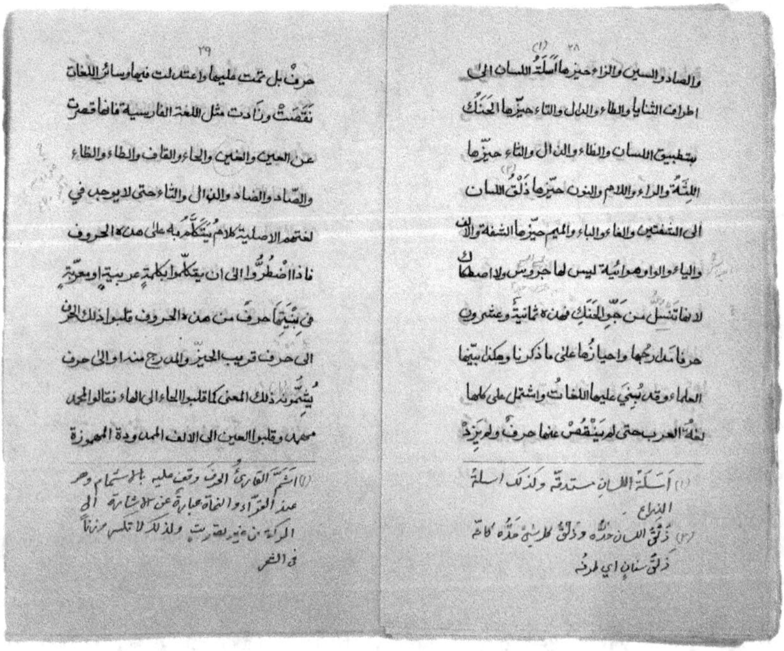

Figure 5.3 Double page from the 'proto edition' IIS London, Zahid Ali Collection, MS 1290, pp. 28–29, with footnotes beneath the main text.

A Comparison of Formal Features of the London Copies

While Saʿīd al-Ghānimī's speaking of 'siblings' referred to the text contained inside the manuscripts, I will focus first on codicological and formal characteristics. The two most obvious of these are dating and provenance: All manuscripts were produced or at least kept on the Indian subcontinent[54] before their transfer to London and all were written in the late 19th or early 20th century CE. I am not qualified to elaborate on the culture of manuscript production within the Ismaili communities in India over the last centuries, but it seems safe to assume that those recent copies of the *Kitāb al-Zīna* form the latest—if not last, for the time being—witnesses of the handwritten transmission of this extensive text among Ismailis.

In the following tables, an asterisk marks when there are major lacunae in the manuscripts which would distort the comparability of features related to writing space like the total number of folios. The dating information is given only in CE.

The following tables compare basic codicological data, both within the London copies and later in contrast to the older witnesses of the text. As can be seen, these codicological features are indicative, at best, of manuscript production and book culture on the Indian subcontinent or within the respective communities. Still, it should not be forgotten that these outward characteristics influence our understanding of the

Table 5.1 Dates and provenance.

	ZAC MS 1269	ZAC MS 1270	ZAC MS 1271	ZAC MS 1290	ZAC MS 1317	HC MS 1410	HC MS 1411
Parts of the book contained	I*	I	II	I	II	I+II	I+II
Dating (year or century)	Late 19th or early 20th	1897	Late 19th or early 20th	1945	Early 20th	1888	Late 19th or early 20th
Place of origin	India	India	India	India	India	India	India

Table 5.2 Basic codicological data.

	ZAC MS 1269	ZAC MS 1270	ZAC MS 1271	ZAC MS 1290	ZAC MS 1317	HC MS 1410	HC MS 1411
Parts of the book	I*	I	II	I	II	I+II	I+II
Size (h × w) in cm	24 × 13	23 × 14	26 × 14	23 × 15	23 × 15	23 × 17	22 × 14
Folios (incl. blank pages)	241*	267*	270	445	296	198	680
Lines per page	17	14	17–18	11	15	21–34	15

text, too. After all, the notion of the *Kitāb al-Zīna* being an encyclopaedia in two parts is based first and foremost on practical considerations of manuscript production—not to mention that Saʿīd al-Ghānimī's edition also consists of two volumes, although they do not correspond to the division from the manuscripts.

Understanding these characteristics as indicative of manuscript culture becomes more obvious when they are contrasted with some of the older copies. I have here relied on Ḥusayn al-Hamdānī's description of the Yemeni copies and the one from Baghdad.[55] As can be seen, the only roughly comparable category is lines per page which still shows the same variation. The older manuscripts are more often fragmentary, with the Leipzig copy (no. 1 in my list) and Sanaa 2119 (no. 5) being the least complete. The percentages are very rough estimations, based on the descriptions by al-Hamdānī (especially in the case of Sanaa 2119 of which I do not possess a reproduction) and comparisons with complete copies in terms of text quantity. Double asterisks mark manuscripts which are incomplete both at the beginning and end (see Table 5.3).

The next table (see Table 5.4) compares selected paratextual elements of the manuscripts, thus connecting the main text with codicological features which, at least to some extent, transcend the individual copy. By the term 'paratexts' I refer here to all written text which is not part of the main text.[56] In the case of the *Kitāb al-Zīna* manuscripts, there are at least two kinds of paratexts which allow the drawing of different

Table 5.3 Data related to writing space and completeness.

	ZAC MSS (average values)	**HC MS 1410**	**HC MS 1411**	**San. 2119**	**San. 45 lugha**	**San. 46 lugha**	**Leipzig Ms.or.377**	**Bagh. 1306**
Completeness	c. 50 %*	100 %	100 %	c. 49%	c. 50 % (?)**	50%	c. 31 %**	c. 85 (?) %**
Size (h × w) in cm	24 × 14	23 × 17	22 × 14	30 × 19	25 × 20	?	17 × 13	?
Folios (incl. blank pages)	240–290	198	680	115	76	220	165	238
Lines per page	11–17	21–34	15	23 (average)	24–30	17	17–19 (1st hand) 13–15 (2nd hand)	23
Date (year or century)	19th–20th	1888	19th	17th (?)	15th–16th	13th (?)	11th (?)	12th (?)

conclusions. Marginal headings and emphases, that is, the repetition of headings and noteworthy terms (mostly categories of lexicographical proof, like *shiʿr*, *ḥadīth*, *kalām* etc.) in the outer margins of the manuscript, appear to be aids for not only reading but actively working with the text. The same is true of the two cases of lists of content which, despite not having page numbers, still help with navigating through the encyclopaedia. The list in MS 1411 is remarkable not least because it is followed by Abū Ḥātim al-Rāzī's foreword which in itself includes an extensive list of chapter headings. Both the marginal emphases and the lists of content are largely absent in the older manuscripts of the *Kitāb al-Zīna*. Of these only the Leipzig copy, which is the most familiar to me, has been included in the following table for the sake of comparison.

Eulogies are the second kind of paratext which I have recorded here. As I have not prepared an extensive statistical analysis, the following reflects merely my impression from working with the manuscripts. It could be stated that each of the oldest copies has its own and unique pattern of eulogies, while among the London copies they appear slightly more uniform. In general, eulogies change depending on the time and place in which they are written and probably also the scribe's religious conviction; the latter could thus leave a more or less individual footprint on the manuscript. For instance, the eulogies in UB Leipzig Ms.or.377 are given, aside from God, only to the prophets, the Shiʿi revolutionary al-Mukhtār and the Ismaili line of imams. The eulogies for the Prophet Muhammad almost always include a prayer for blessings upon his family (*ṣallā-llāhu ʿalayhi wa-ʿalā ālihī*), which indicates a Shiʿi background, too. These eulogies are given less frequently in e.g. the Baghdad manuscript, although still occasionally with blessings for the family. In Sanaa 46 lugha, the eulogies for the Prophet only read *ṣallā -llāhu ʿalayhi*, which does not clearly point to Shiʿi influence. The London copies show both versions but tend to abbreviate them, especially in the Zahid Ali Collection manuscripts, as can be seen in the following table. ʿAlī ibn Abī Ṭālib is almost always given a eulogy in UB Leipzig Ms.or.377—more often than in other witnesses of the text—mostly *ʿalayhi al-sallām*, but also *ṣalawāt Allāh ʿalayhi*,[57] but less frequently in the other manuscripts. As can be seen below, the more recent copies tend to use *karrama-llāhu wajhahū* instead, which I otherwise only found in

Table 5.4 Idiosyncrasies of the scribes regarding paratext.

	ZAC MS 1269	**ZAC MS 1270**	**ZAC MS 1271**	**ZAC MS 1290**	**ZAC MS 1317**	**HC MS 1410**	**HC MS 1411**	**Leipzig UB Ms.or.377**
Marginal headings	Rare	Rare	No	No	Yes	Yes	Yes	No
Marginal emphases	Yes	No	No	No	No	Yes	No	No
Table of contents	No	No	Yes	No	No	No	Yes	No
Eulogy for the Prophet Muhammad	صلعم	ص/صلع	صلعم (rare)	صلع	صلع	صلى الله عليه و آله	صلى الله عليه	صلى الله عليه و على آله
Eulogy for ʿAlī	كرَّم الله وجهه	كرَّم الله وجهه	صلعم (rare)	كرَّم الله وجهه	كرَّم الله وجهه	كرَّم الله وجهه	كرَّم الله وجهه	صلوات الله عليه/عليه السلم
Eulogy for Imams	صلوات الله عليه	رضوان لله عليه	None	ص ا	None	عليه السلم (rare)	None	عليه السلم

Sanaa 46 lugha where it occurs less frequently. It is my impression that the London copies still betray the Ismaili conviction of their scribes. This seems plausible given that the book had an Ismaili author and was transmitted in Ismaili communities. The latter could also explain the higher degree of uniformity among the London copies, as they were all produced in a relatively short time frame and probably in the same region. However, scribal individuality in this respect is still visible e.g. with a change of hands in MS 1410, p. 226 (see no. 8 in my list above), where eulogies for the Prophet's family become less frequent. In the table (see Table 5.4), only the most common eulogies in the respective manuscripts are given, based on random samples.

A Comparison of the Main Text in the London Copies

In order to be able to verify Saʿīd al-Ghānimī's suggestion that MS 1410 from the Hamdani Collection and its 'siblings' from London share a common set of variant readings, it would be necessary to undertake a full-scale collation. This would be a major step towards preparing an independent edition of the text and was thus out of the question for the present chapter. Instead, the following remarks are again based on selected samples. From my own edition of the heresiographical chapters and through frequent comparisons with al-Ghānimī's edition, I have learned that he has not documented all variants from the manuscripts, e.g. in the chapter on non-Islamic innovations *(aṣḥāb al-bidaʿ)* of section IX or in the following example.

A passage that shows actual textual differences in the IIS manuscripts are three verses by the poet Labīd. Abū Ḥātim al-Rāzī cites them in the chapter on *al-fajūr* to prove a point about the meaning of the root f-j-r. As can be seen (see Table 5.5), there are minor differences between the manuscripts, not only regarding the actual text (variants marked by shading) but also its placement, as it was sometimes added only afterwards in the margins, indicating at least two variants in the manuscript models. Here the London copies were not completely identical.

The inaccuracies in al-Ghānimī's edition make it difficult to rely on his suggestion about the relation between the London copies. In fact, the only tangible evidence for their stemmatological relation—or between any extant text witnesses of the *Kitāb al-Zīna*, for that matter—is the list

Table 5.5 Examples of textual variance

	First verse	Second verse	Third verse
HC MS 1410	فإن تتقدَّم تغش منها مقدَّماً غليظاً وإن أخَّرتَ فالكِفل فجر	فقلت ازدجر أحناء طيرك واعلمن بأنك إن قدمتَ رجل عاثر	فأصبحت أنَّى تأتها تبتئس بها كلا منكبيها تحت رجلك شاحر
ZAC MS 1271	فإن تتقدَّم تغشو منها مقدَّماً غليظاً وإن أخَّرتَ فالكِفل فجر	فقلت ازدجر أحناء طيرك واعلمن بأنك إن قدمتَ رجلك عاثر	فاصبحت انى تأتها تلبس بها كلى منكبيها تحت رجليك شاحر
ZAC MS 1317	Identical	Added in margin	Added in margin
HC MS 1411	فإن تتقدَّم تغش منها مقدَّماً غليظاً وإن أخَّرتَ فالكِفل فاجر	فقلت ازدجر أحناء طيرك واعلمن بأنك إن قدمتَ رجلك عاثر	Identical
Lp. Ms.or.377	Identical	Missing	Missing
Bagh. No 1306	Identical	Missing	Missing
San. 46 lugha	Identical	Added in margin	Added in margin

of models used for ZAC MS 1290 (no. 15 in my list above) which relied, among others, on ZAC MS 1270.

I believe there is more to gain through contrasting the London manuscripts with the remaining other copies. As could be seen, the older manuscripts are mostly fragmentary. The Leipzig copy, for instance, would have the most peculiar text, and probably the most defective, if it was not for the many later corrections. From my own work on the heresiographical chapters I can state that both it and the Baghdad manuscript often have minor variants in common which distinguish them from e.g. IIS London, HC MS 1410, which I used for comparison. These variants usually show a different wording or grammatical structure but are not related to content. Sanaa 46 lugha (no. 3 in my list), which al-Hamdānī considered to be of a roughly similar age, is already closer to MS 1410 and, I feel confident to argue based on a few selected samples, also to the other more recent copies of the *Kitāb al-Zīna*. Without having inspected the other two Yemeni manuscripts, I cannot say, however, if the London manuscripts show a more correct text or simply one recension.[58] In general, they seem to preserve a more intact text than the older witnesses that I have seen. Their textual consistency among one another, I assume, has more to do with that intactness than with their relation in terms of the stemma.

Conclusion

The six manuscript copies of the *Kitāb al-Zīna* preserved in the Ismaili Special Collections Unit at The Institute of Ismaili Studies in London are undoubtedly united in their origin of the Indian subcontinent and their relatively recent dates of production between the latter half of the 19th and the first half of the 20th century CE. This is reflected in their codicological and palaeographic features like the recent *naskh* script style and their strikingly similar page size, but also in paratextual elements like additional indices, marginal emphases of headings and key terms, as well as eulogies. None of the copies, however, shows all of these characteristics. On the level of the text, it is difficult to argue for or against their close relation—as suggested by al-Ghānimī's calling them 'siblings' (*akhawāt*)—without a new extensive collation. Selected samples indicate that they contain variants that cannot be caused only by scribal errors. However, when measured against some of the older and often less intact copies, they appear almost uniform and thus, indeed, give the impression of being related in a stemmatological sense. At this point it is little more than an educated guess whether or not the reason for this can be seen in their common origin within the Ismaili communities in South Asia.

NOTES

* The research for this chapter was carried out at the Sonderforschungsbereich 950 'Manuskriptkulturen in Asien, Afrika und Europa', University of Hamburg, funded by the German Research Foundation (Deutsche Forschungsgemeinschaft, DFG) and was part of the general work carried out by the Centre for the Study of Manuscript Cultures (CSMC). I am grateful to Wafi Momin and the anonymous peer-reviewer for their help with this chapter.

1 I included a discussion about the issue in my PhD dissertation, published as C. Berthold, *Die Häresiografie im Kitāb az-Zīna des Abū Ḥātim ar-Rāzī. Textanalyse, Edition und deutsche Zusammenfassung* (Wiesbaden 2019).

2 Claude Gilliot, 'Abū Ḥātim al-Rāzī', *EI3* (Leiden, 2011), pp. 11–18. Some of the manuscript catalogues mentioned below ascribe the *Kitāb al-Zīna* to Muḥammad ibn Idrīs al-Rāzī.

3 Samuel M. Stern, 'The Early Ismāʿīlī Missionaries in North-West Persia and in Khurāsān and Transoxania', *Bulletin of the School of Oriental and African Studies*, 23 (1960), p. 61.

4 Monique Bernards, 'Thaʿlab', *EI2*, vol. 10, p. 433.
5 Rudolf Sellheim, 'al-Mubarrad', *EI2*, vol. 7, p. 279.
6 Jamal Ali, *Language and Heresy in Ismaili Thought: The Kitab al-Zina of Abu Hatim al-Razi* (Piscataway, NJ, 2008), pp. 28–29.
7 Stern, 'Early Ismāʿīlī Missionaries', pp. 65–67.
8 Ismail K. Poonawala, 'al-Nasafī', first paragraph, *EI2*, vol. 7, p. 968.
9 An edition was published by Salah al-Sawy (Tehran, 1977). For a partial translation of the debates, see Lenn E. Goodman, 'Rāzī vs. Rāzī—Philosophy in the Majlis', in Hava Lazarus-Yafeh et al., ed., *The Majlis: Interreligious Encounters in Medieval Islam* (Wiesbaden, 1999), pp. 84–107. A bilingual version (Arabic–English) was published as *Abū Ḥātim al-Rāzī: The Proofs of Prophecy: A Parallel English-Arabic Text*, tr., Tarif Khalidi (Provo, UT, 2011).
10 Ibn al-Nadīm, *Fihrist*, ed., Gustav Flügel (Leipzig, 1871), p. 189, line 22–23.
11 Abū Ḥātim al-Rāzī, *Kitāb al-Zīna*, ed. Saʿīd al-Ghānimī (Beirut and Baghdad, 2015), vol. 1, p. 564, lines 19–20.
12 Ibn al-Nadīm, *Fihrist*, p. 189, lines 21ff.
13 al-Rāzī, *Kitāb al-Zīna*, ed., Saʿīd al-Ghānimī, p. 83, line 5.
14 Ali, *Language and Heresy*, p. 52.
15 This list was first published in this form in C. Berthold. 'The Leipzig Manuscript of the *Kitāb al-Zīna* by the Ismaili Author Abū Ḥātim al-Rāzī (d. 322/933–934)', *Journal of Islamic Manuscripts*, 5 (2014), pp. 25–26.
16 Abū Ḥātim al-Rāzī, *Kitāb al-Zīna*, ed., Ḥusayn al-Hamdānī (Sanaa, 1994), p. 38. The 'sixth part' is mentioned on f. 91r.
17 Ibid., p. 38.
18 I have noted this phenomenon, along with attempts of modern scholarship to structure the text, in Berthold. 'The Leipzig Manuscript of the *Kitāb al-Zīna*', p. 26ff. Ismail K. Poonawala. 'Note on *Kitāb al-Zīna* of Abū Ḥātim Aḥmad b. Ḥamdān al-Rāzī (d. 322/934)', *Chroniques du manuscrit au Yémen*, New Series 2/21 (Jan. 2016), pp. 128–129, considers my remarks 'confused', even though he arrives at the same conclusions later on.
19 For a detailed account of the circumstances cf. Poonawala, 'Note on *Kitāb al-Zīna*', pp. 131–132. I am here correcting my own statement from 'The Leipzig Manuscript of the *Kitāb al-Zīna*', p. 27, where I gave a different distribution of the sections within al-Hamdānī's two fascicles.
20 Jamal Ali presumably uses it in this sense in his *Language and Heresy*, p. 132. In fact, even one manuscript copy, IIS London MS 1290 (Zahid Ali Collection)—one of the two existing 'edition draft' manuscripts—contains a potential secondary title on the outer leaf (in absence of a real cover): *fī gharīb al-qur'ān wa-l-ḥadīth (mimma yaḥtāju al-fuqahā' ilā maʿrifatihī wa-lā yastaghnā al-udabā' ʿanhu)* which is clearly inspired by and partly copied from Abū Ḥātim al-Rāzī's own foreword.
21 Berthold, 'The Leipzig Manuscript of the *Kitāb al-Zīna*', pp. 28–36.
22 Unlike what I have stated in Berthold, 'The Leipzig Manuscript of the *Kitāb al-Zīna*', p. 33, the order of chapters on the first nine folios is most probably correct, the only damages being mechanical lacunae at the beginning and end. I had been misled by the transpositions in the Baghdad copy which I had thought to be more intact than the Leipzig manuscript. As it turned out, the opposite is true. A more detailed account can be found in Berthold, *Die Häresiografie im Kitāb az-Zīna des Abū Ḥātim ar-Rāzī*, pp. 25–27 and 89–92.
23 I had stated this already in Berthold, 'The Leipzig Manuscript of the *Kitāb al-Zīna*', p. 35. However, in his reply to this article, Poonawala, 'Note on *Kitāb al-Zīna*', p. 135, still followed the previous account of Verena Klemm, 'Obvious and Obscure Contexts: The Leipzig Manuscript of the *Kitāb al-Zīna* by Abū Ḥātim al-Rāzī (d. 322/934)', in Andreas Christmann and Jan-Peter Hartung, ed., *Islamica: Studies in Memory of Holger Preißler*

(1943–2006) (Oxford, 2009), p. 57, that the colophon could be used to date the *Kitāb al-Zīna* sections of the codex.

24 I am grateful to Professor Thomas Fuchs, Head of the Special Collections at Leipzig University Library, as well as Dr Bernd Kromer and Dr Ronny Friedrich from the Curt-Engelhorn-Zentrum Archäometrie in Mannheim (Germany) for their support in this endeavour.

25 For more details, see Berthold, *Die Häresiografie im Kitāb az-Zīna des Abū Ḥātim ar-Rāzī*, pp. 26–27.

26 I am afraid the microfilm copy I am using is too bad in terms of quality for me to give folio numbers. It is most likely a copy of the one kept in Cairo's Dār al-Kutub al-Miṣriyya which might be identical to or a copy of the microfilm copy at Cairo University Library which Ḥusayn al-Hamdānī reports as no. 26401 and which is, in turn, a copy of the Arab League Institute of Arabic Manuscripts' microfilm copy. Cf. al-Rāzī, *Kitāb al-Zīna*, ed., al-Hamdānī, p. 38ff.

27 Berthold, 'The Leipzig Manuscript of the *Kitāb al-Zīna*', p. 32.

28 E.g. al-Rāzī, *Kitāb al-Zīna*, ed., al-Ghānimī, p. 301, n. 4.

29 Abū Ḥātim al-Rāzī, *Kitāb al-Zīna*, ed., ʿAbdallāh Sallūm al-Sāmarrāʾī (Baghdad, 1972), p. 20.

30 al-Rāzī, *Kitāb al-Zīna*, ed., al-Ghānimī, p. 66.

31 al-Rāzī, *Kitāb al-Zīna*, ed., al-Hamdānī, p. 39.

32 I am thankful to Daniel Kinitz and David Hollenberg for clarifying the circumstances of manuscript storage at the Great Mosque in Sanaa. The ministry also acted as the publisher of a 1984 catalogue where this manuscript is listed; see Aḥmad ʿAbd al-Razzāq Ruqayḥī, ʿAbdallāh Muḥammad al-Ḥibshī and ʿAlī Wahhāb al-Ānisī, *Fihrist Makhṭūṭāt Maktabat al-Jāmiʿ al-Kabīr*, 4 vols. (Sanaa, 1984). The manuscript can be found in vol. 3, p. 1416 (no. 1900), where the *Kitāb al-Zīna* is incorrectly attributed to Abū Ḥātim Muḥammad ibn Idrīs al-Rāzī. I am grateful to the anonymous reviewer who made me aware of this catalogue.

33 al-Rāzī, *Kitāb al-Zīna*, ed., al-Hamdānī, p. 38. The collation involved correcting e.g. several cases of *saut du même au même*. The 1984 catalogue takes the year 924 as the date of the entire manuscript.

34 A. Ruqayḥī et al., *Fihrist Makhṭūṭāt Maktabat al-Jāmiʿ al-Kabīr*, vol. 3 (Sanaa, 1984), p. 1415 (no. 1897).

35 al-Rāzī, *Kitāb al-Zīna*, ed., al-Hamdānī, pp. 37–38. He erroneously gives the microfilm's shelf-mark as 336 jīm. I am deeply grateful to Davidson MacLaren who helped me in obtaining digital copies of the two microfilms (i.e., 4336 and 4337 jīm), which also cleared up the confusion about the wrong shelf-mark.

36 The Dār al-Makhṭūṭāt apparently now contains all manuscripts from the Western Library. For two catalogues of its manuscript holdings, see Muḥammad Saʿīd al-Malīḥ et al., *Fihris Makhṭūṭāt al-Maktaba al-Gharbiyya bi'l-Jāmiʿ al-Kabīr bi-Ṣanʿāʾ* (Sanaa, 1978) and Aḥmad Muḥammad ʿĪsawī et al., *Fihris al-Makhṭūṭāt al-Yamaniyya li-Dār al-Makhṭūṭāt wa'l-Maktaba al-Gharbiyya bi'l-Jāmiʿ al-Kabīr Ṣanʿāʾ*, 2 vols (Qum, 2005).

37 ʿĪsawī et al., *Fihris al-Makhṭūṭāt al-Yamaniyya*, vol. 1, p. 942. Here the book is wrongly attributed to Muḥammad ibn Idrīs al-Rāzī too. The manuscript can also be found in the slightly older catalogue by al-Malīḥ et al., *Fihris Makhṭūṭāt al-Maktaba al-Gharbīya*, p. 438.

38 al-Rāzī, *Kitāb al-Zīna*, ed., al-Hamdānī, p. 37.

39 Poonawala, 'Note on *Kitāb al-Zīna*', pp. 133–134.

40 Ismail Poonawala, *Biobibliography of Ismāʿīlī Literature* (Malibu, CA, 1977), p. 38; Ali, *Language and Heresy*, p. 9.

41 The Hamdani Collection copies are described by François de Blois, *Arabic, Persian and Gujarat Manuscripts: The Hamdani Collection in the Library of The Institute of Ismaili Studies* (London, 2011), pp. 18–20.

42 al-Rāzī, *Kitāb al-Zīna*, ed., al-Hamdānī, p. 36.

43 de Blois, *Arabic, Persian and Gujarati Manuscripts*, p. 19. I cannot verify the change of hands he notices between pp. 234 and 235; instead I notice one at the end of p. 226. The eulogies for the prophet's family become less frequent after this point; concerning eulogies also see below.

44 The Zahid Ali Collection copies are described by Delia Cortese, *Arabic Ismaili Manuscripts: The Zāhid ʿAlī Collection in the Library of The Institute of Ismaili Studies* (London, 2004), pp. 84–87, on which I will rely here.

45 Ibn Ḥajar al-ʿAsqalānī, *Lisān al-Mīzān*, ed., Dāʾirat al-Muʿarraf an-Niẓāmīya, vol. 1 (Beirut, 1390/1971), p. 164 (no. 523).

46 The secondary entries in the manuscript (ff. 1r and 1v) actually use the term *jild* for 'volume' unlike other manuscripts which refer to one half of the book as a *juzʾ* or *niṣf*.

47 The catchword on f. 2v is not repeated at the beginning of f. 3r, which should have been the case for the list of chapters to be complete.

48 al-Rāzī, *Kitāb al-Zīna*, ed., al-Ghānimī, p. 67.

49 Poonawala, *Biobibliography*, p. 38, gives the shelf-mark as F 2412; al-Ghānimī speaks of Tehran University as the owner and gives No. 1005 as a shelf-mark in his edition, p. 67.

50 Berthold, 'The Leipzig Manuscript of the *Kitāb al-Zīna*', p. 32.

51 After the pages reserved for the introduction (pp. 1–49, including blank pages), the pagination starts anew for the main text.

52 IIS London, Zahid Ali Collection, MS 1290, pp. 26 (in the introduction) and 890 (at the end of the main text), respectively.

53 IIS London, Zahid Ali Collection, MS 1290, Introduction, pp. 27–30.

54 It is difficult to say whether or not MSS 1410 and 1411 were truly linked to Yemeni copies of the text as Ḥusayn al-Hamdānī stated (see nos. 8 and 9 in my list) and/or if they were produced in India from a Yemeni copy that had been brought there.

55 al-Rāzī, *Kitāb al-Zīna*, ed., al-Hamdānī, pp. 36–39.

56 The issue is, of course, more complex when e.g. paratextual elements are over time considered part of the actual book, mark recensions of it or when they consist of other elements than just text.

57 I know one example in UB Leipzig Ms.or.377 of a *karrama-llāhu wajhahū* for ʿAlī, that is on f. 18v.

58 Concerning this issue, I have not been able to identify actual recensions of the *Kitāb al-Zīna* whose characteristics exceed the usual amount of variant readings in the manuscripts.

SECTION III

EXPLORING TWO EARLY ṬAYYIBĪ WORKS AND THEIR TRANSMISSION

6

The *Majmūʿ al-tarbiya* between Text and Paratext: Exploring the Social History of a Community's Reading Culture

Delia Cortese

In general terms, the manuscripts of the *Majmūʿ al-tarbiya* (henceforth MT) in The Institute of Ismaili Studies, London (henceforth IIS) can be described as multiple-text manuscripts featuring a content-wise homogeneous, miscellaneous work belonging to the Ismaili Ṭayyibī literary tradition of the 12th century. As literary objects the manuscripts belong to the handwritten heritage of the Dāʾūdī Bohra community of, mostly, the 19th century. Recently an edition of part one of the MT was published based on a manuscript in Tübingen University library[1] while the second part of this work is still extant only in manuscript form. Altogether, selected extracts of this work have been published in recent years or been the subject of study. Many copies of this work are to be found in several public and private libraries worldwide. The MT is perhaps best known for including the earliest known extract of a letter allegedly sent by the Fatimid caliph al-Āmir (d. 524/1130) to the Yemeni Queen al-Sayyida al-Ḥurra (d. 532/1138) announcing the birth of his son al-Ṭayyib, a document that played a foundational role in the establishment of Ṭayyibī Ismailism.[2]

The manuscripts considered in this chapter are exclusively those in the IIS collection. These are 8 MSS of volume 1, cat. nos: B (121), A (263) (Gacek); 937, 953, 961, 1012 (Cortese 2000); 1163 (Cortese 2003); 1502 (de Blois) and 4 of volume 2, cat. nos: C (122) (Gacek); 867, 932 part only (Cortese 2000); 1503 (de Blois).[3] Content-wise the MT includes 51 different texts of various lengths, some consisting of complete short treatises and many being extracts from or abridgments of larger treatises. The oldest *dated* copy of the MT in this collection is that of MS 937 dated 20 Rabīʿ al-awwal 1121/30 May 1709. All of these manuscripts are the product of individual strands of transmission of the work as none show any indication of having served as master copy for another item in this collection.

A Ṭayyibī Work, its Bohra Manuscripts and their Paratextual Apparatus

The apparently straightforward description of 'miscellaneous manuscript' often used to describe works transmitted in handwritten form such as the MT betrays a number of complexities, with implications for the analysis of the text it contains, its manuscripts and its cataloguing criteria.[4] In order to address these complexities it will be useful to consider in some depth the generic description given at the start of this paper. As literary objects the MT manuscripts are late multiple-texts manuscripts. However, the literary content of these late MT manuscripts consists of miscellaneous medieval textual material, it being a collection of individual texts (*majmūʿa* lit. a bringing together, an assemblage, in this specific case) of various lengths, by various authors, from short extracts to full-length treatises, internally arranged according to no self-evident system. Unlike most *majmūʿa*s, the MT features an originally given overall title; has one identifiable compiler (or a consensually agreed attribution to a particular one) and a preface indicating the compiler's purpose in producing the work and his generic criteria for selecting texts the work contains. This makes the MT a textual product unit, that is an identifiable single work whose content consists of many, separate texts. The texts forming this unit—though by various authors and in different genres—are thematically coherent. As such the multiple-text manuscripts of the MT can be defined as late literary objects featuring a homogeneous medieval textual miscellany. In physical terms, most of the MT manuscripts—all written on paper—occasionally might feature added pages of different size and quality as well as writing by different hands, in different inks and added at different times. However, none of the MT manuscripts examined can be said to be 'composite', that is material objects that feature multiple texts as a result of the collection—over a period of time and by different people—of formerly independent units.

Many *majmūʿas* result from the personal intellectual pursuits of individuals and are destined for personal use. Since in many instances the copyist and the compiler are one and the same person, *majmūʿas* are often only extant in unique manuscripts and are known to have had limited circulation. By contrast, in the case of the MT, its literary contents came to be accepted as a canonical work whose texts came to be repeated in the same sequence across many multiple-text manuscripts over a long period of time. However, variants in the texts reproduced and the paratextual elements[5] featured in each copy render each manuscript textually unique, irrespective of their identical literary content. The considering of these variants and paratextual elements helps us to bridge the gap between the multiple-text manuscript as literary production and the miscellaneous manuscript as textual entity. The relationship between paratext and main text is variable: dependent elements can be integrated as part of the main text in the course of its life, while individual elements of the main text can become paratext. Manuscripts by their very nature favour such flexible divisions and inclusions, particularly the process of transmission by copying. In the case of the manuscripts of the MT this fluidity between text and paratext can be noted for example in the variant ways in which each copyist chooses to introduce each work forming the miscellany. In some cases the titles and authors of entries can be absent in the main text, but added later in the margin (e.g. MS 121 and MS 1052). In other cases these details appear within the main text, indicating that to the copyists in charge they were considered an integral part of the work being reproduced, probably replicating what was found in the master copy used by the scribe.

Beyond the original intentions of the compiler, the paratextual apparatus in some of the MT copies shows signs of varied reading practices and aids that either the copyists had provided in redacting their works or that subsequent users had created for themselves. For example, in some instances we see that users attempted to draw a list of contents. In several manuscripts the headings of titles and chapters are written in the margins by a different hand as well as in the text by the copyist; often headings are written in different colours, an ornamental device but also a practical 'finder' tool. In some manuscripts these 'finders' devices in the margins are particularly visible, with the titles of some works indicated by initials (e.g. *'t' al-ṣalāt* for *Ta'wīl al-ṣalāt*)—thus implying that readers were expected to be already familiar with the full title of what they would read, and, occasionally, the title of the compilation and that of the specific work featured in the page being written in the upper margins by the side of the page numbering, also added at a later stage. This practice of reproducing running headings imitates similar occurrences in printed books. In these cases paratexts indicate a desire to establish a sense of order, enabling the texts to be structured in line with different needs. The adoption of some of these devices goes back to the 14th century when authors were increasingly using techniques to increase the searchability of texts resorting to layout of headlines, different size of letters, various colours, etc., to ease visual orientation.[6]

Preferences on the physical arrangement of the content of a book can have a significant impact on its literary fortunes. For example, the text of the MT is conventionally transmitted in two volumes. As a result of this practical choice the texts in the MT had different fortunes and circulation depending on whether they were in volume 1 or volume 2. In the IIS collection there are more 'complete/comprehensive' manuscript copies of volume 1 than of volume 2,[7] with only one two-volume set written by the same copyist (MS 121 and MS 122).[8] Copies of volume 1 are often heavily annotated unlike copies of volume 2 which only rarely show sign of use and engagement with the text on the part of the prospective user. The fact that many of the MT two-volume sets appear to have become split apart over time is not unusual. A. Tritton commented that, when it came to books, it was the typical way in India that, on the death of the original owner, each heir would get a volume of multi-volume books.[9] To that effect, a clear statement of inheritance appears for example on a paratextual note at the beginning of MS 1502, that is, volume 1 of the MT in the Hamdani collection while the matching volume 2 from the same set is absent. The past practice of dispersing volumes among heirs in the Hamdani family was confirmed to me by the late Professor Abbas Hamdani: his ancestor, Safiyya, was instructed to distribute the volumes in the family library among her younger brothers following the death of their father. This form of dispersal of multi-volume manuscripts points to an understanding of their value in the eyes of their owners resting not so much or only on the literary content but in the volumes being assets that became symbols of family scholarly pedigree and cultural capital to be (physically) transmitted and perpetuated from generation to generation. In such cases the manuscript becomes an object with agency in that its endowment was intended to reinforce familial bonds and community attachment where its possession bestowed on each new owner in turn the role of keepers of secret knowledge and heritage. However, even when an MT two-volume set did not get split such as the one example in the IIS collection we note that volume 1 is heavily annotated and corrected—often by a different hand—while volume 2 of the same set shows almost no sign of subsequent engagement. This may be an indication that even when belonging to the same set and sharing the same journey, over time the volumes must have enjoyed separate destinies and uses.

Author or Compiler?

In literary terms, the character of the MT is compilatory.[10] The 'author' is in fact a compiler who does not engage with the texts he reproduces, except for adding formulaic notes of praise (for example, to Muḥammad, to al-Ṭayyib) to indicate the end of a text and the beginning of the next. Beyond the obvious educational intentions reflected in the consensually assigned title given to this work, as a compilation the MT satisfied two practical purposes in view of its intended readership: (1) the preservation and perpetuation, but also the claiming (even monopolising) for the Ṭayyibīs of a Fatimid Ismaili-based literary tradition and (2) the functioning as a 'two-volume library'[11] by making these texts more readily available to readers, while maintaining strict religious secrecy and control over their teachings and complying to rigorous academic supervision. Within the Ṭayyibī Ismaili tradition, the MT constitutes the first major example of a form of composition that was to be followed by subsequent *majmūʿas*. In many ways it can be said that, in the context of Ismaili literature, the MT inaugurated a literary genre that acquired a distinctive status in the Bohras' written heritage.

The term 'compiler' to describe the author of a Ṭayyibī work raises a number of questions. With the establishment in the 6th/12th century of the *dāʿī muṭlaq* as the Ṭayyibī supreme religious leader whose authority rested on him being recognised as the exclusive holder of the highest possible degree of esoteric knowledge after the hidden imam, the hierarchically organised Ṭayyibī scholarly élites exercised the strictest control over the access to doctrinal learning by Ṭayyibī adherents. Bearing this in mind, to be an author—provided one had the right credentials—was not a problem if the purpose of writing was to repeat and perpetuate Ismaili teachings as elaborated during the Fatimid period. But the act of 'compiling', in a Ṭayyibī context, carried implications, being a potentially doctrinally-endorsing activity based on the ostensibly subjective choice of literary pieces to be included in the collection.[12] On the basis of which or whose authority was a scholar allowed to 'compile' texts in first place? On the basis of which criteria did the compiler select some material at the exclusion of other? As literary innovator within the Ṭayyibī tradition the compiler here becomes for the first time an editor who pre-selects what *he* deems to be best for his audiences with the deliberate (or by default) effect of influencing the trajectory of their learning and thinking. Who was the originally intended audience of the MT? Was it intended for a selected group of learners with potential to join the highest rank within the Ṭayyibī scholarly élite? Was it written for adherents in pursuit of knowledge and answers to doctrinal questions? Was the MT intended to promote a specific religious scholarly line? In most copies texts at the end are said to be followed by other texts and a statement in the preface of the MT states that the work was intended to be read. But was the text intended to be read sequentially or was it meant to be used as a resource from where teacher and learner could 'pull out' selected readings to cover specific themes or answer specific issues? Were these texts intended to be read out during learning sessions or did the reader have some degree of autonomy?

Insights into the organisation of multiple-text manuscripts can reveal important clues about the function of texts and textual knowledge. The works featured in these types of manuscripts may in some cases reflect in turn access to a collection of manuscripts on the part of the compiler. In the case of the MT we are dealing with a high-ranking scholar who, in order to make his selection of texts, must have had access to manuscripts containing secret texts exclusively reserved for the religious leadership. This point raises questions about the method of the compiler as 'researcher' in view of the production of his work. For example, in the case of the second treatise in volume 1 of the MT—*Ta'wīl al-ṣalāt*—the compiler hints at drawing the treatise from a '*majmūʿ al-thānī*', a 'second compilation' that must have been at his disposal. Some texts of the MT are fragments or extensive paragraphs: in such cases did the compiler source his material from other fragments available to him, *hypomnema*, that is, draft notes and notebooks, or did he have at his disposal whole works from which he selected parts to quote? Many texts are reproduced in full but, with few exceptions, they are only thus far known to us through the transmission via the MT. Did the compiler copy them from a collection of manuscripts that was exclusively available to him? If, as stated in the preface of the MT, the works contained were must-reads, how come then we do not have other copies of them, either as independent manuscript units or in other *majmūʿas*, instead of being—with few exceptions—uniquely circulated via the MT?

The compiler of the MT is commonly identified as Muḥammad b. Ṭāhir al-Ḥārithī (d. 583/1188). He was a close associate of the 2nd and 3rd *dāʿī muṭlaq*s—respectively Ibrāhīm al-Ḥāmidī and his son Ḥātim[13]—and teacher of the 5th *dāʿī*, ʿAlī b. Muḥammad b. al-Walīd (d. 612/1215) who dedicated a eulogy to him. He was a close associate of the scholar ʿAlī b. al-Ḥusayn b. Jaʿfar b. Ibrāhīm b. al-Walīd (d. 554/1159) who, according to Ḥasan b. Nūḥ al-Bharūchī (d. 939/1533), in volume 2 of his *Kitāb al-Azhār*, had been Muḥammad's mentor. Three works by ʿAlī b. al-Ḥusayn are included in the MT. The 19th Ṭayyibī *dāʿī muṭlaq* and historian Idrīs ʿImād al-Dīn (d. 872/1468) in his *Nuzhat al-afkār* says that al-Ḥārithī was the author of many works on the imamate of ʿAlī b. Abī Ṭālib and on many aspects of knowledge.[14] There is however in the *Nuzhat* no specific reference to al-Ḥārithī as the compiler of MT. Likewise, while there are several references to al-Ḥārithī in Ḥātim's *Tuḥfat al-qulūb*, no mention is made of him as the compiler of the MT. Bohra scholars of the 19th century, such as Quṭb al-Dīn Burhānpūrī (author of *Muntazaʿ al-akhbār*) and Muḥammad b. ʿAlī (author of *Mawsim-i bahār*), provide information on Muḥammad b. Ṭāhir but neither refer to him as the author of the MT. In the MSS of the MT in the IIS collection al-Ḥārithī's authorship is consistently indicated only in the paratextual parts of the manuscripts, that is, in later/subsequent annotations by owners or scribes written on initial flyleaves or inserted in the colophons. In MS 1502 late paratextual annotations in the initial flyleaves include a short biographical note on al-Ḥārithī.

Indeed, al-Ḥārithī does not announce himself or is openly stated as the 'author' or compiler of the MT within the text of the compilation. Among the texts included in this miscellany, a number of works are indicated as authored by al-Ḥārithī.[15] But while the compiler of the MT speaks in the first person in his preface to his work, al-Ḥārithī is always referred to in the third person in those copies where his name is spelt out. Also, when it occurs, al-Ḥārithī's name is often followed by laudatory formulae suited for a dead person. In short, it is not self-evident—based on the MSS of MT at the IIS—where, when and how the identification of al-Ḥārithī as compiler of the *majmūʿ* (in addition to being a contributor to it) came about. The earliest direct attribution of the MT to al-Ḥārithī I could find occurs in the 18th-century bibliographical work commonly known as *Fihrist* by the Bohra scholar Ismāʿīl al-Majdūʿ.[16]

Pedagogical Practices: Copying and Reading the MT

The word '*tarbiya*' in the title by which the MT is best known needs some comment.[17] First of all, its presence gives an indication of what the work was understood to have been conceived for: that is, to be a summa for the purpose of instruction, education, nurturing. According to a statement in the preface of the work, its pedagogical value was intended to be that of serving as an introduction to what were the must-read books of the *daʿwa*. Reported experiences by Ṭayyibī scholars when confronted with the study of the MT as well as paratextual annotation in the manuscripts available, give us some clues of how this work as an educational tool was used in practice.[18] The MT occupies a special place in the history of Ṭayyibī learning and, subsequently, Bohra religious instruction. The very title given to the compilation and its conferred authoritativeness by the strong association to al-Ḥārithī points to the fact that it was understood to be as a compendium for practical use in the transmission of knowledge. In the preface of the MT the compiler explains his purpose for assembling the texts stating:

> 'I have gathered (*jamaʿtu*) in this book the sciences (*ʿulūm*) the reading of which is necessary for the knowledge of the matters of the rightful *daʿwa*, the worship (*ʿibāda*) and the acquisition of . . . happiness and I have placed (*jaʿaltu*) [in it] from that, both the

> summary and the detailed. It is the gateway (*madkhal*) to what must be read from among the books of the rightful *daʿwa* and I have called it the Book of Essences (or Jewels) (*Kitāb al-jawāhir*) because its making (*kawni-hi*) consists of (*mushtamilan*) the choicest (*zubda*) Arabic expressions and wondrous meanings'.[19]

With regard to the practical, educational uses of Ṭayyibī literature, the acquisition of religious learning was gradual and progressive, from the exoteric to the esoteric. The religious scholar was the gatekeeper of this knowledge. He would judge which student should advance, based on the intellectual skills of the pupils and their desire to advance in mastering the *ḥaqāʾiq*. Accordingly, works would be read in a particular order.[20] The Bohra religious leadership enforced a secretive approach to their literature to ensure that it would be exclusively accessible to sworn community members.[21] In addition to that, based on level of sophistication, doctrinal texts were only disclosed to seekers of knowledge within the community proportionally to their intellectual abilities and level of advancement in knowledge. It is therefore not surprising to find that the copies of texts were executed, when known, by people who belonged to scholarly families and/or achieved formal recognition of their learning by being allowed to act as religious teachers at various levels. In the IIS manuscripts of the MT we come across scribes whose names are accompanied by titles like '*mullā*', '*shaykh*' and '*mālik*' which, in Dāʾūdī Bohra context, indicate formal positions that individuals occupied at the service of the community. For example, a *shaykh* would officiate in large centres and teach *ḥaqāʾiq* at an intermediate to advanced level. A *mullā* would be leader of worship in small centres and teacher of esoteric knowledge for seekers at beginners' level. Because of the strict control imposed over the circulation of knowledge, it is likely that these copies were initially made for personal use, either to preserve knowledge capital with the family and/or for teaching purposes in the case of those who were authorised to do so. The style of writing of the IIS MSS of the MT, while mostly clear, tends to be rather unsophisticated and inconsistent, occasionally with changes of hands indicating that the scribing process was a pursuit conducted over a lengthy period of time, probably in a domestic setting, that might have seen the participation of presumably other family members or very close associates of equal rank, given the secrecy surrounding the text.

The act of copying the book was in itself a learning process as we gather, again, from the colophon of MS 937 where the scribe adds a post-scriptum dedication to his scholar mentor. According to Professor Abbas Hamdani, his great-great grandfather Muḥammad ʿAlī (cf. MS 1502 and MS 1503) organised learning circles during which attendants would be asked to copy manuscripts in two copies: one copy for themselves and one for Muḥammad ʿAlī.[22] The fact that several MSS show little to no internal sign of engagement with the text by lacking annotations or corrections may be indicative of engaging in the act of copying as a learning technique that would make the manuscript a copybook for the personal use of its copyist—almost the product of an act of devotion—rather than a tool solely intended for the propagation and dissemination of knowledge. In such cases we can say that the manuscripts as objects carried a degree of 'agency' as the testament of a social practice that would be expected of a learned Bohra with a specific educational role within his community. Scholarly communities and élite households employed cultural practices in order to build up and sustain their status.[23]

In general, the act of copying at a time when printing was by then available as a device for learning and transmitting knowledge, acquires particular significance when considered within the attitude to accessibility to knowledge held by the Bohras. Copying, when seen in light of a community bent on scholarly élitism and secrecy, became a method to ensure and enforce control over who could be entrusted (and trusted) with acquiring knowledge that was (and still is, in conservative Bohra quarters) only meant to be shared among a few.

In Volume 1 of his *Kitāb al-Azhār*, the Indian Ṭayyibī *dāʿī* al-Bharūchī describes his early training.[24] Upon being inducted into the Ismaili faith as formulated by the Fatimids, he was sent to Yemen to learn the doctrine directly from the reigning *dāʿī muṭlaq*, al-Ḥasan b. Idrīs (d. 918/1512). Having progressed to earn the trust of his master, al-Bharūchī was allowed to learn hidden sciences. He lists 37 titles of books that he had to master to demonstrate his proficiency. In this latter list the MT is ranked no. 2, after *al-Risāla al-waḍʿiya fī maʿālim al-dīn* by Ḥamīd al-Dīn al-Kirmānī (d. 5th/11th century). He states that only after completing their reading attentively and absorbed their meaning, was he allowed to progress with reading other books such as

Asās al-taʾwīl by al-Qāḍī al-Nuʿmān (d. 363/974) which he also read according to a pre-established plan and method. Al-Bharūchī describes his experience of being handed a copy of the MT by the *dāʿī* himself and reading it back to him in a psalmodising manner (*biʾl-tartīl*), 'letter by letter', and with the *dāʿī* explaining what he could not grasp.[25] The *dāʿī* ordered that the books should be read time after time continuously, something that necessitated their study day and night. What al-Bharūchī appears to imply is that he read the content of the MT during sessions with his master to be followed by further private study.[26]

In the *Masāʾil Miyān Shamʿūn* we have another indication of the list of must-reads as specified again by the 20th *dāʿī muṭlaq* al-Ḥasan b. Idrīs. In his answer to a question about the books to study to rise through the ranks of knowledge, the *dāʿī muṭlaq* answers: Start with the books on *sharīʿa*, and then go to those on *taʾwīl*. Among the books listed in this latter category MT is ranked no. 3, after *Tanbīh al-ghāfilīn* by Ḥātim al-Ḥāmidī and *Tanbīh al-hadī waʾl-muhtadī* by al-Kirmānī but before al-Nuʿmān's *Asās al-taʾwīl*. By comparing the reading list that al-Ḥasan b. Idrīs had devised for al-Bharūchī and the one that he prescribed for his contemporary, the scholar Miyān Shamʿūn b. Muḥammad al-Ghūrī we can see that the MT consistently occupies a high position in the programme of study devised for both. Though sharing many similarities, there are however some significant additions and omissions in the other recommended books for each of the two seekers of knowledge, an indication of a certain degree of adaptation of the curriculum to match the abilities of the students and, presumably, their different accessibility to texts and learning contexts. Al-Bharūchī studied at the 20th *dāʿī muṭlaq*'s headquarters, on books given to him by his master and, as he explained, he verbally and directly interacted with the *dāʿī* who explained to him secret teachings and expounded to him sciences to be kept secret.[27] We don't know about Miyān Shamʿūn's learning context or level of proficiency but the changes in his list, compared to al-Bharūchī's, show that the *dāʿī*—besides core books—also tailor-made the reading list for this pupil.

It appears that the 20th *dāʿī muṭlaq* al-Ḥasan b. Idrīs might have been instrumental in securing a formal role for the MT as compulsory reading for advanced seekers of knowledge. In a paratextual note found in one of the initial leaves of MS 1502 it is stated that the text 'on the back (that is, back of the leaf on which the paratextual note is written) is a copy of the book MT and it was written (the copy) during 'the days of Sayyid-nā Nūr al-Dīn—blessed may be his soul—*for* al-Ḥasan b. Idrīs al-Anf'. Based on this claim the main bulk of MS 1502 would have to date sometime during the lifespan of al-Ḥasan b. Idrīs. This dating however is highly unlikely as the MS does not appear to have been produced in Yemen as one would expect for this period. Instead the MS is written in an 'Indian' Arabic script and ends with a Persian expression typically used for concluding the writing of texts, again, a feature that links the MS to the Indian Persianate world as already observed by F. de Blois.[28] Nevertheless the paratextual note is important here in that, at least according to the knowledge held by its scribe, a copy of MT was especially commissioned at some point for or by this *dāʿī muṭlaq* which might evidence his personal investment in the MT to the point of eventually declaring it mandatory reading. Another paratextual note at the beginning of MS 937 of the MT consists of a quote of few verses attributed to al-Ḥasan b. Idrīs in praise of the MT. This reinforces the view of the strong connection (whether real or perceived) between this text and this particular *dāʿī*.

In his *risāla* the Shaykh Luqmānjī (12th/18th century) gives an account of the course of his studies under the direction of the 37th *dāʿī* Nūr Muḥammad Nūr al-Dīn (d. 1130/1718) in 1711. This *dāʿī* at the time had several students but Luqmān and another pupil, Chand Khān, were the more advanced. Unlike others, Luqmān and Chand were taught the MT. This is further indication that the MT was considered a text for intermediate-to-advanced level to be taught selectively.[29] Luqmānjī b. Ḥabīb Allāh (d. 1760) went on to become a highly ranked Ismaili scholar and author of numerous treatises.[30]

According to A.A.A. Fyzee in the *Majālis Sayfiyya* by Ibrāhīm al-Sayfī (d. 1236/1821) we find an account of the education of the 18th century scholar ʿAbd Mūsā, son of the 38th *dāʿī* Badr al-Dīn (d. 1150/1737). Fyzee says that al-Sayfī gives the usual list of books but, summarising the list in his article, he does not mention the MT specifically.[31] However we have proof that the MT was definitely part of ʿAbd Mūsā's learning pedigree because MS 937 was originally his copy as demonstrated by the presence of his ownership seals.[32] Paratextual evidence on the flyleaves in ʿAbd Mūsā's copy also shows that his manuscript of the MT came to be used in collective study sessions.

In his *Fihrist*, al-Majdūʿ classifies the MT in the second part of his work, among the *bāṭinī* books that must be read according to a prescribed order. In his catalogue he ranks the MT 'only' as the sixth must-read work but wedged, as in al-Bharūchī's list, between al-Kirmānī's *al-Waḍʿiya* and al-Nuʿmān's *Asās al-ta'wīl*.[33]

In the early 19th century however, we note a twist of fate for the MT. A *Risāla* by the 45th *dāʿī muṭlaq* Sayyidnā Ṭayyib Zayn al-Dīn (d. 1252/1837), contains specific and authoritative directions regarding the manner in which instruction should be imparted. While giving the usually comprehensive list of books that formed the standard reading list for the curriculum and the order in which they should be read (*tartīb fī qirā'at al-kutub*), it is interesting to note that the MT is no longer included. This exclusion however is in stark contrast to the fact that the majority of the MT MSS at the IIS (and most of those in other collections as far as one can tell) were produced in India between the mid 19th century and the early 20th century. The circulation at this time and place of a work that had been a landmark tool of traditional advanced education in character and purpose since Ṭayyibī times, captures some of the cultural tensions that dominated the intellectual life of the Bohra community in modern times.

The conservative scholarly élites, protectors of traditional educational practices through selective delivery of esoteric knowledge found themselves challenged by those community members who called for opening for Bohras access to modern, western-style education. The 50th *dāʿī*, ʿAbd Allāh Badr al-Dīn (d. 1333/1915), had opposed the spread of western-style education whereas some Bohras were determined to establish educational institutions for the community. The situation for progressive education improved somewhat under the 51st *dāʿī*, Ṭāhir Sayf al-Dīn (d. 1385/1965), though with mixed fortunes. The reformist movement gathered again momentum in 1928 with the control of pious donations that the reformists wanted to be under the *waqf* board rather than the absolute control of the *dāʿī*. It might be that it was thanks to the effects of the actions of this reformist movement and the excommunications that in some instances they generated that copies of the MT (and many other manuscripts) made the transition from being books secreted and circulated within closely-knit learning circles to become available to a broader readership. MS 263 could be taken as an example of how the reformists' hold over pious donations, caused a less stringent control over the physical availability of books. Originally held in the library of the *dāʿī muṭlaq*, MS 263 was given away as *waqf* to become at some point property of the Sarkariyya library. From there it changed hands again, ending up outside Bohra learning circles. The Hamdani and the Ali families, both originally owners of copies of the MT, became enthusiastic supporters of the reform movement, following their excommunication. Fayḍ Allāh b. Muḥammad ʿAli al-Hamdānī (d. 1969), who by opposing the 51st *dāʿī,* Ṭāhir Sayf al-Dīn, had precipitated his family's exclusion from the community, had been entrusted with preserving part of the family collection of Ismaili MSS. Being ostracised, it meant that the Hamdanis were no longer bound by the rule of secrecy surrounding the literature in their MS collections and made their manuscripts available to scholars.[34] Other copies of the MT found their way, probably under similar circumstances, to the library of the Ismaili Society in Mumbai and the book trade. For example, MS 1012 of the MT might have come into the possession of its likely previous owner—the Syrian scholar Mustafa Ghalib—while the latter was touring India during a research trip in 1973. Beside the copies of MT at the IIS, there are several other examples following this pattern of dissemination in other libraries.

The early 20th-century Bohra dissident Mian Bhai Abdul Husain provided a vitriolic account of the Bohra religious teachings as exposed in literature: 'They talk of essences, far-fetched analogies, quiddities, theosophies, speculations about names, letters & numbers in this connection. This sort of hair-splitting which they call Tavil and Haqiqat is unattractive and incomprehensible for a European reader but the Ismaili Shiʿa realizes their quiddities with astonishing tact and incomparable skills. . .'.[35] This passage exemplifies how, in some learned quarters, works such as MT, while valued as historical and literary documents for the sake of academic research, had lost their charisma for doctrinal and religious purposes. Therefore, the greater public availability from the 19th century onwards of the MT manuscripts does not point so much to it having become more used for educational purposes but rather that restrictions to its access had been relaxed in some circles.

Conclusions

In conclusion, what is the MT? Started probably as an informal collection of notes, fragments, annotations and texts that might have served as a resource to help produce sermons and/or for use as religious instruction tools—in conjunction with oral guidance—in time this collection came to be elevated to the status of a systematised, 'canonical' corpus-organiser[36] with a specific place in the Ṭayyibī, and later, Bohra learning curriculum. The presence of a preface in this gathering of texts testifies to the shift in the way in which the MT came to be conceived and how its use should be understood. Content-wise, the MT reflects the themes, debates, concerns and polemics that were dominant within the 12th century Ṭayyibī community. In particular, part of the selection of texts forming the MT testifies to the establishment of a Ṭayyibī religious identity and the subsequent scholarly transition that took place with the transfer of religious and scholarly authority from the al-Ḥāmidī family to that of the al-Walīd.

How relevant was the MT as text to its readers? Its compiler in his introduction makes a grand claim for the MT to contain essential reading for those who wish to engage in the *daʿwa*. But to what extent does the selection of works forming the MT constitute must-read material for intellectually and scholarly advancing *dāʿī*s? Most of the full texts featured in the MT are, thus far, only known to have been transmitted through this compilation. At a glance, many do not even seem to have received mention in other Ṭayyibī works. The MT is obviously a treasure trove for textual preservation, even when abridged, but if the works it contains were really so important for the formation of the *dāʿī*s wouldn't one expect to find them more widely available as stand-alone texts and/or included in other *majmūʿa*s? Are we here witnessing the efforts of a compiler bent on pushing a doctrinal-political agenda by raising the status of otherwise obscure works that nevertheless carried distinctive messages on sensitive issues (*naṣṣ*, imamate of al-Ṭayyib, anti-Nizārī polemics)? The MT did indeed become mandatory reading for the scholarly formation of *dāʿī*s at intermediate/advanced levels but there is no evidence so far of the work having made a direct and overt impact on the writings of those figures known to have read it in great depth. Even al-Bharūchī does not quote or display evidence of having used the MT as a source for his seven-volume *Kitāb al-Azhār*. For example, when reporting the story of the letter sent by al-Āmir to al-Sayyida al-Ḥurra announcing the birth of al-Ṭayyib and therefore his designation as al-Āmir's heir apparent, al-Bharūchī relies on Idrīs ʿImād al-Dīn's account with no mention of the MT's version. By the late 18th–early 19th century the MT disappears from the list of mandatory readings sanctioned by the *dāʿī muṭlaq*. However, the falling out of favour of this text among Bohra's scholarly élites broadly coincides with the popularisation of this work through the relatively copious production of its manuscripts. The fact that the MT contained several authoritative sections on sensitive issues such as *naṣṣ* might have prompted the ruling scholarly élites to curb the authoritativeness of this work at a time when dissent over matters of leadership succession dominated and divided the Bohra community. At the same time its popularisation and dissemination through the production of many manuscript copies was in many cases spearheaded among or through Bohra reformist families who, among other things, challenged the exclusive hold on knowledge that the Bohra scholarly ruling élites strived to preserve for themselves. In light of this polarised use of the MT one can argue that the MT became officially both 'demoted' and 'declassified': 'demoted' because it advertised doctrines that could be used to challenge the authoritativeness of *dāʿī muṭlaqs* whose entitlement to leadership was disputed and 'declassified' because, by becoming widely circulated by or through reformist families, the text had lost 'potency' as a work that should be handled in secrecy and exclusivity.

Not only is the MT made up of many texts but, in turn, the majority of texts it contains are 'polyphonic' treatises, consisting as they do of their authors' choice of voices by a number of Fatimid thinkers in order to communicate ideas and teachings in matters of law, ritual and cosmology. Questions of authorship of multiple-text manuscripts, miscellaneous texts and multi-voice treatises in the context of a closely guarded literary production such as the Ṭayyibī/Bohra are yet to be addressed in this emerging field of research in Islamic Studies. The many 'voices' involved in sourcing, conception, assembling, writing, copying, distributing, reading, annotating and cataloguing the MT make its multiple-text manuscripts living documents that testify to the nature of manuscripts as being 'processes' rather than products.

NOTES

1 Cf. *Kitāb Majmūʿ al-tarbiya*, ed. Ḥ. Khaḍḍūr (Damascus, 2011).

2 Cf. S.M. Stern, 'The Succession to the Fatimid Imam al-Āmir, the Claims of Later Fatimids to the Imamate, and the Rise of Ṭayyibī Ismailism', *Oriens*, 4 (1951), pp. 193–255.

3 Respectively in the following catalogues: A. Gacek, *Catalogue of Arabic Manuscripts in the Library of The Institute of Ismaili Studies* (London, 1984), vol. 1, entry 86; D. Cortese, *Ismaili and Other Arabic Manuscripts* (London, 2000); D. Cortese, *Arabic Ismaili Manuscripts: The Zāhid ʿAlī Collection* (London, 2003); F. de Blois, *Arabic, Persian and Gujarati Manuscripts: The Hamdani Collection in the Library of The Institute of Ismaili Studies* (London, 2011).

4 While there is extensive literature on the study of multiple-text medieval European manuscripts, the subtleties of 'miscellanies' have yet to be fully investigated within the field of study of Islamic manuscripts. For a survey of the state of art in this area of research see the introduction in Michael Friedrich and Cosima Schwarke, ed., *One-Volume Libraries: Composite and Multiple-Text Manuscripts* (Berlin, 2016), pp. 1–26. See also A. Bausi. 'A Case for Multiple Text Manuscripts being "Corpus-Organizers"', *Manuscript Cultures,* Newsletter, no. 3, pp. 34–36. The limited, dedicated literature on conceptual analyses revolving around multiple-text manuscripts within an Islamic framework includes Franz Rosenthal, 'From Arabic Books and Manuscripts, V: A One-Volume Library of Arabic Philosophical and Scientific Texts in Istanbul', *Journal of the American Oriental Society*, 75 (1955), pp. 14–23; N. Martínez de Castilla Muñoz, 'Manuscritos musulmanes misceláneos y facticios del Aragón del siglo XVI', *Manuscritos para comunicar culturas* (2102), pp. 141–150; Konrad Hirschler. '"Catching the eel"—Documentary Evidence for Concepts of the Arabic Book in the Middle Period', *Journal of Arabic and Islamic Studies*, 12 (2012), pp. 224–234, and his recent 'The Development of Arabic Multiple-Text and Composite Manuscripts: The Case of *ḥadīth* Manuscripts in Damascus during the Late Medieval Period', in Alessandro Bausi, Michael Friedrich, and Marilena Maniaci, ed., *The Emergence of Multi-Text Manuscripts* (Berlin, 2020), pp. 275–302 and Gerhard Endress, '"One-Volume Libraries" and the Tradition of Learning in Medieval Arabic Islamic Culture', in *One-Volume Libraries: Composite and Multiple-Text Manuscripts*, pp. 171–205. I take this opportunity to thank Arianna D'Ottone, University of Rome 'La Sapienza', and Verena Klemm, University of Leipzig, for some valuable bibliographic suggestions.

5 That is, textual forms that exhibit physical and/or content-related dependencies on the main text, such as later, marginal annotations, glossae, colophons, interlinear annotations, ownership inscriptions, certificates, different handwritings within the same manuscript, etc. On the value of paratextual notes for the documentary study of Islamic manuscripts see A. Görke and K. Hirschler, ed, *Manuscript Notes as Documentary Sources* (Beirut, 2011).

6 K. Hirschler, *The Written Word in Medieval Arabic Lands: A Social and Cultural History of Reading Practices* (Edinburgh, 2012), p. 18.

7 At a glance the discrepancy in the greater availability of volume 1 compared to volume 2 can be observed across sets in other known library collections.

8 The copyist in question was Ghālib b. ʿAlī Ḥusayn Muḥsin al-Jabalī al-Yaʿburī. He also inscribed himself as the owner of the volumes. This may indicate that the MSS were at least initially intended by the copyist to be primarily for his personal use. He is also the copyist of Ḥasan b. Nūḥ al-Bharūchī's *Kitāb al-Azhār* MS 21, MS 22, MS 23 and 26 also in the IIS collection. From the colophon of MS 23 of *al-Azhār* we learn that this copyist was based in Surat.

9 A. Tritton, 'Notes on some Ismaili Manuscripts', *Bulletin of the School of Oriental Studies*, 7 (1933), pp. 35–39.

10 For a general discussion on the compilation as a literary device see N. Hathaway, 'Compilatio: From Plagiarism to Compiling', *Viator*, 20 (1989), pp. 19–44.

11 I echo here the definition 'One-volume library' devised by F. Rosenthal in 1955.

12 Rosenthal's appreciation for the compiler's 'courageous willingness to make his choice of literary works with a remarkable disregard of religious barriers and traditions' would not apply here, Rosenthal, 'From Arabic Books and Manuscripts', p. 15. For questions about the concept of authorship in the context of compilatory works within the Islamic literary tradition see L. Behzadi's introduction to L. Behzadi and J. Hameen-Antilla, ed., *Concepts of Authorship in Pre-Modern Arabic Texts* (Bamberg, 2015), pp. 9–22.

13 Ḥātim b. Ibrāhīm al-Ḥāmidī. *Risālat Tuḥfat al-qulūb wa-furjat al-makrūb, aw, Kitāb Tuḥfat al-qulūb: fī tartīb al-hudāh wa'l-du'āh fī Jazīrat al-Yaman*, ed. A. Hamdani (London, 2012), p. 44.

14 See the section of Idrīs' *Nuzhat al-afkār* published in A. Hamdani's edition of *Tuḥfat al-qulūb*, pp. 178, 188. Several manuscripts of works by al-Ḥārithī can indeed be found in the IIS MS collection.

15 Six short treatises and another two are attributed. They are all featured in volume 1 only.

16 Ismā'īl b. 'Abd al-Rasūl al-Majdū'. *Fahrasat al-kutub wa'l-rasā'il wa-li man hiya min al-'ulamā' wa'l-a'imma wa'l-ḥudūd al-afāḍil*, ed. 'Alī Naqī Munzawī (Tehran, 1966), pp. 129-134.

17 MT is the title that features in the heading and paratexts of most manuscripts and it is by this title that the work has been known to its readers and cataloguers. However, within the work itself this title is never mentioned. Instead in the preface it is stated that the work is called *Kitāb al-Jawāhir* (*Book of Essences or Jewels*). To my knowledge only al-Majdū' names also this title along with MT.

18 On the materialistic philology that renders a multiple-text manuscript an historical artefact for socio-anthropological insight into patronage or readership see Michael Friedrich and Cosima Schwarke, ed., *One-Volume Libraries*, p. 4.

19 Extract from the preface found in MS 121, MS 961, MS 953, MS 1163 and MS 1502. In his edition, Khaḍḍūr considers this preface to be the introduction of *Kitāb ta'wīl al-ṣalāt*, that is the first treatise featured in the MT. However evidence from the IIS MSS shows that the piece was intended as an introduction to the whole compilation.

20 A.A.A. Fyzee, 'The Study of the Literature of the Fatimid Da'wa', in G. Makdisi, ed., *Arabic and Islamic Studies in Honour of Hamilton A.R. Gibb* (Leiden, 1965), pp. 232–249, 233.

21 On the role of the Bohra manuscript library as a sacred locus for social codicology, see Olly Akkerman, 'The Bohra Manuscript Treasury as a Sacred Site of Philology: A Study in Social Codicology', *Philological Encounters*, 4 (2019), pp. 182–201.

22 Conversation with Professor A. Hamdani held at the IIS, London, 10 June 2016.

23 Hirschler, *The Written Word*, p. 22.

24 'A. al-'Awwā, *Muntakhabāt Ismā'īliyya* (Damascus, 1958), pp. 183–250 for the edition of Volume 1 of al-Bharūchī's *Kitāb al-Azhār*.

25 On the obligation of supporting reading with the shaykh's oral authority in medieval Islamic learning practices, see Badr al-Dīn b. al-Jamā'a, *Tadhkirat al-sāmi' wa'l-mutakallim fī adab al-'ālim wa'l-muta'allim* (Hyderabad, 1353/1934), pp. 172–177. Here the pedagogy described follows in the footsteps of classical Islamic learning characterised by the close link between textual transmission and a personal teaching tradition. See Endress, 'One-volume Libraries', p. 171.

26 About the pedagogical understanding of some reading techniques in the medieval Islamic world see J. Berkey, *The Transmission of Knowledge in Medieval Cairo: A Social History of Islamic Education* (Princeton, NJ, 1994), p. 27.

27 On the possible reasons for the special student status granted to al-Bharūchī, see S. Traboulsi, 'Transmission of Knowledge and Book Preservation in the Ṭayyibī Ismā'īlī Tradition', *Intellectual History of the Islamicate World*, 4 (2016), pp. 22–35, 26.

28 Cf. F. de Blois. *Arabic, Persian and Gujarati Manuscripts: The Hamdani collection* (London, 2011), p. 111.

29 Fyzee, 'The Study', pp. 244–245.

30 cf. I.K. Poonawala, *Biobibliography of Ismāʿīlī Literature* (Malibu, CA, 1977), pp. 201–204.

31 Fyzee, 'The Study', p. 246.

32 It should be noted that the text in the manuscript of *Majālis Sayfiyya* in the IIS collection (MS 1274 ArI ZA), while reflecting other aspects of what is stated by Fyzee regarding the most important works of the *daʿwa*, does not nevertheless contain the list of books studied by ʿAbd Mūsā as described by Fyzee who must have therefore consulted a manuscript of these *majālis* with a somewhat different content.

33 Al-Majdūʿ, *Fahrasat*, pp. 127, 134.

34 The Hamdani and ʿAli manuscript collections are good examples of collections that developed outside the strict control of the *daʿwa*. Cf. Traboulsi, 'Transmission', p. 24.

35 See Mulla Mian Bhai Abdul Husain, *Gulzare Daudi for the Bohra of India* (Ahmedabad, 1920; repr., Surat, 1977); cited in J. Blank, *Mullahs on the Mainframe: Islam and Modernity among the Daudi Bohras* (Chicago and London, 2001), p. 167.

36 I adopt here a concept that has been devised by A. Bausi in his discussion of Ethiopian multiple-text manuscripts. What is meant by this expression is texts belonging to an identifiable religious-cultural tradition being organised into the physical space of the manuscript. See 'A Case for Multiple Text Manuscripts being "Corpus-Organizers"'.

7

Textual, Orthographic Variations and Scribes' Annotations: A Possible Tool for the Transmission Analysis of the Text?

Monica Scotti

This chapter is based on some of the occurrences that I observed during the analysis of the *Mukhtaṣar al-uṣūl*, an interesting treatise by the Ṭayyibī thinker ʿAlī ibn Muḥammad ibn al-Walīd (d. 1215). For the sake of brevity, I will only share some background information and references about the author, his main works and the community he belonged to.

We may infer from his complete name and family lineage that Ibn al-Walīd claimed an illustrious past.[1] Moreover, he had a very good reputation as a learned and pious member of the independent *daʿwa* that had been established in Yemen after the schism that took place in 1130 among the Mustaʿlī branch of the Fatimids (when the 10th imam al-Āmir bi-Aḥkām was murdered and a dispute broke out over his succession).[2] The new community, known as the Ṭayyibīs, was entrusted to a *dāʿī muṭlaq*, appointed by *naṣṣ* ('designation'),[3] who led a hierarchy of ranks on behalf of the imam in hiding.[4]

Ibn al-Walīd held increasingly important roles within this religious group. In fact, at first, he studied under his uncle ʿAlī ibn al-Ḥusayn (d. 554/1159), who held the rank of *ma'dhūn* under the second *dāʿī muṭlaq*.[5] After his death, Ibn al-Walīd became a disciple of Muḥammad ibn Ṭāhir al-Ḥārithī (d. 584/1188),[6] whom he succeeded as *ma'dhūn* of Sanaa for want of the third *dāʿī muṭlaq*, Ḥātim al-Ḥāmidī, who also made him the mentor of his son, ʿAlī ibn Ḥātim al-Ḥāmidī. Actually, it was on Ibn al-Walīd's recommendation that Ḥātim designated his son to succeed him as the fourth *dāʿī*.

Finally, he himself became the next *dāʿī*[7] in 1209 and died at the age of ninety, having set the foundation of a distinguished family of *dāʿī*s that took the place of the Ḥāmidī dynasty and maintained a continuous leadership of the *daʿwa* in Yemen for approximately three centuries with only two brief interruptions.

Ibn al-Walīd was a prolific writer, whose works were held in high esteem among the Mustaʿlī-Ṭayyibī community, which explains why most of them have been preserved, either in the form of manuscripts or published books.[8]

With respect to the *Mukhtaṣar al-uṣūl*, it should be pointed out that, although it is presented as a polemical work about the issue of the so-called Names of God, the treatise addresses a great variety of themes. In the introduction, the author states that he wants to refute the positions held by his adversaries (*khuṣamāʾ*, *khuṣūm*), whom he groups into three main categories:

1. the Ḥashwiyya,[9] that is to say the *aṣḥāb al-ḥadīth* ('men of tradition', which means 'experts of transmitted traditions'), who are identified with the Sunni schools, Shāfiʿīs, Ḥanafīs, Mālikīs and with the Jabarīs;
2. the *aṣḥāb al-raʾy* ('partisans of [personal] opinion'), namely the Muʿtazilīs and Zaydīs;
3. the philosophers (*falāsifa*), the misbelievers (*mulḥidūn*), the dualists (*zanādiqa*)[10] and those who deny the divine attributes (*muʿaṭṭilūn*)[11] and the Prophecy.

The elements that make the *Mukhtaṣar* interesting for scholars are both the formal approach (i.e., the use of different argumentative techniques; Ibn al-Walīd even resorts to the same strategies adopted by his adversaries in order to prove them wrong) and the implied purpose of the text, since there seems to be an apologetic intent in making the readers infer, by elimination, that the only way to salvation is the one followed by the author himself.[12]

During my studies, I tried to gain access to as many manuscripts as I could,[13] and I was able to consult the microfilm of six specimens that are housed at The Institute of Ismaili Studies in London. These manuscript copies are relatively recent, but nonetheless represent a unique source of information about the Ismaili–Ṭayyibī community and their literary heritage.[14]

During my researches, I also tried to gather as much information as I could about the manuscripts in order to perform a proper codicological analysis. However, since it was not possible to access the originals, which were preserved in a different location (not available for consultation), I focused on making observations on the text and its orthography, morphology, syntax, scribal interventions and mistakes as a way to better understand the object of my studies and detect whether it was possible to address the issue of the transmission of the text.

Manuscripts of the *Mukhtaṣar al-uṣūl*

In the table on the next page (see Table 7.1) the main 'reference points' of each manuscript and the names by which I am going to address them in this chapter are listed.

With respect to the manuscripts, I am going to address the features that I was able to gather with respect to the textual/orthographic variations and scribes' annotations.

Manuscript A[19] is characterised by some preliminary annotations bewilderingly disposed on the first pages (pp. 6–7 and 9) containing the name of the author, the name of the treatise (in red ink), the name of the copyist and an invocation to the reader, who is called *akhī*, 'my brother', 'to listen to the teachings of the master of a clear night and of a dark day disclosing mysterious signs (twice)' (see Figure 7.1).[20] Notes and intra-text clarifications, used to explain some words/expressions (i.e., by paraphrases or synonyms), are written either above or below the line and in the margins of the page. The eulogies of the Prophet Muhammad, praises to his family, to the imams and to the previous Messengers in the history of mankind are often rendered *in extenso*, sometimes with an eccentric handwriting, probably for decorative purposes. Like in all the other specimens the eulogies are abundant and randomly shortened or given by logographs.

There are frequent episodes of cacography (i.e., ink blot in at least 50 cases, one of them extensively affects the reading on pp. 129–130) and frequent corrections and/or additions across the whole text. Actually, the copyist chooses different ways to work on the manuscript: usually

Table 7.1 Manuscripts of the *Mukhtaṣar al-uṣūl* housed at The Institute of Ismaili Studies.

Name Given in the Chapter	Manuscript Number	Previous Owner	Copyist	Date	Place
A	MS 142	*Ismaili Society of Bombay*	Nūr Lār-Khān Khīrghawnī	Daras Sayyidinā Wajīh,[15] 17th night of Jumād Ākhir (!), year not given (12th/18th century)	Not given
D	MS 141		ʿAlī-bhāʾī ibn (. . . .?) al-ʿAlī of (sākin) Halwad	1314/1896	Not given
E	MS 678	*Chhotu Lakhani*	Muḥammad Ṣāliḥ Shafaqat Ḥusayn Sārangpūrī	13th day of Ramaḍān 1353/1934	Bābarah, district (*ḍal*ʿ) Kāthiyāwār[16]
F	MS 269		Muḥammad ibn Fidā Ḥusayn	Jumādā al-Ukhrā 1359/1940	Partābgarh[17]
B	MS 1288	*Zāhid ʿAlī*	Unknown	4 Rabīʿ al-awwal 1267/6 January 1851	Not given
C	MS 1204		Unknown	19 Rajab 1280/29 December 1863[18]	Not given

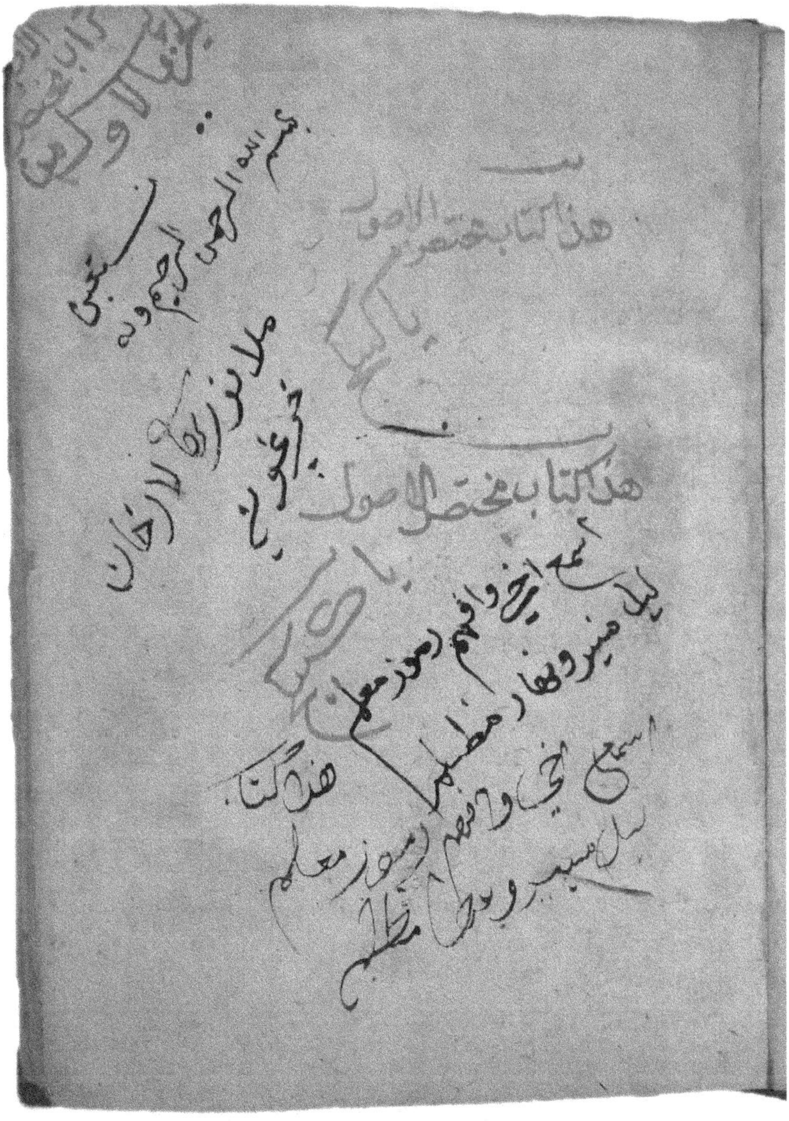

Figure 7.1 MS 142, p. 7(r).

the wrong word is crossed out in the body of the text and the correction is written above the line or, less frequently, in the margin; sometimes the symbols ٢ (*bā hindiyya*) and صح or ص, which stand for the verb *ṣaḥḥa* and/or the adjective *ṣaḥīḥ*, are added next to the correct word whereas a little cross is put above the wrong word; on a few occasions

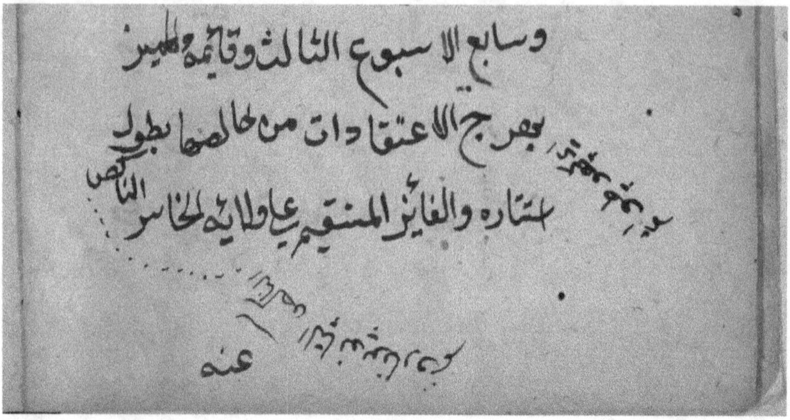

Figure 7.2 MS 142, p. 15(r).

the scribe uses what looks like a collation symbol—a small circle with a trait below—or a letter (it might be م, which stands for *matn*, 'body of the text') in between the lines (i.e., p. 9, between the lines 3–4 and 6–7); once he draws a sequence of dots which lead to a phrase written upside down at the left-hand bottom corner on p. 15 (see Figure 7.2).

With regard to the numbering of quires, the number is placed in the left-hand upper corner (head margin of the recto side) and it is given with the ordinal number spelled out in full letters. This is a common device in use from the second half of the 5th/11th century, which took the place of the numbering in abjad employed until the end of the 4th/10th century.[21] Each time the signature, which is accompanied with the addition of the complete title of the book, is written diagonally (downwards) in red ink.[22]

The device known as *réclame* or catchwords is steadily used in all manuscripts. It implies the anticipation of the first word of a page (usually a recto) written at the bottom of the previous page (a verso). The scribes, or more probably the artisans who cured the layout of the manuscript, resorted to it for the whole length of the text, in order to help maintain the right order of the pages.[23]

Finally, the chapter headings (*bāb*, *faṣl*) are rubricated, which means that they are written in red ink, and sometimes they are accompanied by strokes/logographic signs to catch the reader's attention.

Manuscript B (see Figure 7.3) is almost free from episodes of cacography (only once an ink blot slightly affects the reading on

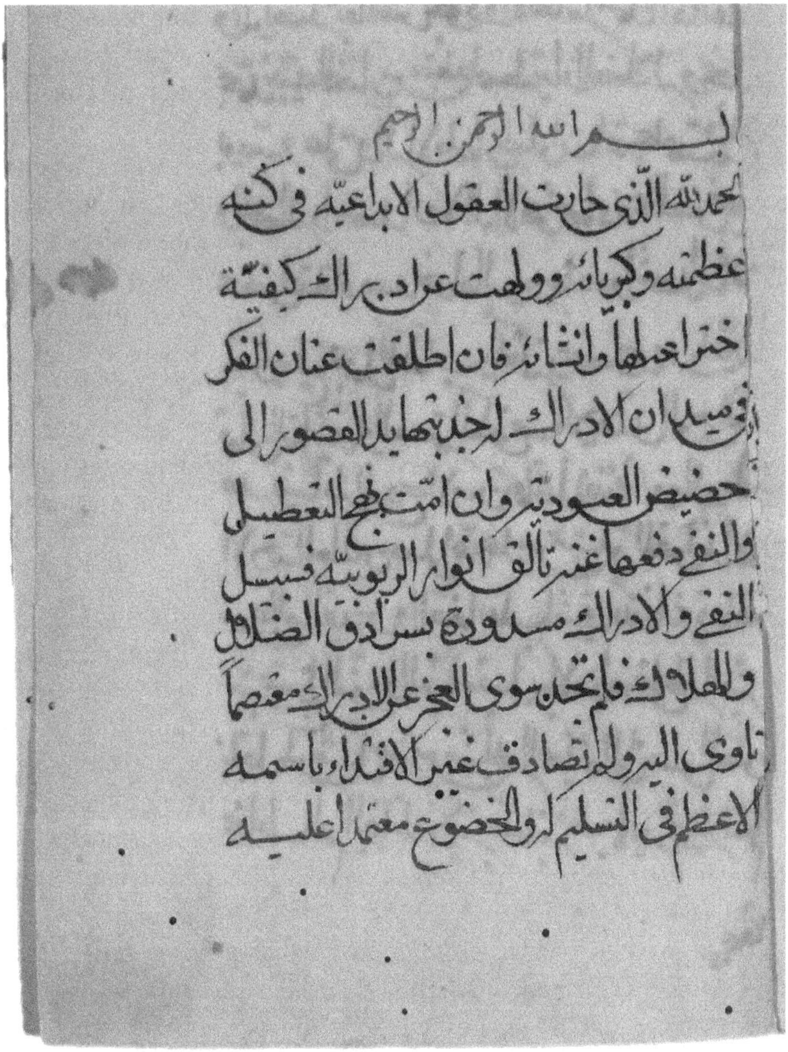
بسم الله الرحمن الرحيم
الحمد لله الذي حارت العقول الابداعيه في كنه
عظمته وكبريائه وولهت عن ادراك كيفية
خنس اعملها وانشائه فان اطلقت عنان الفكر
في ميدان الادراك لرجت بها ايد القصور الى
حضيض العبودية وان امتنع فهم التعطيل
والنفي دفعها غشر تالق انوار الربوبيه فسبل
النفي والادراك مسدودة بسر ادق الضلال
والهلاك فلم تجد سوى العجز عن الادراك معتصما
تاوي اليه ولم تصادف غير الاقتداء باسمه
الاعظم في التسليم له والخضوع معتمدا عليه

Figure 7.3 MS 1288, p. 1(r).

pp. 12–13) but it shows some signs of corrections and additions on the part of the scribe: for instance, the copyist sometimes puts the symbol v, Latin *caret*, in the body of the text to point to omissions, then he writes the missing word/phrase in the margin accompanied by the symbol ٢ (*bā hindiyya*).

In this case, to help maintain the right order of the pages, the device known as *pagination*[24] is employed: the numbers (following the Eastern

Arabic-Indic style of writing numerals) appear on both sides—recto and verso—in the centre of the upper margin. Apart from the rubrication of the chapter headings, punctuation and part of the colophon also appear to be in red ink.

Manuscript C is characterised by some episodes of cacography and corrections; on a few occasions, some lengthy additions can be found in the margin of the text. Again, apart from the rubrication of the chapter headings, the colophon is also given in red ink (see Figure 7.4).

Manuscript D is characterised by some episodes of cacography (i.e., ink blots in at least thirteen cases) and some corrections/additions. Like in manuscript B the device of *pagination* is used, with numbers (following the Eastern Arabic-Indic style of writing numerals) appearing on both sides—recto and verso—in the middle of the upper margin. The chapter headings (*bāb*, *faṣl*), which are rubricated, sometimes cannot be properly read, so either the ink used was too clear, or the rubrication is incomplete (see Figure 7.5).

Manuscript E is characterised by the presence, on the first folio, of the caption 'Chhotu Lakhani collection' followed by the number 134, maybe a reference to a previous cataloguing system. Like in Manuscripts C and D, only a few episodes of cacography can be found (i.e., three small ink blots on ff. 35, 50, 77).

The *sūras* are signalised in the text: the scribe writes the name of the *sūra* in the margin next to a symbol that looks like ۶ with a trait below, whereas the number of the verses is given in Eastern Arabic-Indic style (see Figure 7.6).

The copyist also makes some interventions to amend the text: he uses the symbol *caret* both in the body of the text and above the missing words/phrase that appear in the margin; the symbol ۲ (*bā hindiyya*) also appears and the expression لا is used to point out an error.

Here the device known as *foliation* is used, with the numbering of folia given in Arabic (European) numbers.[25] The chapter headings (*bāb*, *faṣl*), like for Manuscript A, are often accompanied by strokes/logographic signs to catch the reader's attention.

Manuscript F is characterised by the presence of the decorative invocation '*yā 'Alī*' written on the first page (see Figure 7.7) and the presence of the invocation '*yā kabīkaj*' written on the last page.[26] There are also two blank pages found in the middle of the manuscript, maybe for rebinding requirements (ff. 64, 65).

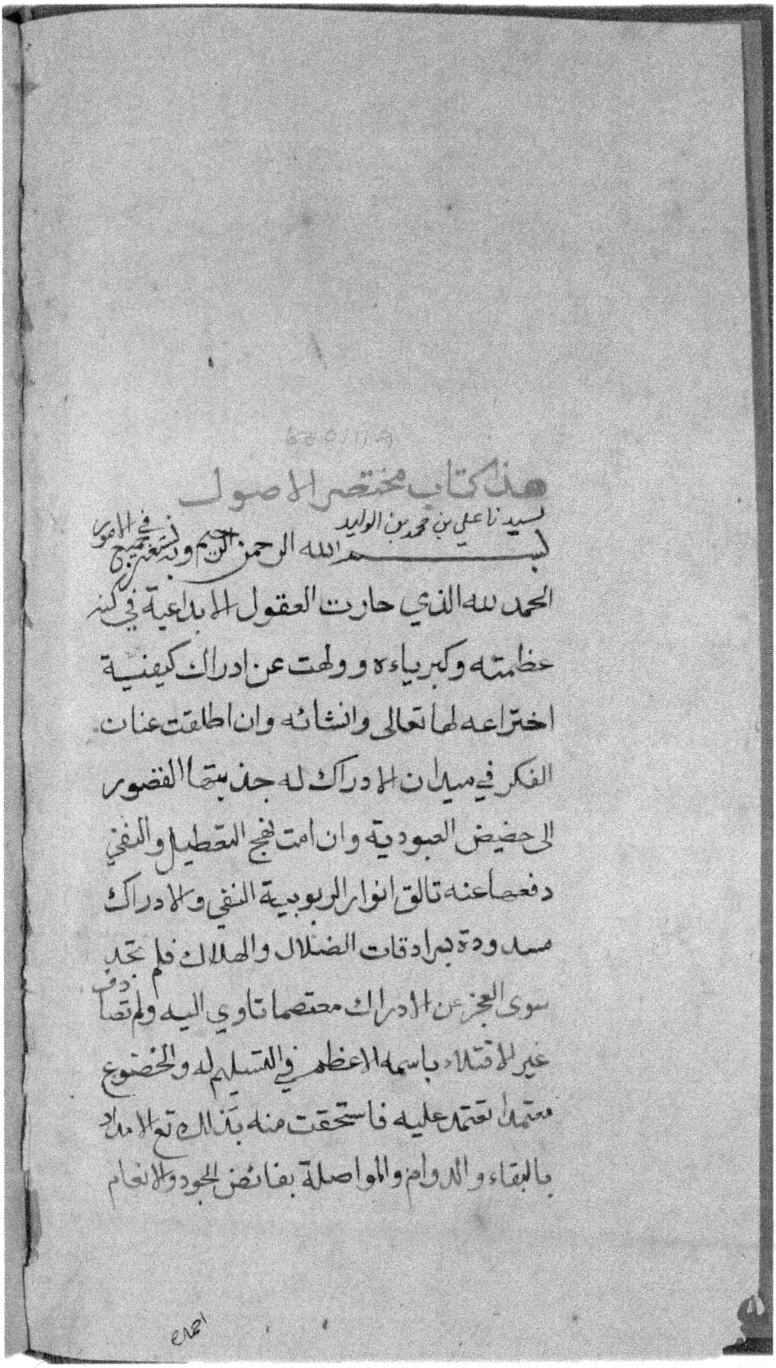
هذا كتاب مختصر الاصول
لسيدنا علي بن محمد بن الوليد
بسم الله الرحمن الرحيم وبه نستعين في جميع الامور
الحمد لله الذي حارت العقول الابداعية في كنه
عظمته وكبريائه وولهت عن ادراك كيفية
اختراعه لها تعالى وانشائه وان اطلقت عنان
الفكر في ميدان الادراك له جذبتها القصور
الى حضيض العبودية وان امت نهج التعطيل والنفي
دفعها عنه تالق انوار الربوبية النفي والادراك
مسدودة بسرادقات الضلال والهلاك فلم تجد
سوى العجز عن الادراك معتصما تاوي اليه ولم تعا
غير الاقتداء باسمه الاعظم في التسليم له والخضوع
معتمدا تعتمد عليه فاستحقت منه بذلك تمام الامداد
بالبقاء والدوام والمواصلة بفائض الجود والانعام

Figure 7.4 MS 1204, f. 1r.

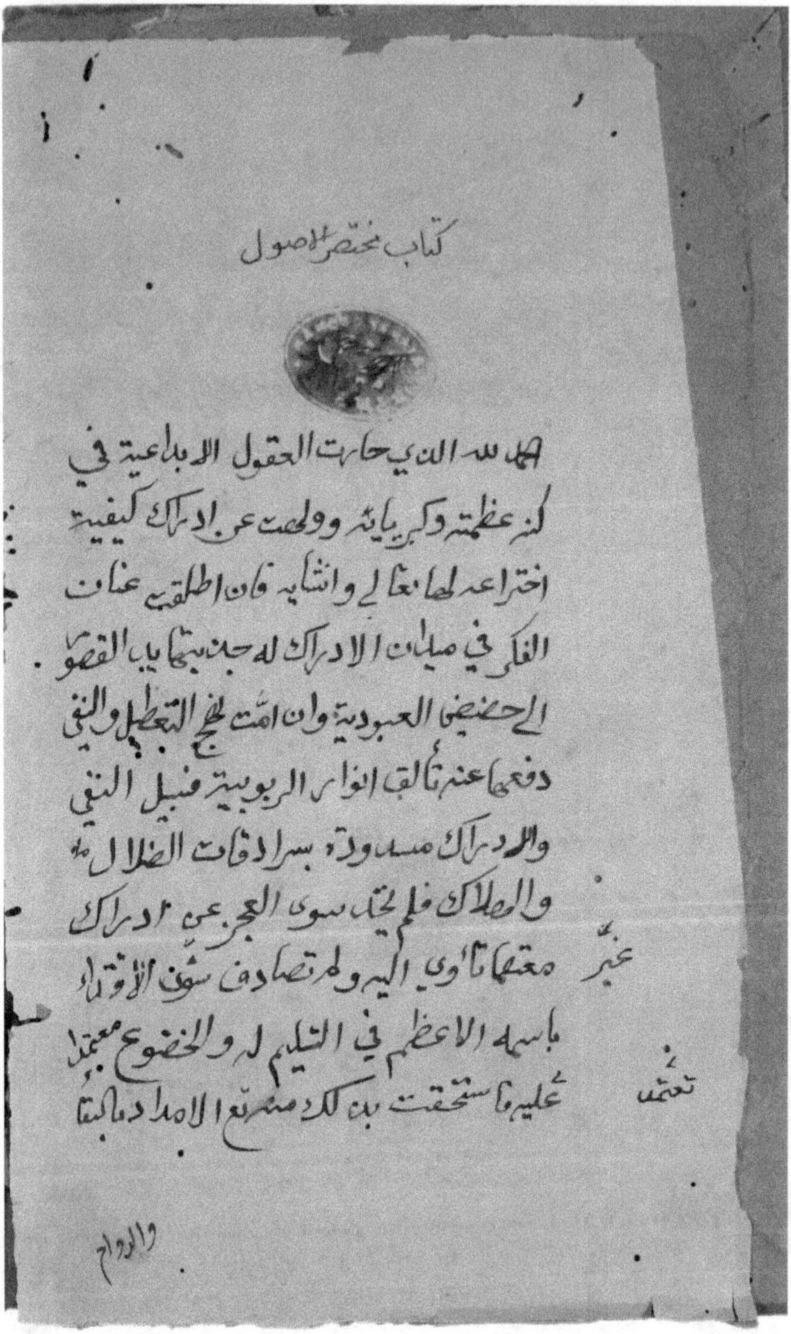
كتاب مختصر الاصول

الحمد لله الذي حارت العقول الابداعية في
كنه عظمته وكبريائه وولهت عن ادراك كيفية
اختراعه لما نعالى واشيائه فان اطلق عنان
الفكر في ميدان الادراك له جذبتها يد القصو
الى حضيض العبودية وان امت لجج التعطيل والنفي
دفعها عنه تألق انوار الربوبية فسبيل النفي
والادراك مسدودة بسرادقات الظلال
والهلاك فلم تجد سوى العجز عن ادراك
معرفتها تأوي اليه ولم تصادف شيئا الا التمسك
باسمه الاعظم في التسليم له والخضوع معتمدا
عليه واستحقت بذلك مشرع الامداد مايثبتا

Figure 7.5 MS 141, p. 1(r), with stamp.

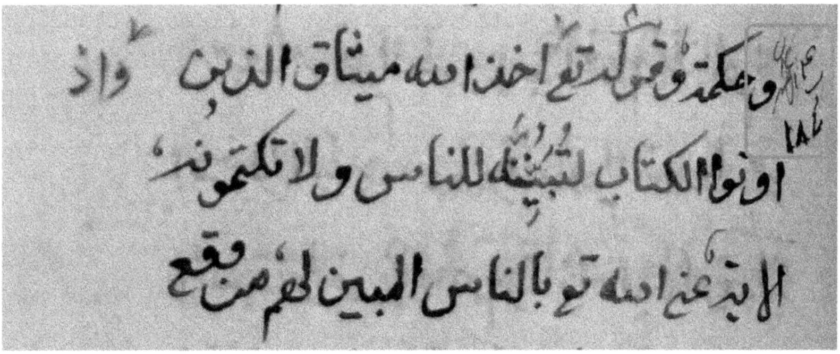

Figure 7.6 MS 678, f. 86, *Sūra* 3:184; transcription: *wa-idha akhadha allāhu mīthāqa alladhīna ūtū al-kitāba la-tubayyinunnahu li'l-nāsi wa lā taktumūnahu*; in the margin: *al-ʿImrān*.

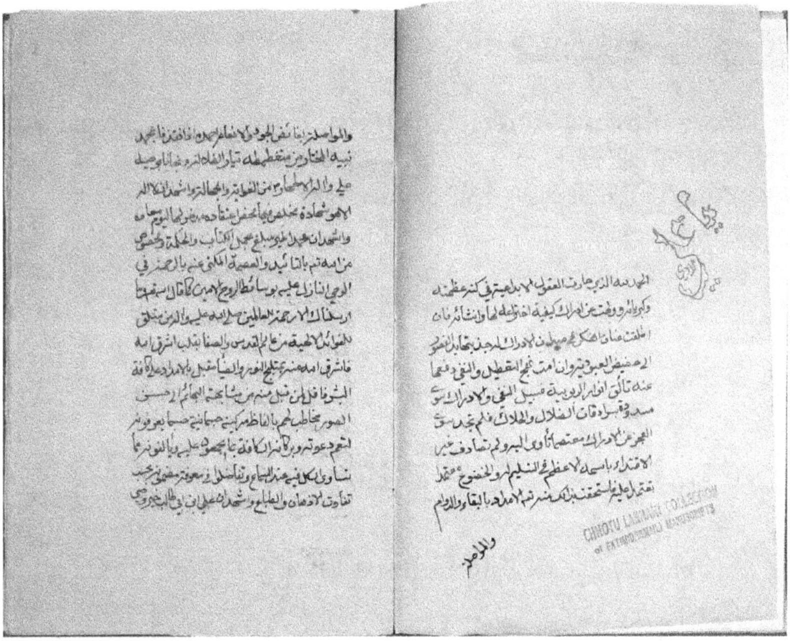

Figure 7.7 MS 269, f. 1, with stamp.

I took notice in F of frequent corrections and additions put in the margin and of recurrent cases of *saut du même au même*, which is an omission similar to haplography,[27] happening when a word or group of words are repeated at a short distance in the text (proximity) and the scribe writes what follows the first occurrence after the second occurrence.

This kind of mistake is frequent also when two close words have the same ending (homoeoteleuton) or beginning (homeoarchy).[28] When a mistake is amended, the scribe puts a small trait above the wrong word in the body of the text, whereas the right word is written in the margin.

The Linguistic Idiosyncrasies

As a way to better work on the collation of the text, I tried to take notice of the linguistic idiosyncrasies that can be observed among the manuscripts. In the following pages these features are grouped into different categories: nouns, verbs, eulogies, alternate notations, mistakes. The numbers among the brackets refer to how many times each occurrence is observed in the corresponding specimen.

Nouns

- Reverse order of words, occurring in all manuscripts except for A: B (2), C (2), D (3), E (1), F (2).
- Use of different cases in all manuscripts (i.e., from the direct to the indirect case).
- Use of feminine instead of masculine and *vice versa*:
  - feminine instead of masculine in A (2), B (3), C (5), D (6), E (2), F (3);
  - masculine instead of feminine in A (2), B (6), C (5), D (4), E (1), F (2).
- Use of singular instead of plural and *vice versa*:
  - singular instead of plural in A (3), B (14), C (20), D (17), E (13), F (23);
  - plural instead of singular in A (4), B (7), C (8), D (12), E (9), F (5).
- Elimination or addition of the article *al-*:
  - elimination of the article in A (6), B (12), C (7), D, (5), E (6), F (8);
  - addition of the article in A (4), B (12), C (12), D (11), E (8), F (6).
- Use of different terms for the same meaning: *khalq* instead of *khilqa* (1), *wasā'iṭ* instead of *wasāṭa* (1), Qur'ān instead of *Kitāb* (1) in F; *al-mursil* instead of *al-rasūl* (1) in C; *al-mulḥidūn* instead of

al-mal[ā]ḥida in B (1) and C (1); *al-mal[ā]ḥida* instead of *al-mulḥidūn* in D (1).

Verbs

The use of different persons, modes and tenses occurs frequently and in all manuscripts. Verbal forms are sometimes substituted with participles; for instance, the form *qā'il* or even *qawluhu* instead of *qāla, yaqūlu* is found in A (*qā'il* instead of *yaqūlu*, p. 162) and in E (*fī qawlihi* instead of *yaqūlu*, p. 65).

Eulogies

The eulogies are very frequent in all manuscripts, so they clearly represent a distinctive stylistic aspect of the treatise. Among the praises addressed to God, the following forms should be mentioned: *taʿālā* and *subḥānahu* (recurrent in all manuscripts); *ʿazza wa-jalla* (found twice in A, and once in D and E); *jalla wa-taʿālā* (not very frequent in all manuscripts); *jalla jalālahu* (found only once in all the manuscripts). As to the way the Prophet Muhammad is referred to in the treatise, he is mainly addressed as *al-nabī* and secondly as *al-rasūl*.

The appearance of these eulogies is far from being consistent in the copies, since they are randomly written *in extenso*, abbreviated, accompanied by logographic signs, etc.

It might be of interest to notice that only in F, the names of the two caliphs Abū Bakr and ʿUmar ibn al-Khaṭṭāb are followed by the despising exclamation 'he be damned', respectively once and three times.

Alternate Notations

They are very frequent. Each of the manuscripts has its proper style of writing words, though various features are common to several, and sometimes even to all of them. Here there is a list of the main variations.

- *Scriptio plena* (*alif* with *madda*). In A it is hardly ever rendered and even when the scribe chooses to write it down, he is not consistent. For example, with regard to the word *āl*, 'family', 12 occurrences over 26 are with *alif madda*; with regard to the name

Ādam, only 2 occurrences over 11 are with *alif madda*; with regard to the word Qur'ān, over 34 occurrences, 9 times the copyist uses *alif madda* and 25 times he does not (in one case the word is even rendered with both spellings on the same page, p. 135). Also in B and in C the *scriptio plena* is not consistently rendered: with regard to the word *āl*, 11 occurrences over 17 are with *alif madda* in B, whereas 10 occurrences over 12 are with *alif madda* in C; with regard to the name Ādam, over 11 occurrences in both B and C, 8 are with *alif madda* in B, but none of them has a *scriptio plena* in C; with regard to the word Qur'ān, over 34 occurrences in both B and C, 18 times are with *alif madda* in B, whereas 11 times the scribe uses a double *alif* and only once there is *alif madda* in C. On the other hand, in D, E and F the *scriptio plena* is always consistently rendered in the text with a double *alif.*

- Long *alif* instead of *alif maqṣūra:* A (6), B (6), C (1), D (6).
- *Alif maqṣūra* instead of *long alif:* D (3), E (1), F (3).
- Lack of *alif maqṣūra* at the end of the word: A (1), B (1), C (2), D (1), E (1), F (1).
- Addition of *alif maqṣūra* at the end of the word: B (2), C (1).
- Addition of *yā'* at the end of the word: A (3), B (3), C (3), D (2), E (3), F (3).
- Lack of *alif* at the end of a 3rd plural person verb: A (14), B (5), C (9), D (4), E (2), F (3).
- Lack of *nūn* at the end of a 3rd plural person verb: C (1), F (2).
- Sometimes composite words are either written separately instead of being rendered as a single word or they are rendered as a single word instead of being written separately. For instance, the scribe usually writes *inkāna* and *inkānat* instead of *in kāna* and *in kānat* in B (once he even writes *qā'ilinna* instead of *qā'il inna*).
- Lack of final *hamza*: A (2), B (3), C (2), D (2), E (1), F (2).
- Lack of final *tā' marbūṭa*: C (2), D (1), E (1), F (2).
- Coupling *wa* often written at the beginning of the line: A (361), B (315), C (254), D (337), E (364), F (267).
- Coupling *wa* written at the end of the line: A (13), B (13),[29] C (71),[30] D (63),[31] E (9), F (34).[32]
- Words are frequently split in two over the lines in A (clearly a stylistic mistake), it happens over 120 times. On one occasion the word is split in two over two different pages (pp. 232-233).

- *Hamza* is not always consistently rendered in the manuscripts. With reference to the word *mu'min*, 'believer', in all its forms (singular, plural, feminine, etc.), over 27 occurrences the scribes only use *hamza* 3 times in A, 2 times in B and 7 times in C. Instead, in F the copyist always writes the *hamza*, in E he uses the *hamza* 24 times over 27 and in D he only omits it once on p. 137.
- *Alif maqṣūra* in A is usually written with diacritic dots below, as if it were a common letter *yā'* (it happens also with regard to the *hamza ʿalā kursī*).

Mistakes

The most frequent mistakes are:

- Metathesis: A (2), B (7), C (4), D (7), E (1), F (1).
- Misplacement of diacritic dots (*taṣḥīf*), especially frequent in B, where some cases can be identified: i.e., the dots above the letters *tā' marbūṭa* and *ḍād* are omitted. Moreover, it is interesting to notice that the diacritic dots above letters such as *tā* and *qāf* are sometimes vertically oriented.
- *Lapsus calami*: *al-shaʿrīʿa* instead of *al-sharīʿa* ('the religious law'), *al-zanāqa* instead of *al-zanādiqa* ('the dualists') and *akluhu* instead of *ʿaqluhu* ('his intellect') in A; *ṭirāṭā* instead of *ṣirāṭā* ('road') in B; *manāl* instead of *manāzil* ('houses') in C, D and E; *al-arḍ* instead of *al-ʿarḍ* ('the offering') in D and F. These mistakes are caused by the assonance between two words and could be interpreted as an evidence either of the fact that at least part of the text was being written by dictation and the reader's pronunciation was not correct, or that the scribe himself was misled by his own mispronunciation.

Conclusion: Is the Collection of Such Data a Possible Tool for Understanding the Transmission of the Text?

As a general remark, it should be noticed that the kind of data that can be gathered by the mere observation of the manuscripts—even when the scholar only possesses a digital version of the text—are extremely varied and potentially of wide range.

Further thinking is due also with respect to the different implications of conveying the same text through mediums such as a manuscript, a print edition, or a digital version.

Moreover, regardless of their 'origin', it is not easy to categorise the gathered data and to rigorously synthetise their implications, especially because there is no established practice and no extended collection to turn to with respect to Arabic manuscripts in general and Ismaili manuscripts in particular.[33]

Having to deal with a limited number of sources in the case of the *Mukhtaṣar al-uṣūl* (sources that have grown now that I am working on a seventh copy of the *Mukhtaṣar al-uṣūl* and also on five copies of the *Ḍiyāʾ al-albāb*,[34] a treatise by the same author) I tried to make at least some general observations.

I noticed, for instance, that in some cases all manuscripts share readings different from those found in the specimen that I had chosen as a reference (A). On the other hand, all manuscripts frequently differ from each other in their readings, even if the many additions and corrections made by the scribes nullify the differences among them in the majority of cases.

Actually, it might be of interest to point out that the presence of symbols that look like small circles with dots (inside or outside) in A suggests the possibility that this copy is itself the product of collation.[35]

Among the general considerations that could be deduced by the analysis of the data gathered in so far, there is the remark that these manuscripts often show similarities in the way the scribes worked on the text. For instance, at the beginning of the third chapter of the second book, there is an addition in A, B and E that could be a digression not belonging to the original text or, more probably, a slightly different repetition of a passage:

> [This chapter is] about their saying that the acts of men (*al-ʿibād*) please the Creator (*al-Bārī*), be He exalted, and [that they] displease Him, and [it is about] their inference of what they had inferred from the verses mentioned [in the previous chapter].[36] They have imposed to the Creator (*al-Bārī*), be He exalted, free movement in relation to the states (*al-taṣarruf ʿalā al-ḥālāt* [which are] different and transient, because of His alteration from pleasure to displeasure [addition][37] when an act of

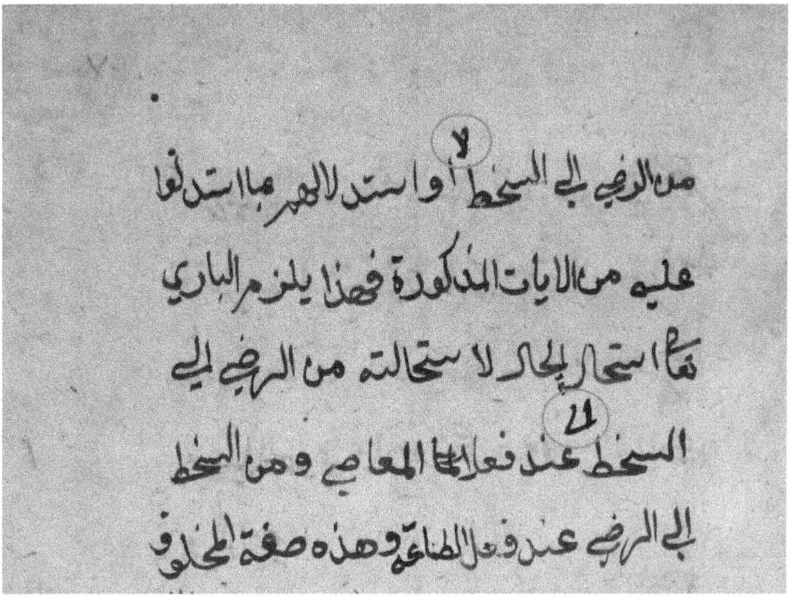

Figure 7.8 MS A.

> disobedience [is performed], and from displeasure to pleasure when an act of obedience [is performed].

The addition seems to have been erased both in A (see Figure 7.8), since the scribe writes *lā* at the beginning and at the end of the sentence, and in E (see Figure 7.9), where the scribe uses a horizontal stroke to cross it out.

Again, in the fourth chapter of the second book there is an addition in D, E and F, '. . . avoiding great sins is assigned to them and this implied the wiping out of their offences and their admission to a Gate of great honour', that seems to be the explanation of Qur'ān 4:31 (35) 'If ye (but) eschew the most heinous of the things which ye are forbidden to do, we shall expel out of you all the evil in you and admit you to a Gate of great honour'.[38]

In the fourth chapter of the first book in A, B, C the copyist added the relative pronoun *alladhī* in the text by error, only in A it is erased (p. 58). Likewise, in the second chapter of the second book there is a common mistake in A, B, C: the scribe wrote *naqḍ* instead of *ba'ḍ*, only in A it is corrected (p. 76). Finally, in the third chapter of the fourth book, a different choice of word has been made: we find

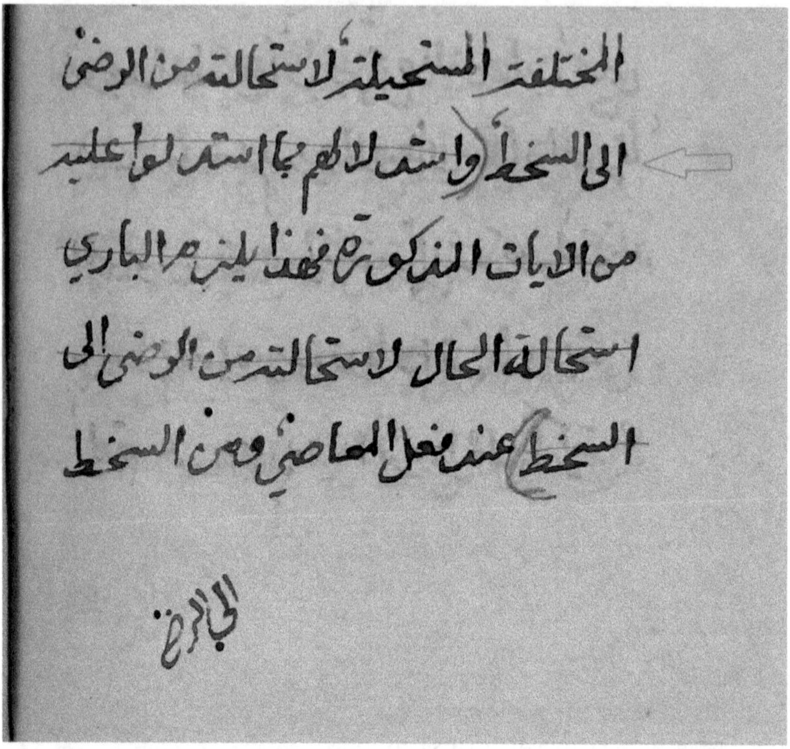

Figure 7.9 MS E.

al-thamara, *al-thamarāt* ('fruit, fruits') in C and D, whereas there is *al-tamra*, *al-tamarāt* ('date, dates') in A, B, E, and F.

Such occurrences, together with the evidence that the content of the *Mukhtaṣar* stays the same in all the texts, may suggest the existence of a very small group or even just one standard/normalised version of the treatise, which was accepted and circulated among the community various centuries after its composition.

Unfortunately, all the facts mentioned in the present contribution, in spite of being abundant, do not suffice to hypothesise any definite line of transmission or *stemma codicum* yet or to clarify the purpose for which the treatise has been copied.[39]

My hope is that these kinds of observations could prove useful for future studies, especially thanks to the introduction of new tools and formalised approaches to the research that is focused on the analysis of digital texts.

NOTES

1 He came from the family of Banū al-Walīd al-Anf that traced their genealogy back to the noble Quraysh tribe through ʿAbd Manāf ibn Quṣayy, who was the father of Ḥāshim ibn ʿAbd al-Manāf, Prophet Muhammad's great-grandfather. The main primary sources and first-hand testimony about his biography are: Ḥātim al-Ḥāmidī, *Tuḥfat al-qulūb*; Idrīs ʿImād al-Dīn, *Nuzhat al-afkār wa-rawḍat al-akhbār*, microfilm, American University in Beirut. See also Ḥasan ibn Nūḥ al-Bharūchī, *Kitāb al-azhār*, ed., ʿĀdil al-ʿAwwā, in *Muntakhabāt Ismāʿīliyya* (Damascus, 1982); Quṭb al-Dīn Burhānpūrī, *Muntazaʿ al-akhbār fī akhbār al-duʿāt al-akhyār*, ed., Sāmir Fārūq Ṭarābulusī (Beirut, 1999); Ismāʿīl ibn ʿAbd al-Rasūl al-Majdūʿ, *Fihrist*, ed., ʿAlī Naqī Munzawī (Tehran, 1966); Ḥusayn al-Hamdānī, *al-Ṣulayḥiyyūn wa'l-ḥaraka al-Fāṭimiyya fī al-Yaman* (Cairo, 1955); see I. K. Poonawala, "Alī b. al-Walīd', *EI3* (online edition).

2 In fact, when the Fatimid reign passed to al-Āmir's cousin, ʿAbd al-Majīd al-Ḥāfiẓ, the local community of Yemen, ruled by the Ṣulayḥid queen al-Sayyida al-Ḥurra, decided to continue the *daʿwa* on behalf of al-Ṭayyib Abī al-Qāṣim (al-Āmir's son), who was only a child at the time of his father's death and was thought from then on to be in hiding.

3 Etymologically: what is apparent to the eye; as a technical term, in Shiʿi doctrine, it designates the principle according to which the Prophet had designated ʿAlī to be his successor. Cf. A. J. Wensinck, 'al-Naṣṣ', *EI2*, p. 1029.

4 Apart from the three higher ranks (the *nāṭiq*, the *waṣī*—or *asās*—and the *imam*), there are seven *ḥudūd:* the *bāb* (the chief administrative head of the *daʿwa);* the *ḥujja* (a high-ranking *dāʿī* who was put in charge of the lands among the twelve regions in which the earth was divided); three *dāʿīs*—the *dāʿī al-balāgh* (who acted as *liaison* between the central and local headquarters), the *dāʿī al-muṭlaq* (who was the chief functionary acting with absolute authority in the absence of the regional *ḥujja* and of the *dāʿī al-balāgh*), the *dāʿī al-maḥdūd* (chief assistant of the *dāʿī al-muṭlaq*); two assistants titled *al-ma'dhūn* (lit. 'licentiate')—*the ma'dhūn al-muṭlaq* and *the ma'dhun al-maḥdūd* (or *al-maḥṣūr*), eventually designated as *al-mukāsir* (lit. 'persuader'), whose authority was limited and was mainly concerned with attracting new converts. Cf. F. Daftary, *The Ismāʿīlīs: Their History and Doctrines* (2nd ed., Cambridge, 2007), pp. 217-219.

5 Cf. I. K. Poonawala, "Alī b. al-Ḥusayn b. al-Ḥusayn b. 'Alī al-Qurashī', *EI3* (online edition).

6 Cf. I. K. Poonawala, 'Muḥammad b. Ṭāhir b. Ibrāhīm al-Ḥārith', *EI2*, p. 411.

7 Ḥātim al-Ḥāmidī stated that all the qualifications of a *dāʿī* described by the *dāʿī* Aḥmad al-Nīsābūrī (d. after 386/996) in his *al-Risāla al-mūjaza al-kāfiya fī ādāb al-duʿāt* were to be found in ʿAlī b. Muḥammad (Ḥātim al-Ḥāmidī, *Tuḥfat al-qulūb*, manuscript in the private collection of Mullā Qurbān Ḥusayn Godhrawala, f. 152r). Cf. I. K. Poonawala, "Alī b. al-Walīd', *EI3* (online edition).

8 Cf. F. Daftary, *Ismaili literature: A Bibliography of Sources and Studies* (London, 2004), pp. 118–119 and, for a comprehensive list of works by ʿAlī ibn al-Walīd and sources on him, see I. K. Poonawala, *A Bio-bibliography of Ismāʿīlī Literature* (Malibu, 1977), pp. 156–161.

9 This term derives from *ḥashw* ('farce' and hence 'prolix and useless discourse'). Sometimes it is associated with the expression *ghuthā'* (lit. 'wastes') to address scholars of little worth who recognised the coarsely anthropomorphic traditions as genuine and interpreted them literally, without criticism (*bi-lā kayfa*). Cf. 'Ḥas͟hwiyya', *EI2*, p. 269.

10 This term is used in the narrow sense to address the Manichaean community (i.e., followers of the gnostic religion founded in the 3rd century CE by the Iranian prophet Mānī); in fact, on account of their creed, which was based on a dualistic system revolving

around the continuous struggle between the cosmological principles of light and darkness, they were denied the *status* of *ahl al-dhimma* by the Muslim law. This term (sing. *zindīq*) is also loosely used as a synonym of *murtadd*, *kāfir* or even *mulḥid*, and, in general, to refer to the 'hypocrites'. Cf. F.C. de Blois, 'Zindīḳ', *EI2*, pp. 510–513.

11 Actually this expression usually refers to the act of denying the attributes of God as perpetrated by the Muʿtazilīs, although they had justified their position on the matter in terms of *tanzīh*, 'purification', and not *taʿṭīl*, 'deprivation'.

12 At the end of the treatise Ibn al-Walīd says: 'if God, be He exalted, wants it, I will single out the explanation of the discourse of the fourth group, which is the group of the people of truth, in another treatise titled "*Jalā' al-ʿuqūl wa zubda al-maḥṣūl*" (the Epistle on the splendour of intellects and the cream of proceeds)'.

13 Poonawala provides the following data about some existing examples of the manuscript: a copy is mentioned in Ṭāhir Sayf al-Dīn's *Asmā' al-kutubi al-maktūba bi-yaday al-duʿāt allatī hiya mawjūda ilā alāna fī khizāna al-daʿwa al-hādiya* (which is part of the *al-Risāla al-Ramaḍāniya*, pp. 354–56) as having been transcribed by the 13th *dāʿī* ʿAlī Shams al-Dīn; two copies are found in Muʿizz Goriawala's *A Descriptive Catalogue of the Fyzee Collection of Ismāʿīlī Manuscripts* (1965), collection housed at the University of Mumbai; two copies are cited in the *Ismāʿīlī Manuscripts in the Collection of Ismailia Association of Pakistan*, Karachi (which I believe are among those housed at the IIS); a copy is said to be cited in the *Ismāʿīlī Manuscripts in the Collection of Shaykh ʿAbd al-Qayyum ibn ʿĪsābnā'ī*, located in Mumbai; two copies are mentioned in the *Qā'ima bi'l-makhṭūṭā al-ʿarabiya al-muṣawwira bi'l-mīkrūfilm min al-jumhūriya al-ʿarabiya al-yamaniya*, Cairo. See I. K. Poonawala, *A Bio-bibliography of Ismāʿīlī Literature*, pp. 159–158.

14 See A. Gacek, *Catalogue of Arabic Manuscripts in the Library of The Institute of Ismaili Studies* (London, 1984), vol. 1, pp. 78–79; D. Cortese, *Ismaili and Other Arabic Manuscript: A Descriptive Catalogue of Manuscripts in the Library of The Institute of Ismaili Studies* (London, 2000), pp. 77–78; D. Cortese, *The Arabic Ismaili Manuscripts: The Zāhid ʿAlī Collection in the Library of The Institute of Ismaili Studies* (London, 2003), p. 121. List of manuscripts: MS 142 (18th century), MS 141, MS 878, MS 1288 and MS 1204 (19th century), MS 678 and MS 269 (20th century).

15 i.e., Wajīh al-Dīn Ibrāhīm (d. 1168/1756), 39th *dāʿī muṭlaq* of the Ṭayyibī Dā'ūdī Bohra, who operated in India during the 12th/18th century.

16 The place name comes from that of a local ruling dynasty, the *Kathi*, from the Rajput clan. It is a peninsula of western India in the Gujarat state.

17 The name could refer to a town in the Rajasthan state, in the northwest of India. Pratapgarh was also a princely state in British India until 1949. More unlikely, it could be a reference to a place located in the Punjab region (meaning 'five rivers'), which comprises vast territories of eastern Pakistan and northern India.

18 At the time of Najm al-Dīn ibn Zayn al-Dīn, who is mentioned in the colophon.

19 I counted 293 pages. If we put aside the preliminary annotations, that clearly do not belong to the original text, and the colophon at the very end of this copy, we are left with 285 pages instead of the 277 pages reported in Gacek's *Catalogue of Arabic Manuscripts*, vol. 1, p. 78.

20 All English translations in the present chapter are my own.

21 The numbering by abjad appears to be more frequent in works dealing with scientific issues than in those about religious sciences. Cf. F. Déroche et al., *Islamic Codicology. An Introduction to the Study of Manuscripts in Arabic Script* (London, 2006).

22 I counted 18 quires, the first of which is pointed out by an arrow. Since I could not examine the original copy I cannot provide a more accurate codicological description. Anyway, it might be of interest to note that the most common formula for quires of manuscripts made of paper is the *quinion*, and that the quires at the beginning and/or at the end of the text are usually rare (*binion*, *ternion*, single *bifolio*) or with an odd number of folios. Cf. F. Déroche et al. *Islamic Codicology*, p. 92.

23 The *réclame* is a system whose importance is demonstrated by the number of technical terms used in various periods and regions of the Arabic world (e. g., *taʿqība, waṣla, wāṣila, rābiṭa, taṣfīḥ, sāʾis, taqyīda* and *raqqāṣ*, the last one literally meaning 'dancer'). The downwards orientation and the fact that the word is spaced with regard to the last line are typical features of oriental manuscripts, whereas in the Maghrebian specimen (at least until the end of the 9th/15th century) it is usually written horizontally and next to the line. Cf. F. Déroche et al. *Islamic Codicology*, p. 106. Gacek gives the following definition of catchwords in his *Vademecum*: 'the last word of a text on the b-page (verso), usually written on its own, below the last line, and repeated as the first word of the next page (a-page or recto)', which actually corresponds to what Déroche calls *contre-réclame* and notices to be especially found in Maghrebian manuscripts of the 8th/14th century. Cf. A. Gacek, *Arabic Manuscripts: A Vademecum for Readers* (Leiden and Boston, 2009), p. 50.

24 *Pagination* is a system that manuscript writers began to currently use only in recent times (13th/19th century), when printing started to gain ground in the Arab world. Gacek also states that it is not infrequently used in Ismaili manuscripts, cf. A. Gacek', *Catalogue of Arabic Manuscripts*, vol. 1, p. xii.

25 A more widespread use of *foliation*, as opposed to quire signatures, is attested only from the 10th/16th century, cf. A. Gacek, *ibid.*, p. 106.

26 The expression '*yā kabīkaj*' is a somewhat mysterious invocation which can be found on the first or the last folio of a codex and is thought to have the power to protect the paper against worms and insects. This word, that seems to be of Persian origin, could refer at the same time to: different plants such as crowfoot (according to Wehr's *Dictionary of Modern Written Arabic*) or a kind of wild parsley, a deadly poison, the king of cockroaches, the patron angel of reptiles (according to Steingass's *Persian-English Dictionary*) and, less likely, the name in Syriac of a king who had command over insects (according to Dihkhudā's *Lughatnāmah*). Cf. A. Gacek, 'The Use of "*kabīkaj*" in Arabic Manuscripts', *Manuscripts of the Middle East I* (Leiden, 1986), pp. 49–53.

27 This is the error of writing a sequence of letters or a word once, when they should have been written twice.

28 Cf. A. Gacek, 'Taxonomy of Scribal Errors and Corrections in Arabic Manuscripts', in *Theoretical Approaches to the Transmission and Edition of Oriental Manuscripts*, ed. Judith Pfeiffer and Manfred Kropp (Würzburg, 2007), p. 222.

29 On three occasions it is placed at the end of a line and repeated again at the beginning of the following line.

30 Once it is placed both at the end of a line and at the beginning of the following line.

31 On three occasions it is placed both at the end of a line and at the beginning of the following line (pp. 93, 94, 111), whereas once it is written at the end of a page and repeated at the beginning of the next page (p. 99).

32 Once it is placed both at the end of a line and at the beginning of the following line.

33 New developments can be found in recent studies. See L.W.C. van Lit, *Among Digitized Manuscripts: Philology, Codicology, Paleography in a Digital World* (Brill, 2019).

34 See A. Gacek, *Catalogue of Arabic Manuscripts*, vol. 1, pp. 14–15; D. Cortese, *Ismaili and other Arabic Manuscripts*, pp. 75–76; D. Cortese, *The Arabic Ismaili Manuscripts*, pp. 38–39; F. de Blois, *Arabic, Persian and Gujarati Manuscripts: The Hamdani Collection* (London, 2011), pp. 120–121. List of manuscripts: MS 246, MS 972, MS 870, MS 1216, MS 1512 (20th century).

35 The Sunni historian al-Khaṭīb al-Baghdādī (d. 463/1071) used to say *al-dāra al-ijāza*, 'the circle is the authorisation'.

36 Ibn al-Walīd refers to the way the so-called *aṣḥāb al-ḥadīth* interpret the Qurʾānic verses that seem to attribute anthropomorphic features to the Creator. In the second chapter of the second book the author had actually denied the thought that God has limbs, by refuting two of the most common explanations given by his adversaries: (i)

the limbs are either an indication of diversification in the essences, which is necessarily implied by the multiplicity of signs, or (ii) they belong to a unique essence whose parts are impossible to be distinguished from each other. The option (i) is denied thanks to a simple demonstration: if any diversification of the parts (*al-ajzāʾ*) were existent in the essence, the composition of its diversifications would demand an intervention from God, since the essence cannot do that on its own. With regard to the option (ii), the mere demonstration that the essence is unique makes the reference to its separated parts pointless.

37 'And their inference of what they had inferred about Him from the [previously] mentioned verses is that they have imposed the mutation of state (*istiḥāl al-ḥāl*) to the Creator (*al-Bārī*), be He exalted, because of His mutation from pleasure to displeasure'.

38 Qur'ān 4:31 (35). See Y. ʿAlī, *The Holy Quran: Text, Translation and Commentary* (Lahore, 1938).

39 In this regard, considering the numerous interventions that were needed to amend the text, the kind of errors that suggest a lack of familiarity in the use and/or understanding of the Arabic language on the part of the scribes, it was implied that these manuscripts were copied for educational purposes. Since they belong to a community that is renowned for their secretive approach to knowledge, we may infer that this specific text was either included in a more 'open/early-stage' programme of learning or that its content was deemed cryptic enough to be safely approached by apprentices.

SECTION IV

REVISITING NIZĀRĪ HISTORY OF ALAMŪT TIMES

8

Alamūt and Badakhshān: Newly Identified *Sargudhasht-i Sayyidnā* Manuscripts and their Background

Miklós Sárközy

The present chapter aims to throw light on 'newly' discovered versions of the so-called *Sargudhasht-i Sayyidnā*, a biography of Ḥasan-i Sabbāḥ, the founder of the Nizārī Ismaili state in Northern Iran. In this chapter I try to give a detailed analysis of the circumstances, content and context of these newly found Central Asian manuscripts.[1] First, I will attempt to situate the *Sargudhasht-i Sayyidnā* in the Persian Nizārī and non-Ismaili historiography. Furthermore, I will try to give an overview of the already known *Sargudhasht-i Sayyidnā* manuscripts possessed by The Institute of Ismaili Studies (IIS) and the Library of the Parliament of the Islamic Republic of Iran. In the second half of the chapter I will try to make a detailed analysis of the hitherto little explored and newly discovered *Sargudhasht-i Sayyidnā* texts from Ismaili populated Badakhshān, of their origin, and characteristics as well as different historical and spiritual aspects which significantly shaped the content of these *Sargudhasht-i Sayyidnā* versions.

Part I: *Sargudhasht-i Sayyidnā* and the Nizārī Historiography

Introduction: Nizārī Ismaili Historical and Doctrinal Sources of the Alamūt Period

As far as Nizārī Ismaili sources are concerned, it is a well-known fact that the number of inner-Nizārī works and other sources relating to the 160 years of the Nizārī Ismaili period is extremely limited. Due to the complete lack of administrative records, correspondence, epigraphic materials and the existence of only a very limited amount of numismatic data, the mainstay of research must rely on two main groups of Nizārī sources relating to the Alamūt period: historical chronicles and doctrinal works by Nizārī authors.

As for the historical works focusing on the history of the Alamūt period, one needs to stress the fact that none of these chronicles have survived completely. Farhad Daftary thinks that a lack of interest in historiography might have played some role in the very limited number of historical works produced in the Nizārī period. A hostile political atmosphere and unwelcoming conditions often caused the Nizārīs to live clandestinely and it should also be pointed out that they regularly practised *taqiyya* or dissimulation in order to conceal their identity, thoughts and perhaps written testimonies as well. This has resulted in the very limited number of genuine historical works, chronicles and annals throughout their history. Had they written openly about their manners, customs and the lives of their rulers, this could have endangered the very existence of the Nizārī communities.[2]

It is said that the most important Nizārī source from the early Nizārī period is the biography of Ḥasan-i Sabbāḥ, entitled *Sargudhasht-i Sayyidnā,* which is partly an official chronicle of the early decades of Ḥasan-i Sabbāḥ's rule and partly a doctrinal biography of the first *dāʿī* of Alamūt.[3] The author or authors of this work remain completely unknown, but the *Sargudhasht-i Sayyidnā* seems to be a very popular work among Nizārīs and it appears that it could have survived both as an independent text and in paraphrase among Nizārīs and Sunnis. As part of the 6th–7th/13th–14th century Īlkhānid Sunni chronicles of Kāshānī, Juwaynī and Rashīd al-Dīn, the *Sargudhasht-i Sayyidnā* could have circulated widely in the Persianate world after the fall of the Nizārī Ismaili state.

As recognised, the *Sargudhasht-i Sayyidnā* has exerted a significant influence over the study of the period of the early Nizārī Ismaili history, traces of which can be found in hitherto unpublished materials of later variants of the *Sargudhasht-i Sayyidnā* preserved in manuscripts and forming part of the Ismaili Special Collections Unit at The Institute of Ismaili Studies. The importance of the *Sargudhasht-i Sayyidnā* as a semi-historical and religious-doctrinal text within Ismaili communities from the 6th/12th century until the present appears as fascinating as aspects pertaining to its wider non-Ismaili reception in Sunni historiography as well.

Nizārī Ismaili Doctrinal Works of the Alamūt Period as Sources of Nizārī Ismaili History

As for our second group of Nizārī sources relating to the Alamūt period, non-historical Nizārī works can also be mentioned, such as the *Dīwān-i Qāʿimiyyāt*, a recently-discovered and published autochthonous Nizārī work.[4] The *Dīwān-i Qāʿimiyyāt* is a collection of *qaṣīdas* dedicated to the *Qiyāma* declaration of 559/1164 of Ḥasan *ʿalā dhikrihiʾl-salām*, an event of huge religious and political importance. Albeit a predominantly religious and literary work, the *Dīwān-i Qāʿimiyyāt* nevertheless contains fascinating historical material on Mongol-Nizārī links prior to the Mongol conquest of Alamūt in 654/1256. It is noticeable that the *Dīwān-i Qāʿimiyyāt* was also the product of the pre-1256 period similar to the *Sargudhasht-i Sayyidnā* and its later fate; its survival as an independent manuscript also shares similarities with the biography of Ḥasan-i Sabbāḥ.

Besides this work, there is another group of doctrinal sources possibly dating back to the Nizārī period (487–654/1094–1256). Among these we can mention the *Haft bāb* of Ḥasan-i Maḥmūd-i Kātib, which contains interesting material about the historical circumstances of the *Qiyāma* declaration. In addition, some aspects of the *Rawḍat al-taslīm* by the great 13th-century Iranian philosopher and politician Naṣīr al-Dīn Ṭūsī (1201–1274) are of historical importance when looking at the issue of political ideologies recurrent among Nizārī elites in their last years. Ṭūsī himself played a highly active role in Nizārī politics, and his time as an influential adviser to the last imams of Alamūt as well as a transmitter of Nizārī traditions in the early Īlkhānid period could be more significant than previously believed.

Apart from these texts, there are a few doctrinal letters in Persian attributed to Ḥasan *ʿalā dhikrihiʾl salām* (557-561/1162-1166). These documents were addressed to various high-ranking Nizārī officials in northern Iran. These texts (including a dialogue between Ḥasan *ʿalā dhikrihiʾl salām* and Dihkhudā ʿAlī Abū Shujāʿ and a letter in the name of Nūr al-Dīn Muḥammad) are thought to have been composed prior to the declaration of the *Qiyāma* in 559/1164—and while they seem authentic texts, they would benefit from more careful philological study.[5]

The *Sargudhasht-i Sayyidnā* and Persian Historiography

Though most of our medieval Sunni Persian sources show a marked enmity towards the Nizārīs, they nevertheless preserved a significant amount of valuable data re-used from these earlier Nizārī sources, none of which has survived completely however.

As is well known, the works of Rashīd al-Dīn, Juwaynī and Kāshānī all contain common elements which are either excerpts from surviving Nizārī texts or which represent recycled information. Juwaynī, Rashīd al-Dīn and Kāshānī succeeded in accessing original Nizārī Ismaili manuscripts containing the story of *Sargudhasht-i Sayyidnā*, and all of them cited it.

On the other hand, significant differences can be detected in the three versions cited by these authors. Juwaynī himself claimed to have a copy of the *Sargudhasht-i Sayyidnā* which he acquired during his visit to the fortress of Alamūt. Juwaynī, an active participant in the Mongol military campaign against the Nizārīs in 1256–1257, who was himself allowed to collect some written sources from the library of Alamūt before the latter's demolition, omitted several important parts, apparently out of his anti-Nizārī zeal or because of his pro-Īlkhānid political sympathies in his *Tārīkh-i Jahāngushāy*.[6] Meanwhile, Rashīd al-Dīn, the highly influential grand vizier of later Īlkhānid rulers showed a much more balanced view in his *Sargudhasht-i Sayyidnā* version and in general proved to be more neutral in his *Jāmiʿ al-Tawārīkh*.[7] Rashīd al-Dīn's own *Sargudhasht-i Sayyidnā* version is more balanced, which shows less hostility against the Nizārīs than the narrative of Juwaynī. He preserved events and historical facts pertaining to Ḥasan-i Sabbāḥ, allegedly deleted by Juwaynī, such as important chronological data about Ḥasan-i Sabbāḥ's visit to Egypt. He also included the legendary story of the three schoolfellows on the friendly relationship of Ḥasan-i Sabbāḥ, Niẓām al-Mulk and ʿUmar Khayyām. Furthermore, Rashīd al-Dīn retains honorific titles reserved for Ismaili political figures such as the usage of *Sayyidnā* (our lord) for Ḥasan-i Sabbāḥ, while Juwaynī does not.[8] Kāshānī, the third author to cite the *Sargudhasht-i Sayyidnā*, was originally an assistant to Rashīd al-Dīn working for the scholarly team of the great Īlkhānid statesman as a possible co-author of the famous *Jāmiʿ al-Tawārīkh*. His own chronicle, the *Zubdat al-tawārīkh*, which was rediscovered roughly sixty years ago for modern scholarship, also included the story of the *Sargudhasht-i Sayyidnā*.[9]

Sadly, none of these Īlkhānid versions of the *Sargudhasht* are extant now, but it could have been a well-known source and could have been popular since it caught the eye of these three major Īlkhānid historians. Due to the lack of Īlkhānid variants of the *Sargudhasht* it is impossible to assess the sources of the three main authors. Hence, questions such as to what extent the *Sargudhasht-i Sayyidnā* version used by Juwaynī was different from that of Rashīd al-Dīn remains an unsolved mystery, perhaps forever.

Besides the *Sargudhasht-i Sayyidnā*, there are other chronicles composed in the early Nizārī period in Northern Iran; yet all of these works perished in the post-Alamūt period with only a few excerpts surviving in the chronicles of Juwaynī, Kāshānī and Rashīd al-Dīn in the Īlkhānid period (654–735/1256–1335). One of these lost works was the so-called *Kitāb-i Buzurg Ummīd*, itself a biography of the second *dāʿī* of Alamūt, Kiyā Buzurg Ummīd (r. 518–532/1124–1138), part of which was incorporated in later Īlkhānid accounts of the Nizārīs. Another possible Nizārī chronicle could have been composed under Muḥammad b. Buzurg Ummīd (532–557/1124–1162), the third *dāʿī* of Alamūt, authored by Dihkhudā b. ʿAbd al-Malik Fashandī, fragments of which also survived in later Īlkhānid accounts. However, after Muḥammad b. Buzurg Ummīd's time, there is a lack of evidence of any court chronicles, though it is conceivable that there were later continuations of these early Nizārī sources (though none of these has survived).[10]

Apparently, Juwaynī, Rashīd al-Dīn and Kāshānī and later authors such as Ḥamd Allāh Mustawfī,[11] Ḥāfiẓ-i Ābrū[12] and others who relied on Juwaynī, Rashīd al-Dīn and Kāshānī used these perished Nizārī sources extensively, and the tenor of their writing changes noticeably when these authors have exhausted such Nizārī sources. It appears that for the early Nizārī period, up until the reign of Muḥammad b. Kiyā Buzurg Ummīd (r. 532–557/1138–1162), one relies more on Nizārī sources in the works of these later Sunni authors than for the years following this time.[13]

Sources related to contemporary Saljūq and Khwārizmian sultans also cover large parts of Nizārī history, especially episodes of their diplomatic relations and missions. The accounts of Ibn al-Athīr (d. 630/1233) on the Iranian and Syrian Nizārīs are of great importance, offering a rare insight into some otherwise unknown events. As for its importance, one can note that Ibn al-Athīr's account represents the most detailed biography of Ḥasan-i Sabbāḥ in the Classical Arabic historiography.[14]

The Tehran *Sargudhasht-i Sayyidnā*

As noted, the *Sargudhasht-i Sayyidnā* was used extensively by Sunni authors in the Īlkhānid and Timurid periods. Yet, the original manuscripts containing the text of the *Sargudhasht-i Sayyidnā* (and other Nizārī historical chronicles from the pre-1256 period) did not survive from the Alamūt or from the post-Alamūt period. Therefore the most difficult question is how to fill the long chronological gap between the 13th–15th-century *Sargudhasht-i Sayyidnā* versions of medieval Persian historiography (Juwaynī, Rashīd al-Dīn and others) and the recently discovered largely Central-Asian *Sargudhasht-i Sayyidnā* manuscripts dating back to the 19th–20th centuries.

Due to the lack of independent manuscripts before the 19th century, the transmission of *Sargudhasht-i Sayyidnā* is hardly detectable. Between the medieval Persian historiography and the modern Ismaili *Sargudhasht-i Sayyidnā* texts we know only one manuscript containing a very shortened version of the *Sargudhasht-i Sayyidnā*. This variant is from 1678, was copied in Safavid Persia, and is now in the Kitābkhāna-i Majlis-i Shūrā-yi Islāmī (Library of the Parliament of the Islamic Republic of Iran) in Tehran, Iran. The text entitled *Sargudhasht Ḥasan-i Ṣabbāḥ*, is itself part of a Persian *Majmūʿa*.[15] After a closer look, however, it appears that the Tehran *Sargudhasht-i Sayyidnā* is only a very distant relative of other *Sargudhasht-i Sayyidnā* texts. The main emphasis of the Tehran variant is on the tale of the three schoolfellows while other details of earlier *Sargudhasht-i Sayyidnā* versions are either missing or are mentioned in an extremely abbreviated form. In two aspects, however, the Tehran manuscript is similar to the later Badakhshāni *Sargudhasht-i Sayyidnā* variants. Both versions end with the conquest of Alamūt by Ḥasan-i Sabbāḥ and stop short of describing its rule; also, both versions largely focus on imaginative elements, tropes and anecdotes on Ḥasan-i Sabbāḥ and historical facts are of secondary interest.

Despite the differences and its brevity, the Tehran manuscript does somehow suggest the popularity and interest in the *Sargudhasht-i Sayyidnā* as an independent text in the Persianate world.

Part II: The *Sargudhasht-i Sayyidnā* Manuscripts at The Institute of Ismaili Studies

The fact that *Sargudhasht-i Sayyidnā* as an independent text never ceased to exist is supported by an increasing group of independent manuscripts discovered and registered in the past few years. It appears that these manuscripts all belong or once belonged to the Nizārī Ismaili communities of the Pamir area in Badakhshān and were produced either in present-day India or in Badakhshān itself. The discovery and evaluation of these manuscripts are of paramount historical importance, since these hitherto little known manuscripts not only represent the continued interest in the *Sargudhasht-i Sayyidnā* among early modern and modern Ismailis but also hint to a possibly unbroken independent *Sargudhasht-i Sayyidnā* manuscript transmission since the 13th century—although the content of these Indo-Iranian *Sargudhasht-i Sayyidnā* manuscripts has been partially transformed.

The Ismaili Special Collections Unit at the IIS currently holds no fewer than nine manuscripts of the *Sargudhasht-i Sayyidnā*. The discovery of these independent *Sargudhasht-i Sayyidnā* manuscripts also implies that this text could have been more widely circulated in the post-Alamūt period, and the existence of surviving manuscripts may question somewhat its 'discovery story' in Alamūt by Juwaynī.

Currently we can separate three groups of independent manuscripts of the *Sargudhasht-i Sayyidnā*: 1. The nine manuscripts owned by The Institute of Ismaili Studies; 2. The three Central-Asian manuscripts mentioned by Bertel's and Baqoev;[16] 3. The Tehran manuscript housed in the Kitābkhāna-i Majlis-i Shūrā-yi Islāmī.

Since late 2014, I have been engaged in the examination of the *Sargudhasht-i Sayyidnā* manuscripts forming part of the IIS collections. This task was undertaken in multiple stages. First, I worked with the digital copies of MS 162 and MS 177,[17] and then in 2016 I received and examined copies of the texts MS BT 1, MS BT 22, MS BT 103, MS BT 192, MS BT 287, and MS BT 295. In late 2020 I received digital copies of two more manuscripts (MS BA 61, MS BA 154) containing versions of the *Sargudhasht-i Sayyidnā*. These manuscripts became part of the IIS repository at different times. In all cases, I worked with digital copies of the manuscripts. All the digital copies are of very good quality, which made my evaluation work more efficient, except for MS BT 287, the deciphering of which proved little difficult due to its poorer quality.

Assessment of Manuscripts 162 and 177 of the *Sargudhasht-i Sayyidnā*

Both of these manuscripts are unpublished, catalogued and now in the possession of the IIS. It appears that these manuscripts once belonged to the Ismaili Society in Bombay. Their acquisition by the Ismaili Society could not possibly have been earlier than 1959, the year when the distinguished Ismaili scholar Wladimir Ivanow left Bombay and moved to Tehran, because Ivanow does not appear to mention these two manuscripts of the *Sargudhasht-i Sayyidnā*.[18]

The initial flyleaf of the MS 177 features the number '1961' in Gujarati numbers and this could refer to the year of its accession by the Bombay Ismaili Society after the departure of Ivanow, according to Delia Cortese who worked extensively on these manuscripts in her excellent paper.[19]

Ivanow does not mention the existence of these two manuscripts in his bibliographic survey of Ismaili literature;[20] however he does refer to another manuscript also called *Sargudhasht-i Sayyidnā* (no. 741). In his entry Ivanow describes it as a short text produced during Safavid dynasty (1501–1722 AD). In our opinion Ivanow could possibly be describing the unique Tehran manuscript of the *Sargudhasht-i Sayyidnā* (penned in 1678), which is also mentioned by Ismail K. Poonawala.[21] This Iranian *Sargudhasht-i Sayyidnā* manuscript seems to be the same as that mentioned above, now in the collection of the Kitābkhāna-i Majlis-i Shūrā-yi Islāmī (Library of the Parliament of the Islamic Republic of Iran) in Tehran, Iran.

As far as the two manuscripts of the Ismaili Society of Bombay are concerned, they were transferred to the manuscript collection of The

Institute of Ismaili Studies in London at a later time after 1977 (however, the exact date of their transfer remains unknown).

The language used by the author(s) of both manuscripts of the *Sargudhasht-i Sayyidnā* of the IIS manuscript collection is exclusively classical Persian. No other language can be identified in the text (except some Arabisms, religious terms which are very common in Classical Persian texts). As to the scripts of the two manuscripts, one can detect significant differences between them. MS 177 was written with a clearly recognisable Indian style, while MS 162 has an entirely different character to its appearance and it could have been donated to the Ismaili Society of Bombay possibly from a Central-Asian Ismaili source. Both manuscripts relate the life and deeds of the young Ḥasan-i Ṣabbāḥ (1050s–1124 AD), the famous Iranian *dāʿī* and founder of the Nizārī Ismaili State in northern Iran (in 1094 AD).

The scribe of MS 177 was a certain 'Khwāja Muʾmin' according to the colophon of the manuscript, which is dated Sunday 22 October 1916, and it was copied in Bombay (Mumbai). This manuscript has been preserved completely and has forty pages. The copyist of the second manuscript (MS 162) remains unknown; the manuscript is in a fragmentary condition, from its thirty-one pages, six (pp. 12–17) are currently missing. According to Delia Cortese MS 162 can probably be dated to the end of the 19th century.[22]

It is important to note that both manuscripts contain the same text despite the fragmentary status of MS 162. There are only minor differences, limited numbers of interpolated words between the two versions (such as the additional colophon of MS 177).

In my opinion the predecessors of the two manuscripts (or their precursors which were then copied and augmented several times) now in the IIS manuscript collection were originally composed in northern Iran as some historical events in the manuscripts suggest (mainly place names referring to the area of Rayy and Rūdbār) not found elsewhere in Rashīd al-Dīn and Juwaynī. Both manuscripts show more similarities to the version preserved by Rashīd al-Dīn than to that of Juwaynī. For instance, the tale of the three schoolfellows is a common element in these mansucripts and that of Rashīd al-Dīn while this story is completely missing from Juwaynī's variant.

As for their differences, one can see thematic and factual differences between these IIS manuscripts and the variants of Juwaynī or Rashīd al-Dīn. As far as the thematic differences are concerned, the IIS *Sargudhasht-i Sayyidnā* manuscripts are of a more imaginative character, where anecdotes, miracles, and dreams play a major role and in general there is less resemblance to a historical chronicle. The narrative of these IIS *Sargudhasht-i Sayyidnā* manuscripts is significantly shorter and ends with the conquest of Alamūt by Ḥasan-i Ṣabbāḥ not mentioning events of later decades.

As for the factual differences, apart from the occurrence of a few differing names, places as well as alternative sequences of events, there are a few more important changes in content when comparing it with Juwaynī's and Rashīd al-Dīn's versions. One of the most significant differences is that in these two IIS manuscripts Ḥasan's lineage is traced back to the fifth Shiʿi imam, Muḥammad al-Bāqir. Among the further differences one can notice the following: the residence of Ḥasan's childhood was not exactly in Rayy but a place called Muḥammad Ābād according to these two IIS manuscripts.

In these two IIS manuscripts slightly more emphasis is put on the northern Iranian areas in terms of geography: for instance the place where Ḥasan met ʿAbd al-Malik b. ʿAṭṭāsh is given as Rūdbār (a place not far from Alamūt in Rūyān) rather than Rayy (mentioned in the Sunni paraphrases); Ḥasan's relationship with ʿAbd al-Malik b. ʿAṭṭāsh is described as one of *khidmat* (servitude) rather than *nayabāt* (deputyship), an unknown position in Ismaili *daʿwa* hierarchies. Interestingly, the date given in the two IIS *Sargudhasht-i Sayyidnā* manuscripts is Rajab AH 484/September 1091, as the year of Ḥasan's takeover of Alamūt, instead of 481/1088 featured in other historical sources for this event. Otherwise, the nearly total lack of dates in the IIS manuscripts once again reinforces that the anonymous editors attempted to transform the text from a historical biography to a more religious-doctrinal one. Finally, the IIS manuscripts end with the legendary account of Ḥasan receiving news of al-Mustaʿlī's usurpation of the throne in Egypt and the arrest of his elder brother Nizār. It is important to stress that MS 162 and MS 177 are practically identical with those other seven *Sargudhasht-i Sayyidnā* manuscripts recently discovered in Tajikistan and Afghanistan.

However, in later times some further elements of Badakhshānī cultural milieu were added to the text (literary and rather non-historical notes connecting Ḥasan-i Sabbāḥ with Nāṣir-i Khusraw). It can be supposed that the spiritual awakening of the Ismailis in the late 18th century under the Qāsim-Shāhī imamate may have contributed to the popularity and the transformation of these manuscripts, all of which were produced in Badakhshān in the modern period (mainly in the 20th century). These early modern influences partly reshaped these manuscripts which both retained the core of their original medieval content, and at the same time included new chapters during the reworking process in Badakhshān. This might hint at the active role of the Ismaili communities of Badakhshān in the preservation of the two texts and the traces left by them show the active and perhaps broad usage and knowledge of the manuscripts of the *Sargudhasht-i Sayyidnā*.[23]

As far as the genre of the two manuscripts is concerned, these can be characterised as shorter historical texts, containing the biography of the young Ḥasan-i Ṣabbāḥ. In some cases, however, the two texts (which are almost completely identical) contain pseudo-historical elements, miracles, tales and visionary interpolations. These could be later additions, though it is not exactly known when and where the core of these texts was written down for the first time. These pseudo-historical elements (such as the virtues of Ḥasan-i Ṣabbāḥ, and the story of his meeting with Nāṣir-i Khusraw) are mainly of a religious character and therefore partly transform the genre of the original historical-doctrinal text into a religious-doctrinal treatise. In general, the two manuscripts can still be perceived primarily as historical sources containing, however, a significant amount of literary and religious-doctrinal elements as well.

As was noted these two manuscripts of the *Sargudhasht-i Sayyidnā* show strong similarities to the variants of the *Sargudhasht-i Sayyidnā* mentioned in Juwaynī and Rashīd al-Dīn and by other medieval Persian historians proving that all of these traditions may go back to a certain 'Urtext', which makes its discovery all the more important.[24]

A 'New' Group of *Sargudhasht-i Sayyidnā* Copies and their Importance

The other group of hitherto little known *Sargudhasht-i Sayyidnā* manuscripts originate from Central Asia in Tajikistan and Afghanistan and once belonged to local Ismailis, though the exact location (both before and after their discovery) of these new findings remain unknown to me. These manuscripts were discovered during various field trips over the last few years. Since I had no direct access to these manuscripts and could work only with the digital copies of these texts, my knowledge is limited on the circumstances of the discovery of these manuscripts (either Badakhshān of Tajikistan or Afghanistan).

Time and Homeland of the New *Sargudhasht-i Sayyidnā* Versions

According to our data there are seven 'new' manuscripts in the collection of ISCU (MS BT 1, MS BT 22, MS BT 103, MS BT 287, MS BT 295, MS BA 61, MS BA 154) containing versions of the *Sargudhasht-i Sayyidnā*, while another manuscript in the holding of the IIS (MS BT 192) contains a *qaṣīda*, which is unrelated to the other versions listed below, though it is attributed traditionally to Ḥasan-i Sabbāḥ.[25]

As for the origin of these seven *Sargudhasht-i Sayyidnā* MSS, five of them (MS BT 1, MS BT 22, MS BT 103, MS BT 287, MS BT 295) appear to originate from present-day Tajikistan, allegedly from the Ismaili populated Badakhshān autonomous area, while two other manuscripts (MS BA 61, MS BA 154) are from Badakhshān of present-day Afghanistan. Besides the Ismaili areas of Tajikistan and Afghanistan the exact location of these new findings are not known to the present author, but perhaps information about copyists can give us clues about the possible regions within Badakhhsān. As will be demonstrated later, scribes of MS BT 1, MS BT 103, and MS BT 295 are from different villages of Shughnān, but in my view this fact does not necessarily mean that the manuscripts were also held in the same village(s) where the copyist(s) was/were born or lived.

It is very probable that one or two of these little-known manuscripts had been already studied and briefly described by Bertel's and Baqoev. The two Soviet scholars mention three Ismaili works in their catalogue: one of them was called *Qiṣṣa-yi Sarguẓasht-i ḥaẓrat-i Bābā Sayyid-nā*, the second *Kitāb-i ḥaẓrat-i Bābā Sayyidnā*, while the third is *Kitāb-i aḥwālāt-i ḥaẓrat-i Bābā Sayyidnā*, titles which show close resemblance to those of MS BT 287 and MS BT 295.[26] All of this data suggests that the Badakhshānī variant of the *Sargudhasht-i Sayyidnā* could have been a well-known text among local Ismaili religious communities which could have had many more copies.

As for the chronology of these manuscripts, most of them were copied in the 20th century according to our data. Among those dated manuscripts that we have, it is MS BT 192 which appears to be the oldest one; according to our data it was completed on 28 Jumādā al-awwal 1310/17 January 1893. Others were copied in the Soviet period; MS BT 295 was completed in 1345/1926–1927 in the early Soviet period right before the official alphabet reform and the prohibition of the Arabic script in 1928 in Soviet-ruled Central Asia; MS BT 1 was copied in 1385/1965, while MS BT 103 was completed on Dhū'l-Ḥijja 1392 / January 1973. MS BT 287 lacks a date. As for the Afghanistan manuscripts, MS BA 154 was completed in Bangala of Ḥasanābād (Mumbai, India) Rabiʿ al-awwal 1328/27 March 1910. MS BA 61 lacks a date.[27]

The Manuscripts

Except for MS BA 154 which was copied in India, all the other manuscripts are of Badakhshānī origin, from either the Tajik or the Afghan part. In all cases these manuscripts are *colligatums*, i.e. these MSS were copied together with other works. The other works of these *colligatums* are sometimes well-known Ismaili spiritual works such as the *Pandiyāt-i Jawānmardī* (MS BT 1), but in some cases are lesser known *risālas* such as the *Tārīkh-i Amīr-i Sīstān* (MS BA 61)[28] or the *Nūr-nāma* (MS BA 154) among others. It is remarkable that versions of the *Tārīkh-i Amīr-i Sīstān* were copied together with the *Sargudhasht-i Sayyidnā* in not less than three of our Badakhshānī manuscripts (MS BT 103, MS BT 287, MS BA 61), the reasons for which (a possible interconnection and high status of these two texts) require further investigation in the future. It is also interesting that the copies of *Tārīkh-i Amīr-i Sīstān* always directly follow the text of the *Sargudhasht-i Sayyidnā* in these three manuscripts, raising further questions on their transmission and contextualisation. It is also important to stress that these *colligatums* were penned exclusively in Persian, and no other languages such as local Pamiri languages or Indian languages spoken or written by Ismaili communities are detected in these manuscripts. Nevertheless irregularities in the Persian orthography can be detected in some cases.

For instance, MS BT 103 appears to be a somewhat hastily copied version, where there is no colophon and there is no reference to the scribe(s) or copyist(s) of the manuscript. The style of the script seems to be a simplified *nastaʿlīq*. Certain peculiarities suggest that the copyist did not completely master the classical Persian orthography, for irregularities of the orthography are visible; some examples include: خاهد instead of خواهد, مروبانی instead of مهربانی, خذمت instead of خدمت, خاب instead of خواب. This however is an exception. This manuscript was copied into an exercise book of allegedly Soviet origin which means that it was produced in a period when the Soviet education system was introduced in Badakhshān. The fact that here, unlike in the other manuscripts, we have no basic information on the scribe, and that there are errors in the orthography, are all signs pointing to the hastiness of the copyist's work. It clearly points to the post-1928 period when the Soviet education system was gradually being established in Badakhshān and the use of the Arabic script and books written in the Arabic alphabet (in any language) were prohibited and scribes/copyists were punished by the Soviet authorities. This manuscript is an exception since it represents the clandestine copying of Ismaili texts in a period when both religious activities and books written in Persian with the Arabic alphabet became illegal in Soviet Badakhshān. This hastily copied manuscript represents the survival of knowledge of the Arabic script among some Ismaili communities in rural Badakhshān. The orthographical errors are probably the result of the unwelcoming conditions, and perhaps secretive copyist activities of Ismailis aiming at preserving their traditions. On the other hand, manuscripts copied or preserved south of river Panj in present-day Afghanistan, an area where Soviet cultural influences were limited, appear to be of higher quality, undoubtedly due to the prevalence of the Arabic script among non-Soviet ruled Ismaili areas. These manuscripts, besides maintaining a firm knowledge of Arabic script, reveal their possible Indo-Persian background due to the style of script used by the copyists.

All of these manuscripts were written in either *nastaʿlīq-i khūsh* or *nastaʿlīq* script, although the quality of the *nastaʿlīq* script often varies, as mentioned above. As for their physical appearance, they were written mostly on European paper (MS BT 1, MS BT 22, MS BT 103, MS BT 287, MS BA 154), while one, MS BA 61 (allegedly the oldest extant one) was written on Oriental paper. The number of lines varies between 11 and 16 per page in each of these manuscripts. They are simple works with no decorative elements, miniatures, or paintings that clearly suggests that they were intended for use by rural communities rather than well-to-do owners. A notable exception is MS BT 103 where the first page has a handwritten decorated character where floral motifs in black ink can be seen below the title of the text. Catchwords also vary; in some cases we find catchwords, but usually catchwords are avoided in these manuscripts. Unlike the two manuscripts analysed by Cortese, these newly identified *Sargudhasht-i Sayyidnā* variants have no stamps of ownership at all presumably for several reasons. First, in order to protect the identity of their owners, the use of stamps could have been deliberately avoided; secondly, I assume, these manuscripts may have been used by several members of these Ismaili communities implying that they were composed for a community rather than a private person. I personally think that these modern versions of the *Sargudhasht* are not entirely conceived as historical or doctrinal works by their readers or listeners, but that their complex spiritual or perhaps sacred values were more important in the eyes of Ismaili communities in Badakhshān.[29]

Copyists

As for the copyists, in some cases we do have some information on the copyists and the social status they enjoyed in local Ismaili communities. It seems to be that there is a significant difference between the social background of the copyists of the manuscripts of Tajikistan and Afghanistan. This difference was undoubtedly caused by modern political changes. The Russian, then Soviet, border divided the Ismaili communities of Badakhshān from the late 19th century. This meant that those communities who became part of the Tsarist empire and later the Soviet Union had to rely on their own scribes and copyists and their foreign contacts were limited, especially after 1922 when the Red Army reoccupied the former Tsarist areas. Copyists of the Tajikistan manuscripts do not always appear completely professional. Negative circumstances such as Soviet political repression, the prohibition of the Arabic alphabet after 1928, religious persecution as well as the closure of the border towards

Afghanistan and British-ruled India (later Pakistan) all resulted in these Soviet-ruled Ismailis being forced to rely on their own local scribes, since they were largely unable to maintain contact with Ismailis beyond the southern borders and thus the purchase of non-local manuscripts might have been nearly impossible for them. On the other hand, one of the two *Sargudhasht-i Sayyidnā* versions (MS BA 154) from present-day Afghanistan was copied in India, in Bangala of Ḥasanābād (Mumbai, India). In most cases the names of the scribes can be found in the colophon of the manuscripts.[30]

As for the identification and social background of the copyists of the Tajikistan manuscripts, in some cases we have more information at our disposal. In all cases we see that these copyists hail from local Ismaili communities, though we are not always in a position to identify the exact location of their activity. However, it is clear that these manuscripts were copied by members of local Ismaili families of Pāmirī origin (such as the area of Shughnān as it appears in some cases). Despite their Pāmirī roots, all the identifiable copyists bore Persian or Islamic Turco-Persian names, where a Persian (like *shāh*) or Turkic (such as *bik*) suffix is added to an Islamic Persian-Arabic name. In no case, including those copied in Soviet Badakhshān, can signs of Russification be detected in the names of the copyists. Obviously, these persons officially had a tripartite name corresponding to Soviet custom (first name—*otchestvo*/father's name—surname with the Russian -ev/-ov suffix) in their personal documents issued by local Soviet Tajik authorities. However, here one can see the total avoidance of these Russifying tendencies which suggests the wonderful perseverance and surviving traditionalism of these Ismaili communities that successfully resisted Sovietisation.

For instance, MS BT 1 was copied by a certain Nawrūzshāh, the son of Naẓarshāh. MS BT 103 was copied by a certain Ḥaqdād, the son of Mamadnaẓarbik (Muḥammadnaẓarbik), while MS BT 295 was copied by a Sayyid (a descendant of the Prophet Muhammad) called Shāhzādamurād and by a certain Ghulām Ḥaydar-i Shāhdawlat. MS BT 287 was copied by a certain Sayyid Nāṣir ʿAlī Shāh at the request of one of his friends, a certain Muhammad. Sayyid Nāṣir ʿAlī Shāh hails from the village of Ḥasanābād, Sarikul in China, though the place of his activity remains unknown; the manuscript comes from present-day Tajikistan. In the case of other manuscripts, we do not have available data regarding the copyists. In one case (MS BT 295) there are a few scattered marginalia, corrections or commentaries of the main text (pp. 3, 15, 28). On p. 42 of this manuscript there is a personal note on the margin written by a certain Sayyid Kāẓimzāda from a place called Qishlāq-i Kūshk who wrote in red ink and commemorated this 'good writing (*khaṭṭ-i khūb*)' of 'one hundred years ago' (along with Shiʿi blessings). This note was dated also where three types of calendars (Hijrī, Jalālī and Western: 1404/1362/1984) can be observed. The place Qishlāq-i Kūshk suggests that this manuscript was copied in the same village or community where MS BT 1 was written. There is a brief religious-poetical excerpt in this manuscript.

As for the social background of these few copyists, it is now known that the copyist of MS BT 1 Nawrūzshāh lived in the village of Kushk of Pārshinīv district of Shughnān, and he was an accomplished Ismaili *maddāh-khān* (a person reading religious blessings during ceremonies) and astronomer. As a copyist he was also very active and copied many *Bayāḍ*s that contain religious and devotional poetry. Nawrūzshāh died in the same village of Kushk some time after 1970. The copyist of MS BT 103 Ḥaqdād the son Mamadnaẓarbik lived in the village of Rāzh of Suchān in Shughnān and was a well-known *khalīfa*, i.e. a religious leader of local Ismailis. Further details of his life are unknown to me. The copyist of MS BT 295 Sayyid Shāhzādamurād was from the village called Sarāy-i Bahār of the Pārshinīv region of Shughnān and he was originally a local physician, and Ghulām Ḥaydar-i Shāhdawlat was his disciple who came originally from Rāshtqalʿa region of Shughnān.[31] All this data suggests that these persons were not only copyists but rather community leaders, distinguished local Ismailis who possibly played an active role in religious ceremonies. Therefore we can presume that these persons both copied and actively used, explained and taught these manuscripts during various private or religious occasions, though the circumstances of the usage of these texts definitely require further analysis.

As for MS BA 154, its copyist was a certain Sayyid Iʿtibār Shāh from Bangala of Ḥasanābād, Mumbai. This means that the Ismailis of present-day Afghanistan succeeded in maintaining good contacts with their coreligionists in India and unlike Soviet-ruled Ismailis, the Ismailis of Afghanistan had access to Ismaili religious literature produced in India.

The Titles

As for the titles of our Badakhshānī *Sargudhasht-i Sayyidnā* texts, there is a great variety. It is important to emphasise that these modern Ismaili manuscripts do not exclusively use the title of *Sargudhasht-i Sayyidnā*, but often prefer other titles such as *Qiṣṣa* or *Qiṣṣa-yi ahwālāt*, *Safarnāma*, *Kitāb* or a combination of these titles. Here the importance of Nāṣir Khusraw's popularity in Badakhshān can be felt which eventually could have played some role in selecting or using some of these titles. On the other hand, the title *Sargudhasht-i Sayyidnā* may also have played some role in local Ismaili written memories. For instance, there is a popular Ismaili text entitled *Sargudhasht-i Nāṣir Khusraw*. Although the analysis of the *Sargudhasht-i Nāṣir Khusraw* is beyond the scope of the present paper, this relatively late work from Badakhshān is an important tale on the legendary 11th-century Ismaili thinker. The deliberate use of the title '*Sargudhasht*' in this case is perhaps a reference to the *Sargudhasht-i Sayyidnā* in order to elevate the sacredness of the biography of Nāṣir Khusraw to the level of Ḥasan-i Sabbāḥ as represented by the *Sargudhasht-i Sayyidnā*. This all hints at the efforts of Badakhshānī Ismailis to equate the two early founding fathers of the two strongholds of Ismailis in Alamūt and in Badakhshān or at least to enhance the importance of Badakhshān as being comparable with that of Alamūt.

Content

As far as the content of these seven 'new' manuscripts is concerned, it is almost completely identical with that of MS 162 and MS 177 except a few opening and closing sentences.[32] Therefore, I will discuss here the nature of the content of the *Sargudhasht-i Sayyidnā* as it appears in MS BT 1.

The version of the *Sargudhasht-i Sayyidnā* in MS BT 1, referred to as *Kitāb-i Mustaṭāb-i Haḍrat-i Bābā Sayyidnā*, is a short treatise on the life and legends of Ḥasan-i Ṣabbāḥ. The manuscript is a *colligatum* containing different genres of Ismaili texts. On the first page before the title of our text (p. 130) a different Persian text (perhaps a last will/testament of a person) unrelated to the *Sargudhasht-i Sayyidnā* can be read, which could have been copied by the same hand, since there is no difference in the style of the script.

The text covering pp. 130-161 is a legendary and incomplete biography of Ḥasan-i Ṣabbāḥ (until his arrival to Alamūt), the founder of the Nizārī Ismaili state in 487/1094, penned by an anonymous author. The text has several parts, most of which were excerpted from famous historical and literary works relating to the life of Ḥasan-i Ṣabbāḥ.

The first part (p. 130) is written in Arabic and dedicated to the origin of Ḥasan-i Ṣabbāḥ emphasising his descent from Imam Muḥammad Bāqir.[33] The subsequent pages (pp. 131–135) are concerned with the story of Ḥasan-i Ṣabbāḥ's youth, education, his conversion to Ismailism from Twelver Shiʿism and the role of the *dāʿī* al-Aṭṭāsh. Then there is a detailed account of the so-called tale of the three schoolfellows, i.e. Ḥasan-i Ṣabbāḥ's encounters with ʿUmar Khayyām and Niẓām al-Mulk, a story of completely legendary character. This version of the three schoolfellows is very close to Rashīd al-Dīn, but none of these versions are fully identical with it. The main subject of this part is the rivalry of Ḥasan-i Ṣabbāḥ with Niẓām al-Mulk on financial issues in the court of the Saljūq ruler Malikshāh. It is important to note that apart from the lineage of Ḥasan-i Ṣabbāḥ, Ḥasan-i Ṣabbāḥ himself is the narrator of the whole text. One should note that the inner structure of this opening part shows remarkable parallels with the structure of a text found at the beginning of MS BA 61 which appears to be a variant of Luṭf Alī Bīg Ādhar's *Ātashkada,* itself a biography of Nāṣir-i Khusraw. The opening eulogies, the genealogy of Ḥasan-i Ṣabbāḥ and Nāṣir-i Khusraw and partly the later narrative appear to follow the same style in case of both texts which in general refers to a common literary attitude applied for biographies by Badakhshānī Ismailis.[34]

Pages 136–147 are dedicated to the wanderings of Ḥasan-i Ṣabbāḥ from Iran to Egypt. According to this chapter Ḥasan-i Ṣabbāḥ was a mendicant when travelling to Egypt. This chapter is also dedicated to several miraculous persons who were the envoys of Fatimid caliph al-Mustanṣir. At the beginning, Ḥasan-i Ṣabbāḥ had a dream where divine inspiration tells him to seek the truth and to leave Khurāsān. He then travels widely and joins different caravans to travel to Egypt. Another divine inspiration tells him (when he was sitting at a spring) how to find the financial means for his trip. Then one can read a longer legend about his encounter with a miraculous boy near Urūmia (a town and a salt lake in present-day northwestern Iran) whom Ḥasan-i

Ṣabbāḥ saw near a tent. Ḥasan-i Ṣabbāḥ was amazed by the divine beauty and eloquence of this child and wishes to buy him from his father. Later he follows the boy and tries to catch him jumping on the top of a tree, but he fails.[35] Eventually it becomes clear that the miraculous boy was also a messenger of the Fatimid caliph. Later Ḥasan meets an old man who is also an envoy of the caliph helping Ḥasan-i Ṣabbāḥ towards Egypt.

Pages 147–152 are dedicated to Ḥasan-i Ṣabbāḥ's journey and stay in Egypt. This part has two main subjects: first, Ḥasan-i Ṣabbāḥ's discussion with Fatimid caliph al-Mustanṣir where the Fatimid ruler informs Ḥasan-i Ṣabbāḥ that all of the miraculous envoys had been sent by him.

The text in the present version emphasises al-Mustanṣir's revelation to Ḥasan that his elder son, Nizār, would be his *bāṭin* (esoteric) heir apparent, following the Ismaili doctrine whereas his other son, Aḥmad al-Mustaʿlī would be the *ẓāhir* (exoteric) caliph. A fascinating fictive element in the narrative is that Ḥasan's encounters with al-Mustanṣir are consistently presented in the context of a dream vision (*khiyāl-ḥairān*) suggesting that Ḥasan-i Ṣabbāḥ never personally met the Fatimid ruler as noted by Cortese.[36] Further, Ḥasan-i Ṣabbāḥ meets Nāṣir-i Khusraw, the famous Ismaili philosopher and traveller; they stay in the same building and plan together to make the *ḥajj* to Mecca.

The next part (pp. 152–162) of this text focuses on Ḥasan's return to Iran from Egypt, giving a vivid and heroic description of his adventures on his sea journey. This episode is echoed, to varying degrees, in all the versions of the *Sargudhasht*. During this dangerous journey, Ḥasan converted his companions en masse to Ismailism, who were all convinced by Ḥasan's account of al-Mustanṣir's miraculous intervention. According to the version of the present text, before leaving Egypt for good, Ḥasan-i Ṣabbāḥ was arrested in a fortress of Dumyāt (Damietta), but one tower of the fortress unexpectedly collapsed—by divine intervention—where Ḥasan was incarcerated and therefore he succeeded in escaping from the hands of Amīr al-Juyūsh. Here, the text more or less follows Rashīd al-Dīn's account. Then we hear about the rivalry of the sons of the ageing al-Mustanṣir, Nizār and al-Mustaʿlī, and the plot of the Amīr al-Juyūsh (Badr al-Jamālī) and al-Mustaʿlī for power, the imprisonment of Nizār by the Amīr al-Juyūsh of Egypt after the death of Caliph al-Mustanṣir. The following episode of this text is concerned with the wanderings of Ḥasan in Iranian lands and his takeover of Alamūt. Here the narrative is enriched with folkloric elements but roughly follows historical facts about Ḥasan-i Ṣabbāḥ's dealings with a certain Mahdī, the owner of Alamūt and the role of Ra'īs Muẓaffar, the Ismaili commander of Girdkūh in buying Alamūt from Mahdī. Finally, we are informed about the arrival of Hādī, the son of Nizār to Alamūt whose identity however remains hidden before the Ismailis at his request. This element hints to the concept of the *Qiyāma* and the emergence of Nizārī Imams in 557/1162.

The text in MS BT 1 ends with an anachronistic account of Ḥasan receiving news of al-Musta'lī's usurpation of the throne in Egypt and his attempts to save the lives of Nizār and Nizār's son. All of these episodes are missing from the 'official' version of the *Sargudhasht-i Sayyidnā* of Juwaynī, Rashīd al-Dīn and Kāshānī. However, the above-mentioned IIS *Sargudhasht-i Sayyidnā* manuscripts (MS 162 and MS 177) do contain these rather ahistorical elements. Therefore, MS 162 and MS 177 represent the same Ismaili tradition preserved in the present manuscript. MSS 162 and 177 apparently seem to have a common origin with the newly identified seven manuscripts and they represent an early modern variant of the *Sargudhasht-i Sayyidnā* tradition, which was finalised either in India or Badakhshān. Authors or editors of this transformed *Sargudhasht-i Sayyidnā* variant remain completely unknown. None of our manuscripts mention them.

The Badakhshāni Milieu and its Influences on *Sargudhasht-i Sayyidnā* Versions

One of the main differences between the *Sargudhasht-i Sayyidnā* versions of Juwaynī, Rashīd al-Dīn and those of Badakhshān is the chapter on the encounter of Ḥasan-i Ṣabbāḥ with Nāṣir-i Khusraw. Apparently in these Badakhshānī *Sargudhasht-i Sayyidnā* versions Nāṣir-i Khusraw plays a significant role. Nāṣir-i Khusraw's appearance and encounter with Ḥasan-i Sabbāḥ in our manuscripts from Badakhshān are of primary importance. Of course Nāṣir-i Khusraw never met Ḥasan-i Sabbāḥ in his lifetime but in this Badakhshānī milieu where the local Ismaili adherence towards Nāṣir-i Khusraw is very strong, local Ismaili narrators may have thought it important to include Nāṣir-i Khusraw in local Ismaili literary works.

It is also a matter of debate how the local Ismailis regarded the *Sargudhasht-i Sayyidnā*? What was the genre of this text in their eyes? How can we understand the prestige of this text in Badakhshān among the Ismailis, keeping in mind that this text was used independently and not as part of a medieval Persian chronicle? For what purpose was the *Sargudhasht-i Sayyidnā* used in Badakhshān?

As for the genre of this text, in my opinion it can be characterised as a *sīra* or rather a *qiṣṣa* of Ḥasan-i Sabbāḥ, the word *qiṣṣa* (story, tale) itself being used among the titles of our texts.[37] Definitely these religious Ismaili communities regarded this short prosaic text as part of their religious education, the story of a pious man, the founder of Alamūt where the main importance was placed on the legendary story of Ḥasan-i Sabbāḥ, his heroic life and deeds which served the Ismaili community. Historical accuracy was perhaps less important in the transmission of this text where traces of compilation also appeared. This legendary and doctrinal treatment of the text in Badakhshān possibly may have allowed a transformation of the text whereby legendary elements of Nāṣir-i Khusraw as well as anecdotes, and imaginative elements became intertwined with the biographical data of Ḥasan-i Sabbāḥ at some point by an unknown editor or editors. However, the core of the text remained largely untouched, being part of an official chronicle of the life and rule of Ḥasan-i Sabbāḥ.

Despite tendencies of compilation one can exclude the possibility that the Badakhshān versions of the *Sargudhasht-i Sayyidnā* were simply extractions from a Sunni chronicle, such as Rashīd al-Dīn or a later Timurid author, because the larger part of the IIS *Sargudhasht-i Sayyidnā* texts shows different textualisation from those of Juwaynī and Rashīd al-Dīn.[38] As another proof of its independent origin, no anti-Ismaili doctrinal influences are detected in the *Sargudhasht-i Sayyidnās* of Badakhshān unlike in other contemporary Ismaili books preserved in the region.[39]

But when and how did Nāṣir-i Khusraw find his way into the *Sargudhasht-i Sayyidnā*? Daniel Beben notes that Nāṣir-i Khusraw is briefly mentioned by Rashīd al-Dīn in his *Sargudhasht-i Sayyidnā* version as a forerunner of Ḥasan-i Sabbāḥ while the versions in Juwaynī and Kāshānī do not mention Nāṣir-i Khusraw at all.[40] Apart from this sole mention there is no chapter dedicated to Nāṣir-i Khusraw in the pre-Badakhshānī versions of the *Sargudhasht-i Sayyidnā*.

It appears that in the pre-Badakhshānī versions of the *Sargudhasht-i Sayyidnā* Nāṣir-i Khusraw was a rather marginal figure. In Juwaynī there is no occurrence of Nāṣir-i Khusraw, while in the *Sargudhasht-i Sayyidnā* variant preserved by Rashīd al-Dīn he is briefly mentioned at one point in the narrative,[41] and the apocryphal alliance and encounter of Ḥasan-i Sabbāḥ and Nāṣir-i Khusraw in Egypt is not mentioned (the visit of Nāṣir-i Khusraw to Cairo in 1052 itself predates by twenty-five years than that of Ḥasan-i Sabbāḥ). On the other hand in the early modern period, approximately since the 16th century signs of an emerging folkloric tale appears in several Ismaili works, where the legendary (and fictional) encounter of Ḥasan-i Sabbāḥ and Nāṣir-i Khusraw appears.

It is perhaps the non-Ismaili 16th-century work entitled *Khulāṣat al-ashʿār* and the 17th-century non-Ismaili work *Dabistān-i madhāhib* which refer for the first time to the encounter between Nāṣir-i Khusraw and Ḥasan-i Sabbāḥ. The first genuine Ismaili work to mention the meeting of Nāṣir-i Khusraw and Ḥasan-i Sabbāḥ is the *Kalām-i pīr*, a work of great importance and with a complicated origin in light of the recent researches of Daniel Beben.[42] According to Beben the *Kalām-i pīr* or parts of it were written much later than had been thought by Ivanow, and the so-called *Sargudhasht-i Nāṣir-i Khusraw*, an 18th-century Ismaili treatise on the life of Nāṣir-i Khusraw, could have heavily influenced the *Kalām-i pīr*.[43] In the *Kalām-i pīr* Nāṣir-i Khusraw encounters Ḥasan-i Sabbāḥ first in Alamūt and recognises him as his true teacher. Then the two travel to Egypt to the court of Fatimid caliph al-Mustanṣir, where the caliph assigned Nāṣir-i Khusraw as the *ḥujjat* of the *daʿwa* in Badakhshān, and sent him to Badakhshān to spread Ismailism.[44] Thus, the *Kalām-i pīr* represents the first hagiographic attempt to create a connection between Nāṣir-i Khusraw and Ḥasan-i Sabbāḥ. In the case of the *Kalām-i pīr* the emphasis is put on Ḥasan-i Sabbāḥ as a master of Nāṣir-i Khusraw while in our newly identified Badakhshāni *Sargudhasht-i Sayyidnā* versions it is Ḥasan-i Sabbāḥ who becomes the pupil of Nāṣir-i Khusraw and follows his advice.

Similar tendencies can be detected in several 18th-century Ismaili works such as the *Silk-i guhar-rīz*[45] or the *Baḥr al-akhbār* where the story of the apocryphal relationship of Nāṣir-i Khusraw and Ḥasan-i Sabbāḥ was further developed. In these texts the encounter of Nāṣir-i

Khusraw and Ḥasan-i Sabbāḥ is depicted in a more elaborate form, where the two persons are depicted as disciples of al-Mustanṣir, and the two founding fathers of two important strongholds of the Ismaili *daʿwa*: Daylamān and Badakhshān. These texts clearly put forward the idea of twin pillars of Ismaili missionary activity, where the merits of Nāṣir-i Khusraw are equal or slightly superior to those of Ḥasan-i Sabbāḥ. The same story can be found in our *Sargudhasht-i Sayyidnā* variants as well on the encounter and missionary activity of Nāṣir-i Khusraw and Ḥasan-i Sabbāḥ. Therefore our manuscripts have ties to the circle of this newly identified Badakhshānī Ismaili religious literature, as represented by the *Sargudhasht-i Nāṣir-i Khusraw*, the *Kalām-i pīr*, the *Silk-i guhar-rīz*, and the *Bahr al-akhbār*. In all cases the adherence to Nāṣir-i Khusraw is very strong and Nāṣir-i Khusraw is regarded equal or perhaps superior to Ḥasan-i Sabbāḥ.[46]

The Qāsim-Shāhī Renaissance and Badakhshānī Ismaili Literature

The earliest dated *Sargudhasht-i Nāṣir-i Khusraw* manuscript is 1144/1731–1732 implying that all the other works where the transformation of the Nāṣir-i Khusraw myth can be found, were composed or reworked after the early decades of the 18th century. However, it is also important to address the question of the reasons for the intensified Nāṣir-i Khusraw cult in Badakhshān. Is there any reason behind these new works allegedly composed or rewritten in the 18th century? Beben believes that the emergence of the Qāsim-Shāhī branch of the Nizārī Ismaili imamate could have been behind this literary activity. After centuries of suppression the Nizārī Ismaili movement under the leadership of the Qāsim-Shāhī imams became successfully reorganised in post-Safavid Persia during the Afshārid, Zand and Qājār dynasties. Beben suggests that the Qāsim-Shāhī imams, in order to exert a more unified religious influence over their Badakhshānī followers tried to promote the revived adherence toward Nāṣir-i Khusraw.

While the merits of Nāṣir-i Khusraw as the founding founder of the Ismaili community in Badakhshān in the 11th century cannot be denied, however the second half of the 18th century coincides with Qāsim-Shāhī efforts to reassert their authority in Badakhshān. These attempts in strengthening the Qāsim-Shāhī branch of the Nizārī Ismaili imams (as opposed to the declining Muḥammad-Shāhī branch in the 18th century) sought to canonise the myth of Nāṣir-i Khusraw. The selection of perhaps the most popular local Ismaili holy man, as well as the founder of the first ever Ismaili communities in Badakhshān was a careful decision to appeal to local Ismailis and to further their religious-political allegiance for the Qāsim-Shāhī *daʿwa* in Badakhshān. This Qāsim-Shāhī missionary activity resulted in producing new literary works, according to Beben, who thinks the eminent Ismaili treatises such as *Kalām-i pīr*, *Sargudhasht-i Nāṣir Khusraw* or *Silk-i guhar-rīz* were all the literary products of this Qāsim-Shāhī literary renaissance in Badakhshān before and after 1800. Beben claims that the possibly earliest copy of the transformed versions of *Sargudhasht-i Sayyidnā* dates back to the end of the 18th century.[47] In this regard, the revised version of the *Sargudhasht-i Sayyidnā* with its lengthy chapter dedicated to Nāṣir-i Khusraw (and his encounter with Ḥasan-i Sabbāḥ) could have been produced in the same period before 1800. The author or authors of this re-editing activity, however, remain unknown. Details of these Qāsim-Shāhī textualisation and canonisation activities as well as the early reception history of these new texts are not yet well understood but these decades appear to have significantly contributed to the enrichment of the Nizārī Ismaili literary tradition. The new Qāsim-Shāhī *Sargudhasht-i Sayyidnā* variants represent this new and promising age of the Nizārī Ismailis under the Qāsim-Shāhī imamate.

Conclusion and Future Prospects

The identification of the nine *Sargudhasht-i Sayyidnā* versions is a very important step which has several promising consequences. The extraordinary fact of the rediscovery of independent *Sargudhasht-i Sayyidnā* texts further helps Ismaili-related research in the field of Ismaili written heritage especially in the Alamūt period which is not too well represented in terms of extant Ismaili sources, as we know. It appears that the *Sargudhasht-i Sayyidnā* was a relatively popular text among Central-Asian Ismailis in modern times as was attested by its numerous copies. These little-known manuscripts shed an important light on the *Sargudhasht-i Sayyidnā* transmission in the past two centuries and the eminent role Ismailis living in Badakhshān and India played in its survival.

Unlike other Ismaili works penned in Badakhshān in the early modern period, the *Sargudhasht-i Sayyidnā* is, however, much older, the origins of which go back to the Alamūt period. These newly identified variants of the *Sargudhasht-i Sayyidnā*, however are of a more doctrinal or religious character, where anecdotes, miracles, and fictive stories are intertwined with inherited older historical materials. The local Badakhshāni milieu also exerted a remarkable influence on the content of these manuscripts, with the re-emerging popularity of Nāṣir-i Khusraw in Badakhshān allegedly introduced by the Qāsim-Shāhī imamate in the late 18th century which partly transformed the content of the *Sargudhasht-i Sayyidnā*.

However, it would be fascinating to know more about the older manuscripts. When and where were the oldest *Sargudhasht-i Sayyidnā* versions copied? Is there any trace of *Sargudhasht-i Sayyidnā* copies before the 19th century or perhaps before the late 18th century? Also, we need to have a better understanding of the role the *Sargudhasht-i Sayyidnā* may have played among local Ismailis of Badakhshān; what type of status it enjoyed among local Ismailis; how its content was treated during religious or non-religious ceremonies, and festivals. Another important aspect of future *Sargudhasht-i Sayyidnā* related research is the relationship this text maintained with other religious Ismaili works, some of them little known, especially those copied together with the *Sargudhasht-i Sayyidnā* in our manuscripts. All these new discoveries hopefully will pave the way for more research on the history of the Ismaili written heritage in the forthcoming decades.

NOTES

1 I would like to express my deepest gratitude to Wafi Momin, Nourmamadcho Nourmamadchoev and their colleagues in the Ismaili Special Collections Unit (ISCU) at the IIS for their immense help and for sharing copies of manuscripts with me.

2 Farhad Daftary, 'Persian Historiography of the Early Nizārī Ismailis', *Iran*, 30 (1992), p. 91.

3 Ibid., p. 96.

4 Ḥasan Maḥmūd Kātib, *Dīwān-i Qā'imiyyāt*, ed., S. J. Badakhchani (Tehran, 2011).

5 See Persian MS 32, f. 42r and a fragment from an uncatalogued Persian manuscript, ff. 39–40. These two texts along with a brief prayer entitled *Du'ā dar hangām-i shab*, attributed to Kiyā Buzurg Ummīd, are held in the manuscript collection of The Institute of Ismaili Studies; see D. Cortese, *Eschatology and Power in Mediaeval Persian Ismailism*

(PhD Dissertation, School of Oriental and African Studies, 1993), pp. 141–142, 161 nos. 57–58.

6 ʿAṭā Malik Juwaynī, *Tārīkh-i Jahān-gushāy*, ed., M. Qazwīnī (Leiden and London, 1912–1937), vol. 3, pp. 186–216, 269–273.

7 Rashīd al-Dīn Faḍl Allāh, *Jāmi ʿal-Tawārīkh: Qismat-i Ismaʿiliyān*, ed. M. T. Dānishpazhūh and M. Mudarrisi-Zanjānī (Tehran, 1338 Sh./1959), pp. 97–137, 149–53.

8 H. Bowen, 'The *Sar-gudhasht-i sayyidnā*, "The Tale of the Three Schoolfellows" and the *Wasaya* of the Niẓām al-Mulk', *Journal of the Royal Asiatic Society*, 4 (1931), pp. 771–782.

9 Abū'l-Qāsim ʿAbd Allāh b. ʿAlī Kāshānī, *Zubdat al-tawārīkh: Bakhsh-i Fātimiyān wa Nizāriyān*, ed., M. T. Dānishpazūh (Tehran, 1366 S/1987), pp. 133–172, 186–190.

10 F. Daftary, *Ismaili Literature: A Bibliography of Sources and Studies* (London and New York, 2004), pp. 46–48.

11 Ḥamd Allāh Mustawfī, *Tārīkh-i Guzīda*, ed. ʿAbd al-Ḥusayn Nawāʾī (Tehran, 1339 Sh./1960), pp. 445–446, 518–521.

12 ʿAbd Allāh Ḥāfiẓ Ābrū, *Majmaʿ al-tawārīkh al-sulṭāniya: qismat-i khulafā-yi ʿAlawiya-yi Maghrib wa Miṣr wa Nizāriyān*, ed., M. Mudarrisī-Zanjānī (Tehran, 1364 Sh./1985), pp. 191–226.

13 Daftary, 'Persian Historiography of the Early Nizārī Ismailis', pp. 95–97.

14 C. Hillenbrand, 'A Neglected Source on the Life of Hasan-i Sabbah, the Founder of the Nizari "Assassin" Sect', *Iran*, 55 (2017), p. 3.

15 A copy of this manuscript was accessed by me in late 2014 by the courtesy of the late Mohsen Jaʿfari-Madhab, an excellent Iranian scholar and a manuscript expert of the National Library of Iran whose sudden and tragic death in 2017 is regretted by all manuscript experts in the field of Iranian studies. Details of the Tehran *Sargudhasht-i Sayyidnā* manuscript are: *Majmūʿa* no. 901, 54; total leaves 387; the *Sargudhasht-i Sayyidnā* runs from leaf 199 to 223.

16 A. Bertel's and M. Baqoev, *Alphabetic Catalogue of Manuscripts Found by 1959–1963 Expedition in Gorno-Badakhshān Autonomous Region* (Moscow, 1967), nos. 175, 176, 177, pp. 75–76. As we will see at least one of the manuscripts held by the IIS may be identical to one of the three manuscripts accessed and described by Bertel's and Baqoev.

17 Both manuscripts are catalogued in the IIS; their catalogue numbers are Persian MS 162 and MS 177. Neither of the two IIS manuscripts of the *Sargudhasht-i Sayyidnā* has been published so far. The only major secondary source to assess their origin and problems was penned by Delia Cortese; see her 'Lost and Found: The *Sargudhasht-i Sayyid-nā*. Facts and Fiction of Ḥasan-i Ṣabbāḥ's Travel to Egypt vis-à-vis the Political and Intellectual Life of 5th/11th Century Fatimid Cairo,' in Eva Orthmann and Petra G. Schmidle, ed., *Science in the City of Fortune: The Dustūr al-Munajjimīn and its World* (Berlin, 2017), pp. 201–203.

18 Cortese, 'Lost and Found: The *Sargudhasht-i Sayyid-nā*', p. 202.

19 Ibid.

20 W. Ivanow, *Ismaili Literature: A Bibliographical Survey* (Tehran, 1963), p. 741.

21 I. K. Poonawala, *Biobibliography of Ismāʿīlī Literature* (Malibu, 1977), p. 253.

22 Cortese, 'Lost and Found: The *Sargudhasht-i Sayyid-nā*', p. 201. n. 6.

23 See further below.

24 For the parallels and similarities between the IIS *Sargudhasht-i Sayyidnā* manuscripts and the accounts of Juwaynī and Rashīd al-Dīn, see Cortese, 'Lost and Found: The *Sargudhasht-i Sayyid-nā*', pp. 204–205.

25 This *qaṣīda*, traditionally attributed to Ḥasan-i Sabbāḥ, was copied on Saturday 28 Jumāda al-Awwal 1310/1894–1895 and consists of fifty lines (14 couplets); two odes attributed to Nāṣir-i Khusraw are recorded after this text.

26 Bertel's and Baqoev, *Alphabetic Catalogue of Manuscripts*, pp. 75–76.

27 According to the information provided to me, the undated MS BA 61 is identical with the one mentioned by Daniel Beben in his dissertation; see D. Beben *The Legendary Biographies of Nāṣir-i Khusraw: Memory and Textualization in Early Modern Persian Ismaiʿilism* (PhD dissertation, Indiana University, 2015), p. 364. n. 38. Beben found this *Sargudhasht-i Sayyidnā* manuscript in the archives of Khorog Research Unit, IIS with catalogue number: n. 66. Its title is *Aḥwālāt-i Haḍrat-i Bābā Sayyidnā*. This manuscript is undated according to Beben but besides the *Sargudhasht-i Sayyidnā* manuscript it contains a pseudo-biography of Nāṣir-i Khusraw which is an excerpt from the *Ātashkada* of a certain Luṭf ʿAlī Bīg Ādhar at the beginning of the manuscript (the structure of this text shows interesting textual parallels in its opening parts with our Badakhshānī *Sargudhasht-i Sayyidnā* texts). Beben believes the manuscript was copied in the late 18th century or somewhat later which, if it proves to be true, makes this the hitherto earliest Badakhshānī variant of the *Sargudhasht-i Sayyidnā* manuscripts. The present author expresses his gratitude to Dr. Daniel Beben for his support in the present research by sharing his doctoral dissertation and other papers.

28 The unpublished *Tārīkh-i Amīr-i Sīstān* written by an unknown author is a little-known Ismaili source allegedly dating back to the Alamūt period which also contains fascinating material for the study of pre-1256 Nizārī Ismaili history. The still unpublished text was kindly made accessible to me by Shafique Virani whose generosity is much appreciated here.

29 This phenomenon, a rather complex doctrinal-religious Badakhshānī attitude with remarkable Sunni and Sufi influences is also strengthened by Beben's recent paper on modern Badakhshānī Ismaili religiosity and its Sufi connections. See D. Beben, 'Aḥmad Yasavī and the Ismāʿīlīs of Badakhshān: Towards a New Social History of Sufi–Shīʿī Relations in Central Asia', *Journal of the Economic and Social History of the Orient*, 63 (2020), pp. 643–681.

30 I received these biographical details through the courtesy of ISCU.

31 I am grateful to ISCU for supplying information on these matters.

32 Its inner title is half-Arabic-half-Persian, MS BT 1, p. 130: هدا کتاب مسطتاب احوالات حضرت بابا سیدنا . . . .

33 MS BT 1, p. 131: از نسل محمد باقر

34 See fn. 27.

35 A somewhat entertaining excerpt from the text MS BT 1, p. 143: و خود را بر آن درخت چسپانیدم بر زحمت تمام بر آن فراز آن درخت برآمدم و رفتم جائی که همان طفل بود

36 Cortese, 'Lost and Found: The *Sargudhasht-i Sayyid-nā* ', pp. 207–208.

37 The term *qiṣṣa* occurs in one case as part of the title of our *Sargudhasht-i Sayyidnā* texts (MS BT 287), but other works copied together with the *Sargudhasht-i Sayyidnā* are also called occasionally *qiṣṣas*. For instance the so-called *Qiṣṣa-yi chihil tanan* (The Story of Forty Persons) in MS BT 103, or the *Qiṣṣa-i dukhtar-i Shaykh Manṣūri Ḥallāj* (The story of Shaykh Manṣūri Ḥallāj's Daughter) in MS BT 295.

38 In order to compare a medieval variant of the *Sargudhasht-i Sayyidnā* and a Badakhshānī variant, I copy here Rashīd al-Dīn's version and a variant of MS BT 1 on the departure of the Alawite Mahdī from Alamūt, the former owner of Alamūt. In Rashīd al-Dīn we read: بعد از مدتی الحال به دامغان افتاد. آن برات امتحان را پیش رئیس مظفر برد. در حال خط ببوسید و زر بداد. ; see Rashīd al-Dīn Faḍlallāh, *Jāmiʿ al-tawārīkh: Qismat-i Ismaʿiliyān*, ed., M. Rawshan (Tehran, 1387/2008), p. 104. Meanwhile in MS BT 1, on p. 160 we read: بعد لا علاج شده علوی مهدی از قلعه الموت رفت به سمت گردکوه دامغان و سه هزار طلا را از رئیس مظفر گرفته.
It is clear that the content of the two sentences is almost the same, but the textualisation is different.

39 For traces of anti-Ismaili tendencies found in Badakhshānī Ismaili literature, see Beben, *The Legendary Biographies of Nāṣir-i Khusraw*, p. 323. n. 43.

40 Ibid., pp. 123–124.

41 Rashīd al-Dīn, *Jāmiʿ al-tawārīkh: Qismat-i Ismaʿiliyān*, ed., M. Rawshan, p. 98.

42 D. Beben, 'The *Kalām-i Pīr* and its Place in the Central Asian Ismaili Tradition', *Journal of Islamic Studies*, 31 (2020), pp. 93–95.

43 Ibid., pp. 90, 98.

44 A similar statement is found in the Badakshānī *Sargudhasht-i* Sayyidnā, for instance, in MS BA 154 f. 220. :سید ناصر تو را حجت جزائر خراسان و بدخشان نمودم

45 I had the opportunity to come across the text of the *Silk-i guharriz* by courtesy of Nourmamadcho Nourmamadchoev.

46 For the importance of Nāṣir-i Khusraw in the above mentioned Badakhshānī works, see Beben, *The Legendary Biographies of Nāṣir-i Khusraw*, pp. 357–365.

47 Beben 'The *Kalām-i Pīr* and its Place', pp. 89–90, 96; for the importance of the Qāsim-Shāhī imams and their influence on Badakhshān in the 18th–19th centuries, see pp. 98–99.

9

ʿ*Ahd-i Sayyidnā*, a Newly Discovered Treatise on the Consolidation of the Nizārī *Daʿwa* in Alamūt

Karim Javan

Introducing the Text

During my evaluation of a manuscript from Badakhshān, I came across a text which contained detailed information about the early confrontation of Nizārī Ismailis with the Saljūq armies in Alamūt. It covers the early years of Nizārī *daʿwa* after the seizure of Alamūt castle by Ḥasan-i Ṣabbāḥ (d. 518/1124), or 'Sayyidnā', as he is referred to here, in 483/1090 and the following periods of siege by the Saljūq sultan, Muḥammad Tapar (d. 511/1117). The text has no title, but for ease of reference we will refer to it here as 'ʿ*Ahd-i Sayyidnā*' ('the covenant of Sayyidnā'), since the main reason for writing it was to remind a friend of the *ʿahd* of Sayyidnā Ḥasan-i Ṣabbāh. The reference to Nāṣir al-Dīn Muḥtasham (r. 626–654/1228–1256) as the *Shahanshāh-i mashriqī* ('The King of the East') at the end of the work indicates that the work was written when he was ruling Quhistān during the reign of Imam ʿAlāʾ al-Dīn Muḥammad (d. 653/1255) in Alamūt. The *ʿAhd-i Sayyidnā* is a short treatise written for a friend who had been subject to some kind of disciplinary ruling by Nāṣir al-Dīn Muḥtasham so that he would endure the ruling faithfully. The identity of both the author and his friend is unknown to us.

By introducing this newly discovered text, this chapter aims to explain in what way this text can expand our knowledge of the Nizārī community during the most challenging period of its formation after the seizure of Alamūt castle in 483/1090. Before presenting a summary of its content which contains historical as well as doctrinal topics, different manuscript versions of this work will be introduced, and then the question of its authorship will be discussed. Since the author is not known to us, using different indications and references within the text and the available literature of the period, the possible author will be introduced.

Manuscripts of the *ʿAhd-i Sayyidnā*

There are three known manuscripts of this text in the manuscript collections of The Institute of Ismaili Studies. The text has major differences in each of these manuscripts. Among these three manuscripts, only one of them has the full text and the rest include parts of the text. The complete version of the text is in a manuscript from Badakhshān, MS BT 9, with miscellaneous contents, in which different texts follow each other without any clear indication that a new text has started. Therefore, the beginning of the text of *ʿAhd-i Sayyidnā* is not quite clear. However, the context of the text indicates a general logical flow, which has been instrumental in identifying the beginning.

The second manuscript, MS BA 59, lacks the beginning, but it presents the most reliable version of the text. The final copy, MS BA 46, includes only short passages of this text. The detailed differences of our three manuscript copies will be discussed after reviewing the content of the work. But, it is important to introduce the manuscript copies before going into the discussion of the content.

MS BT 9

The first manuscript that has the full text of the *ʿAhd* comes from Badakhshān. It is written in black *nastaʿlīq* on Western paper and is bound in a soft brown leather cover. It contains 197 folios and 20 titles in total. The text of the *ʿAhd* starts from f. 93a and ends at f. 125b. According to the colophon on the final page of the manuscript, the completion date seems to be Monday, Rajab 1119/1707. However, there are some ambiguities in the reading of the date. There is a big gap between 119 and a '3' on top of the word '*sana*' which could also be read 1193/1779. However, there are some other notes on the margins of f. 6a that record different dates regarding the birth or the death of certain individuals that have dates earlier than 1193, which cannot be possible. Most of these dates are in three digits such as 114, 118 or 119. Therefore, it is possible that number 3 stands for the day, and 119 is in fact a short form of 1119/1707. This is more likely as the rest of the dates in full format on the same page show 1110, 1114 and 1132, which are in the same hand as the rest of the manuscript. Therefore, these notes could not have been written decades before the completion of the manuscript, and 1119/1707 should be the correct date.

MS BA 59

The second version of the text is within another *majmūʿa* which is written in black *nastaʿlīq* and bound in a brown leather cover, containing 174 folios in total. The text of the *ʿAhd* is between fr. 714 and fr. 721.[1] There are two colophons in this manuscript with two different dates. The first colophon is on fr. 810 which records the date as Friday 12 Rabīʿ al-Awwal 875/8 September 1470. The other colophon is at the end of the manuscript and carries the date of Rabīʿ al-Awwal 1293/ April 1876. Both colophons are in the same handwriting which belongs to the copyist Tashrīf Khudā b. Muḥammad Lāyiq. There is a four-century gap between these two dates which is confusing. The only possible resolution of this discrepancy is to consider the first date as part of the colophon in the original source that this manuscript was copied from, and the second the actual colophon in this manuscript which contains the correct date.

MS BA 46

The third copy only records a fragment of this story. This copy is part of a large *majmūʿa* that contains over 300 folios. Only four folios of this manuscript contain parts of the account of the *ʿAhd*, starting from p. 65 to p. 69. The actual manuscript was not available to me for close examination, but based on the available digital copy, this manuscript seems to be formed of a number of manuscripts from various time periods attached together. It is in different hands and folio sizes, but a big section in which our text is included is written in black *nastaʿlīq* with an average of 12 lines per page. The name of the copyist is mentioned as Mullā Mīr Ḥasan b. ʿAbd al-Fayḍ. The date is written in a confusing way, but based on my best judgement it should be Muḥarram 1121/March 1709.[2]

The Content of the *ʿAhd-i Sayyidnā*

According to the only copy that contains the full account of the *risāla,* the source of the account of the *ʿAhd* is a letter by Raʾīs Muẓaffar (ʿImād Allāh wa al-Dīn Muẓaffar b. ʿAlī b. Muḥammad), sent to Quhistān, in which he had recorded the conversations between Raʾīs Abū al-Faḍl and Ḥasan-i Ṣabbāḥ based on the account of Raʾīs Abū al-Faḍl himself (*bar sabīl-i istishhād*). There were two Raʾīs Muẓaffars who flourished during the Alamūt period and therefore the identity of this particular one is not quite clear. However, according to the *kunya* of ʿImād al-Dīn, he should be the Ismaili *dāʿī* and the vizier of ʿAlāʾ al-Dīn Muḥammad (r. 618 to 652/1221 to 1255) whom Nasawī, the historian and Khwārazm-shāhī official, met in Alamūt in 626/1228.[3] The author explains the source of the *ʿAhd* as follows:

> As Mawlānā had ordered [Sayyidnā] to proselytise first Raʾīs-i Iṣfahānī, he came first to Iṣfahān. During this time, Raʾīs Abū al-Barakāt Tāj al-Dīn Abū al-Faḍl, May he be graced in compassion, was the head of [taxation] of Iṣfahān. He had expressed these blessed words in testimony, based on what was mentioned before, ʿImād Allāḥ wa al-Dīn Muẓaffar b. ʿAlī b. Muḥammad Amīr had written in a letter and a copy was sent to the *mustajīb*s of Quhistān.[4]

The circumstances in which this letter was sent to Quhistān is not explained in our text.

Based on this copy, the following topics are the order of discussions in the text:

Waʿda-hā *and Predictions of Mawlānā*

As was said before, the beginning of the *ʿAhd* is not marked. The only way to identify the beginning is the change in the rhetoric and the theme of the text. Judging by the course of discussions and themes in MS BT 9, the beginning of the text should be where the previous text ends with the concluding prayer of '*bi-ḥaqq-i muḥammad wa āl-i muḥammad*', and a new sentence begins by addressing the fellow faithful brothers (*barādarān-i dīn wa dūstān-i ahl-i yaqīn*). It starts with explaining the reasons for different seditions (*fitna-hā*) and upheavals that were happening in various parts of the world during the life of the author. To his view, these seditions are the predictions (*waʿda-hā*) of '*Mawlānā Malik al-Salām*', which occur when people do not follow the orders of God. He believes that disobedience leads to spiritual disease which needs to be cured. Similar to physical disease, spiritual disease also requires undesirable and bitter medicines to be cured. This introduction is clearly laid out according to the situation of the author's friend who was subject to an undesirable ruling in Quhistān. He wants to remind him that the hardship in people's life is a result of their own actions and disobedience.

Proselytising Raʾīs Abū al-Faḍl

The account of the '*Ahd*-i *Sayyidnā* and the meaning of the 'covenant' comes right after this introduction. Following the previous argument on the need for curing spiritual disease, the author recalls the hardship of the Nizārīs at the time of Ḥasan-i Ṣabbāḥ and the way they overcame the hardship. This '*ahd* is explained in the form of a story in which Sayyidnā set out the conditions for his few followers at the beginning of his *daʿwa* in the fortress of Alamūt, and the way they confirmed their allegiance to the conditions.

According to this account, after returning from Egypt in 473/1080, Sayyidnā goes to Iṣfahān and proselytises Raʾīs Abū al-Faḍl to the Ismaili faith. There is a detailed account of the discussions and theological debates between the two before Raʾīs Abū al-Faḍl's conversion to the Ismaili faith. Finally, it explains how Raʾīs Abū al-Faḍl took refuge in Alamūt after his association with the Nizārīs and Ḥasan-i Ṣabbāḥ was revealed to Muḥammad Tapar, the Saljūq Sultan.[5] According to this account, he came to Alamūt secretly accompanied by a servant, travelling by night. In this account, when Sayyidnā noticed Raʾīs had left all his wealth behind and came to Alamūt disguised as a Sufi, he asked him:

> What has happened to Raʾīs, and what has been the reason for you to come here in this way? Raʾīs cried heartily and said: I have come here in the hope that Sayyidnā with his grace and kindness

> forgive me for my wrong thoughts of his character in the past, so that Mawlānā may not hold me responsible hereafter for that.[6]

This is a reference to the episode in Sayyidnā's *Sargudhasht* in which Ra'īs Abū al-Faḍl cast some doubts on Sayyidnā's mental health during their conversation in his house in Iṣfahān, when Sayyidnā expressed his thought to give the Saljūq Sultan and his vizier a hard lesson if he could find two true friends.[7]

The ultimate fate of Ra'īs Abū al-Faḍl's family members who were executed and burnt in his house in Iṣfahān is also something that only we find in the account of this *risāla*. It also records the death of Ra'īs at Alamūt during the siege by the armies of Sultan Muḥammad Tapar.

Life during the Blockade

The hardship of Ra'īs Abū al-Faḍl in Alamūt in his old age and his help to the *da'wa* is carefully highlighted here in order to make the point of personal sacrifice more clearly to the author's friend. The story of the early struggles of the Nizārīs in Alamūt and the way Sayyidnā encouraged his few followers to hold on to their positions is the central point of the *'Ahd*. Rashīd al-Dīn has also a brief account of those conditions in his history.[8] However, the *'Ahd* presents a detailed eye-witness account of Ra'īs Abū al-Faḍl's life during this period in Alamūt which is a good illustration of the hard conditions that the Nizārīs were living in. This information cannot be found in any other source. In the historiographical tradition of this age, the daily life of ordinary people is rarely reflected as it generally focuses on political and military aspects. From this point of view the information of this text seems more valuable. As an example, in one of the passages of the story we read:

> Sayyidnā—*qaddasa allāh rūḥahū*—ordered the rooms of the fortress to be divided into two/three meters (*gaz*) and five/six meters for the Rafīqs. And because Ra'īs was wealthy, old and fragile, [Sayyidnā] ordered an entire room to be left for him, and designated a man with daily rations to take care of him. Ra'īs wept in complaint saying: 'kindly tell [Sayyidnā] that I have not come from Iṣfahān to blockade Sayyidnā and his people (*jamā'at*). It is obvious how much space each person can have in this fortress. Were I to occupy a room solely for myself, I would

> impose a blockade on everybody. And [on the issue of] the man assigned to my care, I take refuge in God from having a servant of Mawlānā in my service with Mawlānā's cost of food and clothes. If I do this, I will be Mawlānā's antagonist and not his servant. I expect that my space should be the same as others. Since I am old and weak, and cannot do much work, I would like to be assigned to caring for patients, the sick and those who have nobody to care for them, so that I can provide them with drink or water.[9]

The account goes into more details about how he took part in breaking rocks and carrying bricks and timbers to the fortress with the others. The astonishing episode of the story is where it explains how Ra'īs Abū al-Faḍl did not eat a portion of his ration of walnuts, and instead planted them at the bottom of Alamūt fortress, where the walnut trees were still standing at the time of writing the text.

Ḥasan-i Ṣabbāḥ's Letter to Malikshāh

Right in the middle of the story of Ra'īs Abū al-Faḍl, there are two separate accounts in MS BT 9 that do not exist in the other copies. One of them is the letter of Ḥasan-i Ṣabbāḥ to Malikshāh and the other is the story of threatening Sultan Sanjar in his resting place. Based on our knowledge, the letter to Malikshāh was quoted for the first time in the *Majālis al-mu'minīn* of Qāḍī Nūr Allāh Shūshtarī (d. 1019/1610).[10] Although scholars have cast doubt on the authenticity of the letter, most of the information in the letter corresponds with other known sources on the biographies of Sayyidnā and Niẓām al-Mulk. Furthermore, the language of the text looks older than Shūshtarī's era and it corresponds more to the time of Ḥasan-i Ṣabbāḥ.

The other story is the account of threatening Sultan Sanjar by plunging a dagger into the floor next to his bed, which Rashīd al-Dīn also mentions in his history. It is believed that after this incident Sanjar ultimately changed his policies towards the Ismailis.[11] However, the flow of events in the text of *ʿAhd* and its absence in the older copy of the text indicate that these two accounts are later additions by another person.

These differences will be further elaborated on later when we discuss the variations of the account of the *ʿAhd-i Sayyidnā* in different manuscripts.

The Siege of Alamūt by Muḥammad Tapar

In the subsequent passages, the text in MS BT 9 provides a detailed account of the siege of Alamūt by Sultan Muḥammad Tapar, who is mentioned only as Tapar or Tapar *ʿalayhi al-laʿna* (May God curse him). There is a claim in the account of MS BT 46 that Sultan Muḥammad Tapar died as a result of Sayyidnā's prayers, during his siege of Alamūt, which ended the siege. Although this kind of narrative seems to be an extension of the account in later periods, the known historical sources confirm that the reason for ending the siege was the death of Sultan Muḥammad Tapar in 511/1117.[12] At this time Sayyidnā was in old age and seven years later he passed away.

According to Rashīd al-Dīn, Sultan Muḥammad continued his campaign against the Ismailis for eight years in the first decade of the 6th/12th century by sending armies to Alamūt, burning their crops and imposing long blockades on their castles. Life became very difficult for the Nizārīs, such that each person had to rely on a small portion of barley (walnuts in the *ʿAhd's* account) daily, eating it on the walls of the fortress. Nevertheless, they were quite persistent and did not lose their strength. In the meantime, Sultan Muḥammad passed away. After his death in Muḥarram 511/May 1117, the armies heard the news and panicked and quarreled with one another. Finally, they dispersed and left all their supplies behind, to the benefit of the Nizārīs.[13]

The details provided in the text of the *ʿAhd* about the daily life of the Nizārī community during the siege of Alamūt is not found in other known sources. According to this account, each person had a ration of seven walnuts per day during those difficult times as there was not enough food to go around. There was also a shortage of space in the castle for the one thousand inhabitants. Therefore, Sayyidnā had to divide the rooms into smaller ones to accommodate them. Among the people defending the Alamūt castle, there were some who lived there with their families and others who were single. Unfortunately, there is no information in the text about other well-known Nizārī figures in the fortress at that time.

The Content of the Covenant (ʿAhd or Zinhārī)

The actual *ʿahd* or the pledge that Ḥasan-i Ṣabbāḥ required from his followers comes towards the end of the *risāla* after the account of Raʾīs

Abū al-Faḍl and his final fate. This *ʿahd* was a set of three conditions that Ḥasan-i Ṣabbāḥ's followers, numbered around one thousand, were required to accept to be able to remain in the fortress and be part of the Nizārī *daʿwa*. Three different scenarios are explained here that could happen in the future, along with Sayyidnā's expectations of his people in these circumstances.

The first condition dealt with the enemies (*khaṣmān*) of the Nizārīs. Sayyidnā asked them to remain strong in situations of attack or blockade through remembrance of Mawlānā and to be fearless in defending the castle. If they thought they could not keep up with this condition, he would provide them with their travel money and they could leave the castle.

The second condition was about the relations of Sayyidnā and his people who had their families in the castle. He warned them that what happened to the family of Raʾīs Abū al-Faḍl could happen to theirs as well or even worse!

The third and the final condition was about the responsibility of the Nizārīs towards each other. He obliged them to keep their solidarity and to help each other in hardship with extra effort.

These conditions symbolise the principles of the strategy that Ḥasan-i Ṣabbāḥ designed during the early stages of his control of Alamūt to strengthen solidarity among the Nizārīs and to encourage them to stay committed to their cause in order to defend the new *daʿwa*. Later developments prove that his strategy was quite successful as it was able to lay the foundation of a state that lasted for one hundred and seventy years.

Concluding Remarks

At the end of the conditions of the *ʿahd*, the author explains his reasons for writing this *risāla* for his dearest brother (*barādar-i aʿazz*). He aims to comfort his friend and writes that 'he should not be too upset about what Nāṣir al-Dīn (Muḥtasham) as the representative of the imam and the appointed "*muʿallim*" had imposed over him by which he may have suffered'. He reminds him that 'we should not forget the allegiance (*ʿahd wa zinhārī*) that we have on our shoulder'.[14] These final passages are significant as they provide important information about the context or reasons for writing this text as well as the circumstances in which the text was produced. They also provide some historical references about the author and the date he wrote the *risāla*.

Authorship

The author of this *risāla* is not known to us. However, based on different references in the text we can speculate in what period he was living and who were his contemporaries. The most important passage that contains this information is at the end of the text, where the author discusses the context of writing the text:

> My aim in writing these words is that the dearest brother, May God protect and help him, knows the condition of such great allegiance (*ʿahd*) that we have on our yoke. And if in the noble court of Nāṣirī-yi Qādirī, the Shahanshāh of the East, the Khusraw of horizons (*āfāq*), May God extend his shadow and expand his glory, who is the representative and the appointee of the Lord Sublime (*ḥaḍrat-i jallat*) there, the religious and the worldly instructor of the servants imposes on him a rule or task in the way that was explained in the introduction, he should consider it his best interest in both worlds and endure it.[15]

In this passage, 'Nāṣirī-yi Qādirī' and the 'Shahanshāh of the East' seem to be references to Nāṣir al-Dīn ʿAbd al-Raḥīm Muḥtasham who ruled Quhistān from 624/1226 to 654/1256 during the reign of Imam ʿAlāʾ al-Dīn Muḥammad (r. 618/1220–653/1255). The most famous Nizārī authors that we know from this period are Ṣalāḥ al-Dīn Ḥasan-i Maḥmūd and Khwāja Naṣīr al-Dīn Ṭūsī. The genre and the style of the *risāla* does not fit within Ṭūsī's domain, but there are many indications that strongly suggest the author of the *ʿAhd* could be Ḥasan-i Maḥmūd. According to the information in Ṭūsī's *Sayr wa sulūk*, Ḥasan-i Maḥmūd first served Shihāb al-Dīn Muhtasham in Girdkūh and Quhistān.[16] In the account of the *ʿAhd*, we read that the information about the early blockade of the fortress of Alamūt in the text comes from a letter sent to Quhistān by Raʾīs Muẓaffar, which corresponds to Ḥasan-i Maḥmūd's time and place of work. According to his *Dīwān*, Ḥasan-i Maḥmūd travelled to Alamūt in 631/1233, and presented his book of poetry to Imam ʿAlāʾ al-Dīn Muḥammad.[17]

There are a number of other reasons that support the authorship of Ḥasan-i Maḥmūd for this work. First of all, the language and the writing style used in this text are very close to the writings of Ḥasan-i Maḥmūd. The dialect used in the text of the *ʿAhd* is the dialect of the Rūdbār and Daylam area in which *Haft bāb* (wrongly known before as *Haft bāb-i Bābā Sayyidnā*), the introductions to poems in the *Dīwān-i qāʾimiyyāt* and *Taṣawwurāt* are written.[18] The most important feature of this dialect is the use of *hā* before the verbs and sometimes before the object. For example, in the *ʿAhd* it comes: '*man ʾū rā rah-nafaqa, jāma wa chahār-pāy hā-daham*.' In another place we read '*az dīnārī panj dāng hā khaṣmān dahīd*.' This feature shows that these texts could have been written by an author who was from the region of Rūdbār and Daylam.

Apart from the language and the rhetoric in the text, there are certain terms and phrases in this work that we see in no other works but those of Ḥasan-i Maḥmūd. As an example, at the beginning of this text, the author talks about the 'good tidings' of Mawlānā Malik al-Salām[19] that were proved to be true by the spread of the '*fitnahā-yi ākhir al-zamān*' (seditions of the end of time) at the time of the author. This very idea is repeated throughout the *Dīwān-i qāʾimiyyāt*, whenever Ḥasan-i Maḥmūd refers to the Mongol invasion and the safety of the Nizārī territories in the early stages. In the introduction of the poems no. 72 and 124 in the *Dīwān-i qāʾimiyyāt* this idea is repeated:

> This obedience (*ʿubūdiyyat*) was written on the praise of the Lord-Sublime . . . within which some good tidings (*waʿda-hā*) of the Lord of the Truth, ʿAlā Dhikrihi al-Salām have been mentioned . . . .[20]

In another poem (no. 124) that was written on the events of the year 621/1224, the same term is repeated and the armies of Genghis Khan are referred to as the Yaʾjūj and Maʾjūj, signs of the 'seditions of the end of time' (*fitna-yi ākhir zaman*).[21]

Another similarity in the writing of this text and that of Ḥasan-i Maḥmūd is his reference to the living imam in his time, who was ʿAlāʾ al-Dīn Muḥammad. Furthermore, the term that he uses here for referring to the imam is *ḥaḍrat-i jallat*. The only other place where we can find this particular term in reference to the imam is within the *Dīwān-i qāʾimiyyāt*. In the introduction to poem no. 81, he writes:

> This obedience [is] on awakening, self-advice and encouragement on obeying the Lord-Sublime (*ḥaḍrat-i jallat*), and on the good

> tidings (*wa'dahā*) which are fulfilled in this auspicious time, May God extend it to Eternity.

The next trend of thought in the *'Ahd* that could be traced in the works of Ḥasan-i Maḥmūd is the use of particular terms for describing the evolution of souls. The first passage of the *'Ahd* is written on the gradation of souls and the purpose of their creation. The same idea with similar terms could be seen in the introduction of *Dīwān-i qā'imiyyāt*. Although the passage in each text is on a slightly different topic, the foundation of the proposed idea in both texts is common. Explaining the difference between different souls and modes of creation, in the *'Ahd* we read:

> Since the human being is the noblest and the most perfect among all created, and the intellect that is the absolute essence (*jawhar-i kull*) initiates in him, turning from potential to actual . . . and it is known that stones do not have vegetal souls (*jān-i nabātī*), and vegetables do not have animal souls (*jān-i ḥaywānī*) and animals do not have human souls (*jān-i insānī*). . . ."[22]

In this passage, human beings have been identified as the noblest of creation because of the intellect as the total essence being potent in them. They should conduct themselves based on the purpose of their creation. Similarly the souls in the lower levels: *sang* or *jimād* (objects), *jān-i nabātī* (vegetal soul) and *jān-i ḥaywānī* (animal soul) are also destined to function purposefully. This idea is comparable to a passage in the introduction of *Dīwān-i qā'imiyyāt*, where it comes:

> Extremism (*ghuluww*) is applied where someone does not contain himself within his limits and claims ascendance to a world (*kawn*) which would be his misadventure (*balā'*); the inanimate [soul] claims ascending to the vegetal (*nabāt*) world, the vegetal world claims ascending to the perfection of the animal (*ḥaywān*) grade, and the animal claims ascending to the noble level of human (*insān*) . . . .[23]

Although this gradation theory of souls may be a well-known Ismaili idea in this period, using it in the introduction of two works with many other similarities indicates a certain trend of thought that could originate from the same mind.

As mentioned before, this text bears no title and the title of *ʿAhd-i Sayyidnā* has been given here on the basis of the information within the text. In some Persian and Arabic Ismaili manuscripts, we come across similar texts such as the *ʿAhd* or *Mīthāq* of Imam ʿAlāʾ al-Dīn Muḥammad that is attributed to the same period.[24] However, the only references to the *ʿAhd-i Sayyidnā* are again found in the works of Ḥasan-i Maḥmūd. There is no reference to such ideas in other works, either in this or later periods. In the *Dīwān-i qāʾimiyyāt*, Ḥasan-i Maḥmūd refers to "*ahd-i Sayyidnā*' and states that it needs to be always remembered and kept as the measure for ever:

> *Shukr-i niʿmat ān buwad kaz mā bih awwal har yikī / rūy az-īn dunyā-yi dūn bā dāwar-i dayyān kunad*
> *ʿahd-i Sayyidnā kih bar aḥbāb-i mawlānā girift / āwarad bā yād-u ān rā tā abad mīzān kunad*[25]

Which means:

> Being thankful to the grace is that each one of us first turns his face from this lowly world to the Unexampled Judge (God). Remember the 'covenant (*ʿahd*) of Sayyidnā' which was witnessed by friends of Mawlānā and make it the eternal measure!

In conclusion, the above evidence and indications show that it is highly possible that the author of the text of *ʿahd-i Sayyidnā* was Ḥasan-i Maḥmūd who wrote it for a friend who lived in Quhistān.

Reason for Writing the *Risāla*

There is clear evidence in the text that this *risāla* was written for a friend of the author who had been subject to an unfavorable ruling by Nāṣir al-Dīn Muḥtasham. There is no information about the identity of this friend in the text or the reasons for the disciplinary ruling. Judging by the overall context of the *ʿAhd* and its focus on loyalty and the temporary nature of the worldly aspects of life, it is possible that this friend was subject to such rulings by way of confiscation of belongings or properties. There are reports in some sources that Khwāja Naṣīr al-Dīn Ṭūsī who was also a friend of Ḥasan-i Maḥmūd was imprisoned by Nāṣir al-Dīn Muḥtasham, but it is very unlikely that the friend specified here would be him, as the rhetoric in the text indicates that his friend was not a high profile scholar of Ṭūsī's calibre.[26]

In the historiography of the period, we have some evidence that shows that in that particular period of time, there were some major policy changes in the leadership of Quhistān in the 620s/1221–1231, which could have resulted in such circumstances. The author of *Ṭabaqāt-i Nāṣirī*, Minhāj-i Sirāj who visited Quhistān in this period and met Muḥtasham Shihāb al-Dīn has a passage on the political situation of Quhistān in his *Ṭabāqāt*. During this period, the Ismailis in Iran were at the peak of their power, whereas the eastern parts of Muslim lands such as Khurasan and Upper Oxus were experiencing a devastating period due to the first wave of the Mongol invasion. According to the observations of Minhāj-i Sirāj, due to the security of Quhistān under the leadership of Muḥtasham Shihāb al-Dīn and Nāṣir al-Dīn, many scholars from those areas escaped to the Ismaili castles of Quhistān. He writes that the generous gifts from the Nizārī treasury to the new arrivals by Muḥtasham created resentments among ordinary members of the Nizārī community. He describes the situation in the following passage:

> Since Muḥtasham's favour and companionship with the Muslims increased, the community of the *mulḥids* conveyed the stories to Alamūt, saying Muḥtasham Shihāb is going to offer nearly all the resources of the *daʿwatkhāna* to the Muslims. An order came from Alamūt that he should go to Alamūt, and Muḥtasham Shams al-Dīn Ḥasan was sent to Quhistān.[27]

It is possible that as a result of these complaints, there were some consequences for those who benefited from the generous policies of Muḥtasham Shihāb in later periods, and as a result a friend of the author also suffered such consequences. The fact that the story of Raʾīs Abū al-Faḍl is reminded to him, and the way he left his wealth and family behind for the sake of religion is stressed here, prove that there were some similarities between his friend's case and the case of Raʾīs Abū al-Faḍl. However, he has to remind his friend of those sacrifices and the pledge that the *fidāʾīs* of Sayyidnā made so that he does not lose direction.

Variation in the Account in Manuscript Copies

As was said before, the only copy that has the full text of the *ʿAhd* is MS BT 9. However, the beginning of the text is not clearly marked. Therefore, the beginning of the text of the *ʿAhd* was determined based on the change in the theme and the flow of the narrative. For example, the opening sentence of 'O, brothers in religion and friends by faith' (*barādarān-i dīn wa dūstān-i ahl-i yaqīn*) indicates that a new text has started. The previous text which is on the creation of the worlds ends with a prayer and closing phrase *bi-ḥaqq-i muḥammad wa āl-i muḥammad*. However, the end of the *ʿAhd* is clearly marked in the conventional way with the closing prayer: *wa al-salām mawlānā bi-ḥaqq-i ḥaqqihī* and the next text begins the next page. The following text is *Jang-nāmah-yi Sīstān* which is very close in language and time frame to the events discussed in the text of *ʿAhd*. There are traces of *Jang-nāmah-yi Sistān* in some passages of the *ʿAhd* in MS BT 9 that shows the copyist also used information from these texts in his spontaneous modification. For example, in the discussion between Raʾīs Abū al-Faḍl and the Saljūq Sultan in the *ʿAhd* text, there is a phrase that could exactly be found in the text of *Jang-nāmah-yi Sīstān*:

> *tamām-i wilāyat-i ʿirāq az pas-i īshān shamshīr dar ghalāf karda-and, chirākih īshān bi-quwwat-i āl-i muḥammad nishasta-and.*[28]

The language used in the texts of this manuscript is not always consistent. It seems that the copyist has not been completely loyal to his original source, as there are many indications that he has tampered with the text. This is a very common feature among some manuscripts in the Badakhshān region. One possible reason for this could have been the language barrier, because most of these texts were written in the dialect of Alamūt and Rūdbār, which was not sometimes easy to understand for people in Badakhshān. That is why different scribes took the liberty to modify texts according to their choice. Furthermore, in many other cases we come across instances that the copyist has skipped a sentence or a word which he did not understand like Arabic words or phrases. For this reason, some passages of the above text in all the copies are sometimes difficult to understand and occasionally have grammatical mistakes as well.

Furthermore, there are two separate sections in this copy that are clearly later additions to the main text. It is not clear why the scribe decided to insert them within this text and from what original source he included them. Although it is clear that these texts are not fabricated by him, by comparing the two copies (MS BA 59 & MS BA 46) we find that these two accounts obstruct the flow of events in the original text.

The second manuscript, MS BA 59, is also a *majmūʿa*. The text of *ʿAhd* starts after *Ṣaḥīfat al-nāẓirīn*, and ends before the *Dīwān-i qāʾimiyyāt*. However, it lacks the beginning. Compared to MS BT 9, this copy looks more trustworthy in language and the sequence of the events with fewer signs of modification, but it is defective at the beginning. It starts right in the middle of the discussion between Ḥasan-i Ṣabbāḥ and Raʾīs Abū al-Faḍl on the issue of the Imamate.

This copy does not contain the letter of Ḥasan-i Ṣabbāḥ to Malikshāh and the account of the *Fidāʾīs*' mission at the court of Sultan Sanjar. There are a few other noticeable differences between MS BA 59 and MS BT 9. In reference to Ḥasan-i Ṣabbāḥ, MS BA 59 writes *Sayyidnā qaddasa Allāh rūḥahū*, whereas in MS BT 9 *Bābā Sayyidnā* alone is used.

The Qurʾānic verses or Arabic quotations are also preserved more accurately in this copy, whereas in MS BT 9, these parts are sometimes completely omitted, or recorded with many mistakes.

The version within MS BA 46 is a fragmented one of the *ʿAhd*. It only provides some passages of the account and a different version of Raʾīs Abū al-Faḍl's life story. There is a short passage from the final section of the *ʿAhd* in this copy before the story of Tapar and his blockade of Alamūt. However, this blockade episode is also different from that of the other copies as it comes with other components such as the communication of Sayyidnā with Imam Nizār and his sons which is not found in the other copies. It seems that one of the scribes probably combined different sections from number of sources into one text without mentioning the original source.

The passages related to the *ʿAhd* in this copy begin with the promise of Sayyidnā that ʿAlā Dhikrih al-Salām will appear (*ẓuhūr khwāhad kard*) to complete all the *Sharīʿas*. Then it goes to the siege of Alamūt by the armies of both ʿIrāqs (ʿIrāqayn) and Māzandarān. Here, a summary of the story of Abū al-Ḥasan-i Saʿīdī who brings the sons of Imam Nizār is repeated. The account of the resistance of the small group of *fidāʾīs* against Muḥammad Tapar is followed by the sacrifice of Raʾīs-i Iṣfahānī who was martyred in fighting the Tapar army. Finally, Sayyidnā asked the *fidāʾīs* to pray that Tapar may be burst! It claims that Tapar burst to death as a result of their prayer, and they could take back all the treasures that Raʾīs-i Iṣfahānī had brought with him from Iṣfahān.

As is clear, the details of this account are different from the other two. It is not clear how much of the story is according to its original version by the author and how much is the result of different scribes who revised and rephrased the text. Nevertheless, there is no doubt that this copy is a version revised in later periods.

In summary, here is a brief demonstration and a general picture of the similarities and differences between these copies:

Features shared by all versions: The only part that exists in all three of these copies is the passage in which the summary of theological reforms during the Alamūt period is outlined, starting with Ḥasan Ṣabbāḥ and ending at the time of the author which should be the era of Imam ʿAlāʾ al-Dīn Muḥammad's reign, where it says:

> *wa maʿlūm ast kih maqṣūd az āmadan-i Sayyidnā qaddasa allāh rūḥahū ān būd tā bi-farmān-i Mawlānā asās-i daʿwat-i mubārak binahand wa jamāʿat rā bā dast āwarad wa dīdār-i īshān dar-afkanad kih ʿAlā Dhikrihi al-Salām ẓuhūr khwāhad kar.*

Features in only two versions: The passage on the siege of Alamūt by one of the commanders of Muḥammad Tapar and the account of his execution in his camp is recorded in MS BA 46 and MS BT 9. The most trusted copy, MS BA 59, does not have this account.

Features in only one copy: Finally, MS BT 9 is the only copy that has the introduction, Sayyidnā's letter to Malikshāh and the story of the threatening of Sanjar by *fidāʾīs*.

Conclusion

ʿAhd-i Sayyidnā is a unique work that presents valuable information about the life of Nizārī Ismailis during the Alamūt period. In the known historiography of the age, there is little information about the social history of the Ismailis. The works produced by the Nizārīs themselves are also more concerned with doctrinal and ideological topics. The *ʿAhd-i Sayyidnā* is one of the rare works that provides some information about the daily life of ordinary Nizārīs in the early periods.

This *risāla* also explains how important the legacy of Ḥasan-i Ṣabbāḥ was during the Alamūt period. When this *risāla* was written towards the end of the Alamūt state, the Nizārīs had gone into a long period of ideological and political transformation; from the Proclamation of Qiyāma by Ḥasan ʿAlā Dhikrihi al-Salām to the ending of the Qiyāma era by Jalāl al-Dīn Ḥasan and making alliances with the Sunni world; from making peace with the Mongols and Khwārazmshāhīs to fighting against them. After all those years of austerity and prosperity, the *ʿAhd-i Sayyidnā* is remembered in order to remain committed to the promise they made at the beginning of the *daʿwa*. Although the author has not mentioned his name in the text, there are strong indications within the text of the *ʿAhd* that suggest that the actual author is Ṣalāḥ al-Dīn Ḥasan-i Maḥmūd Munshī.

NOTES

1 The manuscript is not paginated. Therefore numbers represent the last three digits of the frame numbers (fr.) of the digital copy.

2 The date is recorded as *dar māh-i muḥarram sāl-i mār sana-yi* 112172 [?] ('in the month of Muḥarram in the Snake year').

3 See Muḥammad b. Aḥmad Nasawī, *Sīrat-i Jalāl al-Dīn Munkabirnī,* ed., Mujtabā Mīnuwī (Tehran, 1384 Sh./2005), vol. 1, p. 185.

4 MS BT 9, ff. 95b–96a. It seems that the scribe has missed some words as some sentences look incomplete, but it does not affect hugely the overall meaning of the passage.

5 See Faḍl Allāh Rashīd al-Dīn, *Jāmiʿ al-Tawārīkh; qismat-i Ismāʿīlīyān wa Nizārīyān wa dāʿīyān wa rafīqān,* ed., M. Rawshan (Tehran, 1387 Sh./2008), p. 112.

6 MS BT 9, ff. 116a–116b.

7 Rashīd al-Dīn, *Jāmiʿ al-Tawārīkh*, p. 112.

8 Ibid., p. 107.

9 MS BT 9, ff. 116b–117a.

10 See Qāḍī Nūr Allāh Shūshtarī, *Majālis al-muʾminīn* (Tehran, 1377 Sh./1998), pp. 310–316. Also, Murtaḍā Rāwandī, *Tārīkh-i ijtimāʿī-yi īrān* (Tehran, 1354 Sh./1975), pp. 199–204.

11 ʿAlāʾ al-Dīn ʿAṭā-Malik Juwaynī, *Tārīkh-i Jahangushāy* (Leiden, 1958), vol. 3, p. 214.

12 Rashīd al-Dīn, *Jāmiʿ al-Tawārīkh*, p. 129.

13 Ibid., p. 129.

14 MS BT 9, f. 125a.

15 MS BA 59, fr. 720.

16 See *Contemplation and Action: The Spiritual Autobiography of a Muslim Scholar; a New Edition and English Translation of Sayr wa Sulūk*, ed. and tr., S. J. Badakhchani (London and New York, 1998), p. 4.

17 See *Dīwān-i qā'imiyyāt* of Ḥasan-i Maḥmūd, ed., S. J. Badakhchani (Tehran, 1390 Sh./2011), pp. 3, 58.
18 Although the content and the ideas of *Taṣawwurāt* are believed to be those of Naṣīr al-Dīn Ṭūsī, the presentation and compilation of the text is attributed to Ḥasan-i Maḥmūd.
19 Malik al-Salām could be a misreading of ʿAlā Dhikrihi al-Salām by one of the copyists.
20 *Dīwān-i qā'imiyyāt*, p. 199.
21 Ibid., p. 327.
22 MS BT 9, ff. 93b–94a.
23 *Dīwān-i qā'imiyyāt*, p. 2.
24 See *al-Dustūr wa daʿwat al-mu'minīn li'l-ḥuḍūr*, in ʿĀrif Tāmir (ed.) *Arbaʿa rasā'il Ismāʿīliyya* (Beirut, 1978), pp. 52–74.
25 Ibid, p. 180.
26 Raḍawī Mudarris, *Aḥwāl wa āthār-i qudwat al-muḥaqqiqīn wa sulṭān al-ḥukamā wa al-mutakallimīn, ustād al-bashar wa ʿaql-i ḥādī ʿashr, Abū Jaʿfar Muḥammad ibn Muḥammad ibn al-Ḥasan al-Ṭūsī, mulaqqab bih Naṣīr al-Dīn* (Tehran, 1354 Sh./1975), p. 11.
27 Minhāj-i Sirāj Jawzjānī, *Ṭabaqāt-i Nāṣirī*, ed.,ʿAbd al-Ḥayy Ḥabībī (Tehran, 1363 Sh./1984), vol. 2, p. 183.
28 MS BT 9, f. 112a, and *Jang-nāmah* in MS 916, f. 2.

10

The Discovery, Description and Publication of the Manuscripts of Two Major Nizārī Ismaili Texts from the Alamūt Period: The *Haft Bāb* and the *Dīwān-i Qā'imiyyāt* of Ḥasan-i Maḥmūd-i Kātib

S. J. Badakhchani

Contextualising the *Haft Bāb* and the *Dīwān-i Qā'imiyyāt*

Ḥasan-i Maḥmūd-i Kātib, author of the books introduced here, was, until the publication of his compendium of poems, namely the Poems of the Resurrection (*Dīwān-i Qā'imiyyāt*)[1] and his Seven Chapters (*Haft bāb*),[2] an enigmatic[3] or more precisely an 'unknown' figure among the Ismaili authors and the classical Persian poets.[4] He was born in the second half of the 6th/12th century probably around the year 555/1160, since the date of the compilation of his *Haft bāb* is 595/1199, compiled during the imamate of Nūr al-Dīn Muḥammad II (d. 607/1210). At the time, judging from the contents of the *Haft bāb* and his notes on Nizārī Ismail history,[5] he must have been well versed in Ismaili history and theology of his time and in particular the doctrine of the Resurrection (*da'wat-i qiyāmat*). In the *Haft bāb* he speaks of the doctrine of the *Qiyāmat* in a vague and elusive manner hinting to his being either present when the doctrine was launched, or at least being born before the event,[6] that is, 17 Ramaḍān 559/8 August 1164. Marshall Hodgson describes the *Haft bāb* as a text that '[r]epresents the full blown *Qiyāma* doctrine, as developed under the son of 'Alā-Dhikri-his-Salām and unchanged as yet by the grandson's policies of Satr.'[7]

A talented poet, he might have composed poems very early in his life but apart from his compendium of poetry and a few scattered quotations resembling his style,[8] so far nothing has come to light from him, which implies that either he did not bother to preserve them, or if he did, he may have destroyed them at a later stage.[9] It is in the *Qā'imiyyāt* that we face a master poet, comparable only to Nāṣir-i Khusraw among the Ismaili poets,[10] and more importantly, a poet whose output represents the best poetic specimens of 7th/13th-century Iran.[11] Being well informed about the doctrine of the *Qiyāmat*, he not only witnessed its dismissal by Jalāl al-Dīn Ḥasan (d. 618/1221), but also its refinement and gradual return as a dominant, and wide-ranging theological norm during the imamate of ʿAlā al-Dīn Muḥammad (d. 653/1255). Composed at various times, the poems of the *Qā'imiyyāt*[12] reflect Ḥasan's involvement in the shaping of what Hodgson describes as the doctrine of *satr*. It is apparent that *satr* or transition from the *Qiyāmat* to the *Sharīʿa*, while maintaining a balance between the two,[13] did not take place instantly or without an insightful preparation demanding the input of the highest ranks of the *daʿwat* organisation and the competent scholars living in Alamūt, or other Ismaili fortresses scattered over a wide territory from present day Afghanistan to the Mediterranean Sea.

At the time, around the year 630/1233, while Alamūt housed one of the best libraries in the Islamic world and notable figures such as al-Muẓaffar b. Muḥammad,[14] Manṣūr b. Abū'l-Fuṭūḥ[15] and Muḥtasham Shihāb al-Dīn were residing there, it was the court of Nāṣir al-Dīn Muḥtasham in Quhistān that sheltered a number of both Ismaili and non-Ismaili scholars who were qualified to take part in the refinements of the doctrine. In all probability this was the reason that around the year 643/1245, Naṣīr al-Dīn Ṭūsī, Ḥasan-i Maḥmūd and Muḥtasham Nāṣir al-Dīn were summoned to Alamūt.[16] Ṭūsī's stay in Alamūt lasted twenty years and Ḥasan-i Maḥmūd stayed there until his last days around the year 644/1246.

Apart from Nāṣir al-Dīn Muḥtasham,[17] who was born into an Ismaili family, both Ṭūsī[18] and Ḥasan-i Maḥmūd[19] were new converts to the Nizārī Ismaili mission (*daʿwa*). Their backgrounds, talents and expertise also differed. Nāṣir al-Dīn Muḥtasham was an experienced scholar-politician, Ṭūsī was a talented scientist-philosopher and Ḥasan-i Maḥmūd a gifted poet with secretarial expertise who preferred to express himself in poetry.[20]

Summoning scholars to the presence of the imam, when crucial decisions were anticipated, had its precedent in the pre-Fatimid and Fatimid times. For example, during the reign of the Fatimid caliph al-Ḥākim (386/996–411/1021), Ḥamīd al-Dīn al-Kirmānī was summoned to Cairo;[21] similarly al-Mu'ayyad fī al-Dīn al-Shīrāzī joined the court of Imam Mustanṣir bi'llah[22] and this may have been the case of anonymous authors[23] who compiled the pamphlets (*rasā'il*) of the Ikhwān al-Ṣafā' in the formative years of the rise of the Ismaili faith as an independent branch of Shi'i Islam usually described as the first period of *satr*.[24]

Ten to fifteen years before leaving Quhistān for Alamūt, Naṣīr al-Dīn Ṭūsī (597/1201–654/1276) had joined the *Jamā'at*,[25] that is, the Ismaili community, and had produced several books and treatises promoting the tenets of the Ismaili faith.[26] His colleague and companion[27] Ḥasan-i Maḥmūd, of whom Ṭūsī speaks as the chief of *dā'īs* (*sayyid al-du'āt*),[28] was also an expert on the subject. Their summoning to Alamūt in order to execute what the imam of the time and the Ismaili *da'wat* were expecting, was a historical event that led to the compilation of the most comprehensive book on Nizārī Ismaili thought in the middle ages;[29] it has survived to our time bearing the title of *Taṣawwurāt* or the *Rawḍa-yi taslīm*. It echoes some of the issues discussed by the Ikhwān al-Ṣafā' and other classical Ismaili authors such as Abū Ya'qūb al-Sijistānī and Nāṣir-i Khusraw.[30] But more significantly it is a precise elaboration on the doctrine of the *Qiyāmat* which, while maintaining similarities, was not intended to be a complete representation of the doctrine of *satr*.[31]

In Alamūt, Ḥasan-i Maḥmūd did not compose any prose material of his own but collaborated with Ṭūsī in the production of the *Rawḍa-yi taslīm*[32] to the degree that in the three main chapters of the *Rawḍa*[33] we can identify quotations from the *Haft bāb*, albeit in much-improved language, which evidently had been rephrased and improved upon by Ṭūsī.[34] Reciprocally, Ḥasan-i Maḥmūd also took on board Ṭūsī's ideas and scholarly rendering of Ismaili theology, that is, the refined version of the doctrine of the *Qiyāmat*, in his compendium of poetry.[35] Comparison between the three texts, namely, the *Haft bāb*, the *Rawḍa-yi taslīm* and the *Dīwān-i Qā'imiyyāt* reflects the nature and extent of the collaboration between the two authors. In the course of time, the *Rawḍa-yi taslīm* assumed the status of the most comprehensive text covering a large spectrum of Ismaili theology of the Nizārī period. The *Haft bāb* became an immensely popular text, judging from the enormity of available manuscripts and probably because of its unsophisticated language. But in the aftermath of Alamūt's destruction by the Mongols, the *Dīwān-i Qā'imiyyāt* disappeared from the public eye for seven centuries.[36]

The combined legacy of Ṭūsī and Ḥasan-i Maḥmūd, as far as the survival and preservation of their written heritage is concerned, are a number of books and short treatises reflecting the 'Preachings of the Resurrection' (*Daʿwa-i Qiyāmat*) and subsequently the 'post *Qiyāmat*' Ismaili tenets of faith that have survived to our time. The Mongol invasion of Islamic lands, the fall of Alamūt and the protracted destruction of Ismaili fortress-libraries subdued the spirit and zeal of knowledge-seeking among the Iranian Ismailis for two centuries. During this period which happens to be the most obscure phase of the Nizari Ismaili history, the time when they were facing the most threatening blow to their survival, the only available alternative to them was to hide their books in the cracks of walls, as in the case of the *Qāʾimiyyāt*, or make multiple copies of them, as in the case of the *Haft bāb-i Ḥasan-i Maḥmūd* and a number of short treatises by Ṭūsī.[37] It was the preservation of these short treatises that enabled Abū Isḥāq, an Ismaili author to write his *Haft bāb*, almost two hundred years later, which in turn became a pattern for producing a number of other books and treatises in the Persian language.

Manuscripts of the Texts and their Editing

Haft bāb

I have highlighted the circumstances that preceded the publication of the *Haft bāb* in my introduction to the edited text.[38] It is worth mentioning that the *Haft bāb* seems to have had a more fortunate destiny than the *Qā'imiyyāt* since multiple manuscript copies of the text have survived, not only in Iran, but also in Tajikistan, Afghanistan, India, and the northern regions of Pakistan, where it seems to have been translated into vernacular languages. In 1933, an incomplete and corrupt version of the treatise wrongly entitled *Haft bāb-i Bābā Sayyidnā* was published by Wladimir Ivanow (1886–1970) who was aware of its false attribution to Bābā Sayyidnā, that is, Ḥasan-i Ṣabbāḥ, the founder of the Nizārī Ismaili movement in Iran.[39] It is most probable that the existence of a number of quotations from Bābā Sayyidnā,[40] and the fact that in some manuscripts the name 'Ḥasan' appears as the author,[41] may have convinced Ivanow to reach such a conclusion. Ivanow, however, does not identify the manuscripts that he used for his edition. In his *A Guide to Ismaili Literature*, he writes: '*Haft bābi Bābā Sayyid-nā*, said to exist in Central Asia, a small booklet (?).' On p. 103, no. 641a, however, he attributes it to Abū Isḥāq: '*Haft-bābi Abū Isḥāq*, an interesting work, obviously of the strict Alamuti school, though copies of it are common in Badakhshān.'[42] The manuscript relied upon by Ivanow is most probably MS 64, pp. 2–35, currently housed at the Ismaili Special Collections Unit of The Institute of Ismaili Studies, but the multitude of copies of the text available in various Ismaili localities leave little doubt that he himself, or his assistants, had access to several other manuscripts.

For the preparation of a new edition of the *Haft bāb*, apart from many handwritten copies of Ivanow's edition which have been occasionally corrected and improved upon by scribes, I have consulted eighteen other manuscripts. Of these, except for the three briefly described below, all are incomplete and end at a similar point. This remains a puzzle to this date, and I cannot find a meaningful explanation for it. The only justifiable explanation may be to assume that the original complete copy of the text survived in the possession of the Murād Mīrzā family[43] in Sidih, a small town near Birjand in southern Khurasan. At some point, someone prepared a copy, assuming the remaining pages were not important,[44] or did not have time to finish the task, and this copy became the source of all incomplete copies since the collection of Ismaili manuscripts in Sidih was tightly guarded and copying from them was extremely difficult. Fortunately, MS 32 (described below), with minor lacunae and mistakes, is almost complete. It was copied by Muḥammad Ḥusayn Ghufrānī, a close companion and representative of the Murād Mīrzā family in Zamānī, a village sixty kilometres south of Birjand. I am told that in the aftermath of the Iranian Islamic Revolution of 1979, the collection of manuscripts owned by the Murād Mīrzā family was looted, and no one has any further information about it.[45] The three manuscripts (all housed in the Ismaili Special Collections at the IIS), described below, are complete with relatively correct text of the *Haft bāb*:

MS 32, no date, in the handwriting of M. H. Ghufrānī; part of a collection, 20 folios (62v–82r), in broken *nastaʿlīq* script; folio size 18 × 15 cm, text size 16.5 × 11.5 cm, 14 lines to a page. Judging from the paper and handwriting, it might be over one hundred years old. This manuscript was kindly made available to me by Walī Muḥammad Ghufrānī and as requested by him, it was donated to the then library of The Institute of Ismaili Studies in 1981.

MS BT 171, scribe unknown, no date, belonged to Sayyed Nawrūz Shāh b. Sayyid Kāẓim. It is complete, part of a collection of which pp. 1–35 is the *Haft bāb*. Written on handmade paper in broken *nastaʿlīq* script; folio size 19.5 × 17 cm, text size 8 × 14 cm, 15 lines to a page; pp. 23–24 and 27–32 are in a different paper, blue in colour, but in the same handwriting. This manuscript is the oldest, copied either during the imamate of Mustanṣir II (d. 885/1480) or Mustanṣir III (d. 904/1498) since in the colophon the name of *Qāʾim-i Qiyāmat* Ḥasan has been replaced by 'al-Mustanṣir bi'llāh'. Judging from the fully coloured digital copy, its script, paper colour and physical appearance, it must be over five hundred years old.

MS BT 157, dated in the year of the rooster, Monday 12?9 (probably 1219/1804), scribe unknown. It belonged to Sayyid Shams al-Dīn b. Sayyid Ibrāhīm. It is complete, part of a collection in which pp. 1–58 is the *Haft bāb*. Written in broken *nastaʿlīq* script on handmade paper. Although the calligraphy is good, apparently the scribe did not know Persian well. There are numerous lacunae, discrepancies and many sentences are left incomplete. Folio size 23.5 × 18 cm, text size 7.5 × 13cm, 12 lines to a page.

Dīwān-i Qāʾimiyyāt

I have described the circumstances and background that preceded the publication of the *Dīwān-i Qāʾimiyyāt* in my introduction to the edited version of the text, and with minor improvements, in a subsequent paper.[46] In brief, after the destruction of the Nizārī Ismaili libraries in Iran by the Mongols in 654/1256, and the hostile environs in which the Ismailis found themselves, they took extreme measures to ensure the survival of copies of their literature in personal collections. In the case of the *Dīwān-i Qāʾimiyyāt*, in order to safeguard it from enemies, a copy prepared on 10 Ramaḍān 1105/5 April 1694 was buried in the crack of a wall and plastered over. This copy was eventually recovered almost three hundred years later (see Figure 10.1). Surprisingly, the last mention of the existence of the book in Persian literary chronicles dates to the compilation of the *Zubdat al-tawārīkh* by Abū al-Qāsim Kāshānī (d. 718/1318), almost 700 years ago.

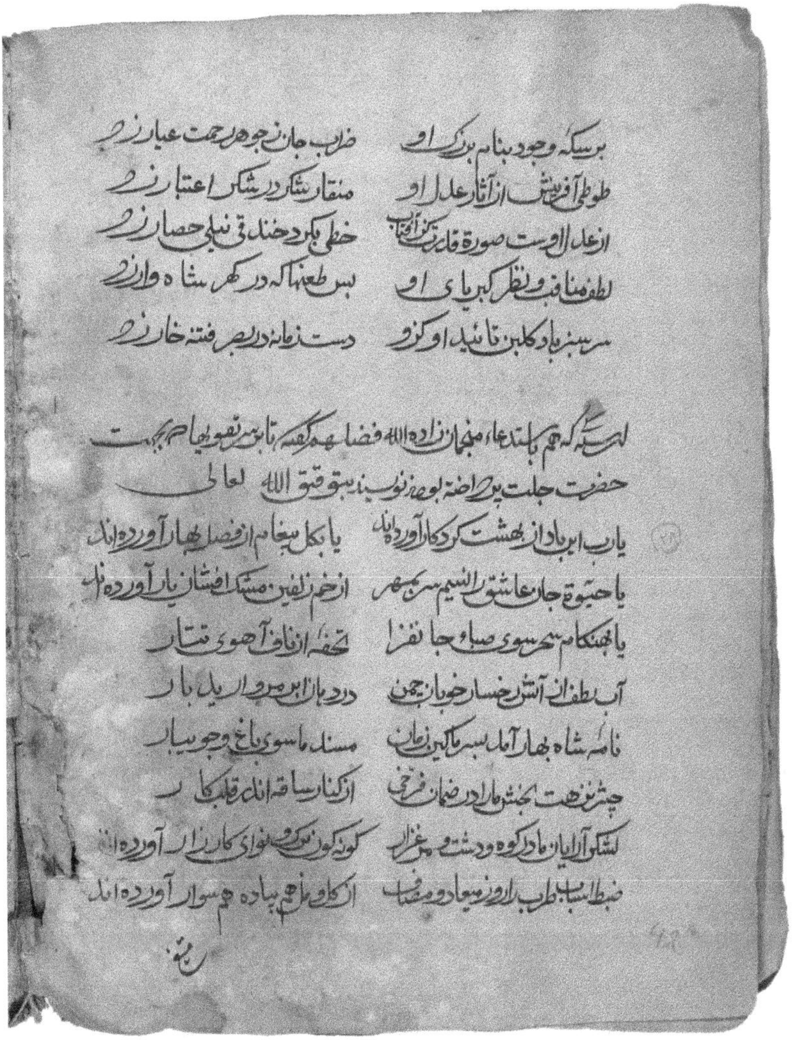

Figure 10.1 Page from the manuscript MS Per 113 that had lain hidden for over three hundred years in Iran.

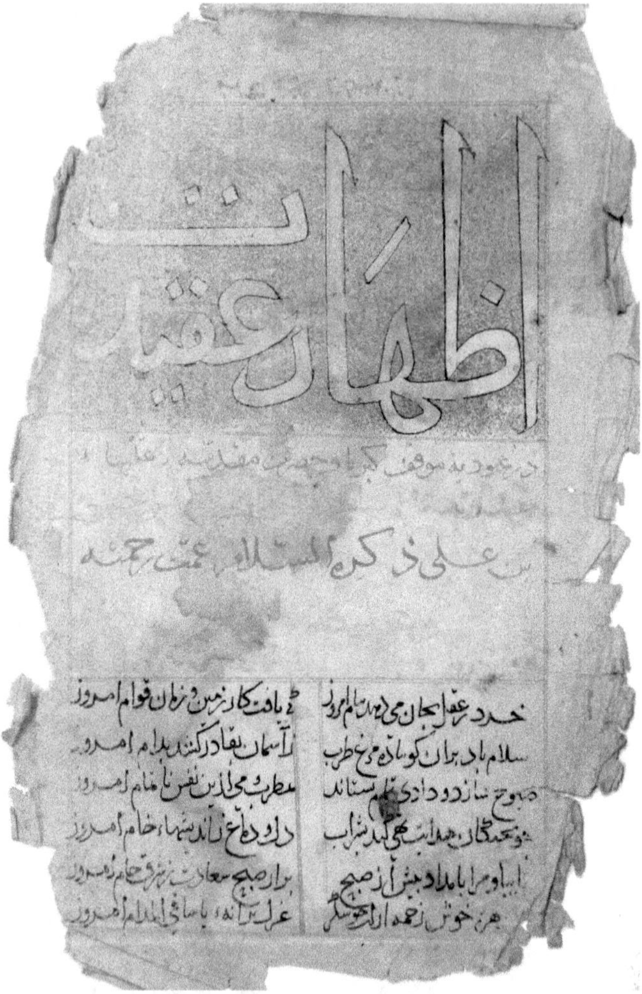

Figure 10.2 Title page of the *Dīwān* (from MS Per 99), which includes six lines from Ode 91; it reads: 'Expression of Belief, in Servitude to the Holy and Exalted Presence of our Lord Muḥammad b. Ḥasan b. ʿAlā Dhikrihi al-Salām, may his Bounty Endure and his Mission prevail'.

The edition of the *Dīwān-i Qāʾimiyyāt* was based on three manuscripts. The oldest manuscript (see Figures 10.2 and 10.3) is made up of two different parts bound together with part one dated 29 Shaʿbān 806/13 March 1404, and part two dated 832/1428. In both cases the scribe is unknown. This manuscript, I am told, survived among the remote offspring of Aga Khan I, Ḥasan ʿAlī Shāh, who migrated to India in the latter part of the 19th century. A second manuscript,

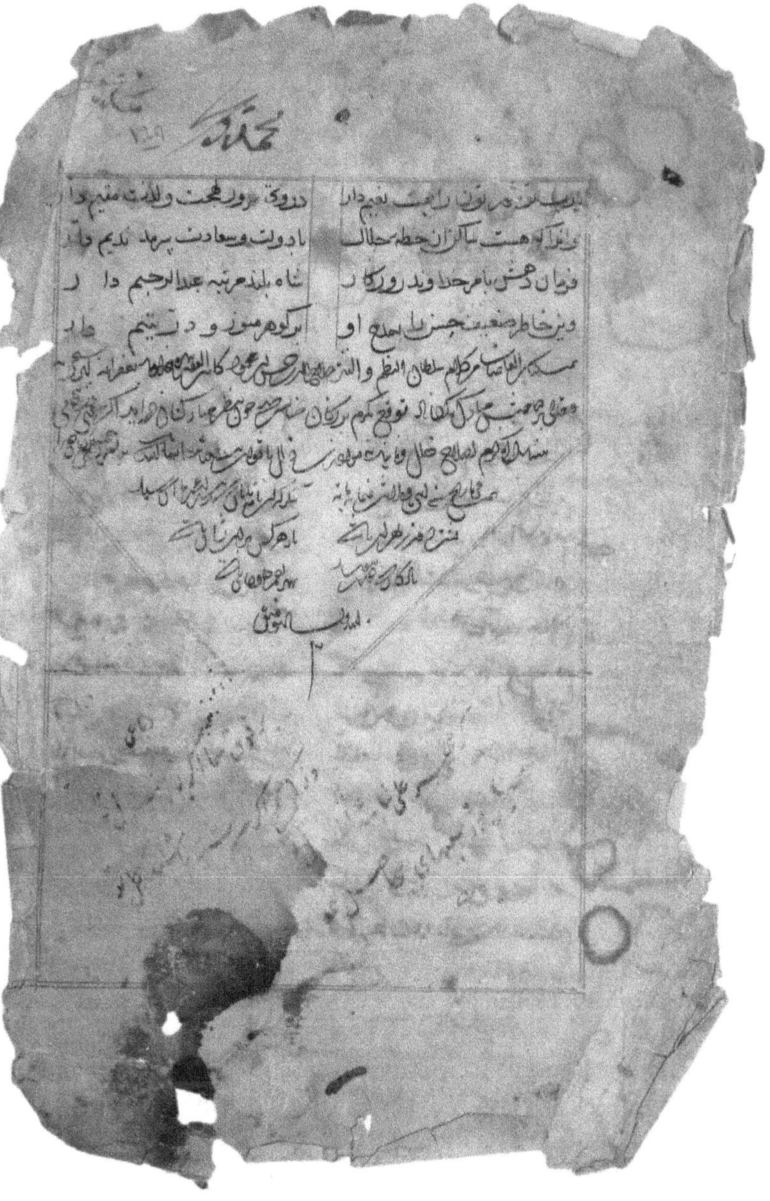

Figure 10.3 Page from the manuscript MS Per 99 (dated 832/1428) that survived among distant family members of Aga Khan I, Ḥasan ʿAlī Shāh in Mumbai.

discovered in Iran, is dated 10 Ramaḍān 1105/5 April 1694, in the handwriting of Mīrzā ʿAlī, son of ʿAbd al-Mu'min. And the third manuscript is in the hand of Muḥammad Ḥusayn b. Mīrzā ʿAlī ʿArabī-dūz-i Sidihī and dated 25 Muḥarram 1101/8 November 1689.[47]

The published version, based on the above manuscripts, consists of two volumes with 157 odes and a total of 4,784 couplets. Reflecting on the importance of the *Dīwān*, Prof. Shafīʿī Kadkanī in his comprehensive introduction to the edition writes:

> The appearance of the *Dīwān-i Qā'imiyyāt* in published form is a great historical event for the Iranian culture, and the Persian poetry that at the same time displays hundreds of new pieces of information concerning the Ismaili faith, its history and the social life and politics of the time. With all apprehension and sensitivity that I always have in relation to Persian poetry and its problems, I must confess that until the time when I had the *Dīwān* at my disposal, apart from few odes that has been quoted in Kāshānī's *Zubdat al-tawārīkh,* I knew nothing at all about this book. In the landscape of the history of Persian poetry and its several styles, the *Qā'imiyyāt* is a different genre, unlike all other poetical compendia and [within the Ismaili poetical corpus] it is only comparable to the *Dīwān* of Nāṣir Khusraw. . .The importance of the *Qā'imiyyāt* is such that it deserves many monographs and studies. [For example,] how much of our poetical heritage in Iran has been produced by Ismaili poets? What about Rūdakī's compendium of poems? Perhaps, it would have been an Ismaili text, if there was a complete version of it.[48] What about Kasā'ī,[49] admired so much by Nāṣir-i Khusraw? In fact, with many Persian poets, even though the printed version of their *dīwāns* may not contain Ismaili elements, it is extremely difficult to distance them from the creative circle of the Ismaili poets. [In conclusion he adds:] In all cultures 'poetry' is the substance of culture. And in comparison to the non-poetical heritage of the Ismaili thinkers in Iran, which is outstanding, it does not seem feasible that their poetical heritage may not have been as comprehensive. Here we need to be cautious, as it may be possible that most of the poets whom the author of *al-Naqḍ*[50] mentions as being Imāmī (Twelver Shiʿi) poets, were in fact Ismailis and for that reason their *dīwāns* are untraceable! One example is Abū al-ʿAlā' Ganjawī[51] whom Khāqānī[52] dislikes because he entertained Ismaili sentiments.[53]

Concluding Remarks

Preparing a critical edition of the Alamūt and post-Alamūt Ismaili texts is a daunting task. Apart from all the difficulties that W. Ivanow highlights,[54] the very nature of Persian script is such that a wrong diacritical sign or a dot can change the meaning of a word, a sentence, or an entire paragraph; not to mention the interpolations, deletions and corrections by scribes that need to be corrected with care and occasionally seeking expert advice. The outcome however is rewarding. First of all, it enables the students to have access to a better version of a text, until such time when the original autographed copy becomes known. More important is the correction of misunderstandings and falsifications. The discovery of the *Dīwān-i Qā'imiyyāt* and its publication alongside the critical edition of the *Haft bāb* enables us not only to have a clear idea of the development of Ismaili theology and its parameters,[55] but also correcting two extremely important issues in the history of the Nizārī Ismailis, namely, the accusation of discarding or abolishing the Islamic religious law and the claim that the Ismaili imams were not legitimate Shiʿi imams as we see mainly in the classical Persian books of history.

In the *Qā'imiyyāt*, Ḥasan-i Maḥmūd elaborates on the above mentioned subjects and speaks of the 'Preaching of the Resurrection' (*daʿwat-i qiyāmat*) as a step towards the perfection (*ikmāl*) of the *sharīʿa*,[56] and in the *Haft bāb* he speaks about Nizār and his offspring's who ruled Egypt.[57] The case of Nizār's appointment as the heir of al-Mustanṣir is recorded in the *Dustūr al-Munajjimīn*, by an anonymous author who probably lived at the time in Cairo and moved to Alamūt a few years before the death of Ḥasan-i Ṣabbāḥ.[58] Further elaborations about Nizār's offspring are attested by Egyptian historians of the time[59] in conformity with the classical books on genealogy such as Ibn ʿInaba's (d. 828/1425) *ʿUmdat al-ṭālib*.[60] Such evidence exposes the stories fabricated by Juwaynī concerning the genealogy of the Nizārī Ismaili imams of Alamūt and their supposed setting aside of the Islamic religious law.[61]

Further, the publication of the *Qā'imiyyāt*, as noted by Shafīʿī Kadkanī, opens up several new fields of investigation, namely, the potential discovery of other Nizārī Ismaili books hidden in personal collections, or Ismaili poetical works that were either completely destroyed or defaced and marketed as non-Ismaili works.[62]

Kadkanī's prediction concerning the discovery of other works proved to be correct, since on my last visit to Iran I came across a newly discovered *Dīwān* by Darwīsh Quṭb al-Dīn who lived in the 17th century. Two copies of the *Dīwān* have been identified. The *Dīwān* reflects the height of the Ismaili-Sufi relationship at the time when the Ismaili Imams disguised themselves as Sufi masters in the Safavid period of the Iranian history.

In the context of the 'Ismaili written heritage' there are other factors at work which should be kept in mind, such as Ismaili texts having been attributed to other faith communities;[63] authors pretending to be ex-Ismailis and writing anti-Ismaili works;[64] interpolations and amendments made by lay Ismaili enthusiasts who changed the implications of a text while preparing a copy for themselves;[65] and above all writing and contributing to Ismaili theology under duress,[66] not to mention misunderstandings that the publication of a corrupt text may cause, as indicated in the comments of M. G. Hodgson about Ivanow's edition of the *Haft bāb*.[67]

NOTES

1 Ḥasan-i Maḥmūd-i Kātib, *Dīwān-i Qā'imiyyāt*, with Persian introduction by M. R. Shafī'ī Kadkanī, ed. Sayyed Jalal Hosseini Badakhchani (2nd ed., Tehran, 2016).

2 Ḥasan-i Maḥmūd-i Kātib, *Haft bāb*, ed. and tr., S. J. Badakhchani as *Spiritual Resurrection in Shi'i Islam: An Early Ismaili Treatise on the Doctrine of Qiyāmat* (London, 2017).

3 Wladimir Ivanow, who first published the *Haft bāb* (in 1933), attributes it to Bābā Sayyidnā, i.e., Ḥasan-i Ṣabbāḥ, the founder of the Nizārī Ismaili movement in Iran, and in his article 'An Ismaili Poem in Praise of Fidawis', *Journal of the Bombay Branch of the Royal Asiatic Society*, New series, 14 (1938), pp. 63–72, which includes the Qaṣida 75 *Dīwān-i Qā'imiyyāt*, pp. 205–208, attributes the *Qaṣida* to Ra'īs Ḥasan or Ra'īs-i Ajal, another Ismaili poet of the Alamūt period who lived a generation earlier. The same attribution is also found in Abū al-Qāsim Kāshānī's *Zubdat al-tawārīkh: bakhsh-i Fāṭimiyān va Nizāriyān*, ed., Muḥammad Taqī Dānishpazhūh (2nd ed., Tehran, 1987), pp. 201–202.

4 Shafī'ī Kadkanī's introduction to *Qā'imiyyāt*, p. 12.

5 Rashīd al-Dīn Faḍl Allāh, *Jāmi' al-tawārīkh*, ed., Muḥammad Raushan (Tehran, 2008), p. 151; Daftary, *The Ismā'īlis: Their History and Doctrines* (2nd ed., Cambridge, 2007), p. 380.

6 In the *Haft bāb*, pp 25–26§47, while reiterating Sayyidnā's words he says: 'We have witnessed all these glad tidings in Mawlānā', that is, Ḥasan 'Alā Dhikrihi al-Salām.' The word 'We', in some manuscripts is 'I' and in some 'They.'

7 Marshall G. S. Hodgson, *The Order of Assassins: The Struggle of the Early Nizari Isma'ilis Against the Islamic World* (The Hague, 1955), p. 279. For more details see my introduction to the *Haft bāb*, pp. 1–10.

8 For example, *Faṣl dar bayān-i shinākht-i imām*, ed. W. Ivanow (Cairo, 1947), pp. 9 and 15.

9 This is possible since in the colophon of the *Haft bāb* (§111), he mentions the name of Ḥasan [for Jalāl al-Dīn] as heir apparent of Muḥammad [for Nūr al-Dīn, better known as Aʿlā Muḥammad] but in the *Qā'imiyyāt* we cannot find any explicit reference to Jalāl al-Dīn Ḥasan who publicly denounced the *Qiyāmat* doctrine. Feasible explanations would be: (a) the poet treated Jalāl al-Dīn's act of abolition of the doctrine as a temporary incident motivated by political measures aimed at creating a united front with Abbasid caliphate against the Mongol threat, or (b) the poet's aim was to collect poems about the *Qiyāmat* only, so he did not include his other poems, and (c) he personally was more inclined to the *Qiyāmat* doctrine because in the *Qā'imiyyāt*, ode 90, he is jubilant when in 633/1236, Imam ʿAla' al-Dīn Muḥammad permits the chief *dāʿī* Muẓaffar b. Muḥammad to read and explain the *Fuṣūl* of ʿAlā Dhikrihi al-Salām, which entailed conditional return to the doctrine.

10 Shafīʿī Kadkanī's introduction in *Qā'imiyyāt*, pp. 9–24.

11 Ibid. pp. 12–14.

12 The word *Qā'imiyyāt* is also used in a generic sense, i.e., in reference to a bulk of literature both in poetry and prose aimed at explicating and popularising the Preaching of the Resurrection.

13 Preparation for the Preaching of the Resurrection seems to have begun immediately after Hasan-i Ṣabbāḥ's return from Cairo because the main trends of the *Qiyāmat* doctrine can be detected in the writings of Muḥammad b. ʿAbd al-Karīm al-Shahrastānī—an Ismaili theologian and heresiographer contemporary with Ḥasan-i Ṣabbāḥ—such as *Mafātīḥ al-asrār wa maṣābīḥ al-abrār*, ed., M. Ādharshab (Tehran, 2008) and his written sermon in the Persian language delivered in Khawārazm (*Majlis-i maktūb-i Khawārazm*). For details see Toby Mayer, 'Introduction', in his *Keys to the Arcana: Shahrastānī's Esoteric Commentary on the Qur'ān* (Oxford, 2009), pp. 7–10 and Naṣīr al-Dīn Ṭūsī, *Rawḍa-yi taslīm*, ed. and tr., S. J. Badakhchani as *Paradise of Submission: A Medieval Treatise on Ismaili Thought* (London, 2005), pp. 157–159§475–482.

14 Naṣīr al-Dīn Ṭūsī, *Sayr wa sulūk*, ed., and tr. S. J. Badakhchani as *Contemplation and Action: The spiritual Autobiography of a Muslim Scholar* (2nd ed., Tehran, 2017), p. 23§1.

15 *Qā'imiyyāt*, author's preamble, p.1.

16 At about this time, there are some indications that scholars from Syria and probably other places were also present in Alamūt. In the colophon of an Arabic treatise called *Al-Dustūr was daʿwat al-mu'minīn li al-ḥuḍūr*, the scribe Aḥmad b. Yaʿqūb al-Ṭayyibī writes that he heard the text from the illustrious *dāʿī* Naṣīr al-Dīn Ṭūsī, who heard it from lord Imam ʿAlā al-Dīn Muḥammad. See *al-Dustūr* in *Arbaʿa Rasā'il Ismāʿīliyya*, ed., ʿĀrif Tāmir (Salamiyya, 1952), p. 101.

17 On Nāṣir al-Dīn Muḥtasham, see Daftary, *The Ismāʿīlīs*, pp. 378–379, 393, and M. Fārūq Furqānī, *Tārīkh-i Ismāʿīliyān-i Quhistān* (Tehran, 2002), pp. 267–269.

18 Ṭūsī, *Sayr wa sulūk*, §1–4.

19 *Haft bāb*, §4.

20 Ibid., p. 91§109.

21 Daftary, *The Ismāʿīlis*, pp. 186–189.

22 On al-Mu'ayyad, see Verena Klemm, *Memoirs of a Mission: The Ismaili Scholar, Stateman and Poet al- Mu'ayyad fī al-Dīn al-Shīrāzī* (London, 2003); and Daftary, *The Ismāʿīlīs*, pp. 203–204.

23 Authorship of the Ikhwān al-Ṣafā is one of the most debated issues, unless we accept that it was a commissioned work, compiled by different authors promulgating the Ismaili *Daʿwat*.

24 Two major periods of *satr* are recorded in the Ismaili history, the first started with the hiding or disappearance of Ismāʿīl b. Jaʿfar al-Ṣādiq and the second with the death of Nizār b. Mustanṣir, the Fatimid caliph.

25 Ṭūsī, *Sayr wa sulūk*, pp. 31–32§16.

26 For example, *Sayr wa suluk*, *Āghāz wa anjām*, *Tawallā wa tabarrā*, *Akhlāq-i Muḥtashamī*, *Akhlāq-i Nāṣirī*, *Risāla dar ni'mat-hā khushī-hā wa ladhat-hā* and a few short treatises yet unpublished.

27 Probably for the first time, Ḥasan-i Maḥmūd met Ṭūsī in Gird Kūh near Dāmghān in the court of Muḥtasham Shihāb al-Dīn who later became the governor of Quhistān in 621/1224, since the letter inviting Ṭūsī to meet the Muḥtasham was in Ṣalāḥ al-Dīn Ḥasan's [i.e., Ḥasan-i Maḥmūd's] handwriting. Being almost 27 years older, Ṭūsī may have looked at him as his mentor. See *Sayr was sulūk*, p. 30§15,

28 Ṭūsī, *Rawḍa-yi taslīm*, p. 170§518.

29 Daftary, *Ismaili Literature: A Bibliography of Sources and Studies* (London, 2004), p. 57.

30 See Hermann Landolt, 'Introduction' to Ṭūsī, *Rawḍa-yi taslīm*, pp. 6–11.

31 See Daftary, *Ismaili Literature*, p. 158.

32 *Rawḍa-yi taslīm* or *Taṣawwurāt* was first edited and published by W. Ivanow in 1950. A critical analysis of the text, detailed manuscript variants, glossary of technical terms and partial English translation constituted part of my DPhil. thesis at the Faculty of Oriental Studies at Oxford University in 1989. The complete text, English translation and introduction by Professor Herman Landolt and philosophical commentary by Christian Jambet was published in 2005.

33 Ṭūsī, *Rawḍa-yi taslīm*, chapters 21, 24 and 26.

34 For more detail see Landolt, 'Introduction', in Ṭūsī, *Rawḍa-yi taslīm*, pp. 1–11.

35 S. J. Badakhchani, 'Introduction' in *Qā'imiyyāt*, p. 108.

36 Kāshānī, a 13th-century historian, quotes a few odes from the *Qā'imiyyāt* in his *Zubdat al-tawārīkh* and apart from that, we do not find any mention of Ḥasan-i Maḥmūd in the chronicles of the Persian poets.

37 For example, *Sayr wa sulūk*, *Āghāz wa anjām* and *Maṭlūb al-mu'minīn*, in S. J. Badakhchani, *Contemplation and Action* (London, 2005) and *Shi'i Interpretations of Islam* (London, 2010).

38 Ḥasan-i Maḥmūd, *Haft bāb*, pp. 1–10.

39 On Bābā Sayyidnā, see Daftary, *The Ismā'īlīs*, pp. 310–344; idem, 'Ḥasan-i Ṣabbāḥ and the Origin of the Nizārī Ismaili Movement', in F. Daftary, ed., *Mediaeval Ismaili History and Thought* (Cambridge and New York, 1996), pp. 181–204; and the following articles by W. Ivanow: 'al-Ḥasan b. Ṣabbāḥ' in *The Encyclopaedia of Islam*, ed. M. Houtsma et al. (London, 1913–1938), vol. 2, p. 276; 'al-Ḥasan b. Ṣabbāḥ' in *Handwörterbuch des Islam*, ed., A. J. Wensinck and J. H. Kramers (Leiden, 1941), pp. 170–171; and 'al-Ḥasan b. Ṣabbāḥ', in *Shorter Encyclopaedia of Islam*, ed., H. A. R. Gibb and J. H. Kramers (Leiden, 1953), pp. 136–137.

40 In the *Haft bāb*, there are 12 references to Bābā Sayyidnā Ḥasan-i Ṣabbāḥ, see *Haft bāb*, §20, 46, 47, 48, 52, 53, 64, 73, 76, 91, 106 and 108.

41 Ibid., pp. 38–39.

42 I am in the process of publishing a new edition and English translation of Abū Isḥāq's *Haft bāb* which was compiled in the 8th/15th century.

43 After the fall of Alamūt until late in the 19th century, Sidih, a small town north of Birjand, was the dwelling place of the leaders of the Ismaili community in Khurasan and the Murād Mīrzā family, being offspring of Naṣīr al-Din Ṭūsī, were venerated and functioned as 'Instructors' (*mu'allim*) and guardians of the Nizārī Ismaili literature.

44 Ivanow also entertained this view and did not include chapter seven in his edition (published in 1933). Marshal Hodgson compared Ivanow's edition with a manuscript at his disposal and added one page to the text, i.e., §101–103 of my 2017 edition.

45 For the other manuscripts used for the edition of *Haft bāb*, see my edition of *Haft bāb*, (London, 2017). pp. 40–41.

46 S. Jalal Badakhchani. *Poems of the Resurrection*: Ḥasan-i Maḥmūd-i Kātib and his *Dīwān-i Qā'imiyyāt*, in Omar Alí-de-Unzaga, ed., *Fortresses of Intellect: Ismaili and other Islamic Studies in Honour of Farhad Daftary* (London, 2011), pp. 431–442.

47 All of the above-mentioned manuscripts are housed at the Ismaili Special Collections Unit, The Institute of Ismailis Studies.
48 Rūdakī Samarqandī, Abū Ja'far b. Muḥammad, also known as father of Persian poetry. His *Dīwān* of around 1200 hemstitches is believed to have originally contained over a million hemstitches. He flourished during the reign of the Sāmānid king Naṣr b. Aḥmad (r. 914–943).
49 A talented Shi'i poet; for Nāṣir Khusraw's mention of his name, see *Dīwān-i Nāṣir-i Khusraw*, ed., Mīnuwī and Muḥaqqiq (Tehran, 1387 Sh./2008), pp. 23, 92, 101, 262, 332, 423, 430, 487 and 497.
50 Compiled some fifty years after the death of Ḥasan-i Ṣabbāḥ, *al-Naqḍ* provides a comprehensive inventory of Shi'i institutions of learning, scholars, poets, and the type of religious debates current at the time.
51 Abū al-'Alā' Ganjawī, an Ismaili poet. His anthology of poems has not survived to our time.
52 Afḍal al-Dīn Badīl b. Ibrāhīm Khāqānī (1122–1190), born in Azerbaijan, married the daughter of Niẓāmī Ganjawī. He is better known for his poems in praise of the Prophet Muhammad and his satirical writings.
53 Shafi'ī Kadkanī's introduction in *Qā'imiyyāt*, pp. 12–14.
54 For Ivanow's comments and obstacles in the editing of the Nizārī Ismā'īlī texts, see *A Guide to Ismaili Literature* (London, 1933); and his *Ismā'īlī Literature, a Second Amplified edition of Guide to Ismaili Literature* (Tehran, 1963).
55 For an overview of different phases of the development of Ismaili theology, i.e., the period of Revelation; the inner meaning and exegesis (*bāṭin and ta'wīl*); the appearance of the authoritative instruction (*ta'līm*) and the preaching's of the Resurrection (*Qiyāmat*), see Jalal Hosseini Badakhchani, *The Paradise of Submission: A Critical Edition and Study of the Rawḍa-yi taslīm commonly known as Taṣawwurāt by Khwāja Naṣīr al-Dīn Ṭūsī* (DPhil dissertation, Oxford University, 1989), pp. 68–123 and idem, 'Introduction', in *Haft bāb*, pp. 4–16.
56 Ṭūsī uses *istikmāl*, see *Rawḍa*, §79,192,251 and 399, see also Christian Jambet's foreword to *Haft bāb*, p. xvii.
57 *Haft bāb*, p. 64§38.
58 See *Dustūr al-Munajjimīn* (*ca*. 500/1106), facsimile ed. (Tehran, 2019), f. 343.
59 *Haft bāb*, p. 70§52.
60 Ibn 'Inaba, Jamāl al-Dīn b. Aḥmad. *'Umdat al-ṭālib fī ansāb-i āl Abī Ṭālib* (Najaf, 1961), p. 237.
61 Juwayni, 'Alā' al-Dīn 'Aṭā Malik. *Tārīkh-i Jahāngushā*, ed., M. Qazwīnī (Leiden, 1936–1964), pp. 222–240.
62 *Qā'imiyyāt*, introduction, p. 15.
63 This trend appears to be the consequence of the precautionary dissimulation (*taqiyya*) employed to cover up the Ismaili orientation of a text. For its practice in Badakhshān, see Maryam Moezzi, *Ismā'īliyya-yi Badakhshān* (Tehran, 2016), pp. 193 and 203–225.
64 See Muḥammad Karīm Khurāsānī, *al-Tanbīhāt al-jaliyya fī kashf asrār al-bāṭiniyya* (Najaf, 1351/1932). For more detail see Mas'ūd Mīrshāhī, *Wāqi'a-yi Ismā'īlīhā-yi Nishābūr*, Kaweh, no. 126 (Berlin, 2009), pp. 74–75 and 82.
65 This phenomenon is visible in some manuscripts of the *Haft bāb*.
66 Daftary, *The Ismā'īlīs*, pp. 379–380 and his foreword to the 2nd edition of *Sayr wa sulūk* (Tehran, 2017), p. 8.
67 *Haft bāb*, p. 42, n.114.

SECTION V

COMMUNAL SCRIPT, SCRIBAL ELITE, AND SATPANTH MANUSCRIPT CULTURE

11

Khwājah Sindhi (Khojki): Its Name, Manuscripts and Origin*

Shafique N. Virani

Like musk are the wise, their wisdom its fragrance
  Else like mountains they are, the hidden gold, their wisdom
Fragrance divorced from its musk is naught but guile
  Once you extract gold from its ore, what's left but worthless
    rock?
Where is this gold hidden along with that musk?
  Let me seek that jewel box of inherent value!
Thence I stirred, setting out on my journey
  Forgetting the comforts of home, garden, and all that
    appeared fair
From Persian and Arab, from Hindi and Turk
  From Sindhi, Byzantine, and Hebrew, from all bar none
From philosopher and Manichean, from atheist and Sabian
  I asked for what I sought, inquiring incessantly[1]

From All Bar None: Recovering South Asian Islam

Applauded as both 'a genius and a visionary', Marshall Hodgson (d. 1968) transformed the study of Islam like few others.[2] In his time, he decried the 'Arabistic. . .bias' that he saw 'reflected in book after book and article after article; not least in the *Encyclopaedia of Islam*'.[3] Acknowledging that earlier editions of this erudite and indispensable *Encyclopaedia* had the 'Arabic textual tradition' as a 'primary focus', the preface of the current third edition, promises that:

> While adhering to the rigorous scholarly standards of its predecessors, this third edition is explicitly innovative in a

> number of respects. First, the entire compass of the Muslim world is being taken seriously, both geographically and chronologically. Moving further in the direction already adopted in the more recent sections of the second edition, EI3 will devote full attention to such areas as South and Southeast Asia, Sub-Saharan Africa, and indeed the Muslim presence in wider areas of the world.[4]

Such declared aims are promising and aspire to address critiques *à la* Hodgson. However, the *Encyclopaedia*'s 'Instructions for Authors' belie these vigorous avowals by providing only four transliteration tables, all for the Arabic script. Even a table supposedly for 'Urdu, Hindi, and Punjabi', inexplicably ignores the Devanagari and Gurmukhi scripts, both of which have rich traditions of Muslim literature. The instructions completely overlook countless other scripts, languages, and literatures of South Asia, Sub-Saharan Africa, and elsewhere.[5]

Nāṣir-i Khusraw extolled the virtues of seeking knowledge 'From Persian and Arab, from Hindi and Turk, from Sindhi, Byzantine, and Hebrew, from all bar none.' Such cosmopolitanism would go a long way toward addressing Marshall Hodgson's withering assessment of Islamic studies and his deeply held conviction that it was imperative to adopt a global approach to Muslim and world history.

One of the earliest Western references to South Asian Ismaili literature 'in the Sindhi character and Cutchi language' mirrors the strong Middle Eastern bias in Islamic Studies.[6] In the 'Case of the Khojahs,' an 1847 lawsuit about inheritance customs, Chief Justice Sir Thomas Erskine Perry wrote: 'Nor have they any scholars or men of learning among them, as not a Khojah could be quoted who was acquainted with Arabic or Persian, the two great languages of Mahomedan literature and theology.'[7] The overt racism of the judge's assessment may gall modern sensitivities, but it underscores the type of chauvinism expressed toward non-Middle Eastern forms of Muslim expression.[8] The judge's sentiments reflected the condemnation of the Indian cultural milieu by certain members of the *ashrāf*, the foreign-born Muslim 'elite'. As Asani writes, their 'desire to maintain the "pristine" purity of Islam led them to disparage everything Indian — from Indian languages which they considered unworthy of recording Islamic religious literature to even the native Indian Muslims whom they contemptuously called *ajlāf*, "mean," "ignoble," "wretches".[9] Scholarship and learning, by definition, were the preserve of Arabic and Persian. Hence, the significant achievements of Muslim literatures in Indic languages such as Hindi, Bengali, Panjabi, Sindhi, Gujarati, and others were summarily dismissed. As Gottschalk has trenchantly pointed out, 'The British Orientalists of South Asia paid far more attention to Hinduism, opting to rely on their Middle Eastern-assigned colleagues to describe Islam from the supposed heartland'.[10]

The Khwājah Sindhi (Khojki) manuscript collection is among the most significant holdings of the Ismaili Special Collections Unit of The Institute of Ismaili Studies. This corpus records the literary legacy of the South Asian Ismailis, most prominently the *ginān*s, along with significant samples of literature from sister communities. Thus, we find verses of the most illustrious mystic poets of Sindh, Shāh ʿAbd al-Laṭīf and Sachal Sarmast; passages from the works of renowned *bhaktī* and *sant* poets such as Kabīr, Mīrābāī, Nānak, Ravīdās, and Narsīṃh Mahetā; selections from the *Spiritual Couplets* (*Mathnawī-yi maʿnawī*) of Jalāl al-Dīn Rūmī in both the Persian original and in Sindhi translation; and *ghazals* composed by Amīr Khusraw and Shaykh Saʿdī.[11]

The community called its script 'Sindhi', a name also applied to other scripts from Sindh. An important section of the South Asian Ismaili community was identified by the Persian honorific title Khwājah or Khojā (the common pronunciation in many parts of Sindh and Gujarat, respectively).[12] Therefore, when necessary to distinguish its script from others, the community would employ terms such as 'Khwājah Sindhi'. We adopt the same practice in this chapter when necessary to differentiate from other Sindhi scripts or from the Sindhi language. As we will discuss below, in recent times, scholars have widely adopted the name 'Khojki', though the origins of this neologism have hitherto been little known.

Before the age of the printing press and the era of official language standardisation, a variety of scripts and literatures held sway in regions and communities across South Asia. However, as Salomon laments, such scripts:

> . . . are not well documented, and little published information is available about their current status. Many of them have fallen out of use within the last century, largely due to the standardizing

> effect of printing technology and of the language policy of the republic of India since independence, which has favoured the propagation of the official languages of the individual states, and along with each of them, a standard script.[13]

Following this introductory section entitled 'From All Bar None: Recovering South Asian Islam', this chapter analyses three questions related to the study of Khwājah Sindhi and its manuscript tradition. 'From Sindhi to Khojki: The Evolution of a Name' explores how the modern name Khojki has almost displaced the original names used by the community itself, such as Sindhi and Khwājah Sindhi.[14] 'Ancient Manuscripts, Modern Neglect' documents the survival, and possible loss, of several Khwājah Sindhi manuscripts of greater antiquity than the oldest known text currently in an institutional collection. Lastly, 'Pīr Ṣadr al-Dīn and Khwājah Sindhi: From Attribution to Tradition' questions the widely held scholarly consensus that Ismailis attributed the creation of Khwājah Sindhi to the 14th-century Ismaili luminary Pīr Ṣadr al-Dīn. It also introduces and assesses a hitherto unnoticed tradition regarding the script's origin.

From Sindhi to Khojki: The Evolution of a Name

> *Khudawadi. . . .commonly and erroneously called the Sindhi*
>
> Sir Richard Burton[15]

Abū Rayḥān al-Bīrūnī (d. after 442/1050) bequeathed to posterity one of the most valuable works on Indology ever written. This was his *Book of India* (*Kitāb taḥqīq mā li'l-Hind*), based in part on his personal observations when he visited the region. He mentions eleven scripts current in the Subcontinent, three of which were prevalent in particular parts of Sindh: Ardhanāgarī, Malwārī, and Saindhava.[16]

Centuries later, in 1851, Richard Burton, then a lieutenant in the imperial British army, wrote his well-known *Sindh, and the Races that Inhabit the Valley of the Indus*. In Burton's time, two primary families of scripts existed in the region. One was based on the abjad characters of the Arabic alphabet and the other on the ancient Abugida or 'alphasyllabary' characters of the indigenous Brāhmī script.[17] We know the latter from the Ashokan inscriptions, the oldest definitively dateable engravings in India, which hail from the third century BCE.[18]

In describing Brāhmī's Sindhi descendants, Burton opines disdainfully: 'But however numerous these alphabets may be, they are all, in their present state, equally useless.'[19] The prevailing colonial attitude toward the Sindhis, manifest in the chauvinistic tone of Burton's Preface, may help to explain his cavalier comments about Sindhi scripts:

> . . . the author has striven to the utmost to avoid all unnecessary indelicacy; but in minute descriptions of the manners and customs of a barbarous or semi-civilized race, it is, as every traveller knows, impossible to preserve a work completely pure.[20]

The so-called 'barbarous or semi-civilized' users of the closely related Brāhmic scripts, including two of its most prominent exemplars, now often referred to as Khudāwādī and Khojki, called their scripts 'Sindhi'.[21] Burton was convinced that the native speakers erred in their terminology. Modern scholars needn't be so dismissive. While the term 'Khojki' has become almost universal in scholarship to refer to the script of the South Asian Ismailis, few realise that this usage is of comparatively recent coinage. In fact, its Romanised form with the conjunct *jk* is impossible with most transliteration systems current in academia. The script's *halant* or *virām* sign, which suppresses the inherent vowel and facilitates conjuncts such as the *jk* in the word Khojki, is normally Romanized as a short 'i' or, as we have done in this chapter, as a lowercase dotless i 'ı'.[22] Some researchers seem to have recognised this incongruence. Therefore, they have devised terms that appear more 'correct'. These include 'Khojakī,' or 'Khwājakī'—a sort of 'academic folk etymology'—an attempt to justify the neologism 'Khojki' with an origin that was linguistically possible within the tradition.[23] While such forms existed in the community tradition (albeit rarely), they were generally used adjectivally, not as a proper name for the script. We may trace the evolution from the traditional term 'Sindhi' to the neologism 'Khojki' quite handily.

Murādh: ʿAli: Bhāī: Jumā, an Ismaili poet and publisher, regularly described his lithograph publications of the mid- through late-1800s as being in 'Sindhi', the most prevalent name for the community's script. The script was related to the Sindhi language, but was not used exclusively for it, much as the Arabic abjad script is also employed for languages such as Persian, Ottoman Turkish, and Urdu and the Devanagari script for languages like Sanskrit, Hindi, and Marathi.

Juma's *Ten Sindhi Dirges* (*Sındi: ḍohı marāsiā*) is one example among many.[24] That the word 'Sindhi' in the publication's title refers to the script and not the language is clear from the book's contents, comprising elegies in both the Urdu and Sindhi languages, but all recorded in the 'Sindhi' script. The Ismailis established the 'Khojā Sındhi' printing press in Mumbai in the early 1900s, in which Sindhi referred to the script, and not necessarily the language, of the publications.[25] In around 1904, the compiler of the injunctions (sg. *farmān*) of His Highness Āghā Khān III regretted the inadequacies of the 'Sindhi' moveable metal typeface (*bībā*) available to him.[26] Similarly, writing in Gujarati in 1917, Vīrajī Premajī Pārapīā tells of a family history handwritten in 'Sindhi characters' by his maternal grandfather's paternal cousin, Kāmaḍīā Jāpharabhāi Dhālāṇī.[27] The following year, in the Gujarati publication of the *Tale of Light* (*Nur nāmu*), Hājī Neṇashībhāī Nathu of Mumbai noted that he had transcribed the book from 'an ancient manuscript written in Sindhi characters' (*purātan Sindhī akṣharanā hast lekh*).[28] In his Introduction to the first Gujarati script edition of the ginān *Tales of Truth*, majora (*Sataveṇī Moṭī*), published in 1919, Mukhī Lalajībhāī Devarāj writes in some detail about how Ismaili publications in the Gujarati script came about, supplementing publications in the traditional community script, which he also refers to throughout as 'Sindhi'.[29] Such examples illustrating that the script was known simply as 'Sindhi' could be multiplied many times over.

Schools where Ismailis taught their religious literature in the community script were called 'Sindhi' schools. The textbooks bore the titles *Sindhi Book One* through *Sindhi Book Four*. While the earliest lithograph editions of these textbooks published in the mid-1890s were in the Sindhi language transcribed in Khwājah Sindhi script, the textbooks produced from 1909 onward were in the Gujarati language transcribed in Sindhi script and still titled 'Sindhi Books'.[30] Thus, Mujtaba Ali writes in 1936, 'Sindhi schools are evening schools situated in the Jamā'at Khāna [the Ismaili congregation centre] where Khojāh boys receive religious training and learn to read the Sindhi language in which the gināns are written'.[31] Mujtaba Ali is clearly referring to the Khwājah Sindhi script, rather than the Sindhi language, *per se*, as the vast majority of gināns are not in the Sindhi language.[32] The community referred to the script as 'Sindhi' almost exclusively until at least the late

1940s. The titles of children's school books, such as later editions of the aforementioned four *Sindhi Books* (*Sındi Chopaḍī 1-4*), as well as *A Garland of Sindhi Children's Lessons* (*Sindhīḇāḷaḇodamāḷā*), and *Sindhi Children's Picture Lessons* (*Sındi bāḷ chitraḇod*) bear witness to this.[33]

The proceedings of several court cases also reflected community usage. For example, Justice Perry's aforementioned remarks of 1847 describe the recording of an Ismaili religious work in 'Sindhi character and Cutchi language.'[34] Approximately two decades later, Edward Howard, counsel for the defence in the Aga Khan Case, in a speech about the Khwājahs at the Bombay High Court, referred to 'their old books. . .written in the Sindhi characters and in a mixed language of Kutchi and Gujerati.'[35] In his judgement on the case, Sir Joseph Arnould said of the Khwājahs, 'Their language is Scindi or Cutchee—a cognate dialect—and such ancient religious works as they possess are written in the Scindi language and character'.[36] These remarks were repeated verbatim in the so-called 'Haji Bibi Case' of 1905-1908.[37]

Unlike justice officials, the British administrative bureaucracy needed to distinguish the Sindhi script of the Khwājahs from other related scripts, and thus added variations of the word 'Khwājah' to describe it. For example, Captain George Stack (1849), followed by George Grierson (1919), described it as the Sindhi of the 'Khwājās', Richard Burton (1851) as 'that used by the Khwajah tribe', and Edward Aitken (1907) as 'the "Khoja" character'.[38] This was also the practice adopted by some pioneering scholars who examined Ismaili printed books and manuscripts. For example, in 1893, in his catalogue of Hindi, Panjabi, Sindhi, and Pashtu books in the Library of the British Museum, and then in 1905 in his account of Indic manuscripts in the same museum, James Blumhardt described several books recorded in the 'Khoja-Sindhi character' and a manuscript from Zanzibar 'written in a character of the type of Ḵẖwājah Sindhi'.[39]

Occasionally, the Ismailis also found it necessary to distinguish their own Sindhi script from Sindhi preserved in the abjad script. To specify that the script they were referring to was specific to the Khwājah or Khojā community, they added the suffix *ī*, common to both Persian and several Indic vernaculars, generating a qualitative adjective. After the sound 'ah', an epenthetic *k* (rather than the more common *g*) was added to create words such as 'Khojakī' or 'Khojıki', an adjective to qualify Sindhi.[40] This adjective was, however, not originally used as a substantive noun. Its usage was strictly adjectival. For example, the 1926 report of the annual meeting of the Khoja Ismaili Library of Karachi accounted its book holdings by language, noting that there were 985 titles in Gujarati, 473 in English, 89 in 'Sīndhī Khojakī', 26 in 'Sīndhī Phārasī' (i.e., Sindhi in the abjad or 'Farsi' script), 18 in Urdu, 13 in Persian, and 4 in Arabic.[41] The first instance I'm aware of in which a Gujarati author uses a similar word as a substantive comes not from the Khwājah community itself, but from the sister Ismaili community, the Momnās. Momīn Miyāñjī Nuramahamad wrote in 1936, 'Pīr Ṣadr al-Dīn has written many books in the Khojākī language, most of which are in poetic form'.[42] However, the popularisation of the word as a substantive in academia is clearly due to the influence of Wladimir Ivanow, a Russian scholar of Ismailism who had close relationships with the Ismailis in India. Early on, he seems to have adopted the adjectival usage of the word from the community. Thus, in 1936 he noted that the gināns were 'written down in Sindhi (Khojki) characters' and in 1938 described the 'Khojki Sindhi' inscriptions on a slab and gravestones dating between 1722 and 1810 at the mausoleum of Imam Nizār (d. 1134/1722) in Iran.[43] However, in the same 1938 article, like Nuramahamad before him (who innovates Khojākī rather than Khojakī), he used the term as a substantive, a proper noun to name the script. He explained that he was providing the inscriptions in Nagari transliteration as 'Khojki type is not available.'[44] He maintained this novel usage in his edited volume *Collectanea* in 1948, in which he captioned an image of a page of printed text: 'in Gujrati (in Khojki characters)' and writing in a footnote, 'Printed in Bombay (in Gujrati, but in Khojki script)'.[45] Ivanow's usage of Khojki as the script's proper name was quite foreign to Ismaili practice. However, later scholars who cited him followed his practice, such as Hollister in his *Shiʿa of India*.[46]

Later, Ghulam Ali Allana's 1963 work, 'Sindhi poetry of the Sumra era' (*Sūmran je daur jī Sindhī shāʿirī*) made the natural addition *Khwājakī Sindhī*, reflecting the name of the community as pronounced in parts of Sindh and the aforementioned usage *Sindhī Khojakī*. He also added the name *Forty-lettered* (*Chālīha akharī*), which technically refers to the 'garland of sounds'-style charts (*varṇamālā*) found in the manuscripts, and known by this title.[47] The following year, in his *Sindhi Scripts* (*Sindhī ṣūratkhaṭṭī*), he included the previously undocumented form *Khwājiko* (which he omits in a later publication).[48] In an English publication, he uses 'Khuwaja Sindhi', mirroring the early British usage, and notes, likely recording current practice at the time of his writing in the 1980s, that 'In Sindh it is also called "Khuwajiki Sindhi" but in India and Africa it is simply known as "Sindhi".'[49]

From the 1940s onward, in Ismaili literature itself, we witness the importation of the newly coined term 'Khojki', not as an adjective describing a type of Sindhi, but as a proper noun. For example, in the third edition of the aforementioned *Tales of Truth*, majora (*Sataveṇī moṭī*), published in 1949, in contrast to the first edition, the editor precisely imitates Ivanow's usage, writing about the 'Sindhi (Khojki) script'.[50] The same is true in the *Khojki Urdu Primer* (*Khojıki Uradu pırāimar*), a 1950 elementary schoolbook for Urdu speakers with new editions appearing afterward, and translated from its counterpart, ironically named *Khojki Sindhi Primer* (*Khojıki Sındi pırāimar*), with the word 'Sindhi' no longer referring to the script, but to the language spoken by the schoolchildren.[51] The popularisation across the region of the abjad script for Sindhi was a factor in this shift. However, the traditional nomenclature of 'Sindhi' continued in the community alongside the new term. For example, in his Introduction to the sixth Gujarati edition of the *Words of the Lord* (*Kalāme Maulā*), published in 2009 VS/1953 CE, Vali Nanji Hooda writes of the three 'Sindhi' editions of the book and of the 'Sindhi type[face]'.[52] By the 1980s, the neologism had made inroads into Gujarati Ismaili literature, though Ismailis still did not widely accept the Anglicised usage of 'Khojki' by itself without 'Sindhi'. Thus, we read in Abdul Husen Alībhāi Nānajī's *The Pir Has Graced Our Threshold* (*Pīr Padhāryā Āpaṇe Dvār*) about the anthology of gināns published 'in Sindhī Khojakī script' (*Sindhī Khojakī lipi*).[53]

By contrast, Ivanow's 1938 usage of the word 'Khojki' divorced from 'Sindhi' was adopted by most scholars writing in Western languages. With few exceptions, such as Zawahir Moir's article, 'Khwajah Sindhi Literature', specialist literature since the 1970s, while occasionally acknowledging alternative terms, has followed Ivanow's innovation of 'Khojki' by itself, or variant Romanizations.[54] Those who lived through the evolution of the nomenclature, though, were well aware that 'Khojki' was a neologism. Thus, in an English-language article published in 1990, one Ismaili preacher (*wāʿiẓ*), born in 1919, wrote of 'the script now known as Khojki'.[55]

Ancient Manuscripts, Modern Neglect

> *. . . it is possible that [the writings of the Ismailis] constitute the oldest extant literary expression of Sindhi. . .parts of the later Ismaili literature in Kachchhi, Gujrati, and a few pieces in Sindhi are of so archaic a character that we may accept some of them as genuinely ancient witnesses of the language of the Lower Indus Valley.*
>
> Annemarie Schimmel[56]

There are gināns that refer to a written tradition at the time of their composition and to the transcription of copies from originals.[57] Take, as one example among many, this passage from the 15th/16th-century Ismaili mystic Sayyid Nūr Muḥammad Shāh's *Vine of the Tale of Truth*, majora (*Satavenī moṭī nī vel*), in which he describes his encounter with the Kaṇbīs, an agricultural community that had accepted Ismailism:

Overcome was I with pity then
  And said to that congregation:
'With all your entreaties now
  That knowledge shall I bestow upon you
This knowledge is named *The Account of Truth*
  Conduct your religious works by its injunctions
The innermost essence of all knowledge it is
  In which is written what shall ferry you across the ocean of existence
Countless narratives shall it contain
  The secrets of the saints and prophets
All the mysteries of the faith are in it
  The manners and ways of the path of truth
All the ancient tales of the world
  Have manifested themselves in a venerable form'
None of the world's knowledge can compare
  To what was bestowed upon the believers there
From the original which had been recorded
  A copy was transcribed
Placed in their hands this was:
  'Together, follow its injunctions

Enter the religion and adopt its ways
  Propagate the mysteries of worship and goodness
In this are all the practices of religion
  Which will be limitless'
Such was the knowledge I bestowed
  Upon those who had love for the guide
O you, my beloved, the true master is none other than you!
  Taking it, they all departed
    Those who follow its injunctions
  The true guide says:
    They shall be blessed with gnosis[58]

Unfortunately, local South Asian communities, whether Hindu, Muslim, or otherwise, rarely had the means or the expertise to preserve manuscripts. Academics did not give the vernacular literatures the same attention they gave to Sanskrit, Arabic, and Persian, resulting in tremendous neglect and the loss of countless works.

Scholars generally consider the earliest extant manuscript evidence of Sindhi poetry to be seven verses of a certain Qāḍī Qādan (d. 958/1551), as recorded in the Persian *Account of the Gnostics* (*Bayān al-ʿārifīn*), composed by Muḥammad Riḍā of Thatta, the medieval capital of Sindh, in 1038/1629.[59] The oldest extant manuscript in Gujarati script dates to 1592.[60] Khwājah Sindhi manuscripts of even greater antiquity existed in recent memory, but it is not clear whether these still survive.

In the case of Haji Bibi vs. The Aga Khan at the High Court of Bombay, Juma Jan Muhammad Ismail, whose family had traditionally looked after the shrine of the Ismaili Pīr Tājdīn (fl. 9th/16th c.) in Sindh, presented a Khwājah Sindhi manuscript of gināns dated 1622 VS/1565 CE.[61] Another manuscript of gināns dated *ca.* 1531 VS/1474 CE was also submitted.[62] The latter predates the oldest known abjad Sindhi and Gujarati manuscripts by over a century. A report from 1924 indicates that several ginān manuscripts dating from the 1600s onward were available in Ismaili prayer houses (*jamāyatakhānā*) in India.[63] The Kaṭhiyāvāḍ Ismaili Literature Promulgation Society (*Ismāilī Sāhity Prachārak Maṇḍaḷ*) of Bhāvnagar, represented by Nuradīn Mīṭhābhāī Budhavāṇī, Valīmahamad Nānajī Ghīvāḷā, Gulāmahusen Ḍī. Anīl and Valī Nānajī Hudā, exhibited several of these, dating to the early 1700s, at the *Seventh Gujarati Literature Conference* held in 1924.[64] The manuscript used for the edition of the ginān *Tales of Truth*, majora (*Sataveṇī moṭī*) was dated between 1669 and 1719.⁶⁵ In more recent times, an independent researcher identified Khwājah Sindhī manuscripts in personal collections dated 1594 VS/1538 CE and 1608 VS/1552 CE, along with others of significant antiquity.⁶⁶

Unfortunately, none of the owners of these older manuscripts appear to have donated them to institutional collections, and it is unclear whether these copies still exist.⁶⁷ The oldest known Khwājah Sindhī manuscript preserved at an academic institution is KH 25 in the Ismaili Special Collections Unit of The Institute of Ismaili Studies, which dates to 1793 VS/1736 CE.⁶⁸ The oldest of the aforementioned Khwājah Sindhī inscriptions mentioned by Ivanow is on the grave of a certain Āqā Nihāl, dated 1135/1722.⁶⁹ However, several accessible manuscripts were clearly copied from much earlier exemplars. For example, manuscript KH 38 in the Ismaili Special Collections Unit, copied in 1886 VS/1829 CE for Megaji: Manajiāṇi mentions 'Pir Dādu who left, with all well-being, from Nagar for Bhuj in 1641 VS/1584 CE.'⁷⁰ As Nanji notes, 'It is quite clear that such an insertion, which is entirely unrelated to the copyist's task of writing down the gināns, shows that his source must either have been a much older manuscript incorporating a contemporary event, or one that contained such early information'.⁷¹ The antecedent of this notice is possibly a manuscript that the scribe tells us belonged to someone from Pīrāṇ Pāṭaṇ (another name for Pāṭaṇ, the ancient capital city of the Chaulukya dynasty, 23.85°N 72.125°E), which, the scribe relates in some detail, was copied by Rāi: Rehemān: Somajiāṇi, which was copied by Kāmaṇiā Virapār: Sajaṇāṇi, which was copied by his son Vali Virapārāṇi, which was the immediate source of the present text.⁷²

Pīr Ṣadr al-Dīn and Khwājah Sindhī: From Attribution to Tradition

Don't delay in reading the books,
Burst forth from the flaming pillar, like the man-lion Narsiṃh
Pīr Ṣadr al-Dīn⁷³

Virtually all modern scholars of Khwājah Sindhī maintain that an Ismaili belief credits the charismatic figure of Pīr Ṣadr al-Dīn with the invention of the script.⁷⁴ What strikes an odd note is that researchers have never adduced evidence of such a tradition from the extensive written record of the community written in Gujarati and Khwājah Sindhi, nor the British gazetteers that recorded countless oral narratives of communities across the Subcontinent. While it is possible that such documentation exists, no scholar has ever offered a source for it, to the best of my knowledge.

No mention of such a tradition exists in the sections dedicated to the life of Pīr Ṣadr al-Dīn in the early writings of Khwājah Ismaili authors, such as Jaffer Rahimtoola's 1905 work *The History of the Khojas* (*Khojā kom no itihas*), Hāsham Boghā Māstar's 1912 *Origins of the Khojas* (*Asalīyate Khojā*), or Alimahomed Janmahomed Chunara's voluminous *Noorum-Mobin: Or the Sacred Cord of God* (*Nūram mobīn: Yāne Allāhanī pavitr rasī*), with its first edition in 1935 and its fourth and final one in 1961.[75] While the aforementioned Momnā author alludes to Pīr Ṣādr al-Dīn's writing his works in the 'Khojākī language', nowhere does he credit him with the invention of the script.[76] This tradition is also absent in the traditions of sister communities, such as in the *Chronicles of the Pīrs* (*Tavārikhe pīr*), authored in 1934 by the Imāmshāhī Sayyid, Sadaradīn Daragāvālā.[77]

The earliest written record of a tradition attributing the development of the Khwājah Sindhi script to Pīr Ṣadr al-Dīn may go back no earlier than a scholarly article by the Sindhi academic Ghulam Ali Allana in the 1960s.[78] By the 1970s, the idea of Pīr Ṣadr al-Dīn's having developed the Khwājah Sindhi script had gained some currency in the Ismaili community, likely as a result of Allana's publication. We may note as an example the preface and article on Pīr Ḥasan Kabīr al-Dīn in the English-language work, *The Great Ismaili Heroes*, published in 1973.[79] Tellingly, the article on Pīr Ṣadr al-Dīn in the same publication mentions nothing of his involvement with the script, even though an image of a Khwājah Sindhi manuscript accompanies the piece.[80] Similarly, the 1974 Gujarati book *History of the Pīrs* (*Pīrono itihās*), with a second edition in 1977, lacks any such reference.[81] However, later publications, such as Abdul Husen Nānajī's 1986 Gujarati publication *The Pīrs Have Graced our Threshold* (*Pīr padharya āpaṇe dvār*), take the tradition of Pīr Ṣadr al-Dīn's development of the script as a matter of course.[82]

Where did Ghulam Ali Allana get the idea that Pīr Sādr al-Dīn invented the Khwājah Sindhi script? He or one of his informants possibly referred to the rare and hitherto unstudied text, *The Genealogical Tree of the Secret Path* (*Gupat panthakā shujarā*), or a similar work. The content and style of this Indic composition recalls that of the so-called *Book of Highest Initiation*, which, modern scholarship has established, was a myth devised by the community's enemies that passed as 'the secret doctrine of the Ismāʿīlīs'.[83] The manuscript of the Indic work, the only one yet discovered, apparently belonged to a prosperous member of the Khwājah community of Surat and was published in the Gujarati script by Edalajī Dhanajī Kābā in 1916.[84] As the text refers to Ḥasan ʿAlī Shāh, Āghā Khān I, as the reigning Imam, it would have been composed between 1817–1881. The editor admitted to having no information about the work's authorship or the circumstances of its composition. It contains a passage that states: 'The Sindhi letters used by the Khwājahs of Sindh were established by Sohadev Joshī so that the letters of the secret faith could also remain secret, so that nobody else could understand the secret. Thus, he prepared all the treatises, writing them in the secret letters'.[85] While *The Genealogical Tree* considers Pīr Ṣadr al-Dīn and Sohadev Joshī to have been two different people, the Ismailis generally consider Sohadev to have been one of Pīr Ṣadr al-Dīn's titles.[86] The late tradition of this 'Sohadev Joshī's' creation of the Khwājah Sindhi script was apparently unknown to the vast majority of the Khwājah community until Ghulam Ali Allana popularized it in his work without providing the source of his information. If this was the case, he identified 'Sohadev Joshī' with Pīr Ṣadr al-Dīn.

A different tradition, equally unnoticed by scholars, is a statement in the 1892 work *An Account of the Khwājahs* (*Khojā vṛtānt*) by the well-informed Sachedīnā Nānajīāṇī, the Assistant Revenue Commissioner of Kachchh. Nānajīāṇī writes that the script used by the Khwājah community for recording the gināns was originally from the Panjab. The Lohāṇās, among whose descendants were the Khwājahs, brought it thence to Sindh.[87] Nānajīāṇī does not mention any involvement of Pīr Ṣadr al-Dīn. The Panjabi Ismaili Abualy A. Aziz of Amritsar (d. 2008), citing the notes of his grandfather, Aziz (d. 1928), also suggests a Panjabi origin for the script. Unlike Nānajīāṇī, though, he specifically associates it with Pīr Shams, the ancestor of Pīr Ṣadr al-Dīn, who was active in Panjab. The Panjabi Ismailis apparently called their script Gurmukhi (literally meaning 'from the mouth of the guide'), the same name applied by the Sikhs to their own script.[88] Similar to Sikh Gurmukhi, the literatures preserved in Khwājah Sindhi blend several languages and are representatives of the so-called *sant-bhāṣhā*, or the heterogeneous discourse of the saints. Grierson had cautioned already in 1904, 'It is an error to call Gurmukhi the alphabet of the Panjabi language. It is not peculiar to that form of speech. It is, properly speaking, the language of the Sikh Scriptures, most of which are not in Panjabi'.[89] Khwājah Sindhi was, like Sikh Gurmukhi, a script for a wide range of languages beyond Sindhi. These included Persian, a non-Indic language, and to an extent, Arabic as well.

As with the oft-cited narrative of Pīr Ṣadr al-Dīn's involvement, it is difficult to know how far back we can trace the traditions cited by Nānajīāṇī and Aziz. Khwājah Sindhi graphemes are undeniably much closer to the other scripts of Sindh, such as Khudāwādī, than they are to Sikh Gurmukhi. Beginning in 1958, excavations at a site known as Banbhore (variously spelled as Bhanbhore, Bhambhore, etc.), some sixty-five kilometres east of Karachi, further call into question claims of the script's origin in the Panjab. At the dig, investigators discovered potsherds bearing inscriptions dating back to the eighth century.[90] Of the three images of fragments provided by the expedition, the first and third have been identified as Ardhanāgarī, and the second as Lohāṇakī or Lāṛī.[91] The letters of the second fragment bear an obvious resemblance to characters in Khwājah Sindhi and her sister scripts, such as Khudāwādī, demonstrating the clear antiquity of the direct ancestor of these writing systems in Sindh itself.[92] This fact and the presence of graphemes representing the Sindhi implosives strongly suggest an ancient Sindhi rather than a more recent Panjabi provenance.[93]

Afterword: Questions and Conundrums

'Questioning dispels conundrums (puchhaṇā na munjhaṇā). . .'
Sindhi Proverb

A Sindhi proverb advises, 'one who asks won't be entangled', or simply put, 'questioning dispels conundrums' (𑈟𑈯𑈏𑈷𑈘𑈬 𑈞 𑈤𑈯𑈴𑈐𑈘𑈬 or پُڇڻا نه منجهڻا). In this chapter, three questions were posed. The first was regarding the original name of the script now frequently referred to as Khojki. As the evidence from the mid-1800s onward shows, those who wrote in the script, like those who used its sister Khudāwādī, called it Sindhi. When necessary to distinguish it from the abjad or Arabic script, they added adjectives to give formulations such as 'Khwājah Sindhi' (the variant used in this paper) or 'Sīndhī Khojakī'. The Russian scholar Wladimir Ivanow popularized the word 'Khojki' as a noun in an article written in 1936, the same year a Momnā Ismaili scholar writing in Gujarati used the word Khojākī. Ivanow's usage influenced academic works on the subject and in turn, the coinage made inroads into the community. The Arabic abjad script's promulgation as the official script of Sindh hastened the adoption of the new term. However, the community never completely abandoned earlier usages.

The second question was related to the antiquity of the Khwājah Sindhi manuscript tradition. While the oldest known manuscript in an institutional collection dates to 1793 VS/1736 CE, there is extensive documentation of much older exemplars surviving at least until colonial times. Some of these predate the most ancient extant Gujarati and abjad Sindhi manuscripts. If they still survive, they would be extremely valuable for understanding not only Ismailism but the development of vernacular literatures of many sister communities in the Subcontinent.

The third question concerned the origins of the tradition connecting Pīr Ṣadr al-Dīn with the development of the Khwājah Sindhi script. Scholars who refer to this tradition have not adduced it from the extensive written material produced by the community itself or the oral traditions recorded in government gazetteers. Influential Ismaili histories of Pīr Ṣadr al-Dīn in Gujarati do not connect him with the script at all. So if such a tradition existed, it was either not known to or not given credence by the leading intellectuals in the community. Like the name 'Khojki' itself, the tradition of Pīr Ṣadr al-Dīn's involvement possibly entered the community through an academic article, this one published in a Sindhi language journal. The 'tradition' recorded in that article may have come from a little-known 19th-century work, which itself does not clearly state that the originator of the script was Pīr Ṣadr al-Dīn. Meanwhile, a previously undocumented Ismaili tradition concerning the connection of the script with Panjab was also discussed and evaluated.

Beyond these three questions, there are many more conundrums yet to be solved about Khwājah Sindhi and its manuscript heritage. As the Sindhi proverb assures us, with further questioning, these can surely be dispelled as well.

NOTES

* This chapter is dedicated to the memory of the late Alwaez Rai Akberali Babul (d. 2016) and his family.

1 Ḥakīm Abū Muʿīn Nāṣir-i Khusraw, *Dīwān-i Ḥakīm Nāsir-i Khusraw: Matn-i intiqādī hamrāh bā sharḥ*, ed. Jaʿfar Shiʿār and Kāmil Aḥmad-nizhād (Tehran, 1378 Sh./1999), *qaṣīdah* 100, pp. 273–274; Ḥakīm Abū Muʿīn Nāṣir-i Khusraw, *Dīwān-i ashʿār-i Ḥakīm Nāṣir-i Khusraw Qubādiyānī*, ed. Mujtabā Mīnuwī and Mahdī (Mehdi) Muḥaqqiq (Mohaghegh), reprint ed., 2 vols., vol. 1 (Tehran, 1357 Sh./1978 CE); (Originally published, Tehran, 1353 Sh./1974 CE), *qaṣīdah* 242, pp. 509–510; Ḥakīm Abū Muʿīn Nāṣir-i Khusraw, *Dīwān-i Nāṣir-i Khusraw*, ed. Naṣr Allāh Taqawī and Mujtabā Mīnūwī (Tehran, 1373 Sh./1994 CE); (Originally published, Tehran, 1304–1307 Sh./1925–1928 CE), *qaṣīdah* 105, p. 233. All translations in this paper are the author's own, unless otherwise indicated. The meaning of the third couplet cited here is somewhat obscure, as noted in Nāṣir-i Khusraw, *Dīwān-Shiʿār and Aḥmad-nizhād, qāṣīdah* 242, p. 510; Nāṣir-i Khusraw, *Dīwān-Mīnuwī and Muḥaqqiq*, vol. 1, *qaṣīdah* 100, p. 273. The word *mukhabbar* used in the verse has the same sense as *makhbar* and is contrasted with its opposite, the word *manẓar* in the following verse.

2 Bruce B. Lawrence, 'Genius Denied and Reclaimed: A 40-Year Retrospect on Marshall G.S. Hodgson's *The Venture of Islam*', *Marginalia: Los Angeles Review of Books*, November 11, 2014. http://marginalia.lareviewofbooks.org/retrospect-hodgson-venture-islam/.

3 Marshall G.S. Hodgson, *The Venture of Islam: Conscience and History in a World Civilization; The Classical Age of Islam*, 3 vols., vol. 1 (Chicago, 1974); repr., Digital, 2009, p. 40.

4 Marc Gaborieau et al., 'Preface', in *Encyclopaedia of Islam*, ed. Kate Fleet, et al., Online, 3rd ed., (Leiden, 2016).

5 'Instructions for Authors: *Encyclopaedia of Islam, Third Edition*', ed. Kate Fleet, et al. (Leiden, n.d.), pp. 8–11. In this chapter, the transliteration protocols developed jointly by the Policy and Standards Division at the Library of Congress and the Cataloging and Classification Section of the American Library Association, commonly referred to as the ALA-LC Romanization Guidelines, have been followed with the following exceptions: The unvoiced palatals are represented as *cha* and *chha* in preference to *ca* and *cha* and the palatal and cerebral sibilants are represented as *sha* and *ṣha* in preference to *śa* and *sha*. Word-final inherent *a* is dispensed with for all New Indo-Aryan (NIA) languages. The Khwājah Sindhi transliteration system employed, in contrast to many in current use, makes use of the appropriate roman characters for the implosive phonemes. Khwājah Sindhi *halant* is represented as a lowercase dotless i, i.e., ı (Unicode U+0131), following the useful innovation introduced by Christopher Shackle and Zawahir Moir, *Ismaili Hymns from South Asia: An Introduction to the Ginans*, 2nd revised ed. (Richmond, 2000), p. 37. Adopting a strict transliteration system with Khwājah Sindhi is absolutely necessary, but leads to unusual renderings. For example, 𑈧𑈬𑈧𑈬𑈐𑈭 𑈡𑈬𑈂 and 𑈛𑈬𑈦𑈤𑈈 must be transliterated Lālaji bāi (rather than Lālaji bhāi) and *dāramık* (rather than *dhāramık*). This is because, in the current state of our knowledge, at least in the majority of manuscripts, the aspirated phonemes *bha* and *dha* are represented by the graphemes 𑈡 and 𑈛.
In this chapter, broad language categories are sometimes employed. Hence the word Hindi includes its various 'dialects', as the word Sindhi encompasses a range of 'dialects', including Kachchhi.

Randall K. Barry, Library of Congress, and American Library Association, 'Arabic', in *ALA-LC Romanization Tables: Transliteration Schemes for non-Roman Scripts*, Online ed., (Washington: Cataloging Distribution Service, Library of Congress, 2012) http://www.loc.gov/catdir/cpso/romanization/arabic.pdf; Randall K. Barry, Library of Congress, and American Library Association, 'Persian', in *ALA-LC Romanization Tables: Transliteration Schemes for non-Roman Scripts*, Online ed., (Washington: Cataloging Distribution Service, Library of Congress, 2012) http://www.loc.gov/catdir/cpso/romanization/persian.pdf; Randall K. Barry, Library of Congress, and American Library Association, 'Gujarati', in *ALA-LC Romanization Tables: Transliteration Schemes for non-Roman Scripts*, Online ed., (Washington: Cataloging Distribution Service, Library of Congress, 2011) http://www.loc.gov/catdir/cpso/romanization/gujarati.pdf; Randall K. Barry, Library of Congress, and American Library Association, 'Sindhi (in Arabic script)', in *ALA-LC Romanization Tables: Transliteration Schemes for non-Roman Scripts*, Online ed., (Washington: Cataloging Distribution Service, Library of Congress, 2013) http://www.loc.gov/catdir/cpso/romanization/sindhi.pdf; Randall K. Barry, Library of Congress, and American Library Association, 'Hindi', in *ALA-LC Romanization Tables: Transliteration Schemes for non-Roman Scripts*, Online ed., (Washington: Cataloging Distribution Service, Library of Congress, 2013) http://www.loc.gov/catdir/cpso/romanization/hindi.pdf; Randall K. Barry, Library of Congress, and American Library Association, 'Urdu (In Arabic Script)', in *ALA-LC Romanization Tables: Transliteration Schemes for non-Roman Scripts*, Online ed., (Washington: Cataloging Distribution Service, Library of Congress, 2012); Randall K. Barry, Library of Congress, and American Library Association, 'Sanskrit and Prakrit (in Devanagari script)', in *ALA-LC Romanization Tables: Transliteration Schemes for non-Roman Scripts*, Online ed., (Washington: Cataloging Distribution Service, Library of Congress, 2012) https://www.loc.gov/catdir/cpso/romanization/sanskrit.pdf; Randall K. Barry, Library of Congress, and American Library Association, 'Panjabi (in Gurmukhi script)', in *ALA-LC Romanization Tables: Transliteration Schemes for non-Roman Scripts*, Online ed., (Washington: Cataloging Distribution Service, Library of Congress, 2011) https://www.loc.gov/catdir/cpso/romanization/sanskrit.pdf.

6 Erskine Perry, *Cases Illustrative of Oriental Life and the Application of English Law to India, Decided in H.M. Supreme Court at Bombay* (London, 1853), p. 114.

7 Ibid. 'Kojah' emended to 'Khojah'. The presence of several Persian works preserved in Khwājah Sindhi manuscripts raises questions about Perry's assumption. Of particular note is the *Counsels of Chivalry* (*Pīr Pandiyāt-i Javānmardī*), preserved in several copies, including KH 25, which dates to 1793 VS/1736 CE. See Zawahir Moir, 'A Catalogue of the Khojki Manuscripts in the Library of the Ismaili Institute', London, 1985, pp. [1, 6-7]. For the succeeding period, we also find a lengthy Sindhi translation in Khwājah Sindhi script of the *Guidance for Seeking Believers* (*Hidāyat al-Mu'minīn al-Ṭālibīn*) by Muḥammad ibn Zayn al-ʿĀbidīn Fidāʾī Khurāsānī (d. 1342/1923). See Shafique N. Virani, *The Ismailis in the Middle Ages: A History of Survival, A Search for Salvation* (New York, 2007), p. 27. Gravestones of South Asian Ismailis buried at the Imam's residence in Iran between 1722 and 1810 confirm the community tradition of frequent travel between India and Iran, which would have been facilitated by knowledge of Persian, particularly for those South Asian Ismailis who served at the Imam's *darkhānah*, or place of residence. These gravestones are described below.

8 It is not that the Ismailis were necessarily singled out from among their peers by the British. Hughes quotes Burton and Pottinger as writing, respectively, 'The Sindhi is. . .idle, apathetic, notoriously cowardly and dishonourable, addicted to intoxication, unclean in his person, and immoral in the extreme'. He is 'avaricious, full of deceit, cruel, ungrateful, and such a stranger to veracity, that among bordering nations the term "Sindian dog" is synonymous with "treacherous liar"'. His own assessment is similar, 'In religion the Sindi is a Sūni (sic), though some of them belong to the Shia

sect. There are few learned men among them, notwithstanding that the course of study pursued by their Akhūnds (or instructors) lasts from fifteen to twenty years'. See Albert William Hughes, *Gazetteer of the Province of Sindh*, 2nd ed. (London, 1876); (Originally published, 1874), pp. 86–87. Justice Perry's critique apparently played a role in motiving Kāsam Sumār Thārīyāṇī, a young Khwājah, to pursue higher education, and, in 1898, to succeed Mīrzā Hairat as chair and professor of Persian Literature at the prestigious Elphinstone College in Mumbai. He was elected as head of Arabic and Persian language at the college and was appointed as a fellow of the senate. See Phidāhusen Yusuph Varatejavāḷā, *Phārasī bhāṣhānā pahelā prophesar marhum Kāsam Sumār Thārīyāṇī nuṃ ṭuṅk jīvan vr̥tānt: Athavā Khojā juvāno ne chīmakī* (n.p., 1916), p. 34 et passim; Jāfarabhāī (Jaffer) Rematulā (Rahimtoola), *Khojā kom no itihās* (Mumbai, 1905), pp. 276–278, 283–284. See also University of Bombay, *The Bombay University Calendar for the Year 1887-88* (Bombay, 1887), pp. 205, 404, 449.

9 Ali Sultaan Ali Asani, 'Sufi Poetry in the Folk Tradition of Indo-Pakistan', *Religion & Literature*, 20 (1988), p. 82.

10 Peter Gottschalk, *Beyond Hindu and Muslim: Multiple Identity in Narratives from Village India* (Oxford, 2000), p. 28.

11 See, for example, Zawahir Noorally, 'Catalogue of Khojki Manuscripts in the Collection of Ismailia Association for Pakistan', Karachi, 1971, manuscript nos. 1, 5, 9, 18, 28, 34, 51, 99.

12 In Kachchh, both pronunciations were current. See James Burgess, *Archaeological Survey of Western India: Report on the Antiquities of Kāṭhiāwāḍ and Kachh; Being the Result of the Second Season's Operations of the Archaeological Survey of Western India, 1874-75* (London, 1876), p. 194. Several other spellings besides Khwājah and Khojā are commonly found as well. The influential *Cyclopaedia of India* by Edward Balfour is representative in moving seamlessly between Khwaja, Khwajeh, Khwajo, Khoja, Khojah, Khojo, Khajah, Kojah, Khoaja, and Cojia. See *The Cyclopaedia of India and of Eastern and Southern Asia: Commercial, Industrial, and Scientific; Products of the Mineral, Vegetable, and Animal Kingdoms, Useful Arts and Manufactures*, 3rd ed., vol. 2 (London, 1885); (Originally published, 1857), pp. 54, 106, 168, 190-191, 205, 229, 249, [5]37, [5]54. See also Edward Granville Browne, *A Literary History of Persia: From Firdawsī to Sa'dī*, 4 vols., vol. 2 (Cambridge, 1906), p. 460. As the word comes from the Persian خواجه, and the pronunciation Khwājah is commonly used, particularly in Sindh, this Romanization is preferred in this chapter, though variants will abound in quotations, due to the diverse spellings found in the sources. For Khwājah, see also Anjuman-i Ismā'īlīyah, *Marāsilāt: Khwājah Ithnā 'asharī jī 12 sherātīn jā jawāb* (Hyderabad, Sindh, 1920). An early use of the term may be found in Saiyaḍ Imāmashāhā, *Janat puri*, 2nd ed. (Mumbai, 1976 VS/1920 CE), vv. 85–88; Vali Mahomed Nanji Hooda, 'Some Specimens of Satpanth Literature', chap. 2, in *Collectanea*, ed. Wladimir Ivanow, vol. 1 (Leiden, 1948), p. 131.

13 Richard G. Salomon, 'Writing Systems of the Indo-Aryan Languages', chap. 3, in *The Indo-Aryan Languages*, ed. Dhanesh Jain and George Cardona (London, 2003), p. 69.

14 For the prevailing current opinion on the name, see Azim Nanji, *The Nizārī Ismā'īlī Tradition in the Indo-Pakistan Subcontinent* (Delmar, NY, 1978), p. 8.

15 Richard Francis Burton, *Sindh, and the Races that Inhabit the Valley of the Indus: With Notices of the Topography and History of the Province* (London, 1851), pp. 154, 401n48. Burton's endnote has been interpolated following the ellipses.

16 Muḥammad ibn Aḥmad Bīrūnī, *Fī taḥqīq mā li'l-Hind min maqūlah maqbūlah fi'l-'aql aw mardhūlah*, ed. C. Eduard Sachau (Hyderabad, 1377 AH/1958 CE), p. 135; Muḥammad ibn Aḥmad Bīrūnī, *Fī taḥqīq mā li'l-Hind min maqūlah maqbūlah fi'l-'aql aw mardhūlah*, ed. and tr. Eduard C. Sachau, *Alberuni's India: An Account of the Religion, Philosophy, Literature, Chronology, Astronomy, Customs, Laws and Astrology of India, about A.D. 1030*, vol. 1 (London, 1887), p. 173. The names of the scripts are Romanized as per Sachau's rendering.

17 Throughout this chapter I use 'abjad' script rather than 'Perso-Arabic script'. With regard to this term, see Azartash Azarnoosh, 'Abjad', in *Encyclopaedia Islamica*, ed. Wilferd Madelung and Farhad Daftary, Online ed., (Leiden, 2015); Georg Krotkoff, 'Abjad', in *Encyclopaedia Iranica*, ed. Ehsan Yarshater, Online ed., (New York, 2011) http://www.iranicaonline.org/articles/abjad; Azarnoosh, 'Abjad', in *Encyclopaedia Islamica*; Gustav Weil and Georges S. Colin, 'Abdjad', in *Encyclopaedia of Islam*, ed. Peri J. Bearman, et al., tr. Rahim Gholami, Online, 2nd ed., (Leiden, 2012). The term abugida is derived from the first four consonants and vowels of the Ethiopic script. Each character of an abugida 'denotes a consonant accompanied by a specific vowel, and the other vowels are denoted by a consistent modification of the consonant symbols, as in Indic scripts'. See Peter T. Daniels, 'The Study of Writing Systems', chap. 1, in *The World's Writing Systems*, ed. Peter T. Daniels and William Bright (New York, 1996), p. 4.

18 Richard G. Salomon, 'Brahmi and Kharoshthi', chap. 30, in *The World's Writing Systems*, ed. Peter T. Daniels and William Bright (New York, 1996), p. 373.

19 Burton, *Sindh, and the Races*, p. 153.

20 Ibid. vi.

21 This is, in fact, how Stack, writing in 1849, refers to the Khudāwādī variety of the script. George Stack, *A Grammar of the Sindhi Language* (Bombay, 1849), pp. 1-2. See also Kanhaiyalal P. Lekhwani, *Sindhī ḇolī aiṉ adab jī tārīḵh* (Mysore, 2011), p. 36; Anshuman Pandey, 'A Roadmap for Scripts of the Landa Family', Ann Arbor, Michigan, University of Michigan, February 9, 2010. ISO/IEC JTC1/SC2/WG2 (N3766 L2/10-011R), pp. 1-2; Anshuman Pandey, 'Proposal to Encode the Sindhi Script in ISO/IEC 10646', Ann Arbor, Michigan, University of Michigan, August 2, 2010. ISO/IEC JTC1/SC2/WG2 (N3871 L2/10-271), pp. 1-3; Arvind Vijaykumar Iyengar, 'A Diachronic Analysis of Sindhi Multiscriptality', *Journal of Historical Sociolinguistics* (November 27, 2020): p. 11.

22 I intend to publish a study of the Khwājah Sindhi vowel and consonant systems, which will explain these nuances in greater detail.

23 For an example of Khojaki and Khojakī, see Gulshan Khakee, *The Dasa Avatāra of the Satpanthi Ismailis and the Imam Shahis of Indo-Pakistan* (PhD dissertation, Harvard University, 1972), p. 6 et passim; Ali Sultaan Ali Asani, 'The Khojkī Script: A Legacy of Ismaili Islam in the Indo-Pakistan Subcontinent', *Journal of the American Oriental Society*, 107 (1987), p. 239; Anshuman Pandey, in collaboration with Shafique N. Virani, 'Final Proposal to Encode the Khojki Script in ISO/IEC 10646', Ann Arbor, Michigan, University of Michigan, January 28, 2011. ISO/IEC JTC1/SC2/WG2 (N3978 L2/11-021), p. 1. For 'Khwajakī' (sic, likely Khwājakī) see Ali Sultaan Ali Asani, 'At the Crossroads of Indic and Iranian Civilizations: Sindhi Literary Culture', in *Literary Cultures in History: Reconstructions from South Asia*, ed. Sheldon I. Pollock (Berkeley, CA, 2003), p. 624.

24 See, for example, [Khojā:] Murād-ʿali: [Bhāi:] Jumā:, ed. *Sındi: ḍohı marāsiā* (Mumbai: [Khojā:] Murād-ʿali: [Bhāi:] Jumā:, 1952 VS/[1896 CE]).

25 It is noteworthy that the usage of 'Khojā Sındhī' in Khoja Sindhi Printing Press here differs from the way the expression would come to be used some decades later. Whereas in the early 1900s, parallel expressions such as 'Khojā jamātakhānā' (Khojā community centre) and 'Khojā kabarasatān' (Khojā cemetery) indicate that the phrase was understood to mean the Sindhi printing press of the Khojās, later usage of Khojā or Khwājah and Sindhi together indicated a particular type of Sindhi, something that only became necessary when the abjad Sindhi script gained widespread acceptance.

26 Sulṭān Muḥammad Shāh Āghā Khān III, *Savant 1959-60 nī (Gu. Kā. tathā Kachh parānt khātenī) musāpharīmāṃ thayalā sarī dhaṇī salāmat dātāranā pharamāno:*, Bhāg trījo-Kachh parānt ([Mumbai]: n.p., [*ca.* 1904]), p. 4.

27 Vīrajī Premajī Pārapīā, *Kābā Timir Bhāskar: Urphe Khojā Ibhalāṇi vanshanuṃ vṛttānt ane Vakil (Pir) Dhādhu* (Mumbai, 1335 AH/1973 VS/1917 CE), p. 4.

28 *Nur nāmu* (Mumbai, 1974 VS/1918 CE).

29 Mukhī Lālajībhāī Devarāj, 'Prastāvanā', in *Sataveṇī moṭī*, ed. Mukhī Lālajībhāī Devarāj, 1st ed. (Mumbai, 1975 VS/1919 CE), pp. 2-3. He also emphasizes that the name of the printing press itself was the 'Khojā Sīndhī chhāpakhānuṃ'. As mentioned, the word 'Khojā' in the name of the press is part of a pattern for all the South Asian Ismaili institutions of the time, such as the 'Khoja Library', the 'Khoja Jamatkhana', and so-forth, and so was not used specifically to identify the type of Sindhi script among others. This becomes particularly clear given the use of the word 'Sindhi' without any adjective in general discussions of the script in this publication, among others. Similarly, writing in 1918, an Ithnā ʿasharī author of Khwājah ancestry noted that the gināns were originally written in Sindhi script, which he was transliterating in Gujarati script (*muḷ Sīndhī līpi uparathī Gujarātī līpimāṃ*). See Edalajī Dhanajī Kābā, ed. *Satapanth shāstr*, 1st ed., vol. 1 (Amreli, Kathiawad, 1918), front cover, pp. 5–6. In another work, he writes of genres of literature known as *jaṅganāmuṃ* and *phatenamuṃ* being written in Kachchhī language and Sindhi script (*Kachchhī bhāṣhā ane Sīndhī līpimāṃ*), and of the Persian work *Pandiyāt-i jawānmardī* being published in Sindhi translation written in Sindhi script by Mukhi Laljibhai Devraj (*Sīdhī (sic) līpi tathā Sīndhī tarajumāmāṃ chhapāvyuṃ chhe*). See his *Khojā Sarv Sangrah*, 1st ed., 2 vols. (Amreli, Kathiawad, 1918), vol. 1, pp. 153, 156, 194.

30 See, for example, [Khojā:] Murād-ʿali: [Bhāi:] Jumā:, *[Sindia peri chopaḍi]* ([Mumbai], [1952 VS/1896 CE]); *Sīndī ḇījī chopaḍī* (Mumbai, 1952 VS/1896 CE) and Sındi ṭekṣhaṭ ḇuk kamiṭi, *Sındi paheli chopaḍi*, 1st ed., 4 vols., vol. 1 (Mumbai, 1966 VS/[1909 CE]); Sındi ṭekṣhaṭ ḇuk kamiṭi, *Sındi ḇiji chopaḍi*, 1st ed., 4 vols., vol. 2 (Mumbai, 1967 VS/[1910 CE]); Sındi ṭekṣhaṭ ḇuk kamiṭi, *Sindi triji chopaḍi*, 1st ed., 4 vols., vol. 3 (Mumbai, 1968 VS/[1911 CE]); Sındi ṭekṣhaṭ ḇuk kamiṭi, *Sındi chothi chopaḍi*, 1st ed., 4 vols., vol. 4 (Mumbai, 1968 VS/[1911 CE]). This style of textbook nomenclature was already ubiquitous in the vernacular literature. See, for example, Munshī Udhārām Thānvardās (Moonshee Oodharam) Mīrchandāṇī, *Sindhī pahriyoṃ kitāb*, 7th ed. (Karāchī, 1877); Ṭī. Sī. (T.C.) Hop (Hope), *Gūjarātī pehelī chopaḍī, Gujarāti First Book*, 11th ed. (Mumbai, 1876).

31 Syed Mujtaba Ali, *The Origin of the Khojāhs and their Religious Life Today*, vol. 8 (Bonn, 1936), p. 105 n. 25, see also pp. 67–68, 74.

32 For a breakdown of language prevalence in the Ginans, see Shackle and Moir, *Ismaili Hymns*, pp. 42–44.

33 Ālījāh Valībhāī Nānajī Hudā, *Sindhīḇāḷaḇodamāḷā*, 6th ed. (1980 VS/1924 CE); *Sındi bāḷ chitraḇod*, 24th ed. (Mumbai, 1949); Sındi ṭekṣhaṭ ḇuk kamiṭi, *Sındi paheli chopaḍi*, 7th ed., 4 vols., vol. 1 (Mumbai, 1984 VS/1928 CE). The use of the term *ḇāḷaḇod* by Hudā is interesting. The term is frequently used in Western India to refer to a variety of the Devanagari script, and currently often denotes Marathi. See, for example, Savāībhāī Rāmachand, *Āṅkanī chopaḍī: muḷākṣhar, bārākhaḍī, nāmāṃ, kāgaḷ, khat, hu[ṇ]ḍī, ka[ṅ] kotrī, hisābanī kuñchīyo, moḍhe gaṇvānā hīsāb, sa[ṅ]khyā, saravāḷā, bādabākī, guṇākār, kāṣhṭako, ane bāḷabodhī muḷākṣharo tathā mahīnā tathā iṅgrejī e. bī. sī. ḍī. sudhī* (Ahmedabad, [*ca.* 1900]), p. 32. To the best of my knowledge, the earliest European attestation of the word *bālabodh* is in the writings of Maturin Veyssière La Croze (d. 1739), the French Benedictine historian and orientalist. See James Fuller Blumhardt and Alfred Master, *Catalogue of the Gujarati and Rajasthani Manuscripts in the India Office Library*, 2nd ed. (Oxford, 1954), p. 6; George Abraham Grierson, *Indo-Aryan Family: Southern Group; Specimens of the Marāṭhī Language* (Calcutta, 1907), p. 16. Based on Hudā's usage in the title of his primer, one wonders if this term was applied to Khwājah Sindhi as another name for the script.

34 Perry, *Cases Illustrative of Oriental Life*, p. 114.

35 Edward Irving Howard, *The Shia School of Islam and its Branches, Especially that of the Imamee-Ismailies: A Speech Delivered by E.I. Howard, Esquire, Barrister-at-Law, in the Bombay High Court, in June, 1866*, ed. H. Wynford Barrow (Bombay, 1866), p. 71.

36 Joseph Arnould, *Judgment by the Hon'ble Sir Joseph Arnould in The Kojah Case otherwise known as The Aga Khan Case heard in the High Court of Bombay, during April and June 1866 (Judgement delivered, 12th November 1866)* (Mumbai, 1867), p. 11.

37 'Haji Bibi v. H.H. Sir Sultan Mohamed Shah, The Aga Khan, Suit No. 729 of 1905', *The Bombay Law Reporter*, 11 (1908), p. 430.

38 George Stack, *A Grammar of the Sindhi Language* (New Delhi, 2001); (Originally published, Bombay, 1849), pp. 3–6, 8; George Abraham Grierson, *Indo-Aryan Family: North-Western Group; Specimens of Sindhī and Lahndā* (Calcutta, India, 1919), pp. 15–17; Burton, *Sindh, and the Races*, p. 153; Edward Hamilton Aitken, *Gazetteer of the Province of Sind* (Karachi, 1907), p. 161.

39 James Fuller Blumhardt, *Catalogue of the Marathi, Gujarati, Bengali, Assamese, Oriya, Pushtu, and Sindhi Manuscripts in the Library of the British Museum* (London, 1905), p. 40; James Fuller Blumhardt, *Catalogues of the Hindi, Panjabi, Sindhi, and Pushtu Printed Books in the Library of the British Museum* (London, 1893). He writes of the latter, 'There are only eleven Sindhi manuscripts. . . . The last manuscript is particularly interesting from a philological point of view. It contains a collection of religious works in a form of Sindhi in which there is a large admixture of Persian and Arabic words, written in a type of the Khwājah character, which it has been impossible to reproduce in type. The Gujarati character has therefore been employed' (vi).

40 This formation is likely what also gave rise to names such as that for the language 'Sirāikī', which Shackle describes as 'most plausibly explained as "the language of the north" (< Sindhi *siro* "up-river, north")' *The Sirāikī Language of Central Pakistan: A Reference Grammar* (London, 1976), p. 2. Thus, using the same logic, the coinage 'Khojki' refers to the script, or language, of the Khojāhs.

41 'Dhī Khojā Īsamāilī Lāyabrerī Karāñchīnī vārṣhik janaral sabhā: Navī menejīṅg kamiṭīnī chuṇṭaṇī', *Dhī Ismāīlī*, April 18, 1926, p. 10.

42 Momīn Mīyāñjī Nuramahamad, *Isamāilī Momin komano itihās*, 1st ed. (Mumbai, 1354 AH/1936 CE), p. 119. Note that the word here is Khojākī rather than Khojakī.

43 Wladimir Ivanow, 'The Sect of Imam Shah in Gujrat', *Journal of the Bombay Branch of the Royal Asiatic Society*, 12 (1936), p. 29; Wladimir Ivanow, 'Tombs of Some Persian Ismaili Imams', *Journal of the Bombay Branch of the Royal Asiatic Society*, 14 (1938), pp. 57–59.

44 Ivanow, 'Tombs', pp. 57–59.

45 Wladimir Ivanow et al., eds., *Collectanea*, vol. 1 (Leiden, 1948), figure 6 after p. 68, p. 122 n.1. These notes appear to be by Ivanow, and not the authors of the individual contributions.

46 John Norman Hollister, *The Shiʿa of India* (London, 1953), p. 335.

47 Ghulām ʿAlī (Ghulam Ali) Alānā (Allana), *Sindhī Ṣūratkhaṭṭī*, 3rd ed. (Hyderabad, Pakistan, 1969); (Originally published, 1964), pp. 23–24; G̱hulām ʿAlī (Ghulam Ali) Alānā (Allana), 'Maqālo: Sūmran je daur jī Sindhī shāʿirī', *Ṭamāhī Mihrāṇ* 9, no. 1–2 (1963), p. 152. For more detailed information on these tabular syllabries, also pronounced *chāri akhari*, see Shackle and Moir, *Ismaili Hymns*, p. 35.

48 Alānā (Allana), *Sindhī Ṣūratkhaṭṭī*, pp. 23–24. He attributes the form *Khwājiko* to Stack, *A Grammar of the Sindhi Language*, but does not provide a page reference. Khubchandani does the same in at least two different works, spelling the name *Khuwājiko* in the older work and *Khwajiko* in the more recent, but again without a page reference to Stack's work, *Sindhi Studies* (Pune, 1981), p. 13; 'Sindhi', chap. 17, in *The Indo-Aryan Languages*, ed. Dhanesh Jain and George Cardona (London, 2003), p. 634. Asani gives the same name, but no reference is cited. See Asani, 'At the Crossroads', in *Literary Cultures in History: Reconstructions from South Asia*, p. 622. Google's digitization of Stack's 1849 work, rendered easily searchable by OCR, reveals that he never used this term. In any case, the term is formed in a manner similar to the name of various related Indo-Aryan dialects known as 'Hindko', spoken in Northwest Pakistan, and 'Vāṇiko', 'the script of

the merchants'. Both Stack, *A Grammar of the Sindhi Language*, p. 122 and Ernest Trumpp, *Grammar of the Sindhi Language, Compared with the Sanskrit-Prakrit and the Cognate Indian Vernaculars* (London: Trübner, 1872), pp. 62, 73 discuss the adjectival suffix *-ko*. While acknowledging other theories, Shackle suggests that 'Hindko' likely means simply 'the Indian language', to distinguish it from neighbouring Pashto, and hence Khwājiko (if the prevalence of such a term can be more convincingly documented) would simply mean the script, or language, of the Khwājahs. Christopher Shackle, 'Hindko in Kohat and Peshawar', *Bulletin of the School of Oriental and African Studies, University of London* 43, no. 3 (1980): p. 482. I am grateful to my colleague Arvind Iyengar for the insights about the *-ko* suffix.

49 G̱ẖulām ʿAlī (Ghulam Ali) Alānā (Allana), *The Arabic Element in Sindhi* (Lahore, [after 1984]), p. 35. No publication date is provided, but the latest date mentioned in the author's biography on the dust cover of the book is 1984. This is the published form of the author's MA thesis, 'The Arabic Element in Sindhi' (Master's thesis, School of Oriental and African Studies, University of London, 1963). Yelena Shlyuger of the library of the School of Oriental and African Studies informed me that the library does not make theses available through Interlibrary Loan, and hence I could not consult the original thesis (personal communication by email of 21 November 2018).

50 Saiyad Nuramahamadshāh bin Imāmashāh, *Sataveṇī moṭī*, 3rd ed. (Mumbai, 1949), p. 4.

51 On. Mishanari Sulıtān-ali Nazar-ali, On. Mishanari Kāsam-ali Mahamadajāphar, and Māsatar Hāshım Moleḍinā, *Pākısatān je dāramık isakulan je lāe Khojıki Sındi pırāimar (Pırāimari darajā 1 khāṃ 4)* (Karachi, 1950); On. Mishanari Sulıtān-ali Nazar-ali, On. Mishanari Kāsam-ali Muhammadajāphar, and Māsıtar Hāshım Moleḍinā, *Pākısatān je dāramık isakulan je lāe Khojıki Sındi pırāimar (Pırāimari darajā 1 khāṃ 4)* (Karachi, [n.d., after 1950]); On. Vāiz Sulıtān-ali Nazar-ali, On. Vāiz Kāsam-ali Muhammadı Jāpharı, and Māsıṭar Hāshımı Moleḍinā, *Pākısıtān je dārımıkı isıkulanı je lāe Khojıki Sındi pırāimarı (Pırāimari darıjā 1 khāṃ 4)*, 4th ed. (Karachi, 1957); On. Vāiz Sulatān-ali Nazar-ali, On. Vāiz Kāsam-ali Muhammaḍ Jāphar, and Māsıṭar Hāshım Moleḍinā, *Pākısatān ki Isamāiliyā ḍini isakuloṃ ke lie Khojıki Uraḍu pırāimar (Barāe ḍarajā 1 se 4)*, tr. Sher-alī Mukhī Mahar-alī Isamāili Pıshāvaravālā, 5th ed. (Karachi, 1964); On. Vāiz Sulatān-ali Nazar-ali, On. Vāiz Kāsam-ali Muhammaḍ Jāphar, and Māsiṭar Hāshım Moleḍinā, *Pākısatān ki Isamāiliyā ḍini isakuloṃ ke lie Khojıki Uraḍu pırāimar (Barāe ḍarajā 1 se 4)*, tr. Sher-alī Mukhī Mahar-alī Īsamāīlī Pishāvaravālā, 6th ed. (Karachi, 1966).

52 ʿAlī ibn Abī Ṭālib (attrib.), *Kalāme Maulā*, 6th ed. (Mumbai, 2009 VS/1953 CE), p. [i].

53 Hujhuramukhī Abdul Husen Ālījāh Mishanarī Alībhāi Nānajī, *Pīr padhāryā āpaṇe dvār: Tavārīkhe Ismāīlī Pīr*, 1st ed., 2 vols., vol. 1 (Mumbai, 1986), p. 302.

54 See, for example, Noorally, 'Catalogue of Khojki Manuscripts in the Collection of Ismailia Association for Pakistan'; Moir, 'A Catalogue of the Khojki Manuscripts in the Library of the Ismaili Institute'; Zawahir Moir, 'Khwajah Sindhi Literature', *Sind Quarterly*, 14, 2 (1986); Zawahir Moir, 'Khojki Manuscripts', *South Asia Library Group Newsletter*, 44 (January 1997); Shackle and Moir, *Ismaili Hymns*; Khakee, *Dasa Avatāra of the Satpanthi Ismailis;* Gulshan Khakee, 'The Dasa Avatāra of Pir Shams as Linguistic and Literary Evidence of the Early Development of Ismailism in Sind', chap. 17, in *Sind Through the Centuries: Proceedings of an International Seminar held in Karachi in Spring 1975 by the Department of Culture, Government of Sind*, ed. Hamida Khuhro (Karachi, 1981); Nanji, *Nizārī Ismāʿīlī Tradition*, p. 8, Ali Sultaan Ali Asani, *The Būjh Nirañjan: An Ismaili Mystical Poem* (Cambridge, MA, 1991); Ali Sultaan Ali Asani, 'The Khojkī Script: A Legacy of Ismaili Islam in the Subcontinent', chap. 6, in *Ecstasy and Enlightenment: The Ismaili Devotional Literature of South Asia* (London, 2002); Asani, 'The Khojkī Script and its Manuscript Tradition', in *Ecstasy and Enlightenment: The Ismaili Devotional Literature of South Asia*; Ali Sultaan Ali Asani, *The Harvard Collection of Ismaili Literature in Indic Languages: A Descriptive Catalog and Finding Aid* (Boston, MA, 1992); Shafique

N. Virani, 'Symphony of Gnosis: A Self-Definition of the Ismaili Ginān Literature', chap. 55, in *Reason and Inspiration in Islam: Theology, Philosophy and Mysticism in Muslim Thought*, ed. Todd Lawson (London, 2005); Shafique N. Virani, 'The Voice of Truth: Life and Works of Sayyid Nūr Muḥammad Shāh, A 15th/16th Century Ismā'īlī Mystic' (Master's thesis, McGill University, 1995); Pandey, in collaboration with Virani, 'Final Proposal to Encode the Khojki Script in ISO/IEC 10646'; Michel Boivin, 'A Note on the Khudāwādī – A Vanishing Script of Sindh', *Journal of the Pakistan Historical Society*, 63 (2015); Arvind Vijaykumar Iyengar, 'Sindhī Multiscriptality, Past and Present: A Sociolinguistic Investigation into Community Acceptance' (PhD dissertation, University of New England, 2017); Virani, *Ismailis in the Middle Ages*; Zahir Bhalloo and Iqbal Akhtar, 'Les manuscrits du sud de la vallée de l'Indus en écriture khojkī sindhī: état des lieux et perspectives', in *Asiatische Studien - Études Asiatiques* (2018). This has also become common in Sindhi scholarship itself, influenced directly by Ivanow. See, for example, Nabī Bakhshu Khān (Nabi Baksh Khan) Balochu (Baloch), *Sindhī ḇolī 'ain adaba jī tārīkh: Qadīm daura khān 1860 tā'īn* (3rd ed., Jāmshoro, Pakistan, 1990); (Originally published, 1962), p. 195.

55 Abualy Alibhai Aziz, 'On the Origin of the Khojki Script', in *Proceedings of the S.O.S. Khojki Coference: January 20th–21st, 1990, Toronto, Canada*, ed. Salim Juma and Nagib Tajdin (Montreal, 1990), p. 47. He further notes that it had earlier been known as Sindhi 'until a few decades ago when the name Khojki (i.e. pertaining to Khojas) came into common use', ibid. p. 48.

56 Annemarie Schimmel, *Sindhi Literature* (Wiesbaden, 1974), vol. 9, pp. 45.

57 Virani, 'Voice of Truth', p. 36.

58 Nūr Muḥammadshāh, *Vel sataveṇi vaḍi ji (Sataveṇī moṭī nī vel)*, in manuscript M2, Personal Collection of Alwaez Abdulrasool Mawji, Calgary, Canada, canto 167.

59 A facsimile edition of the Persian text, along with a Sindhi translation and commentary, is available in Muḥammad Riḍā ibn 'Abd al-Wāsi', *Bayān al-'ārifīn wa tanbīh al-ghāfilīn*, ed. and tr. 'Abd al-Ghaffār Sūmro, *Sayyid 'Abd al-Karīm Shāh Bulṛī wāre je malfūẓāt*, Facsimile ed. (J̌ām Shoro, Sindh, 1428 AH/2007 CE). Asani, 'At the Crossroads', in *Literary Cultures in History: Reconstructions from South Asia*, pp. 615-621 examines the available scholarly literature on Qāḍī Qādan.

60 P.J. Mistry, 'Gujarati Writing', chap. 32, in *The World's Writing Systems*, ed. Peter T. Daniels and William Bright (New York, 1996), p. 391. Mistry does not provide any information about the whereabouts of the manuscript or other details, unfortunately. It should also be recalled that the so-called 'Gujarati' script was only adopted in Gujarat in the nineteenth century, Colin P. Masica, *The Indo-Aryan Languages* (Cambridge, 1991), p. 143.

61 *Evidence Taken on behalf of the First Defendant in the High Court of Judicature at Bombay; Suit no. 729 of 1905*, (Bombay, 1908), p. 242 as cited in Nanji, *Nizārī Ismā'īlī Tradition*, p. 11. The title Nanji refers to is not available through the union catalogue 'WorldCat'. Shah Hussain of the Aga Khan Library also indicates that they do not possess a copy of this work. For additional details see also Māstar Hāsham Boghā, *Taphasīre Dhuā* ([Mumbai], 1909), pp. 8, 16; Mukhī Lālajībhāī Devarāj, 'Prastāvanā', in *Tarabīyate duā: Manavantā bodh guru Pīr Sadaradīne Shīyā Īmāmī Isamāilī Khojāo māṭe khās racheli rojīndā bandagī "duā" ane tenī puratī samajaṇ sāthe*, ed. Mukhī Lālajībhāī Devarāj (Mumbai, 1915), pp. 2–3; Mumtaz Ali Tajddin Sadik Ali, *101 Ismaili Heroes: Late 19th century to Present Age* (Karachi, 2003), vol. 1, p. 230. This is the same witness referred to as Joomabhai and Jumabhai Ismail in 'Haji Bibi Case', pp. 441, 448; *The Hon'ble Mr. Justice Russell in The Aga Khan Case heard in the High Court of Bombay from 3rd February to 7th August 1908 (Judgement delivered 1st September 1908)* (Bombay, 1908), pp. 30, 40.

62 Anil Gulāmahusen refers to this in his 'Isamāīlī sāhity', chap. 7, in [*Sātamī Gujarātī Sāhitya Pariṣhad*] (n.p., 1924), p. 121. Note: A photocopy of this single chapter from the

book is available to me. The publication information is taken from handwritten notes in the copy.

63 Ibid. p. 122.

64 Ibid.; 'Sātamī Gujarātī Sāhity Pariṣhadd (sic): Ismāilī Sāhity Prachārak Maṇḍaḷ taraphathī gayeluṃ ḍepyuṭeshan', *Īsamāilī Satapanth prakāsh* 8, 8 (Jyeṣhṭh chandrākī 1980 VS/1924 CE), p. 467.

65 Devarāj, 'Prastāvanā', in *Sataveṇī moṭī*, p. 4; Virani, 'Voice of Truth', pp. 101–102.

66 Mumtaz Ali Tajddin Sadik Ali, 'Ginans in Khojki Manuscripts' (Karachi, n.d.). Mr. Sadik Ali informs me that he identified these and other manuscripts prior to 1975. When he returned to various villages in Sindh in 1998–1999 to find the owners, he was dismayed to find they had either passed away or moved to other places. He has therefore not been able to obtain copies of the manuscripts he had seen earlier, and is not certain that they are still in existence (personal email communication, 6 November 2018). The images of two Khwājah Sindhi manuscripts in *Sind Through the Centuries: An Introduction to Sind, a Progressive Province of Pakistan* (Karachi, 1975), p. 46 are mislabelled as dating from the 17th–18th century. The first image dates to the reign of the Imam Ḥasan ʿAlī Shāh (r. 1232–1298/1817–1881), while the second was copied in 1912 VS/1855 CE.

67 In this regard, see Jafferali H. Lakhani, 'Pir Sadar Din', in *The Great Ismaili Heroes: Contains the Life Sketches and the Works of Thirty Great Ismaili Figures* (Karachi, 1973), p. 89. Mr. Lakhani had worked extensively to collect Arabic, Persian and Khwājah Sindhi Ismaili manuscripts, and was quite familiar with the various collections in India.

68 Moir, 'A Catalogue of the Khojki Manuscripts in the Library of the Ismaili Institute', p. 1; Noorally, 'Catalogue of Khojki Manuscripts in the Collection of Ismailia Association for Pakistan', np. Note that the pagination for the colophons given in these two draft catalogues is not the same. The volume is described in some detail in Khakee, *Dasa Avatāra of the Satpanthi Ismailis*, p. 5 et passim. In 1974, the Ismailia Association Pakistan published a *Ginan Souvenir* with a picture of a Khwājah Sindhi manuscript on the front cover with the caption, '300 years old Khojki manuscript of Pir Hasan Kabirdin's Ginan found in Muscat and preserved at the Ismailia Association', *Ginan Souvenir: 1974*, (Karachi, 1974). However, there is no indication of the existence of a manuscript dated to approximately 1674 in the two catalogues of Zawahir Moir (née Noorally). While the image on the cover is extremely unclear, from the few words that are legible, I believe the *ginān* to be the *Sat vachan* of Pīr Ḥasan Kabīr al-Dīn, which has been published in *100 Gınānani chopaḍi: Venati moṭi maher karo tathā Sat vachan ne Sataguranuranā vivānuṃ nānuṃ gınān tathā bijā gınāno vāli*, 5th ed., vol. 1 (Mumbai, 1990 VS/1934 CE), pp. no. 1, 1–4. This ginān is present in Khwājah Sindhi manuscript 25, and it is possible that this is the text from which the image was taken, and not from any other manuscript. See Moir, 'A Catalogue of the Khojki Manuscripts in the Library of The Library of The Institute of Ismaili Studies', p. 6.

69 Ivanow, 'Tombs', p. 58. Romanization corrected to Āqā from Aqā. Unfortunately, Ivanow only provides the text of the Khwājah Sindhi inscription (in Devanagari script) for the latest of the graves, dated 1217/1803. The translation of the inscription provided is incorrect.

70 Nagar is perhaps a reference to Thatta, the medieval capital of Sindh, and Bhuj is a municipality and the current headquarters of the Kachchh district in Gujarat. On Nagar as an alternative name for Thatta, see Ahmad Hasan Dani, *Thatta: Islamic Architecture* (Islamabad, 1982), p. 199. A poem by Khālū Maḥmūd, a later Iranian contemporary of Pīr Dādū (d. 1650 VS/1594 CE), notes that Daiwal (the port of Thatta) was an important Ismaili centre in Sindh. See Shafique N. Virani, 'The Scent of the Scarlet Pimpernels: Ismaili Leaders of the 11th/17th Century', in *The Renaissance of Shiʿi Islam in the 15th-17th Centuries: Facets of Thought and Practice*, ed. Farhad Daftary and Janis Esots (London, 2022). However, as *nagar* can also simply mean city or town, this may possibly be

another location. This is suggested in Valībhāī Nānjī Hudā, *Asaty ārop yāne Khojā jñātinuṃ gaurav*, 1st ed. (Dhorājī, Kathiawad, 1927), p. 114, which indicates that Pīr Dādu had already left Sindh in 1606 VS/1549. On the other hand, a portion of Khwājah Sindhi manuscript KH 25 housed at The Institute of Ismaili Studies, transcribed in 1813 VS/1756 CE, indicates that it was copied in the *jamāʿat khānah* (Ismaili community centre) of Nagar. The language of the scribe is Sindhi, indicating that Nagar was in Sindh. See Moir, 'A Catalogue of the Khojki Manuscripts in the Library of the Ismaili Institute', p. 27.

71 Nanji, *Nizārī Ismāʿīlī Tradition*, pp. 10-11. Manuscript KH 38, Ismaili Special Collections Unit, Institute of Ismaili Studies, London, f. 11r.

72 KH 38, ff. 2v, 104r-104v. The manuscript is described in Moir, 'A Catalogue of the Khojki Manuscripts in the Library of the Ismaili Institute', pp. 94-103.

73 Pīr Saḍaraḍīn, 'Alakh achheḍ abhed aparamapar', in *100 Gınānani chopaḍi: Ebi taie tame pāṭh 183 tathā tenā joḍilā (6) tathā Pırem Pāṭaṇ moṭo ane Sutakanā moṭā gınānavāḷi chopaḍi*, 5th ed., 6 vols., vol. 2 (Mumbai, 1993 VS/1936 CE), no. 21, p. 57.

74 Shackle and Moir, *Ismaili Hymns*, p. 34; Asani, 'The Khojkī Script: A Legacy of Ismaili Islam', in *Ecstasy and Enlightenment: The Ismaili Devotional Literature of South Asia*, p. 101; Nanji, *Nizārī Ismāʿīlī Tradition*, p. 8.

75 Rematulā (Rahimtoola), *Khojā kom no itihās*, pp. 212, 219–222; Vajhīr Alīmāmad Jānamahamad (Vazir Alimahomed Janmahomed) Chunārā (Chunara), *Nūram mobīn: Yāne Allāhanī pavitr rasī; Īsamāīlī Īmāmono Jvalant Ītihās*, ed. Jāphar-alī Māhamad Suphī, *Noorum-Mobin or The Sacred Cord of God: A Glorious History of Ismaili Imams*, 4th ed. (Mumbai, 1961); (Originally published, Mumbai, 1935), pp. 321–325; Māstar Hāsham Boghā, *Asalīyate Khojā: Yāne asal kharekharā Khojāo Koṇ?* (Mumbai, 1912 CE/1330 AH), passim.

76 Nuramahamad, *Isamāilī Momin komano itihās*, pp. 117–119.

77 Pīrajhādā Saiyad Sadaradīn Ech. Daragāvālā, *Tavārīkhe-Pīr*, 1st ed., vol. 2 (Mumbai, 1354 AH/1934 CE), pp. 83–99. Similarly, writing in 1912, a Twelver author of Khwājah ancestry makes no mention of the Khwājah Sindhi script in his section on Pīr Ṣadr al-Dīn. See Edalajī Dhanajī Kābā, *Khojā Komanī Tavārīkh, The History of the Khojas* (Amreli, Kathiawad, 1330 AH/1912 CE), p. 277.

78 See Alānā (Allana), 'Sūmran je daur', p. 152.

79 In this regard, see Abdul Rehman Kanji, 'Preface,' in *The Great Ismaili Heroes: Contains the Life Sketches and the Works of Thirty Great Ismaili Figures* (Karachi, 1973), p. 1; Abualy Alibhai Aziz, 'Pir Hasan Kabiruddin', in *The Great Ismaili Heroes: Contains the Life Sketches and the Works of Thirty Great Ismaili Figures* (Karachi, 1973), p. 92.

80 Lakhani, 'Pir Sadar Din', in *The Great Ismaili Heroes: Contains the Life Sketches and the Works of Thirty Great Ismaili Figures*, pp. 87-90. A slightly later abridged version of the same article also omits any reference to Khwājah Sindhi, Jafferali H. Lakhani, *Life and Works of Pir Sadardin* (Karachi, 1974), pp. 13–15.

81 Akabar Dāmāṇī, *Pīrono Itihās*, 2nd ed. (Mumbai, 1977); (Originally published, 1974), pp. 44–59.

82 Hajhūramukhī Abdul Husen Ālījāh Mishanarī Alībhāī Nānajī, *Pīr padhāryā āpaṇe dvār: Tavārīkhe Ismāīlī Pīr*, 1st ed., 2 vols. (Mumbai, 1986), vol. 2, p. 326.

83 Samuel Miklos Stern, 'The "Book of the Highest Initiation" and other Anti-Ismāʿīlī Travesties', chap. 4, in his *Studies in Early Ismāʿīlism* (Leiden, 1983), p. 58; Farhad Daftary, *Ismaili Literature: A Bibliography of Sources and Studies* (London, 2004), pp. 85–87.

84 Edalajī Dhanajī Kābā, 'Prastāvanā', in *Gupat panthakā shujarā: Ek juno hast likhit lekh*, ed. Edalajī Dhanajī Kābā (Amareli, Kathiawar, 1916), p. [i].

85 Kābā, *Gupat panthakā shujarā*, p. 8.

86 For an example of this title used for Pīr Ṣadr al-Dīn, see *Pīr Hasan Kaḇīradīn ne Kānīpāno saṃvāḍ*, (Mumbai, 1905), p. 14. While acknowledging this tradition, the

somewhat confused narrative of *The Genealogical Tree* makes Pīr Ṣadr al-Dīn and Sohadev Joshī two separate individuals. See Kābā, *Gupat panthakā shujarā*, pp. 1–2, 7, 17.

87 See Sachedīnā Nānajīāṇī, *Khojā vṛtānt* (Ahmedabad, 1948 VS/1892 CE), p. 4. Rematulā (Rahimtoola), *Khojā kom no itihās*, p. 220 criticizes Nānajīāṇī's theory of the origin of the Khwājahs in Panjab.

88 Aziz, 'Origin of the Khojki Script', in *Proceedings of the S.O.S. Khojki Coference: January 20th-21st, 1990, Toronto, Canada*, p. 48. Of course, it is generally accepted that both Sikh Gurmukhi and the various Sindhi scripts, including Khwājah Sindhi, are descendants of Brāhmī through one of the variants of the Shāradā script, Masica, *The Indo-Aryan Languages*, p. 143. The development of Sikh Gurmukhi is traditionally ascribed to Guru Angad (d. 1552). See Harjeet Singh Gill, 'The Gurmukhi Script', chap. 33, in *The World's Writing Systems*, ed. Peter T. Daniels and William Bright (New York, NY, 1996), p. 395.

89 George Abraham Grierson, 'On the Modern Indo-Aryan Alphabets of North-Western India', *Journal of the Royal Asiatic Society of Great Britain and Ireland* (1904), p. 68. Pañjābī and Gurmukhī replaced by Panjabi and Gurmukhi.

90 F.A. Khan, *Banbhore: A Preliminary Report on the Recent Archaeological Excavations at Banbhore*, 4th ed. ([Karachi?], 1976); (Originally published, 1960), pp. 15–16.

91 Ibid. 16; Alānā (Allana), *Sindhī Ṣūratkhaṭṭī*, pp. 21–22. Allana's numbering of the potsherds is based on an earlier edition of Khan's publication, and so differs from the numbering provided here.

92 Alānā (Allana), *Sindhī Ṣūratkhaṭṭī*, pp. 21–22; Boivin, 'A Note on the Khudāwādī', p. 11.

93 With regard to the presence of graphemes to represent the Sindhi implosive sounds, it must be noted that Aziz mentions the script as written in Panjab differed from its more common Sindhi variety, Aziz, 'Origin of the Khojki Script', in *Proceedings of the S.O.S. Khojki Coference: January 20th-21st, 1990, Toronto, Canada*, p. 48. Only once the relevant manuscripts have been examined will a clearer picture emerge.

12

A Forgotten Voice: The Agency of the Scribal and Literate Elite and the Satpanth Manuscript Culture

Wafi A. Momin

The Problem: Questioning an Image

From the first half of the 19th century, a specific set of images concerning the Khojas have dominated the administrative, legal and ethnographic studies produced by colonial officials and other observers in India. These images portray the Khojas largely in terms of a caste or tribe of Muslim merchants, traders and cultivators, long settled along the north-western regions of the erstwhile British Indian territories, in what are now the provinces of Punjab and Sindh in Pakistan, and the states of Gujarat and Maharashtra in India. A number of these studies also venture into questions of their origins, history and customs. On these issues, their assessments are particularly devoted to establishing the connections of the Khoja community with their religious leaders, known widely as the Ismaili imams who previously resided in Iran before settling in India from the 1840s onwards. Through these leaders, the observers (notably the earlier ones) further linked the community to what they oftentimes label as the 'Ismaili heresy'.

This cluster of depictions have remained influential in how the Khojas and their religious beliefs have largely been viewed in the colonial and public imagination. In this chapter, I seek to interrogate these images and discuss the socio-literary configuration of some segments among the Khojas and the larger group of literate gentry to which they belonged. I first probe into the nature and implications of this imagination—aspects of which have also been internalised by modern scholarship—through an examination of its constitutive elements, together with the rationale that has undergirded and perpetuated it. In doing so, I hope to recover fragments of a now largely forgotten voice that played an important role in the shaping of the religious culture to which the Khojas belonged.

First taking a look at some early depictions, Captain James MacMurdo, who served (among other appointments) as Resident at the court of the Rao of Kutch, in his account of that region described the Khojas of Kutch as 'Mahomedan cultivator[s]', who traced their origins to Persia and 'frequently [made] a pilgrimage to a spot eight days march to the N.W. of Ispahan, where they [worshiped] a living *peer*, or *saint*'.[1] Similarly, Richard Burton, in his comprehensive survey of the land and inhabitants of Sindh, considered the Sindhi Khojas of Persian origin, observing that they probably 'fled the country when the Ismailiyeh heresy (to which they still cleave) was so severely treated by Holaku Khan'. He further declared the Sindhi Khoja to be 'rarely a well-educated man', and (on this point) he found him to be 'inferior to his brethren settled in India and Muscat', adding that in Sindh 'they have progressed just sufficiently to invent a character for themselves, and to write out the Koran in it'.[2] And, finally, in a photographic account of the races and tribes found in Bombay (and other localities of the Bombay Presidency), William Johnson devoted a section to the Bombay Khojas, noting that they were 'principally employed as merchants and petty dealers'. Although, in his brief description, he hinted at a reformist party among them, as well as its charitable activities for the cause of education, including the running of a newspaper, the representative portrait chosen for the community highlighted one Nansi Parpia, a 'shopkeeping celebrity in Bombay', and an unnamed companion whose claim to fame was the founding of 'one of the Khojah firms recently established in London'.[3]

Arguably, at the heart of such early colonial portrayals of the Khojas lay the interconnected facets of their religious identity and the entrepreneurial character that has become a hallmark of the community's social stature within and beyond South Asia over the last two centuries. The vexed question of their religious identity—along with the legal contestations that hinged on this issue, culminating (in some ways at least, but far from being conclusively resolved) in the well-known Aga Khan Case of 1866—has been rigorously debated by scholars. On this matter, the Khojas (including other groups forming part of the Satpanth tradition)[4] have long borne a kind of double burden. On the one hand, the supposed 'Ismaili' substructure undergirding the edifice of the Satpanth (long maintained by a dominant group of scholars) readily contributed to the community's image of belonging to a sect of Islam considered by many to be a heresy (as the above depictions show). This was further entrenched, on the other hand, by the portrayal of the religious beliefs and practices of the Khojas (and, indeed, those of other Satpanth communities) in terms of an amalgamation of 'Hindu' and 'Muslim' worldviews, which rendered them short of practising the kind of ideal Islam that the proponents of this view had in mind.[5]

But the construction of this image of their religious identity has equally been a consequence of their portrayal as an exclusively merchant community. This becomes evident from how observers have time and again deemed the Khojas (almost as a logical extension) to have lacked a class of knowledgeable people who could bring their religious doctrines in line with what were held to be the normative teachings of Islam. A compelling example of how this connection was drawn may be seen in a legal dispute, centred on the rights of female inheritance among the Khojas, which was presided over by Justice Erskine Perry in the Bombay Supreme Court in 1847. The case proceedings and the judgement set the tone of how the Khojas were henceforth imagined in colonial and public discourse. In the judgement issued by Perry, he described them as follows:

> The Kojahs [*sic*] are a small cast [*sic*] in Western India . . . who, by their own traditions . . . were converted from Hinduism about four hundred years ago. . . Their language is Cutchí; their religion Mahomedan; their dress, appearance, and manners, for the most part, Hindu. . . [They] are now settled principally amongst Hindu communities, such as [those in] Cutch, Kattiawar, and Bombay. . . [and] constitute, at this [latter] place, apparently about two thousand souls, and their occupations, for the most part, are confined to the more subordinate departments of trade. Indeed the cast [*sic*] never seems to have emerged from the obscurity which attends their present history, and the almost total ignorance of letters, of the principles of their religion, and of their own status, which they now evince, is probably the same as has always existed among them since they first embraced the precepts of

> Mahomed. Although they call themselves Mussalmans, they evidently know but little of their Prophet and of the Koran; and their chief reverence at the present time is reserved for Agha Khan... To use the words of one of themselves, they call themselves Shías to a Shía, and Sunníys [*sic*] to a Sunníy, and they probably neither know nor care any thing as to the distinctive doctrines of either of these great divisions of the Mussalman world. They have, moreover, no translation of the Koran into their vernacular language, or into Guzaratí their language of business... Nor have they any scholars or men of learning among them, as not a Kojah could be quoted who was acquainted with Arabic or Persian, the two great languages of Mahomedan literature and theology.[6]

Perry's judgement and the legal dispute from which it ensued came to have far reaching consequences for the public image of the Khojas. Despite upholding the position that the Khojas had traditionally followed the custom of disinheriting daughters, which he considered 'nearly analogous to the Hindu rule of succession', and despite finding confusion in their ranks about their religious tenets (as the excerpts above show), he nonetheless acknowledged them as Muslims of some sort. But the larger question of the perceived eclectic, and thus ambiguous, tenor of their religious identity which cast doubt on their 'Muslim' credentials in the first place—the logic for which Perry found in such factors as the 'total ignorance [on their part about] the principles of their religion', and the absence of 'scholars or men of learning among them ... acquainted with Arabic or Persian'—continued to haunt the community's image for a long time.[7]

It reached yet another tipping point in the Aga Khan Case of 1866 when it got paired with a dispute about the ownership of property and assets administered by the Khojas of Bombay. To be sure, the issue this time (as far as the religious identity of the Khojas was concerned) did not concern the admixture of 'Hindu' elements in their beliefs and practices, something that was acknowledged and reinforced throughout the trial proceedings. Rather, it premised on the form of Islam—whether Shiʿi or Sunni—that the Khojas were first converted to. A noteworthy departure in the much-cited trial judgement by Sir Joseph Arnould was the characterisation of Ismaili tenets which he found to be at the foundation of the doctrines followed by the Khojas.

Arnould presided over lengthy debates and exhaustive evidence presented by the contending parties, and resorted to a mass of historical and other documents. Considering all of this, he did not accept (like others before him) the construction 'Ismaili heresy' as given and unproblematic, rather he found its rationale in the adverse portrayal of Ismaili doctrines on the part of Sunni rulers who considered the adherents of these doctrines a political threat. However, as far as the social position of the Khojas was concerned, he considered them 'originally Hindoos of the trading class' and (like others) presented them 'all, as a rule, engaged either in retail trade or commerce, [who] frequently prosecute both with considerable success'.[8]

What we therefore see after the 1866 trial is a gradual transformation in the portrayal of the Khojas and their religious culture—that is, a shift from their representation as belonging to 'Ismaili heresy' to their delineation as the 'disciples of the old man of the mountain', or (better still) as the Nizārī Ismailis.[9] This shift and the consequent equation of the Khojas with the Assassins, in many ways, were a product of the advancements in how the 'Ismaili' dispensation came to be understood and appreciated in the wider context of the history of Islam from the second half of the 19th century onwards, something that was to unfold (in the decades to come) in a major break from the earlier modes of imagining the Ismailis, that is to say, in light of the kind of fanciful accounts fostered by Muslim and European writers.[10] But, more importantly, they were also a result of the internal contestations and debates that erupted among the Khojas and other Satpanthī groups, which hinged on varied interpretations of their history, and in turn were rigorously expressed through public platforms and courtrooms.[11]

Notwithstanding this gradual shift in how the Khojas were viewed in legal and public discourse around this time, their wholesale depiction as traders and merchants continued unabated. For example, in a volume of the exhaustive *Gazetteer of the Bombay Presidency*, dedicated to the Muslims of Gujarat, the Khojas (together with some other Muslim groups) were plainly classified as 'Hindu converts' making up 'trading communities'.[12] It is noteworthy that in consequence of the aforementioned epistemological transformation, we rarely encounter the kind of rhetoric that Perry's judgement fostered, connecting the 'ambiguity' in the Khojas' religious doctrines with a lack of knowledgeable experts in Islamic precepts and so on. But modern scholarship has largely internalised this logic by its incessant representation of the Khojas as an exclusively merchant community, being oblivious to its grave implications. Thus, it is ironic that despite producing some nuanced analysis of the interplay of diverse religious currents forming part of the Satpanth worldview, scholars have hardly asked how the ramifications of such an interplay were engaged with and negotiated on the part of the adherents of the tradition (to which the Khojas belonged), not just using courtrooms but through other spaces too. I argue that it is in part this internalised logic of Khojas-equal-a-merchant-community that has concealed other important literary-intellectual facets of the community that were critically involved in shaping its multi-layered religious identity in premodern times and through the period of transformation in colonial India.[13]

Against the backdrop of these long-drawn images of the Khojas, I foreground in this chapter the agency, social roles and ideological affinities of a forgotten scribal class which, in turn, formed part of a larger group of literate gentry. This class included in its ranks those who self-consciously identified themselves as Khojas, as well as the literati of other clusters who participated in the practice of Satpanth. This learned gentry was at the forefront of producing and cultivating a vibrant manuscript culture and disseminating a variety of textual and other materials through this medium. The voices of the many agents who formed part of this literate segment are inscribed in these manuscripts, as well as in the practices associated with the materials copied therein. Moreover, in addition to the scribal and literate class, this manuscript culture drew a variety of audiences and publics to its ambit, including patrons, congregations, performers and singers, diviners, healers and their clients, not to speak of the community members at large. The manuscripts in question are primarily transcribed in a script now generally referred to as Khojkī, while a large number of them are also copied in Gujarati and Devanagari scripts.[14] Since these manuscripts were cultivated among different circles of the larger Satpanth nexus, I refer to them as forming part of the Satpanth manuscript culture.[15] Before discussing pertinent materials and salient aspects of the agency of scribal and literate group, it is important to situate its role in the context of Satpanth historiography, and that of the literate classes in South Asia and beyond.

Probing a Silence: Locating the Satpanth Scribal and Literate Elite

If the scribes and literati (which included many Khojas) were so important in shaping the world of Satpanth (as I will show later in this chapter), how might we explain a conspicuous silence about them in previous studies? Why has the voice of this group largely been ignored? The dominant image of the Khojas as merchants, traders and shopkeepers, as outlined in the previous section, has clearly been a driving force. But I shall offer here some further observations behind this silence, before moving on to locate this group in the larger setting of the functions of similar classes in South Asian society and beyond.

The history of the Satpanth tradition, especially in its premodern phase, has largely been approached with reference to the proselytising mission of some charismatic figures, revered as Pīrs and Sayyids, who are widely believed to have been despatched for this task by the Nizārī imams. They are thus regarded as the key agents in the propagation and dissemination of Satpanth teachings to their audiences mainly through the medium of the *Ginān* literature—a body of poems (with some prose texts) composed in a combination of Indic languages, notably Gujarati, Hindi, Sindhi and Punjabi. In some studies, the role of their supposed disciples is obliquely acknowledged, but the onus of initiating the Satpanth practice and formulating its teachings is singularly placed on the shoulders of these Pīrs and Sayyids, who are thereby seen as a crucial link between the seat of the Nizārī imamate and its Indian followers.[16] This presents a far-fetched and simplified picture of a long and multi-layered process. Holding a group of preachers mostly hailing from outside India (especially in the earlier stages of the propagation), along with their Indian descendants—collectively forming a class of charismatic saints—as largely responsible for building the edifice of the Satpanth is, to say the least, not a convincing enough explanation of the entire phenomenon spread over several centuries. Furthermore, there is hardly anything concrete that we learn about the life and circumstances of these charismatic saints beyond what we find in the *Ginān*s ascribed to some of these figures, or what is recounted about them in relatively recent 'communal' accounts produced within different clusters of the tradition, whose value for other purposes cannot of course be discounted.

Moving away from an exclusive focus on the charismatic class, it is important to foreground the part played by other actors in this process, or to acknowledge them even when our sources do not permit us to take full stock of their contribution. By this approach, I seek to interrogate a prevalent historiographical trend that envisages the evolution of Satpanth mainly as a product of missionary activity. It is against this backdrop that the part played by the largely forgotten or downplayed agency, namely the scribal and literate class, becomes important.

Another reason why the seminal role played by the scribes and literate class, especially in the premodern history of the tradition (as will be discussed in the next section), has hardly received any attention in previous scholarship is the kind of sources that scholars have largely relied upon in approaching the questions of the historical formation of Satpanth.[17] Such groups seldom figure independently in the usual pool of much drawn upon sources, namely the *Ginān*s, hagiographic stories and oral traditions concerning the mission of the charismatic figures, and communal accounts. Even when such groups do appear on rare occasions in this pool of sources, they are more often overshadowed by the Pīrs and Sayyids. The position and contribution of the scribal/literate class are thereby *assumed* at best, rather than *problematised* and *explored*. As noted, we learn a great deal about this class from the manuscripts they cultivated, as well as from the cultural practices they were engaged in, all of which collectively shed valuable light on the configuration of premodern Satpanth religiosity and its transition to modern times.

The quintessential role and contribution of the scribal and secretarial classes in the functioning of medieval and early modern polities and the structuring of caste communities in India has been amply documented. Such classes commanded respect because of their knowledge of writing and languages, familiarity with the norms of governance and the relevant socio-religious codes. They brought their skills to bear in a wide array of domains from fiscal administration and accountancy to epistolography and varied tasks of record keeping. Being highly mobile and itinerant, these classes were especially attracted to the opportunities offered by ruling states, which in turn heavily relied on them to administer their bureaucratic procedures. The example of Kāyastha and Khatrī castes is a relevant case in point, wherein we see how literate Hindus came to occupy important administrative positions within the state apparatus during the time of Muslim political dominance. The mobility of such groups engendered in them a cosmopolitan outlook, connecting them to a wider circle of scribal and literate groups throughout India and beyond. In short, with their much sought-after skills and access to courtly and religious environments, these classes wielded power and formed the elite segment of their societies.[18]

For the time period with which this chapter is primarily concerned—namely, the early modern and the colonial era—the scribes and the larger group of literate gentry forming part of the Satpanth tradition share many of these functions.[19] Their position in their respective communities ought to be viewed against the backdrop of the prestige and power the scribal and secretarial groups commanded in South Asia. In addition to examining the agency of this collective gentry, I seek to show that the Satpanth literate groups were not just confined to transcribing materials handed down from earlier generations. Rather, their role needs to be conceived more broadly in the context of the patronage-clientele complex, as well as in a cultural setting where access to knowledge was mediated by such classes. Hence, many of them also need to be seen as scholars and learned individuals closely invested in spreading the teachings and cherished ideals of Satpanth, including what they found resonating with these ideals in their immediate environment. Also, as I argue elsewhere, this scribal/literate class infused a kind of 'popular' ethos into the social practices of the concerned groups that endowed the tradition with a multi-layered personality, which, in turn, was to have major ramifications for its modern history.[20]

Before moving on to present relevant materials from our manuscripts, it must be highlighted by way of a caveat that our analysis is constrained by the fact that the oldest manuscripts at our disposal date from the first half of the 18th century. Hence, any generalisation or deductions about the social roles, ideological orientations and other aspects of the scribal craft and connected matters, beyond the period of the (known) production of these manuscripts, must be drawn with caution. Nevertheless, the larger patterns emerging out of these manuscripts suggest that the scribes were working within well-established norms associated with this profession the roots of which lay much deeper in time than what the physical evidence itself would otherwise suggest.

With these remarks, I now turn to examine different features of the concerned Khojkī/Gujarati manuscripts, such as colophons, scribal notations, patterns of textual transmission and a selection of textual materials copied in them. From these features, I argue, one learns a good deal about those involved in the production of the manuscripts, and the cultivation and dissemination of the materials transmitted through them. They further allow us to recover 'voices' of those involved in the practices embedded in these materials. By 'voices', I do not merely mean what they *said* through colophons, scribal notations and so on. Rather, I seek to probe into many other domains like their position in society, their ideological and religious predilections, their literary tastes and the kind of audiences they catered to. It is also through these aspects that the scribal and learned agents *speak* to us when we try to make sense of their role in creating the multivalent universe of Satpanth.

Fragments of a Forgotten Voice

As noted, our primary sources of information for the scribes and the larger group of literate elite active within the network of the communities concerned are the very manuscripts they transcribed, which (together with the literary and other materials copied in them) were circulated and consumed along varied channels of the client-patron circuit. As far as the scribes are concerned, their voices are particularly inscribed in such places in the manuscripts as the colophons and marginal notations (where available), prefatory/terminal declarations appearing frequently at the beginning/conclusion of the texts copied therein, as well as occasional information of historical and social import, at times embodying popular lore or individual perceptions on certain issues. All these fragments collectively constitute a key site where the scribal agency is configured. They allow us to understand, through the scribes' own voices, such matters as the social background, ideological predilections, literary tastes, as well as the status and roles not only of the scribes themselves but the learned classes engaged in the cultivation of these manuscripts more broadly, and (from these aspects) the larger world of Satpanth.

Upon a closer inspection of these manuscripts, we notice that the scribes consistently followed a pattern in transmitting the multitude of literary genres and other materials they transcribed. In the prefatory declaration, with which a manuscript or a given text opens, the copyist generally commences with the formula *Alā toāhāra* ('reliance is upon God') or *Basmallāh* (opening verse of the Qur'ān invoking God's benevolence)—at times, these two formulas occur together—or occasionally some other invocations (see further on).[21] These invocatory formulas are then followed by a brief mention of the nature or genre of the text and its (supposed) composer, where known. We often find this basic information being augmented, taking on the form of what may be called a 'colophon', especially before the commencement of major works. The colophon thus adds such details as the patron and scribe involved in the production of the manuscript, the place and date of its copying coupled with information about the source manuscript, as well as benedictions invoking the assistance of higher or mediating agencies (see below), and sometimes even a brief comment on the theme or character of the text itself. Moreover, somewhat similar details are at times produced in a colophon at the conclusion of the texts, particularly after the major ones, where the scribe asks for forgiveness, again invoking certain agencies, and humbly pleading with the readers to correct any errors that may have crept into the text.[22] It must be stressed here that the pattern of these declarations and colophons, notwithstanding some unique features, is not necessarily peculiar to the Satpanth manuscripts, but encountered across different manuscript cultures in South Asia and beyond.[23]

A few examples will be useful to illustrate the pattern outlined above. In one manuscript, after invoking *Alāhatohāra*, the scribe thus commences the copying of a text ascribed to Jaʿfar al-Ṣādiq (see Figure 12.1):

> Risālo:haẕarata:emāmi:jāphara:sādhaka:jo:asala:bolī:phārasī: amijāṁ:thī:utāreo:āhe:so:megajī:devarāja:je:akhare:ma[. . .]ṇa: shuru:keāṁsī

> I now start [transcribing] the *Risālo* (*Risāla*) of Haẕrat Imām Jaʿfar al-Ṣādiq, originally copied from the Persian language, and [now being produced] from the handwriting of Megajī Devarāj.[24]

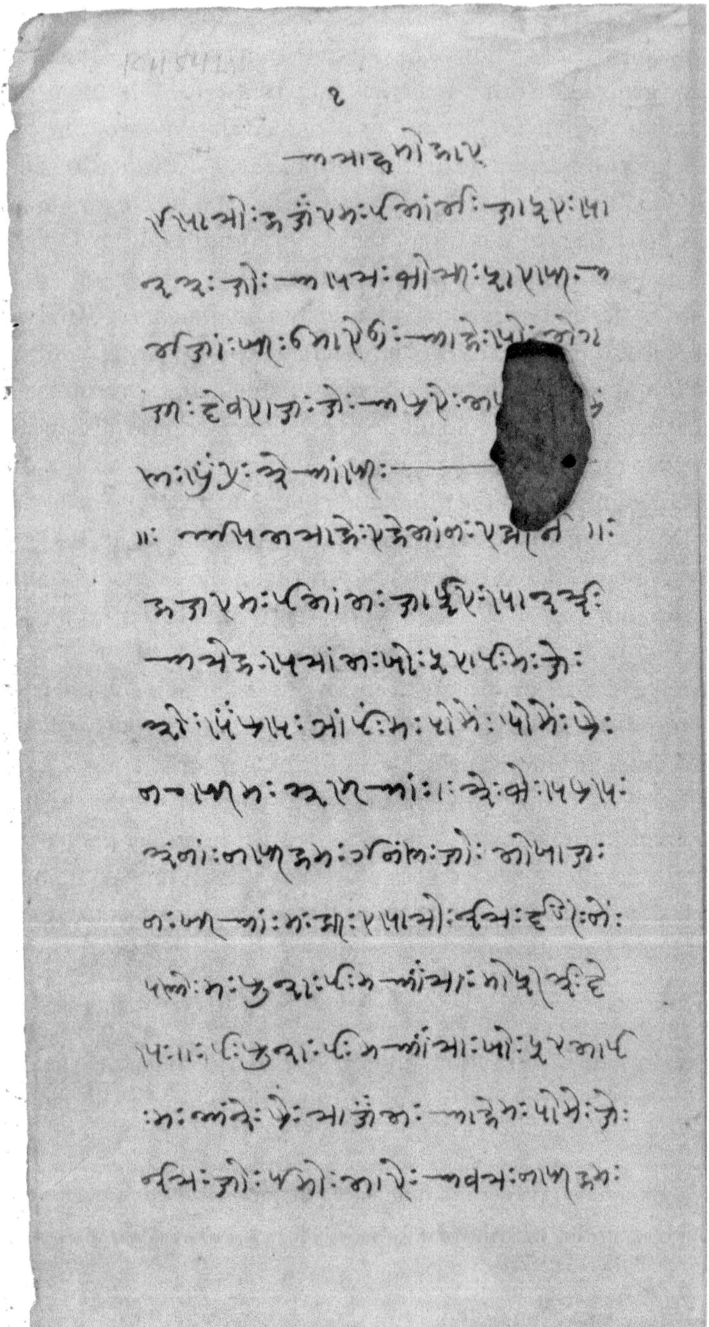

Figure 12.1 KH 541, f. 1v, scribal note before the copying of *Risālo*, ascribed to Jaʿfar al-Ṣādiq.

In another manuscript, the scribe concludes the copying of a *Ginān* text with these words (see Figure 12.2):

> Janājo:pīra:hasanakabhīradhīnajo:‖:so:pīra:emāmashāhā:bhākhe u:so:sapuraṇa:huo:bhula:cuka:nabhī:karīma:māphakare:‖:hīgirat ha:sā:akhare:mathā:akhara:utāreo:āhe:sahī:

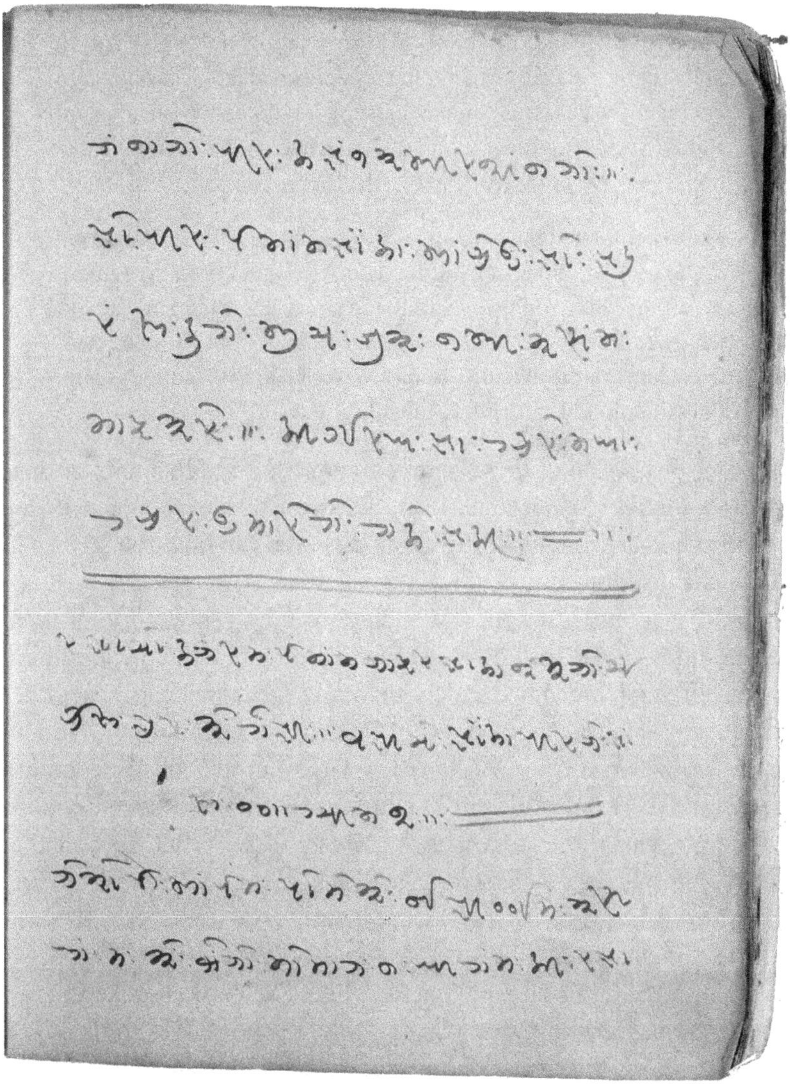

Figure 12.2 KH 431, f. 85r, scribal remarks at the conclusion of *Janājo*, ascribed to Imām Shāh.

[The text of] *Janājo* (*Janāza*) of Pīr Ḥasan Kabīrdīn, which was narrated by Pīr Imām Shāh, concludes now; may *nabī karīm* (the 'blessed prophet', i.e., Prophet Muhammad) forgive any errors; I have copied this text (*graṁth*) word for word.[25]

Finally, a scribe finishes up the copying of a manuscript with these remarks:

Copaṇī:likhakari:tamāmi:kīhae:vāribhirisapati:jumerāti:samati:1942:visākhi:5:hisābhi:saṁkarātijo:=sana:hijarī:1304:isavī:1886:likhī:visana:dāsi:valadi:ratanā:sākana:seālakoṭa:jokoi:kitābhi:curāe:usike:pāsase:jaramānā:līā:jāegā:dasati:khati:visana:dāsi:mālakivī:visadāsi:gunegāri:bhaṁdāe:puritakasīrikā:salāmi:vājeā:ho:‖

I have completed the copying of this book (*copaḍī*) on Thursday, VS 1942, 5 Vaisākha, coinciding with AH 1304, CE 1886; written by Visana Dāsa, son (*walad*) of Ratanā, resident (*sākin*) of Siālkoṭ; whoever tried to steal this book (*kitāb*), a fine would be extracted from him; undersigned, Visana Dāsa Mālakivī Visadāsī, accept the salutation of this sinful and failing servant.[26]

A closer inspection of these sample fragments and other similar ones yields a number of insights. First, although the texts copied in the manuscripts are, linguistically speaking, wide ranging, the scribes of these manuscripts use certain languages more frequently, to judge from the idiom used in the colophons and prefatory/terminal declarations. These include Kacchī (a 'dialect' of Sindhi, which I have by far encountered more widely than any other language), or other varieties of Sindhi, together with Gujarati and Hindustani, and in some cases Persian too. As noted, a large number of the Satpanth communities (Khojas included) hail from the north-western regions of India where these languages are widely spoken. But the fact that many an inspected manuscript have Kacchī as the predominant scribal idiom would suggest that a greater segment of the scribal elite engaged in the cultivation of these manuscripts originated from Kutch (or adjacent areas in Sindh and Gujarat where Kacchī was spoken), even if their actual copying took place in urban centres like Bombay and Karachi, as was the case with many of these manuscripts.[27]

In this context, it is worth recalling that in the communal traditions transmitted among the Khojas (and other Satpanthī circles), it was a figure named Dādū who supposedly settled many Khoja families from Sindh to Kutch sometime in the second half of the 16th century. And while the exact circumstances leading to the migration are unclear (perhaps caused by the animosity between the local ruler of Sindh and the saint, as maintained in some communal accounts), Kutch was indeed identified by the early 19th century as the main homeland and a key centre of the Khojas, despite the fact that their sizeable pockets and other Satpanthī groups by then also lived in Kathiawar (Saurashtra) and other parts of Gujarat, Sindh and beyond. The evidence of scribal idiom from our manuscripts thus also supports the eminence the region of Kutch had acquired around this time as a major communal centre of the Khojas.[28]

But what particularly deserves our attention, as far as the linguistic features of the Satpanth manuscript culture are concerned, is the impressive command of languages exhibited by the scribes (and, in many cases, by the patrons for which they were produced), as is evident from the multilingual character of the literary corpus transmitted through it.[29] This is a remarkable feat that would have required the scribes and others involved to have attained some degree of familiarity with this rich mix of literary and religious materials, together with a facility in the accompanying polyglot idiom, rather than merely copying the corpus *passively*.

At this juncture, it is important to observe how, despite advocating linkages between the Nizārī imamate and Satpanth mission, some scholars have ironically doubted, or otherwise remained incognizant of, the existence of a group of literati who must have, in effect, brought the traditions of the two worlds together in meaningful ways. W. Ivanow, in particular, has categorically stated—in explaining the dearth of reliable historical sources in the aftermath of the fall of Alamūt—that the Indian followers lacked 'the necessary command of language' which would have allowed them to record events in Iran during their sojourns to the headquarters of the imams.[30] Leaving aside the issue of 'historical' records and what is left of them, if the very premise of some connection between the traditions in India and Iran is accepted (the evidence for which, however meagre, has been amply brought to light),[31] then it necessitates the presence of a group of 'intermediaries', operating at various levels and, above all, well-versed in the pertinent languages of the two worlds, in order to consummate this relationship in any meaningful sense. In other words, Persian was indeed a key language, the knowledge of which was confidently disclaimed by Ivanow among the Indian followers of Nizārī imams, that these intermediaries would have required. And the scribal and literate elites who are the focus of our discussion were one such group that possessed the required competence in it alongside other languages, thus mediating between the religious and cultural idioms of the two worlds.

The evidence for this observation is borne first by the kind of literary and religious corpus transmitted via the manuscripts. This includes many Persian texts transcribed in Khojkī, like the *Pandiyāt-i Javānmardī*, containing the admonitions of the Nizārī imam Mustanṣir bi'llāh (d. *ca.* 885/1480),[32] together with its Sindhi/Gujarati renditions which indicate the requirements of a different audience not familiar with Persian, and a plethora of prayers, poems, 'occult' material etc., composed/transcribed in Persian and Arabic and copied widely in the manuscripts. It must be added that in recording Arabic prayers or fragments, we oftentimes find an effort on the part of the scribes to represent certain features of the Arabic phonetic system through a combination of dots or diacritical marks, like the *shadda*, in the Khojkī alphabet much before the script supposedly became standardised and evolved with the advent of printing, again showing their familiarity (even if at a basic level) with the intricacies of Arabic sound system in transcribing these texts.[33] But, more significantly, the observation for the scribes' knowledge of Persian is also borne out by the colophons and occasional notes penned in Persian that we encounter in quite a few manuscripts, testifying to the scribe's working knowledge of Persian.[34] Moreover, given the political and cultural power exerted by Persian in premodern India, it is not implausible to suggest that the scribes of these manuscripts, especially those who demonstrate a good familiarity with Persian, had sufficient opportunities in their own local contexts to learn the language, which was widely understood among the educated circles in India during early modern and even early colonial times when these manuscripts were produced.

Many of the Satpanth manuscripts (on closer observation) may be classified into two broad categories, those primarily used (or meant to be used) in congregational spaces (mainly referred to as *khānā*) to facilitate the practical needs of the congregation (see Figure 12.3), and

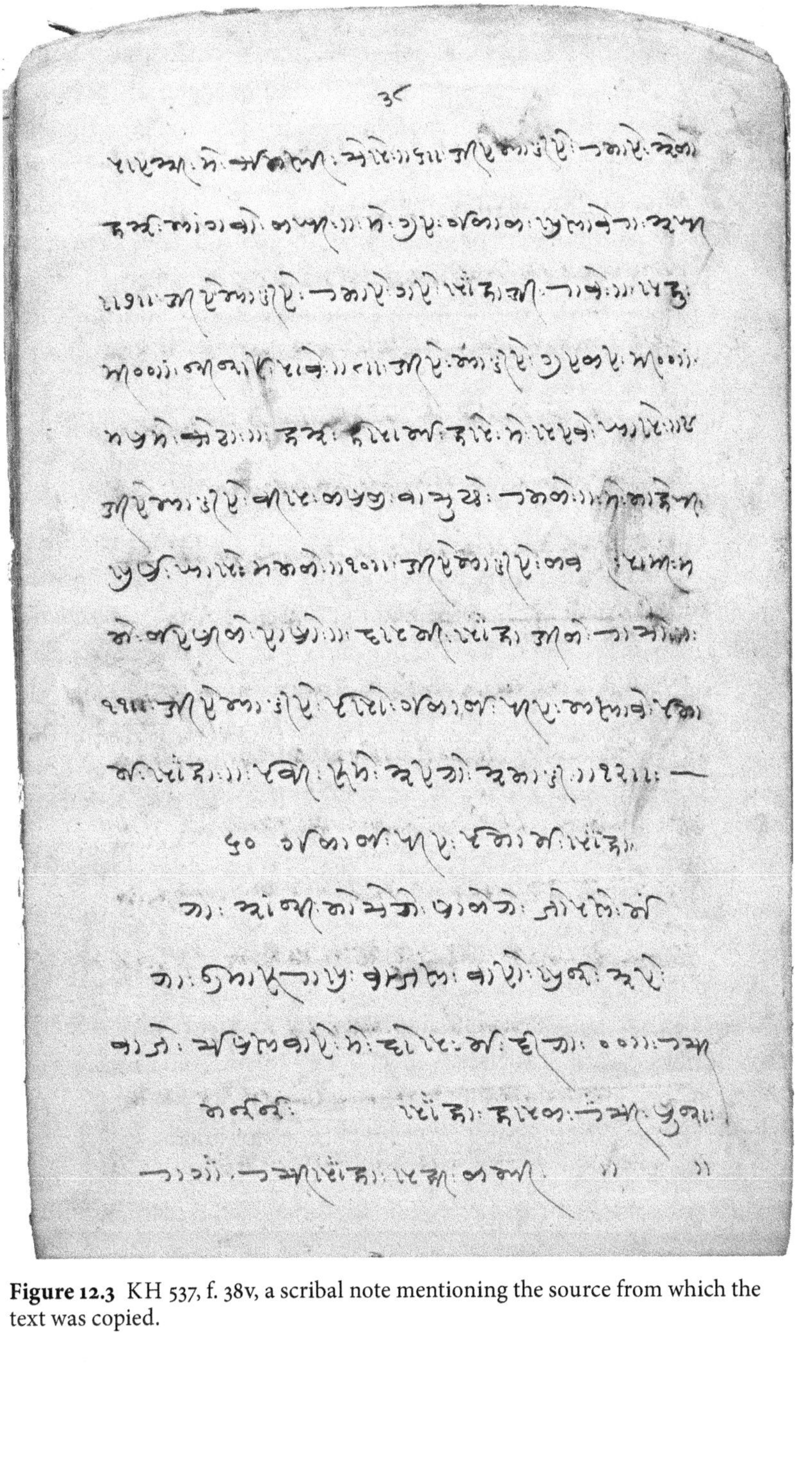

Figure 12.3 KH 537, f. 38v, a scribal note mentioning the source from which the text was copied.

those copied for and belonging to individual patrons. The exact context of the manuscripts, as falling in one or the other of these categories, is generally evident from the kind of materials copied in them, and/or from the colophons (where available), and consequently dictates the flavour that pervades the transcribed texts. It is therefore not surprising to find quite a wide-ranging body of material, going beyond the supposed congregational needs of the concerned communities, copied throughout the manuscripts, reflecting the personal tastes of the patron/scribe, audience needs, and the wider religio-literary trends in the immediate social milieu.[35] Also, whereas the boundaries between the composer of a given text and the copyist transcribing it are often clearly marked, at times we see these functions combined in one person, when a composer transcribes his own literary works in a given manuscript, and it is this aspect of the Satpanth literary culture that makes it a dynamic one, entwining the literate elite and its audience through a dialectical process.[36] Another important aspect of the scribal craft worth highlighting is the performative role evident from a number of texts in the 'story' genre, often referred to as *kiso* (from *qiṣṣa*). This would suggest that many of the texts in this genre were meant to be recited or read to audiences in a gathering, rather than being read silently by individuals on their own. The 'performative' aspect of the craft of scribes and literate gentry becomes even more vivid when we consider the existence of 'occult' material and prognostic texts in the manuscripts which must have been employed by the concerned members of the group when consulted by visitors for prognostic or healing purposes, forging a kind of clientele relationship between them.[37]

Based on the patterns of names borne by members of the literate class (scribes, patrons, owners etc.), as evident from colophons, scribal notations, ownership notes and even some genealogical lists, we can distinguish two broad groups. One group predominately bears Indic names, while the other carries mainly Arabic/Persian ones. In the former case, attested far more than the latter, we find many of the scribes and their patrons identified by the honorific titles Khojā, Kāmaḍīā and so on, titles that continued to be borne by what became known as the Nizārī Ismailis from among the adherents of the Satpanth tradition. The Arabic/Persian names, on the other hand, generally carry the honorific titles *vakīl*, *bāvā* and the like, representing some functional roles that came to be formed among the Satpanthī communities as their organisational structure became more bureaucratic.[38] In between these two broad categories of names, we come across others of a hybrid nature, combining Indic names with Arabic/Persian ones. As names are important markers of identity, based on the patterns of names encountered in the manuscripts, one may postulate that certain members of the concerned literate/bureaucratic elite either hailed from outside India (possibly Iran or Central Asia) and became indigenised, or underwent a process of 'Islamisation' to an extent that is sufficiently evident from their Arabic/Persian names as compared to the names of other members.[39]

In the manuscripts, the terminology frequently employed to designate the task of 'copying' or 'transcribing' by the scribes includes *likhatang*/*lakhatang*, and some other compound words formed by the prefix *likh*/*lakh-* (like *lakhaṇ vāro*), or in few instances *dast-khaṭ*, *be-dast* etc. These terms convey the sense of one who 'writes', 'transcribes', or the one 'undersigned'. In addition, the names of some copyists and their patrons often bear the title Khīāte, which has been taken to mean 'known as, named, called', following apparently the generally understood meaning of the term *khyāta*. As the term Khīāte often appears between the personal and family names of the scribes, this has thereby been taken to imply that some scribes were known by their surnames.[40] Indeed, the Sanskrit root *khyāti* ('renown', 'fame') does suggest this possibility, but we cannot take it as a rule. For one, we occasionally find the names of some bureaucratic elites (*vakīl*s) copied in the manuscripts suffixed with this title too. Furthermore, in Rajasthani the term *khyāta*, it may be recalled, has evolved from its Sanskrit root to signify 'that which is told or proclaimed' and 'an account or description'. Based on this further semantic possibility, it may be inferred that the Khīāte of Satpanthī manuscripts may have originally meant those associated with the task of writing/recording—the scribal class, so to speak—possibly signifying a mark of social standing or an acknowledged status. I shall therefore argue that titles like Khīāte allow us to further imagine the learned groups as forming a class of their own in the network of concerned communities.[41]

Finally, a relevant question for us to consider before concluding our discussion is what, if anything, we learn about the religious proclivities of the scribes from these manuscripts. There are indeed some significant insights that the manuscripts offer on this score with particular bearing on the kind of images about the Khojas that I mentioned in the first section of this chapter. The colophons and prefatory/terminal declarations, as noted earlier, invoke certain higher or mediating agencies, from whom the scribes either seek assistance or plead forgiveness from them for any errors that may have remained in transcribing the texts, which are clearly considered sacred. These agencies, for the most part, are God (referred to as *Khudā*, *Allāh* and occasionally by other terms), *Panjtan-i pāk* (the Holy Five, referring collectively to Muhammad and his immediate family, namely, ʿAlī, Fāṭima, Ḥasan, Ḥusayn), the names of Muhammad and ʿAlī (with titles like *nabī*, *maulā* as may be applicable) on their own, or some imams revered in the Nizārī tradition (flourishing when the manuscripts in question were copied), as well as simply the term Shāh Pīr—a compound term often taken as referring (as per some interpretations) to the bearer of the offices of 'imamate' and 'Pīrship'—or Dhaṇī Pīr ('lord Pīr') etc.[42]

What is interesting to note here is that in the colophons and scribal notations, we hardly come across the agencies associated with the 'Hindu' tradition, such as the deities Rām, Krishna, Viṣṇu or the more generic Harī and Sāmī (from *svāmī*), a feature that is the hallmark of the *Ginān* literature more generally.[43] This is moreover not just the case with the scribal notations, but with much of the 'occult' material transmitted via the manuscripts. Similarly, at the beginning or conclusion of many texts, we often find the scribes producing the Muslim profession of faith, *Lā ilāha illallā muḥammad rasūl allāh* ('there is no god but Allāh, and Muhammad is his messenger'), or similar Arabic formulas.[44] In short, the aforementioned elements from the Satpanth manuscript tradition collectively bear a noteworthy imprint of the religious and ideological leanings of the scribes/patrons, which were structured largely by the symbols and agencies associated with the Muslim tradition, rather than those of the 'Hindu' one.

Another relevant point to underscore here pertains to the use of dating system by the scribes. Where the manuscripts provide dates, this is usually done in the Vikram Saṁvat era which was prevalent in western India. However, the Vikram Saṁvat era is often combined with the Hijri dating system in quite a few manuscripts.[45] The occasional use of the Hijri system, it may be argued, implies some level of Muslim consciousness on the part of the scribes, for it would hardly have served the functional purpose of providing dates to potential readers who would be mainly familiar with and must have utilised the Vikram Saṁvat era.

Concluding Observations

Using the lens of manuscripts and associated cultural practices, this chapter has sought to recover the voices of and examine the role of the scribal/literate gentry in the formation of the Satpanth tradition, which has hitherto been primarily envisaged as a product of missionary activities as far as its premodern history is concerned. In premodern societies, in the absence of widespread literacy, it was mainly through the mediating groups of literati and performers (such as scribes and narrators) that textual and other genres (like those transmitted through Satpanth manuscripts) were made available to the concerned audiences, until the advent of printing redefined in critical ways the modes of engagement with texts. It was at this juncture that the manuscript culture gradually gave way to the print culture, and scribes became less prominent and relevant, disappearing conspicuously in our case from the early decades of the 20th century.

To scholars and observers of the Satpanth tradition, who are more familiar with the multi-faceted doctrinal vision of the *Ginān*s, the overtly 'Muslim' orientation of the Satpanth literate gentry, as shown here through a variety of features in the manuscripts they cultivated, might seem to suggest a degree of incompatibility between the two worlds—that of the supposed composers of *Ginān*s (Pīrs and Sayyids) and the scribal/literate class. However, despite their conspicuous supra-sectarian attitude, the *Ginān*s do at times depict a concern with what may be called inter-religious dialects.[46] These fragments of *Ginān*ic articulations and the further concrete evidence from the manuscripts allow us to postulate a pronounced transition of the Satpanth worldview and the religious identity of its adherents to a new mode in which many an adherent from these communities (and certainly the scribal and literate gentry examined in this chapter) were more self-consciously aware of their 'Muslim' identity. Furthermore, as the evidence in the present chapter shows, many members of this scribal and literate class hailed from the Khoja communities whose incessant portrayal as merchants and traders, at least since the first half of the 19th century, downplays their agency and voice in being at the forefront of shaping the contours of their religious beliefs, worldviews and practices during premodern and colonial times.

NOTES

1 MacMurdo's account of Kutch appeared in *Transactions of the Literary Society of Bombay*, vol. 2 (London, 1820), pp. 205–241; the description of the Khojas is offered on p. 232. Some decades later, Dalpatrām Prāṇjivan Khakhar, in his 'Castes and Tribes in Kachh', found the Khojas (like MacMurdo) to be 'chiefly cultivators in Kachh, but [were] enterprising merchants in Bombay and Zanzibar, China, [etc.]'. He further identified the Khojas of Kutch as 'Shiah Muhammadans', most of them being 'originally Hindus of the Bhâṭia caste', and provided additional observations on their mixed religious tenets; see *The Indian Antiquary, A Journal of Oriental Research*, 5 (1876), pp. 167–174, at 171.

2 Richard Burton, *Sindh and the Races that Inhabit the Valley of the Indus* (London, 1851), pp. 248–250. Amelia Cary (wife of Lord Falkland, the governor of Bombay) thus remarked about the Khojas around the same time as Burton penned his observations on them: '[They] are a kindred tribe of Mahomedan heretics. They do not usually, like the Bohras, travel about as pedlars, but in Bombay, and other seaport towns of Western India, and in Cutch, they have a great share in the local trade; and in Scinde, where they are very numerous, I am told they cultivate land, and are distinguished for their enterprise and industry'. She then goes on to underscore the eclectic nature of their religion and its connection with the 'Ismalite heresy' through their spiritual head, the Aga Khan; see her *Chow-Chow; being Selections from a Journal Kept in India, Egypt, and Syria* (London, 1857), vol. 2, pp. 18–19.

3 William Johnson, *The Oriental Races and Tribes, Residents and Visitors of Bombay: A Series of Photographs, with Letter-Press Descriptions*, vol. 1: *Gujarât, Kutch, and Kâthiawâr* (London, 1863), pp. 97–99.

4 Literally meaning the 'True Path', *Sat-panth* is a key idea (along with some others) employed in the *Ginān* literature for the religio-moral dispensation propagated in it. Khojas were among the many groups who were preached the teachings of Satpanth, with the *Ginān*s being an important medium for it.

5 For a survey of the issues involved on the question of the religious identity of Khojas, see Ali S. Asani, 'From Satpanthi to Ismaili Muslim: The Articulation of Ismaili Khoja Identity in South Asia', in Farhad Daftary, ed., *A Modern History of the Ismailis: Continuity and Change in a Muslim Community* (London, 2011), pp. 95–128.

6 Sir Erskine Perry, *Cases Illustrative of Oriental Life, and the Application of English Law to India* (London, 1853), pp. 112–114.

7 One may immediately recognise that Perry's observations about the Khojas' practice of Islamic precepts were (partly) countered by observers like Burton who, for example, noted that the Khojas of Sindh had a practice of writing the Qur'ān in their communal script. Also, in a reprint of the judgement originally delivered by Perry in 1847, he rectified certain factual inaccuracies earlier made about the Khojas; see ibid, p. 113 (note a). The key point here is that, despite having differences and counterpoints in how certain details about the Khojas were brought to light by these accounts, there was a degree of uniformity in the manner certain overarching images about them were perpetuated.

8 See *Judgment by the Hon'ble Sir Joseph Arnould in the Kojah Case, otherwise known as the Aga Khan Case, heard in the High Court of Bombay, during April and June, 1866* ([Bombay], 1866), esp. pp. 7, 11–12.

9 See, for example, H. B. E. Frere, 'The Khojas: The Disciples of the Old Man of the Mountain', *Macmillan's Magazine*, 34 (1876), pp. 342–350, 430–438. Frere introduces the Khojas as 'the present representative' of the 'old man of the mountain', who 'though now peaceful merchants and cultivators, are the successors in unbroken descent of the Assassins of the Middle Ages'. His paper produces long excerpts from Arnould's judgement. See also R. E. Enthoven, *The Tribes and Castes of Bombay* (Bombay, 1922), vol. 2, pp. 217–230, where after identifying the Khojas as 'Ismáiliás of the Nazárian sub-division', it provides such details as their history, customs, religious practices etc., finishing the account with their achievements in the sphere of commerce and business in India and beyond.

10 Farhad Daftary discusses these advancements in his *The Ismāʿīlīs: Their History and Doctrines* (2nd ed., Cambridge, 2007), pp. 1–33.

11 Zawahir Moir, 'Historical and Religious Debates amongst Indian Ismailis 1840–1920', in Mariola Offredi, ed., *The Banyan Tree: Essays on Early Literature in New Indo-Aryan Languages* (New Delhi, 2000), vol. 1, pp. 131–153; and Wafi Momin, *The Formation of the Satpanth Ismaili Tradition in South Asia* (PhD diss., The University of Chicago, 2016), esp. pp. 212–253.

12 James Campbell, ed., *Gazetteer of the Bombay Presidency*, Vol. 9, Part 2: *Gujarát Population: Musalmáns and Pársis* (Bombay, 1899); for Khojas, see pp. 36–50. It may be noted that similar to the Khojas, the Bohras represented yet another group who were by and large depicted as traders and merchants despite having a long tradition of intellectual and literary activities, as is evident (for example) through the manuscript culture cultivated among them.

13 For example, W. Ivanow saw the split within what he called the sect of Satpanth (in the beginning of 10th/16th century) as a clash between the interests of the 'trading newcomers' (that is, the Khojas) and 'converts from the local farmers' of Gujarat and Konkan (who remained known as Satpanthīs); see his *Ismaili Literature: A Bibliographical Survey* (2nd ed., Tehran, 1963), p. 12. It must be pointed out that some earlier accounts, while dwelling on various meanings of the term 'Khoja', did hint at other possibilities alongside the conventional 'lord' and 'master'. Hence, Burton considered the term 'Khwajeh' (as he applied it to the Khojas of Sindh and other parts) a Persian 'titular appellation' which signified 'a bard, a teacher, and a merchant' without discussing its implications; see his *Sindh and the Races*, p. 412, n. 26.

14 On Khojkī script see Ali Asani, 'The Khojkī Script: A Legacy of Ismaili Islam in the Indo-Pakistan Subcontinent', *Journal of the American Oriental Society*, 107 (1987), pp. 439–449; and Christopher Shackle and Zawahir Moir, *Ismaili Hymns from South Asia: An Introduction to the Ginans* (Richmond, 2000), pp. 34–42.

15 There are at present two known institutional collections of these manuscripts, namely those of The Institute of Ismaili Studies and Harvard University, with many in private possession; for the Harvard manuscripts, see Ali S. Asani, *The Harvard Collection of Ismaili Literature in Indic Languages: A Descriptive Catalog and Finding Aid* (Boston, 1992). This chapter is mainly based on observations drawn from the Institute's collection, a catalogue of which is forthcoming.

16 For some of the works exhibiting this trend, see W. Ivanow, 'The Sect of Imam Shah in Gujrat', *Journal of the Bombay Branch of the Royal Asiatic Society*, New Series, 12 (1936), pp. 19–17; and his *Ismaili Literature*, pp. 11–12, 174–181; Azim Nanji, *The Nizārī Ismāʿīlī Tradition in the Indo-Pakistan Subcontinent* (Delmar, NY, 1978), pp. 33–96; and Shackle and Moir, *Ismaili Hymns from South Asia*, pp. 6–8.

17 An important exception here is Asani, *The Harvard Collection*, esp. pp. 48–51; Asani's observations on the scribes are based on relevant manuscripts housed at Harvard.

18 For some relevant studies discussing the role of this class, see Muzaffar Alam and Sanjay Subrahmanyam, 'The Making of a Munshi', *Comparative Studies of South Asia, Africa and the Middle East*, 24 (2004), pp. 61–72; Kumkum Chatterjee, 'Scribal Elites in Sultanate and Mughal Bengal', *The Indian Economic and Social History Review*, 47

(2010), pp. 445–472; Rosalind O'Hanlon, 'The Social Worth of Scribes: Brahmins, Kāyasthas and the Social Order in Early Modern India', *The Indian Economic and Social History Review*, 47 (2010), pp. 563–595; Daud Ali, 'The Image of the Scribe in Early Medieval Sources', in Kesavan Veluthat and Donald R. Davis, Jr., ed., *Irreverent History: Essays for M.G.S. Narayanan* (Delhi, 2014), pp. 167–187; and Rajeev Kinra, *Writing Self, Writing Empire: Chandar Bhan Brahman and the Cultural World of the Indo-Persian State Secretary* (Oakland, CA, 2015).

19 During the course of my research and fieldwork in different parts of South Asia, I have come across many documents and manuscripts, copied in both Khojkī and Gujarati, which contain mainly administrative and financial records, suggesting that the concerned scribes were also engaged in various bureaucratic functions.

20 Momin, *The Formation of the Satpanth Ismaili Tradition.*

21 The invocatory formula *Alā* (from *Allāh) toāhāra*, which is a characteristic feature of the Satpanth manuscripts transcribed in Khojkī and Gujarati scripts, often occurs with slight variations, such as *Alā tohāra* and *Alāha tohāra*. For an example of its occurrence together with *Basmallāh*, see KH 404, pp. 1, 208. It seems to have been in vogue widely in Sindh and the adjoining regions beyond those who cultivated these manuscripts. For its occurrence in some versions of the Sindhi romantic tale of *Sassuī Punhun* (popular in Baluchistan and Sindh), see Burton, *Sindh and the Races*, p. 95; and [F. J. Goldsmid,] *Sáswí and Punhú: A Poem in the Original Sindi; with a Metrical Translation in English* (London, 1863), p. 15 (Sindhi), p. 9 (English). Goldsmid describes it as 'a cry often heard among Mahomedans, especially Sindis and Belúchis, on the departure of caravans or detachments. It is expressive of trust in Providence' (p. 27, n. 18).

22 At the beginning of a text, this information accompanies terms like *likhaṇ shuru keāsī / shuru kiī āhe / shuru karīo tā* ('I have started writing') or similar phrases, indicating the commencement of transcribing/copying. On the other hand, at the end of a text the colophon bears a combination of terms such as *tamat tamām / tamām shud / puro theo / sampuraṇ samāpta*, indicating that 'the task has been completed'. In some manuscripts, we find the practice of beginning and finishing the texts with the terms *atha* and *iti*, a convention widely observed in Indian manuscripts. For example, in KH 431 (dated VS 1940/*ca.* 1884), the scribe thus commences the popular tale of Sudāmā (Śrīdāmā): 'Atha:sadāmā:purī:likhīche' ('now transcribed is *Sadāmā Purī*') (f. 152v); and ends it with these words: 'Itī:sirī:sadāmā:purī:samāpata' ('so completed *Sadāmā Purī*') (f. 188v).

23 See, for example, Gérard Colas, 'The Criticism and Transmission of Texts in Classical India', *Diogenes*, 47 (1999), pp. 32–33, 41 (fn. 11).

24 KH 541 (dated VS 1927/*ca.* 1871), f. 1v; it was not possible to read some words as the folio has been eaten into where this note appears. The scribe thereafter commences *Risālo* with the formula *Basmallāh* (which is also the case with many other texts copied in the manuscript); for the *Risālo*, see Asani, *The Harvard Collection*, p. 11. It seems that the scribe in this manuscript used many different sources, for example, after finishing another text, he notes, 'I have copied [the text] verbatim from the handwriting of Khojā Alārakheā Korajī; if there are any mistakes then correct them before reading it' (182r). While transcribing selections from Khojkī here, I have disregarded the tendency of 'over-nasalisation' encountered frequently in the manuscripts, so as not to encumber the transcription.

25 KH 431 (dated VS 1940/*ca.* 1884), f. 85r. The *Ginān Janājo* is also known as *Janat Purī*; for its translation, see Vali M. Hooda, tr., 'Jannatpuri, or the City of Paradise', in W. Ivanow, ed., *Collectanea* (Leiden, 1948), pp. 122–137.

26 KH 55, p. 136.

27 This observation is further supported by the colophons of some manuscripts where the place of their copying is identified as some place in Kutch; see, for example, KH 508, f. 65r (Bhuj); KH 621, f. 296v (Nāgalpur).

28 For communal traditions about Dādū's role in settling the Khojas to Kutch, see Sacedīnā Nānajīāṇī, *Khojā Vṛttānt* (Ahmedabad, 1892), pp. 241–242; Vīrajī Premajī Pārapīā, *Kābā Timir Bhāskar urphe Khojā Ibhalāṇī Vaṁshanuṁ Vṛttānt ane Vakīl (Pīr) Dhādhu* (Mumbai, 1917), pp. 9–12; and Alīmāmad Jānamāmad Cunārā, *Nurūn Mobīn athavā Allāhanī Pavitra Rasī* (Mumbai, 1935), pp. 573–575. On the identification of Kutch as the homeland of the Khojas in the 19th century, see Perry, *Cases Illustrative of Oriental Life*, p. 112; and *A Voice from India. Being an Appeal to the British Legislature, by Khojahs of Bombay, against the usurped and oppressive domination of Hussain Hussanee, commonly called and known as 'Aga Khan'* (London, 1864), p. 9.

29 See Asani, *The Harvard Collection*, pp. 5–22ff.

30 See W. Ivanow, 'Tombs of Some Persian Ismaili Imams', *Journal of the Bombay Branch of the Royal Asiatic Society*, New Series, 14 (1938), pp. 49–50. In the same article, Ivanow mentions the visit of some Indian followers to Kahak in Iran, a residence of the Nizārī imams from roughly the end of the 17th to the middle of the 18th century, and points to the existence of their graves, some bearing inscriptions in Khojkī script. He, however, does not discuss the question of linguistic knowledge on the part of some of these Indian visitors which the existence of the graves throws open.

31 See, for instance, Nanji, *The Nizārī Ismāʿīlī Tradition*, esp. Part I; and Momin, *The Formation of the Satpanth Ismaili Tradition*, pp. 61–81ff.

32 For the Persian text of *Pandiyāt-i Javānmardī* transcribed in Khojkī, see, for instance, KH 25 (vol. 1), pp. 142–211; W. Ivanow edited and translated the Persian text in his *Pandiyat-i Jawanmardi or 'Advices of Manliness'* (Leiden, 1953).

33 See, for example, KH 131 and KH 419 where Arabic sounds are represented by the scribe in copying the Arabic and other texts with a combination of dots and the marker for *shadda*. In fact, on some occasions, scribes were conscious that to transcribe the Arabic text, it was 'Khojkī' rather than the Gujarati script which was a suitable option, implying that provision in the former was supposedly available through modifications to adapt the script for Arabic (see Momin, *The Formation of the Satpanth Ismaili Tradition*, p. 44).

34 The use of Persian (in Perso-Arabic script) in the colophons etc. may be seen in KH 31 (beginning); KH 508 (VS 1926/*ca.* 1870), f. 65r where the scribe begins and concludes the colophon with the Persian couplet, *har ke khvānad doʿā ṭamʿa dāram, ze-ānke man banda-i guneh kāram* ('I seek prayers from those who read [it], for I am a sinful servant') which generally occurs in Persian manuscripts.

35 This classification, it may be stressed, is more suggestive than exhaustive, as there are many textual genres that overlap between these two categories. For examples of the manuscripts copied from those kept in congregational spaces or those belonged to other individuals, see KH 537 (undated), f. 38v, where the scribe copied sixty *Gināns* of Imām Shāh from a book of the congregation space of Kāṇḍī Mohallā (in Bombay) (kāṁdhī:moleje:khāneje:copaṇe:miṁjā) (see Figure 12.3); also, the source of another thirty *Gināns* of Imām Shāh that the scribe copies in the same manuscript is mentioned as the volume (*pothī*) of Khojā Ṭālib Kāmaḍīā (f. 66v).

36 For example, see KH 121 where the scribe, Khojā Khamīs Māmadāṇī, copies his own poetic works (*kāfīs*) in praise of God, Prophet Muhammad, Imam ʿAlī and other imams of his time.

37 I discuss this diverse range of literary and religious genres, and their ramifications in forging the complex tenor of the Satpanth epistemic order in Momin, *The Formation of the Satpanth Ismaili Tradition*.

38 Nanji, *The Nizārī Ismāʿīlī Tradition*, pp. 89–90.

39 In the hybrid cases, it is often the surnames that remain Indic while the forenames show the Arabic/Persian trend (like Khoāje Nur Māmad Khīāte Manjīāṇī), but some names depart from this pattern too. The above observations on the patterns of names of the members of the scribal/literate class are preliminary ones, and it will be worthwhile comparing these patterns (as prevalent among the Khojas and other Satpanth

communities more widely) from the larger pool of available sources to come up with a comprehensive picture of this phenomenon.

40 This has been suggested in Asani, *The Harvard Collection*, p. 50.

41 The line of *vakīl*s who are referred to as *khīāto* appears in KH 25, vol. 2, p. 198. For the use of this title with the names of scribes/patrons, see KH 431 (dated VS 1940/*ca.* 1884) (towards the end, on a differently numbered page); KH 612 (VS 1909/*ca.* 1853), f. 24; KH 640 (on an unnumbered page in the beginning, producing 'table of contents'). See also the example mentioned in Asani, *The Harvard Collection*, p. 50. For the Rajasthani *khyāta* genre, see Norman P. Ziegler, 'The Seventeenth Century Chronicles of Mārvāṛa: A Study in the Evolution and Use of Oral Traditions in Western India', *History in Africa*, 3 (1976), pp. 131–132. A further case in point is the title Ākhūnd (comparatively more widespread in Sindh) added to the names of some scribes in the Satpanth manuscripts, marking their 'learned' status.

42 See the following examples; for God (referred to as *Allāh*, *Khudā* etc.), KH 203, f. 18v; KH 515, f. 1; for *Panjtan-i Pāk*, KH 431, f. 2r; KH 509, p. 1; KH 541, f. 69; for 'Alī (using different titles), KH 507, f. 50; KH 508, f. 16; for *Shāh Pīr*, KH 526, f. 5b; KH 537, f. 38; KH 549, f. 1; KH 557 (unpaginated folio); KH 619, f. 1; for *Dhaṇī Pīr* (the lord Pīr), KH 507, f. 1; KH 533, f. 111; KH 538, p. 59; for the name of Ḥasan 'Alī (Aga Khan I), KH 623, f. 166, and Sulṭān Muḥammad Shāh (Aga Khan III), KH 625, p. 70, the last two being the Nizārī imams.

43 The exceptions in the manuscripts are some Indic popular tales associated with certain mythological figures where Hindu deities are of course invoked. But at the commencement of such texts, the agencies that the scribes invoke are not those of the Hindu tradition. See also Wafi Momin, 'On the Cusp of "Islamic" and "Hindu" Worldviews? The *Ginān* Literature and the Dialectics of Self and Other', in Orkhan Mir-Kasimov, ed., *Intellectual Interactions in the Islamic World: The Ismaili Thread* (London, 2020), pp. 427–451; and idem, 'The Idea of Evil and Messianic Deliverance in the Satpanth Ismaili Tradition of South Asia', in Natasha Mikles and Joseph Laycock, ed., *Religion, Culture, and the Monstrous: Of Gods and Monsters* (Lanham, MD, 2021), pp. 63–77.

44 The Muslim *shahāda* is produced in, among others, KH 431, f. 107v; KH 530, f. 53r and KH 560, f. 300r.

45 For the use of Hijri dates in the manuscripts, see KH 55, p. 136 and KH 413, ff. 132v–133r. In some rare cases, the Gregorian dating is also combined with Vikram Saṁvat and Hijri eras.

46 See Momin, 'On the Cusp of "Islamic" and "Hindu" Worldviews?'.

SECTION VI

IDENTITY, CULTURAL INTERACTIONS, AND ESOTERIC INTERPRETATION AMONG CENTRAL ASIAN ISMAILI COMMUNITIES

13

Ismaili–Sufi Relationships in the Light of the Niʿmat Allāhī Manuscripts in the Holdings of The Institute of Ismaili Studies*

Orkhan Mir-Kasimov

Shāh Niʿmat Allāh Walī (d. 834/1430–1431) was a famous Sufi master and the founder of an influential Sufi order.[1] It is well known that the Ismailis and the Niʿmat Allāhīs had a long history of close and friendly relationships.[2] However, while the historical aspect of this relationship has attracted some scholarly attention, our knowledge concerning its intellectual aspect, that is, each group's awareness of the other's doctrines, is still very limited. The present paper aims at addressing this latter point by focussing on some manuscripts attributed to Shāh Niʿmat Allāh Walī and preserved in the Ismaili Special Collections Unit at The Institute of Ismaili Studies (IIS) in London. These manuscripts, which include prose and poetry, come from private Ismaili libraries in Badakhshān (Tajikistan and Afghanistan).[3] Ismaili communities of these regions regard Shāh Niʿmat Allāh Walī as their co-religionist and his works, especially the poetry attributed to him, are still popular and are recited during religious ceremonies.[4] This seems also confirmed by the existence of very recent (20th century) copies among the manuscripts collected and preserved at the IIS. Is there anything in the nature and contents of these works attributed to Shāh Niʿmat Allāh Walī that explains their incorporation as part of the Ismaili spiritual and intellectual heritage? Information concerning the reception and transmission of the Niʿmat Allāhī texts in Ismaili milieus could provide some useful highlights to complement our knowledge of historical relationships between the Ismailis and Niʿmat Allāhis.

I will begin this chapter by briefly discussing the reasons for the rapprochement between the Ismailis and Sufis in general and the Ismailis and Niʿmat Allāhīs in particular. I will then focus on the manuscripts attributed to Shāh Niʿmat Allāh Walī in the collection of The Institute of Ismaili Studies, on their description, identification, and when relevant, comparison with the existing editions. While discussing the contents of these works, I will highlight the points that, in my opinion, are particularly close to the Ismaili doctrinal positions and could therefore explain the popularity of Shāh Niʿmat Allāh Walī's works in the Ismaili milieu.

Doctrinal and Historical Links between Niʿmat Allāhīs and Ismailis

Sufism and Shiʿism are two esoteric currents of Islam and, as such, they share many common features. In the course of history this similarity generated, on the one hand mutual sympathy and collaboration and, on the other, rivalry and competition. For example, some major branches of the Shiʿis, such as the Twelvers and the Ismailis, adhere, like the Sufis, to the idea of divinely inspired guide. However, for the Twelvers and the Ismailis, this guide must belong to the particular line of the prophetic family, that of the Imams, in which the prophetic knowledge is preserved and transmitted from father to son. In contradistinction, for the Sufis spiritual leadership is not limited to the prophetic family and belongs to the Shaykhs, spiritual masters who attained the highest degree of enlightenment.

The contradiction between these two potentially conflicting conceptions of authority was somewhat flattened in Twelver Shiʿism, where the Sufi shaykh could be seen as a representative of the hidden Imam during the prolonged absence of the latter.[5] We know that some Niʿmat Allāhī dervishes made this claim in the past, and it seems that this is presently the understanding that the Twelver Shiʿi followers of the Niʿmat Allāhiyya have concerning the relationship between the hidden Imam and their shaykh.[6] But such a solution was obviously not applicable to the Ismaili cause. Indeed, there was no major occultation in the Ismaili branch of Shiʿi Islam and therefore the Ismaili Imam was always more or less present and accessible to his community.[7] In addition, it seems that Shāh Niʿmat Allāh Walī never explicitly presented himself as a champion of the Ismaili, or even more broadly Shiʿi, cause.

However, in spite of these circumstances, it seems that the Ismailis, like the Twelvers, did have some authentic interest in the Niʿmat Allāhī doctrine, and this interest was not limited to tactical dissimulation (*taqiyya*), that is, to the adoption of a Sufi appearance in order to avoid persecution. This is probably due to the following reasons.

First, the rapprochement between Shiʿism and Sufism, especially in the period following the Mongol invasions and the end of the Nizārī Ismaili state in northern Iran created a context, marked by the works of such prominent Shiʿi thinkers as Ḥaydar Amulī (d. after 787/1385), in which Sufi doctrines could be perceived as authentic esoteric teachings of the Shiʿi Imams.[8] This was facilitated by the fact that Sufism at that time was becoming more and more impregnated by Shiʿi ideas and symbolism, including the veneration of ʿAlī b. Abī Ṭālib and of the prophetic family, and emphasis on the *walāya* as the inner dimension of the prophecy.[9] In this atmosphere of Sufi/Shiʿi eclecticism, it is not surprising that the Nizārī Ismailis could discern and incorporate in their tradition the ideas resonating with their own doctrines not only from Shāh Niʿmat Allāh Walī, but also from Persian mystical poets, such as Sanāʾī (Majdūd b. Adam al-Ghaznawī, d. 525/1131), Farīd al-Dīn ʿAṭṭār (d. 586/1190 or 627/1230) or Jalāl al-Dīn Rūmī (d. 672/1273), and from mystical thinkers such as ʿAzīz al-Dīn Nasafī (d. *ca.* 700/1300) or famous Ibn ʿArabī (d. 638/1240).[10] Another strong argument for the incorporation of the Sufi literature in the Persian language into the Persianate Nizārī Ismaili tradition is that the Nizārī written heritage was severely diminished after the destruction of the libraries in Ismaili strongholds in northern Iran. Recognition of the Sufi literature as expressing the same esoteric truths as the teachings of the Imams could have been seen as a remedy to the loss of the Ismaili libraries in the fire of the Mongol invasions.

Second, Shāh Niʿmat Allāh Walī belonged to this specific generation of post-Mongol spiritual leaders, such as Faḍl Allāh Astarābādī (d. 796/1394), Muḥammad Nūrbakhsh (d. 869/1464), Muḥammad Ibn Falāḥ (al-Mushaʿshaʿ) (d. 870/1465–1466) and the Safavid leaders Junayd (d. 864/1460), Ḥaydar (d. 893/1488) and Shāh Ismāʿīl (d. 930/1524), who had a particularly strong awareness of their mission as divinely guided leaders, often marked by more or less strongly expressed messianic claims. These kinds of spiritual guides were particularly close to and, at least in some cases could be inspired by, the Nizārī Ismaili conception of *qiyāma*, the messianic age placed under authority of the divinely guided Imam.[11] The poetry of Shāh Niʿmat Allāh Walī contains many elements that are usually associated with Shiʿi tenets, such as the centrality of ʿAlī b. Abī Ṭālib, the names of several Shiʿi Imams, mention of the 'five of the cloak', of the 14 Immaculate ones, of the tragedy of Karbala, and so on.[12] Some verses attributed to Shāh Niʿmat Allāh Walī also suggest that he was believed to be divinely protected from error.[13] Other verses mention 'universal rite' and divine guidance.[14] Apparently, the explicit inspiration of Shāh Niʿmat Allāh was the theory of the Seal of the Sainthood of Ibn ʿArabī.[15] Whether Shāh Niʿmat Allāh was familiar with the Nizārī Ismaili doctrine of the *qiyāma* remains a question, but the image of an infallible divinely guided leader who ushers in a universal religion of the messianic age resonates very strongly with the Nizārī Ismaili description of the Imam of the *qiyāma*.

The third argument that is usually mentioned as one of the possible explanations of the close historical relationships between the Ismailis and Niʿmat Allāhīs is the genealogy of Shāh Niʿmat Allāh Walī. According to some accounts, he was a descendant of Ismāʿīl b. Jaʿfar al-Ṣādiq.[16]

Such is the background against which the historical relationships between Qāsim-Shāhī branch of the Nizārī Ismailis and the Niʿmat Allāhī Sufi order should be considered. It will be remembered that some kind of association between these two groups existed apparently since the 32nd Imam of the Qāsim-Shāhī Ismailis, Mustanṣir biʾllāh II (d. 885/1480) and continued until the middle of the 20th century.[17]

This could also explain why the Sufi literature, including poetry and doctrinal works, and in particular the poetry and works of Shāh Niʿmat Allāh Walī not only circulated, but was and, as some of the recently copied manuscript material shows, still is popular among the Ismailis. There are also probably some more specific links between the figure of Shāh Niʿmat Allāh Walī and Ismailism in Badakhshān, since some traces of Shah Niʿmat Allāh Walī's influence can be discerned in *Chirāgh-rawshan,* the local tradition of the Ismaili communities of Badakhshān.[18]

Manuscripts of Works Attributed to Shāh Niʿmat Allāh Walī in the Collection of the IIS

As mentioned, the works attributed to Shāh Niʿmat Allāh Walī in the collection of The Institute of Ismaili Studies include poetry and doctrinal treatises in prose. Poetry is part of the miscellaneous compilations of poetry (MS BA 71, MS BA 126, MS BA 141, MS BT 130, MS BT 134, MS BT 173, MS BT 185, MS BT 197, MS BT 282, MS BT 285). The poetry attributed to Shāh Niʿmat Allāh Walī occupies a few folios in each of these manuscripts. MS BA 86 is a voluminous collection of Shāh Niʿmat Allāh's doctrinal treatises (*rasāʾil*). As mentioned, all these manuscripts come from the private libraries of Ismaili families of Badakhshān region of Tajikistan and Afghanistan.[19]

Poetry

The compilations of poetry include older looking manuscripts (MS BA 71 (1367/[1947–1948]), MS BA 141 (1365/[1946]), MS BT 197 (n.d.), MS BT 134,[20] MS BT 130,[21] and more recently copied manuscripts written in what look like Soviet-era school notebooks and address books (MS BA 126 (n.d.), MS BT 173 (n.d.), MS BT 185 (n.d.), MS BT 282 (1963?), MS BT 285 (1380/[1960–1961]). The significant number of manuscripts written on modern supports suggests that this poetry is still popular and circulates widely among the Ismailis of Badakhshān.

A few notes about the contents of these fragments of poetry: Shāh Niʿmat Allāh Walī's kind of mystical messianic ethos, combined with a more or less clearly expressed claim to divinely guided leadership and interwoven with Shiʿi-sounding references, did appeal to the Ismailis. One of the recently copied manuscripts (MS BA 126, copied on a Soviet-era school notebook) (see Figure 13.1) contains poetry ascribed to Shāh Niʿmat Allāh where he calls himself the locus of manifestation of sincerity (*maẓhargāh-i ṣidq*), infallible (*maʿṣūm*), and light of ʿAlī b. Abī Ṭālib (*nūr-i ʿAlī*). He is the cupbearer of God (*sāqī-yi khudā*), he is the minstrel of God (*muṭrib-i khudā*) in this cycle (*dar īn dawr/ dar īn qarn/ dar īn ʿaṣr*) for the friends of Jaʿfar's station (*dustān-i maqām-i Jaʿfarī*) and divinely appointed representative of the Twelver Mahdi Muḥammad ibn ʿAskarī in this age (*nāʾib be-khudā manam dar-īn ʿaṣr/ ān mahdī-yi ibn ʿAskarī-rā*). He is the sun of the Real and

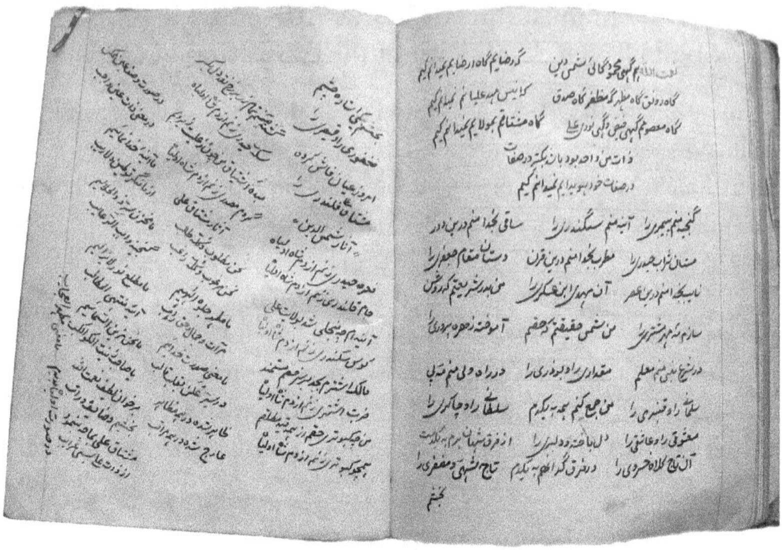

Figure 13.1 Poetry ascribed to Shāh Niʿmat Allāh from MS BA 126.

the Real itself (*man shams-i ḥaqīqatam ke ḥaqqam*). He is the teacher of the prophetic law, and he is the guide on the paths of sainthood. He is the mirror reflecting the *walāya* of ʿAlī b. Abī Ṭālib; he is the locus of manifestation of the divine splendour (*maẓhar-i jilwa-yi ilāhī*); he is the metaphysical meaning of the divine form (*maʿnā-yi ṣūrat-i khudā*).

This kind of claim comes very close indeed to the image of a Shiʿi, and in particular Ismaili Imam. Even if there is little doubt that any explicitly Shiʿi elements in Shāh Niʿmat Allāh's poetry refer to the Twelver and not the Ismaili Shiʿi tradition, they obviously also resonated with the Ismaili Shiʿi worldview. Among our fragments, there are verses where Shāh Niʿmat Allāh praises ʿAlī b. Abī Ṭālib, his family and the 14 impeccable ones.[22] These verses can be found in the following manuscripts: MS BT 173 (modern notebook) contains praise of ʿAlī and the famous phrase which describes ʿAlī as the prototype of Islamic chivalry,[23] 14 impeccable ones, *walāya* and *walī*; and MS BT 197 contains a piece of poetry titled 'the Qasida of Shāh Niʿmat Allāh Walī' (*qaṣīda-yi Shāh Niʿmat Allāh Walī*), where ʿAlī is described as the supreme Imam and the *walī* of the two worlds,[24] and the author of the *qaṣīda* (Niʿmat Allāh Walī?) claims to possess ʿAlī's seal (*muhr*). The *qaṣīda* also expresses loyalty to the family of ʿAlī. MS BT 134 contains praise of ʿAlī as well.

Manuscripts MS BT 282 and MS BT 185 (modern notebooks) contain fragments of 'philosophical' poetry of Shāh Niʿmat Allāh Walī, mentioning universal Intellect, universal soul, planets, nature and so on, which resonates with the Ismaili cosmogonical and cosmological doctrines.

One fragment of poetry in manuscript MS BA 71 is related to the particular status of the Timurid line. It describes Tamerlane (d. 807/1405) as the Lord of Conjunction (*ṣāḥib-i qirān*), then mentions Mīrānshāh (one of the sons of Tamerlane, d. *ca.* 810/1408) and Bābur (Ẓāhir al-Dīn Muḥammad, d. 937/1530, a fourth-generation descendant of Mīrānshāh). This same manuscript contains some eschatological predictions, mentioning several dates, the end of the world (*ākhir zamān*) and the coming of Jesus.

The remaining fragments mainly contain Sufi poetry, lyrical passages which do not seem to be linked with any specifically Ismaili doctrinal topic.

Doctrinal Works

As mentioned, manuscript MS BA 86 titled 'the Epistle of Shāh Niʿmat Allāh Walī' (*Risāla-yi Shāh Niʿmat Allāh Walī*) (see Figure 13.2) is more interesting from the point of view of the Ismaili reception of the Niʿmat Allāhī doctrines. The manuscript contains about 300 folios, that is, 600 pages. In spite of its title, it is not a single epistle, but a collection of some 45 *rasāʾil*. According to the colophon, the manuscript was completed on *chahārshamba* 14 *Rajab* 1238 (Wednesday 26 March 1823) by Mullā ʿAlī Muḥammad.[25]

I compared the contents of this manuscript with one of the existing editions of Shāh Niʿmat Allāh's works, namely Javad Nūrbakhsh's edition titled *Risālahā-ye ḥaḍrat-i sayyid Nūr al-Dīn Shāh Niʿmat Allāh Walī,* 4 vols. (Tehran, 1357 Sh. [1978-1979]). This edition contains 94 treatises ascribed to Shāh Niʿmat Allāh. The results of this comparison are presented in the reconstructed table of contents of the manuscript MS BA 86 below (titles published in the Nūrbakhsh edition are in bold).

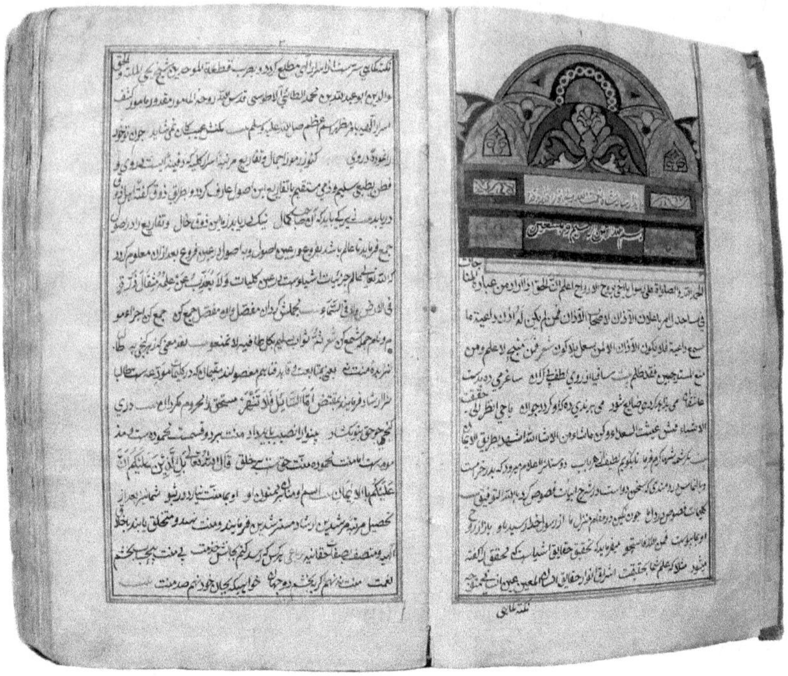

Figure 13.2 *Risāla-yi Shāh Niʿmat Allāh Walī* in MS BA 86.

1. **(1b–11b), Text of the *Risāla-yi sharḥ-i abyāt-i Fuṣūṣ al-ḥikam*** [this is only part of the text published in the Nūrbakhsh edition, 4:436–522. The manuscript diverges from the printed text of the Nūrbakhsh edition starting from the p. 485].
2. (11b–58b) Unidentified untitled text divided into chapters corresponding to the letters of the alphabet (*bāb al-ḍād* etc.), however not in alphabetical order.
3. (58b–95b) *Sharḥ-i lamaʿāt-i ʿIrāqī*.
4. **(95b–107a) untitled section introduced by *basmala*,** apparently identical with the *Marātib-i rindān* **in Nūrbakhsh 1:229–269.** This is a metaphysical treatise with passages on the meaning of letters.
5. **(107a–127a) *Sharḥ-i faṣṣ-i awwal min Fuṣūṣ al-ḥikam* [=Nūrbakhsh 4:319–389].** Contains passages on the human being as locus of manifestation of the divine names and attributes which could be read as related to the Shiʿi concept of Imam.
6. (127a–138a) *Tarjuma-yi nuqūsh-i fuṣūṣ al-ḥikam.*

7. **(138a–147a) *Dar taḥqīq-i Fuṣūṣ al-ḥikam* [=Nūrbakhsh 4:286–318].** Contains comments on prophetic figures starting with Adam.
8. **(147a–152a) *Risāla-yi ḥurūf-i muʿjam wa muḥmala,* [=Nūrbakhsh *Risāla-yi taḥqiqāt-i ḥurūf* 3:325–341].** Apparently the same as the *Risāla-yi ḥurūf* 222a–228a.
9. **(152a–153b) *Risāla-yi ḥurūf-i yushār bihi* [=Nūrbakhsh *Risāla-yi ʿayniyya* 3:396–400].** A metaphysical treatise on the significance of letters of the alphabet.
10. **(153b–159a) *Risāla-yi sharḥ-i rumūz* [=*Risāla-yi rumūz* Nūrbakhsh 3:36–57].** A treatise on the properties of vision and of the names and of perception.
11. **(159a–165a) *Risāla wa bihi nastaʿīnu hidāyāt* [=*Risāla-yi hidāyat* in Nūrbakhsh 2:188–208].**
12. **(165a–168a) *Risāla-yi muqaddimāt-i khamsa* [=Nūrbakhsh *Risāla-yi uṣūl-i khamsa* 2:142–152].**
13. (168a–171b) *Risāla-yi janāniyya.*
14. (171b–174b) *Risāla-yi wāridāt.*
15. (174b–180a) *Su'āl wa jawāb* (is not identical to the *Risālya-yi su'āl wa jawāb* in Nūrbakhsh 2:1–23).
16. (180a–199b) *Risāla dar jawāb wa su'āl* (is not identical to the *Risāla-yi su'āl wa jawāb* in Nūrbakhsh 2:1–23).
17. **(199b–201a) *Risāla-yi dhawqiyāt* [=*Risāla dhawqiyya* Nūrbakhsh 3:262–267].**
18. (201a–203a) Untitled text introduced by a *basmala.*
19. **(203a–210a) *Risāla-yi nukāt* [=*Risāla-yi nukāt* in Nūrbakhsh 3:237–260].**
20. **(210a–212b) *Risāla-yi taḥqīq al-īmān* [=Nūrbakhsh 1:104–111].**
21. **(212b–222a) *Risāla-yi ḥurūfāt* [=Nūrbakhsh *Risāla fī asrār al-ḥurūf* 3:350–379, MS text has a short continuation after Nūrbakhsh's final lines].**
22. **(222a–228a) *Risāla-yi ḥurūf.* Apparently the same as *Risāla-yi ḥurūf-i muʿjam wa muḥmala* 147a–152a.**
23. **(228a–229a) Untitled, the same as 152a–153b, *Risāla-yi ḥurūf-i yushār bihi* [=Nūrbakhsh *Risāla-yi ʿayniyya* 396–400].**
24. (229a–236a) *Risālahā-yi wa bihi nastaʿīnu.*
25. (236a–238a) *Risāla dar bayān-i sūrat al-tawḥīd.*
26. (238a–240b) *Risāla-yi sajda-yi tilāwat.*
27. (240b–241b) *Risāla dar bayān-i kalima-yi ṭayyiba.*

28. (241b) *Risāla dar bayān-i miʿrāj* [= Nūrbakhsh 1:74].
29. (241b–242a) *Risāla dar bayān-i islām.*
30. (242a–246b) Untitled section introduced by *basmala.*
31. (246b–248a) *Risāla-yi ḥūzā'iyya.*
32. (248a–251a) *Risāla-yi amānāt.*
33. (251a–254a) *Risāla-yi hidāyat li-l-salamayn.*
34. (254a–256b) *Risāla-yi maḥabbat-nāma* [= *Maḥabbat-nāma* Nūrbakhsh 1:208–215 text somewhat longer at the end in the MS]
35. (256b–259a) A section introduced by *Ka-mā qāla al-Imām ʿAlī Abī Ṭālib al- ʿilm nuqṭa,* followed by a *basmala.*
36. (259a–262a) *Risāla-yi ījādiyyat* [=Nūrbakhsh *Risāla al-ījādiyya* 2:25–36].
37. (262a–269a) *Risāla-yi fuṣūl.*
38. (269a–273a) *Risāla dar bayān-i aqṭāb* [= Nūrbakhsh 1:142–155 (*quṭbiyya*)].
39. (273a–274b) *Risāla-yi barāzikh* [is part of the *Risāla-yi barāzikh* in Nūrbakhsh 2:277–307, 302–307].
40. (274b–275a) Untitled section introduced by *basmala.*
41. (275a–276a) *Risāla-yi khalwat* [= Nūrbakhsh 1:226–7].
42. (276a–277b) *Risāla-yi naṣā'iḥ* [= *Naṣīḥat-nāma* Nūrbakhsh 1:381–386].
43. (277b–278a) *Risāla-yi bayān-i sūrat al-ikhlāṣ.*
44. (278a–279a) *Risāla-yi sharḥ-i Allāh nūr al-samawāt wa-l-arḍ.*
45. (279a–285b) *Risāla-yi maʿārif.*
46. (285b–293a) *Risāla-yi sharḥ-i asma'.*
47. (293a–294b) *Risāla-yi sharḥ-i asma'-i Allāh.*

Of course, this is only a preliminary attempt at identifying the contents of the manuscript MS BA 86. As can be seen from the list above, sometimes untitled treatises from the manuscript appear with a title in the printed edition (no. 4), sometimes the same work has different titles in the manuscript and in the printed edition (nos. 8, 9, 11, 12), and sometimes different works appear under the same title (no. 15). Therefore, a closer examination of the text of the manuscript and a comparison with other printed editions and manuscripts of the works of Shāh Niʿmat Allāh Walī will certainly yield a more accurate identification of the contents of this manuscript. Until then, the question whether MS BA 86 contains any significant differences compared to the printed versions of Shāh Niʿmat Allāh's works, and whether it contains any previously unknown works attributed to Shāh Niʿmat Allāh Walī remains open.

I was unable to discern any particular intention behind the selection of Shāh Niʿmat Allāh Walī's works included in the manuscript MS BA 86. The manuscript contains treatises reflecting various aspects of Shāh Niʿmat Allāh's thought: commentaries on Ibn ʿArabi's *Fuṣūṣ al-ḥikam*, works on the metaphysical properties and meanings of the letters of the alphabet, works on various aspects of the Sufi spiritual doctrine, commentaries on the Qur'ānic suras and symbolism, interpretations of Islamic rituals, treatises on the symbolism of divine names, doctrinal discussions in the form of questions and answers, and works on specific points of Shāh Niʿmat Allāh's thought.

But it is true that many of the ideas expressed in these treatises have close parallels in Ismaili doctrine. For example, the treatise *Sharḥ-i faṣṣ-i awwal min Fuṣūṣ al-ḥikam* (MS BA 86 ff. 107a–127a, Nūrbakhsh 4:319–389) contains several passages on the human being as locus of manifestation of the divine names and attributes which could be read as related to the Shiʿi concept of Imam:

> 'Adam was created as vicegerent (*khilāfat*) [of God], and the vicegerent is like a mirror which reflects [. . .] the secrets of the divine names and the lights of the truths from the world of infinity.' (Nūrbakhsh 4:321)

> 'The supreme purpose of creation of the human world is manifestation (*ẓuhūr*) [of the divine truths] [. . .] and vision of the essence of the Real (*ru'yat-i dhāt-i ḥaqq*) through this essence itself in the comprehensive mirror of humanity.' (Nūrbakhsh 4:323).

> 'Manifestation of the divine secrets is concealed in names and attributes, and the comprehensive locus of manifestation of the divine secrets is human being.' [Nūrbakhsh 4:332]:

> 'Sufis call the universe "the greater man" (*insān-i kabīr*), because the universe in its entirety is contained in the human constitution (*nash'at-i insāniyya*), and the entities [that fill] the universe are articulations (*mafṣil*) of the human constitution, while the human being is the macrocosm (*ʿālam-i kabīr*).' (Nūrbakhsh 4:334).

These passages resonate, in particular, with the outlook on the original nature, purpose of creation and relation to the universe of the human being proper to the Nizārī Ismaili tradition and reflected in its extant works:

> 'It was the wish of God that He should be recognised and worshipped. He chose [for this] man, from all creation, and favoured him with His own form and attributes, and this [man's] form is His personal form.'[26]
>
> 'Thus, in relative terms, mankind is scattered [all over] the universe and, as such, universe is said to be the macrocosm (*insān-i kabīr*) and mankind the microcosm (*insān-i ṣaghīr*). But in reality the universe is the microcosm and mankind the macrocosm. Thus, universe is the human being dispersed, and human being is the sum of the entirety of the universe.'[27]

The *Risāla dar bayān-i aqṭāb* (MS BA 86, 269a–273a; Nūrbakhsh 1:142–155) contains passages on the status of the Pole (*quṭb*) of the spiritual hierarchy that are close to the Shiʿi concept of Imam. Of course, the mention of the 12 Poles brings Shāh Niʿmat Allāh's theory closer to the Twelver conception of the imamate, but the idea of Imam as perfect human being and the perfect leader of the Muslim community, without whom the community could not exist, is shared by Twelvers and Ismailis. Below is an extract from the *Risāla dar bayān-i aqṭāb* which strongly resonates with the Shiʿi conception of the Imamate:

> 'It is necessary to observe obedience to the head of the saints (*vālī-yi valāyat*). [. . .] The purpose in [creation] of the human being is service to God the Most High [. . .] but the perfection of this servitude is only realised in perfect human beings. The non-perfect human beings, even if they are human, are human animals (*insān-i ḥayvān*) [. . .], speaking animals (*ḥayvānan nāṭiqan*). And the Poles (*aqṭāb*) are from the perfect. [. . .] Learn that the Poles of the Muhammadan era are of two kinds: the Poles following his [Muhammad's] mission and the Poles preceding this mission. [The latter] consist of 313 Messengers (*rusul*), while the Poles following [the prophetic mission] and up to the day of Resurrection are 12. There are two Seals who are not included in this count, they are Jesus and the Mahdi, peace be upon them. These two are the unique ones (*mufridayn*), not the Poles. The 12

> Poles constitute the axis of the [Islamic] community until the day of Resurrection. Without them, the community would become confused.' [Nūrbakhsh 1:142–3].

It is therefore understandable that the treatises attributed to Shāh Niʿmat Allāh Walī could be read as an expression of the Ismaili esoteric doctrines, and this could explain the preservation of a substantial collection of Shāh Niʿmat Allāh Walī's theoretical works such as those copied in MS BA 86 in Ismaili private libraries.

Conclusion

While the study of the Ismaili manuscripts is our main source of knowledge on the Ismaili tradition itself, the study of the non-Ismaili manuscripts preserved in Ismaili collections gives us an insight into relationships between the Ismailis and other Islamic groups. In spite of its obvious relevance to the area of Ismaili and broader Islamic studies, this topic has not been systematically researched yet. A more substantial exploration of the non-Ismaili literature circulating in Ismaili milieus would therefore be highly desirable.

The presence of poetry and doctrinal works attributed to Shāh Niʿmat Allāh Walī among the manuscripts preserved by the Nizārī Ismaili communities of Badakhshān and Afghanistan can be explained by the long history of friendly relationships between the Ismailis and the Niʿmat Allāhīs, as well as by the deep intellectual and doctrinal affinities that stimulated the Ismaili interest for the thought of Shāh Niʿmat Allāh Walī. Substantial work remains to be done in order to consistently identify the manuscripts attributed to Shāh Niʿmat Allāh Walī in Ismaili collections, to address the issue of their authorship, and to compare them with other extant copies or with printed editions. Given the significant duration of association between the Ismailis and Niʿmat Allāhīs, it could be expected that more Niʿmatullahi manuscripts will be discovered in the Ismaili collections.

According to Shozodamamad Sherzodshoev: 'Shāh Niʿmat Allāh's versified works have been widely disseminated in Badakhshān. His gnostic odes (*qaṣīdas*) have been copied in about twenty *bayāḍs* (collections of religious poetry) kept in private collections by the residents of Badakhshān of Tajikistan and Badakhshān of Afghanistan.'[28] However, it seems that in present-day Ismaili communities of Badakhshān and Afghanistan the knowledge of the doctrinal aspects incorporated into Shāh Niʿmat Allāh Walī's poetry and, even more so, of his doctrinal works, has significantly diminished. According to Shozodamamad Sherzodshoev, ordinary members of these communities have hardly any idea of Shāh Niʿmat Allāh Walī's identity and teachings. Some older people refer to him as their *pīr-i maʿrifat* (literally 'master of knowledge', ultimate teacher). Still, as mentioned, Shāh Niʿmat Allāh's poetry continues to be recited at the religious festivals and ceremonies such as *Chirāgh-rawshan* and *madāḥ-khānī*, even if some reciters in Badakhshān are now unfamiliar with the Arabic script and have their copies transcribed in Cyrillic.

NOTES

* My thanks to Wafi Momin, for his enthusiastic support and for providing me with the manuscript material and information concerning the collection of the manuscripts used in this study.

1 There is still no comprehensive monograph on Shāh Niʿmat Allāh Walī, his work and his thought in any western language. For general information on him and on the Niʿmat Allāhī Sufi order, see Hamid Algar, 'Niʿmat-Allāhiyya', *EI2*, vol. 8, pp. 44–48 and references there. In Persian, see Ḥamīd Farzām, *Taḥqīq dar aḥwāl wa naqd-i āthār wa afkār-i Shāh Niʿmat Allāh Walī* (Tehran, 1374 Sh./1995).

2 See Farhad Daftary, *The Ismāʿīlīs: Their History and Doctrines* (Cambridge, 2007, first printed in 1990), pp. 456–467, 477–480, and Nasrollah Pourjavady and Peter Lamborn Wilson, 'Ismāʿīlīs and Niʿmat Allāhīs', *Studia Islamica*, 41 (1975), pp. 113–135.

3 According to Shozodamamad Sherzodshoev, who is Head and Senior Research Fellow at the Khorog Manuscript Unit, Tajikistan, these libraries mostly belong to the Ismaili nobility families related to the Pīrs (spiritual guides) and Khalīfas (Pīr's deputies, religious leaders), and were not largely accessible. I am indebted to Mr Sherzodshoev for information regarding the provenance and circulation of the texts attributed to Niʿmat Allāh Walī in the present-day Ismaili communities of Badakhshān and Afghanistan. My thanks go also to Wafi Momin and Nourmamadcho Nourmamadchoev for their help in organising an interview (on 21 July 2020) with Shozodamamad Sherzodshoev and for forwarding to me his written notes which are used in this paper.

4 Such as *Chirāgh-rawshan* and *madāḥ-khānī,* which involve the recitation of poetry. On these ceremonies, see Nourmamadcho Nourmamadchoev, 'Ismaili-Sufi and Ismaili-Twelver Relations in Badakhshān in the Post-Alamūt Period: The *Chirāgh-nāma,*' in Orkhan Mir-Kasimov, ed., *Intellectual Interactions in the Islamic World: The Ismaili Thread* (London, 2020), pp. 355–380.

5 According to Twelver Shiʿi beliefs, the twelfth Imam, Muḥammad b. al-Ḥasan al-ʿAskarī, has been hidden since 260/874 and had no generally recognised representatives since 329/941, the year when his major occultation started. See D. B. MacDonald [M.G.S. Hodgson], 'Ghayba', *EI2*, vol. 2, p. 1026.

6 According to Algar, Nūr ʿAlī Shāh Iṣfahānī maintained that the Sufi master is the representative (*nāʾib*) of the hidden Imam. Nūr ʿAlī Shāh was a disciple of Maʿṣūm ʿAlī Shāh Dakkanī (d. 1212/1797–1798), the Niʿmat Allāhī master who reintroduced the order into Iran in the 13th/18th century. See Algar, 'Niʿmat-Allāhiyya', *EI2*, vol. 8, pp. 44–48. A similar point of view is expressed by Nūr ʿAlī Tabandeh (Majdhūb ʿAlī

Shāh), the present *Quṭb* (head) of the Gunābādī branch of the Niʿmat Allāhī order. According to him, the Shiʿi Imams, persecuted by the ʿAbbasids, appointed some Sufi masters as their representatives, and authorised them to designate their own representatives. One of these Sufi masters was Maʿrūf al-Karkhī (d. 200/815–816), who was the spiritual ancestor of the Niʿmat Allāhī line. See Nūr ʿAlī Tabandeh, 'Opening Statement', *Celebrating a Sufi Master: A Collection of Works on the Occasion of the First International Symposium on Shah Nematollah Vali* (San Jose, CA, 2002), p. 11 (my thanks to Alessandro Cancian for bringing this work to my attention). See also O. Scharbrodt, 'The *Quṭb* as Special Representative of the Hidden Imam: The Conflation of Shiʿi and Sufi *Vilāyat* in the Niʿmatullāhī Order', D. Hermann and S. Mervin, ed., *Shiʿi Trends and Dynamics in Modern Times (XVIIIth–XXth Centuries)* (Beirut, 2010), pp. 33–49.

7 There were periods when the Ismaili Imams were hidden, but during these periods they had representatives who ensured the contact with their followers. See F. Daftary, 'Satr', *EI2*, vol. 12, pp. 712–713.

8 For the analysis of Ḥaydar Amulī's thought concerning the relationships between Shiʿism and Sufism, see Henry Corbin, *En Islam Iranien*, vol. 3 (Paris, 1972), pp. 178–190. Amulī continued a tendency that was developed in the Twelver Shiʿi milieus of Bahrain, by thinkers such as ʿAlī b. Sulaymān (d. *ca.* 672/1273) and Maytham al-Baḥrānī (d. 689/1290). On them, see Ali al-Oraibi, *Shīʿī Renaissance: A Case Study of the Theosophical School of Bahrain in the 7th/13th Century* (PhD dissertation, McGill University, 1992), especially pp. 172–217; and his 'Rationalism in the School of Bahrain: A Historical Perspective,' in L. Clarke, ed., *Shīʿite Heritage* (Binghamton, NY, 2001), pp. 331–343.

9 For an outline of Shiʿi/Sufi eclecticism in 8th/14th and 9th/15th centuries see Marshall G.S. Hodgson, *The Venture of Islam: Conscience and History in a World Civilization*, vol. 2 (Chicago and London, 1974), pp. 495–500.

10 See Daftary, *The Ismāʿīlīs*, p. 420.

11 On the Nizārī Ismaili theory of the *qiyāma*, see M. Hodgson, *The Order of Assassins: The Struggle of the Early Nizārī Ismāʿīlīs against the Islamic World* (The Hague, 1955), pp. 143–185. On the possible influence of this theory on the post-Mongol mystical and messianic movements see Orkhan Mir-Kasimov, 'The Nizārī Ismaili Theory of the Resurrection (*Qiyāma*) and Post-Mongol Iranian Messianism,' in Mir-Kasimov, ed., *Intellectual Interactions in the Islamic World*, pp. 323–352.

12 See, for example, Shāh Niʿmat Allāh Walī, *Kuliyyāt-i ashʿār*, ed. Jawād Nūrbakhsh (Tehran, 1358 sh./[1979]), pp. 754 ff. This, however, is not by any means an indication of Shāh Niʿmat Allāh's adherence to Shiʿism. Praise of ʿAlī b. Abī Ṭālib, of the prophetic family and of the twelve Imams was common in the Sunni literature of his time. See, for example, Matthew Melvin-Koushki, *The Quest for a Universal Science: The Occult Philosophy of Ṣāʾin al-Dīn Turka Iṣfahānī (1369–1432) and Intellectual Millenarianism in Early Timurid Iran* (PhD dissertation, Yale University, 2012), p. 70 ff.

13 *Sayyidam az khuda ke maʿṣūm ast*, cited from the *Dīwān* of Shāh Niʿmat Allāh Walī in Kāmil Muṣṭafā al-Shaybī, *al-Ṣila bayna-l-taṣawwuf wa-l-tashayyuʿ* (Beirut, 1982, first published 1963–1966), vol. 2, p. 221, note 6.

14 *Madhhab-i jāmiʿ az khudā dāram / īn hidāyat ma-rā būd azalī*, no. 5, ibid.

15 On Ibn ʿArabī's theory of the Seal of sainthood, see Michel Chodkiewicz, *Le Sceau des saints: prophétie et sainteté dans la doctrine d'Ibn Arabî* (Paris, 2012, first published 1986). The influence of Ibn ʿArabī, and in particular of his theory of the Seals of Prophethood and Sainthood, is clearly visible and explicitly acknowledged in the work of Shāh Niʿmat Allāh Walī. See Ḥamīd Farzām, *Shāh Walī wa daʿwā-yi mahdawiyyat* (Isfahan, 1348 Sh./[1969]).

16 For the sources mentioning the genealogy of Shāh Niʿmat Allāh Walī, see Daftary, *The Ismāʿīlīs*, n. 57, p. 651, and Farzām, *Taḥqīq*, pp. 17-21.

17 See n. 2 above. On the close association between the Niʿmat Allāhīs and Nizārī Ismaili Imams see also Nile Green, *Bombay Islam: The Religious Economy of the West Indian*

Ocean, 1840–1915 (New York, 2011), especially pp. 155–178. My thanks to Wafi Momin for attracting my attention to this work.

18 See Nourmamadcho Nourmamadchoev, *The Ismāʿīlīs of Badakhshān: History, Politics and Religion from 1500 to 1750* (PhD thesis, School of Oriental and African Studies, University of London, 2014), pp. 221 ff., 230–234.

19 The letters BT and BA in the manuscript code indicate the provenance of the manuscripts: 'BT' stands for Badakhshān of Tajikistan, while 'BA' stands for Badakhshān of Afghanistan.

20 I was unable to access this manuscript directly and found it difficult to date on the basis of scans that I had at my disposal. The field report mentions several dates ranging from 1360/[1941] to 1390/[1970].

21 Ditto. The dates mentioned in the field report are based on two different colophons and provide two possible dates, 1309/[1892] or 1390/[1970].

22 That is, the Prophet Muḥammad, his daughter Fāṭima, and the twelve Imams.

23 'There is no [chivalrous] young man like ʿAlī, there is no sword like *Dhū'l fiqār*' (*lā fatā illā ʿAlī lā ṣayf illā dhū'l-fiqār*). For the first part of this tradition see Muhammad Jaʿfar Mahjub, 'Chivalry and Early Persian Sufism', Leonard Lewisohn, ed., *The Heritage of Sufism*, vol. 1 (Oxford, 1999), pp. 549–582, p. 554. For the full text of this statement, ascribed either to the Prophet Muhammad or to a supernatural voice heard during the battle of Uhud (3/624), see Christoph Heger, 'Yā Muḥammad – kein "oh Muhammad", und wer ist ʿAlī?' in Markus Groß and Karl-Heinz Ohlig, ed., *Schlaglichter: die beiden ersten islamischen Jahrhunderte* (Berlin, 2005), pp. 278–292, at p. 286.

24 *Ḥaqqan ke ʿAlī imām-e ʿālī ast / Dar mamlakat-e dū kawn walī ast.*

25 According to Shozodamamad Sherzodshoev (written communication, 21 July 2020), 'This treatise and his [that is, Shāh Niʿmat Allāh Walī's] other versified works have been brought with high probability from India, at a time when the Ismailis of Badakshan had connection with their Imams in Bombay (present day Mumbai). As we know, in the 19th and early 20th century, Ismailis of Badakhshān such as Ḥājjī Yārbek (d. 1949), Sayyid Farrukh Shāh (d. after 1890) and Sayyid ʿUlfaṭ Shāh (d. after 1890) travelled to India to meet their Imams of the Time. These people brought with them many religious books from Bombay. It is apparent from the manuscripts of Sayyid ʿUlfaṭ Shāh that he has resided for a number of years in Bombay and has copied some rare Ismaili treatises and brought them to Badakhshān.'

26 Abū Isḥāq Quhistānī, *Haft Bāb-i Abū Isḥāq*, ed. and tr. Wladimir Ivanow (Bombay, 1959), English translation p. 37, original text p. 36.

27 Ḥasan-i Maḥmūd-i Kātib, *Haft Bāb*, ed. and tr. Jalal Badakhchani as *Spiritual Resurrection in Shiʿi Islam: An Early Ismaili Treatise on the Doctrine of Qiyāmat* (London and New York, 2017), paragraph 61, English translation pp. 73–74, original text p. 32.

28 Private communication, 21 July 2020.

14

Poems of Allegiance: Shāh Ḍiyāʾī-i Shughnānī's *Salām-nāma**

Nourmamadcho Nourmamadchoev

Introduction

Badakhshān, a landlocked country in the foothills of the Hindu Kush and the Pamir mountains, is well known for its precious and semi-precious stones. In the south it is dominated by the Hindu Kush mountains while in the east and the north the Pamir mountains are located. It forms a distinct geographic unit, only opening in the west to the plains of Tāliqān and Qundūz[1] that lead to Herat, Balkh and Bukhara. The famous Oxus River, *Āmū daryā,* rises in the upper reaches of Badakhshān where the semi-independent principalities of Shughnān, Darwāz, and Wakhān are located. These small mountainous principalities, at one time subordinate to mainland Badakhshān, enjoyed their semi-independence until the end of the 19th century.

Several factors contributed to the semi-independence of Badakhshān, particularly the northern mountainous principalities of Shughnān, Wakhān, and Darwāz. Firstly, this is a landlocked region surrounded by a range of high mountains, and it would be difficult for anyone governing the region to impose authority beyond these natural lines of demarcation. Secondly, its remote location made it difficult to govern from a distance as vassals put in charge could not inculcate loyalty to the ruler whose seat was far from the region. Thirdly, it was not an urban centre like Herat, Balkh, or Bukhara that offered the ruler panoptic control. And, fourthly, the local population were either of Ismaili persuasion or were sympathetic to Shiʿi Islam. Therefore, the mountain dwellers were 'loyal' to the political rulers because of fear and at the same time showed their true loyalty to the line of Shiʿi imams that traced their lineage to the *Ahl al-bayt*, the Family of the Prophet.

The term *Ahl al-bayt*, 'the People of the House', is used to express reverence for and devotion to the 'Five Members of the Prophet's Family'. I should mention that the term *Ahl al-bayt* is used in a broader Ismaili context as a reference to the extended line of imams from Imam ʿAlī b. Abī Ṭālib (d. 40/661) to the present day. Similarly, the Ismailis of Badakhshān use the term *Panj tan-i pāk*, as an equivalent of the term *Ahl al-bayt*, meaning the 'Five Pure Figures' while the term *Panj-tanī* is used to refer to the Ismaili branch of Shiʿi Islam.[2]

The focus of this chapter is to introduce Shāh Ḍiyāʿī, a hitherto unknown author from the northern mountainous region of Shughnān, and analyse his poetic composition known as *Salām-nāma*.[3] It is important to mention at the outset that the history of Shughnān in the 16th century is shrouded in mystery. Hence, due to the absence of historical data about the political and social history of Shughnān, I will provide a short historical overview of Badakhshān of the 16th century to contextualise the life and work of Shāh Ḍiyāʾī-i Shughnānī.

The Politics of Rule in Badakhshān in the 16th Century

In the first half of the 16th century, with the incursion of the Safavid and Shaybānīd dynasties into Mā warā al-nahr,[4] Ḥisār and Badakhshān were merged and remained under the control of the last Timurids. After the loss of Mā warā al-nahr to the Shaybānīds, the Timurids faced internal and external challenges in their wider domain including Badakhshān. The internal challenge to their rule was a rivalry between the princes who exercised a territorial ambition and desired Badakhshān to be part of their realm.[5] Mention could be made of princes that traced their line to Sulṭān Abū Saʿīd b. Mīrān Shāh (r. 855–873/1451–1469) who subjugated Badakhshān and ordered the execution of Shāh Sulṭān Muhammad, the last ruler of Badakhshān, and his family in 872/1467–1468.[6] The last Timurid contenders to power in Badakhshān in the first half of the 16th century were: Nāṣir Mīrzā (891–921/1486–1521) and Mīrzā Khān, also known as Sulṭān Ways (d. 926/1520), the former being Ẓahir al-Dīn Muhammad Bābur's (888–937/1483–1530) brother while the latter was his first cousin.[7] It was Mīrzā Khān whose bid for power in Badakhshān was eventually successful. The external challenge to the Timurid power in Badakhshān came from the Shaybānīds who ousted the Timurids out of Mā warā al-nahr at the turn of the 15th century and desired Badakhshān to be part of their domain. Another external challenge to the Timurid rule came from a certain Shāh Raḍī al-Dīn.[8] We learn from the *Ta'rīkh-i Rashīdī* that Shāh Raḍī al-Dīn or Raḍī al-Dīn II b. Ṭāhir was the leader of the Nizārī Muhammad-Shāhī Ismailis.[9] He was invited to Badakhshān, from Sīstān, a region in the southeast of Persia, as stated in the *Ta'rīkh-i Rashīdī*:

> Someone [from the local population] was sent to Seistān [i.e. Sīstān] to bring Shāh Raḍī al-Dīn, the hereditary spiritual leader of these people, to whom and to whose ancestors they had never failed to pay their annual tithes.[10]

The interplay of politics and religion becomes visible at this point, as religion seems to have been used as a tool to mobilise not only the local Ismailis but all those sympathetic to Shiʿi Islam who, under the leadership of Raḍī al-Dīn II b. Ṭāhir, took control of Badakhshān in the early 16th century.[11]

Several factors might be the cause of Shāh Raḍī al-Dīn's success: the first factor is evidently a political one, whereby the local rulers of Badakhshān attempted to retain their semi-independent status with the help of Shāh Raḍī al-Dīn. This attempt resulted in Badakhshān remaining partially outside the realm of the ruling powers but becoming the point of contention for the Shaybānīds and the Timurids. Secondly, the religious affiliation of the local population seems to have been different from that of the invading powers that kept them apart from their overlords. Hence, Badakhshān and its local ruling elite found themselves outside mainstream political power. Thirdly, neither the Shaybānīds nor the Timurids would have liked a condominium division of authority in their realm. Being outside the Tīmūrid's and Shaybānīd's control and Shāh Raḍī al-Dīn, the Nizārī Muhammad-Shāhī Ismaili leader, becoming an effective ruler of Badakhshān reveals that there was a remotely located opposition to the established regime, which is demonstrated in the following:

a) a remote mountainous region difficult to control
b) local ruling elite not tracing their ancestry to both contending ruling houses

c) an external figure in power tracing his lineage to the line of Shiʿi imams who could mobilise the local population and rebel at any time

Therefore, Vladimir Bartol'd (1869–1930), a prominent Russian Orientalist of the 20th century, surmises that Shāh Raḍī al-Dīn controlled the region from 912/1507 to 915/1509 only. It was in 915/1509 that he was beheaded, and his head was presented to Mīrzā Khān at *Qalʿa-i Ẓafar.*[12]

The brutal killing of Shāh Raḍī al-Dīn opened a new opportunity for the internal contender, Mīrzā Khān (r. 915–926/1510–1520), who with military support from Emperor Bābur brought Badakhshān under Tīmūrid control. With this gesture Mīrzā Khān cemented his position and from then onwards sought to defend his newly conquered territories from internal riots and external military campaigns.

Mīrzā Khān was the son of Sulṭān Maḥmūd b. Abū Saʿīd (d. 926/1520–1521). We learn from the *Ta'rīkh-i Rashīdī* and *Tadhkīrat al-shuʿarā* as well as from modern studies that Mīrzā Khān had claimed the throne of Badakhshān.[13] This mountainous region, along with Ḥisār and Khuttalān, was controlled by Sulṭān Maḥmūd Mīrzā for almost 26 years (from 873/1469 to 899/1494).[14] Quite surprisingly, Shāh Begim, Mīrzā Khān's grandmother, who was the daughter of Shāh Sulṭān Muhammad (d. 870/1466–1467), the last ruler of Badakhshān, supported his claim. Hence, Shāh Begim claimed the region for Mīrzā Khān.[15]

The 16th-century sources propose a hypothesis according to which Mīrzā Khān was elevated to a position of authority in Badakhshān with the assistance of Shāh Ismaʿil I (Abū al-Muẓaffar, r. 907–930/1501–1524)—the Safavid monarch. Most obviously, Bābur and later Humāyūn depended on military aid from the Persians in order to help them reinstate their political authority in Mā warā al-nahr and Badakhshān. Thus, Bābur sent envoys, led by Mīrzā Khān, to the Safavid court to negotiate the conditions of the aid of the Safavids. Therefore, the rise of Mīrzā Khān to power in Badakhshān had a direct link with Safavid interest in the region.[16] One of the conditions of the Safavids was that Bābur should accept the Shiʿi faith and recite the *khuṭba* in the name of the Persian monarch using the Shiʿi formula. Consequently, Bābur minted coins in the name of Shāh Isma'il I and with the names of the Twelve Shi'i imams imprinted on them.[17]

It should be mentioned that the Timurid sources, including the *Bābur-nāma* and the *Ta'rīkh-i Rashīdī*, provide only a limited insight into the activities of Mīrzā Khān, particularly for the last decade of his life (917–926/1511–1520). Even the birth of Sulaymān Mīrzā, the future ruler of Badakhshān, in 920/1514 was only noted *en passant*. Nonetheless, after the death of Mīrzā Khān in 926/1520, Bābur decided to take his son—Sulaymān Mīrzā—to his court in Kābul. By this gesture, Bābur clearly demonstrated his interest in the affairs of Badakhshān. To reinforce such a strategic and political move, he sent his son and future successor—Humāyūn (913–963/1508–1556)—to rule Badakhshān on behalf of Mīrzā Khān's son, Sulaymān Mīrzā. Thus, Humāyūn was intermittently in charge of Badakhshān from 926/1520 to 934/1529.[18] By the above gesture Bābur clearly showed this region to be the *de facto* possession of his ancestors—the Timurids—who had directly controlled it since 872/1467–1468.

We learn from historical sources that in 937/1530 Humāyūn (r. 937–947/1530–1540 and 962–963/1555–1556) succeeded his father, Emperor Bābur and, as predicted, he installed the young Sulaymān Mīrzā to the throne of Badakhshān. Hence, Sulaymān Mīrzā and his son Ibrāhīm Mīrzā controlled Badakhshān for over five decades (from 937/1530 to 994/1585).

The northern mountainous principalities of Shughnān, Wakhān and Darwāz possibly remained relatively peaceful during this turbulent period. This was mainly due to their isolation and harsh climatic conditions. Local hagiographic sources as well as oral tradition tell of the arrival of certain *darwīshes* to the region of Shughnān in the second half of the 16th century. The names of these *darwīshes* are given as Sayyid Muhammad Iṣfahānī, known as Shāh Kāshān, Sayyid Shāh Malang, and Shāh Burhān Walī. Their arrival heralded a change in the religious and political life of Shughnān. One can assume that their arrival marked a *coup d'état* that led to the change in the ruling house of Shughnān to which Shāh Ḍiyā'ī traced his lineage. It was in this turbulent period of the 16th century that Shāh Ḍiyā'ī was born in Shughnān and later, for unknown reasons, left for Balkh.

The Biography of Shāh Ḍiyā'ī-i Shughnānī

Shāh Ḍiyā'ī's life remains shrouded in mystery. This is mainly due to the paucity of historical sources as well as the absence of biographical records about him. We learn from his *nisba* that he was born in the northern mountainous region of Shughnān. Nothing is known about his childhood except some oral stories prevalent among the local population of Shughnān. He records his name as Shāh Ḍiyā but later became famous under his *nom de plume*, Ḍiyā'ī or Shāh Ḍiyā'ī. The term Shāh, i.e. *prince*, affixed to his name refers to his social status. In one of his *qaṣīda*s known as *Panj tan-i pāk*[19] he affirms this by referring to himself as 'a scion of the local rulers of Shughnān' as he says:

Ba aṣlu nasl zi shāhān-i mulki Shughnānam,
Chū la'l jāyu makān ast dar Badakhshān.[20]

By birth and origin, I am the scion [*shāh*] of rulers of Shughnān,
My residence and place, like the ruby, is in Badakhshān.

The fragmented pieces of poetry that reached us testify that Shāh Ḍīyā'ī was a well-educated man. He was praised for his talent by his contemporaries and later poets. For instance, Naẓmī-i Shughnānī, an 18th-century poet from Shughnān includes his name among the luminaries of classical Persian literature such as Jalāl al-Dīn al-Rūmī (d. 672/1273), Ḥāfiẓ-i Shīrāzī (792/1390) and many others.[21] Shāh Ḍiyā'ī was also a contemporary of Imām-Qulī, a 17th-century Ismaili poet and preacher from Dizhbād (b. after 1056/1646), who wrote his poetic compositions under the pseudonym, Khākī-i Khurāsānī.[22] The religious and didactic *qaṣīda*s composed by Shāh Ḍiyā'ī are still sung by *madāḥ-khāns*[23] in Badakhshān. It is highly likely that Shāh Ḍiyā'ī's mother tongue was Shughnānī.[24] However, he composed his poems in Persian, the *lingua franca* and the language of the educated elite of the region. He was evidently well versed in the science of religion, particularly the study of Qur'ān and *ḥadīth* (i.e. Prophetic tradition) as well as the history of Islam in general and Shi'i Islam in particular.

The fragmented poetic pieces that have reached us testify that Shāh Ḍiyā'ī flourished in the 16th century and possibly passed away some time in the first half of the 17th century. In the context of the political history of Badakhshān, as discussed earlier, he was a contemporary of Sulaymān Mīrzā, Ibrāhīm Mīrzā, and his son Shāhrukh Mīrzā, the last of the Timurid rulers of Badakhshān. Sulaymān Mīrzā and his successors ruled the region as vassals of the Mughals of India. In the religious context, however, Shāh Diyāʾī was a contemporary of two or possibly three Nizārī Qāsim-Shāhī as well as Nizārī Muhammad-Shāhī imams as shown in Table 14.1.

His exact date of birth is recorded neither by him nor by his contemporaries. Modern scholars provide three contradicting dates of his birth: for instance, in an interview with Gabrielle van den Berg, Sultonnazar Sayyidnazarov (d. 2008), a famous *madāḥ-khān* from the north-west of Badakhshān of Tajikistan, provides his date of birth as 932/1525.[26] Ḥusayn-i Hasanyār-i Shughnānī, an Afghan scholar, argues that he was born in the first half of the 18th century. According to him, Shāh Ḍiyāʾī was born either in 1136/1724 or 1138/1726.[27] Amirbek Habibov, a Tajik scholar, argues that Shāh Ḍiyāʾī was alive in 1012/1603-1604. Hence, in Habibov's view Shāh Ḍiyāʾī was born sometime in or after 963/1556.[28] Evidently, Habibov and Ḥasanyār-i Shughnānī, derived the date of Shāh Ḍiyāʾī's birth from the same *qaṣīda* known as *Panj tan-i pāk*. In stanza 16 of this *qaṣīda*, Shāh Ḍiyāʾī talks about the completion of this *qaṣīda* and uses a Persianised Arabic numeral *sabʿa-i ʿarba* to

Table 14.1 Contemporaries of Shāh Ḍiyāʾī-i Shughnānī.

Mughal Emperors	Rulers of Badakhshān	Nizārī Qāsim-Shāhi Imams	Nizārī Muhammad-Shāhī Imams
Ẓahīr al-Dīn Muhammad Bābur (d. 936/1530)	Sulaymān Mīrzā (d. 997/1589)	Murād Mīrzā (d. 981/1574)	Shāh Ṭāhir b. Raḍī al-Dīn II al-Ḥusaynī Dakkanī (d. *ca.* 956/1549)
Nāṣir al-Dīn Muhammad *Humāyūn* (r. 937–947/1530–1540 and 962–963/1555–1556)	Ibrāhīm Mīrzā (d. 967/1560)	Dhū al-Faqār ʿAlī (d. 1043/1634)	Ḥaydar b. Shāh Ṭāhir (d. 994/1586)
Abū l-Fatḥ Jalāl al-Dīn Muhammad *Akbar* (r. 963–1014/1556–1605)	Shāhrukh Mīrzā (d. 1607)	Nūr al-Dīn known as Nūr al-Dahr (d. 1082/1671)[25]	Ṣadr al-Dīn Muhammad b. Ḥaydar (d. 1032/1622)

refer to his age. Hasanyār-i Shughnānī incorrectly reads the above expression as 74 while Habibov puts it correctly as 47. It is also evident from Habibov and Ḥasanyār-i Shughnānī's writings that both researchers had access to only three *qasīda*s of Shāh Ḍiyā'ī. The stanza 16 provided by both scholars is identical as shown below:

Zi sālu mahi tū raftast sabʿa-i arbaʿ
Chū rukh namūd az īn saqf gunbad-i ʿarfa.
Az īn qaṣīda biguftam man az īn maṭlaʿ.
Ba waqt-i chāsht bishud khatm, khatm-i in maqṭaʿ.
Muhammad astu ʿAlī Fāṭima Ḥasanu Ḥusayn.

As your age in terms of years and months has reached forty-seven,
It was in a time when the sun had risen and lighted the world.
That I composed the first line (*matla*ʿ) of this *qaṣīda*,
While the final verse (*maqta*ʿ) was completed before the mid-day.
[Praise be to] Muhammad, ʿAlī, Fāṭima, Ḥasan and Ḥusayn.[29]

In light of this, Ḥusaynyār-i Shughnānī's hypothesis can be dismissed on the ground of incorrect reading of the date provided in stanza 16 of the *qaṣīda*. G. van den Berg and Habibov's hypothesis, on the other hand, awaits further research and the discovery of new sources could provide a different date to what they have proposed.

A manuscript containing two more *qaṣīda*s of Shāh Ḍiyā'ī was recently discovered in the private collection of Shāh-i Kalān b. Shāhzādamuammad (1921-2015), a famous Ismaili *khalīfa* from the village of Kushk[30] in Badakhshān of Tajikistan. This manuscript provides a different reading of the stanza 16 which reads:

Zi sāli tisʿa miʾa tāsiʿūn dīgar arbaʿ,
Chū rukh namūd az īn saqf gunbad-i ʿarfa.
Az īn qaṣīda biguftam man az īn maṭlaʿ.
Ba waqt-i chāsht bishud khatm, khatm-i in maqṭaʿ.
Muhammad astu ʿAlī Fāṭima Ḥasanu Ḥusayn.

From the year nine hundred and ninety-four,
At a time when the sun had risen and lighted the world.
I composed the first line (*matla* ʿ) of this *qaṣīda*,
The final verse (*maqta* ʿ) was completed before the mid-day.
[Praise be to] Muhammad, ʿAlī, Fāṭima, Ḥasan and Ḥusayn.[31]

It is evident from the extract above that Shāh Ḍiyā'ī composed this *qaṣīda* in the year 994/1585–1586. If we take the date recorded in the newly discovered manuscript at face value, it would mean that Shāh Ḍiyā'ī was born sometime in 954/1538. This can be considered correct if Shāh Ḍiyā'ī was 47 years old as recorded by Habibov. Hence, logic compels us to conclude that this famous *qaṣīda* must have had two versions of the stanza 16 recorded in different manuscript traditions. However, we do not know which of these versions was the original one.

Even though Shāh Ḍiyā'ī was born to the ruling family of Shughnān, he does not specify his place of residence. Historical sources as well as oral tradition refer to the residence of the rulers of Shughnān as *Bar-panja qal'a,* the Bar-panja Castle, which was located on the left bank of the Panj river.[32] Another line of rulers of Shughnān resided in the region of Shākh-dara and their residence is known as *Rāsht-qal'a*, the Red Castle. The rulers of Shākh-dara are the splinter group that separated from the rulers of Shughnān. Both lines of the ruling houses of Shughnān, however, traced their descent to a certain Sayyid Mīr Ḥasan Shāh, better known as Shāh Khāmūsh (d. 531/1136) who arrived in Shughnān in the second half of the 11th century.[33]

It is evident from Shāh Ḍiyā'ī's *qaṣīda*s that he left his hometown and travelled to Balkh. Habibov argues that he travelled to Balkh to study[34] which is partly convincing. In one of his *qaṣīda*s dated 993/1585, Shāh Ḍiyā'ī laments about his difficult departure from Badakhshān.[35] Similar lamentations are also expressed in his other *qaṣida*s including the *Salām-nāma* where he says:

Zi mulki Badakhshān ba Balkham kunūm rah,
Tu dādī bashārat ba kuyat amīrā!

As I am travelling from Badakhshān to Balkh,
Oh Lord, you are the one who guided me to you.[36]

The precise location of Shāh Ḍiyā'ī's residence in Balkh also remains unknown to us. It is likely that he resided in the village of Khwājah Khayrān, a rural place to the east of Balkh city, where today's Mazār-i Sharīf, the noble shrine attributed to Imam 'Alī b. Abī Ṭālib, is located.[37]

We do not have any information as to whether he returned to his hometown, Shughnān. The oral tradition narrates that he lived in Balkh near the shrine attributed to Imam ʿAlī. The oral tradition recounts that he expressed his wish to be buried near this shrine. We learn from the *Salām-nāma* (lines 75 to 82) that he fell ill in Balkh. Writing about this period of his life, he clearly expounds, 'he had no true companion save sorrow' there.[38] No precise information is available about the last years of his life. Therefore, one might infer that he passed away in Balkh sometime in the first half of the 17th century.

The Manuscripts of *Salām-nāma*

The full corpus of Shāh Ḍiyā'ī's poetic composition in the form of a *dīwān* has not reached us. Fragments of his poetry, namely five *qaṣīda*s, are preserved in various anthologies known as *Bayāḍ*.[39] The *bayāḍ*, as a technical term, is used to refer to a sort of anthology in the form of an informal notebook with poetical fragments. Physically, they are of different form and can include various poetic compositions as well as short treatises. As the *bayāḍ* was of either a small or medium size, it was easy to carry out and was used to copy poems from word of mouth or from another manuscript.

The *Salām-nāma,* which is briefly discussed below, consists of 70 *bayt*s (140 lines) and found in four manuscripts only. The title, *Salām-nāma,* can be translated as 'A Poem of Allegiance.' The description of the manuscripts provided below is based on the digital copies of selected folios from three manuscripts to which I had access.

The *Salām-nāma* is a long *qaṣīda* composed in the genre of *madḥ*, panegyric. As is evident from the opening line, the *qaṣīda* is in praise of Imam ʿAlī b. Abī Ṭālib and the imams from the *Ahl al-Bayt*. The language of the *qaṣīda* is couched in a way that requires a solid understanding of the history of Islam during the lifetime of the Prophet. The form, genre and imagery employed by the author makes the *qaṣīda* engaging and readable. However, a reader not well grounded in the era of the life of the Prophet would find it hard to decipher the text.

A copy of this *qaṣīda* was found in *Bayāḍ-i ashʿār-i Naẓmī,* a collection of poetry of Naẓmī-i Shughnānī. The *Bayāḍ* is preserved in the collection of manuscripts of the Academy of Sciences of Tajikistan which was not accessible to me. Another copy of this *qaṣīda* was discovered by Andreĭ Bertel's (d. 1995) and Mamadvafo Baqoev (d. 1972) during an expedition to Badakhshān of Tajikistan in 1962 which appears under record number 140 as MS 1962/17b.[40] A copy of selected folios from this manuscript containing the text of *Salām-nāma* was provided to me by Dr Sultonbek Aksakolov in 2010.[41] The selected pages/folios do not have any colophons and therefore it is difficult to determine the place and date of its copying.[42]

The second copy of the *Salām-nāma* was found in a *Majmūʿa* currently numbered MS BT 105. The digital copy of this manuscript is preserved in the Ismaili Special Collections Unit (ISCU) at The Institute of Ismaili Studies, London. This manuscript has more than 10 titles in prose and poetry. On the first page, it states that the manuscript was copied by Sayyid Munīr b. Muhammad Qāsim al-Badakhshānī (1882–1957)[43] and is dated 1357/1938. The text of *Salām-nāma* appears on pages 155 to 159.

The third copy of the *Salām-nāma* is found in another *Bayāḍ*, numbered MS BT 173, and a digital copy of this manuscript is preserved in ISCU. This manuscript was copied by Muqair-Shāh, the son of Dilāwar-Shāh. This is a very recent manuscript that has been copied onto a modern paper notepad and may tentatively be dated to the 1960s or 1970s.

The text of *Salām-nāma* found in MS 1962/17b and MS BT 105 are almost identical. The full text of the *qaṣīda* in these two manuscripts consists of 70 couplets (140 lines). However, the same text with various reading is found in MS BT 173, which, due to some scribal insertions, is a bit longer. The sequence of the couplets in the *qaṣīda* is not identical to MS BT 105 or the text found in MS 1962/17b. As the text of *Salām-nāma* copied in MS 1962/17b is less corrupt, it has therefore been chosen as the basis for this analysis.

Apart from this, two other *qaṣīda*s of Shāh Ḍiyā'ī recently found in a *Bayāḍ* from the collection of *khalīfa* Shāh-i Kalān, have been consulted for this research. As the manuscript is not numbered, I tentatively refer to it as MS S *Bayāḍ*. This manuscript was copied by Shāhzādamuhammad b. Sayyid Farrukh-Shāh (d. 1889) and dated 25 Dhū al-Qaʿda 1350/2 April 1932.

The *Salām-nāma*: A Poem of Allegiance

Composing a panegyric, *madḥ*, in praise of Shiʿi imams, particularly Imam ʿAlī b. Abī Ṭālib is a prevalent genre in Arabic and Persian literature.[44] The luminaries of Persian literature portray the figure of Imam ʿAlī b. Abī Ṭālib as the just ruler, or the archetypal hero, whose rule is based on his impeccability and justice, i.e. *ʿiṣma* and *ʿadl*. The application of literary imagery to the life of Imam ʿAlī created a wide range of expressions that made him 'a distinct and extremely influential literary and artistic persona' in history.[45] Similar to the famous poets of the Persian literature, Shāh Ḍiyāʾī also composed *qaṣīda*s in praise of imams from the *Ahl al-bayt*. Although the *qaṣīda*s reached us in scattered form without any titles, it is assumed that they are part of a larger corpus. Habibov proposed a theory that the *Salām-nāma* or 'A Poem of Allegiance' seems to be part of a larger *Diwān*, collection of poems, probably consisting of more than 300 couplets.[46] Unfortunately, no copies of a *Diwān* attributed to Shāh Ḍiyāʾī have reached us.

Shāh Ḍiyāʾī composed his *qaṣīda*s inspired by historical events that took place during the lifetime of the Prophet Muhammad and Imam ʿAlī b. Abī Ṭālib. The framework of these poetic composition is based on historical as well as legendary events. Hence, the *Salām-nāma* can be divided into three sections:

1. Narratives based on Qurʾānic verses and the Prophetic *ḥadīth*s
2. Narratives expressing devotion to the imams
3. Biographical data about the life of the author

The opening and closing lines of the *Salām-nāma* are identical. This sets the themes of the *qaṣīda* whereby Shāh Ḍiyāʾī starts his praise by paying homage to imams from the noble and pious line. Although the main object of Shāh Ḍiyāʾī's praise is Imam ʿAlī b. Abī Ṭālib, his name is not explicitly mentioned in the *Salām-nāma*. In so doing, the author extends his praise to imams that trace their lineage to the Prophet Muhammad through Imam ʿAlī. The core of his narrative in this *qaṣīda* is based on verses from the Qurʾān and selected *ḥadīth*s of the Prophet which will be discussed in the next section.

The Use of Qurʾān and *Ḥadīth* in *Salām-nāma*

Shāh Ḍiyāʾī's relation to the subject of his elegy remains multifaceted and has a complexity that stems from the explicit and implicit use of the Prophetic tradition as well as verses from the Qur'ān. The use of various Arabic concepts expressed in the Persian language and adapted to the context of the *qaṣīda* gives it a distinctive tone. The author evidently uses classical conventions, including form, genre, imagery and diction to promote a politico-religious claim for the ʿAlid legitimacy that is supported by carefully selected maxims from the Qur'ān and the *ḥadīth*. Shāh Ḍiyā'ī employs more than 20 verses of the Qur'ān in the composition of *Salām-nāma*.[47] In constructing his narrative, he uses expressions from a given Qur'ānic verse and Prophetic *ḥadīth* to contextualise his argument. For instance, in lines 5 to 10 Shāh Ḍiyā'ī sets up the context of his *qaṣīda*. He explicitly combines the Prophetic *ḥadīth*s where the Prophet refers to Imam ʿAlī as a brother and as a *walī* (legatee), the spiritual master of every believer, where he says:

Tu'ī jānishīni Muhammad ki hastī,
Walī-i khudāwu barādar nabīrā.

Indeed, you are the deputy of Muhammad,
And the legatee of God and a brother to the Prophet.[48]

This is followed by praise of Imam ʿAlī's qualities, particularly his knowledge that made him the master of believers *par excellence* and the master of the angels and spirits (lines 9–10). With these opening statements, Shāh Ḍiyā'ī explicitly raises the notion of loyalty and fidelity to Imam ʿAlī, which is conventionally expressed in the concept of *walāya*. The concept of *walāya* here is used in a broader religious context and denotes the spiritual authority of the imam which is considered the *sine qua non* in Shiʿi theology. Hence, in lines 6, 17, 31, 70 and 96 Shāh Ḍiyā'ī employs various derivations of the term *walī* such as *walī-i khudā*, *walāyat*, *walī-i walāyat* and *wālī*, which he uses interchangeably to express his devotion to the imams from the Ahl al-bayt.

As the Shiʿi theologians considered the concept of *walāya* 'to be an essential part of every prophetic mission,'[49] Shāh Ḍiyā'ī alludes to the presence of the *walī* or *imam* with every prophet from the time of Adam down to the Prophet Muhammad (lines 27 to 36). In this context, the author brings forward the relationship between the concept of *nubuwwa* (prophethood) and *imāma* (imamate) employing the term *walāya*. Therefore, *walāya* in a broader Shiʿi context is seen as a complement to the *nubuwwa* simply because the Prophet provided the esoteric interpretation of the Revelation (*tanzīl*) while the imam explicates the hidden spiritual meaning (*ta'wīl*) of the revelation to the believers. With this setting in mind, Shāh Ḍiyā'ī succinctly encapsulates the event of Ghadīr Khum by evoking the Prophetic *ḥadīth*, where he states:

Walāyat zi tū gasht dar dahr mashhūr,
Nubuwwat zi tū yāft naṣran naṣīrā.

It was because of you that *walāyat* became known in the world,
And the prophethood found stronger support.

The interpretation of the above passage shows a link to several Qur'ānic verses and which, as Shi'i theologians argue, have a direct link to the event of the Ghadir Khum (Qur'ān 5:3 and 5:67). In other words, the pinnacle of the Prophet's mission was to announce the *walāya/imāma* of Imam 'Alī b. Abī Ṭalib as stated in Qur'ān 5:67.[50]

Another important event discussed in the *Salām-nāma* is the Treaty of Hudaybiya. It has been reported that the Prophet and his companions, who wanted to perform the pilgrimage, waited for permission to enter Mecca and 'Uthmān ibn 'Affān (d. 36/656) was sent to negotiate. A false rumour reached the Prophet that 'Uthmān had been killed and hence, he summoned everyone to take pledge with him, known as *Bay'at al-riḍwān* or the Pledge under the Tree. It is believed that this event took place in Dhū al-qa'dah 6/February 628 in a place known as al-Ḥudaybiya.[51] Shāh Ḍiyā'ī uses verses from *Sūrat al-Fatḥ* (the Victory) and blends them with the Prophetic tradition using poetic imagery. This allows him to expand his discussion on the relationship of the Prophet Muhammad and Imam 'Alī. Therefore, in line 51, he quotes the opening line of verse 18, the Victory, to emphasise the importance of being loyal to the Prophet, as he says:

Laqad raḍīya Allāhu 'an al-mu'minīn' guft,
Khudā dar ḥaqqī dūstānat amīrā.

Indeed, Allah was pleased with the believers,
When he said, it was revealed to you for the sake of your friends.[52]

Furthermore, Shāh Ḍiyā'ī once again stresses the position of Imam 'Alī in relation to the Prophet Muhammad describing him as 'the one who is closest to the Prophet' and hence he refers to him as a legatee and deputy.

In the *Salām-nāma*, Shāh Ḍiyā'ī refers to God by two Arabic terms and one Persian term: *khudā*, *Allāh* and *ḥaqq*. For instance, in line 15, he used the term *ḥaqq* twice: in the first instance, he used it to refer to God and in the second instance, he used it as part of an expression, *dar ḥaqqi*, meaning for the sake of. To create a long-lasting effect, Shāh Ḍiyā'ī masterfully uses Qur'ānic expressions and swiftly switches to Persian, or vice versa, to express his devotion to the Imams as shown below:

> *Zi ḥaq dar ḥaqq-i dūstān-i tu āmad,*
> *Lahum maghfirat wa ajran ʿaẓimā.*
>
> From God it was revealed about your friend that,
> Theirs will be forgiveness and immense reward.[53]

It is evident from the above examples that Shāh Ḍiyā'ī engages with Qur'ānic verses in a creative way to emphasise his points. Such an engagement allows him to use some of the Arabic terms in the spiritual as well as the physical context. Therefore, the passage above can be a reference to at least three Qur'ānic verses where the expression *lahum maghfira wa ajr ʿaẓima*, 'theirs shall be forgiveness and a great reward', is fully used.

Expressing Devotion to the Imams

The religious affiliation of Shāh Ḍiyā'ī-i Shughnānī remains open for speculation. As noted above, Shāh Ḍiyā'ī referred to himself as the 'scion of rulers of Shughnān'. Historical sources and modern studies show that Badakhshān, particularly the northern parts of the region, including the semi-independent principalities of Shughnān and Wakhān, had been a bastion of the Ismaili branch of Shiʿi Islam since the 11th century.[54] Shāh Ḍiyā'ī's ancestors could have been the followers of either the Twelver Shiʿi or the Ismaili branch. The application of terms such as the Twelver Shiʿi and Ismaili reflects the modern notion and usage of these terms seems to have been different in our author's lifetime. In the context of Badakhshān, the Ismailis used the term *Panj-tanī* to express their affiliation to the Ismaili branch of Shiʿi Islam. Praise of the Twelver Shiʿi imams by Ismaili poets was a prevalent theme in the post-Alamūt period of Ismaili history. Mention could be made of Imām-Qulī, also known as Khākī-i Khurāsānī, whose poems provide ample evidence to support this argument.[55] To ascertain the religious affiliation of Shāh Ḍiyā'ī at this point is difficult due to the absence of the larger corpus of his poetic compositions. This difficulty has been exacerbated by scribes copying his poems and introducing new lines to his original compositions as will be shown below.

It is evident from Shāh Ḍiyā'ī's writings that he was acquainted with the works of Nāṣir-i Khusraw, who is referred to as the founder of the Ismaili communities in Badakhshān. A close reading of Shāh Ḍiyā'ī's *Salām-nāma* reveals that he composed this *qaṣīda* in imitation of Nāṣir-i Khusraw's poem:

> *Darakhti tū gar bāri dānish bigirad,*
> *Ba zīr ovarī charkha nīlufarīrā.*
>
> If a tree of your life acquires a fruit of knowledge,
> You will be able to bring down the circle of the sky.

Shāh Ḍiyā'ī, like Khākī-i Khurāsānī, also praises the Twelver Shiʿi imams in his poems. The difficulty herein lies in ascertaining whether these *qaṣīdas* represent Shāh Ḍiyā'ī's composition or whether these elements are later additions to his original text. The *Salām-nāma* is a good example to support this argument.

It is evident from the *Salām-nāma* that Shāh Ḍiyā'ī pays homage to the imams commonly accepted by the Twelver Shiʿis and the Ismailis. In lines 87 to 97 he praises the Imams from Imam Ḥasan b. Alī (d. 49/669-70) to Imam Jaʿfar al-Ṣādiq (d. 148/765). These lines are present in all manuscripts I have consulted. From line 98 onwards the text reveals a strange pattern of change. For instance, in the copy of *Salām-nāma* found in MS 1962/17b and MS BT 105 Shāh Ḍiyā'ī praises Imam Ismāʿīl b. Jaʿfar as he says:

> *Ba Shāh Ismāʿīl shāh-i muḥibbān,*
> *Ki ū rahbarī rāh shud mu'minīrā.*
>
> [Praise is] to Shāh Ismāʿīl, the king of the lovers,
> Who became the guide of the faithful believers.

The passage above can be interpreted in two ways: for the Ismailis this is a reference to Imam Ismaʿil b. Jaʿfar al-Ṣādiq. Strangely, it can also be a reference to the Safavid monarch, Shāh Ismaʿil I (Abū al-Muẓaffar, r. 907–930/1501–1524). As was discussed earlier, the Safavids helped the early Mughal rulers to regain control over the territories they lost to the Shaybānīds. In return, the Mughals helped in the spread of Shiʿi doctrine in their domain. Similarly, an anonymous *qaṣīda*, *Ākhirzamān-nāma,* attributed to Nāṣir-i Khusraw, was found in Badakhshān in which the author praises the Safavid rulers and presents them as the saviour of the world.[56]

It is important to note that the extract quoted above is missing in MS BT 173. A close reading of the *qaṣīda* in MS BT 173 shows that an additional six lines in praise of the Twelver Shiʿi imams have been added to the *qaṣīda*. A similar version of these verses is quoted by Mariam Moezzi in her book.[57] It is possible that the praise of the Twelver Shiʿi imams from Imam Mūsā al-Kāẓim (d. 183/799) to Imam Muhammad al-Mahdī (entered major occultation in 329/940) is a later addition to the *Salām-nāma* and other poems of Shāh Ḍīyāʾī which remains a topic for further discussion.

Conclusion

Shāh Ḍīyāʾī-i Shughnānī's life remains shrouded in obscurity. In the absence of a larger corpus of his writing it is difficult to establish his exact date of birth and death. We can conclude that Shāh Ḍīyāʾī was born in the first half of the 16th century and possibly passed away in the first quarter of the 17th century. Even though Shāh Ḍiyāʾī traces his lineage to the ruling elite of Shughnān, he left his home town under unknown circumstances and travelled to Balkh. It is highly likely that he passed away in Balkh.

The larger corpus of his poetic composition, possibly in the form of a *dīwān*, did not reach us. The fragments of his poems that have reached us are scattered and preserved in different collections. Most of his poems, including the *Salām-nāma* are found in Badakhshān of Tajikistan. There is a possibility that copies of his poems can be found in archives in Balkh in Afghanistan.

The *Salām-nāma* is a long poem in praise of the imams from the *Ahl al-bayt*. It is evident from the above discussion that Shāh Ḍiyāʾī wrote this *qaṣīda* based on Qurʾānic verses and Prophetic *ḥadīths*. The core of this *qaṣīda* rotates around the notions of Prophethood (*nubuwwa)* and the imamate (*imāma*). Shāh Ḍiyāʾī commemorated two events from the early Islam in this *qaṣīda*: the Treaty of Hudaybiya also known as *Bayʿat al-riḍwān* and the event of the last pilgrimage that took place in Ghadir-i Khum.

The original length of the *Salām-nāma* is not known. This *qaṣīda* seems to be in a state of flux since additional lines have been added to this *qaṣīda* by scribes. As discussed earlier, the genealogy of the Twelver Shiʿi imams was added to the *qaṣīda* in some manuscripts but is absent from other copies. This can be an indication that the Ismaili elements have been removed from the *qaṣīda* and the Twelver Shiʿi elements are added to it by copyists. The life and literary activity of Shāh Ḍiyāʾī are an important part of the history of Shughnān and Badakhshān in a broader context. Therefore, a further systematic study of his life based on new manuscript sources found in Badakhshān of Afghanistan and Tajikistan remains a desideratum.

NOTES

* This article is dedicated to the loving memory of my father Tolibsho Nurmamadshoev (d. 2015).

1 For the geography of Tāliqān and Qundūz, see W. L. Adamec, ed., *Historical and Political Gazetteer of Afghanistan*, vol. 1: *Badakhshān Province of Northeastern Afghanistan* (Graz, 1972), pp. 116–117 and 176–177.

2 A. Shokhumorov, 'Khāna-i Payravānī Rāstī,' in A. Shokhumorov, *Pamir – Strana Ariev* (Dushanbe, 1997), pp. 116–152; A. Iloliev, '*Panjtani* Tradition: A Set of Traditional Beliefs and Practices of the Shiʿi Ismailis of Badakshan,' in *Proceedings of the Fifth Annual International Conference on Shiʿi Studies* (London, 2020), pp. 45–61; K. S. Vasil't͡sov, "*Alam-i Sagir:* K Voprosu o Simvolike Tradit͡sionnogo Pamirskogo Zhilischa,' in R. R. Rakhimov and M. E. Revan, ed., *T͡sentral'nai͡a Azii͡a: Tradit͡sii͡a v Uslovii͡akh Peremen*, 2 (St Petersburg, 2009), pp. 150–179; N. Nourmamadchoev, *The Ismāʿīlīs of Badakhshān: History, Politics and Religion from 1500 to 1750* (PhD diss., School of Oriental and African Studies, 2014), pp. 147–149.

3 I am grateful to Hidoyatulloh Sherzodshoev for kindly sharing a manuscript from his private collection that contained poems of Shāh Ḍiyāʾī-i Shughnānī. I will refer to this manuscript as MS S: *Bayāḍ*. I express my gratitude to Otambek Mastibekov for his feedback on the rhyme and meter of the text of *Salām-nāma*.

4 The term Mā Warāʾ al-Nahr means 'the land which lies beyond the river', i.e. beyond the Oxus or Āmū-Daryā. See V. Barthold, 'Mā warā al-nahr', *EI2*, pp. 852–859.

5 Dawlatshāh Samarqandī, *The Tadhkīratu 'sh-shuʿarā: "Memoirs of the Poets"*, ed., E.G. Browne (London, 1901), p. 453; Mīr ʿAlī Shīr Nawāī, *Majālis un-nafāis: Galaxy of Poets*, ed., ʿAlī Asghar Ḥekmat (Tehran, 1945), p. 209; Mīrzā Muhammad Ḥaidar Dughlāt, *Taʾrīkh-i Rashīdī*, ed., A. Ghaffārī Fard (Tehran, 1383 Sh./2004), pp. 136–139; A. Habibov, *Ganji Badakhshon* (Dushanbe, 1972), pp. 5–6, 20–21 and 38–39.

6 V. Gardner, 'Abū Saʿīd b. Muhammad b. Mirānshāh,' *EI3*, vol. 2 (2013), pp. 1–4.

7 Ẓahīr al-Dīn Muhammad Bābur, *Bābur-nāma*, tr., W. M. Thackston (New York and Oxford, 1996), pp. 182–184; B. A. Akhmedov, 'Poslednie Timuridy i Bor'ba za Badakhshān,' in P. G. Bulgakova and I. Karimov, ed., *Issledovanii͡a po Istorii Nauki i*

Kul'tury Narodov Sredneĭ Azii, (Tashkent, 1993), pp. 87–88. N. M. Lowick, 'Coins of Sulaymān Mīrzā of Badakhshān,' *Numismatic Chronicles*, 7/5 (1965), pp. 221–229.

8 F. Daftary, 'Šāh Ṭāher Ḥosayni Dakkani,' *Encyclopaedia Iranica*, online edition; F. Daftary, 'Shāh Ṭāhir and Nizārī Ismaili Disguises,' in Todd Lawson, ed., *Reason and Inspiration in Islam: Theology, Philosophy and Mysticism in Muslim Thought: Essays in Honour of Hermann Landolt* (London, 2005), pp. 395–406; Nourmamadchoev, *The Ismāʿīlīs of Badakhshān*, pp. 67–75.

9 The Qāsim-Shāhī Nizārīs are of the opinion that the Muhammad-Shāhī Nizārīs are not the rightful bearers of the mantle of the Imamate, which resulted from the Qāsim-Shāhī–Muhammad-Shāhī schism of the 13th century. Nourmammadchoev, *The Ismāʿīlīs of Badakhshān*, pp. 152–193.

10 Mīrzā Muhammad Ḥaidar Dughlāt, *Ta'rīkh-i Rashidī: A History of the Khans of Moghulistan*, tr., W. M. Thackston (Cambridge, MA, 1996), pp. 146 and 152.

11 Ibid., p. 147.

12 V. Bartol'd, 'Badakhshān,' in *Sochenenii͡a*, vol. 3: *Raboty po Istoricheskoĭ Geografii* (Moscow, 1965), p. 345; B. Iskandarov, *Sot͡sial'no-Ėkonomicheskie i Politicheskie Aspekty Istorii Pamirskikh Kni͡azhestv (X v. – Pervai͡a polovina XIX v.)* (Dushanbe, 1983), pp. 46–49; Habibov, *Ganji Badakhshon*, p. 8; Dughlāt, *Ta'rīkh-i Rashīdī*, ed., Fard, p. 152; Daftary, 'Shāh Ṭāhir and the Nizārī Ismāʿīlī Disguise,' pp. 395–406.

13 Samarqandī, *The Tadhkīratu 'sh-shuʿarā'*, p. 535; Habibov, *Ganji Badakhshon*, p. 6.

14 Bartol'd, 'Badakhshān', p. 345; Akhmedov, 'Poslednie Timuridy', p. 82; N. N. Tumanovich, *Gerat v XVI–XVII vekakh* (Moscow, 1989), pp. 76–78; Lowick, 'Coins of Sulaymān Mīrzā of Badakhshān', pp. 221–229.

15 'It [i.e. Badakhshān] has been my hereditary kingdom for three thousand years. Although I am a woman and not entitled to rule, Mīrzā Khān is my grandson. The people will not deny me and my offspring'; see Dughlāt, *Ta'rīkh-i Rashīdī*, ed., Fard, p. 137.

16 Ibid., pp. 219–221; See T. G. Abaeva, *Ocherki Istorii Badakhshana* (Tashkent, 1964), pp. 101–102; M. B. Dickson, *Shāh Tahmasb and the Uzbeks: The Duel for Khurasan with ʿUbayd Khan: 1524–1540*, (PhD diss., Princeton University, 1958), pp. 48–49.

17 R. Islam, *Indo-Persian Relations: A Study of the Political and Diplomatic Relations between the Mughal Empire and Iran* (Tehran, 1970), pp. 192–195.

18 Dughlāt, *Ta'rīkh-i Rashīdī*, tr., Thackston, pp. 232–241; Dickson, *Shāh Tahmāsb and the Uzbeks*, pp. 46–49; S. Digby, 'Humāyūn,' *EI2*, vol. 3 (1971), pp. 575–577; A. Asani, 'Humāyūn,' in J. W. Meri, ed., *Medieval Islamic Civilisations: An Encyclopaedia* (London, 2006), vol. 1, pp. 333–335; Habibov, *Ganji Badakhshon*, p. 8.

19 For the definition of the term *Panj tan-i pāk*, see the references in footnote 2 above.

20 MS S: *Bayāḍ*, ff. 44b–47a. Habibov, *Ganji Badakhshon*, p. 155; L. Mirzohasan and A. Charoghabdol, ed., *Tazkirai Adiboni Badakhshon* (Dushanbe, 2005), p. 18; G. van den Berg, *Minstrel Poetry from the Pamir Mountains: A Study of the Songs and Poems of the Ismāʿīlīs of Tajik Badakhshān* (Wiesbaden, 2004), p. 286; Nourmamadchoev, *The Ismāʿīlīs of Badakhshān*, p. 183.

21 Habibov, *Ganji Badakhshon*, p. 184.

22 J. Badakhchani, 'Ḳāki Ḳorāsāni, Emāmqoli,' *Encyclopaedia Iranica*, vol. XV, p. 356.

23 The term *madāḥ-khanī* literally means singing devotional poetry and it stems from the Arabic word *madḥ* meaning 'to praise'. The person who performs the singing of devotional poetry is known as *madāh-khān*.

24 The Shughnānī language, also known as *Khughnāni*, is one of the Pamiri languages of the southeastern Iranian language group prevalent in the Gorno-Badakhshān Autonomous Region (GBAO) of modern Tajikistan and in the Badakhshān Province of Afghanistan.

25 For the genealogy of the Qāsim-Shāhī Nizārī imams, see F. Daftary, *The Ismaili Imams: A Biographical History* (London, 2020). For the genealogy of the Muhammad-Shāhī

(Mu'minī) Nizārī imams, see F. Daftary, *The Ismāʿīlīs: Their History and Doctrines,* (Cambridge, 2007), pp. 509–510.

26 G. van den Berg, *Minstrel Poetry*, p. 286.

27 Husayn-i Hasanyār-i Shughnānī, *Shāh Ḍiyā'-i Ḍiyā'ī: Shāʿir-i Shūrīda Ḥāl az Tabāri Shāhān-i Shughnān* (9 March 2011); Ẓuhūr ʿAlī Shāh-i Ẓuhūrī, *Shāh Ḍiyā'ī wa Mullā Lāchīn* (21 September 2018). Both articles are available online at www.shughnan.com/?page_id=4300 (Accessed on 2 January 2019).

28 If we deduct 47 from 1603 it yields the year 1556, which corresponds to 932 in the Islamic calendar.

29 Habibov, *Ganji Badakhshon*, p. 156; L. Mizohasan, and A. Charoghabdol, ed., *Tazkira-i Adiboni Badakhshon* (Khorog, 2007), p. 18; G. van den Berg, *Minstrel Poetry*, p. 286; Nourmamadchoev, *The Ismāʿīlīs of Badakhshān*, p. 183.

30 The village of Kushk is part of the Shughnān region, which is about 15 kilometres north-west of Khorog, the capital of the GBAO.

31 MS S: *Bayāḍ*, ff. 44b–47a.

32 The remnants of *Bar-Panja Qalʿa*, the Bar-Panja Castle, are still in place and located in the village of Bahshār of the Badakhshān Province of Afghanistan. See Adamec, ed., *Historical and Political Gazetteer of Afghanistan*, vol. 1, p. 45.

33 Mīrzā Sangmuhammad Badakhshī and Mīrzā Fażlʿalībek Surkhafsar, *Ta'rīkh-i Badakhsān* (Moscow, 1997), ff. 119a–119b and ff. 123b–124a, Russian tr., pp. 100–106; J. Gross, 'Foundational Legends, Shrines and Ismāʿīlī Identity in Gorno-Badakhshān, Tajikistan,' in M. Cormack, ed., *Muslims and Others in Sacred Space* (Oxford, 2013), p. 169; Nourmamadchoev, *The Ismāʿīlīs of Badakhshān*, pp. 196–204. Sayyid Farrukh-Shāh, *Tā'rīkh-i shāhān-i Shughnān*, in MS S *Bayāḍ* (folio number is missing).

34 Habibov, *Ganji Badakhshon*, pp. 156–157.

35 MS S: *Bayāḍ*, ff. 47b–49b.

Chū laʿl az kān barāmad az Badakhshān bā dil-i purkhūn,
Ba ṣad ḥasrat, ba ṣad mihnat, ba ṣad kulfat, ba ṣad savdā.

As a ruby was taken out from Badakhshān with heavy heart,
With hundreds of difficulties, sorrows, and bargains.

36 MS BT 105, *Bayāḍ*, pp. 155–159; MS BT 173, *Bayāḍ*, ff. 65b–68a; Habibov, *Ganji Badakhshon*, p. 157.

37 R. D. McChesney, *Waqf in Central Asia: Four Hundred Years in the History of a Muslim Shrine, 1480–1889* (Princeton, 1991), pp. 3–45.

38 MS BT 105, *Bayāḍ*, pp. 155–159; MS BT 173, *Bayāḍ*, ff. 65b–68a.

39 See *EI2*, vol. 13, p. 185.

40 A. Bertel's and M. Bakoev, *Alfavitnyĭ Katalog Rukopiseĭ Obnaruzhennykh v Gorno-Badakhshanskoĭ Avtonomnoĭ Oblasti Ekspiditsieĭ 1959–1963 gg.* (Moscow, 1967), p. 66. Bertel's and Baqoev incorrectly state that Ḍiyā'ī or Shāh Ḍiyā'ī-i Shughnānī is an 18th century poet from Badakhshān. Ibid. p. 34 and p. 66.

41 I am grateful to Sultonbek Aksakolov, from the University of Central Asia, who brought the text of *Salām-nāma* from this manuscript to my attention.

42 Shāh Ḍiyā'ī-i Shughnānī, *Salām-nāma*, in MS 1962/17b, ff. 5b-20b.

43 For a biography of Sayyid Munīr, see M. Zoolshoev, 'Forgotten Figures of Badakhshān: Sayyid Munir al-Din Badakhshani and Sayyid Haydar Shah Mubarakshahzada,' in D. Dagiev and C. Faucher, ed., *Identity, History and Trans-Nationality in Central Asia: The Mountain Communities of Pamir* (London, 2019), pp. 145–155.

44 F. Haj Manouchehri (tr. M. Melvin-Koushki), "ʿAlī b. Abī Ṭālib: Imam ʿAlī in Persian Literature and Folklore,' *Encyclopaedia Islamica* (Leiden, 2011), vol. 3, pp. 560–565.

45 Ibid., pp. 560–565.

46 Habibov, *Ganj-i Badakhshon*, p. 157.

47 Qur'ānic verses used in the *Salām-nāma* are: 2:126; 3:162; 3:180; 4:128; 4:146; 5:9; 5:55; 8:16; 9:72–73; 16:7; 22:72; 36:62; 44:53; 48:18; 48:28; 57:5; 57:15; 67:13; 76:7; 76:13; 89:27.

48 R. Shah-Kazemi, *Imam 'Alī: From Concise History to Timeless Mystery* (London, 2019), p. 153; see also his "Alī b. Abī Ṭālib', *Encyclopaedia Islamica* (Leiden, 2011), vol. 3, p. 485.

49 D. Mohammad Poor, "Alī b. Abī Ṭālib: Theological Doctrines,' *Encyclopaedia Islamica*, (Leiden, 2011), vol. 3, pp. 518–522.

50 'O Messenger! Convey that which has been sent down unto thee from thy Lord, and if thou dost not, thou wilt not have conveyed His message. And God will protect thee from mankind. Surely God guides not disbelieving people'; see S. H. Nasr, *The Study Quran: A New Translation and Commentary* (New York, 2015), pp. 313–314.

51 W. Montgomery Watt, 'al-Ḥudaybiya', *EI2*, vol. 3, p. 539.

52 'God was content with the believers when they pledged allegiance unto thee beneath the tree. He knew what was in their hearts and sent down Tranquility upon them and rewarded them with a victory nigh'; see Nasr, *The Study Quran*, p. 1252.

53 Qur'ān 5:9; 33:35; 49:3.

54 Nourmamadcheov, *The Ismā'īlīs of Badakhshān*, pp. 194–214.

55 MS Per 81 [MS 901] and MS Per 82 [MS 902] *Dīwān-i Khākī-i Khurāsānī*, in the collection of The Institute of Ismaili Studies, London.

56 G. van den Berg, 'Ismā'īlī Poetry in Tajik Badakhshān: A Safavid Connection?', *Persica*, 17 (2001), pp. 1–9; Nourmamadchoev, *The Ismā'īlīs of Badakhshān*, pp. 234–235.

57 Mariam Moezzi quotes this passage from a manuscript in the collection of the Institute of Humanities in Khorog, Tajikistan. M. Moezzi, *Ismā'īlīya-i Badakhshān* (Tehran, 1395/2016), p. 180.

15

The *Ṣaḥīfat al-nāẓirīn*: Reflections on Authorship and Confessional Identity in a 15th-Century Central Asian Text*

Daniel Beben

The history of Ismailism in the Persianate world in the centuries following the Mongol conquests remains among the least explored areas in the field of Ismaili studies today. This is particularly the case for the Central-Asian Ismaili tradition, as research in this area until recently has been severely hampered by a lack of access to source materials, the vast bulk of which remain held in private collections in the highland Badakhshān region.[1] However, in recent years a significant quantity of Ismaili manuscript materials from Badakhshān have come to light, many of which have now been collected and made available by The Institute of Ismaili Studies (IIS). Among the more prominent texts of the Central Asian Ismaili tradition is one titled *Ṣaḥīfat al-nāẓirīn* (Pages for the Readers), also known under the titles *Sī ū shish ṣaḥīfa* (Thirty-Six Chapters) and *Tuḥfat al-nāẓirīn* (Gift for the Readers), which is the subject of reassessment in this chapter. The *Ṣaḥīfat al-nāẓirīn* is an important yet understudied work covering a series of topics related to Ismaili theology and doctrine, and is noteworthy for being the first Ismaili text known to have been composed within Badakhshān after Nāṣir-i Khusraw (d. after 462/1070). While the text undoubtedly deserves further study on several counts, in this chapter I will pursue the more limited objective of re-examining the matter of the authorship of the text and, by extension, the implications of it for the history of Ismailism in Central Asia.

In the majority of its known manuscripts, the *Ṣaḥīfat al-nāẓirīn* is attributed to an author named Sayyid Suhrāb Walī, a legendary *pīr* or religious leader within the Central-Asian Nizārī Ismaili tradition, and it was to his name that the work was attributed in the publication of the text and in subsequent scholarship. In more recent years, however, a range of new materials have come to light that call for a reassessment both of the attribution of the work to Sayyid Suhrāb and of its historical significance within the Central-Asian Ismaili tradition. In particular, since its initial publication nearly a dozen new manuscripts of the work have been identified. While the majority of these copies are likewise attributed to Sayyid Suhrāb, there have also appeared several copies attributed to a different author, Ghiyāth al-Dīn ʿAlī Iṣfahānī, a scholar who is known to have been in the service of several of the Timurid governors of Badakhshān in the second half of the 15th century. In this chapter I contend that Ghiyāth al-Dīn was most likely the original author of the *Ṣaḥīfat al-nāẓirīn*. Moreover, I examine some of the possibilities that may explain the apparent shift in the text's attribution to Sayyid Suhrāb, which in turn may shed some additional light on the biography of this important yet enigmatic figure within the history of Central Asian Ismailism.

The Historical Context: Ismailism in Badakhshān to the 15th Century

The history of Ismailism in Badakhshān following the death of Nāṣir-i Khusraw in the late 11th century down to the Timurid conquest in the mid 15th century remains almost entirely obscure.[2] While Nāṣir-i Khusraw may be credited with the introduction of Ismailism into the region, following his death we find no direct evidence of Ismaili activity in Badakhshān again until the 15th century.[3] In 1150 the Badakhshān region was conquered by the Ghūrids, who were renowned opponents of the Ismailis.[4] Consequently, it is likely that any Ismaili community that had been established by Nāṣir-i Khusraw in this region would have suffered persecution or been driven underground, which may explain the absence of any references to Ismailis in the sources of this period. The Mongol conquests in the 13th century likewise dealt a devastating blow to Ismaili communities and institutions throughout the Muslim world. While it has often been assumed that Badakhshān was spared from the Mongol conquests due to its mountainous territory, in fact the region was indeed conquered and became part of the patrimony of Chinggis Khan's son Chaghatay.[5] At some point after the death of Chaghatay in 1244 we see the emergence in the region of an autonomous dynasty of obscure origin who claimed descent from Alexander the Great, whose members continued to rule the region for nearly two centuries under Mongol and later Timurid vassalage.[6]

The sources throughout the Mongol era are entirely silent on the question of Ismaili activity in the Badakhshān region. In consequence, there remains an open question as to the date of the introduction of the Nizārī *daʿwa* in Badakhshān, as Nāṣir-i Khusraw died prior to the death of Imam Mustanṣir bi'llāh I in 487/1094 and the ensuing schism within the Ismaili community.[7] The earliest direct attestation of Nizārī activity in Badakhshān is found in an early-15th century text titled *Haft nukta*, or 'Seven Aphorisms,' containing a series of discourses believed to be from the Nizārī Imam Islām Shāh, in which reference is made to *murīd*s residing in Badakhshān.[8] The *Ṣaḥīfat al-nāẓirīn* itself is also a key piece of evidence for the expansion of the *daʿwa* in Badakhshān in the 15th century, being the earliest known Ismaili text to have been composed within Badakhshān since the death of Nāṣir-i Khusraw. The 15th century is a period more broadly associated with a vigorous expansion of the Nizārī *daʿwa* into new areas, particularly in South Asia, culminating with the shift of the seat of the imamate to the town of Anjudān in central Iran during the time of Imam Mustanṣir bi'llāh II (d. 885/1480), a move taken most likely for the purpose of situating the imamate closer to its increasing body of followers in India.[9] It is entirely possible, of course, that a smaller, undocumented Ismaili presence had been found in Badakhshān in earlier centuries. However, the fact that an Ismaili presence in Badakhshān appears in the historical sources again only in the 15th century, and not earlier, speaks at least to a significant expansion of the *daʿwa* in Badakhshān in this period.

In 871/1466–1467, the last member of the dynasty of autonomous rulers of Badakhshān, Shāh Sulṭān Muḥammad, was overthrown and executed by the Timurid ruler Abū Saʿīd, and the Badakhshān region was thereafter annexed to the Timurid empire.[10] The Timurids are known for having taken very harsh measures towards the Ismailis in their domains.[11] Among other incidents, the Timurid governor Sulṭān Ways Mīrzā is recorded as having violently suppressed an Ismaili uprising in Badakhshān in 913/1508.[12] It is important to keep this historical context in mind for the subsequent discussion of the *Ṣaḥīfat al-nāẓirīn*, as the text was composed at a time when the Nizārī *daʿwa* maintained an expanding yet still precarious position in Badakhshān.

The *Ṣaḥīfat al-nāẓirīn* and its Manuscripts

The *Ṣaḥīfat al-nāẓirīn* is a didactic treatise consisting of thirty-six (or thirty-five in some copies) chapters covering various aspects of Ismaili theology and cosmology. The date of composition of the work is generally given as 856 or 857/1452–1453. The earliest printed version of the text, issued under the title *Tuḥfat al-nāẓirīn*, was published in 1960 by the Pakistani scholar Qudratullāh Beg, although copies of this are extremely rare and were not available to me. The following year, an edition of the text was produced by Hūshang Ujāqī, a student of Wladimir Ivanow, with an introduction written by Ivanow.[13] Both editions attribute the composition of the text to an author named Sayyid Suhrāb Walī.

Ujāqī's edition of the *Ṣaḥīfat al-nāẓirīn* was based on three manuscripts, the oldest dated 1137/1725 (to date the oldest known manuscript of the work), with the other two dating to the late 19th century (1312/1894 and 1277/1861). The latter copy is most likely the same as IIS MS 176 (discussed below). The present location of the other two manuscripts is unknown. Nine copies in total are held in the IIS archives. Seven of these copies represent the same redaction as the Ujāqī and Ivanow edition. These include MS 176, evidently one of the copies consulted for the Ujāqī and Ivanow edition, which was copied on 19 Ramaḍān 1277 (30 March, 1861) by Sayyid Muflis Shāh. MS 196 is undated but appears to be a rather recent copy. This copy is also incomplete, ending with *ṣaḥīfa* ten. MS 821 is directly copied from Ujāqī's edition (including the footnotes), as is MS BT 74. Neither of these copies are dated but were obviously produced after the text's publication in 1961.[14] MS BA 101 was copied on the tenth of Ṣafar 1293 (5 March, 1876). MS BT 98 was copied on a Tuesday of Rabīʿ al-thānī 1333 (February–March 1915) by ʿĀlim Shāh walad-i Sayyid Muḥammad. MS 15095 omits the introduction and is undated, with the colophon mentioning only that it was completed on a Thursday in the beginning of the month of Shawwāl, but it also appears to be a relatively recent copy. Two other copies, MS BA 59 and MS BA 159, represent a second redaction of the text, which I will discuss later.

Aside from the copies held in the IIS there are also four copies in the Bertel's and Bakoev collection at the Rudaki Institute of Oriental Studies in Dushanbe, Tajikistan. Two of these are incomplete but the two complete copies represent the second redaction of the text, which I will discuss further below. Finally, there are two other manuscripts of the work preserved in St Petersburg. The first is a copy collected by Aleksandr Semenov, representing the redaction published by Ujāqī, dated 1333/1915, copied by Shāhzāda Muḥammad b. Farrukhshāh.[15] Another copy, defective in the beginning and dated 1281/1864–1865, was collected by Ivanow prior to his exile from Russia.[16] Both of these copies are currently held at the Institute of Oriental Manuscripts in St Petersburg (formerly the St Petersburg branch of the Institute of Oriental Studies of the Russian Academy of Sciences).[17]

Sayyid Suhrāb Walī and the *Ṣaḥīfat al-nāẓirīn*

The majority of the recovered manuscripts of the *Ṣaḥīfat al-nāẓirīn* attribute the work to an author named Sayyid Suhrāb Walī Badakhshānī. Since the publication of Ujāqī's edition, subsequent scholarship has largely accepted the attribution of Sayyid Suhrāb as the author of the work.[18] But very little is known of this individual. Most of what has been stated thus far in the scholarship on him has been based on a few autobiographical details taken from the conclusion to the *Ṣaḥīfat al-nāẓirīn*, which states only that the author converted to Ismailism at the age of 12 and provides a brief account of the theological questions that prompted his search and conversion. The author of the *Ṣaḥīfat al-nāẓirīn* also refers to a number of his previous compositions, including a cosmological work titled *Risāla-i asrār al-nuṭfa*, a work on Ismaili doctrine titled *Risāla-i ḥudūdiyya*, and another *daʿwa* text titled *Rawḍat al-mutaʿallimīn*.[19] To date none of these texts have been identified or recovered.

The brief notices on Sayyid Suhrāb found in current scholarship, with the exception of the work of Abdulmamad Iloliev, have largely ignored the far more voluminous body of material on this figure that is found in the hagiographical corpus of the Central Asian Ismailis. Granted, much of this material is of an obviously legendary quality and is preserved only in relatively late compositions, dating to the 19th century or later. Nonetheless, from this material we can at least obtain a sense of his significance and legacy within the Central Asian Ismaili tradition, which in turn might help us to better understand the nature of his connection with the *Ṣaḥīfat al-nāẓirīn*. The chief and earliest source in this regard is a text titled the *Silk-i guhar-rīz*, which I have discussed at greater length elsewhere.[20] The work was composed in the town of Jurm in present-day Afghan Badakhshān *ca.* 1251/1835 and survives in multiple copies throughout Tajikistan and Afghanistan. The text was authored by a descendant of Sayyid Suhrāb named Khwājah Aḥrār, who also employed the *takhalluṣ* Kūchak or 'Little One' in his poetry, along with the pen-name *Guhar-rīz* or 'Jewel-spreader'. The title thus implies a double entendre, as the term *silk* (meaning 'string' or 'thread') may signify a collection or 'threading' of poetry (referring to the author's composition) as well as the 'string of jewels' that comprises the author's genealogy extending back to Sayyid Suhrāb and thence to the Prophet Muḥammad. The text covers a broad array of topics, including chapters dedicated to aspects of Ismaili theology and doctrine, but it also includes a series of historical and hagiographical narratives concerning the Nizārī imams and, more importantly for our purposes, the lineages of Ismaili *pīr*s of the Badakhshān region extending from Nāṣir-i Khusraw.

The *Silk-i guhar-rīz* was produced and transmitted within a family of *pīr*s who claimed both a genealogical and initiatic line of descent from Sayyid Suhrāb, who is depicted in the text as having been one of the two chief disciples of Nāṣir-i Khusraw. The text, along with other evidence from this period points to a sharp rivalry in the 19th century between representatives of the lineage of Sayyid Suhrāb and those of other lineages claiming spiritual descent from Nāṣir-i Khusraw, most notably that of 'Umar Yumgī, who is depicted in the *Silk-i guhar-rīz* as the second and lesser disciple of Nāṣir. Therefore, it must be kept in mind that the biographical and hagiographical materials available on the figure of Sayyid Suhrāb were composed within a competitive environment, in which individuals laying claim to his ancestry vied for positions of authority and recognition within the Ismaili community of Badakhshān.

According to the account in the *Silk-i guhar-rīz*, Sayyid Suhrāb was a descendent of Mūsā al-Kāẓim, through whom he traced his sayyid ancestry.[21] His ancestors were rulers of the town of Yazd in Iran and were originally followers of the line of Imam Ismāʿīl, but then outwardly switched their allegiance to the Ithnāʿasharī imams, whom they recognised as the *mustawdaʿ* or 'entrusted' imams, while the true or 'established' (*mustaqarr*) imams of the line of Ismāʿīl remained in a state of *saṭr* or concealment.[22] Following the conclusion of the line of Ithnāʿasharī imams and the occultation of its last representative, along with the public re-emergence of the Ismaili imams in Northern Africa, the ancestors of Sayyid Suhrāb once again transferred their allegiance to the Ismaili imams. The *Silk-i guhar-rīz* further relates that Sayyid Suhrāb's father, Mīr Sayyid Ḥasan, upon hearing of the repute of Nāṣir-i Khusraw, entrusted his son to a renowned dervish by the name of Bābā Ḥaydar, who was asked to travel to Badakhshān and to deliver Sayyid Suhrāb, then four years old, to the tutelage of Nāṣir, who subsequently raised the child as his chief disciple and successor.

The *Silk-i guhar-rīz* goes on to relate a number of additional narratives regarding the life of Sayyid Suhrāb, emphasising the vast body of knowledge that he obtained from his discipleship with Nāṣir-i Khusraw and his charismatic following amongst the people of Badakhshān. The narratives of Sayyid Suhrāb found in the *Silk-i guhar-rīz* are reiterated and embellished in a number of later hagiographical sources from Badakhshān, particularly an early 20th-century text titled the *Baḥr al-akhbār*.[23] In addition to these hagiographical accounts, the renown of Sayyid Suhrāb within the Central Asian Ismaili community is also reflected in a plethora of genealogical traditions among various families in the Badakhshān region who claim Sayyid Suhrāb as an ancestor and as a key link in an initiatic *silsila* extending back to Nāṣir-i Khusraw.[24]

Despite some of the clearly legendary details reflected in these hagiographical narratives, the extent of Sayyid Suhrāb's presence within the genealogical traditions of the Badakhshān region suggests that his name bears at least some connection to a historical figure. However, there are a number of reasons to question whether Sayyid Suhrāb was in fact the original author of the *Ṣaḥīfat al-nāẓirīn*. First, there is the question of chronology, as the hagiographical tradition maintains that Sayyid Suhrāb was a disciple of Nāṣir-i Khusraw, who died in the late 11th century, while the *Ṣaḥīfat al-nāẓirīn* was composed in the 15th century. Moreover, the autobiographical account presented in the conclusion to the *Ṣaḥīfat al-nāẓirīn* differs in some respects from what is found in the hagiographical narratives surrounding Sayyid Suhrāb. Among other things, the *Silk-i guhar-rīz* claims that Sayyid Suhrāb was from a family who had long been followers of the Ismaili imams, while the autobiographical narrative in the *Ṣaḥīfat al-nāẓirīn* states that the author was a convert to the Ismaili tradition. But perhaps the most significant reason to question the text's attribution to Sayyid Suhrāb is the presence of other manuscripts of the work which bear the name of an entirely different author. I will turn now to a discussion of these manuscripts.

The Second Redaction

In the archives of the IIS there is held another manuscript of the *Ṣaḥīfat al-nāẓirīn*, MS BA 59, dated 1293/1876. This copy differs in a number of respects from the version represented in Ujāqī's edition, chiefly in the fact that the name of the author is given not as Sayyid Suhrāb, but rather Ghiyāth al-Dīn ʿAlī b. Ḥusayn b. ʿAlī Amīrān Iṣfahānī.[25] This copy also bears a different introduction than the version published by Ujāqī. Furthermore, the text of MS BA 59 is composed only of thirty-five chapters, and not thirty-six, and is clearly identified as a thirty-five chapter work in the introduction.[26] However, aside from the difference in the introduction the content of the text is otherwise the same, as the 19th chapter of MS BA 59 has simply been split into two chapters in the version represented in the Ujāqī edition.[27] This redaction is also evidently represented in another undated IIS manuscript, MS BA 159. This copy is defective at the end and moreover omits the introduction, and therefore does not provide any attribution. Instead it proceeds directly with the table of contents, which contains thirty-five chapters and matches the chapter headings of MS BA 59 (similarly omitting the 20th chapter from the Ujāqī redaction). Hence, this copy would appear to be another witness to the second redaction of the text.

Although these two manuscripts in the IIS collection have come to light only recently, two other copies of the *Ṣaḥīfat al-nāẓirīn* bearing the attribution to Ghiyāth al-Dīn were collected already in 1959, during the first of a series of Soviet research expeditions to Badakhshān led by Andrei Bertel's and Mamadvafo Bakoev, and are held today in the archives of the Rudaki Institute of Oriental Studies in Dushanbe.[28] These include MS 1959/8a (copied 1365/1946 by Shāh Fiṭūr Muḥabbat Shāhzāda)[29] and MS 1959/23a (copied 1248/1833 by Sayyid ʿArab b. Sayyid Shāh ʿAbbās). These two copies likewise bear the name of Ghiyāth al-Dīn ʿAlī Iṣfahānī as the author and their introductions are the same as IIS MS BA 59.[30] Aside from their catalogue descriptions, these copies of the text have remained unstudied to date.

Hence, it would appear that these four manuscripts (two in the IIS archives and two in Dushanbe) represent a separate redaction of the work, evidently unknown to Ivanow and Ujāqī. Moreover, there is also a shift in the title of the work between these two redactions. The more specific (and quite likely original) title of *Ṣaḥīfat al-nāẓirīn* is found only in copies of the redaction attributed to Ghiyāth al-Dīn Iṣfahānī. In copies attributed to Sayyid Suhrāb the introduction containing the title *Ṣaḥīfat al-nāẓirīn* has been eliminated and replaced. Instead, in this version the work is generally given the generic title of *Sī ū shish ṣaḥīfa* or, in some cases, as *Ṣaḥīfa-i Sayyid Suhrāb* or some variant thereof.[31]

Ghiyāth al-Dīn ʿAlī Iṣfahānī

While the figure of Ghiyāth al-Dīn ʿAlī Iṣfahānī is also rather poorly known, there is somewhat more historical information available on this figure in comparison with Sayyid Suhrāb Walī, who is known purely through legendary accounts in the Badakhshāni hagiographical tradition. At the very least, the information available on this figure allows us to firmly locate him in time and place. While I have not located any references to Ghiyāth al-Dīn in historical sources, there are a number of other extant treatises attributed to him, from which we know him to have been a polymath in the service of several of the Timurid governors of Badakhshān in the second half of the 15th century. Among the earliest of these is a letterist treatise titled *Asrār al-ḥurūf*, dated 870/1465–1466 and dedicated to Abū Bakr, son of the Timurid ruler Abū Saʿīd, who was appointed by his father as governor of Badakhshān following his conquest of the region.[32] The most well known of Ghiyāth al-Dīn's works is the *Dānish-nāma-i jahān*, a large scientific compendium covering a variety of topics that is dedicated to the Timurid ruler Sulṭān Maḥmūd, who replaced his brother Abū Bakr as the governor of Badakhshān in 873/1469.[33] Another text attributed to him is the *Durrat al-misāḥa*, a text on geometry and measurements written in 890/1485 and dedicated to the same Sulṭān Maḥmūd.[34] Ghiyāth al-Dīn is also credited with a number of works on astronomy, including a work titled *Khulāṣat al-tanjīm va burhān al-taqvīm* and a shorter work titled *Maʿārif al-taqvīm*.[35] A version of the latter has been preserved among the Ismailis of Badakhshān under the title *Nujūm* and was still used in local calendar systems in Badakhshān down to the mid 20th century.[36] A number of other treatises are also attributed to him on such diverse topics as falconry and culinary arts.[37]

None of these other texts attributed to Ghiyāth al-Dīn contain any overt Ismaili content, nor is it likely that Ghiyāth al-Dīn would have found employment as an avowed Ismaili under the Timurids. In fact, the copy of the *Asrār al-ḥurūf* examined by Edward Browne concludes with a quotation from a letter from the 15th-century Naqshbandī shaykh Khwāja Abū Naṣr Pārsā, which Ghiyāth al-Dīn says he obtained from Jāmī, whom he identifies as his 'master and patron'. This note would seem to suggest a connection on the part of Ghiyāth al-Dīn with the Sunni Naqshbandī Sufi order.[38] How then do we account for the existence of an openly Ismaili text (the *Ṣaḥīfat al-nāẓirīn*) composed under the name of Ghiyāth al-Dīn? One possibility is that his career path may have resembled that of Nāṣir al-Dīn Ṭūsī, who earlier in his career had composed several avowedly Ismaili texts before apparently shedding his Ismaili affiliations following the Mongol conquests.[39] It should be noted that the *Ṣaḥīfat al-nāẓirīn* was composed prior to the Timurid takeover of Badakhshān, possibly while in the service of Shāh Sulṭān Muḥammad, the last pre-Timurid ruler of the region, who appears to have been more lenient towards the Ismailis than his Timurid successors. As mentioned above, the author of the *Ṣaḥīfat al-nāẓirīn* also cites several earlier compositions which, although they have not been recovered, by their titles and the context of their citation evidently dealt with Ismaili themes. By contrast, there is no evidence of any open engagement with Ismaili themes in the output of Ghiyāth al-Dīn produced after the Timurid conquest of Badakhshān. Hence, it is conceivable that the Timurid takeover of the region would have led Ghiyāth al-Dīn to conceal any Ismaili affiliations for the purpose of self-protection and for the sake of ingratiating himself with his new employers, although it is possible that he may have continued his *da'wa* activities thereafter by more furtive means. On this possibility I will have more to say below.

On the Authorship of the Text

Is it possible to determine that one redaction of the text might represent an earlier or even 'original' version of the *Ṣaḥīfat al-nāẓirīn/Sī ū shish ṣaḥīfa*? While the attribution to Sayyid Suhrāb predominates and is attested earlier in the manuscript record, it should be noted that all of the known manuscripts of the work are relatively late copies, dating to the 18th century or later. For a number of reasons, I would argue that Ghiyāth al-Dīn was most likely the original author of the work. Firstly, the more generic title of the work found in the redaction attributed to Sayyid Suhrāb may be evidence of a later adaptation. The presence of multiple copies of the work with the introduction omitted (including IIS MS 15095 and MS BA 159, and Dushanbe MSS 1959/24v and 1959/7v) suggests that the introduction may have been lost and reconstructed in at least one line of manuscripts, with its title and attribution shifted.

In addition, the nature of the shift in the attribution of the authorship of the *Ṣaḥīfat al-nāẓirīn* may also provide a clue as to which is the earlier version. There are two possible explanations that may account for the change of attribution. The first is that only one of the two names may refer to the 'true' author of the text and that the presence of the other's name in the manuscript record constitutes a typical example of pseudo-attribution. If this is the case, then circumstantial evidence once again suggests that Ghiyāth al-Dīn was most likely the original author. Sayyid Suhrāb, as I have outlined above, is a renowned figure within the Ismaili community of Badakhshān, whose name is associated with a wide array of hagiographical narratives and genealogical traditions. By contrast, there are no such legacies associated with the name of Ghiyāth al-Dīn. The practice of pseudo-attribution almost universally reflects an effort to attach some measure of added legitimacy and privilege to a text and, by association, to those who transmit or employ the text within a particular social context.[40] Hence, there is no evident reason for why the name of Ghiyāth al-Dīn would have been chosen for a pseudo-attribution. Undoubtedly, any change in attribution between the two authors would have been done in favour of the more well-known author (i.e., from Ghiyāth al-Dīn to Sayyid Suhrāb), representing an effort (presumably by a later member of Sayyid Suhrāb's lineage) to appropriate the text for his legacy and for the prestige of his lineage. As I have noted above, evidence from 19th-century sources such as the *Silk-i guhar-rīz* suggests a pointed contestation for leadership within the Ismaili community of Badakhshān between representatives of the lineage of Sayyid Suhrāb and others, and one may imagine that the attribution of texts such as the *Ṣaḥīfat al-nāẓirīn* may have played a key role in this competition.[41]

There is, however, a second possibility that we might consider, which is that Sayyid Suhrāb and Ghiyāth al-Dīn are actually two different names for the same individual. While, as I have noted above, the hagiographical traditions surrounding Sayyid Suhrāb differ in some key respects from the autobiographical data presented in the conclusion to the *Ṣaḥīfat al-nāẓirīn* and the sparse biographical data available on Ghiyāth al-Dīn, there are some curious points of convergence as well. To begin with, the account of Sayyid Suhrāb in the *Silk-i guhar-rīz* depicts him as a native of Yazd, in Central Iran, while Ghiyāth al-Dīn's *nisba* places his origins in the relatively nearby city of Iṣfahān. Furthermore, the addition of the patronymic al-Ḥusaynī to the name of Ghiyāth al-Dīn in some manuscripts of his works indicates his status as a *sayyid*.

One point of apparent incongruity between the two figures which I outlined earlier is that the author of the *Ṣaḥīfat al-nāẓirīn* clearly identifies himself as a convert to the Ismaili tradition, while the hagiographical record depicts Sayyid Suhrāb as being from a family that had long been followers of the Ismaili imams. As noted in that discussion, however, the *Silk-i guhar-rīz* also goes to some lengths to account for what appears to have been an Ithnāʿasharī connection on the part of Sayyid Suhrāb's ancestors, with the framework of the *mustawdaʿ/mustaqarr* imamate employed as an explanatory device to legitimize these affiliations, in effect retroactively claiming his ancestors as dissimulated Ismailis. Both the autobiographical account in the *Ṣaḥīfat al-nāẓirīn* and the hagiographical tradition connected with Sayyid Suhrāb also share a common narrative of admission to the *daʿwa* at a young age: the *Ṣaḥīfat al-nāẓirīn* records the author's conversion at the age of 12 (by contrast, Nāṣir-i Khusraw encountered the *daʿwa* only after the age of 40), while the *Silk-i guhar-rīz* reports that Sayyid Suhrāb was bestowed to Nāṣir-i Khusraw's tutelage at the tender age of 4.

The autobiographical conversion narrative related in the *Ṣaḥīfat al-nāẓirīn* also suggests some similarities to the account of Sayyid Suhrāb in the *Silk-i guhar-rīz*. The account relates that the author's spiritual search was initiated at the prompting of an unnamed dervish who recited some verses from Nāṣir-i Khusraw, thus planting the seeds of questioning in his mind and initiating an extended process of personal search concluding with his embrace of Ismailism. Hence, while the author of the *Ṣaḥīfat al-nāẓirīn* does not claim to have been Nāṣir-i Khusraw's direct disciple, his narrative does assign a prominent place to Nāṣir's legacy and thought in affecting his conversion. The hagiographical tradition also depicts Sayyid Suhrāb as having been a highly learned individual and a specialist in Ismaili philosophy, having spent several decades studying at the feet of Nāṣir-i Khusraw. This is clearly illustrated in a narrative from the *Silk-i guhar-rīz*, which relates that one day Nāṣir-i Khusraw was leading a *dhikr* circle with his companions, when the people entreated his disciples to pose a question to Nāṣir regarding the origins of the soul. The people turned to Sayyid Suhrāb, telling him: 'You are our leader' (*tū pīshqadam-i māhā'ī*), and begged him to pose the question to Nāṣir. Sayyid Suhrāb posed the question to Nāṣir, who instructed him that he should answer the question for the people himself. Upon this command (*bi-farmān-i pīr*), Sayyid Suhrāb turned to the audience and began a lengthy discourse on cosmology, the nature of the soul, and the need for a spiritual guide. The discourse reveals Sayyid Suhrāb to be fully fluent in the system of Ismaili Neo-Platonic philosophy propounded in the works of Nāṣir-i Khusraw, and which is abundantly represented in the *Ṣaḥīfat al-nāẓirīn*.[42]

Yet all of this potential evidence would seem to be negated by the clear chronological discrepancy between the depiction in the hagiographical tradition of Sayyid Suhrāb as a disciple of Nāṣir-i Khusraw and the dating of the *Ṣaḥīfat al-nāẓirīn*, constituting a nearly four century gap. However, aside from the attachment of his name to the *Ṣaḥīfat al-nāẓirīn*, there is additional evidence to suggest that Sayyid Suhrāb may in actuality have lived in the 15th century. This evidence is attested in the various genealogical traditions among the Ismailis of Badakhshān that are traced back to Sayyid Suhrāb. While there is not space here to discuss these traditions in detail, it suffices to mention that a chronological analysis of these genealogies demonstrates that Sayyid Suhrāb could not possibly have been a contemporary of Nāṣir-i Khusraw; rather, the genealogies largely concur in suggesting a birth date for Sayyid Suhrāb around the early 15th century, which aligns with the attested dates of his literary output in the second half of the 15th century.[43]

Conclusion

The evidence adduced above, demonstrating convergence both in the dates and in some of the key biographical data available for the figures of Sayyid Suhrāb Walī and Ghiyāth al-Dīn Iṣfahānī, suggests that the matter of the authorship of the *Ṣaḥīfat al-nāẓirīn* may constitute something more than a case of mere pseudo-attribution. Accordingly, I put forth here the hypothesis that these two names may in fact refer to one and the same individual; or, more specifically, that Ghiyāth al-Dīn was a Nizārī *dāʿī* who adopted the pseudonym or *nom de guerre* of Sayyid Suhrāb following the Timurid conquest of Badakhshān. Over time, the name and legacy of Sayyid Suhrāb likely took on a number of legendary embellishments, while his original name was evidently obscured, although still preserved to a degree within the manuscript record. Examples of such a wholesale 'replacement' of the identity of a historical figure are not unknown in the history of Central Asia, especially in predominately oral environments, such as that found in Badakhshān in the pre-colonial era, where the lack of written records permitted a much greater degree of creativity in narrative development.[44]

The master–disciple relationship between Nāṣir-i Khusraw and Sayyid Suhrāb depicted in the hagiographical record undoubtedly represents a later effort to reify a symbolic link between the two figures and their legacies. As I have mentioned above, the *Ṣaḥīfat al-nāẓirīn* is the earliest known Ismaili text to have been composed within Badakhshān following the death of Nāṣir-i Khusraw; furthermore, the author of the *Ṣaḥīfat al-nāẓirīn* acknowledges the work of Nāṣir-i Khusraw in spurring his own conversion to Ismailism, and clearly envisioned his *daʿwa* work as a means of continuing or reviving the tradition established by Nāṣir-i Khusraw within the Badakhshān region. It is not difficult to imagine, therefore, how this intellectual relationship between Nāṣir-i Khusraw and Ghiyāth al-Dīn/Sayyid Suhrāb may have, over the course of centuries, become telescoped within the hagiographical imagination into a discipleship relationship, thereby collapsing the gap in the historical record between Nāṣir's career and the later introduction of the Nizārī *daʿwa* in Badakhshān.

The question of Ghiyāth al-Dīn's identification with or relationship to Sayyid Suhrāb remains at this time a matter of speculation, pending further study and the availability of additional evidence. This matter aside, the association of Ghiyāth al-Dīn's name with the *Ṣaḥīfat al-nāẓirīn* nonetheless stands as a significant fact in its own right, as it allows us to state, with great certainty, that Ghiyāth al-Dīn was, for at least one stage of his career, a proponent of the Ismaili *daʿwa*.[45] While he may not have reached the stature of earlier Ismaili intellectuals such as Naṣīr al-Dīn Ṭūsī or Nāṣir-i Khusraw, he was nonetheless a learned scholar of the Timurid period, writing at a time when the classical tradition of Ismaili scholarship is widely believed to have come to an end. Moreover, being a convert to the Ismaili tradition himself, his career would appear to have echoed that of previous converts who went on to become prominent leaders of the *daʿwa*, to include the two most prestigious *dāʿīs* of the Persian Ismaili tradition, namely Ḥasan-i Ṣabbāḥ and Nāṣir-i Khusraw. Accordingly, future research should be focused on a closer study of his works with an eye towards their relationship with the broader Ismaili literary tradition.

NOTES

* I would like to thank Wafi Momin and Nour Nourmamadchoev of the IIS for their assistance with the manuscripts of the *Ṣaḥīfat al-nāẓirīn* that were consulted for this chapter. I dedicate this chapter to the memory of Qudratbek Elchibekov (1938–2020), who generously shared with me his copies and unsurpassed knowledge of the *Silk-i guhar-rīz*, as well as other manuscript materials used in this chapter.

1 The historical Badakhshān region spans across the territories of present-day eastern Tajikistan and north-eastern Afghanistan, and is closely linked as well with the Gilgit-Baltistan region of northern Pakistan and bordering areas in the Xinjiang province of north-western China.

2 For a general survey of Ismaili history in Central Asia with further references, see Daniel Beben, 'The Ismaili of Central Asia', in *The Oxford Research Encyclopedia of Asian History*, ed. David Ludden (New York, 2018), available online at http://asianhistory.oxfordre.com.

3 On Nāṣir-i Khusraw's *daʿwa* career in Badakhshān and its legacy, see idem., 'Islamisation on the Iranian Periphery: Nasir-i Khusraw and Ismailism in Badakhshān', in

A. C. S. Peacock, ed., *Islamisation: Comparative Perspectives from History* (Edinburgh, 2017), pp. 317–335.

4 On Ghūrid rule in Badakhshān see Minhaj al-Dīn Jūzjānī, *Ṭabaqāt-i Nāṣirī*, ed., ʿAbd al-Ḥayy Ḥabībī, 2 vols. (Kabul, 1342 Sh./1963), vol. 1, pp. 384–392. On Ghūrid opposition to the Ismailis see Clifford E. Bosworth, 'The Early Islamic History of Ghūr,' *Central Asiatic Journal*, 6 (1961), pp. 132–133. Among other things, the Ghūrids patronised the heresiographical work of the Ashʿarī theologian Fakhr al-Dīn al-Rāzī, a fierce critic of the Ismailis who sharply condemned Nāṣir-i Khusraw; see his *Iʿtiqādāt firaq al-muslimīn wa'l-mushrikīn*, ed., Ṭaha ʿAbd al-Rawūf Saʿd and Muṣṭafā al-Hawwārī (Cairo, 1398/1978), p. 122.

5 Rashīd al-Dīn, *Jāmiʿ al-tavārīkh*, tr., Wheeler M. Thackston as *Compendium of Chronicles: A History of the Mongols*, 3 vols. (Cambridge, MA, 1998), vol. 1, p. 250; Ghiyāth al-Dīn Khwāndamīr, *Ḥabīb al-siyar fī akhbār afrād bashar*, tr., W. M. Thackston as *Habibu's-siyar Tome Three: The Reign of the Mongol and the Turk* (London, 2012), p. 44.

6 There has been very little scholarship to date on the history of Badakhshān in this period; see further my discussion in Daniel Beben, *The Legendary Biographies of Nāṣir-i Khusraw: Memory and Textualization in Early Modern Persian Ismāʿīlism* (PhD diss., Indiana University, 2015), pp. 101–113.

7 While we do not have any reliable reports on the exact death date of Nāṣir-i Khusraw, it is clear that he was deceased by 485/1092, when he is referenced in the past tense in the heresiographical work of Abu'l-Maʿālī; see his *Bayān al-adyān*, ed., Abbās Iqbāl Āshtiyānī, Muḥammad Taqī Dānishpazhūh and Muḥammad Dabīr Sīyāqī (Tehran, 1375 Sh./1997), pp. 55–56.

8 I have consulted IIS MS 32 (ff. 22a–25a) and MS 37 (ff. 4b–10a). On the text see also Shafique N. Virani, *The Ismailis in the Middle Ages: A History of Survival, a Search for Salvation* (Oxford, 2007), pp. 86–87. While Virani also quotes an earlier text from the late 13th or early 14th century, the *Alfāẓ-i guharbār*, as containing a reference to Ismailis in Badakhshān, this reference most likely constitutes a later emendation in the manuscript cited by him, as the reference to Badakhshān is missing from all other known manuscripts of the work, including those preserved in Badakhshān. On that basis, we may assume that the reference to Badakhshān was probably not original to the text, as it is inconceivable that a Badakhshāni scribe would have intentionally removed such a reference. See further my discussion in Beben, *The Legendary Biographies of Nāṣir-i Khusraw*, pp. 233–40.

9 On this period, termed the 'Anjudān revival' in contemporary scholarship, see Farhad Daftary, *The Ismāʿīlīs: Their History and Doctrines* (2nd ed., Cambridge, 2007), pp. 422–451; Virani, *Ismailis in the Middle Ages*, pp. 109–132.

10 For accounts of Sulṭān Muḥammad, who was also a respected poet to whom a *dīvān* of poetry is attributed, see Dawlatshāh Samarqandī, *Tadhkirat al-shuʿarā*, ed., Fāṭima ʿAlāqa (Tehran, 1385 Sh./2007), pp. 819–820; Amīn Aḥmad Rāzī, *Tadhkira-i haft iqlīm*, ed., Sayyid Muḥammad Riḍā Ṭāhirī, 3 vols. (Tehran, 1378 Sh./1999), vol. 2, p. 605.

11 On Timurid persecution of Ismailis in Iran see Virani, *Ismailis in the Middle Ages*, pp. 102–105.

12 Mīrzā Muḥammad Ḥaydar Dūghlāt, *Tārīkh-i Rashīdī*, ed., ʿAbbāsqulī Ghaffārī Fard (Tehran, 1283 Sh./2004), pp. 346–347.

13 Sayyid Suhrāb Walī Badakhshānī, *Sī ū shish ṣaḥīfa*, ed., Hūshang Ujāqī and Wladimir Ivanow (Tehran, 1961).

14 The practice of creating handwritten copies from printed editions of Ismaili texts appears to have been rather common in Badakhshān in the Soviet period due to the rarity of these publications, as similarly produced copies are known of other texts as well.

15 Aleksandr A. Semenov, 'Opisanie ismailitskikh rukopiseĭ, sobrannykh A. A. Semenovym', *Izvestiia Rossiĭskoĭ Akademii Nauk* (*Bulletin de l'Académie des Sciences de Russie*) ser. 6, 12 (1918), pp. 2191–2192.

16 Wladimir Ivanow, 'Ismailitskiia rukopisi Aziatskogo Muzeia', *Izvestiia Rossiĭskoĭ Akademii Nauk* (*Bulletin de l'Académie des Sciences de Russie*) ser. 6, 11 (1917), pp. 376–377.

17 N. D. Miklukho-Maklaĭ, *Persidskie i tadzhikskie rukopisi Instituta Narodov Azii: kratkiĭ alfavitnyĭ katalog*, 2 vols. (Moscow, 1964), pp. 356–357.

18 The exception in this regard is Abusaid Shokhumorov, who mentions the attribution of copies of the text to Ghiyāth al-Dīn ʿAlī in his *Razdelenie Badakhshana i sud'by Ismailizma* (Moscow, 2008), p. 27. The earliest scholar to mention Sayyid Suhrāb was Aleksandr Semenov who, based on a series of interviews with Ismailis in Central Asia, noted that there is allegedly a biographical account of Nāṣir-i Khusraw that was authored by a certain Sayyid Suhrāb, who was among the chief disciples of Nāṣir. He mentions that copies of this text were maintained among his descendants in the village of Suchān (located in the Gund valley in present-day Tajik Badakhshān) in his time but were not available to him. See Aleksandr A. Semenov, 'Iz oblasti religioznykh verovaniĭ shugnanskikh ismailitov', *Mir Islama*, 4 (1912), p. 550. The text that Semenov describes here is almost certainly not the *Ṣaḥīfat al-nāẓirīn* but rather the *Silk-i guhar-rīz*, which I will discuss further below. Among the more recent notices on Sayyid Suhrāb and the *Ṣaḥīfat al-nāẓirīn* see Delia Cortese, *Eschatology and Power in Mediaeval Persian Ismailism* (PhD diss., School of Oriental and African Studies, University of London, 1993), pp. 237–242; Farhad Daftary, 'Badakhshānī, Sayyid Suhrāb-i Walī', in *Dānish-nāma-i jahān-i Islām* (Tehran, 1369 Sh./1990), pp. 520–521; idem., *Ismaili Literature: A Bibliography of Sources and Studies* (London, 2004), p. 110; idem., 'Badak̲šāni, Sayyed Sohrāb Wali', *EIr*; Kudratbek Ėl'chibekov, 'Ismailizm na Pamire', in *Istoriia Gorno-Badakhshanskoĭ avtonomnoĭ oblasti*, vol. 1: *s drevneĭshikh vremen do noveĭshego perioda* (Dushanbe, 2005), pp. 455–456; Muṣṭafā Ghālib, *Aʿlām al-Ismāʿīliyya* (Beirut, 1964), pp. 304–305, who erroneously attributes a number of anonymous works mentioned by Ivanow in his survey to Sayyid Suhrāb; Abdulmamad Iloliev, *The Ismāʿīlī-Sufi Sage of Pamir: Mubārak-i Wakhānī and the Esoteric Tradition of the Pamiri Muslims* (Amherst, 2008), pp. 33–34; Wladimir Ivanow, *Ismaili Literature: A Bibliographical Survey* (Tehran, 1963), pp. 163–164; Nourmamadcho Nourmamadchoev, *The Ismāʿīlīs of Badakhshān: History, Politics and Religion from 1500 to 1750* (PhD diss., School of Oriental and African Studies, University of London, 2014), pp. 167–169; Ismail K. Poonawala, *Biobibliography of Ismāʿīlī Literature* (Malibu, CA, 1977), pp. 267–268; Virani, *Ismailis in the Middle Ages*, p. 119. In his survey of Ismaili history, Daftary advances the claim that 'the Nizārīs of Badakhshān did not produce any noteworthy authors after Sayyid Suhrāb Valī Badakhshānī'; see Daftary, *The Ismāʿīlīs*, p. 408.

19 These works are cited on pages 19, 46, and 55 (respectively) of the Ujāqī edition.

20 Beben, *The Legendary Biographies of Nāṣir-i Khusraw*, pp. 344–402. See also Iloliev, *The Ismāʿīlī-Sufi Sage of Pamir*, pp. 27–46. My references herein will be to a typescript prepared for an unpublished edition of the text by Qudratbek Elchibekov.

21 The main biographical narrative of Sayyid Suhrāb is given on pp. 88–94 of Elchibekov's edition.

22 The concept of the *mustawdaʿ*/*mustaqarr* imamate is often evoked in Ismaili sources to address cases where there are two living claimants to imamate. The 'entrusted imam' represents the public face of the imamate and in effect serves as a placeholder for the true or 'established imam', who may be concealed from public view, and from whom the true lineage of imamate is transmitted. For more on this concept see further Virani, *Ismailis in the Middle Ages*, pp. 83–86.

23 Saidjaloli Badakhshī, *Bahr-ul-akhbor*, ed., R. Rahmonqulov (Khorogh, 1992).

24 On these familial traditions see John Mock, 'Shrine Traditions of Wakhan Afghanistan', *Journal of Persianate Studies*, 4 (2011), p. 130; M. Nazif Shahrani, *The Kirghiz and Wakhi of Afghanistan: Adaptation to Closed Frontiers and War* (2nd ed., Seattle, 2002), p. 56.

25 The manuscript was copied on Thursday, 1293 Rabiʿ al-awwal/March–April 1876 by Tashrīf-i Khudā b. Mullā Muḥammad Lāʾiq.

26 *Va ān-rā Ṣaḥīfat al-nāẓirīn nām nahāda shud mushtamal bar sī ū panj ṣaḥīfa bi-tartībī ki dar fihrist qalamī mīshavad* (f. 2a). By comparison, the Ujāqī edition here reads: *va īn risāla mushtamal ast bar sī ū shish ṣaḥīfa ki bi-fihrist gufta khwāhad shud* (p. 1).

27 The section starting the 20th chapter in Ujāqī's edition is preceded in MS BA 59 not by a new chapter heading, but rather simply by the word *tanbīh*, indicating an admonishment to the reader.

28 Andreĭ Bertel's and Mamadvafo Bakoev, *Alfavitnyĭ katalog rukopiseĭ, obnaruzhennykh v Gorno-Badakhshanskoĭ avtonomnoĭ oblasti ėkspeditsieĭ 1959–1963* (Moscow, 1967), pp. 69–71. In his report on the first expedition, Bertel's offered a brief note on the importance of the discovery of these manuscripts and the significance of their attribution to Ghiyāth al-Dīn, as the text was previously known at that time only through the earlier copies collected by Semenov and Zarubin, which were attributed to Sayyid Suhrāb; see Andreĭ Bertel's, 'Nakhodki novykh rukopiseĭ v Tadzhikistane', *Problemy vostokvedeniia*, no. 6 (1959), pp. 222–223.

29 The colophon to this copy is dated 867/1462–1463, which is later than other known copies but still before the Timurid conquest, and includes a note that it was written 'at the request of the inhabitants of Badakhshān.'

30 Two other copies in this collection (1959/24v and 1959/7v) are defective in the beginning and hence lack information on the attribution of the work.

31 In his introduction to Ujāqī's edition (p. 9), Ivanow notes, 'Although local tradition preserves its title as "Ṣaḥīfatu'n-Nāẓirīn", this apparently, is never found in known copies.' This remark demonstrates that Ivanow was unaware of the second redaction bearing this title. The title *Tuḥfat al-nāẓirīn* does not appear in any of the manuscripts that I have examined, although it evidently appeared in at least one of the copies consulted by Qudratullāh Beg for his edition.

32 Edward G. Browne, *A Catalogue of the Persian Manuscripts in the Library of the University of Cambridge* (Cambridge, 1896), pp. 219–220 (#133).

33 I have examined MS Per 491 from the collection of the Wellcome Institute in London. The author's name is given here as Ghiyāth al-Dīn ʿAlī b. Amīrān al-Ḥusaynī al-Iṣfahānī. For the catalogue description see Fatemeh Keshavarz, *A Descriptive and Analytical Catalogue of Persian Manuscripts in the Library of the Wellcome Institute for the History of Medicine* (London, 1986), pp. 386–387, with references to MSS in other collections listed therein. On the dating and dedication of the text, see Wladimir Ivanow, 'The Date of the *Dānish-nāma-i-jahān*', *Journal of the Royal Asiatic Society of Great Britain and Ireland*, no. 1 (1927), pp. 95–96. On the work, see also Lutz Richter-Bernburg, 'Medical and Veterinary Sciences. Part One: Medicine, Pharmacology and Veterinary Science in Islamic Eastern Iran and Central Asia', in M. S. Asimov and C. E. Bosworth, ed., *History of Civilizations of Central Asia*, vol. 4, part 2: *The Age of Achievements: A.D. 750 to the End of the Fifteenth Century* (Paris, 1998), p. 314.

34 Charles A. Storey, *Persian Literature: A Bio-bibliographical Survey*, vol. 2.1 (London, 1958), pp. 10–11.

35 Ibid., p. 75.

36 A manuscript of this text was copied by Shāhzāda Muḥammad b. Farrukhshāh in 1925 and was used as the basis for a Cyrillic-script edition of the work prepared by Umed Mamadsherzodshoev, published in Khorogh in 1995. On the use of this text in local Pamiri calendar systems see Karim-Aly Kassam, Umed Bulbulshoev, and Morgan Ruelle, 'Ecology of Time: Calendar of the Human Body in the Pamir Mountains', *Journal of Persianate Studies*, 4 (2011), pp. 146–170.

37 In the United States National Library of Medicine there is preserved a short and apparently undated treatise attributed to Ghiyāth al-Dīn on the topic of foodstuffs (https://www.nlm.nih.gov/hmd/arabic/bioG.html; accessed 22 December 2020), while a manuscript in the library of the School of Oriental and African Studies in London (Phillott collection MS 46482) contains a treatise authored by him on falconry titled

Bāz-nāma. This work was composed in 859/1455 and hence predates the Timurid conquest of Badakhshān (http://www.fihrist.org.uk/profile/work/ff921eb7-af9a-4607-b317-d3704825cf7b; accessed 22 December 2020).

38 On the intellectual circles of the Pārsā family and the Naqshbandiyya in 15th-century Central Asia, see Jürgen Paul, 'The Khwājagān at Herat during Shāhrukh's Reign', in İlker Evrim Binbaş and Nurten Kılıç-Schubel, ed., *Horizons of the World: Festschrift for İsenbike Togan* (Istanbul, 2011), pp. 217–250; Maria E. Subtelny, 'The Making of *Bukhārā-yi Sharīf*: Scholars, Books, and Libraries in Medieval Bukhara (The Library of Khwāja Muḥammad Pārsā)', in Devin DeWeese, ed., *Studies on Central Asian History in Honor of Yuri Bregel* (Bloomington, 2001), pp. 79–111.

39 On the career of Nāṣir al-Dīn Ṭūsī and his shifting communal affiliations, see Farhad Daftary, 'Nasir al-Din al-Tusi and the Ismailis', in his *Ismailis in Medieval Muslim Societies* (London, 2005), pp. 171–182.

40 On the practice of pseudo-attribution in the Ismaili tradition, see further my discussion in 'The *Kalām-i pīr* and Its Place in the Central Asian Ismaʿili Tradition', *Journal of Islamic Studies*, 31 (2020), pp. 70–102.

41 This phenomenon of competition between saintly lineages, often entailing the 'forging' or pseudo-attribution of texts, is well attested across Central Asia and the Islamic world in this period; for one example see Devin DeWeese, 'The Politics of Sacred Lineages in 19th-Century Central Asia: Descent Groups Linked to Khwaja Ahmad Yasavi in Shrine Documents and Genealogical Charters', *International Journal of Middle East Studies*, 31 (1999), pp. 507–530.

42 The discourse covers pp. 78–85 of Elchibekov's edition.

43 This assertion is based on an analysis of eight distinct genealogical texts connected with Sayyid Suhrāb found in private collections in Tajikistan and Afghanistan that have been identified as part of an ongoing research project on genealogical traditions in Badakhshān. To these texts we may also add the lineage descending from Sayyid Suhrāb presented in the aforementioned *Silk-i guhar-rīz*. By back dating from the latest figure mentioned in each of these genealogies and assuming generational gaps of 25–30 years, we can posit birth dates for Sayyid Suhrāb ranging from the mid-14th to the mid-15th century, with the majority clustered around the year 1400. None of the genealogical sources identified thus far suggest a plausible birth date for Sayyid Suhrāb prior to the 14th century. Hence, while the details of these genealogical records are impossible to verify historically, at the very least it is obvious that they were not fabricated for the purpose of depicting Sayyid Suhrāb as a contemporary of Nāṣir-i Khusraw. These genealogical records will be examined in detail in a forthcoming book, *Ismailism in Badakhshān: A Genealogical History*, co-authored with Jo-Ann Gross. Meanwhile, see my preliminary discussion in Beben, *The Legendary Biographies of Nāṣir-i Khusraw*, pp. 376–384.

44 One example of such narrative 'replacement' might be seen in the case of Baba Tükles, a legendary Sufi figure who is credited in the oral traditions of many Central Asian peoples with the conversion to Islam of Özbek Khān (r. 1313–1341), the Mongol ruler of the Golden Horde. As Devin DeWeese has demonstrated, the name Baba Tükles probably represents a mythologised form of a historical figure from the Yasavī Sufi tradition by the name of Sayyid Ata. See Devin DeWeese, *Islamization and Native Religion in the Golden Horde: Baba Tükles and Conversion to Islam in Historical and Epic Tradition* (University Park, 1994).

45 As this chapter was being finalised for publication I received access to additional folios of IIS MS 15095, in which was discovered a previously unknown text attributed to Ghiyāth al-Dīn Iṣfahānī, titled *Hidāyat al-ṭālibīn*. The text is an apologetic work in support of the Ismaili position in relation to the claims of other branches of Shiʿi Islam. While the discovery of this work has no immediate bearing on the matter of the authorship of the *Ṣaḥīfat al-nāẓirīn*, it does provide further evidence of Ghiyāth al-Dīn's

commitment to the Ismaili *daʿwa*. The work may postdate the composition of the *Ṣaḥīfat al-nāẓirīn*, as it is not among the texts cited within it, although it is unclear if it preceded the Timurid conquest of Badakhshān. It is also worthy of note that in the manuscript this work immediately follows the text of a known work titled *Irshād al-ṭālibīn*, dedicated to a defence of the rival Muḥammad-Shāhī line of Nizārī imams, which was composed prior to 915/1509. On this text see Virani, *Ismailis in the Middle Ages*, pp. 77–81. While the author's name is not listed in any of the known copies of this work, the similarities between the titles and content raise the possibility that Ghiyāth al-Dīn may have also been responsible for composing the *Irshād al-ṭālibīn*. I intend to explore further this newly discovered text and its relationship with the *Irshād al-ṭālibīn* in a future study.

16

The Seven Pillars of the Sharīʿa and the Question of Authority in Central Asian Ismaili Manuscripts: An Ismaili Esoteric Discourse

Yahia Baiza

The study of Central Asian Ismaili manuscripts is a relatively new and less explored academic area. These manuscripts rarely feature in modern Ismaili and non-Ismaili scholarly works. Most of them are collections (*majmūʿa*) of treatises and contain a wide variety of themes, such as the Ismaili interpretations of the *sharīʿa*, the Sufi-Ismaili hybrid gnostic texts, devotional poetry, religious education, and religious mythology. This chapter analyses one of the most copied treatises called the *Seven Pillars of the Sharīʿa*, which appears across numerous manuscripts. The presented discussions explore how the examined treatises offer an Ismaili interpretation of the pillars of the *sharīʿa*, in what ways they conceptualise and articulate the notion of authority and mediate it between the text and the members of the community; how the texts of the *Seven Pillars of the Sharīʿa* form and inform the identity of the targeted audience; and what kind of latent and manifest messages the texts convey to their audience. The chapter begins with a concise codicological analysis of the manuscripts in which the treatises are copied, followed by a discussion on the concept of *taʾwīl* in the Ismaili esoteric tradition, and finishes with a detailed analysis of the *Seven Pillars of the Sharīʿa*.

Codicological Analysis

Codicology is an important part of manuscript analysis. It deals with various physical aspects of a text, such as the examination of materials, tools, techniques, ornamentation, pagination, inks, scribes and scripts, and colophon, to name a few. This study also pays attention to the codicology of the examined manuscripts and the concerned treatises. The term codicology and codicological analysis have a broad range of implications. The analysis of a codex, for instance, could vary from a sophisticated scientific examination of the material used for the production of a given codex to the systematic observation of the above-mentioned physical properties of texts.[1] This study is not concerned with a scientific examination of the material because the author has access to digitized copies of the manuscripts only since the originals of most of the copies are held in Khorogh, the capital of Gorno-Badakhshān Autonomous Oblast[2] (GBAO) of Tajikistan.

Codicology is an important aspect of understanding manuscripts. It reveals various key features and aspects of a manuscript, such as a provenance, the time during which a treatise/manuscript was produced and completed, and whether the examined manuscript is an original work or a recent copy. Between the years 2016 and 2018, as part of joint research projects between the Ismaili Special Collections Unit and the Central Asian Studies Unit of The Institute of Ismaili Studies, this author conducted a rigorous codicological analysis of nine manuscripts: MS BT 4, MS BT 7, MS BT 17, MS BT 25, MS BT 34, MS BT 59, MS BT 157, MS BT 189, and MS BT 265. Of these, except MS BT 34 and MS BT 189, all other seven manuscripts contained the treatise of the *Seven Pillars of the Sharīʿa*. Instead of engaging in a full codicological analysis of these nine manuscripts, this chapter uses the space in the following sections to present a concise codicological analysis of the concerned treatises so that the readers get the gist of the complexities and nuances surrounding the manuscripts and the examined treatises.

Overview

Each examined manuscript is a collection of independent treatises. The treatises of the *Seven Pillars of the Sharīʿa* are handwritten texts. The sizes (height and width) of the treatises and their folios are not known. A ruler marked in millimetres is an important part of the digitization process and perhaps the most important tool in the kit for measuring a manuscript's dimensions. However, the digitization process misses placing a ruler with a millimetre scale along the vertical

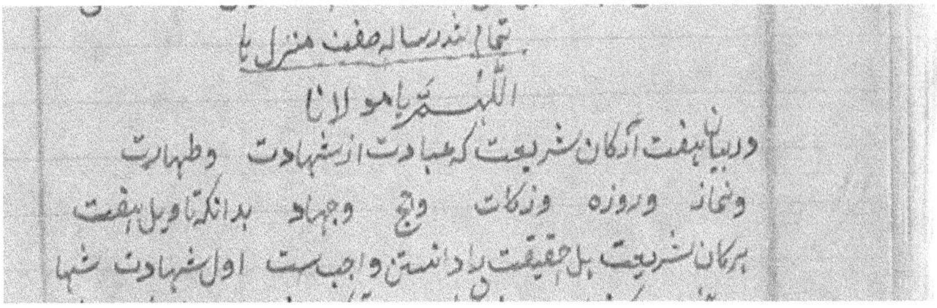
در بیان هفت ارکان شریعت که عبادت از شهادت و طهارت
و نماز و روزه و زکات و حج و جهاد بدانکه اول هفت
ارکان شریعت بل حقیقت یاد داشتن واجب است اول شهادت شها

Figure 16.1 An example of the material used for the manuscripts (MS BT 7, f. 13).

and horizontal lengths of the manuscript's cover pages and the first folio. Therefore, it is not possible to comment on the size of the folios.

The material of all nine manuscripts is made of ordinary papers, produced in a modern stationery factory (see Figure 16.1). The texts are written horizontally from right to the left in black colour. The papers are either plain, horizontal lined or, sometimes, squared. The number of lines on each folio varies between 13 and 18, depending on the size of the folio and the scribe's style of writing. The length of treatises varies between three to five folios. The manuscripts do not follow a single pagination style. In some, pagination is in Persian numerals at the top centre of each folio, while others are not paginated.

Copyists often decorate pages, particularly when the codex has religious importance, such as the Qur'ān and/or any other sacred texts, or texts that generally deal with subjects that are important. The design and style of decorations could be abstract geometrical figures, botanical elements, or architecturally inspired images. The examined treatises do not have any noticeable decorations. The absence of even simple geometrical shapes suggests that the copyists were primarily interested in the subject and the content of the treatise. Also, it suggests that the copyists were neither professionals nor had rich and wealthy patrons.

The scribes create margins (see Figure 16.2), without using them for writing additional notes. It appears as if they are to protect the texts from the gradual erosion of the paper, the effect of fingers turning the folios, and damage caused by water (see Figure 16.3). In the examined manuscripts, the margins are rarely used for commentaries. The only systematic use of the margins the copyists make is the use of the space at the bottom left corner of the verso folio (reading from right to left),

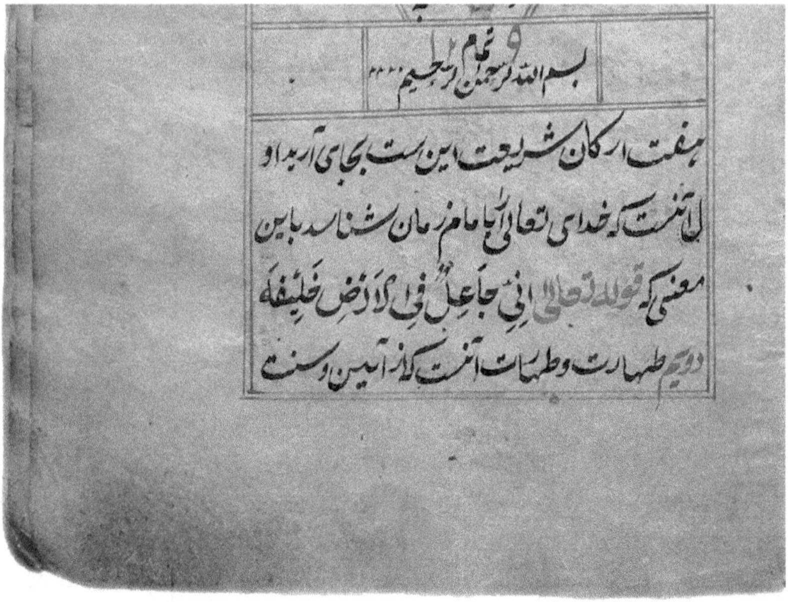

Figure 16.2 An example of margins (MS BT 157, f. 39).

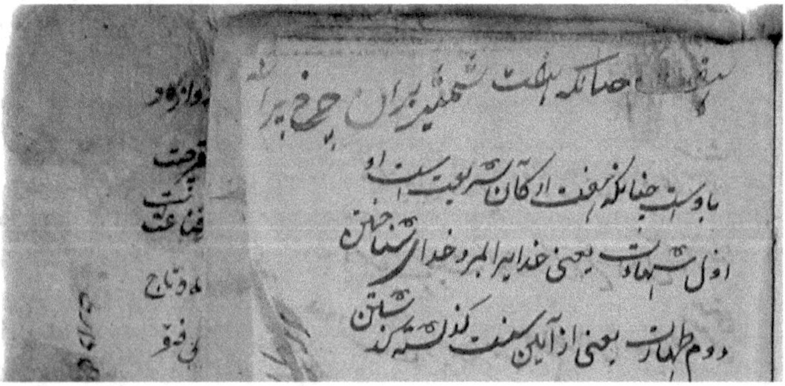

Figure 16.3 Example of gradual erosion (MS BT 25, f. 89).

where the copyists write the first word of the first sentence of the recto folio.

The colophon is another important component of a manuscript. Commonly, the author/copyist writes his name and the date and place he completed the manuscript. Sometimes, it is also possible that the author/scribe writes his name on the cover page, the flyleaf, or in the

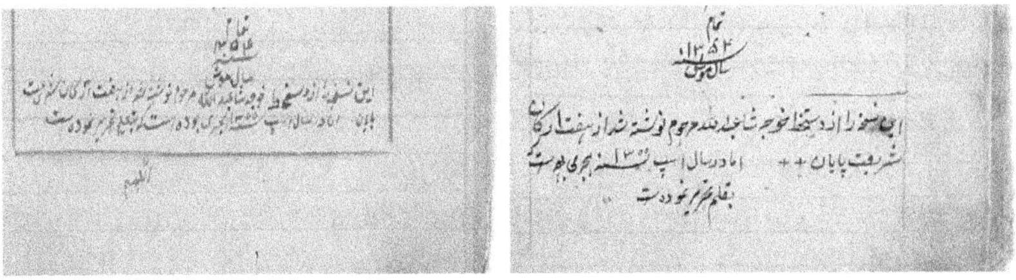

Figure 16.4 MS BT 7, f. 31 (left) and MS BT 17, f. 29 (right).

initial parts of a text. This author has carefully checked all these possibilities for finding useful information about the original author or copyist. In the case of this study, colophons do include names, without specifying whether they are of the original author who penned the manuscript, or they relate to the copyist. Therefore, it is not possible to make a definitive conclusion about the identity of the names that appear in the colophon.

The above colophons (see Figure 16.4) reveal similar information about the treatise of the *Seven Pillars of the Sharīʿa*. A careful analysis of the styles of the writings reveals that the two manuscripts are the works of two different copyists. The two colophons consist of two identical parts and require careful reading, interpretation, and calculation and conversion of lunar, Gregorian and Chinese calendars.

The first part gives the completion date of the examined treatises. It reads: 'completed in the year 1354, the year of the Rat' (*tamām, 1354, sāl-e mūsh*). The year of the Rat refers to the Chinese zodiac symbol. However, the colophons do not specify the month or the day when the manuscripts were completed. Although scribes and writers were customarily using the lunar *hijrī* calendar in their colophons, these do not specify whether the given year corresponds to the lunar or solar *hijrī* year. In this regard, the Chinese zodiac symbol of the year, which is used in many of the examined Persian Central Asian Ismaili manuscripts, helps to clarify the situation. The conversion and calculation of differences between lunar, solar, and Chinese years prove that the year of the Rat 1354 relates to the lunar *hijrī* calendar. Also, it is worth noting that not the entire year of 1354 is the year of the Rat. A further calculation helps to specify the possible time range when the manuscript was penned. Since the Chinese Zodiac year of the Rat starts on 29 Shawwāl 1354, the examined treatises were copied sometimes between 29 Shawwāl and 30 Dhū al-Ḥijja 1354, which corresponds to 24 January–24 March, 1936 of the Gregorian calendar. Hence, one can safely claim that the examined treatises were copied from an original text during the months of Dhū al-Qaʿda and Dhū al-Ḥijja of 1354/25 January–24 March, 1936.

The second part of the two colophons relates to the original copy of the text and provides a name and an additional calendar year. It reads: 'this text (*nuskhah*) is copied from the late Khūjah Shāh ʿAbd Allāh's handwritten text of the *Seven Pillars of the Sharīʿa*, end (*pāyān*). But it was penned in the year 1300 of the Chinese zodiac year of the Horse' (MS BT 7, f. 31; MS BT 17, f. 21). To write the year, all examined manuscripts use Persian numerals. The years written in these two colophons, as has already been examined, are in lunar *hijrī*. The word 'Khūjah', which also spelled as 'Khwājah', is an honorific religious title, often used for a Sufi teacher. It suggests that Shāh ʿAbd Allāh was a local religious teacher. The exact day and month in which Khūjah Shāh ʿAbd Allāh penned the manuscript remain unknown. The colophon does not tell us the date of Shāh ʿAbd Allāh's death. However, it does suggest that he died after 1882–1883. It is important to note that the copyist writes the year 1300 in an unusual numerical style, which can also be read as 1355 (۱۳۵۵). However, the size of the last two digits is larger than zero (۰) and smaller than five (۵). From this author's analysis perspective, the given year is 1300 and not 1355. The obvious reason for rejecting 1355 as a possible date is that the unknown copyist, as analysed in the first part of the colophon, finished copying the manuscript in 1354, meaning that the original work itself, belonging to Khūjah Shāh ʿAbd Allāh, could have not been written a year later in 1355. Also, the mentioned size of the last two digits, larger than zero and smaller than five, is probably because the original author did not want his readers to mistake zero for a dot (۰) nor for five. Besides, the Zodiac animal symbol for the year 1355 is Ox and not Horse. Therefore, the correct reading of the year in the colophon is 1300, which is also the year of the Horse. Again, the tradition of adding the Chinese zodiac animal symbol plays an important role in resolving the ambiguity. Thus, it can safely be claimed that Khūjah Shāh ʿAbd Allāh penned the original copy of the treatise sometime between 1 Muḥarram and 29 Rabī al-Awwal 1300/12 November 1882–7 February, 1883. The presented analysis is the maximum limit one could discern from the two colophons.

To conclude, these presented codicological discussions show some of the complexities and nuances involved in the study of manuscripts in general and the Central Asian Ismaili manuscripts in particular. The presented analysis of the colophons also demonstrates the importance of codicology in decoding complex issues for which there is often no other way of finding a solution. The discussions also demonstrate that a correct understanding of the texts often requires a meticulous reading and analysis of more than one manuscript as one cannot solely rely on a single manuscript for making a definitive conclusion. In analyzing the treatise of the *Seven Pillars of the Sharīʿa*, this author read and compared the texts across all treatises.

The Concept of *Taʾwīl* in the Ismaili Esoteric Tradition

In exploring and analyzing the texts of the examined treatises, it is vital to define and explain the concept of *taʾwīl* in the Ismaili tradition, which provides the intellectual context and space for the articulation of the Ismaili-specific pillars of the *sharīʿa*. This section demonstrates why the science of *taʾwīl* occupies an important position in the Ismaili thought, and how Ismaili *dāʿīs* (summoners) and scholars used to apply it as an intellectual tool to understand and interpret the Qurʾān, the Prophetic traditions, and the *sharīʿa*. The Ismailis have developed a very systematic approach to the esoteric interpretation of the Qurʾān. The key canonical works on the subject were developed during the Fatimid empire (296–567/909–1171). Linguistically, *taʾwīl* (pl. *taʾwīlāt*, to interpret and explain something) is a verbal noun, derived from the second form *awwala* of the root verb *awl* (to bring something back to its source, origin, i.e. to its beginning (*awwal*). The science of *taʾwīl* is an esoteric interpretation that primarily concerns the inner meaning of the Qurʾānic words and verses.

The term *taʾwīl* appears 17 times in the Qurʾān and implies a variety of meanings. Generally, it means interpretation and explanation of the meaning of words, events, or something that is not predictable and explainable by the simple faculty of the human mind. For example, in Chapter 3, verse 7, the Qurʾānic concept of *taʾwīl* refers to the true understanding of the divine scripture (*al-kitāb*). In this verse, the phrase, *wa mā yaʿla-mu taʾwīla-hu illā Allāh-u waʾr rāsikhūn fiʾl ʿilm* (and no one knows its true meaning except Allah and those firmly established in knowledge) (Qur'ān, 3:7). This verse links the term *ta'wīl* with the correct and true interpretation of the divine scripture, *al-kitāb*. In Chapter 12, verses 6, 21, 36, 37, 44, 45, 100–101; and Chapter 18, verses 78 and 82, the term *ta'wīl* refers to 'interpretation of events and dreams' (*ta'wīl al-aḥādīth*), whereas in Chapter 4, verse 59 and Chapter 10, verse 39, the term *ta'wīl* is associated with 'forewarning of an event'. In Chapter 17, verse 35, the term refers to reaching pleasant or fairer results (*aḥsan-u ta'wīlan*), particularly by way of doing something good and just. Since *ta'wīl*, as shall be further explored in this section, is primarily applied to the divine scripture, the term has been understood as tracing the meaning of words to their origin through esoteric interpretation.

The Qur'ān contains both clear and allegorical verses. It refers to the former as *muḥkamāt* (firm in meaning) and describes them as the principal verses (*umm al-kitāb*), and to the latter as *mutashābihāt* (allegorical). Even though it is being revealed in a clear Arabic language (*bi-lisānin ʿarabiyyin mubīn*) (Qur'ān, 26:195) and is a 'clarification of everything' (*tibyānan li-kulli shay*) (Qur'ān, 16:89), the Qur'ānic concept of *ta'wīl* inspired many different intellectual movements and schools in Islam. Each school, from traditionalist, theologist, and jurists to rationalist, mystic, and Shiʿi, developed their own approaches to *ta'wīl*. As a result, many interpretations and explanations of the divine scripture emerged throughout history. Among these different schools, the Ismaili interpretation of Islam developed its science of *ta'wīl*. The need for understanding the true meaning of allegorical verses was the key reason for the rise of all these different *ta'wīlic* approaches. Al-Qāḍī al-Nuʿmān (d. 363/974), the Fatimid chief jurist (*qāḍī al-quḍāt*) and chief *dāʿī* (*dāʿī al-duʿāt*), developed canonical works on the theory of the Ismaili science of *ta'wīl*.[3] On the science of *ta'wīl*, especially the true meaning of allegorical verses about which the Qur'ān states that 'no one knows its true meaning except Allah and those firmly established in knowledge' (Qur'ān, 3:7), al-Qāḍī al-Nuʿmān asserts that the knowledge of *ta'wīl* is the exclusive authority of the Prophet Muḥammad and his successors,[4] i.e. the Ismaili imams of the time. He further elaborates on the concept of *ta'wīl* in his *Tarbiyat al-mū'minīn* (*The Upbringing of the Believers*), better known as the *Ta'wīl daʿā'im al-Islām*,[5] and *Asās al-ta'wīl* (*The Foundation of Ta'wīl*).[6] These works laid the foundation for the Ismaili science of *ta'wīl*, which was then further elaborated and developed by the Ismaili *dāʿīs* and scholars, namely Abū Yaʿqūb al-Sijistānī (d. *ca.* 360/971), Ḥamīd al-Dīn al-Kirmānī (d. 412/1021), al-Mu'ayyad fī'l-Dīn al-Shīrāzī (d. 470/1078) and Nāṣir Khusraw (d. 469/1077 or 486/1093), Naṣīr al-Dīn Ṭūsī (d. 673/1274), and ʿAbd al-Karīm al-Shahrastānī (d. 553/1158), to name a few.

The exoteric tradition often relies on the science of *tafsīr* (pl. *tafāsīr*), whereas the esoteric tradition, especially the Ismailis, employ the science of *ta'wīl*. In al-Shahrastānī's discussion,[7] the closest equivalent to *ta'wīl* is *tafsīr*. On the definition and difference between the two, he states that '*tafsīr*' is the verbal noun from the second form '*fassara*' (the explanation, the commentary, and interpretation of something) of the verb '*fasara*', which means to manifest and to explain something, whereas '*ta'wīl*', from the lexicographers' (*ahl al-lugha*) viewpoint, is derived from *awl*, which means 'returning' or 'going back' (*rujūʿ*) to the origin.[8] Sayyid Suhrāb Walī-Badakhshānī, a 15th-century Ismaili author from Badakhshān, also defines *ta'wīl* as returning something to its origin, by way of returning an expression or an utterance (*qawl*) to its inner meaning (*bāṭin*) and truth (*ḥaqīqat*).[9] While al-Shahrastānī presents a variety of meaning that exegetes and lexicographers attach to both terms, and those meanings often are close to, than different from, each other. However, al-Shahrastānī's understanding of the terms is that *tafsīr* refers to the meaning of words as they are expressed, whereas *ta'wīl* is about taking the meaning of a word back to the original meaning or intention of the speaker, a quality that cannot be attributed to *tafsīr*.[10] Other Ismaili scholars and *dāʿīs* have a similar position and standing on the concept of *ta'wīl*.

From the Ismaili tradition's perspective, the divine revelation (*tanzīl*) has an exoteric (*ẓāhir*) and an esoteric (*bāṭin*) dimension. The comprehension of the former is possible by ordinary human beings, so long as the person is well versed in the Arabic language and grammar. By contrast, the latter is hidden from the ordinary people. This understanding could be viewed across the work of all Ismaili *dāʿīs*. In his works, al-Sijistānī often engaged himself with the esoteric dimension of the divine revelation.[11] Al-Kirmānī also viewed *ta'wīl* as a science of the inner meaning of the divine revelation. He states that everything apparent by its nature, like the universe and everything within it, could be found by human senses; whereas those things that are not apparent by their nature, like the hereafter, or the necessity of the creator (God), could only be found by the power of the intellect and knowledge.[12] He argues that the external dimension of the divine scripture is concerned with actions related to the religious tenets or law (the *sharīʿa*); whereas *ta'wīl* refers to the hidden meanings of the words and actions, such as God's oneness (*tawḥīd*), reward (*ṣawāb*), punishment (*ʿiqāb*), and everything whose existence is not apparent to the senses.[13] Thus these viewpoints demonstrate that the Ismaili scholars believe that the divine revelations embed both exoteric and esoteric dimensions, and *ta'wīl* is an intellectual exercise through which one can unveil the esoteric depth of the divine scripture and message.

The Ismaili *dāʿīs* and scholars also view *ta'wīl* and *tanzīl* as two interdependent, and yet correlated and complementary components of the divine message and prophetic wisdom. They apply *ta'wīl* as a necessary means to penetrate the depth of the divine wisdom and Prophetic traditions. Nāṣir Khusraw defines *ta'wīl* as the inner meaning of the word. He states that words (*lafẓ-hā*) of the Qur'ān are different from each other in the same way as the *sharīʿas* of different prophets are different from one another. The *sharīʿas* are like human bodies which are different from each other and their conditions (*ḥālāt*) change over time. However, the meaning of the divine scriptures and the esoteric interpretation of the prophets' *sharīʿas* are similar to each other, because their *ta'wīl* or esoteric meanings is constant. Therefore, the word (*lafẓ*) is associated with the revelation (*tanzīl*), whereas the esoteric interpretation (*ta'wīl*) is related to the hidden meaning of the divine word.[14] Hence, Nāṣir Khusraw suggests that *tanzīl* and *ta'wīl* remain interdependent as body and soul.

In the Alamūt era (1090–1256), the Ismaili *dāʿīs* viewed the office of imamate as encompassing both *ta'wīl* and *tanzīl*. Naṣīr al-Dīn Ṭūsī's writing suggests that revelation and *ta'wīl* are not only interdependent and complementary to each other, but they also reach their perfection in the era of imamate, to differentiate it from the era of the Prophet. He states that the imam stands at the commencement of the cycle of perfection (*dawr-e kamāl*) and his office encompasses both the origin (*mabdaʿ*) and perfection (*kamāl*).[15] For Ṭūsī, the imam is the perfector of religion or the divine guidance, as he leads things (divine guidance) back to their origin through his knowledge and divine mandate of *ta'wīl*, which Ṭūsī defines as 'restoring things to their origin (*radd al-shay' illā awwalihi*)'.[16] He further refers to a saying of the Prophet that 'if the world were to be devoid of the imam of the time for even an hour (*sāʿah*) the world and its inhabitants would perish'.[17] According to this statement, the Ismailis believe that both the imam and the *ta'wīl* shall exist together until the Day of Judgement—a time by which God's religion and guidance reach its perfection.

The Seven Pillars of the Sharīʿa

The science and concept of *ta'wīl*, as discussed above, stand at the heart of the Ismaili esoteric interpretation of the *sharīʿa* and the Qur'ān. From the Ismaili viewpoint, the daily ritualistic practices, the sum of which is articulated in what is known as the pillars of the *sharīʿa* (*arkān-e sharīʿa*) or the pillars of Islam (*arkān-e Islām*), embed subtle esoteric meanings that can only be discerned through *ta'wīlic* interpretation. While the Sunni exoteric tradition recognizes five pillars for the *sharīʿa*,[18] the Ismaili tradition, as presented in al-Qāḍī al-Nuʿmān's *Daʿā'im al-Islām* (*The Pillars of Islam*), includes seven pillars, namely (i) *wilāya* (ii) *ṭahāra* (iii) *ṣalāt* (iv) *zakāt* (v) *ṣawm* (vi) *ḥajj* and (vii) *jihād*.[19] The pillar of *wilāya* is a fundamental doctrinal and conceptual theme in al-Qāḍī al-Nuʿmān's pillars of the *sharīʿa* as well as in the Ismaili concept of *ta'wīl*. Referring to the importance of this pillar, al-Qāḍī al-Nuʿmān states that 'the *wilāya* is the highest pillar because it is through *walī* (friend, authority, and guardian) that one can attain the knowledge (*maʿrifa*) of other pillars'.[20] In the Ismaili conception of succession to the Prophet, the term *walī* refers to the Ismaili imam of the time and the term *wilāya* (authority and guardianship) is a reference to the office of imamate.

Ṭūsī's *Maṭlūb al-mū'minīn* (*Desideratum of the Faithful*) also includes a treatise on the seven pillars of the *sharīʿa*, *Dar bayān-e haft arkān-e sharīʿat wa ta'wīl ān* (*On the Explanation of the Seven Pillars of the Sharīʿa and its Ta'wīl*). In this treatise, he names the same seven pillars, namely (i) *shahādat* (ii) *ṭahārat* (iii) *namāz* (*ṣalāt*) (iv) *rūzah* (*ṣawm*) (v) *zakāt* (vi) *jihād*, and (vii) *ḥajj*.[21] In Ṭūsī's treatise, the seven pillars start with *shahādat* and not the *wilāya* as it appears in al-Qāḍī al-Nuʿmān's *Daʿā'im*. However, the content of Ṭūsī's *shahāda* is very much the same as the essence of al-Qāḍī al-Nuʿmān's pillar of *wilāya*, with an exception that al-Qāḍī al-Nuʿmān book of *wilāya* is a very detailed discussion surrounding the concept of imamate, whereas Ṭūsī's concept of *shahāda* is just one sentence long. The Central Asian Ismaili manuscripts, which contain Seven Pillars of the *sharīʿa*, and is analyzed and discussed in the next section, follow Ṭūsī's work and not that of al-Qāḍī al-Nuʿmān. The simple reason for that is that the Ismailis of Central Asia had better access to Ṭūsī's works, which were written in Persian Darī, as compared to al-Qāḍī al-Nuʿmān's *The Pillars of Islam*, written in Arabic. The following sections analyse and discuss the esoteric interpretation of the seven pillars of the *sharīʿa* as they appear in the treatise of *Bāb dar bayān-e haft arkān-e sharīʿat* (*A Chapter on the Seven Pillars of the Sharīʿa*), better known as the *Seven Pillars of the Sharīʿa* or simply *Seven Pillars* (*Haft arkān*).

As a brief note on the use of Arabic and Persian Darī terms, all key terms that are directly taken from the examined manuscripts follow Persian Darī spelling and transliteration, such as '*namāz*' (prayer, in Persian Darī) instead of *ṣalāt* (in Arabic), or '*shahādat*' (testimony, Persian Darī) instead of *shahāda* (Arabic). However, when a term is not directly taken from the examined manuscripts, it is written in Arabic transliteration, such as *sharīʿa* and not *sharīʿat* (in Persian Darī).

1. Testimony (*shahādat*)

This first pillar, the *shahādat*, is generally viewed as the foundation of Islam. The declaration of the twin testimony (*shahādatayn*) *Lā ilāha illā Allāh* (There is no God, but Allāh) and *Muḥammad Rasūl Allāh* (Muhammad is the Messenger of Allah) testifies the monotheist nature and message of Islam and establishes the root origin of the Prophet Muhammad's prophetic authority. In the exoteric realm of the *sharīʿa*, anyone who pronounces the testimony, to accept Islam as his/her faith, is a Muslim, regardless of his/her theological and jurisprudential standing, and the rituals he/she practices daily.

The esoteric *ta'wīl* of the text is primarily concerned with the inner meaning of the testimony, and not a mere repetition of it by the tongue. The text of the treatise states that it is necessary for the people of the truth (*ahl-e ḥaqīqat*) to know that the true understanding of *shahādat* is possible only through the knowledge of the imām of the time. The text adds that people ought to know that reaching the spiritual status of being consciously aware of the knowledge (*maʿrifat*) of God is only possible through the knowledge and recognition of the imam of the time (MS BT 4, ff. 33–34). Therefore, a true understanding of *shahādat*, namely the denial (*nafī*) part, saying that 'there is no God' (*lā ilāha*), and the affirmation (*ithbāt*) part, stating that 'but Allāh' (*illā Allāh*), is possible only through the teaching of the imam of the time (MS BT 4, ff. 33–34).

In the view of the examined treatises, a simple declaration by the tongue is not sufficient to understand the true meaning of the testimony. The treatise in MS BT 7 explains that the declaration of the testimony itself does not make a person a Muslim in the true sense of the word (MS BT 7, f. 13). To attain the true meaning of *shahādat*, one needs instructional guidance so that s/he can disavow (*tabarāʾ*) the falsehood (*bāṭil*) and accept (*tawalā*) the truth (*ḥaqīqat*). The denial part (*nafī*) is a general statement, whereas the acceptance (*ithbāt*) part is a special confession and acceptance of the command of God, whose house is the imam of the time (MS BT 7, ff. 13–14). Accordingly, the true knowledge of God and the correct understanding of *shahādat* is possible only through the teaching of the imam of the time.

Comparing '*shahāda*' with that of '*wilāya*' in al-Qāḍī al-Nuʿmān's *Pillars of Religion*, the concept of *shahāda* in the Ismaili esoteric interpretation of the *sharīʿa* is not limited to *shahādatayn* (*tawḥīd* and *nubuwwa*). Rather, it also includes the recognition and acceptance of the office of *wilāya* or the authority of the imam of the time. In Shiʿi tradition of Islam, the office of *wilāya* starts with the imamate of ʿAlī ibn Abī Ṭālib, the Prophet's cousin and son-in-law, and the fourth caliph of Islam (r. 656–661). The doctrine of *wilāya* or imamate in the Shiʿi Ismaili Nizārī interpretation of Islam differs from other Shiʿi groups. The Ismailis believe in the living and present hereditary imam of the time, who is a direct descendent of the Prophet Muhammad, through the lineage of Fāṭima (the Prophet's daughter) and ʿAlī ibn Abī Ṭālib. His Highness the Aga Khan, the 49th living hereditary imam of the Shiʿi Imāmī Ismaili Muslims, explained the position of the Ismaili imamate at the Parliament of Canada in the following words:

> The Sunni position is that the Prophet nominated no successor, and that spiritual-moral authority belongs to those who are

> learned in matters of religious law. As a result, there are many Sunni imams in a given time and place. But others believed that the Prophet had designated his cousin and son-in-law, Ali, as his successor. From that early division, a host of further distinctions grew up—but the question of rightful leadership remains central. In time, the Shia were also sub-divided over this question, so that today the Ismailis are the only Shia community who, throughout history, have been led by a living, hereditary Imam in direct descent from the Prophet.[22]

As the above statement explains the office of *wilāya* or imamate is the most important pillar in the Ismaili tradition and the single most important authority that guides the community throughout history. In the Ismaili conception of succession to the Prophet, the term *walī* refers to the Ismaili imam of the time and the term *wilāya* (authority and guardianship) is a reference to the office of imamate. In the view of examined treatises, 'the testimony (*shahādat*) is about knowing God through the imam of the time so that people may acquire the knowledge of God through the knowledge of him [i.e. the imam of the time]' (MS BT 4, f. 34). Therefore, *shahāda* is the highest pillar because it is also through *walī* or the imam of the time that one can attain the knowledge (*ma'rifa*) of other pillars, which are explained below.

2. Purification (*ṭahārat*)

The subject of the second pillar is *ṭahārat*, the ritual of cleansing. Linguistically, the term means 'purification and cleanliness', which also appears in *Sūra al-Tawba*, saying that 'In it are men who love to purify themselves. Allah loves those who purify themselves' (Qur'ān, 9:108). The exoteric definition of *ṭahārat* is often associated with cleansing oneself before offering prayers, through the necessary performance of *wuḍū* (ablution) or, in certain cases, both *wuḍū* and *ghusl* (complete washing of body). The purifying agent cleans herself/himself with water. In the absence or shortage of water, the ritual of *tayammum*, cleansing oneself by clean dry earth, is also permissible.

The esoteric understanding and interpretation of *ṭahārat* primarily focus on spiritual purification. The spiritual cleaning, as the examined texts narrate, happens through the water of spiritual wisdom that emanates from the teaching of the truthful teacher to remove doubts and uncertainty from one's mind (MS BT 265, f. 13). In doing so, the person is expected to cease all previous religious thoughts, traditions, and practices, while accepting and obeying the instructional guidance of the imam of the time, whom the texts refer to as *muḥiqq* (truthful master) (MS BT 7, f. 15). Therefore, accepting the imam's instruction and teaching, in the view of the examined treatises, leads to the purification of the believer's soul in the same way as water purifies the body (MS BT 4, ff. 34–35; MS BT 7, f. 15). The concept of obedience to the imam of the time represents the core element of the Ismaili doctrine, which is embedded in and emanates from the pillar of *shahādat*, a belief that also forms the core of the Ismaili literature.

3. Prayer (*namāz*)

The third pillar concerns the ritual of daily prayer (in Arabic, *ṣalāt*). On the exoteric level, there are prayers at five set times of the day. The esoteric interpretation of the prayer moves beyond the concept of time and units of prayer. Instead, it accentuates the perpetual state of worship. The perpetual state of prayer is a spiritual state in which the daily prayer exceeds the limitation of time and space. The Ismaili esoteric interpretation of prayer emphasises that the believer ought to not neglect the remembrance and worship of God for a moment. The text of manuscript MS BT 4 quotes several Qurʾānic verses, such as 'those who are constant in their prayer' (Qurʾān, 70:23), meaning that a believer even for a single moment ought not to be negligent of the remembrance of God and his vicegerent. In other words, one ought to remain in a constant and perpetual connection with God and state of prayer.

In the Ismaili esoteric tradition, the Ismaili imam of the time is central to all aspects of religion, including the permanent state of prayer. While the believer deliberately and consciously strives to remain in a permanent state of prayer, the treatises state that the believer's heart, tongue, and action constantly focus on the spiritual direction of the prayer (*qibla*), that is, the true teacher (MS BT 4, f. 35). The Ismaili literature, especially during and after the Alamūt era, employs the term '*muʿalim*' (teacher) for imam because the Ismaili imam is the teacher and the guide for the Ismaili communities. The above expression of 'true teacher' (*muʿalim-e ṣādiq*), which the Ismailis use as a synonym for the Ismaili 'imam of the time', is rooted in the Qur'ān. The Qur'ān says 'O believers! Keep your duties unto Allah and stand with the truthful' (Qur'ān, 9:119). From the examined treatises' viewpoint, the word 'the truthful' (*aṣ-ṣādiqīn*) is a reference to the Prophet Muhammad in his time and the imam of the time in every age. Khwāja Naṣīr al-Dīn Ṭūsī, the prominent scholar and chief *dā'ī* of the Alamūt era, says that the imam is the *khalīfah* (vicegerent) and the true teacher (*mu'alim-e ṣādiq*).[23] The other term that the Ismailis use for their imam of the time is '*mu'alim-e waqt*' (the teacher of the time).

4. Fasting (*rūzah*)

The exoteric dimension of fasting (in Arabic, *ṣawm*) is abstaining from eating and drinking during the daylight hours of the month of Ramaḍān. The Ismaili esoteric interpretation of fasting exceeds the physical and temporal abstinence from eating and drinking. The examined treatise state that true fasting is safeguarding one's apparent and non-apparent limbs from everything that goes against the will and liking of the teacher of the time (*mu'alim-e waqt*) (MS BT 7, f. 16), i.e. the imam of the time.

The treatise also adds the concept of *taqiyya* (precautionary dissimulation of faith) as another aspect of the esoteric interpretation of fasting. It recommends members of the Ismaili community to observe *taqiyya* during their conversations with people who do not admit the authority of the imam. In the context of *taqiyya*, fasting conceptually refers to a *mustajīb* (the ordinary member of the Ismaili community), who abstains from discussing the secrets of the Ismaili doctrine with non-Ismailis, whereas the feast of breaking the fast (*'īd*) represents the days of the teacher (MS BT 4, ff. 35–36). Another treatise in manuscript MS BT 7 states that 'as the exoteric fasting is abstinence from food, the esoteric fasting is abstinence from esoteric food' (MS BT 7, f. 16). Another treatise on *'Īd al-fiṭr* (the festival of breaking of the fast, ff. 67-73) in MS BT 189 further elaborates on *taqiyya* as an esoteric concept of fasting, through a discussion on *fiṭr* (breaking of the fast). The treatise adds that the term *fiṭr* has exoteric and esoteric meanings. From the exoteric perspective, *fiṭr* means the breaking of fast through eating, drinking, and offering charity to others. The esoteric (*bāṭinī*) meaning of the term refers to avoiding any type of discussions on the secrets of the Ismaili doctrine with non-Ismailis. In other words, *mustajībs* are expected not to break their physical and spiritual (*ḥawās-e ẓāhir wa bāṭin*) fasting until they reach their *ḥujjat* or instructor, who will water their thirst with true knowledge and education (MS BT 189, ff. 72–73). In these discussions, esoteric food is the knowledge of the imam of the time and the knowledge of the Ismaili doctrine, which the *mustajībs* learn from their local teachers and are expected to keep secret and for themselves. The text describes the teaching of the teacher as a joyous occasion, a spiritual feast, in the same way as the three-day jubilee (*ʿīd*) at the end of the month of Ramaḍān is a joyous occasion. It is a happy occasion because the teacher opens *mustajībs*' minds and hearts by teaching them the esoteric knowledge of God, the knowledge which the teacher himself acquired from the higher ranks within the Ismaili ranks of faith (*ḥudūd-e dīn*)[24] (MS BT 189, ff. 72–73/136).

The above esoteric concept of fasting is also discussed in other Persian Ismaili literature. In his *qaṣīda* of *īd al-fiṭr*, penned sometime in the 12th/18th century, Mullā Ḥusayn son of Yaʿqūb Shāh son of Ṣādiq Ṣūfī, a Persian *dāʿī* in Quhistān of Iran, states that fasting means (i) not revealing the secret of the Ismaili doctrine to the non-Ismailis, and (ii) getting engaged in the remembrance of the truth. He further adds that fasting is also about keeping one's eye away from everything that is forbidden and becoming a member of the people of purity, whereas the *ʿīd* of the people of purity is the reunion with the beloved (*wiṣāl-e ḥabīb*) (MS BT 189, f. 72/136). The concept of reunion with the beloved is an important event in the Ismaili tradition. As has been discussed, meeting the local teacher and learning the Ismaili esoteric knowledge is a reunion at the lowest level, whereas a physical meeting (*dīdār*)[25] with the imam of the time is the highest occasion for an Ismaili Muslim. Not every physical encounter with the imam of the time is a *dīdār*. The concept of *dīdār* applies only when the imam of the time grants an audience to a single member or a large gathering of his followers to give them blessings and guidance. Hence, *dīdār* is the highest feast for an Ismaili Muslim. The Fatimid chief *dāʿī* al-Muʾayyad fī al-Dīn al-Shīrāzī describes his first *dīdār*, when he met Imam-Caliph al-Mustanṣir biʾllāh on 30 *Shaʿbān* 449/7 November 1057 in Cairo, in the following words:

> I was taken near the place wherefrom I saw the bright light of the Prophethood. My eyes were dazzled by the Light. I shed the tears of joy and felt as if I was looking at the face of the Prophet of God and of the Commander of the Faithful, Ali.[26]

From the examined treatises' perspectives, fasting starts with abstinence from eating and drinking but continues with the esoteric process of teaching and learning, in which unquestionable obedience to, and establishing the spiritual relationship and bondage with, the imam of the time are the key objectives.

5. Alms (*zakāt*)

The exoteric aspect of *zakāt* is the separation of a specific portion of one's wealth and submitting it to either a public treasury (*bayt al-māl*) or directly distributing it to poor and needy people or any other charitable causes. The term is derived from the Arabic verb *z-k-w* (*zakawa*), which means 'to grow, to increase'. In the moral sense, it means to be pure, just, and honest in one's heart.[27] The Qur'ān makes the payment of *zakāt* obligatory, without specifying its exact amount. It says: 'Perform prayer and give alms and bow down with those who bow down' (Qur'ān, 2:43). Therefore, the amount of the *zakāt* varies between different Muslim groups, from 2.5 % in the Sunni to one fifth (*khums*) in the Twelver Shīʿa, and one-tenth (*ʿushur* in Arabic, and *dah-yakah* in Persian Darī) in the Shīʿa Ismaili traditions.[28] The material submission of alms is important but not sufficient for the spiritual alleviation of the soul for which, in the view of the examined treatises, the divine blessing is needed.

The esoteric interpretation of alms concerns the spiritual nourishment and alleviation of the soul to a higher spiritual level. The examined treatises state that alms is about nourishing one's soul with the spiritual food, that is, the word of the truth (*sukhan-e ḥaq*) (MS BT 4, f. 36; MS BT 7, f. 16). The Qur'ān tells the Prophet Muhammad to take Muslims' alms, cleanse and purify them, and pray for them because your prayer is comforting mercy for them (Qur'ān 9:103). In the Ismaili notion of authority, the imam of the time has the authority to collect alms. In the words of Nāṣir Khusraw, almsgiving is a process that purifies the body and soul. The purity of the soul, as he states, depends on the purity of body, and the purity of body is in the purity of food one eats, whereas the purity of food is in the legitimation (*ḥalāl kardan*) of wealth (*māl*), and the legitimation of wealth is in separating the share of God Almighty, whose share is taken from people by the Prophet and those (imams of the time) who have the divine command to stand in his (the Prophet's) place.[29] It is within this esoteric worldview that the Ismailis around the world submit their alms to their imam of the time. This is why the Ismailis refer to their alms as *māl-e imām*, a portion of one's wealth that goes to imam.[30] Like the Prophet's prayer for the Muslims, the imam's prayer is a blessing and comforting mercy, and a source of purification for the Ismaili communities.

6. Pilgrimage (*ḥajj*)

The sixth pillar of the *sharīʿa* is the pilgrimage. The text distinguishes between two types of pilgrimage: exoteric and esoteric. The exoteric pilgrimage refers to the *ḥajj*[31] ceremony which Muslims perform annually in the month of *Dhū al-Ḥijja* in Mecca by visiting and circumambulating the house of Kaʿba, which is the direction of the prayer (*qibla*) and a symbolic representation of the House of God. From the examined treatises' viewpoint, esoteric pilgrimage is the search for the true House of God (MS BT 265, f. 14). They state that the intention of going for a pilgrimage is about abandoning the material life and seeking the eternal life that is founded on divine love and knowledge (MS BT 4, f. 37; MS BT 7, f. 18). The texts further elaborate that the knowledge of God is attainable through the instruction of 'the truthful master of the time' (*muḥiqq-e zamān*), i.e. the imam of the time. The exoteric pilgrims pass through different destinations and stages, such as going through Iraq and Damascus,[32] until they reach the Kaʿba. Similarly, the spiritual pilgrims pass through different levels and stages of knowledge, i.e. the ranks of faith or ranks of knowledge, until they reach their spiritual destination, *that is*, the imam of the time. The texts also describe the esoteric pilgrimage as 'the greatest pilgrimage' (*Ḥajj-e akbar*) (MS BT 4, f. 37), and the imam of the time and the heart of perfect men (*dil-e kāmilān*), those who attained the knowledge of imam and God, as the real House of God. Hence, the treatises make the notion of love, knowledge, and obedience to the imam of the time the key criteria for attaining the spiritual pilgrimage (MS BT 17, f. 16).

7. Striving (*jihād*)

The exoteric aspect of *jihād* is often explained through armed struggle against the enemies of religion. In Western literature, the term is often and mistakenly translated as 'holy war', a concept that is primarily rooted in the history of the Crusades (1096–1291). The examined treatises present an Ismaili esoteric interpretation of *jihād*. They distinguish between physical and non-physical forms of *jihād*. The physical (*jismānī*) *jihād* is a struggle against the enemies of religion, whereas the non-physical *jihād* is divided into three types: spiritual (*rūḥānī*), intellectual (*ʿaqlānī*) and real (*ḥaqīqī*). These three types of *jihāds* are closely associated and are identical with one another, especially when the last two are considered to be one. The texts state that the spiritual *jihād* refers to fighting darkness (*ẓulmat*) with the power of spiritual light (*nūr*). The treatises treat this form of *jihād* as identical to the second and third forms of *jihād*. The treatises define the intellectual *jihād* as equipping oneself with the blade of instructional guidance and teaching (*tīgh-e taʿlīm*) of the imam of the time and the words of wisdom (*sukhanān-e maʿrifat*) of the true teacher (*muʿalim-e ṣādiq*). The third and the *ḥaqīqī jihād* is fighting against one's own whims and temptations (*hawāī khūd*) (MS BT 4, ff. 38–39; MS BT 17, ff. 16–17). The treatises treat the fight against one's temptation as the highest form of *jihād*. Although the second and the third forms of *jihād* are very identical to one another, the latter is indeed the realization of *rūhānī* and *ʿaqlānī jihāds*. In other words, spiritual *jihād* loses its value when one does not apply it to one's daily life. The treatise of the *Seven Pillars of the Sharīʿa* in manuscript MS BT 59 asserts that the real *jihād* is chopping off the head of temptation, whim, and arrogance (*takabbur*), and recognising the imam of the time (MS BT 59, f. 74). The treatises emphasise the spiritual *jihād* over the physical and encourage the Ismaili communities to actively search for and acquire spiritual wisdom.

In the Ismaili literature, the imam's teaching (*Kalimat al-ḥaq*) is the source of spiritual wisdom, which originates from the divine words, i.e. the Qur'ān, and reaches the *mustajīb* through the ranks of faith (*ḥudūd-e dīn*). The examined treatises state that spiritual wisdom emanates from *kalimat al-ḥaq* (the words of truth) and cleanses a believer's soul in the same way as water cleans the body (MS BT 59,

f. 74; MS BT 61, ff. 56–58). On the esoteric level, the physical *jihād* turns into spiritual and intellectual *jihād*, whereas the physical sword turns into the intellectual blade, and the physical enemy or the enemy of religion (*kāfir*) is a person's whim, temptation, arrogance, and all forms of moral and social ills. The practice of spiritual *jihād* requires a continuous process of education, learning, and training. The examined treatises encourage the spiritual *jihād* as the real *jihād*, which ought to be conducted in line with the teaching of the imam of the time, that is, spiritual wisdom and *kalimat al-ḥaq*.

Conclusion

The presented analyses and discussions demonstrated that the *sharīʿa* is a path that shows the direction toward acquiring God's *maʿrifa* and conducting one's daily life by God's instruction. The pillars of the *sharīʿa* (seven in the Ismaili and five in the Sunni traditions) form a ladder in which each pillar is a rung that leads towards the ultimate goal of the *sharīʿa*, that is, living a life of complete submission to Allah. In this sense, the *sharīʿa*, as well as its pillars, are means and not the ultimate goal itself, as the *sharīʿa* is the path toward the destination and not the destination itself. As a text in MS BT 189 states, 'the *sharīʿa* is the path (*sharīʿat rāh ast*), the *ṭarīqa* is walking on that path (*ṭarīqat raftan*), and *ḥaqīqa* is the destination one has to reach (*ḥaqīqat ba manzil rasīdan*)'. Also, it allegorically states that 'the *sharīʿa* is the vessel (*kishtī*), the *ṭarīqa* is the sea (*baḥr*), and the *ḥaqīqa* is the pearl (*dur*) in that sea' (f. 102). These distinctions form an important part of the educational objectives in the examined manuscripts.

In the view of the examined treatises, God, the Qurʾān and its attributes, and soul, all are the secrets of religion and their understanding requires divine knowledge (*maʿrifa*) (MS BT 189, f. 4). The examined texts explicitly and implicitly assert that people need an instructor to correctly utilise the tools, i.e the pillars of the *sharīʿa*, so they can acquire the correct knowledge of God. Also, they assert that it is the imam alone who can correctly teach how to utilise the means of the *sharīʿa* and attain the knowledge of God. Had it not been the case, as Abū Isḥāq Quhistānī states in his *Seven Chapters*, all people, regardless of their levels of knowledge and intelligence, would have had an equal understanding of the divine truth.[33] This is why the examined treatises refer to the imam of the time as the 'teacher'. In the Ismaili tradition, there is no more truthful teacher in matters of religion other than the imam of the time.

The examined treatises' ultimate objective (*maqṣad*) is to convey an educational and intellectual message of the pillars of the *sharīʿa*, which revolve around the centrality of the imam's position and authority and the reinforcement of his spiritual link with the Ismaili communities. The texts make it clear that one cannot attain the knowledge of God without the instruction of the truthful master (*muʿalim-e ṣādiq*).[34] For the Ismaili communities, the Prophet in his time and the Ismaili imam of the time in every age are the most truthful teachers. This is why the concept of imamate and the imam's authority form and inform the Ismaili identity and the core foundation of the Ismaili pillars of the *sharīʿa*.

NOTES

1 Yahia Baiza, *The Sharīʿa in Central Asian Ismaili Manuscripts: Codicological and Content Analysis* (Unpublished, London, 2016), p. 19.

2 'Gorno' and 'Oblast' are Russian words for 'mountainous' and 'province or region' respectively. The term Gorno-Badakhshān Autonomous Oblast (GBOA) literally means Mountainous Badakhshān Autonomous Province. Next to Leninabad and Khatlon oblasts, GBOA is the third province of Tajikistan. It is an autonomous province/region in eastern Tajikistan, with a population of 209,000 as of 1998 (Frank Bliss, *Social and Demographic Change in the Pamirs (Gorno-Badakhshān, Tajikistan)*, tr. Nicola Pacult and Sonia Guss with the support of Tim Sharp [London, 2006], p. 46), the absolute majority of which follow the Shiʿi Ismaili Nizārī interpretation of Islam.

3 Yahia Baiza, 'al-Qāḍī al-Nuʿmān', in *Routledge Medieval Encyclopedia Online* (London, 2021).

4 al-Qāḍī al-Nuʿmān, *Daʿāʾim al-Islām*, ed., Asif b. Ali Asghar Faizi (Cairo, 1963), vol. 1, pp. 22–23.

5 al-Qāḍī al-Nuʿmān, *Taʾwīl al-daʿāʾim*, ed., Arif Tamir (Beirut, 1994).

6 al-Qāḍī al-Nuʿmān, *Asās al-taʾwīl*, ed., A. Tamir (Beirut, 1960). Al-Muʾayyad fīʾl-Dīn al-Shīrāzī translated the book into Persian under the title of *Bunyād-e taʾwīl*. A manuscript of the book is housed at the IIS; see MS 929 (Per I), dated 1883.

7 al-Shahrastānī was one of the prominent 11th–12th century Ismaili scholars and *daʿis* of the Alamūt period. He lived a mysterious life as an Ashʿarite scholar who taught in the Baghdad Niẓāmiyyah and worked as a scholar in the Saljūqid Sulṭān Sanjar's court publically and operated as an Ismaili *dāʿī* secretly. For further details on his life and Ismaili affiliation, see Toby Mayer, ed. and tr., *Keys to the Arcana: Shahrastānī's Esoteric Commentary on the Qurʾān. A Translation of the Commentary on Sūrat al-Fātiḥa from Muḥammad b. ʿAbd al-Karīm al-Shahrastānī's Mafātīḥ al-Asrār wa Masābīḥ al-Abrār* (Oxford, 2009), pp. xiii–xv, 3–19.

8 Ibid., pp. 47–48.

9 Sayyid Suhrāb Walī-Badakhshānī, *Sīyu-shash ṣaḥīfah (Thirty-six Chapters)*, ed., Hūshang Ujāqī (Tehran, 1961), p. 46.

10 Mayer, ed. and tr., *Keys to the Arcana*, pp. 47–50.

11 Abū Yaʿqūb al-Sajistānī, *Kitāb al-Iftikhār*, ed., Mustafa Ghalib (Beirut, 1980), pp. 98–99; ed., Ismail K. Poonawala (Beirut, 2000), pp. 214–215. In his criticism of Ghalib's edition, Poonalwala describes the former's edition as unreliable. In his preface to *Kitāb al-Iftikhār*, Poonawala describes his frustration at the lack of honesty and distortion of scholarly works among publishing houses in Beirut. In the light of Poonawala's criticism, it is important to read Ghalib's and other editions of *Kitāb al-Iftikhār* with great caution.

12 Ḥamīd al-Dīn al-Kirmānī, *Majmuʿat rasā'il al-Kirmānī*, ed., Mustafa Ghalib (Beirut, 1983), p. 151; and Paul Walker, ed. and tr., *Master of the Age: An Islamic Treatise on the Necessity of the Imamate: A Critical Edition of the Arabic Text and English Translation of Ḥamīd al-Dīn Aḥmad b. ʿAbd Allāh al-Kirmānī's al-Maṣābīḥ fī ithbāt al-imāma* (London, 2007), pp. 31–32.

13 al-Kirmānī, *Majmuʿat rasā'il al-Kirmānī*, p. 152.

14 Nāṣir Khusraw, *Wajh-e Dīn* (Tehran, 1969), p. 61.

15 Naṣīr al-Dīn Ṭūsī, *Paradise of Submission*, ed., Sayyed J. Badakhchani (London, 2005), p. 136.

16 Ibid., p. 136

17 Ibid., p. 148.

18 The five pillars of the *sharīʿa* and/or Islam in the Sunni tradition include (i) testimony (*shahāda*) (ii) prayer (*ṣalāt*) (iii) fasting (*ṣawm*) (iv) alms (*zakāt*) and (v) pilgrimage (*ḥajj*).

19 al-Nuʿmān, *Daʿā'im al-Islām*, vol. 1.

20 Ibid., vol. 1, p. 2.

21 Naṣīr al-Dīn Ṭūsī, *Maṭlūb al-mū'minīn*, translated as 'Desideratum of the Faithful' in Sayyed J. Badakhchani, ed. and tr., *Shiʿi Interpretations of Islam: Three Treatises on Theology and Eschatology* (London, 2010), p. 42–42.

22 Aga Khan IV, 'Address to both Houses of the Parliament of Canada in the House of Commons Chamber" (27 February 2014), Accessed: 22 January 2021 at https://www.akdn.org/speech/его-высочество-ага-хан/address-both-houses-parliament-canada-house-commons-chamber.

23 Ṭūsī, *Maṭlūb al-mū'minīn*, op. cit. p.38.

24 The Ismaili ranks of faith (*ḥudūd-e dīn*) include seven ranks which, starting from the top, are: *imām, bāb* (gate), *ḥujjat* (proof), *dāʿī* (summoner), *mā'dhūn-e akbar* (senior licentiate), *ma'dūn-e asghar* (junior licentiate), and *mustajīb* (respondent).

25 There is also spiritual *dīdār* (a glimpse of the light of the beloved), a concept that is commonly shared across most, if not all, spiritual and mystical traditions. Spiritual *dīdār* is a spiritual experience. When it happens, the lover (seeker) experiences the light (*nūr*) of the Beloved (God) in a state of non-awakening. It is a bright light that lasts less than a second (a glimpse) that gives the most satisfying spiritual feeling and satisfaction to the person who experiences it.

26 al-Mu'ayyad fī al-Dīn al-Shīrāzī, *Life and Lectures of the Grand Missionary Al-Muayyad-Fid-Din al-Shirazi*, ed., Jawad Muscati and Khan Bahadur (Karachi, 1966), pp. 28–29.

27 Yahia Baiza, 'Authority and Rituals in the Shia Ismaili Tradition: An Interpretative Analysis', in Abbas Poya and Farid Suleiman, ed., *Unity and Diversity in Contemporary Muslim Thought* (Cambridge, 2017), p. 165.

28 Ibid., p. 166.

29 Nāṣir Khusraw, *Wajh-e dīn*, pp. 176–177.

30 Baiza, 'Authority and Rituals', p. 167.

31 The other form of pilgrimage is 'the ʿ*umra*' (*ḥajj-e* ʿ*umra*) and can be undertaken at any time of the year.

32 Apparently, the author's location at the time of writing the text was Khurasan and Persia, from where pilgrims had to pass through Iraq and Damascus to reach Mecca.

33 Abū Isḥāq Quhistānī, *Haft Bāb* (*Seven Chapters*), ed. and tr., Wladimir Ivanow (Tehran and Bombay, 1955), p. 10.

34 Ṭūsī often refers to the imam of the time as the truthful teacher (*muʿalim-e ṣādiq*). See his *Maṭlūb al-muʾminīn*, op. cit., and *Sayr wa Sulūk* (*Contemplation and Action*), ed., Sayyed J. Badakhchani (Tehran, 2017).

SECTION VII

APPROACHING TEXTUAL TRANSMISSION THROUGH QUR'ĀNIC MANUSCRIPTS AND HOLOGRAPH/AUTOGRAPH COPIES

17

Writing the Qur'ān between the Lines: Preliminary Remarks on Marginalia in the Qur'ān Manuscripts held by The Institute of Ismaili Studies*

Asma Hilali

Introduction

Scriptural sources are at the core of religious thought in Islam because they constitute the object of study as well as the tools of constructing religious authority. The so-called 'foundational' texts in Islam are the Qur'ān and hadith (words and acts of the Prophet). To these two bodies of text are added other material described in hadith narratives as 'something in-between Qur'ān and hadith' that I name 'intermediary genres'.[1] Textual studies have shown that various materials have circulated and have been taught and annotated since the beginnings of Islam in the 7th century.[2]

In Islamic studies scholarship, especially since the pioneering works of Georges Vajda in the 70s and those of George Makdisi in the 80s, the transmission of texts has occupied the attention of some major scholars of the 20th and 21st century such as Gregor Schoeler, Stefan Leder, and Jonathan Berkey. Studies on textual transmission in Islam deal with four themes: the historicity/'authenticity' of the Islamic texts, the textual composition between fiction/history, the edition of manuscripts, and, finally, the canonisation history that includes studying the origins of the texts. However, the field shows three main challenges: the necessity of studying new material and material studied in a new perspective; the meta-textual features, including marginal and interlinear annotations; and, finally, a need to reflect critically on the previous scholarship. This chapter attempts to overcome the three challenges with a special focus on the study of the meta-textual features in Qurʾān manuscripts, and more precisely, the marginal and interlinear annotations within the perspective of analysing the teaching activity and its contribution in shaping the religious literature, in this case, Qurʾān fragments. The same features have been rather explored as part of paleographical studies and as strictly related to the issue of correction and canonisation.[3] By marginal and interlinear annotations, I refer to the fragments of texts, letters, words and sentences, inserted in the margins of the Qurʾān passages and sometimes between the lines.[4] They are sometimes organised in sophisticated way and often inserted occasionally and fragmentarily; they can have various functions such as correcting[5] the passage or mentioning Qurʾānic variants and readings.[6]

My interest in the marginal and interlinear annotations in Qurʾān manuscripts originates in my study of the transmission of the religious material and the interaction between various religious genres in early and medieval Islam.[7] More precisely, I gave particular importance to the margins in the Qurʾān manuscripts since my work on the collections of Qurʾān fragments from Dār al-Makhṭūṭāt, Ṣanʿāʾ, the so-called 'Sanaa palimpsest'. My study allowed me to show the importance of switching the focus of the study from the book to the fragment and from the text to the margins.[8] Since my experience with the Ṣanʿāʾ palimpsest, I extended my examination of the marginal annotations in Qurʾān manuscripts to three collections: The Doha Museum collection,[9] The Institute of Ismaili Studies collection and the Raqqāda museum (Qayrawan, Tunisia) collection.[10] My research on the marginal annotations in the religious manuscripts, including the Qurʾān manuscripts, aims to bring to light new material that will renew our knowledge of the terminology, techniques of transmission and teaching as well as the actors of the teaching sessions in which religious material has been studied and interpreted. The second objective is to compare the early teaching annotations with the theory of transmission elaborated by the Muslim scholars starting from the 10th century. Studying the continuities and discontinuities between practices of teaching and theory of teaching is fundamental; the connections between the two activities are assessed and interpreted in order to understand the evolution of the techniques of annotations that refer to the transmission of knowledge and the teaching activity that considerably affects the religious corpus. Finally, analysing the marginal and interlinear annotations in Qur'ān manuscripts in different collections aims to develop a new approach to the history of the religious genres in Islam that takes into consideration the usage of the texts by their contemporaries. It also takes into consideration the fluctuation between the religious genres within the framework of the transmission and teaching milieu. The same fluctuation appears often as resulting from the presence of marginal annotations. As I will show in this chapter, the marginal annotations bring additional texts into the manuscript and create interaction between various materials such as Qur'ānic material and exegetical material.

The historical framework of my investigation is adapted to the collections under consideration and takes into account the dating of the manuscripts set by the codicological studies. Generally, the historical framework coincides with the first six centuries of Islam, with the expansion of the lands of Islam and the constitution of the corpus of religious texts, mainly the canonisation of the fundamental religious corpora and their consolidation by generations of commentators and exegetes. The 10th century CE coincides with the emergence of colleges (in Arabic: *madrasa*-s)[11] and the pivotal transformation of religious education and the transmission of knowledge from the circle of disciples (in Arabic: *ḥalaqa*) to organised courses in houses and colleges. However, within the specific collection of The Institute of Ismaili Studies, the historical framework of my research extends the limits of the 10th century and, as will be detailed below, enriches the material under study by including samples of manuscripts dated between the 14th and 20th centuries.

The framework of my analysis integrates paleography and codicology as tools of analysis in dating manuscripts and interpreting the empty spaces that announce the presence of teaching annotations; philology as a tool of textual analysis to understand the particularity of each text; intellectual history for situating the teaching activity within the historical Islamic milieu; history of science in order to situate the theory of textual transmission within the wider framework of the evolution of the Islamic sciences; epistemology of textual transmission for interpreting the terminology of transmission and assessing its evolution from early teaching annotations to later theories of transmission.

Qur'ān Manuscripts at The Institute of Ismaili Studies

As stated by Adam Gacek, The Institute of Ismaili Studies possesses a collection of manuscripts that covers a variety of subjects including Qur'ān commentaries, alchemy, etc.[12] They are described as a mixture of codices, small treatises, dated between the 14th and the 20th centuries and most of them are written by scribes of 'Shīʿī persuasion' following the expression of Gacek.[13] This chapter provides an overview of the presence of marginal annotations in the collection on the basis of a sample of seven Qur'ān manuscripts preserved by the Ismaili Special Collections Unit of The Institute of Ismaili Studies. In the following discussion, I describe the marginal and interlinear annotations through the sample under study and attempt to analyse the particularities of the techniques of marginalia. Finally, I identify the specific usage of each manuscript by its contemporaries in the light of the available information the annotations provide. Although I mainly discuss a collection of Qur'ān manuscripts, I also attempt to show that, most interestingly, when there is a Qur'ānic text, there is often more than Qur'ānic text. By this, I refer to the presence of glosses, translations, exegetical quotations, Qur'ānic variants and readings (*qirā'a* pl. *qirā'āt*, *ḥarf* pl. *ḥurūf*) respectively, grammatical remarks, etc. These precisions contribute to defining the very meaning of interlinear and marginal annotations and, as will be discussed later in this chapter, underline the wide range of topics they cover.

Presentation of the Material

MS 909: An Incomplete Qur'ān Codex

The first manuscript is known with the number MS 909 and is an incomplete codex of Qur'ān. In this manuscript, the margins are dedicated to (a) translating the text into Persian; (b) interpreting some key words in Farsi; and finally (c) the missing passages of the Qur'ān text are added. In the middle of the incomplete Qur'ān book, the decoration is modified and suggests that two Qur'ān codices might be at the origin of the manuscript. However, the above description is interrupted in the renovated parts of the manuscript; the renovation does not reproduce the texts inserted in the margins. There is no colophon allowing further conclusions about the identity of the scribe

Figure 17.1 Folio from Qur'ān Codex MS 909.

or the recipient of the manuscript although the presence of Persian suggests the Perso-Islamic context of writing the marginalia.

MS 921: A Qur'ān Codex in Maghribi Script

The codex MS 921, so called '*Maghribi*', is a colourful codex presenting several interesting features related to text-making and textual transmission. The incomplete codex contains a big part, yet not the totality of the Qur'ān text. The Qur'ān chapters are ordered in a different way than in the Cairo edition of the Qur'ān.[14] Moreover, some titles of chapters are also different. In this manuscript, the marginalia consist mainly of corrections inserted by one scribe. He/she dedicates the marginalia to the addition of the missing parts in the Qur'ān text. The

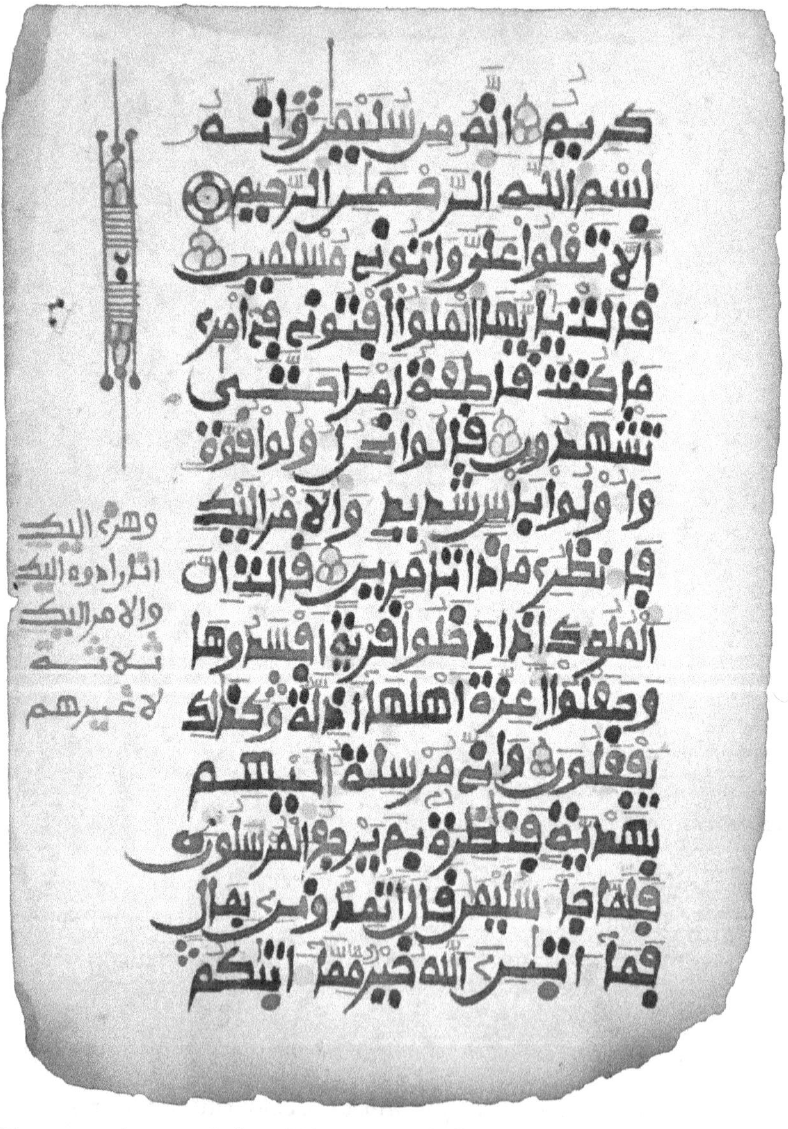

Figure 17.2 An example from MS 921 in *Maghribi* script.

added textual pieces are most of the time entire Qur'ānic verses. The corrections inserted in the margins are linked with a catch sign at the end of the line. There is no colophon allowing the drawing of conclusions about the context of production of the manuscript.

MS 581: An Illuminated Qur'ān Manuscript in Naskhī Hand

Manuscript MS 581 is a codex dated to the early 18th century without a colophon.[15] The manuscript is on laid oriental paper, written in

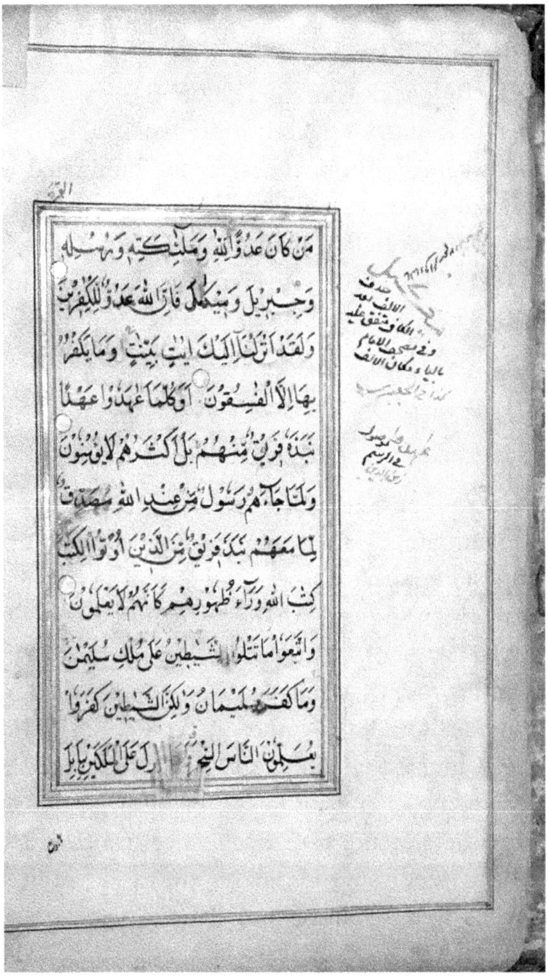

Figure 17.3 Folio from MS 581, an illuminated Qur'ān manuscript in *Naskhī* hand.

'elegant *Naskhī* hand' and illuminated in gold and colours.[16] Some of the margins are illuminated.[17] The marginal annotations can be organized into three categories: (a) grammatical remarks, (b) notes related to the recitation, and (c) notes related to the Qur'ānic variants and readings. The commentaries are introduced by different hands and are sometimes written in Persian; they refer to specific exegetical literature such as al-Bayḍāwī, *Anwār al-tanzīl wa-asrār al-ta'wīl*, one of the most popular and, to some extent, controversial Sunnī Qur'ānic exegetical work composed in the 13th century.[18]

MS 580: A Qur'ān Codex in 'Kashmiri' Style

MS 580 is a Qur'ān codex without a colophon. It is dated to the late 17th or early 18th century.[19] Gacek describes it as being written in 'elegant *Naskhī* hand'.[20] The manuscript is illuminated in gold and colours, Gacek identifies it as a Kashmiri style.[21] The marginalia are mainly dedicated to correcting the mistakes that occurred in copying the Qur'ān text. However, some marginal annotations include invocation such as, for example, on f. 79.

MS 745: An Incomplete Qur'ān Codex in Naskhī Hand

MS 745 is an incomplete Qur'ānic codex written in Naskī hand[22] that does not contain illuminations.[23] The marginal notes are dedicated to listing the Qur'ānic variants and readings in their respective positions in the Qur'ānic passages. Some marginal notes consist of commentaries written in Persian. The particular aspect of this codex relates to the last chapter of the Qur'ān, *al-Nās* (People).[24] The chapter's title, corresponding to the last chapter, is written as *al-Nisā'* (Women), a title that is, in fact, Qur'ān, 4, rather than Qur'ān, 114. However, the content of the chapter is that of Qur'ān, 114 (People). This mistake has not been corrected by any means in the manuscript. This uncorrected mistake suggests that the codex is probably not intended for circulation. Its usage might be dedicated exclusively to the identification of the Qur'ānic variants and readings and to the translation of specific passages into Persian. This remark is of great importance because, by not correcting the content, the decisions made concerning the marginal annotations affect the way the manuscript is meant to be

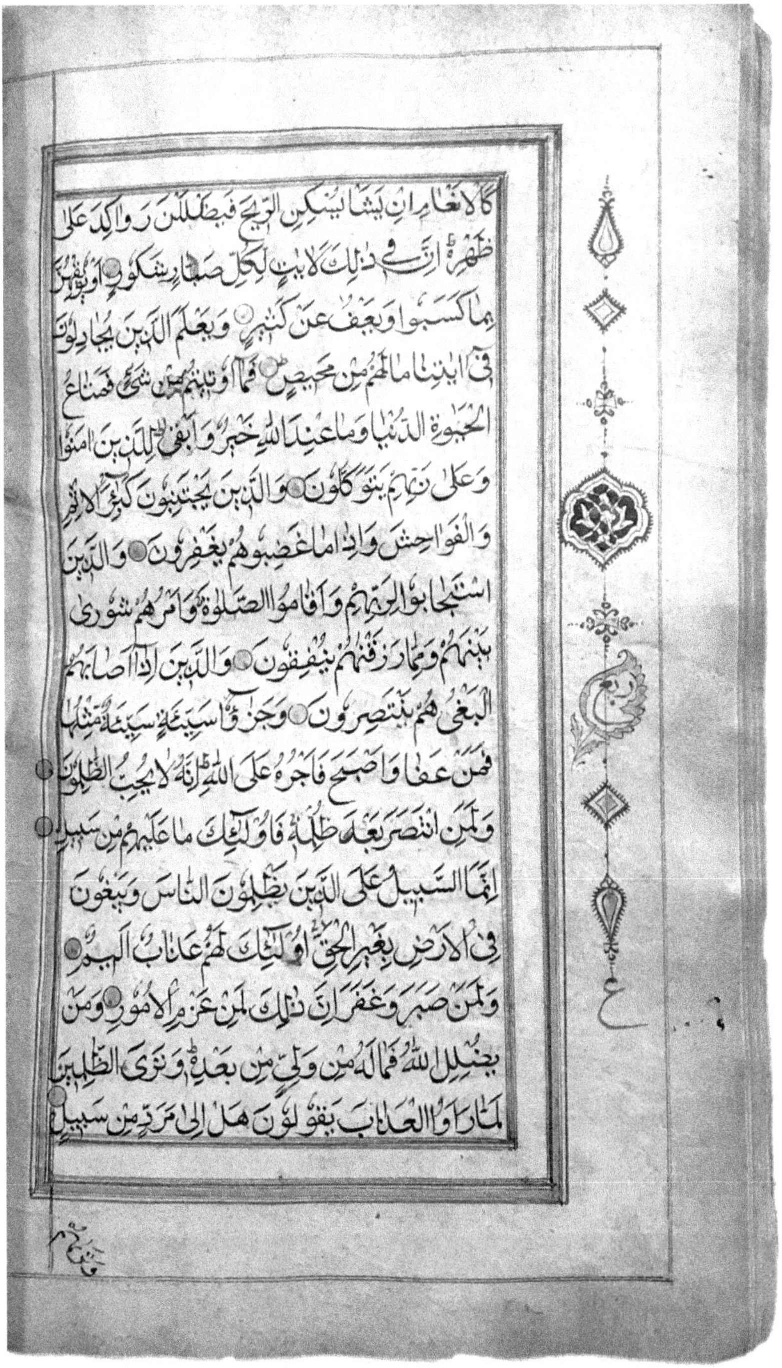

Figure 17.4 Folio from MS 580, a Qur'ān codex in 'Kashmiri' style.

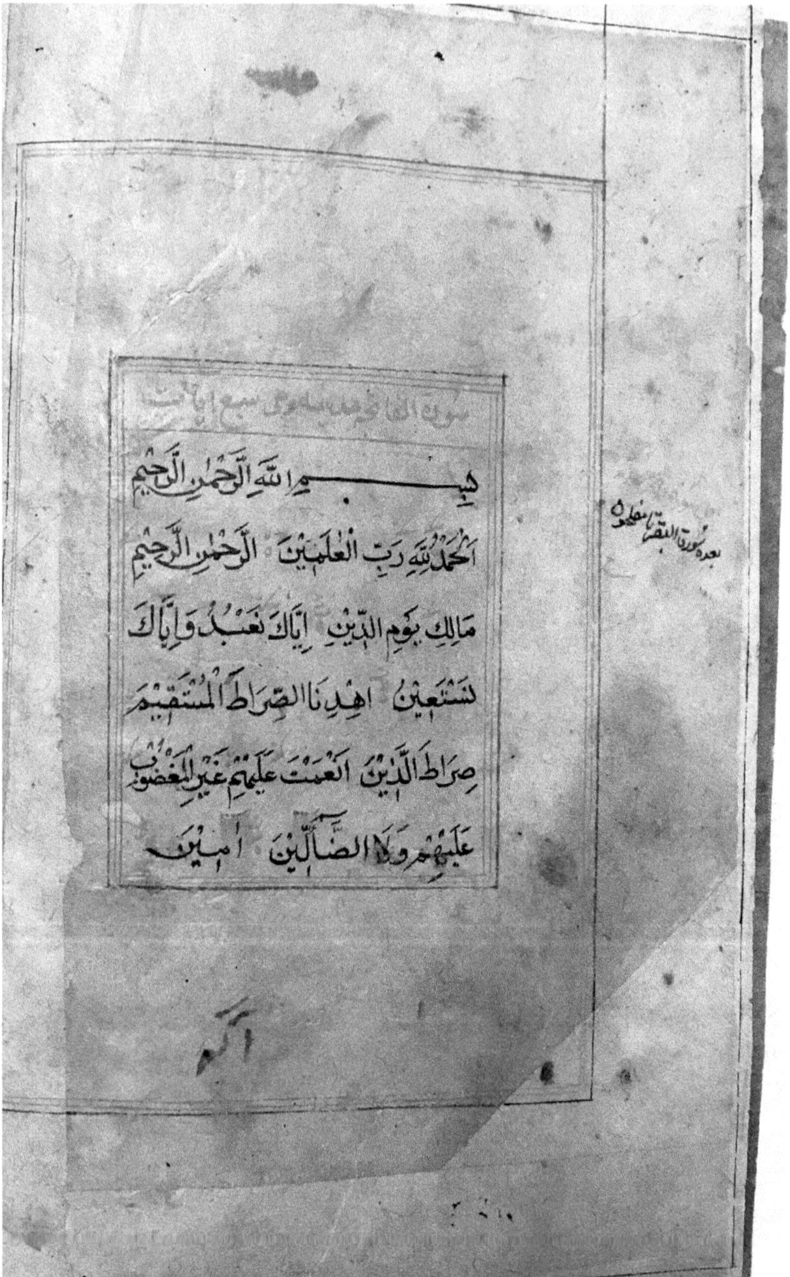

Figure 17.5 Folio from MS 745, an incomplete Qur'ān codex in *Naskhī* hand with the opening chapter of the Qur'ān.

read. The reader is directed to read the margins rather than the Qur'ānic text itself.

MS 1700: A Central Asian Qur'ān Manuscript

This manuscript, a codex being perhaps of 'Central-Asian' provenance, is written by a professional scribe and contains illuminations. Some parts of the manuscript have been repaired. The marginal annotations are dedicated to correcting mistakes that occur in the Qur'ān text and to commenting on the vocalisation and the pronunciation of specific passages and words. The same marginal notes suggest that the codex has been used as a support for the recitation of the Qur'ān.

HDP 19: A Folio from a Qur'ān Manuscript from Mamluk Times

The decorated Mamluk folio is impressive with its rich decoration and does not present any other particularity except one single marginal note consisting of a correction of a mistake that occurred in the Qur'ān text.

Figure 17.6 MS 1700, a folio from a Central Asian manuscript showing the opening chapter of the Qur'ān.

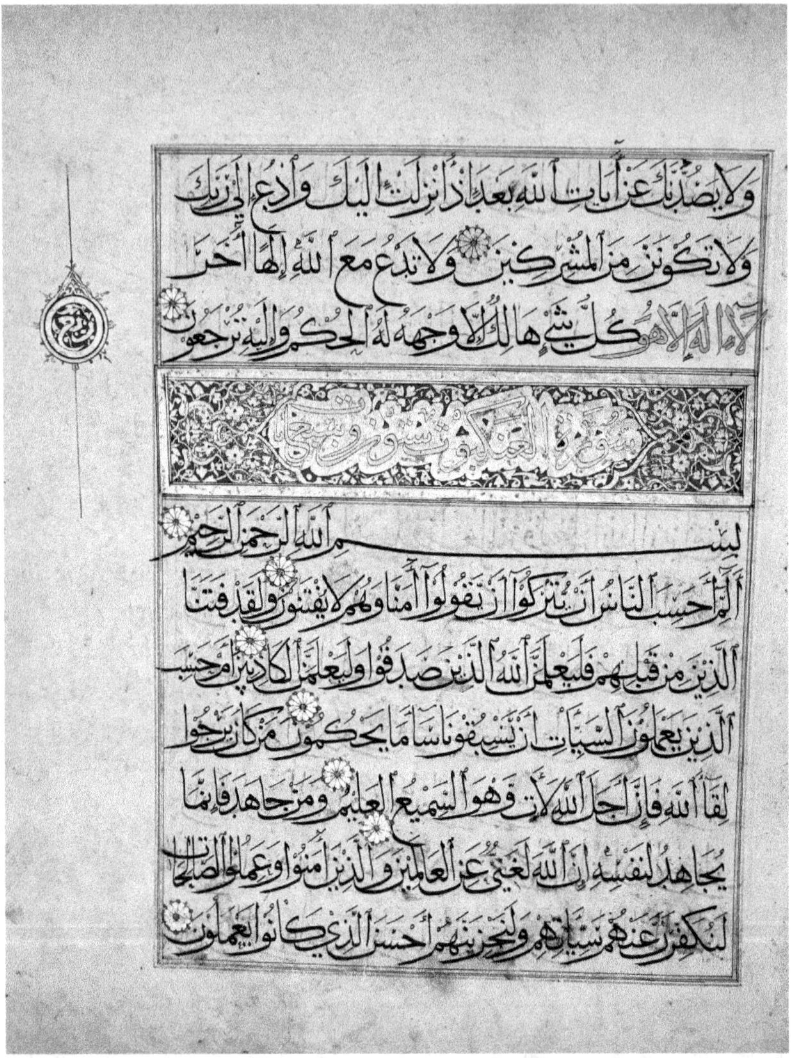
ولا يصدنك عن آيات الله بعد إذ أنزلت إليك وادع إلى ربك
ولا تكونن من المشركين ولا تدع مع الله إلها آخر
لا إله إلا هو كل شيء هالك إلا وجهه له الحكم وإليه ترجعون

بسم الله الرحمن الرحيم
الم أحسب الناس أن يتركوا أن يقولوا آمنا وهم لا يفتنون ولقد فتنا
الذين من قبلهم فليعلمن الله الذين صدقوا وليعلمن الكاذبين أم حسب
الذين يعملون السيئات أن يسبقونا ساء ما يحكمون من كان يرجو
لقاء الله فإن أجل الله لآت وهو السميع العليم ومن جاهد فإنما
يجاهد لنفسه إن الله لغني عن العالمين والذين آمنوا وعملوا الصالحات
لنكفرن عنهم سيئاتهم ولنجزينهم أحسن الذي كانوا يعملون

Figure 17.7 HDP 19, a folio from a Qur'ān manuscript from Mamluk times.

Marginal and Interlinear Annotations and Contexts of Transmission

Any conclusions concerning the contexts for the transmission of the Qur'ān manuscripts held by the Ismaili Special Collections Unit of The Institute of Ismaili Studies depend on definitive assessments of the date and provenance of each manuscript. The following remarks show how the marginalia notes are organised in the Qur'ān manuscripts and propose a few hypotheses about the functions of the marginal and interlinear annotations in relation to the contexts of transmission specific to the manuscripts in the collection. The occurrences of the marginal and interlinear annotations in the seven Qur'ān manuscripts are organised into the following topics:

1) Translation of Qur'ānic expressions (namely into Persian);
2) Interpretation of specific Qur'ānic passages; this includes the insertion of quotations from *tafsīr* works such as Nāṣir al-Dīn al-Bayḍāwī's commentary of the Qur'ān;
3) Corrections of the Qur'ānic passages, which includes adding in the missing pieces of the Qur'ān text;
4) Instructions related to the pronunciation and recitation of Qur'ān vocabulary;
5) Occasional insertion of invocation.

Two functions of the marginalia seem to determine the way in which they are organised in the collection: (a) interpreting and correcting the Qur'ānic passages and (b) setting the rules for pronunciation and recitation of the Qur'ān text. Furthermore, inserting the Qur'ānic variants and readings at the places where they occur in the Qur'ān text appears to be an additional function of the marginal notes, although it does seem to have the same importance as the interpretation and setting of the recitation rules. Nevertheless, the close connection between the two categories of information: inserting the variants and readings on one hand and setting the rules of recitation on the other hand suggests that the former is considered in the marginalia as a sub-category of the latter. Some of the Qur'ānic variants and readings concern the recitation of specific passages of the Qur'ān and specify the way such and such reader of the Qur'ān should pronounce specific passages.[25] The last category of marginalia notes is the one dedicated to translating the Qur'ān text into *Persian*—obviously, a task dedicated to Persian speaking readers.

The particularity of the marginalia notes in the examined Qur'ān manuscripts from the IIS consists of their pragmatic aspect—that is to say their dedication to specific functions that facilitate understanding the Qur'ān text and reciting it by following specific rules. These functions of the marginalia suggest that the manuscripts might have been annotated in order to be transmitted in limited circles given that they answer specific needs. The marginal annotations express an attempt at appropriating the Qur'ān manuscripts and transforming the Qur'ān text to a private object. This particular use of the manuscript may be compared to the observation made by the epigraphist and historian of the Qur'ān Frédéric Imbert who dedicated an important work to studying Qur'ānic graffiti.[26] Imbert calls the Qur'ānic text written by the scribes of the graffiti 'the Qur'ān of the hearts' referring to the personal and almost intimate use they make of the Qur'ānic graffiti. The marginalia in the Qur'ānic manuscripts held by the IIS suggests that the manuscripts have circulated in restricted and perhaps private circles and have been dedicated mainly to liturgical purposes. Despite their organised aspect, the information provided by the marginal annotations is not exhaustive or systematic. For example, the number of Qur'ānic variants and readings provided by the marginalia is limited, as are the instructions related to the rules of recitation. The various functions of the marginalia seem to be directed towards setting the rules of the correct recitation of the Arabic Qur'ānic text and its understanding for non-Arabic readers in order to facilitate its liturgical use. The sample of Qur'ān manuscripts from the IIS collection shows how the study of the marginalia in Qur'ān manuscripts within specific collections contributes to assessing the reception of the Qur'ān manuscripts by the contemporary community of readership.

NOTES

* My thanks to Wafi Momin, Head of Ismaili Special Collections Unit at The Institute of Ismaili Studies, and to all the staff members of the Unit, particularly Nourmamadcho Nourmamadchoev for facilitating my work on the manuscripts.

1 Asma Hilali, 'Coran, ḥadīṯ et textes intermédiaires. Le genre religieux aux débuts de l'islam', *Mélanges de l'Université Saint Joseph*, 64 (2012), pp. 29–44.

2 Ibid.; Fred Donner, *Narratives of Islamic Origins: The Beginning of Islamic Historical Writing* (Princeton, 1998).

3 Keith Small, *Textual Criticism and Qur'ān Manuscripts* (Lanham, 2011); Daniel Alan Brubaker, *Corrections in Early Qur'ān Manuscripts: Twenty Examples* (London, 2019).

4 On the use of the margins in Arabic manuscripts, see Annie Vernay-Nouri, 'Marges, gloses et décor dans une série de manuscrits arabo-islamiques', *Revue des Mondes Musulmans et de la Méditerranée,* special issue *La tradition manuscrite en écriture arabe*, ed. Geneviève Humbert, 99–100 (2002), pp. 117–131.

5 For corrections in the Qur'ān manuscripts, see, Adam Gacek, 'Taxonomy of Scribal Errors and Corrections in Arabic Manuscripts', in *Theoretical Approaches to the Transmission and Edition of Oriental Manuscripts: Proceedings of a Symposium Held in*

Istanbul, March 28–30, 2001, ed. Judith Pfeiffer and Manfred Kropp (Beirut, 2007), pp. 217–236; Adam Gacek, 'Technical Practices and Recommendations Recorded by Classical and Post-classical Arabic Scholars Concerning the Copying and Correction of Manuscripts', in *Les Manuscrits du Moyen-Orient. essais de codicologie et de paléographie. Actes du colloque d'Istanbul*, ed. François Déroche (Istanbul and Paris, 1989), pp. 51–60; see more recently, Brubaker, *Corrections in Early Qur'ān Manuscripts*. On the corrections of the Qur'ān from a theoretical perspective, see Behnam Sadeghi, 'Criteria for Emending the Text of the Qur'ān', in *Law and Tradition in Classical Islam. Studies in Honor of Hossein Modarressi*, ed. Michael Cook, Najam Haider, Intisar Rabb, and Asma Sayeed (New York, 2013), pp. 21–41.

6 Alba Fedeli, 'Relevance of the Oldest Qur'ānic Manuscripts for the Readings Mentioned by Commentaries: A Note on Sura "Ṭā-Hā"', *Manuscripta Orientalia*, 15 (2009), pp. 3–10.

7 Asma Hilali, 'Compiler, exclure, cacher. Les traditions dites forgées dans l'Islam sunnite (VIe/XIIe siècle)', *Revue de l'histoire des Religions*, 2 (2011), pp. 163–174; Hilali, 'Coran, ḥadīṯ et textes intermédiaires'.

8 Asma Hilali, 'Le palimpseste de Ṣan'ā' et la canonisation du Coran: Nouveaux éléments', *Cahiers du Centre Gustave Glotz*, 21 (2010), pp. 443–448; Asma Hilali, 'Was the Ṣan'ā' Qur'ān Palimpsest a Work in Progress?', in *The Yemeni Manuscript Tradition*, ed. Sabine Schmidtke, David Hollenberg, Christoph Rauch (Leiden, 2015), pp. 12–27; Asma Hilali, *The Sanaa Palimpsest: The Transmission of the Qur'ān in the Seventh Century AH* (Oxford, 2017), pp. 39–40; cf. Behnam Sadeghi and Mohsen Goudarzi, 'Ṣan'ā'1 and the Origins of the Qur'ān', *Der Islam*, 87 (2012), pp. 1–129; Elisabeth Puin, 'Ein früher Koranpalimpsest aus Ṣan'ā' (DAM 01-27.1). Part II', in *Vom Koran zum Islam*, ed. Markus Groß and Karl-Heinz Ohlig (Berlin, 2009), pp. 523–681 (esp. p. 547).

9 Asma Hilali, 'Writing the Qur'ān between the Lines: Marginal and Interlinear Notes in Selected Qur'ān fragments from the Museum of Islamic Art, Qatar', in Bradford A. Anderson, ed., *From Scrolls to Scrolling: Sacred Texts, Materiality, and Dynamic Media Cultures* (Berlin, 2020), pp. 51–61.

10 My study includes the analysis of the religious fragments in the collection of 'The Laboratory of Conservation and preservation of Manuscripts in Raqqāda', Qayrawān, Tunisia. The results of this work have been presented at the Conference 'Marginal commentaries in Arabic Manuscripts', Leipzig, 3 December 2019.

11 George Makdisi, *The Rise of Colleges: Institutions of Learning in Islam and the West* (Edinburgh, 1981).

12 Adam Gacek, *Catalogue of Arabic Manuscripts in the Library of The Institute of Ismaili Studies* (London, 1985), p. ix.

13 Ibid.

14 About the history of the different editions of the Qur'ān and the importance of the Cairo edition, see Adrian Alan Brockett, *Studies in Two Transmissions of the Qur'ān* (PhD dissertation, University of St Andrews, 1985); Wizārat al-Awqāf wa shu'ūn al-Azhar, *al-Azhar tārīkhuh wa taṭawwuruh* (Cairo, 1964).

15 For a detailed codicological description of the manuscript, see Gacek, *Catalogue of Arabic Manuscripts*, p. 128.

16 Ibid.

17 Ibid.

18 James Robson, 'al-Bayḍāwī', *EI2* (Brill Online).

19 Gacek, *Catalogue of Arabic Manuscripts*, p. 128.

20 Ibid.

21 Ibid.

22 A detailed codicological description of this manuscript appears in Gacek, *Catalogue of Arabic Manuscripts*, p. 128.

23 Ibid.

24 Following the translation of M.A.S. Abdel Haleem, see his *The Qur'ān: A New Translation* (Oxford, 2004), p. 114.

25 On the history and the meaning of the Qur'ānic variants, see al-Ṣuyūṭī, *al-Itqān fī 'ulūm al-qur'ān*, vol. 1 (Beirut, 2004), p. 139; Viviane Comerro, *Les traditions sur la constitution du* muṣḥaf *de 'Uthmān* (Beirut, 2012), pp. 119–135; Shady Hekmat Nasser, *The Transmission of the Variant Readings of the Qur'ān: The Problem of Tawātur and the Emergence of Shawādhdh* (Boston/Leiden, 2013), pp. 35–65. On the notion of *rasm*, see Frederick Leemhuis, 'Codices of the Qur'ān', *Encyclopaedia of the Qur'ān* (Brill Online).

26 Frédéric Imbert, 'Le Coran des pierres. Statistiques épigraphiques et premières analyses', in Mehdi Azaiez and Sabrina Mervin, *Coran: Nouvelles approches* (Paris, 2013), pp. 99–124.

18

The Making of Holographs/Autographs: Case Studies from the Special Collections of The Institute of Ismaili Studies

Walid Ghali

Introduction

The codicological and textual studies on Islamic manuscripts in the autograph/holograph category do not match the wealth and depth of the material available in libraries and archives, let alone in private collections. Frédéric Bauden and Élise Franssen claim that contrary to what exists for manuscripts of medieval Europe, we do not have a comprehensive study devoted to the specific category of autograph notes, holograph or authorial manuscripts and the problems they pose for the Arabic manuscript tradition.[1]

In addition, there are other reasons for the richness of the manuscript corpus in different Muslim cultures that resulted from the relatively late introduction of the movable printing press, which in most Muslim countries was not widespread until the dawn of the 20th century. However, it is worth mentioning that there is a noticeably growing interest in the study of autograph manuscripts that have been recently discovered in various manuscript collections across the world. While the field is advancing, there is still a long journey to understanding the history of writing practices in the Muslim world. Another challenge is related to terminology and definitions. Adam Gacek has provided precise definitions of holographs, autographs and authorial manuscripts. However, the terminology in Arabic deserves some attention, too. Therefore, this chapter attempts to contribute to this aspect based on the analysis of the holographs in The Institute of Ismaili Studies (IIS) collection.

Recent studies of both the history of writing as well as practical examples of holographs have enabled codicology specialists to explain some of the technicalities in the making of holographs. This adds to our knowledge in terms of philology, textual criticism, codicology and palaeography, as well as being important for enhancing our understanding of the working methods of past scholars, for our comprehension of book culture and the publication process, for our grasp of the transmission of knowledge, and more simply, for highlighting the need to compare these specific manuscripts in order to acknowledge other holograph manuscripts or autograph notes by the same author.[2]

For instance, the recent discovery of al-Maqrīzī's holograph of his magnum opus *al-Khiṭaṭ* is a significant example of the importance of holographs.[3] This is also evident in classical works that dealt with authorship and writing as a profession known as *belles-lettres* or penmanship literature (*adabiyyāt*), where in some cases, it gives a detailed explanation on some technical matters such as how additions, corrections or insertions were made.

Another remarkable advantage of studying holographs is that it can take us back to the era of a manuscript's origins and the history and debates around its subject matter. Signed manuscripts can also confirm the originality of its authorship and other specific features such as plagiarism. It could also help a researcher who wants to look at the unwritten history, such as economic or political circumstances while writing the holograph. For those who study the history of books and writing, a holograph is a significant source of information. Therefore, without making a thorough study of the manuscript tradition and the evidence it contains, we would not be able to trace in full the routes and the individuals through which knowledge was disseminated in the traditional world of Islam.

This chapter aims to contribute to this growing field of study by providing some codicological and textual analysis of holograph/autograph manuscripts in The Institute of Ismaili Studies collection. In addition to the codicological elements, the chapter will address any peculiarities that could confirm the type of the holograph (fair copy, draft, or copybook) in order to bring forward the challenge of terminologies mentioned previously. Particular attention will also be given to the importance of these holographs as part of the manuscript corpus at the Institute's collections and in general. I will begin by giving a brief background of the history of the manuscript collections at The Institute of Ismaili Studies.

The Manuscript Corpus at the IIS

The manuscript collections started to become part of The Institute of Ismaili Studies from 1979 onward, two years after the establishment of the Institute. However, the beginnings of this collection can be traced back to the 1930s and 1940s when the Russian scholar and pioneer of modern Ismaili studies, Wladimir Ivanow (1886–1970), together with other Ismaili scholars, gathered a large number of manuscripts for the Ismaili Society in Bombay. These acquisitions have provided the basis for the Institute's collection. The collection started with 1,000 manuscript volumes, but it has been growing ever since through a rigorous acquisition programme and generous donations.

It is the most extensive known, and accessible, collection of Ismaili works in the world. Although the collection includes some late copies—some of them as late as the 1960s—their value is indisputable because of their rarity and the uniqueness of content.[4] The Arabic portion of the collection is rich in content and covers subjects ranging from commentaries on the Qur'ān to alchemy, with a sizeable number of small treatises, and a proportion of explicitly Shiʿi material. The codicological and paleographical observations about the holographs which follow are based on the data gathered from the Arabic collection described in the catalogues in addition to the analysis that has been recently carried out.

As for the Arabic collection, Adam Gacek, former librarian at The Institute of Ismaili Studies, first published a catalogue of Arabic manuscripts held by the IIS. The two-volume catalogue was published in 1984–1985, focusing on the Arabic manuscripts only. In the year 2000, another catalogue was published by Delia Cortese to supplement the previous two volumes.[5] That said, the catalogue offers different types of information and codicological approaches to the same works. Three years later, Cortese produced another catalogue of Arabic Ismaili manuscripts from the Zahid Ali collection that had been donated to the Institute.[6]

In 2011 François de Blois published a catalogue of the Arabic, Persian and Gujarati manuscripts that have been donated to the IIS in London. The collection previously belonged to Muḥammad ʿAlī Hamdānī and represents a large segment of the Hamdani family's library collected over seven generations by this family of eminent scholars from the Dāʾūdī Bohra community in India and Yemen. The bulk of the manuscripts consist of Ismaili religious writings, but there are also a good number of books of general Islamic and literary content.[7] This catalogue contains detailed descriptions of the manuscripts in the Hamdani collection, discussing both the content of the works and the manuscripts' codicological features. The introduction also contains a comprehensive history of the Hamdani family. It is worth mentioning that the majority of the books are in Arabic, but there are also a small number in Persian and in the Bohra *daʿwa* language (*lisān al-daʿwa*), which is Gujarati written in Arabic script.[8]

In his introduction to the second volume, Gacek pointed to the significance of the Arabic collection evident in the wide range of subjects covered and its diverse provenances and codicological resemblance. He also noted that the collection 'contains at least six holographs (nos. 69, 143, 157, 158, 162, 298 [sic]), five texts transcribed directly from holographs (nos. 63, 87, 165A.6, 117, 170), four collated with holographs (nos. 87, 126, 197, 245) and eight which were specially executed for patrons (nos. 4, 87, 133, 111, 144A, 197, 239, 245)'.[9]

Also, there are other manuscripts in the Hamdani collection marked as unique or holograph (de Blois: MS 1542, MS 1544, MS 1569, MS 1642 and MS 1639). It is worth mentioning that the manuscripts executed especially for patrons (such as MS 4, MS 87, MS 133, MS 111, MS 144A, MS 197, MS 239, MS 245) are not included in this chapter as they are not relevant to the holograph category. Also, manuscripts recorded as unique in the Hamdani collection (such as MS 1487/36a) are not discussed either. Both categories deserve dedicated further study.

In describing these manuscripts, I aim to focus on what is important in them regarding authorship and contents. in addition, I will mention relevant codicological features that could confirm a manuscript's status as a holograph, with emphasis on the type of holograph.

Holograph and its Terminologies

According to *The Oxford English Dictionary*, an autograph is, apart from its meaning as a signature, 'That which is written in a person's handwriting; the author's own manuscript', and '[c]ontains occasional verses, etc., as well as the person's signature.'[10] Holograph, however, is 'of a deed, letter, or a document: Wholly written by the person in whose name it appears'. On the other hand, '[i]n holograph: [it is something] wholly in the author's handwriting'.[11] In *Webster's Third New International Dictionary*, an autograph is 'an original handwritten manuscript, as of an author's or a composer's work',[12] while a holograph is a 'document (as a letter, deed, or will) wholly in the handwriting of the person from whom it proceeds and whose act it purports to be.'[13] More specifically, as per *The Oxford English Dictionary*, 'the word "holograph" comes to us from the Late Latin *holographus*, "entirely written by the signer", but originally from the Greek *holographos*. The same source states that the word "autograph" also comes from Late Latin *autographum*, neuter of *autographus*, and again originally from the Greek (*autographos*), meaning "written with one's own hand".'[14]

Although the two words are often used interchangeably, Gacek provided a distinct definition of a holograph as a manuscript entirely written by the author whereas an autograph is a short inscription by a person bearing his/her name by way of signing colophon, ownership mark or a consultation note.[15] Bauden defines the authorial manuscript as 'a manuscript copied by a scribe and then revised by the author of the text, who left autograph interventions, such as corrections, emendations, cancellations or comments, in the margin or in any other blank space of the manuscript (interlinear space, title page, margin, etc.)'.[16] It is worth noting that the latter definition applies to the case of MS 656 (*Naṣīḥat al-ikhwān*) which will be discussed later in this chapter.

The Arabic terminologies about the manuscript authorship are slightly extended but also convoluted. The autograph manuscripts (*al-makhṭūṭāt al-muwaqqaʿah*) usually mean either the author is the copyist or the manuscript has a short statement signed by him, whereas *bi-khaṭ al-mu'allif* refers to the copies that have been wholly written by the author (holographs). In the latter category, however, one can find two types of works: the draft (*musawwadah*) or fair copy (*mubayyaḍah*).

Simultaneously, the fair copies were scarce because dictation was the predominant way of transmitting religious works in the first four centuries of Muslim history, but there are other related terminologies such as the archetype (*al-nuskhah al-dustūr*), unique copy (*al-aṣl al-waḥīd*), or the attested copy (*taṣdīq*).[17]

The bio-bibliographical references often mention the type of manuscripts used within the learned circles. For instance, many manuscripts were left as draft copies due to the author's death. Most of these works have been completed by the author's students or another scholar. Ibn al-Nadīm mentions in his major corpus *al-Fihrist* that Ibn Durayd (d. 321/933) who wrote a similar work as Ibn Qutaybah's *Adab al-Kātib*, could not copy from the draft (*wa-lam yujarriduhu min al-musawwadah*), but he did not mention the reason.[18] Another example was mentioned in Ibn Abī Usaybiʿah's *ʿUyūn al-Anbāʾ* to the effect that al-Rāzī (d. 311/923) wrote his book *al-Ḥāwī*, but he died before the proofreading (*wa-lam yufsaḥ lahu fī al-ajal an yuḥarrir hādhā al-kitāb*).[19] Moreover, the famous work *al-Aghānī* by Abū al-Faraj al-Iṣfahānī (d. 356/967) was sold as codices in *Taʿlīq* handwriting which was believed to have been the draft copy.[20]

The other type of holograph is the author's fair copy, which is the copy that the author copied from his draft with all mistakes fixed and new contents inserted. However, the author could have decided to revisit the fair copy and make another round of changes on his fair copy before sharing it with the copyists. Alternatively, the same could happen after the distribution of the book and perhaps after some years. In such a case, the author uses his copy or any other copy in hand. For example, Ibn Abī al-Ḥadīd mentioned that when he was working on his *Sharḥ Nahj al-Balāghah,* he found many copies of the original work that included glosses and marginal notes. it was said that one of these copies was a certified autograph that was signed by al-Sharīf al-Raḍī himself.[21]

The holographs in the IIS collection are indicated by terminologies similar to those discussed above. In MS 1639, the title page is in contemporary handwriting with a partial table of contents (f. 1r) where the word (*bi-khaṭṭih)* is mentioned on labels with the title on the front cover and spine. However, it was noticed that the manuscript was attributed to al-Sakhāwī by mistake.[22] The author appears in three places on this manuscript as Muḥammad ibn Muḥammad al-Saḥmāwī including the spine and title page which seems to be added by a different later handwriting. For instance, the following statement is mentioned on the title page, '*bi-khaṭṭ mu'allifihā kamā ḥarrara fī ākhir al-kitāb bi-yadihi mimmā 'unya bi-jam'ihi wa-kitābatihi bi-khaṭṭihi Muḥammad bin Muḥammad al-Saḥmāwī*'.[23] Both the spine and title page are confirmed in the colophon statement in the original handwiting where it reads '*tamma al-kitāb al-mubārak . . . al-musamma bi'l-Farā'id al-Mukhtabarah min Inshā' al-Muwaqqi'īn al-Mu'tabarh*' (see Figures 18.1 and 18.2). It should be noted that the word '*al-Muwaqqi'īn*' was wrongly mentioned as '*al-Muwaffiqīn*' on the title page statement. Perhaps this work deserves further examination to confirm its authorship and content. It is believed that the author's name has always been mixed up with that of al-Sakhāwī.[24]

The second case worth highlighting is that, it was not possible to confirm the status of MS 298—*al-Ṣaḥīfah al-sajjādīyah* by Zayn al-'Ābidīn 'Alī ibn al-Ḥusayn—as a holograph, as asserted by Gacek.[25] Also, in MS 1533, the title and author are indicated in the superscription, and, in a recent hand, on the title page and the label on the front cover; assorted notes also appear on the title page including an acquisition note signed by Muḥammad 'Alī b. Fayḍ Allāh (al-Hamdānī) with the date 1314/1896–1897. Title pages are a common feature in the collection, where the title and the author are recorded along with other useful information that confirms the holograph attribution. These include terms such as *bi-khaṭṭih* (MS 1639), *rāqimihā* (MS 656), *bi-khaṭṭ muṣannifihā* (MS 1533).

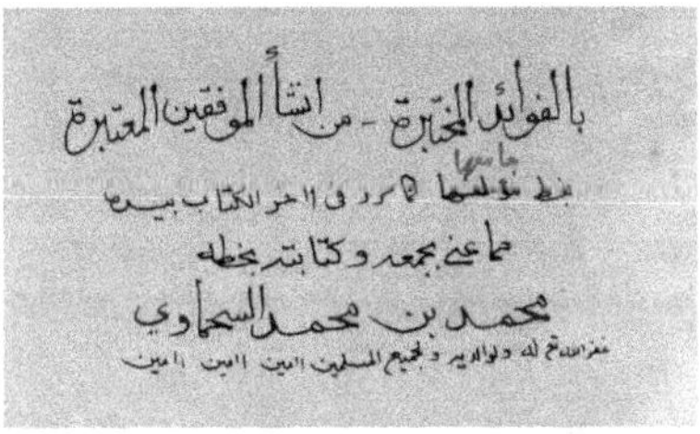

Figure 18.1 MS 1639—From the title page.

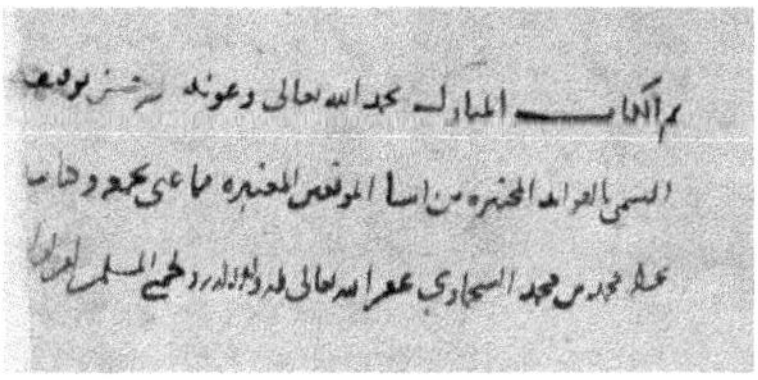

Figure 18.2 MS 1639—Colophon.

Major Physical Characteristics

The following section aims to provide a codicological analysis of twelve Arabic manuscripts that were categorised in the catalogues as holographs (see Table 18.1). In doing so, I will give a brief physical and codicological description of these manuscripts. Also, their contents, their research significance and their position within the IIS collection will be noted. More importantly, working under the assumption that the manuscripts are all correctly attributed to the category of authorial manuscripts, it is essential to distinguish between holographs and autographs showing the particularities of each form.

In terms of the number of folios, the largest manuscript is MS 746 consisting of 441 folios, probably because it is a composition of ten epistles. It is worth mentioning that only four titles are mentioned on the title page: *Jumān al-Jinān*, *al-Wajīzah fī al-Ṣalāh*, *al-ʿAsharah al-Kāmilah* and *Thānī al-Masāʾil*. The second largest manuscript, MS 617, contains 209 folios in a neat *Naskhī* hand, in black ink with a black leather binding without flap. The smallest manuscript in this collection

Table 18.1 List of the Holograph Manuscripts in the IIS Collection.

No.	Collection	Title
MS 1639	Hamdani	*al-Fawāʾid al-mukhtabarah min inshāʾ al-muwaqqiʿīn al-muʿtabarah*
MS 1642	Hamdani	*Rawḍat al-adib wa-tuḥfat al-labīb wa-nukhbat al-ḥasīb li-maʿrifat al-ansāb*
MS 1533	Hamdani	*al-Risālah al-mufradah*
MS 798	Gacek, v.2	*al-Risālah al-Muḥammadīyah fī aḥkām al-mīrāth al-abadīyah*
MS 1544	Hamdani	*Qiṣṣat Ghāyat al-Jamāl*
MS 656	Gacek, v.2	*Naṣīḥat al-ikhwān ʿan shrub al-dukhān*
MS 915/C1	Zahid Ali	*Ḥāshiyat mukhtaṣar al-maʿānī*
MS 617	Gacek, v.2	[*Ḥāshiyah ʿalā sharḥ tahdhīb al-manṭiq*]
MS 746	Gacek, v.2	[*Rasāʾil Muḥammad Riḍā*]
MS 298	Gacek, v.2	*al-Ṣaḥīfah al-sajjādīyah*
MS 1569	Hamdani	Three treatises
MS 621	Gacek, v.2	*al-Rasāʾil wa-al-masāʾil*

of holographs is MS 656 (*Naṣīḥat al-ikhwān*) consisting of 20 folios in neat handwriting with many insertions and corrections that are signed by the author.

As for the writing surfaces, most of the manuscripts are written on laid paper, a few of them have watermarks such as MS 157 and MS 69. MS 157 includes the following watermarks: 'Star [in the circle of flowers]', 'Star of India', 'Made in England for Abdou Hossein Rusoolbhoy'. These two manuscripts were created by Muḥammad Riḍā ibn Muḥammad Jaʿfar al-Rāzī al-Gharawī (fl. 1320/1902). Also, the manuscripts in this collection are provided with catchwords, even though these are not always written below the line of the verso page; sometimes, the catchwords are written in the middle. It was observed that there were no catchwords on MS 1569, f. 22v and f. 44v, but the last word of the page is repeated on the next page; on f. 48b the catchword does not match the first word on the next page and has been crossed out.

The average number of lines in the collection ranges between 10–19 per page with clear lines. The lines in MS 1533 are irregular, and it is believed that it is in two hands (18 or 19 lines in the first hand; 15 or 16 lines in the second hand). The majority of the holographs in this collection are in red and brown leather binding, some with flaps. The only exceptions are MS 1569 (which comes in cloth binding with leather trim), MS 656 (in half cloth binding) and MS 746 (in quarter cloth binding). The present binding of these manuscripts is likely to be original.

The Arabic manuscript collection in The Institute of Ismaili Studies is quite diverse in provenance. Manuscripts were copied in Iraq, Afghanistan, Iran, India, Yemen and Egypt across a wide timespan between the 13th century to even the first quarter of the 20th century. Describing the provenance of Hamdani collection, Abbas Hamdani explains '[t]he authorship of most of these manuscripts is Ismaili, dating from the pre-Fatimid period up to the Ṭayyibī *daʿwa* in India and then to the present day. However, the earlier manuscripts are copies from the post-Ṣulayḥid period. Some old ones might still be found in private libraries in the Yemen'.[26]

The majority of the manuscripts presented in this chapter were copied in Yemen and India. The most notable exception is MS 162 (Gacek, vol. 2), copied in Shiraz (Dār al-ʿIlm Shiraz, Ramaḍān

1155/1744), and MS 1639 (Hamdani) *al-Fawāʾid al-mukhtabara*, known as *al-Tawqiʿāt* by al-Saḥmāwī, which was copied in Egypt. It was difficult to identify the date and provenance of MS 1569 (Hamdani).

This corpus of holographs was copied mainly between the 18th and 19th century and two of them even in the first quarter of the 20th century [9 manuscripts], but there is one manuscript MS 1639/1 dated (or confidently datable) slightly before 1500 AD. One manuscript was difficult to date (MS 1569 Hamdani), but I give an approximate date based on its position in the corpus of Gujarati and Arabic manuscript from the end of the 19th century. The following table (Table 18.2) provides a list of the studied manuscripts organised chronologically noting the Hijrī and Christian years and the place of copying.

Colophons are of great importance to scholars because they include invaluable information such as the date when a manuscript was inscribed. In this connection, Franz Rosenthal has brought to light literary evidence, which seems to indicate that autograph versions (*bi-khaṭṭ muʾallif*) were held in high esteem, as confirmed by several colophons.[27] Before concluding this section, some remarks on the nature of colophons in the mansucripts under discussion are in order.

In this corpus of holographs, the colophon is introduced most frequently by the word *tammat*, and the terms often used to confirm

Table 18.2 Dates and Provenance of the Holographs.

No.	Collection	Provenance	AH	AD
MS 1639/1	Hamdani	Egypt	[857]	[1453]
MS 1642/130	Hamdani	Yemen		1620
MS 1533/3	Hamdani	India	1154	1741
MS 798/162	Gacek v.2	Shiraz	1155	1744
MS 1544/102	Hamdani	Yemen?	1158	1745
MS 656/158	Gacek v.2	Yemen	1173	1759
MS 143	Gacek v.2	Yemen	1231	1816
MS 915	Zahid Ali	India?	1248	1832
MS 617/69	Gacek v.2	India?	[1320]	[1902]
MS 746/157	Gacek v.2	India	[1320]	[1902]
MS 298/185b	Gacek v.2	Yemen?	ND	ND
MS 1569/98	Hamdani	[Yemen?]	[1201?]	[1801?]

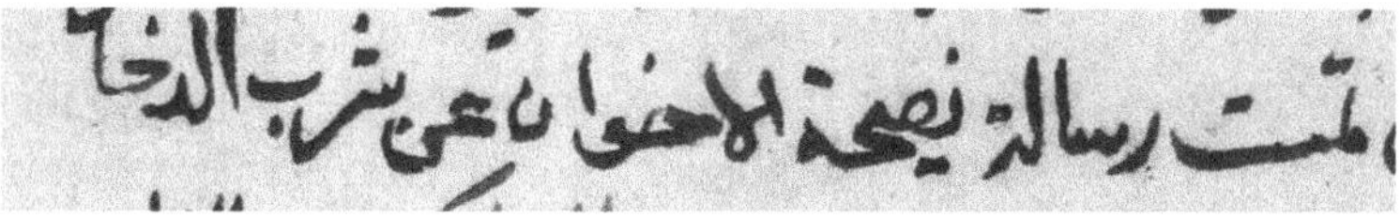

Figure 18.3 MS 656, f. 20r—Colophon.

the status of holograph are *rāqimihā* (its scribe), *katabahā bi-yamīnih* (wrote it by his right hand) and *bi-khaṭṭi muṣannifihā* (in the handwriting of the author). Also, the dates are written either in full or numerals or both. For instance, there are two statements in MS 656 confirming the authorship and holograph status. The first one is from the colophon which reads '*tammat risālat . . . bi-khaṭṭi mu'allifihā . . .*) (see Figure 18.3); the second statetment is mentioned in the lower-left corner of f. 20v which reads: *wa-kāna al-farāgh min raqm hādhihi al-nuskhah bi-khaṭṭi mu'allifihā Hibat Allāh 'Abd al-Rahīm Ja'far fī shahr Muḥarram al-ḥarām la'allahu laylat al-jum'ah.*

The Private Live of the Holographs

Paratextual elements are a significant feature in the Islamic manuscript tradition in general, but are of particular importance for holographs. They include remarks that owners wrote in the manuscripts, as well as any endownment statements (*waqf*) indicating the donation of a given book to a religious, charitable endowment. Some books contain notes from the authors stating that they had reviewed the copy of the book and approved it, while some book owners make notes about those who read or borrowed the manuscripts. In sum, the paratextual features record the lives of a single manuscript or of a collection.

Throughout the centuries, Islamic manuscripts were copied and used either for private use, as donations to someone or an institution, or for sale. So, ownership statements are valuable evidence to indicate the name of the person(s) who owned the manuscript throughout its history and to signpost the provenance. John Carter defines provenance as 'the pedigree of a book's previous ownership.'[28] Generally speaking, ownership statements vary from the simple *ex libris* (*min kutub*) to miniature compositions containing textual formulae like the *basmalah, ḥamdalah* and *taṣliyah.*[29]

There are rich signs of ownership statements and seals in the corpus under study, especially in the Hamdani collection. Some of these statements are basic, and others are detailed in terms of their structure, perhaps because various scholars from the Hamdani family owned items from this collection and travelled between India and Yemen. This is evident from the ownership statements. For example, MS 1642 has a long ownership statement without a date, using the expression *ṣāra fī milk* (became the property of). On the other hand, MS 1530 includes a basic statement: it starts with *fī milkat* (owned by) and ends with a date. More importantly, MS 1533 has an acquisition note signed by Muḥammad ʿAlī b. Fayḍ Allāh (al-Hamdānī) dated 1314/1896–1897 with various seals on different folios (see Table 18.3).

Although the ownership statements are often accompanied by impressions of private seals, this is not the case in this collection of holographs except in MS 1544 and MS 798 where the seal accompanies the ownership statement. There are traces of other seals in the collection that take different shapes (squares, circles and octagons). Most of them include the name of the owner in basic form, except MS

Table 18.3 A Selection of Ownership Statements.

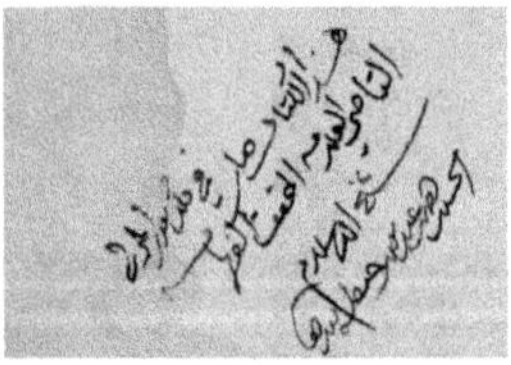	*Hādhā al-kitāb ṣāra fī milk bi-qadar al-Mawlā al-qāḍī al-ʿallāma al-muḥaqqiq al-fahhāma shaykh al-islām* [*al-hasan . . .*] **MS 1642**
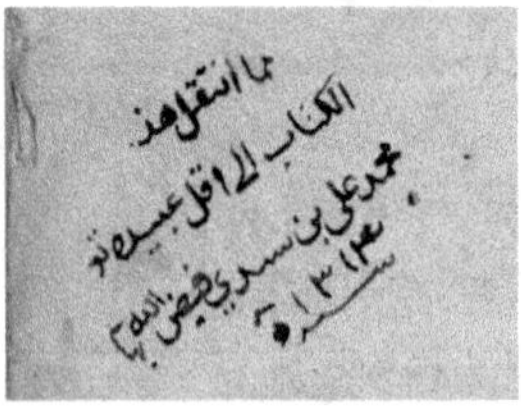	*Mimma intaqala hādhā al-kitāb ila aqall ʿabīduhu taʾāla Muḥammad ʿAlī ibn Fayḍ Allāh (al-Hamdānī) sanat 1314* [1896–1897] **MS 1533**
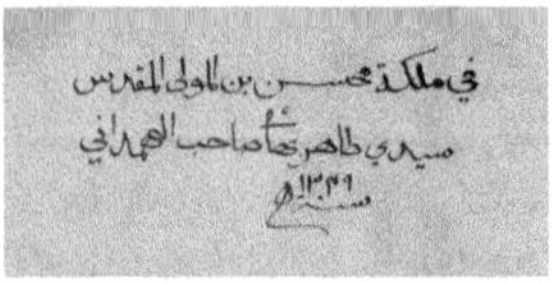	*Fī milkat Muḥsin ibn al-Mawla al-Muqaddas Sayyidī Ṭāhir Bahāʾ Ṣāḥib al-Hamādanī. 1349 AH* **MS 1530**

Table 18.4 A Selection of Seal Impressions.

MS 798	MS 1533	MS 1639	MS 1544	MS 1544

798 which includes the formula *Lā ilāha illā Allāh al-Malik al-Ḥaqq al-Mubīn* [. . .] *ʿabdahu Ḥusayn Muḥammad Sīrra* (see Table 18.4).

The analysis shows that this collection of holographs is rich in marginal notes and glosses. They range from short comments or detailed annotations explaining a word or group of words to a complete annotation *(ḥawāshī)*, which discusses either a different matter or adds a quotation. Most of the corrections are connected with the words omitted in transcription or inserted while proofreading, which are invariably indicated by the word *ṣaḥḥa* or the letter *ṣād* (meaning 'correct'). The two examples below represent different types of glosses in MS 656 and MS 746.

In MS 656, the author uses the word *tanbīh* (alert) to comment on or correct the main text and uses the word *ḥāshiyah* to add a new idea or insert a quotation from another reference. In both ways, he signs his name with the word *ṣaḥḥa* .

MS 746 (see Figure 18.4) includes some lengthy marginal comments written at different angles. However, it is noted that the author used the same pen for corrections and a different pen in faded black for additions and annotations.

It is also noted that the Hamdani collection manuscripts include title pages that were seemingly added later by the owner or another scholar. Most of these pages included paratextual information that is worthy of further study. For instance, MS 1642 has the original title page with ownership statement *(hādhā al-kitāb ṣāra fī milk* [. . .] *al-mawlā al-qāḍī al-ʿallāma al-muḥaqqiq al-fahhāma shaykh al-islām* [name]). MS 1533 has a title page on f. 2r written in different hand with ownership statement dated 1313 AH, and before *Basmalah,* the title and author are mentioned in detail. MS 656 is one of the few manuscripts in this collection with a laid-out title page with different ownership statements and stamps.

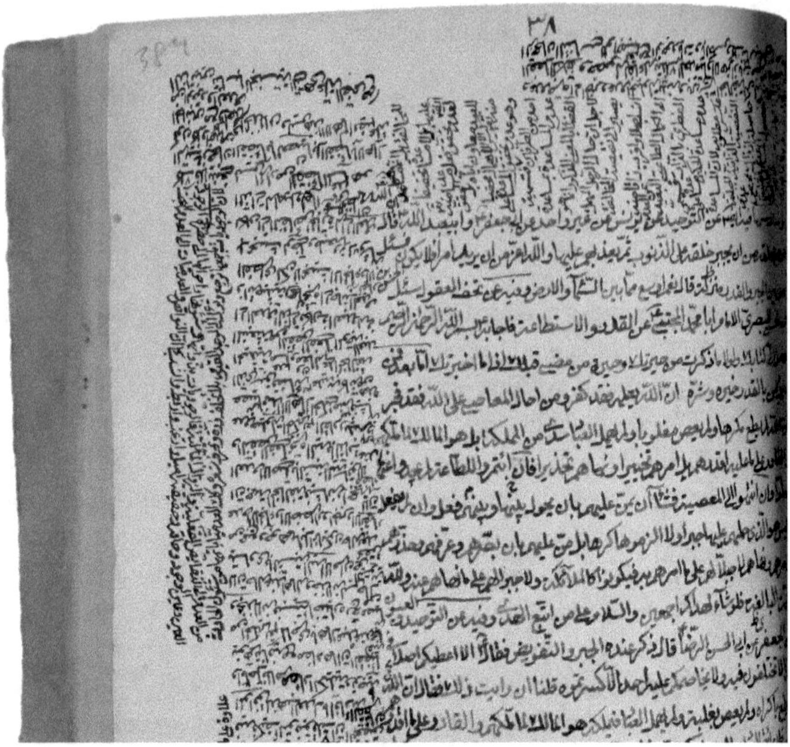

Figure 18.4 MS 746, marginal notes on f. 384r.

Text and Composition

The reasons for copying a text may affect its final appearance, depending also on the circumstances of its production. Earning money was one of the main reasons for scholars and students alike. It sometimes fell to such individuals to copy manuscripts for study purposes, to obtain a copy of a work, or to disseminate it to the wider community to transmit knowledge. However, copying a manuscript is a time-consuming task, and it is difficult to determine the identity of the individual who copied the manuscript regardless of the information available in colophon or any other sources.[50]

It suffices to say that the holographs examined in this chapter have been produced mainly by scholars, and it is difficult to say whether they were mainly copied for money. The chief reason to copy them in my view was to preserve knowledge as part of the scholarly tradition in

Shiʿi Muslim communities. For the Ṭayyibīs, the main concern was to preserve the text contained in the book rather than the book itself. Books are only a medium for preserving knowledge and ideas which are disseminated when the books are copied. Accordingly, the Ṭayyibīs have a strong scribal tradition, which lasted until the late 20th century. Some of the manuscripts were copied by scholars in order to obtain copies, while others were transcribed by students for their educational needs. The Khizāna al-Muḥammadiyya al-Hamdāniyya, which consisted of manuscripts copied by or for Shaykh Muḥammad ʿAlī and Fayḍ Allāh Hamdānī, and the Zahid Ali collection, are good examples of private collections preserved outside the direct control of the central *daʿwa* authority.[31]

Another reason in the production of these manuscripts was to complement an orally transmitted tradition such as MS 1642, *Rawḍat al-Adīb wa-Tuḥtfat al-Labīb wa-Nukhbat al-Ḥasīb li-Maʿrifat al-Ansāb*. This manuscript includes many genealogical trees that must have been preserved orally or in fragments. Unfortunately, we do not have access to this oral tradition, either because it was lost or because it is kept within close confines or closed educational circles within the Ṭayyibī tradition.[32]

The main component in these manuscripts is standard where they begin with *basmalah* ('in the name of God'), followed by *ḥamdalah (Praise to God), salamah* ('peace be upon him') and *baʿdiyah* ('thereafter'*)*. In some cases, the *basmalah* is preceded by the title as is the case in MS 1544. In another case, MS 1642, the *basmalah* was followed by a short prayer in the same line that reads (*rabbī yassir wa-aʿin yā Karīm*), asking for God's help, and a shorter version of the same prayer reads *rabbī yassir* in MS 1639.

Some of the manuscripts seem to be the only recorded complete copies, such as MS 1533. The text is a refutation where it includes long quotations from the treatise under attack, followed by a point-for-point response. The issue in question is the respective claims of the Dāʾūdī and Sulaymānī factions. This particular manuscript happens to have been written in two hands. A note on the title page states that the first half is in the hand of the author, citing the very modest titles which precede the author's name on the first page of the text, but I think that these could have been copied from the archetype and do not necessarily prove that this manuscript is a holograph.

In some cases, the text shifts back and forth between the first person plural (author speaking) and the third person singular (obviously a scribal interpolation). MS 656 is a clear example of this element as it is believed to be the author's fair copy, where he inserted glosses and quotations from different sources. He relied on many references to support his claim on the smoking prohibition; he quoted many passages from other works verbatim. It is worth mentioning that he also ignored some critical resources on the subject, such as Laqqānī's and al-Akhīsārī's works on the prohibition of smoking. The latter adopted the ideas of Ibn al-Qayyim and Ibn Taymiyah and led the debate on the subject in the 17th century.

As mentioned previously, it was difficult to confirm the type of holograph in some manuscripts. It is believed that MS 656 is the author's fair copy evident in the extensive insertions and annotations signed by the author. Moreover, it is mentioned on f. 20 that this is the only certified copy (*wa-hādhihi al-nuskhah hiya muʿtamad mā siwāhā wa-ilayhā al-marjiʿ fī-mā ʿadāhā*). The circumstances behind the composition of MS 1639, the study of its text and its authorship attribution are worthwhile to examine further. This manuscript is an extensive collection of *inshā*, that is, letters, documents and a few extracts from similar writings, compiled as a handbook for professional chancery secretaries from Mamluk Egypt.

According to de Blois, this manuscript's compiler is al-Sakhāwī (from the town of Sakha in Lower Egypt); there is an indication of the title or the compiler's name in the main body of the text. However, there are three lines on the last page (f. 241r), in different handwriting, stating that it is a collection of *tawqīʾāt*[33] with the title *al-Fawāʾid al-Mukhtabarah min Inshāʾ al-Muwaqqiʿīn al-Muʿtabarah,* compiled and written in his own hand (*mimma ʿuniya bi jamʿihi wa katabahu bi khaṭṭih* Muḥammad b. Muḥammad al-Saḥmāwī). The information contained in these three lines is reproduced in a recent hand on the title page and the spine of the manuscript. Al-Sahmāwī is the compiler of an important handbook for chancery secretariats titled *al-Thaghr al-Basim fī Ṣinā'at al-Kātib wa-al-Kātim* 'the Smiling Mouth on the Craft of the Scribe and Secretary'. So, it is likely to be part of al-Saḥmāwī's work as he was one of the famous Muwaqqiʿīn (secretary) in this period.

Conclusion

This chapter has provided a brief analysis of the holograph collection in the IIS manuscript corpus. In doing so, twelve manuscripts (holographs and autographs) were analysed by throwing light on their codicological and textual characteristics. The most prominent finding to emerge from this study is that these holographs are diverse in their physical and textual characteristics. The chapter also tried to demonstrate that a manuscript in the author's hand belongs to a particular category and should command the special attention of anyone editing, studying, or translating the text.

The IIS collection's authorial manuscripts represent significant examples of the holograph categories. However, some of these manuscripts require further analysis and study to confirm their status as holograph, fair copy or archetype. The differences between a working copy and a completed project are already apparent in this collection from the extensive corrections and insertions in one manuscript, and from the clean text in another.

This collection's physical characteristics in terms of the foliation and binding have not been studied before. The majority of these holographs keep the original binding possibly because they were copied in the 19th century. However, the codicological elements could provide more insights about the history and provenance of the collection. External features such as how a script is laid out and the page composed can convey additional data in this regard, though these should be treated with caution. To this end, the collection is rich in ownership statements, marginalia and seals that require further attention. Analysing these aspects will enable us to understand the corpus better. It might be helpful to apply this approach to the IIS collection to establish a knowledge base of external features (*ex libris*) that will shed light on more historical, geographical and biographical aspects of the IIS collection.

On the text criticism side, it is believed that none of these holographs have been published except MS 298 (*al-Ṣaḥīfah al-Sajjādīyah* by Zayn al-ʿĀbidin ʿAlī ibn al-Ḥusayn), which is proved not to be holograph. That said, other texts would benefit from detailed analysis or from their edition and publication. Overall, this study's contribution has been to confirm the authenticity of the holographs in the IIS collection and to invite further analysis of more manuscripts that belong to the same category. Using current technologies to map the collection in order to demonstrate the relationships between different manuscripts and collections is the ideal method to analyse the IIS collection. This might lead to significant discoveries to enhance our understanding of the collection.

NOTES

1 Frédéric Bauden and Élise Franssen, ed., *In the Author's Hand: Holograph and Authorial Manuscripts in the Islamic Handwritten Tradition* (Leiden, 2019), p. 7.
2 Ibid., p. 1.
3 In 2010, Noah Gardiner, then a doctoral candidate in the Department of Near Eastern Studies at the University of Michigan, discovered a holograph fair copy of the third part of *al-Mawāʾiẓ wa-al-iʿtibār fi dhikr al-khiṭaṭ wa-al-āthār* by al-Maqrīzī. After this discovery, many scholars revisited the work and a new critical edition was produced.
4 Adam Gacek, 'Library Resources at The Institute of Ismaili Studies, London', *British Society for Middle Eastern Studies Bulletin*, 11 (1984), pp. 63–64.
5 Delia Cortese, *Ismaili and Other Arabic Manuscripts: A Descriptive Catalogue of Manuscripts in the Library of The Institute of Ismaili Studies* (London, 2000).
6 Delia Cortese, *Arabic Ismaili Manuscripts: The Zāhid ʿAlī Collection in the Library of The Institute of Ismaili Studies* (London, 2003).
7 François de Blois, *Arabic, Persian and Gujarati Manuscripts: The Hamdani Collection in the Library of The Institute of Ismaili Studies* (London, 2011).
8 Ibid.
9 Adam Gacek, *Catalogue of Arabic Manuscripts in the Library of Ismaili Studies*, vol. 2 (London, 1985), p. ix.
10 J. A. Simpson and E. S. C. Weiner, *The Oxford English Dictionary* (2nd ed., Oxford, 1989), vol. 1, p. 803.
11 Ibid, vol. 7, p. 316.
12 Philip B. Gove, ed., *Webster's Third New International Dictionary* (Springfield, MA, 1981), p. 147.
13 Ibid, p. 1081.
14 As quoated in A. Gacek, 'Arabic Holographs: Characteristics and Terminology', in Bauden and Franssen, ed., *In the Author's Hand*, p. 55.
15 Ibid., p. 56.
16 Bauden and Franssen, ed., *In the Author's Hand*, p. 3.
17 Attestations (*taṣdīq*) are another tradition that is related to the making of manuscripts in general, and to autographs in particular. It is that category of notes in manuscripts stating that a particular manuscript or note is indeed in the hand of this or that scholar or scribe.
18 Ibn al-Nadīm, *al-Fihrist*, ed., Muḥammad ibn Isḥāq, Yūsuf ʿAlī Ṭawīl and Aḥmad Shams al-Dīn (Beirut, 1996), p. 92.
19 Aḥmad ibn al-Qāsim ibn Abī Uṣaybiʿah, *ʿUyūn al-Anbāʾ fī Ṭabaqāt al-Aṭibbāʾ*, ed., Nizār Riḍa (Beirut, n.d.), p. 421.
20 Abū al-Faraj al-Iṣfahānī, *Kitāb al-Aghānī*, ed., Dār Iḥyāʾ al-Turāth (Beirut, 1994), vol. 1, p. 5.
21 ʿAbd al-Ḥamīd ibn Hibat Allāh ibn Abī al-Ḥadīd, *Sharḥ Nahj al-balāghah*, ed., Muḥammad ʿAbd al-Karīm Nimrī (Beirut, 1998), vol. 4, pp. 656–700.

22 Shams al-Dīn Muḥammad b. ʿAbd al-Raḥmān al-Sakhāwī (831/1427–902/1496) was one of the students of Aḥmad ibn Ḥajar al-ʿAsqalānī (d. 852/1449). Among his numerous works are *Al-Maqāṣid al-ḥasana* and *Al-Qawl al-Badīʿ fi'l-Ṣalāt ʿ ala 'l-Ḥabīb al-Shafīʿ*.

23 Muḥammad ibn Muḥammad al-Shams ibn al-Badr al-Saḥmāwī al-Qāhirī al-Shāfiʿī al-Muwaqqī (d. 868/1464).

24 For unknown reasons al-Saḥmāwī's name was mixed up with that of al-Sakhāwī despite the fact that he was mentioned in many biographies including al-Sakhāwī's *al-Daw' al-Lāmiʿ li-Ahl al-Qarn al-Tāsiʿ* (Beirut, n.d.), vol. 10, p. 37.

25 Gacek, *Catalogue of Arabic Manuscripts*, vol. 2, p. 15 (Catalogue no. 185/B).

26 de Blois, *Arabic, Persian and Gujarati Manuscripts*, p. xxv.

27 Franz Rosenthal, *The Classical Heritage in Islam* (London, 1992), p. 23.

28 John Carter and Nicolas Barker, *ABC for Book Collectors* (London, 1980), p. 166.

29 Adam Gacek, *Arabic Manuscripts: A Vademecum for Readers* (Leiden, 2009), p. 174.

30 Samer Traboulsi, 'Transmission of Knowledge and Book Preservation in the Ṭayyibī Ismāʿīlī Tradition', *Intellectual History of the Islamicate World*, 4 (2016), p. 29.

31 On the history of the Khizāna al-Muḥammadiyya al-Hamdāniyya, see Abbas Hamdani's remarks in de Blois, *Arabic, Persian and Gujarati Manuscripts*, pp. xxv–xxxiv.

32 As Samer Trabouslsi remarks, '[f]or the time being, we can safely assume that the Ṭayyibī educational oral tradition developed significantly between the days of [Muḥammad b. Ṭāhir al-Ḥārithī] and [Ḥasan b. Nūḥ al-Bharūchī], since the first author's [anthology of different texts] is in two volumes, while the second is in seven. The development in the educational oral tradition was most probably a result of the changes in the constitution of the Ṭayyibī community, with the increased Indian presence and demands resulting from the major political and economic developments in Yemen and later in India' (see his, 'Transmission of Knowledge', p. 30).

33 This word normally means 'signatures', but is used here evidently in the sense of 'signed documents'. In other words, it includes models of different styles developed by chancery secretaries in Mamluk Egypt.

List of Illustrations

Figures

4.1 Title page of the first treatise (*On Arithmetic*) from the Epistles of the Pure Brethren (*Rasāʾil Ikhwān al-*Ṣafāʾ), MS 1040 of the Collection of The Institute of Ismaili Studies, London (f. Ar14/W1v). The manuscript is dated 953/1543. 90

4.2 Pages from IIS MS 1040 showing the end of the shorter version of Epistle 52 *On Magic* followed by the longer version, which is headed by a decorative title (f. Ar690/W683r). 124

5.1 Double page from IIS London, Hamdani Collection, MS 1410, pp. 225–226, showing two chapters on the Muʿtazila and a change of scribal hands (and pen) at the end of p. 226. 147

5.2 Beginning of IIS London, Hamdani Collection, MS 1411, showing the start of a list of chapter headings. 148

5.3 Double page from the 'proto edition' IIS London, Zahid Ali Collection, MS 1290, pp. 28–29, with footnotes beneath the main text. 148

7.1 MS 142, p. 7(r). 187

7.2 MS 142, p. 15(r). 188

7.3 MS 1288, p. 1(r). 189

7.4 MS 1204, f. 1r. 191

7.5 MS 141, p. 1(r), with stamp. 192

7.6 MS 678, f. 86, *Sūra* 3:184; transcription: *wa-idha akhadha allāhu mīthāqa alladhīna ūtū al-kitāba la-tubayyinunnahu li'l-nāsi wa lā taktumūnahu*; in the margin: *al-ʿImrān*. 193

7.7 MS 269, f. 1, with stamp. 193

7.8 MS A. 199

7.9	MS E.	200
10.1	Page from the manuscript MS Per 113 that had lain hidden for over three hundred years in Iran.	263
10.2	Title page of the *Dīwān* (from MS Per 99), which includes six lines from Ode 91; it reads: 'Expression of Belief, in Servitude to the Holy and Exalted Presence of our Lord Muḥammad b. Ḥasan b. ʿAlā Dhikrihi al-Salām, may his Bounty Endure and his Mission prevail'.	264
10.3	Page from the manuscript MS Per 99 (dated 832/1428) that survived among distant family members of Aga Khan I, Ḥasan ʿAlī Shāh in Mumbai.	265
12.1	KH 541, f. 1v, scribal note before the copying of *Risālo*, ascribed to Jaʿfar al-Ṣādiq.	314
12.2	KH 431, f. 85r, scribal remarks at the conclusion of *Janājo*, ascribed to Imām Shāh.	315
12.3	KH 537, f. 38v, a scribal note mentioning the source from which the text was copied.	319
13.1	Poetry ascribed to Shāh Niʿmat Allāh from MS BA 126.	336
13.2	*Risāla-yi Shāh Niʿmat Allāh Walī* in MS BA 86.	338
16.1	An example of the material used for the manuscripts (MS BT 7, f. 13).	391
16.2	An example of margins (MS BT 157, f. 39).	392
16.3	Example of gradual erosion (MS BT 25, f. 89).	392
16.4	MS BT 7, f. 31 (left) and MS BT 17, f. 29 (right).	393
17.1	Folio from Qur'ān Codex MS 909.	419
17.2	An example from MS 921 in *Maghribi* script.	420
17.3	Folio from MS 581, an illuminated Qur'ān manuscript in *Naskhī* hand.	421
17.4	Folio from MS 580, a Qur'ān codex in 'Kashmiri' style.	423
17.5	Folio from MS 745, an incomplete Qur'ān codex in *Naskhī* hand with the opening chapter of the Qur'ān.	424
17.6	MS 1700, a folio from a Central Asian manuscript showing the opening chapter of the Qur'ān.	425
17.7	HDP 19, a folio from a Qur'ān manuscript from Mamluk times.	426
18.1	MS 1639—From the title page.	437
18.2	MS 1639—Colophon.	437

18.3 MS 656, f. 20r—Colophon. 441
18.4 MS 746, marginal notes on f. 384r. 444

Tables

4.1 The place of IIS MS 1040 among the complete dated manuscripts of the *Rasāʾil Ikhwān al-Ṣafāʾ*. 85
4.2 Mention of the Prophet Muhammad and the words that follow. 94
4.3 Number of variants with regard to MS Atif 1681 in which Jīwā Khān's edition coincides with these MSS/editions. 99
4.4 No. of times that MS 1040 coincides with these copies but not with Jīwā Khān's ed.; and that Jīwā Khān's ed. coincides with these copies but not with MS 1040. 99
4.5 Epistles 32 and 33 in IIS MSS 1040 and 83 compared to other manuscripts. 107
4.6 Synoptic view of Epistle 48. 117
4.7 Synoptic view of Epistle 49. 121
4.8 Synoptic view of Epistle 52. 125
5.1 Dates and provenance. 149
5.2 Basic codicological data. 150
5.3 Data related to writing space and completeness. 151
5.4 Idiosyncrasies of the scribes regarding paratext. 153
5.5 Examples of textual variance. 155
7.1 Manuscripts of the *Mukhtaṣar al-uṣūl* housed at The Institute of Ismaili Studies. 186
14.1 Contemporaries of Shāh Ḍiyāʾī-i Shughnānī. 353
18.1 List of the Holograph Manuscripts in the IIS Collection. 438
18.2 Dates and Provenance of the Holographs. 440
18.3 A Selection of Ownership Statements. 442
18.4 A Selection of Seal Impressions. 443

Index

The abbreviation 'b.' for *ibn* ('son of') is alphabetised as written.
The Arabic definite article 'al-' is ignored for the purposes of alphabetisation.
The letter *f* following an entry indicates a page that includes a figure.
The letter *t* following an entry indicates a page that includes a table.
Bold text indicates manuscript numbers.

Abbasid Caliphate, 23, 24, 269 n.9
  anti-Ismaili literary campaigns, 24–5
ʿAbd Allāh b. Maymūn al-Qaddāḥ, 31
ʿAbd Allāh Badr al-Dīn, 175
ʿAbd al-Ḥusayn Ḥusām al-Dīn, 83
ʿAbd Mūsā Badr al-Dīn, 174
Abdul Husain, Mian Bhai, 176
abjad script, 278, 279, 281, 282, 283, 290
Abū al-ʿAlāʾ Ganjawī, 266
Abū Bakr, Timurid governor, 377
Abū Bakr al-Rāzī
  'Destruction of the Religions, The', 50
Abū al-Faraj al-Iṣfahānī, 436
  al-Aghānī, 436
Abū al-Faḍl, Raʾīs, 240, 241–3, 250
Abū Hātim al-Rāzī, 37, 50, 137–8, 145
  Aʿlām al-Nubūwa, 138
  Kitāb al-Iṣlāḥ, 138
  Kitāb al-Jāmiʿ, 138
  Kitāb al-Zīna see *Kitāb al-Zīna*
Abū Isḥāq Quhistānī, 39, 260, 261
  Haft bāb (Seven Chapters), 260, 409
Abū Saʿīd b. Mīrān Shāh, Sulṭān, 348
Abugida, 278
Account of the Gnostics (*Bayān al-ʿārifīn*) (Muḥammad Riḍā), 285
Adab al-Kātib (Ibn Qutaybah), 436
Afghanistan, 216, 217, 218, 219, 220, 221, 222, 223, 258, 260, 439
Aga Khan I, Ḥasan ʿAlī Shāh, Nizārī Imam, 33, 264, 265, 288
Aga Khan III, Sulṭān Muhammad Shāh, Nizārī Imam, 36, 37–8, 280, 348, 371
Aga Khan IV, H.H. Prince Karim, current Nizārī Imam, 41
Aga Khan Case, 33, 281, 304, 306–7
al-Aghānī (Abū al-Faraj al-Iṣfahānī), 436
ʿAhd-i Sayyidnā, 237, 253–4
  Abū al-Faḍl, Raʾīs, 240, 241–3, 250
  Alamūt, 242–3, 244, 252
  authorship, 246–9
  content, 240–6
  covenant, 244–5
  Ḥasan-i Maḥmūd-i Kātib, 246–9, 254

Ḥasan-i Ṣabbāḥ, Ra'īs (Sayyidnā), 237, 240, 241–2, 243, 244–5
manuscripts, 238–40
MS BA **46**, 239–40, 244, 252, 253
MS BA **59**, 239, 252, 253
MS BT **9**, 238–9, 240, 243, 244, 251, 252, 253
Muẓaffar ('Imād Allāh wa al-Dīn Muẓaffar b. 'Alī b. Muḥammad), Ra'īs, 240
Nāṣir al-Dīn Muḥtasham, Amir, 237, 245, 250
reason for writing, 249–50
Siege of Alamūt by Muḥammad Tapar, 244
variation in the account in manuscript copies, 251–3
wa'da-hā and predictions of Mawlānā, 240–1
'Alā'al-Dīn Muḥammad, Imam, 237, 240
Ahl al-bayt (the Family of the Prophet), 347–8, 356, 358, 359, 363
Aḥmad b. Ya'qūb al-Ṭayyibī, 269 n.16
Aḥsan, Sayyida, 52
Aitken, Edward, 281
ajlāf (mean; ignoble; wretches), 277
Ākhirzamānnāma (attrib. Nāṣir-i Khusraw), 363
al-Āmir, Caliph, 163, 178
'Alā-Dhikrihis-Salām, Imam, 257, 263
'Alā'al-Dīn Muḥammad, Imam, 237, 240, 258
A'lām al-Nubūwa (Abū Ḥātim al-Rāzī), 138
Alamūt, 28, 242–3, 244, 252, 258
alā toāhāra, 313, 326 n.21
'Alī b. Abī Ṭālib, Imam, 24, 333, 336, 348, 355, 357–8, 359, 360
Ismaili imamates, 401–2
'Alī, Zāhid, 7, 36, 37, 146–7
Allana, Ghulam Ali, 287–8
'Sindhi poetry of the Sumra era' (*Sūmran je daur jī Sindhī shā'irī*), 282
Sindhi Scripts (*Sindhī ṣūratkhaṭṭī*), 282–3
alms (*zakāt*), 406–7
Almutawa, Shadha, 114
alphabet, 278–9, 289
alphasyllabary, 278
al-Āmir bi-Aḥkām, Caliph, 163, 178, 183
Amīr Khusraw, 277
Āmū daryā (Oxus River), 347
Amulī, Ḥaydar, 333
annotations, 443, 446
Anjudān revival, 38
anti-Ismaili literary campaigns, 24–6
Anwār al-tanzīl wa-asrār al-ta'wīl (al-Bayḍāwī, Nāṣir al-Dīn), 422
Arabic language/script, 29, 219, 220, 278, 279, 289, 290, 318
Encyclopaedia of Islam, 275–6
manuscript corpus, 433–4, 438, 439, 440
manuscript terminology, 431, 435
scholarship, 277, 285
Arabistic bias, 275–6
archaeology, 38
archetype (*al-nuskhah al-dustūr*), 436
Ardhanāgarī, 278
Aristotle
Categories, 57
On Interpretation, 57
Posterior Analytics, 57
Prior Analytics, 57, 78
Arnould, Joseph, 281, 306–7
Asās al-ta'wīl (al-Nu'mān, al-Qāḍī), 172–3, 175, 396–7
aṣḥāb al-ra'y, the, 184

Ashokan inscriptions, 278
ashrāf (foreign-born Muslim 'elite'), 276
Asrār al-ḥurūf (Ghiyāth al-Dīn ʿAlī Iṣfahānī), 377, 378
assassination, 26
Assassins, 325 n.9
etymology, 31
legends, 26, 31
Astarābādī, Faḍl Allāh, 333–4
Ātashkada (Luṭf Alī Bīg Ādhar), 225
ʿAṭṭār, Farīd al-Dīn, 333
attested copy (*taṣdīq*), 436
Aziz, Abualy A., 288

Bābur, Emperor, 348, 350–1
Bābur-nāma, 351
Badakhshān, 9, 34, 216–17, 224, 261, 334, 347–8, 364
16th century politics of rule, 348–51
Ismaili Islam, 361, 370–2
Ismaili Literature, 230–1
Qāsim-Shāhī Renaissance, 230–1
Russian/Soviet rule, 220, 221–2
Sargudhasht-i Sayyidnā, 227–30
Badakhshānī, Sayyid Suhrāb Walī, 370, 373–6, 377, 379–83, 397
baʿdiyah (thereafter), 445
Badr al-Dīn b. al-Jamāʿa
Tadhkirat al-sāmiʿ wa'lmutakallim fi adab al-ʿālim wa'l-mutaʿallim, 180 n.25
al-Baghdādī, 24
Baḥr al-akhbār, 229–30, 375
Bāʾī, Zaynab, 52
Baig, Ḥājī Qudratullāh, 7
Banbhore, 289
Baqoev, Mamadvafo, 218, 356
Bartol'd, Vladimir, 350
basmala, 59, 61, 313, 445
bayāḍ (anthology), 356
Bayāḍ-i ashʿār-i Naẓmī (Naẓmī-i Shughnānī), 356
Bayān al-ʿārifīn (*Account of the Gnostics*) (Muḥammad Riḍā), 285
Bayʿat al-riḍwān (Pledge under the Tree), 360
al-Bayḍāwī, Nāṣir al-Dīn
Anwār al-tanzīl wa-asrār al-ta'wīl, 422
Begim, Shāh, 350
Berchem, Max van, 33
Bertel's, Andrey E., 40, 218, 356
bhakti, 277
al-Bharūchī, Ḥasan b. Nūḥ, 169, 172–3, 177–8
Kitāb al-Azhār, 169, 172–3, 178
Bhāvnagar, 285
Bhuj, 286
bi-khaṭ al-mu'allif, 435, 440
al-Bīrūnī, Abū Rayḥān, 278
Book of India (*Kitāb taḥqīq mā li'l-Hind*), 278
black legend, 24, 25, 31
Blumhardt, James, 281
Bobrinskiy, Count Aleksey A., 34
Boghā Māstar, Hāsham
Origins of the Khojas (*Asalīyate Khojā*), 287
Bohras, 2, 325 n.12
doctrinal learning, 168, 170–1, 172–4, 176
Dā'ūdī Bohras, 2, 171, 434, 445
formal positions, 171
scholars, 36
scribes, 10, 171, 172
secrecy, 172, 288
see also Ṭayyibī Ismailis
Bombay, 6, 433
Bombay High Court, 281, 285
Book of Highest Initiation, 288
Brāhmī, 278–9

Browne, Edward G., 35
Bukhara, 347
Burhānpūrī, Quṭb al-Dīn, 169
Muntaza' al-akhbār, 169
Burton, Richard, 278, 281, 304
Sindh, and the Races that Inhabit the Valley of the Indus, 278–9
al-Bustānī, Buṭrus b. Sulaymān, 57, 82, 96, 110, 111, 112, 123, 126
Buzurg Ummīd, Kiyā, 211
Buzurg Ummīd, Muḥammad b., 211

Cahen, Calude, 40
Cairo, 23
Callataÿ, Godefroid de, 97, 110, 119, 122, 123, 125
Canard, Marius, 40
Caprotti, Giuseppe, 33
Carter, John, 441
Casanova, Paul, 32, 33
Case of the Animals versus Man Before the King of the Jinn, The, 102–3
'Case of the Khojahs', 276
catchwords, 439
Categories (Aristotle), 57
Central Asia (Mā warā al-nahr), 348, 349, 350
Chālīha akharī, 282
Chand Khān, 174
Christian Crusaders, 25–6
anti-Ismaili literary campaigns, 25–6
Chronicles of the Pīrs (*Tavārikhe pīr*) (Daragāvālā, Sadaradīn), 287
Chunara, Alimahomed Janmahomed, 7
Noorum-Mobin: Or the Sacred Cord of God (*Nūram mobīn: Yāne Allāhanī pavitr rasī*), 287
Clay, Jenny Strauss, 52
cloth bindings, 439
codicology, 389–90, 431–3, 438–41, 447
Collectanea (Ivanow, Wladimir), 282
colligatums, 219
colophons, 312, 313, 392–3*f*, 440–1
Composition no. 1 (Saporta, Marc), 116
Corbin, Henry, 9, 39
corrections, 432, 435, 439, 443, 447
Cortázar, Julio
Royuela, 116
court cases, 276, 281
Cutchee, 281 *see also* Kachchhi
Cutchi *see* Kachchhi

Da'ā'im al-Islām (*The Pillars of Islam*) (al-Nu'mān, al-Qāḍī), 36, 399, 400, 401
Dabistān-i madhāhib, 229
Dādu, Pir, 286, 316–7
dā'ī muṭlaq, 167, 169, 172, 173, 174, 175, 176, 178
dā'īs (missionaries; summoners), 23, 27
Dānish-nāma-i jahān (Ghiyāth al-Dīn 'Alī Iṣfahānī), 377–8
Dar bayān-e haft arkān-e sharī'at wa ta'wīl ān (*On the Explanation of the Seven Pillars of the Sharī'a and its Ta'wīl*) (al-Ṭūsī, Naṣīr al-Dīn), 399–400
Daragāvālā, Sadaradīn, 287
Chronicles of the Pīrs (*Tavārikhe pīr*), 287
Darrah-i Ṣūf, 88
Darwāz, 347, 351
Darwīsh Quṭb al-Dīn
Dīwān, 268
da'wa (summons; call), 23–4, 114, 170–1, 439, 445
language, 434
Nizārī, 237, 241, 242, 245, 258, 259, 371–2

Defrémery, Charles François, 32
'Destruction of the Religions, The' (Abū Bakr al-Rāzī), 50
Devanagari script, 276, 279
Devarāj, Mukhī Lalajībhāī, 280
Dhālāṇī, Kāmaḍīā Jāpharabhāi, 280
dīdār (meeting), 405
Dieterici, Friedrich, 33
Dihkhudā b. ʿAbd al-Malik Fashandī, 211
al-Dīn, ʿAbd al-Qādir Najm, 47
al-Dīn, Muḥammad Badr, 47
al-Dīn, Ṭāhir Sayf, 6, 47
Dīwān (Darwīsh Quṭb al-Dīn), 268
Dīwān-i Qāʿimiyyāt (Poems of the Resurrection) (Ḥasan-i Maḥmūd-i Kātib), 209, 247, 248, 249, 257, 259–60, 262–8
Ḍiyāʾī-i Shughnānī *see* Shāh Ḍiyāʾī-i Shughnānī
draft, 432, 435, 436
Durrat al-misāḥa (Ghiyāth al-Dīn ʿAlī Iṣfahānī), 378
Dustūr al-Munajjimīn, 267
Al-Dustūr was daʿwat al-muʾminīn li al-ḥuḍūr, 269 n.16

École des Langues Orientales Vivantes, 29
education, 9, 23, 167–8
  colleges, 417
  doctrinal learning, 168, 170–1, 172–5
  reform, 175–6
  scripts, 280–1, 283
  Sindhi schools, 280–1
  Soviet, 220
Egypt, 439, 440*t*, 446
El-Bizri, Nader, 126
  Epistles of the Brethren of Purity, 82
Encyclopaedia of Islam, 275–6
England, 439
'Epistle of Shāh Niʿmat Allāh Walī, the' (*Risāla-yi Shāh Niʿmat Allāh Walī*) (Niʿmat Allāh Walī, Shāh), 337–43
Epistles of the Brethren of Purity (El-Bizri, Nader [general ed.]), 82
Erskine Perry, Thomas, 276, 281, 305–6
ex libris, 441, 447

Fahrasat al-kutub wa'l-rasāʾil (*Fihrist al-Majdūʿ*) (al-Majdūʿ, Ismāʿīl b. ʿAbd al-Rasūl), 2–3, 53–4, 170, 175
fair copy, 432, 435, 436, 446, 447
Fakhr al-Dīn al-Rāzī, 76
farmān, 280
fasting (*rūzah*), 404–6
Fatimid Caliphate, 23, 24, 258–9
  heritage, 27
  Ismaili law, 27
  Ismailism, 167, 168, 172
  studies, 32–3
  succession dispute, 183
Fatimid Ismailism, 167, 168, 172
fidāʾīs, 26
'figure of the bride', 75–6
Fihrist (Ibn al-Nadīm), 138, 145, 436
Fihrist al-Majdūʿ (*Fahrasat al-kutub wa'l-rasāʾil*) (al-Majdūʿ, Ismāʿīl b. ʿAbd al-Rasūl), 2–3, 53–4, 170, 175
folios, 438, 442
foliation, 190
Franssen, Élise, 431
Fyzee, Asaf A. A., 36, 37, 174

Gacek, Adam, 418, 422, 431, 433, 434, 435
Gazetteer of the Bombay Presidency, 307

gazetteers, British, 287
Genealogical Tree of the Secret Path, The (*Gupat panthakā shujarā*), 288
genealogy, 445
Ghadīr Khum, 360
Ghālib, Muṣṭafā, 8, 40, 176
al-Ghānimī, Saʿīd, 137, 141, 142, 149, 150, 154, 156
al-Gharawī, Muḥammad Riḍā ibn Muḥammad Jaʿfar al-Rāzī, 439
al-Ghazālī, 24–5
  al-Mustaẓhirī, 25
ghazals, 277
Ghiyāth al-Dīn ʿAlī b. Ḥusayn b. ʿAlī Amīrān Iṣfahānī, 370, 376–80, 382–3
  Asrār al-ḥurūf, 377, 378
  Dānish-nāma-i jahān, 377–8
  Durrat al-misāḥa, 378
  Khulāṣat al-tanjīm va burhān al-taqvīm, 378
  Maʿārif al-taqvīm, 378
Ghufrānī, Muḥammad Ḥusayn, 261, 262
Ghulām Ḥaydar-i Shāhdawlat, 222, 223
al-Ghulūw wa'l-Firaq al-Ghāliya fī l-Ḥaḍāra al-Islāmiyya (al-Sāmarrāʾī, ʿAbdallāh Sallūm), 141
al-Ghūrī, Miyān Shamʿūn b. Muḥammad, 173
Ghūrid dynasty, 370
Gibb, Hamilton A. R., 36, 48
*ginān*s (devotional works), 29, 42, 280, 282, 283, 284–6, 309, 323, 324 n.4
  Khwājah Sindhi (Khojki) manuscript collection, 277
  Nānajīāṇī, Sachedīnā, 288
glosses, 436, 443, 446
Goeje, Michael de, 32, 50
Goldziher, Ignác, 50
Goodman, Lenn, 102, 103
Great Ismaili Heroes, The, 287
Grierson, George, 281, 289
Guide to Ismaili Literature, A (Ivanow, Wladimir), 2–3, 4, 53, 261
Gujarati, 277, 280, 282, 283, 285, 287, 288, 290
Gujerati *see* Gujarati
Gujrati *see* Gujarati
Gurmukhi script, 288–9
Guyard, Stanislas, 31

Habibov, Amirbek, 353–4, 355, 358
hadith, 415
Ḥāfiẓ-i Shīrāzī, 352
Haft bāb (Seven Chapters) (Abū Isḥāq Quhistānī), 260, 409
Haft bāb (Seven Chapters) (Ḥasan-i Maḥmūd-i Kātib), 28, 209, 257, 259–62, 267, 268
  MS **32**, 261, 262
  MS **64**, 261
  MS BT **157**, 262
  MS BT **171**, 262
Haft bābi Bābā Sayyid-nā, 260–1
Haft nukta (Seven Aphorisms) (Islām Shāh), 371
'Haji Bibi Case', 281, 285
ḥajj (pilgrimage), 407
al-Ḥākim, Caliph, 259
halant, 279
Halflants, Bruno, 122, 123
Halm, Heinz, 41
ḥamdalah (Praise to God), 445
Hamdani, Abbas, 7–8, 37, 40, 49, 52, 76, 116, 166, 172, 439
al-Hamdānī, ʿAlī b. Saʿīd al-Yaʿburī, 47

al-Hamdānī, Fayḍ Allāh b. Muḥammad ʿAlī, 47, 176
al-Hamdānī, Ḥusayn, 3–4, 36–7, 47, 48, 49, 50–2
Kitāb al-Zīna, 140–1, 143, 150
al-Hamdānī, Muḥammad ʿAlī, 47, 172, 437, 442
Hamdani Collection, 37, 41, 49, 50–4, 144, 166, 434, 439, 442
al-Ḥāmidī, ʿAlī ibn Ḥātim, 183
al-Ḥāmidī, Ḥātim b. Ibrāhīm, 169
Tanbīh al-ghāfilīn, 173
Tuḥfat al-qulūb, 169
Hammer-Purgstall, Joseph von, 32
handwritten books, 9
ḥaqāʾiq, 171
Ḥaqdād, son of Mamadnaẓarbik, 222, 223
al-Ḥārithī, Muḥammad b. Ṭāhir, 169–70, 183
al-Ḥasan b. Idrīs (al-Anf), 173–4
al-Ḥasan b. al-Nuʿmānī al-Ismāʿīlī, 58, 88
Ḥasan, Ḥasan Ibrāhīm, 40
Ḥasan Kabīr al-Dīn, Pīr, 287
Ḥasan-i Maḥmūd-i Kātib, 246–9, 254, 257–8, 259
Dīwān-i Qāʾimiyyāt (Poems of the Resurrection), 209, 247, 248, 249, 257, 259–60, 262–8
Haft bāb (Seven Chapters), 28, 209, 257, 259–62, 267, 268
Taṣawwurāt, 247, 259
Ḥasan-i Ṣabbāḥ, Raʾīs (Sayyidnā), 24, 28, 207, 210, 215, 216, 225–7
ʿAhd-i Sayyidnā, 237, 240, 241–2, 243, 244–5
Haft bāb (Seven Chapters), 260–1
letters of, 209–10
Niẓām al-Mulk, 210, 225
Persian language, 29
ʿUmar Khayyām, 210, 225
see also *Sargudhasht-i Sayyidnā*
Hasanyār-i Shughnānī, Ḥusayn-i, 353–4
ḥāshiyah, 443
Ḥashwiyya, the, 184
al-Ḥāwī (al-Rāzi, Abu Bakr Moḥammad b. Zakariyāʾ), 436
Ḥaydar, Shaykh, 333–4
Hindi, 276, 277, 279, 281
Hinduism, 277, 285, 322
History of the Khojas, The (*Khojā kom no itihas*) (Jaffer Rahimtoola), 287
History of the Pīrs (*Pīrono itihās*) (Dāmāṇī, Akabar), 287
Hodgson, Marshall, 39–40, 257, 258, 268, 275, 276
Hollister, John Norman
Shiʿa of India, 282
holograph manuscripts in the IIS, 431, 432–3, 434, 435, 436–41, 447–8
MS **69**, 439
MS **143**, 440*t*
MS **157**, 439
MS **162**, 439–40
MS **298**, 437, 438*t*, 440*t*, 447
MS **617**, 438*t*, 440*t*
MS **621**, 438*t*
MS **656**, 438*t*, 439, 440*t*, 441*f*, 443, 446
MS **746**, 438*t*, 439, 440*t*, 443, 444*f*
MS **798**, 438*t*, 440*t*, 442, 443*t*
MS **915**, 438*t*, 440*t*
MS **1530**, 442*t*
MS **1533**, 437, 438*t*, 439, 440*t*, 442*t*, 443*t*, *i445*

MS **1544**, 438*t*, 440*t*, 442, 443*t*, 445
MS **1569**, 438*t*, 439, 440*t*
MS **1639**, 436–7*f*, 438*t*, 440*t*, 443*t*, 445, 446
MS **1642**, 438*t*, 440*t*, 442*t*, 443, 445
ownership statements, 441–4
physical characteristics, 438*t*–41, 447
seals, 442–3*t*
text and composition, 444–6
holographs, 431, 435
Hooda, Vali Nanji, 7
Howard, Edward, 281
Huart, Clément, 35
Humāyūn, Emperor, 351
Ḥusayn, Muḥammad Kāmil, 39
'Silsilat Makhṭūṭāt al-Fāṭimiyyīn' series, 39
Ḥusayn, Mullā, 405
Ḥusayn, Ṭāhā, 49–50
al-Ḥusayn, Zayn al-ʿĀbidīn ʿAlī ibn
al-Ṣaḥīfah al-sajjādīyah 437, 447

Ibn Abī al-Ḥadīd, 436
Sharḥ Nahj al-Balāghah, 436
Ibn Abī Usaybiʿah, 436
ʿUyūn al-Anbāʾ, 436
Ibn ʿArabī, 333, 334
Ibn al-Athīr, 212
Ibn Durayd, 436
Ibn Ḥajar al-ʿAsqalānī
Lisān al-Mīzān, 145
Ibn Hāniʾ, 37
Ibn ʿInaba
ʿUmdat al-ṭālib, 267
Ibn al-Nadīm, 138, 436
Fihrist, 138, 145, 436
Ibn Qutaybah, 436
Adab al-Kātib, 436
Ibn al-Rawandī
Kitāb al-zumurrud, 50
Ibn Rizām (Abū ʿAbd Allāh Muḥammad b. ʿAlī b. Rizām al-Kūfī), 24
Ibn al-Walīd, ʿAlī b. al-Ḥusayn b. Jaʿfar b. Ibrāhīm b., 169, 183
Ibn al-Walīd, ʿAlī b. Muḥammad b. 169, 183–4
Mukhtaṣar al-uṣūl see *Mukhtaṣar al-uṣūl*
Ibrāhīm Mīrzā, 351
Idrīs, ʿImād al-Dīn, 48, 169
Nuzhat al-afkār, 169
ʿUyūn al-akhbār, 50
Zahr al-maʿānī, 48
Imām-Qulī (Khākī-i Khurāsānī), 352, 361–2
Imamate, the, 342–3, 348
spiritual authority, 396, 398–410
Imbert, Frédéric, 428
implosives, 289
India, 276–83, 285, 303, 317–18, 434, 439, 440*t*, 442
elite literate classes, 310–11
inscriptions, 435
Institute of Ismaili Studies (IIS), 5, 7–8, 29, 41–2, 128 n.2, 439
Hamdani Collection, 37, 41, 49, 50–4, 144, 166, 434, 439, 442
holograph manuscripts, 436–48
Ismaili Special Collections Unit (ISCU), 128 n.2
Khwājah Sindhi (Khojki) manuscript collection, 277, 286
manuscript corpus, 433–4
Qurʾān Manuscripts, 418–28
Zāhid ʿAlī Collection, 37, 41, 145–8, 433, 445
Iran, 258, 260, 261, 262, 266, 268, 439
Iraq, 439

Isagoge (Porphyry), 57
Iṣfahānī, Ghiyāth al-Dīn ʿAlī b. Ḥusayn b. ʿAlī Amīrān, 370, 376–80, 382–3
Isḥāq b. al-Shaykh al-Fāḍil Sulaymānjī, 58
Islām Shāh, Nizārī Imam,
  Haft nukta (Seven Aphorisms) 371
Islamic manuscripts, 441
Islamic Research Association, 6–7, 37–8
Islamic World, 258
Ismāʿīl I, Shāh, 333–4, 350, 362–3
al-Ismāʿīlī, al-Ḥasan b. ʿAlī al-Nuʿmānī, 88
Ismaili law, 27
Ismaili literature/texts, 2, 4–5, 23, 27, 28
  classical, 27
  destruction of, 4, 260, 262, 333
  limiting access, 9
  literary networks, 7, 8
  transmission, 5
Ismaili manuscripts, 5, 28–9
  transmission, 5
Ismaili Society, 6–7, 38–9
Ismaili studies, 2, 3, 4, 5, 29
  modern scholarship (1931–1945), 35–8
  modern scholarship, consolidation of (1946–1977), 38–41
  orientalist perspectives (1810–1930), 29–35
  progress (1977–present), 41–2
Ismaili theology, 258, 259, 267, 268
Ismaili-Sufi relationship, 268
Ismailis, the, 23, 332–3, 361
  anti-Ismaili literary campaign, 24
  Badakhshān, 34, 361, 370–2
  black legend, 24, 25, 31
  Central Asian, 33–4
  dāʿīs (missionaries), 23, 27
  divine revelation, 397–8
  esoteric tradition, 395–400
  European perception of, 26–7
  Fatimid Ismailism, 167, 168, 172
  fidāʾīs, 26
  as heretics, 24, 303, 304, 307
  imamate, 401–2, 403–4
  military campaigns against, 25
  Niʿmat Allāh Walī, Shāh, 336, 342–4
  Niʿmat Allāhīs, 331, 332–4, 343
  Panj-tanī, 348
  schism, 24, 371
  secrecy, 172, 288
  sharīʿa, 395, 398
  spiritual authority, 332, 333–4
  Sufism, 332–4
  taʾwīl concept, 395–400
  wilāya doctrine, 401
  zakāt (alms), 406
  see also Institute of Ismaili Studies; Nizārī Ismailis; Ṭayyibī Ismailis
'Ismāʿīlīya' (Ivanow, Wladimir), 38
'Ismāʿīliyya' (Madelung, Wilferd), 41
Ivanow, Wladimir, 1–2, 3, 5–6, 34, 35–6, 38–40, 433
  archaeology, 38
  cataloguing, 34, 37, 40
  Collectanea, 282
  copying of texts, 9–10
  Corbin, Henry, 9
  Guide to Ismaili Literature, A, 2–3, 4, 53, 261
  'Haft bābi Bābā Sayyid-nā, 260–1, 268
  Islamic Research Association, 6, 37–8

Ismaili Society, 38–9
'Ismā'īlīya', 38
Khojki script, 282, 283, 286, 290
literacy, 317
Sargudhasht-i Sayyidnā, 214

Jābir b. Ḥayyān, 3
Ja'far b. Manṣūr al-Yaman, 37
Jalāl al-Dīn Ḥasan, 258
Jalāl al-Dīn al-Rūmī, 352
Jamā'at, 259
Jamā'at Khāna, 280, 285
jamāyatakhānā see Jamā'at Khāna
Jāmi' al-Tawārīkh (Rāshid al-Dīn Sinān), 210, 211
jihad (striving), 408–9
Jīwā Khān, Nūr al-Dīn b., 81, 82–3, 114
Johnson, William, 304
Jumā, Murādh: 'Ali: Bhāī:, 279
Ten Sindhi Dirges (*Sındi: ḍohı marāsiā*), 280
Juma Jan Muhammad Ismail, 285
Junayd, Shaykh, 333–4
Juwaynī, 'Atā Malik, 208, 210, 211, 267
Sargudhasht-i Sayyidnā, 208, 210, 211, 215, 227, 228, 229
Tārīkh-i Jahāngushāy, 210

Kābā, Edalajī Dhanajī, 288
Kabīr, 277
Kachchhi/Kacchī script, 284, 316
Kadkanī, Shafī'ī, 266, 267–8
Kalām-i pīr, 229, 230, 231
Kalāme Maulā (*Words of the Lord*) (Hooda, Vali Nanji), 283
Kaṇbīs, the, 284
Kanz al-Walad (al-Ḥāmidī, Ibrāhīm ibn al-Ḥusayn), 9
Karachi, 282
Kasā'ī, 266
Kāshānī, Abū'l-Qāsim 'Abd Allāh b. 'Alī, 208, 210–11
Sargudhasht-i Sayyidnā, 208, 210–11, 227, 228
Zubdat al-tawārīkh, 211, 263, 266
Kaṭhiyāvāḍ Ismaili Literature Promulgation Society (*Ismāilī Sāhity Prachārak Maṇḍaḷ*), 285
Khākī-i Khurāsānī (Imām-Qulī), 352, 361–2
Khāqānī, Afḍal al-Dīn Badīl b. Ibrāhīm, 266
Khayrkhwāh-i Harātī, 39
Khīāte (title), 321
al-Khiṭaṭ (al-Maqrīzī, Taqī al-Dīn Aḥmad b. 'Alī), 432
al-khizāna al-maknūna' (guarded treasure), 27–8
Khizāna al-Muḥammadiyya al-Hamdāniyya Collection, 445
Khojā *see* Khwājah
Khojāh *see* Khwājah
Khojas, 29
colonial portrayal, 303–8, 324
female inheritance, 305–6
Kutch, 316–17
literate classes, 308–12, 317–18, 320–1, 323–4
migration, 317
religious identity, 304–8, 322
Satpanth manuscripts, 308, 312–23
as traders and merchants, 303, 304, 305, 307–8, 324
see also Nizārī Ismailis, Khwājah
Khojki *see* Khwājah Sindhi
Khudāwādī, 279, 289, 290
Khulāṣat al-ash'ār, 229
Khulāṣat al-tanjīm va burhān al-taqvīm (Ghiyāth al-Dīn 'Alī Iṣfahānī), 378

Khusraw, Amīr, 277
Khwājah, 277, 279, 281, 282, 288
Khwājah Aḥrār, 374
Silk-i guhar-rīz, 229–30, 231, 374–6, 380–1
Khwājah Khayrān, 355
Khwājah Sindhi', 277, 281–3, 285–91
'Khwajah Sindhi Literature', (Moir, Zawahir), 283
Khwājah Sindhi (Khojki) manuscript collection, 277
antiquity, 284–6
KH **25**, 286
KH **38**, 286
khyāta (that which is told or proclaimed), 321
khyāti (renown; fame), 321
al-Kirmānī, Ḥamīd al-Dīn, 27, 37, 50, 259
Rāḥat al-ʿaql, 39
al-Risāla al-waḍʿiya fi maʿālim al-dīn, 172, 175
Tanbīh al-hadī wa'l-muhtadī, 173
ta'wīl, 397–8
Kitāb al-Azhār (al-Bharūchī, Ḥasan b. Nūḥ), 169, 172–3, 178
Kitāb Bilawhar wa Budhāsaf, 114
Kitāb al-Iṣlāḥ (Abū Ḥātim al-Rāzī), 138
Kitāb al-jawāhir (*Book of Essences or Jewels*), 171
Kitāb al-Jāmiʿ (Abū Ḥātim al-Rāzī), 138
Kitāb al-Maḥṣūl (al-Nasafī, Muḥammad ibn Aḥmad), 138
Kitāb ta'wīl al-ṣalāt, 165–6
Kitāb al-Zīna (Abū Ḥātim al-Rāzī), 137, 138–41
ʿAlī, Zāhid, 146–7
Berlin copy, 147
eulogies, 152–4
al-Ghānimī, Saʿīd, 137, 141, 142, 149, 150, 154, 156
India, Shaykh ʿAbd al-Qayyūm ʿIsābhā'ī collection, 144
Karachi copy, 146, 147
Labīd verses, 154–5*t*
manuscript comparisons, 149–56
manuscript copies, 141–56
MS **1290**, 140, 146–7
MS Bagh. **1306**, 151*t*, 152, 155*t*
MS HC **1410**, 144, 147*f*, 149*t*, 150*t*, 151*t*, 153*t*, 154, 155*t*, 159 n.43
MS HC **1411**, 144–5, 148*f*, 149*t*, 150*t*, 151*t*, 152, 153*t*, 155*t*, 159 n.43
MS Leipzig Or. **377**, 140, 141–2, 150, 151*t*, 152, 153*t*, 155*t*
MS San. **2119**, 143, 150, 151*t*
MS San. **45** lugha, 143, 151*t*
MS San. **46** lugha, 139–40, 143, 151*t*, 152, 154, 155*t*
MS ZAC **1269**, 145, 146, 149*t*, 150*t*, 153*t*
MS ZAC **1270**, 145, 147, 149*t*, 150*t*, 153*t*, 155
MS ZAC **1271**, 145–6, 149*t*, 150*t*, 153*t*, 155*t*
MS ZAC **1290**, 145, 146–7, 148*f*, 149*t*, 150*t*, 153*t*, 155
MS ZAC **1317**, 145, 146, 149*t*, 150*t*, 153*t*, 155*t*
Mumbai, Asghar Ali collection, 143–4
Kitāb al-zumurrud (Ibn al-Rawandī), 50
Kitāb-i Buzurg Ummīd, 211
Kitāb-i ḥaẓrat-i Bābā Sayyidnā, 218
Kitāb-i Mustaṭāb-i Haḍrat-i Bābā Sayyidnā, 224
Kraus, Paul, 3–4, 37, 49–54
Kutch, 316–17
Kutchi *see* Kachchhi

laid paper, 439
Lakhani, Chottu, 8
languages, 276–8, 316, 317–18
  Arabic, 29
  daʿwa, 434
  Gujarati, 280, 283, 288
  Hindi, 276, 277, 279, 281
  Marathi, 279
  Panjabi, 277, 281, 288–9
  Persian, 29, 276, 277, 279, 281, 282, 285, 289, 318, 434
  Sanskrit, 279, 285
  Turkish, 279
  Urdu, 276, 279, 280, 282, 283
  see also scripts
Lāṛī, 289
leather trim, 439
legal code, 27
legends
  Assassin, 26
  black legend, 24, 25, 31
Lewis, Bernard, 40
Lewy, Hans, 3
Lisān al-Mīzān (Ibn Ḥajar al-ʿAsqalānī), 145
literacy, 308–12, 323
literary networks, 7, 8
lithographs, 279, 280
logical epistles, 57
Lohāṇakī, 289
Lohāṇās, the, 288
Lucknow, 1
Luqmānjī b. Ḥabīb Allāh, 174
Luṭf Alī Bīg Ādhar
  Ātashkada, 225

Mā warā al-nahr (Central Asia), 348, 349, 350
Maʿārif al-taqvīm (Ghiyāth al-Dīn ʿAlī Iṣfahānī), 378
MacMurdo, James, 304
Madelung, Wilferd, 40, 41, 118, 119
  'Ismāʿīliyya', 41
Mahetā, Narsīṃh, 277
Maḥmūd Mīrzā, Sulṭān, 350
Majālis (al-Muʾayyad fi'l-Dīn al-Shīrāzī), 50
Majālis al-muʾminīn (Shūshtarī, Qāḍī Nūr Allāh), 243
Majālis Sayfiyya (al-Sayfī, Ibrāhīm), 174
al-Majdūʿ, Ismāʿīl b. ʿAbd al-Rasūl, 2, 28, 170
  Fihrist al-Majdūʿ (*Fahrasat al-kutub wa'l-rasāʾil*), 2–3, 53–4, 170, 175
Mājid, ʿAbd al-Munʿim, 40
Majmūʿ al-tarbiya (MT), 163–4, 177–8
  ʿAlī b. al-Ḥusayn b. Jaʿfar b. Ibrāhīm b. al-Walīd, 169
  author/compiler, 167–70
  al-Bharūchī, Ḥasan b. Nūḥ, 173
  as canonical work, 165
  al-Ḥārithī, Muḥammad b. Ṭāhir, 169–70
  al-Ḥasan b. Idrīs, 173–4
  copying and reading, 170–6
  copyists, 165, 166, 171–2
  dating, 163–4, 174
  doctrinal learning, 170–3, 174–5, 177–8
  intended readership, 167, 168
  MS **1012**, 176
  MS **263**, 176
  as multi-voice treatise, 178
  multiple-text manuscripts of, 164
  paratextual elements, 165–6, 174
  physical arrangement, 166–7
  reading practices and aids, 165–6
  as textual product unit, 164
  variants, 165

majmūʿas, 165, 167
Makdisi, George, 415
al-makhṭūṭāt al-muwaqqaʿah, 435
Malwārī, 278
Manichaean community, 201 n.10
Manṣūr b. Abū'l-Futūḥ, 258
manuscripts
authorial, 431, 432, 435–6
autograph, 431, 435, 440
Chālīha akharī, 282
codicology, 389–90, 431–3, 438–41, 447
colligatums, 219
colophons, 312, 313, 392–3*f*, 440–1
compilations, 167–8
copying, 172, 444–5
culture of, 323
decoration, 89, 129 n.16, 391
draft copies, 435–6
fair copies, 435–6
foliation, 190
holograph, 431, 432–3, 434, 435, 436–41
homoioteleuton, 62, 64, 65, 66, 67, 68, 69, 71, 72, 73, 74, 77
inheritance dispersal, 166
Khwājah Sindhi (Khojki), 277, 278, 281, 284–6, 288, 290
margins, 391–2*f*
miscellaneous, 164, 165, 178
multi-voice treatises, 178
multiple-text, 165, 168, 178
pagination, 189–90
paratextual elements, 165, 441
preservation, 285
réclame (catchwords), 188
saut du même au même, 193–4
secrecy, 172
textual product units, 164
see also Institute of Ismaili Studies
manuscripts of *Rasāʾil Ikhwān al-Ṣafāʾ* (The Epistles of the Brethren of Purity), 85*t*–7*t*
MS **83**, 106, 107*t*, 108, 109, 110, 111, 112
MS **84**, 103
MS **87**, 115, 117*t*, 119, 121*t*, 122
MS **576** *see* MS **576**
MS **927**, 57, 58, 61, 62–3, 70, 75, 76, 77
MS **1040** *see* MS **1040**
MS Atif Efendi **1681** [ع] *see* MS Atif Efendi **1681** [ع]
MS BnF **2303**, 86*t*, 95*t*, 103, 106, 117*t*, 119, 121*t*
MS BnF **2304**, 86*t*, 94*t*, 108, 117*t*
MS BnF **2305**, 86*t*, 94, 103, 106, 107*t*
MS BnF **2341**, 86*t*, 95*t*, 96, 98, 107*t*, 110, 117*t*, 119, 121*t*
MS BnF **6647–8**, 84, 85*t*, 99*t*, 106, 115, 117*t*, 124
MS Esad Efendi **3637**, 95*t*, 96, 97, 106, 108–9, 116, 117*t*, 119, 121, 122, 125
MS Esad Efendi **3638**, 85*t*, 94*t*, 98, 99*t*, 100, 105, 106, 117*t*, 122
MS Escorial **923**, 95*t*, 96, 97
MS Feyzullah **2130–1**, 85*t*, 94*t*, 96–7, 99*t*, 105, 110, 117*t*, 124
MS Garrett **4263**, 95*t*, 96, 98, 119, 121*t*
MS **1482**, 115, 117*t*, 119–20, 121*t*, 122
MS Hunt **296**, 95*t*, 108
MS Köprülü **870,** 85t, 89, 94t
MS Köprülü **871,** 85t, 94t, 100, 103, 108, 116, 117*t*, 119, 122, 123
MS Laud Or. **255**, 95*t*, 106, 108, 116, 117*t*, 118, 119
MS Laud Or. **260** [خ], 57, 62, 76, 85*t*, 95*t*, 100, 113, 117*t*

MS Mahdavi **7437**, 94*t*, 99*t*
MS Majlis **1278**, 86*t*, 95*t*, 98, 106, 117*t*, 119, 121*t*
MS Marsh **189** [غ], 57, 62, 76, 86*t*, 95*t*, 96, 100, 103, 109, 117*t*
MS Munich arab. **652**, 86*t*, 95*t*, 97, 98, 110, 117*t*, 118, 119, 121*t*
MS Nuruosmaniye **2863**, 86*t*, 95*t*, 97, 117*t*, 119, 121*t*
MS Or. **2359**, 125
MS Ragip Pasha **840**, 89, 124, 125
MS Sālār Jung **41**, 85*t*, 95*t*, 96–7, 98, 99*t*, 106, 116, 117*t*, 118–19, 121*t*, 122
MS SOAS Or. **45812**, 95*t*, 98, 103, 106, 117*t*, 119, 121*t*
MS Sprenger **1946**, 103
al-Maqrīzī, Taqī al-Dīn Aḥmad b. ʿAlī, 432
al-Khiṭaṭ, 432
Marathi, 279
marginal comments, 435, 436, 443, 444*f*
Marquet, Yves, 42, 103, 114
Maslama al-Qurṭubī, 79 n.15
Massignon, Louis, 2, 35, 37, 53, 35, 37
Revue des Études islamiques, 53
Maṭlūb al-mūʾminīn (*Desideratum of the Faithful*), al-Ṭūsī, Naṣīr al-Dīn, 399–400
Mawsim-i bahār (Muḥammad b. ʿAlī), 169
Mednitzki, Hadasa (Leila), 51, 52
Metlitzky, Dorothee, 52
Minhāj-i Sirāj, 250
Ṭabaqāt-i Nāṣirī, 250
Mīr Sayyid Ḥasan, 375
Mīrābāī, 277
Mīrzā Khān (Sulṭān Ways), 348–9, 350–1, 371–2
miscellaneous manuscripts, 164, 165, 178
Momnās, the, 282, 287, 290
Mongol Empire, 250, 260, 262, 333, 370–1
MS **576**, 57, 58, 60–1, 76, 77–8, 89, 102
additions, 61, 67, 73, 76
autocorrections, 65, 66, 73
cacogrophy, 65, 69, 70, 72, 74, 75, 77
catchwords, 61
emendation, 77
ending, 61, 62, 65, 67, 70, 75, 76
Epistle ʻOn Animals', 103
Epistle ʻOn Arithmetic', 95*t*
Epistle ʻOn Astronomy' 97
Epistle ʻOn Doctrines', 102
Epistle ʻOn Geography', 97
Epistle ʻOn Geometry', 96
Epistle ʻOn Languages', 105
Epistle ʻOn Minerals', 102
Epistle ʻOn Music', 97
Epistle ʻOn Pleasure', 104
Epistle ʻOn the *Categories*', 64–5
Epistle ʻOn the Heavens', 101
Epistle ʻOn the *Isagoge*', 62, 100
Epistle ʻOn the *On Interpretation*', 66–7
Epistle ʻOn the *Posterior Analytics*', 72–5
Epistle ʻOn the Practical Crafts', 98
Epistle ʻOn the *Prior Analytics*', 68–70
Epistle ʻOn the Theoretical Crafts', 98, 102
lectio facilior, 65, 72
letters, confusion of, 65, 67, 69, 72, 74
metathesis, 69, 72, 74
mistakes, 61, 65, 66, 67, 69–70, 72, 73, 74–5

omissions, 62, 64, 64, 67, 68–9, 72, 73, 74, 75–6, 78
pagination, 60, 72
peculiar orthography, 61, 64, 66, 68, 69, 72, 73
titles, 60, 62, 66, 69, 72, 73
MS **1040**, 57–60, 76–8, 81–2, 90*f*, 124*f*, 126–8
additions, 60, 64, 66, 67, 68, 70, 71, 78
autocorrections, 64, 65, 68, 71
Buṭrus al-Bustānī print (‘Ṣādir edition), 82, 93, 102, 104, 110–11, 112, 119, 120, 121*t*, 123, 126
cacogrophy, 63, 68, 69, 70, 71, 74, 75. 77
de Callataÿ, Godefroid, 97, 110, 119, 122, 123, 125
description, 84–93
Dieterici edition, 95*t*, 103
El-Bizri, Nader, 93, 96, 97, 98, 126
emendation, 64, 78
ending, 61, 62, 65, 67, 70, 75, 76
Epistle, 32, 106–9
Epistle, 33, 106–9
Epistle ‘On Animals’, 102–3
Epistle ‘On Arithmetic’, 90*f*, 93–6
Epistle ‘On Astronomy’ 96–7
Epistle ‘On Belief’, 113–14
Epistle ‘On Cause and Effect’, 111–12
Epistle ‘On Character Traits’, 98–9*t*
Epistle ‘On Companionship’, 113
Epistle ‘On Definitions’, 112–13
Epistle ‘On Doctrines’, 101–2, 113
Epistle ‘On Geography’, 97, 127
Epistle ‘On Geometry’, 96
Epistle ‘On Governance’, 120–1
Epistle ‘On Intellect and the Intelligible’, 109–10
Epistle ‘On Languages’, 105
Epistle ‘On Life and Death’, 104
Epistle ‘On Magic’, 122–5
Epistle ‘On Matter and Form’, 100
Epistle ‘On Minerals’, 101–2
Epistle ‘On Movement’, 110–11
Epistle ‘On Music’, 97, 126–7
Epistle ‘On Peri Hermeneias’, 100
Epistle ‘On Periods and Cycles’, 110
Epistle ‘On Pleasure’, 104
Epistle ‘On Proportion’, 97
Epistle ‘On Resurrection’, 120
Epistle ‘On Sense and the Sensible’, 109
Epistle ‘On Spiritual Beings’, 118–20, 121*t*
Epistle ‘On the Call to God’, 114–18
Epistle ‘On the *Categories*’, 63–4, 65
Epistle ‘On the Heavens’, 101
Epistle ‘On the Intellectual Principles according to the Pure Brethren’, 106, 109
Epistle ‘On the *Isagoge*’, 61, 62, 99–100
Epistle ‘On the Macrocosm’, 109
Epistle ‘On the *On Interpretation*’, 65–7
Epistle ‘On the Order of the Universe’, 109, 121–2
Epistle ‘On the *Posterior Analytics*’, 70–1, 73–5, 100
Epistle ‘On the Practical Crafts’, 98
Epistle ‘On the *Prior Analytics*’, 67–8, 69–70, 100
Epistle ‘On the Theoretical Crafts’, 97–8, 101–2

Halflants, Bruno, 122, 123
homoioteleuton, 65, 67, 69, 71, 73, 74
Jīwā Khān edition, 81, 82–3, 84, 90, 92, 93, 95*t*, 96, 97, 98–9*t*, 100, 101, 102, 104, 105, 106, 108, 109, 110, 111, 112, 113, 114, 115, 117*t*, 118, 119, 120, 121*t*, 122, 123, 124, 125, 126–7
lectio facilior, 65
letters, confusion of, 65, 67, 74
Madelung, Wilferd, 118, 119
metathesis, 69, 74
mistakes, 59, 63–4, 65, 66, 67, 68, 69–70, 71, 73, 74–5, 78
numeration, 58
omissions, 62, 63, 65, 67, 68, 69, 71, 73, 74, 75–6, 78
peculiar ortography, 59–60, 63, 65, 66, 68, 69, 70, 73
quadrivium, 59
signes-de-renvoi, 60, 64, 68
titles, 62, 66, 68, 69, 70, 73
Traboulsi, Samer, 113
Walker edition, 106, 108, 110
Yūsuf, ʿAlī edition, 83–4, 92, 95*t*, 96, 97, 99*t*, 100, 123
Ziriklī print, 82–4, 96, 100, 101, 104, 110, 111, 112, 123, 126
MS Atif Efendi **1681** [ع], 57, 59, 76, 77, 85*t*, 89
Epistle, 32, 108
Epistle, 33, 108
Epistle ʻOn Arithmetic', 94
Epistle ʻOn Character Traits', 98–9*t*
Epistle ʻOn Companionship', 113
Epistle ʻOn Definitions', 112
Epistle ʻOn Geography', 97
Epistle ʻOn Geometry', 96
Epistle ʻOn Governance', 120
Epistle ʻOn Governance', 120
Epistle ʻOn Languages', 105
Epistle ʻOn Matter and Form', 100
Epistle ʻOn Movement',111
Epistle ʻOn Music', 97
Epistle ʻOn Proportion', 97
Epistle ʻOn Spiritual Beings', 119
Epistle ʻOn the Call to God', 116, 117*t*, 118
Epistle ʻOn the *On Interpretation*', 66, 67
Epistle ʻOn the Practical Crafts', 98
Epistle ʻOn the Theoretical Crafts', 97
MS BT **105**, 357, 362
MS BT **173**, 357, 363
al-Mu'ayyad fi'l-Dīn al-Shīrāzī, 37, 259
Majālis, 50
mubayyaḍah, 435
Mughal Empire, 363
Muhammad, Prophet, 360, 401–2
Muḥammad ʻAlī, 172
Muḥammad b. ʻAlī, 169
Mawsim-i bahār, 169
Muḥammad Ibn Falāḥ (al-Mushaʿshaʿ), 333–4
Muḥammad Riḍā
Account of the Gnostics (*Bayān al-ʿārifīn*), 285
Muḥammad Tapar, Sultan, 237, 244
Mujtaba Ali, 280
Mukhtaṣar al-uṣūl (Ibn al-Walīd, ʻAlī ibn Muḥammad), 183, 184–5, 197–200
eulogies, 195
foliation, 190
linguistic idiosyncrasies, 194–200
Manuscript A (MS **142**), 185–8*f*, 199*f*

Manuscript B (MS **1288**), 186*t*, 188–90
Manuscript C (MS **1204**), 186*t*, 190, 191*f*
Manuscript D (MS **141**), 186*f*, 190, 192*f*
Manuscript E (MS **678**), 186*t*, 190, 193*f*, 200*f*
Manuscript F (MS **269**), 186*t*, 190, 193*f*
manuscripts of, 185–94
pagination, 189–90
réclame, 188
saut du même au même, 193–4
mullā, 171
multiple-text manuscripts, 165, 168, 178
Mumbai, 280
Muntazaʿ al-akhbār (Burhānpūrī, Quṭb al-Dīn), 169
Murād Mīrzā family, 261
Mūsā Khān Khurāsānī, 7
musawwadah, 147, 435
Mustanṣir III, 262
Mustanṣir bi'llāh, Imam-Caliph, 39, 226, 259, 318, 371, 405–6
al-Mustaẓhir, Caliph, 25
al-Mustaẓhirī (al-Ghazālī) 25
Muʿtazilīs, the, 202 n.11
Muẓaffar (ʿImād Allāh wa al-Dīn Muẓaffar b. ʿAlī b. Muḥammad), Raʾīs, 240, 258

Nagar, 286
Nagari, 282
namāz (prayer), 403–4
Nānajī', Abdul Husen Alībhāi
Pir Has Graced Our Threshold, The (*Pīr Padhāryā Āpaṇe Dvār*), 283, 287
Nānajīāṇī, Sachedīnā, 288
Account of the Khwājahs, An (*Khojā vṛtānt*), 288
Nānak, Guru, 277
Nanji, Azim, 42
al-Naqḍ, 266
Narsīṃh Mahetā, 277
Nasafī, ʿAzīz al-Dīn, 333
al-Nasafī, Muḥammad ibn Aḥmad, 138
Kitāb al-Maḥṣūl, 138
Nāṣir al-Dīn ʿAbd al-Raḥīm Muḥtasham, 237, 245, 246, 249, 250, 258
Nāṣir Mīrzā, 348
Nāṣir-i Khusraw, 35, 37, 224, 230–1, 258, 259, 266, 276, 370
Ākhirzamānnāma, 363
almsgiving, 406–7
Persian, use of, 27
Sargudhasht-i Nāṣir Khusraw, 224, 229, 230, 231
Sargudhasht-i Sayyidnā, 225, 226, 227, 228–30, 231
Sayyid Suhrāb Walī, 380–1, 382–3
Shāh Ḍiyāʾī-i Shughnānī, 362
taʾwīl, 397, 398
Wajh-i dīn, 35
Nathu, Hājī Neṇashībhāī, 280
Nawrūzshāh, son of Naẓarshāh, 222, 223
Naẓmī-i Shughnānī, 352
Bayāḍ-i ashʿār-i Naẓmī, 356
Niʿmat Allāh Walī, Shāh, 331, 333
doctrinal works, 337–43, 344
'Epistle of Shāh Niʿmat Allāh Walī, the' (*Risāla-yi Shāh Niʿmat Allāh Walī*), 337–43
genealogy, 334
manuscripts of, 331, 335–43
MS BA **86**, 337–43
MS BA **126**, 335, 336*f*

MS BT **71**, 337
MS BT **134**, 337
MS BT **173**, 336
MS BT **185**, 337
MS BT **197**, 336
MS BT **282**, 337
poetry, 334, 335–7, 343, 344
'Qasida of Shāh Niʿmat Allāh Walī, the' (*qaṣīda-yi Shāh Niʿmat Allāh Walī*), 336–7
Risāla dar bayān-i aqṭāb, 342–3
Sharḥ-i faṣṣ-i awwal min Fuṣūṣ al-ḥikam, 341–2
Niʿmat Allāhīs, 331, 332–4
Niẓām al-Mulk, 25, 210
Nizār, Imam, 282
Nizār ibn al-Mustanṣir, 267
Nizārī Ismailis, 6, 24–5, 28–9, 253–4, 259, 260, 307, 371
'Ahd-i Sayyidnā, 237
Alamūt, 28, 242–3, 244
as assassins, 25, 26, 31, 325 n.9
daʿwa (summons; call), 237, 241, 242, 245, 267, 371–2
Dīwān-i Qāʿimiyyāt, 209
doctrinal works, 208, 209–10
European perception of, 26–7
Haft bāb (Ḥasan-i Maḥmūd-i Kātib), 209
historical chronicles, 207–9, 211–12
libraries, 4, 176, 260, 262, 333
naming, 31
Niʿmat Allāh Walī, Shāh, 336, 342–4
Niʿmat Allāhīs, 331, 332–4, 343
Qāsim-Shāhī renaissance, 230 1
qiyāma, 334
Rawḍat al-taslīm (al-Ṭūsī, Naṣīr al-Dīn), 209
Sargudhasht-i Sayyidnā, 208–9, 210–11
Satpanth, 309, 317
spiritual authority, 332, 333–4
Sufism, 332–4
see also Khojas
Noorum-Mobin: Or the Sacred Cord of God (*Nūram mobīn: Yāne Allāhanī pavitr rasī*) (Chunara, Alimahomed Janmahomed), 287
al-Nu'mān, al-Qāḍī, 27, 37, 396
Asās al-ta'wīl (*The Foundation of Ta'wīl*), 172–3, 175, 396–7
Daʿā'im al-Islām (*The Pillars of Islam*), 36, 399, 400, 401
Ta'wīl daʿā'im al-Islām (*Tarbiyat al-mū'minīni*) (*The Upbringing of the Believers*), 396–7
Nūr al-Dīn Muḥammad II, Ismaili Imam, 257
Nūr Muḥammad Nūr al-Dīn, 174
Nūr Muḥammad Shāh, Sayyid, 284
Vine of the Tale of Truth (*Sataveṇī moṭī nī vel*), 284–5
Nur nāmu (*Tale of Light*), 280
Nuramahamad, Momīn Miyāñjī, 282
Nūrbakhsh, Javad
Risālahā-ye ḥaḍrat-i sayyid Nūr al-Dīn Shāh Niʿmat Allāh Walī, 337–40
Nūrbakhsh, Muḥammad, 333–4
Nuzhat al-afkār (Idrīs, ʿImād al-Dīn), 169

O'Leary, De Lacy Evans, 33
omissions, 75–6
On Interpretation (Aristotle), 57
On Logic: An Arabic Critical Edition and English Translations of Epistles, 10–14 (Baffioni, Carmela), 57, 64, 66, 67, 68, 69, 72, 73, 74, 75, 76–8
orientalists, 29–35, 277

Origins of the Khojas (*Asalīyate Khojā*) (Boghā Māstar, Hāsham), 287
Ormsby, Eric, 104
ownership marks, 435,
ownership statements, 441–3*t*, 447
Oxus River, 347

Pachymeres, Georgios, 75
pagination, 189–90
Pakistan, 260
paleography, 433
Pamir, 347
Pandiyāt-i Javānmardī, 39, 219, 318
Panjabi, 277, 281, 288–9
Panj tan-i pāk (Five Pure Figures), 348, 352
Panj tanī, 348, 361
Pārapīā, Vīrajī Premajī, 280
paratextual elements, 165, 441, 443
Pāṭaṇ, 286
Persia, 58
Persian Ismailis, 30
Persian language/script, 29, 276, 277, 279, 281, 282, 285, 289, 318, 434
Persian historiography, 210–12
philosophy, 27
pilgrimage (*ḥajj*), 407
Pines, Shlomo, 52
  Pir Has Graced Our Threshold, The (*Pīr Padhāryā Āpaṇe Dvār*) (Nānajī', Abdul Husen Alībhāi), 283, 287
plagiarism, 432
Plato
  Republic, 76
Polo, Marco, 26
Poonawala, Ismail K., 41, 109, 143, 144
Porphyry
  Isagoge, 57
Posterior Analytics (Aristotle), 57
prayer (*namāz*), 403–4
Preaching of the Resurrection, 260, 267
printed books
  limited use of, 9
printing, 9, 172, 277–8, 280, 431
  culture of, 323
Prior Analytics (Aristotle), 57, 78
private libraries, 3, 4, 5, 8
proofreading, 436, 443
provenance, 434, 439, 440*t*, 441
Punjabi *see* Panjabi
purification (*ṭahārat*), 402–3
Pythagorean theorem, 75

Qādan, Qāḍī, 285
al-Qāḍī al-Nuʿmān, 173
Qāʾimiyyāt, 258, 260, 266, 267 see also *Dīwān-i Qāʾimiyyāt*
'Qasida of Shāh Niʿmat Allāh Walī, the' (*qaṣīda-yi Shāh Niʿmat Allāh Walī*) (Niʿmat Allāh Walī, Shāh), 336–7
qaṣīdas, 352, 353–9, 362, 363–4
  Panj tan-i pāk (Shāh Ḍiyāʾī-i Shughnānī), 352
  Salām-nāma (A Poem of Allegiance) (Shāh Ḍiyāʾī-i Shughnānī), 355, 356–61, 362–4
Qāsim-Shāhī renaissance, 230–1
qiṣṣa (story; tale), 228
Qiṣṣa-yi Sarguẕasht-i ḥaẓrat-i Bābā Sayyid-nā, 218
qiyāma, 334
Quhistān, 250, 258
Qurʾān, 360, 395–6, 404, 406, 415
  commentaries on, 433
  seven pillars of the *sharīʿa*, 399–400
Qurʾān manuscripts
  annotations, 416–28
  HDP, 19, 425–*f*

meta-textual features, 415–16
MS **580**, 422, 423*f*
MS **581**, 421*f*–2
MS **745**, 422–5
MS **909**, 418–19*f*
MS **921**, 419–21
MS **1700**, 425*f*
transmission, 415–17, 426–8
al-Qurṭubī, Maslama *see* Maslama al-Qurṭubī
Quṭb al-Dīn, 268
Dīwān, 268

Raḍī al-Dīn II b. Ṭāhir, Shāh, 349–50
Rāḥat al-ʿaql (al-Kirmānī, Ḥamīd al-Dīn), 39
Rahimtoola, Jaffer
History of the Khojas, The (*Khojā kom no itihas*), 287
Raʾīs Ḥasan or Raʾīs-i ajal, 268 n.1
Rasāʾil Ikhwān al-Ṣafāʾ (The Epistles of the Brethren of Purity), 33, 42, 57 *see also* manuscripts of *Rasāʾil Ikhwān al-Ṣafāʾ*
Baffioni, Carmela, 100, 101, 110, 111, 112, 120, 121
Buṭrus al-Bustānī print (Ṣādir edition) [Ṣ], 57, 82, 93, 102, 104, 110–11, 112, 119, 121*t*, 123, 126
de Callataÿ, Godefroid, 97, 110, 119, 122, 123, 125
Dieterici edition, 33, 95*t*, 103
El-Bizri, Nader, 93, 96, 97, 98, 126
Epistle, 32, 106–9
Epistle, 33, 106–9
Epistle 'On Animals', 102–3
Epistle 'On Arithmetic', 59, 60, 90*f*, 93–6
Epistle 'On Astronomy' 59, 60, 96–7
Epistle 'On Belief', 113–14
Epistle 'On Cause and Effect', 111–12
Epistle 'On Character Traits', 98–9
Epistle 'On Companionship', 113
Epistle 'On Definitions', 112–13
Epistle 'On Doctrines', 101–2, 113
Epistle 'On Geography', 59, 60, 97, 127
Epistle 'On Geometry', 59, 60, 96
Epistle 'On Governance', 120–1
Epistle 'On Intellect and the Intelligible', 109–10
Epistle 'On Languages', 105
Epistle 'On Life and Death', 104
Epistle 'On Magic', 122–5
Epistle 'On Matter and Form', 100
Epistle 'On Minerals', 101–2
Epistle 'On Morals', 60
Epistle 'On Movement', 110–11
Epistle 'On Music', 59, 60, 97, 126–7
Epistle 'On Number', 59
Epistle 'On Peri Hermeneias', 100
Epistle 'On Periods and Cycles', 110
Epistle 'On Pleasure', 104
Epistle 'On Proportion', 97
Epistle 'On Resurrection', 120
Epistle 'On Spiritual Beings', 118–20, 121*t*
Epistle 'On the Belief of the Pure Brethren', 103
Epistle 'On the Call to God', 114–18
Epistle 'On the *Categories*', 57, 61, 63–5, 77
Epistle 'On the Heavens', 101

Epistle 'On the Intellectual Principles according to the Pure Brethren', 106, 109
Epistle 'On the *Isagoge*', 57, 61–3, 76, 99–100
Epistle 'On the Kinds of Proper Attitude', 76
Epistle 'On the Macrocosm', 109
Epistle 'On the *On Interpretation*', 57, 59, 61, 65–7, 77
Epistle 'On the Order of the Universe', 109, 121–2
Epistle 'On the *Posterior Analytics*', 57, 59, 70–76, 77, 100
Epistle 'On the Practical Crafts', 98
Epistle 'On the *Prior Analytics*', 57, 59, 63, 67–70, 77, 100
Epistle 'On Sense and the Sensible', 109
Epistle 'On the Theoretical Crafts', 97–8, 101–2
fihrist, 92–3
Halflants, Bruno, 122, 123
Jīwā Khān edition, 81, 82–3, 84, 90, 92, 93, 95*t*, 96, 97, 98–9*t*, 100, 101, 102, 104, 105, 106, 108, 109, 110, 111, 112, 113, 114, 115, 117*t*, 118, 119, 120, 121*t*, 122, 123, 124, 125, 126–7
Madelung, Wilferd, 118, 119
On Logic: An Arabic Critical Edition and English Translations of Epistles 10–14, 57, 64, 66, 67, 68, 69, 72, 73, 74, 75, 76–8
OUP editions, 82, 84, 127
stemma codicum, 77
al-Ṭībāwī, ʿAbd al-Laṭīf, 125–6
Traboulsi, Samer, 113
Walker edition, 106, 108, 110
Yūsuf, ʿAlī edition, 83–4, 92, 95*t*, 96, 97, 99*t*, 100, 123
Ziriklī print, 82–4, 96, 100, 101, 104, 110, 111, 112, 123, 126
Rāshid al-Dīn Sinān, 25, 31, 208, 210, 211
Jāmiʿ al-Tawārīkh, 210, 211, 242, 243
Sargudhasht-i Sayyidnā, 208, 210, 211, 215, 227, 228, 229
Ravīdās, 277
Rawḍat al-mutaʿallimīn, 373
Rawḍat al-taslīm (al-Ṭūsī, Naṣīr al-Dīn), 209, 259
al-Rāzi, Abu Bakr Moḥammad b. Zakariyāʾ, 436
al-Ḥāwī, 436
réclame (catchwords), 188
Republic (Plato), 76
Revue des Études islamiques (Massignon, Louis), 53
Riḍā, Muḥammad, 285
Rieu, Charles, 125
Risāla dar bayān-i aqṭāb (Niʿmat Allāh Walī, Shāh), 342–3
al-Risāla al-waḍʿiya fi maʿālim al-dīn (al-Kirmānī, Ḥamīd al-Dīn), 172, 175
Risāla-i asrār al-nuṭfa, 373
Risāla-i ḥudūdiyya, 373
Risālahā-ye ḥaḍrat-i sayyid Nūr al-Dīn Shāh Niʿmat Allāh Walī (Nūrbakhsh, Javad), 337–40
Rosenthal, Franz, 440
Rousseau, Jean Baptiste L. J., 30, 31
Royuela (Cortázar, Julio), 116
Rūdakī, 266
Rūmī, Jalāl al-Dīn, 333
Spiritual Couplets (*Mathnawī-yi maʿnawī*), 277
Ruska, Julius, 49, 51
Russia, 33–34, 221

Russian Institute of Oriental Manuscripts, 34
Rustichello of Pisa, 26
rūzah (fasting), 404–6

Saʿdī, Shaykh, 277
Ṣadr al-Dīn, Pīr, 286–9, 290
Safavid dynasty, 268, 350, 362–3
ṣaḥḥa (correct), 187, 443
al-Ṣaḥīfah al-sajjādīyah (al-Ḥusayn, Zayn al-ʿĀbidīn ʿAlī ibn), 437, 447
Ṣaḥīfat al-nāẓirīn (Pages for the Readers), 369–70
  authorship, 370, 373, 375–6, 379–82
  Ghiyāth al-Dīn ʿAlī b. Ḥusayn b. ʿAlī Amīrān Iṣfahānī, 370, 376–80, 382–3
  historical context, 370–2
  manuscripts, 372–3, 376–7
  Sayyid Suhrāb Walī, 370, 373–6, 377, 379–83, 397
al-Saḥmāwī, Muḥammad ibn Muḥammad, 437, 446
  al-Tawqiʿāt (*al-Fawāʾid al-mukhtabara*), 440
  al-Thaghr al-Bāsim fī Ṣināʿat al-Kātib wa-al-Kātim (the Smiling Mouth on the Craft of the Scribe and Secretary), 446
Saindhava, 278
al-Sakhāwī, Shams al-Dīn Muḥammad b. ʿAbd al-Raḥmān, 437, 446
Salām-nāma (A Poem of Allegiance) (Shāh Ḍiyāʾī-i Shughnānī), 355, 356–61, 362–4
salamah (peace be upon him), 445
Saljūq Empire, 25
Salomon, Richard G. 277–8
al-Sāmarrāʾī, ʿAbdallāh Sallūm, 140–1, 142
  al-Ghulūw waʾl-Firaq al-Ghāliya fī l-Ḥaḍāra al-Islāmiyya, 141
Ṣanʿāʾ palimpsest, 416
Sanāʾī Ghaznawī, 88, 333
Sanjar, Sultan, 243
Sanskrit, 279, 285
sant, 277
santbhāṣhā (heterogeneous discourse of the saints), 289
Saporta, Marc
  Composition no. 1, 116
Sargudhasht-i Sayyidnā, 207, 208–9, 231–2, 242
  Badakhshāni milieu, influences of, 227–30
  content, 224–7
  copyists, 221–3
  genre, 228
  Ivanow, Wladimir, 214
  Juwaynī, ʿAtā Malik, 208, 210, 211, 215, 227, 228, 229
  Kāshānī, Abūʾl-Qāsim ʿAbd Allāh b. ʿAlī, 208, 210–11, 227, 228
  manuscripts at IIS, 213–31
  MS **162**, 214–17, 224, 227
  MS **177**, 214–17, 224, 227
  MS BA **61**, 218, 219, 221, 225
  MS BA **154**, 218, 219, 220, 222, 223
  MS BT **1**, 218, 219, 220, 222, 223, 224–7
  MS BT **22**, 218, 220
  MS BT **103**, 218, 219, 220, 221, 222, 223
  MS BT **192**, 218, 219
  MS BT **287**, 218, 219, 220, 221, 222
  MS BT **295**, 218, 219, 222, 223
  Nāṣir-i Khusraw, 225, 226, 227, 228–30, 231
  Nizārī historiography, 207–13

Nizārī Ismaili doctrinal works of the Alamūt period as sources of Nizārī Ismaili history, 209–10
Nizārī Ismaili historical and doctrinal sources of the Alamūt period, 207–9
Persian historiography, 210–12
Rāshid al-Dīn Sinān, 208, 210, 211, 215, 227, 228, 229
Tehran, 212–13, 214
titles, 224
Sargudhasht-i Nāṣir Khusraw, 224, 229, 230, 231
Sarkariyya library, 176
Sarmast, Sachal, 277
Sataveṇī Moṭī (Tales of Truth), 280, 283, 286
Sataveṇī moṭī nī vel (*Vine of the Tale of Truth*) (Nūr Muḥammad Shāh, Sayyid), 284–5
Satpanth, 304, 309
literate class, 310, 311, 320–1, 323–4
scripts, 318
see also Satpanth manuscripts
Satpanth manuscripts, 308, 312–23
classification, 318–19
copying/copyists, 321–2
dating system, 322–3
formulas, 313–16
languages/scripts, 316, 317–18
names/titles, 320–1
performative aspect, 320
religious culture, 321–2
satr, doctrine of, 258
al-Sayfī, Ibrāhīm
Majālis Sayfiyya, 174
Sayr va sulūk (al-Ṭūsī, Naṣīr al-Dīn), 29, 246
Sayyed Nawrūz Shāh b. Sayyid Kāẓim, 262
Sayyid, Ayman F., 40
Sayyid Iʿtibār Shāh, 223
Sayyid Mīr Ḥasan Shāh (Shāh Khāmūsh), 355
Sayyid Munīr Badakhshānī, 7, 20 n.19
Sayyid Nāṣir ʿAlī Shāh, 222
Sayyid Shāhzādamurād, 223
Sayyid Suhrāb Walī, 370, 373–6, 377, 379–83, 397
Sayyid-nā Nūr al-Dīn, 174
Sayyidnā Ṭayyib Zayn al-Dīn, 175
al-Sayyida al-Ḥurra, Queen, 163, 178, 201 n.2
Sayyidnā, Ḥasan-i Ṣabbāḥ, 260–1
Sayyidnazarov, Sultonnazar, 353
Schaeder, Hans-Heinrich, 49
Schwaebsch, Liselotte (Lilo), 52
scientific orientalism, 29
Scindi *see* Sindhi
scripts, 219, 220, 277–82
abjad, 278, 279, 281, 282, 283, 290
Abugida, 278
Arabic, 318
Ardhanāgarī, 278
Bohra *daʿwa*, 434
Brāhmī, 278–9
Devanagari, 276, 279
Gujarati, 277, 280, 282, 283, 285, 287, 288, 290
Gurmukhi, 288–9
Kachchhi, 284
Khudāwādī, 279, 289, 290
Khwājah, 277, 281–3, 285–91
loss, 333
Malwārī, 278
Persian, 318
Sindhi, 277, 278–91
Saindhava, 278
seals, 442–3*t*
Semenev, Aleksandr A., 34, 35

seven pillars of the *sharīʿa*, 399–400, 409–10
Seven Pillars of the Sharīʿa, 389, 409–10
alms (*zakāt*), 406–7
analysis, 400–9
codicological analysis, 389–95
copyist, 394
dating, 393–4
fasting (*rūzah*), 404–6
pilgrimage (*ḥajj*), 407
prayer (*namāz*), 403–4
purification (*ṭahārat*), 402–3
striving (*jihād*), 408–9
ta'wīl concept, 395–400
testimony (*shahādat*), 400–2
Seventh Gujarati Literature Conference, 285
Shāh ʿAbd Allāh, 394
Shāh ʿAbd al-Laṭīf, Sindhi poet, 277
Shāh Ḍiyāʿī *see* Shāh Ḍiyā'ī-i Shughnānī,
Shāh Ḍiyā'ī-i Shughnānī, 348, 351, 363–4
biography, 352–6
contemporaries of, 353*t*
devotion to the Imams, 361–2
manuscripts of *Salām-nāma*, 356–7
Panj tan-i pāk, 352
Salām-nāma (A Poem of Allegiance), 355, 356–61, 362–4
Shāh Khalīl Allāh, imam, 30
Shāh Khāmūsh (Sayyid Mīr Ḥasan Shāh), 355
shahādat (testimony), 400–2
Shāhjahānpūr, 58
al-Shahrastānī, ʿAbd al-Karīm, 397
Shāhzādamuammad, Shāh-i Kalān b., 354
Shākh-dara, 355
Shams, Pīr, 288
Sharḥ Nahj al-Balāghah (Ibn Abī al-Ḥadīd), 436
Sharḥ-i faṣṣ-i awwal min Fuṣūṣ al-ḥikam (Niʿmat Allāh Walī, Shāh), 341–2
sharīʿa, 258, 267, 395, 398, 410 see also *Seven Pillars of the Sharīʿa*
al-Sharīf al-Raḍī, 436
Shaybānid dynasty, 88, 349
shaykh, 171
al-Shayyāl, Jamāl al-Dīn, 40
Sherzodshoev, Shozodamamad, 343, 344
Shiʿa of India (Hollister, John Norman), 282
Shihāb al-Dīn, Muḥtasham, 250, 258
Shiʿi Islam, 24, 30, 259, 332–3, 334, 361, 445
Niʿmat Allāh Walī, Shāh, 336, 341–3
see also Ismailis, the
al-Shīrāzī, al-Mu'ayyad fi'l-Dīn, 37, 397, 405–6
al-Shirwānī, Aḥmad b. Muḥammad b. ʿAlī al-Anṣārī al-Yamanī, 103
Shughnān, 347, 348, 351, 352, 355, 361, 364
al-Shumūs al-Zāhira (al-Ḥāmidī, Ḥātim), 9
Shūshtarī, Qāḍī Nūr Allāh
Majālis al-mu'minīn, 243
Sī ū shish ṣaḥīfa (Thirty-Six Chapters), 369, 377, 379 see also *Ṣaḥīfat al-nāẓirīn*
Sidih, 261
al-Sijistānī, Abū Yaʿqūb, 27, 37, 259, 397
Sikhs, the, 289
Silk-i guhar-rīz (Khwājah Aḥrār), 229–30, 231, 374–6, 380–1

'Silsilat Makhṭūṭāt al-Fāṭimiyyīn' series (Ḥusayn, Muḥammad Kāmil), 39
Silvestre de Sacy, Antoine Isaac, 29–32
Sinān, Rāshid al-Dīn, 25, 31
Sindh, and the Races that Inhabit the Valley of the Indus (Burton, Richard), 278–9
Sindhi, 277, 278–91
  Khudāwādī, 279, 289, 290
  Khwājah, 277, 281–3, 285–91
'Sindhi poetry of the Sumra era' (*Sūmran je daur jī Sindhī shā'irī*) (Allana, Ghulam Ali), 282
Sindhi Scripts (*Sindhī ṣūratkhaṭṭ*) (Allana, Ghulam Ali), 282–3
Sohadev Joshī, 288
South Asia, 276, 277, 279, 285
  Islam, 275–8
  see also India
Southeast Asia, 276
Soviet rule, 220, 221–2
Stack, George, 281
Star of India, 439
Stern, Samuel Miklos, 40
  'Early Ismā'īlī Missionaries in North-West Persia and in Khurāsān and Transoxania, The', 138
Strauss, Bettina, 52
Strauss, Leo, 52
striving (*jihād*), 408–9
Stroeva, Lyudmila V., 40
Sub-Saharan Africa, 276
Sufism, 331–4, 341 *see also* Ni'mat Allāh Walī, Shāh
Sulaymān Mīrzā, 351
Sulaymāni, the, 445
Sulṭān Maḥmūd, 377–8
Sunni Islam, 24, 399
  anti-Ismaili literary campaigns, 24–5, 26
  Ḥashwiyya, the, 184
  zakāt (alms), 406
Surūr, Muḥammad J., 40

Ṭabaqāt-i Nāṣirī (Minhāj-i Sirāj), 250
Tadhkirat al-sāmi' wa'lmutakallim fī adab al-'ālim wa'l-muta'allim (Badr al-Dīn b. al-Jamā'a), 180 n.25
Tadhkīrat al-shu'arā, 350
tafsīr (explanation), 397
ṭahārat (purification), 402–3
Ṭāhir Sayf al-Dīn, 175
Tājdīn, Pīr, 285
Tale of Light (*Nur nāmu*), 280
Ta'līq, 436
Tāmir, 'Ārif, 40
Tanbīh al-ghāfilīn (al-Ḥāmidī, Ḥātim), 173
Tanbīh al-hadī wa'l-muhtadī (al-Kirmānī, Ḥamīd al-Dīn), 173
Tannery, Paul, 75–6
tanzīl (revelation), 360, 398
taqiyya (precautionary dissimulation of faith), 404
Tarbiyat al-mū'minīn (*The Upbringing of the Believers*) (al-Nu'mān, al-Qāḍī), 396–7
Tārīkh-i Amīr-i Sīstān, 219
Tārīkh-i Jahāngushāy (Juwaynī, 'Atā Malik), 210
Ta'rīkh-i Rashīdī, 349, 350, 351
Taṣawwurāt (*Rawḍa-yi taslīm*) (al-Ṭūsī, Naṣīr al-Dīn), 247, 259
ta'wīl (interpretation; returning), 395
ta'wīl concept, 395–400

Ta'wīl al-ṣalāt, 165–6
al-Tawqiʿāt (*al-Fawāʾid al-mukhtabara*) (al-Saḥmāwī, Muḥammad ibn Muḥammad), 440
al-Ṭayyib Abī al-Qāṣim, Caliph, 163, 178, 201 n.2
Ṭayyibī Ismailis, 9, 27–8, 83, 163, 183
  compilations, 168
  doctrinal learning, 168, 170–1, 172–5, 176
  Majmūʿ al-tarbiya, 167, 170–1
  manuscripts, 445
  see also Bohras
Ṭayyibīs, 167–8, 170, 171, 175, 177–8
testimony (*shahādat*), 400–2
textbooks, 280–1, 283
textual criticism, 432, 447
textual product units, 164
al-Thaghr al-Bāsim fī Ṣināʿat al-Kātib wa-al-Kātim (the Smiling Mouth on the Craft of the Scribe and Secretary) (al-Saḥmāwī, Muḥammad ibn Muḥammad), 446
Thatta, 285
al-Ṭībāwī, ʿAbd al-Laṭīf, 125–6
title pages, 436–7, 438, 443, 445, 446
Timurid dynasty, 348–9, 371–2
transmission, 5, 415–17, 426–8
Treaty of Hudaybiya, 360
Tuḥfat al-nāẓirīn (Gift for the Readers), 369, 372 see also *Ṣaḥīfat al-nāẓirīn*
Tuḥfat al-qulūb (al-Ḥāmidī, Ḥātim), 169
Turkish, 279
al-Ṭūsī, Naṣīr al-Dīn, 28, 39, 209, 246, 249–50, 258, 259–60
  Dar bayān-e haft arkān-e sharīʿat wa taʾwīl ān (*On the Explanation of the Seven Pillars of the Sharīʿa and its Taʾwīl*), 399–400
  imamate, 404
  Ismailism, 378
  Maṭlūb al-mūʾminīn (*Desideratum of the Faithful*), 399–400
  Sayr va sulūk, 28, 246
  Taṣawwurāt (*Rawḍa-yi taslīm*), 209, 259
  taʾwīl, 397, 398–9
Twelvers, 266, 332, 361, 362, 363, 364
  Niʿmat Allāh Walī, Shāh, 342
  zakāt (alms), 406

Ujāqī, Hūshang, 372
ʿUmar Khayyām, 210
ʿUmar Yumgī, 374
ʿUmdat al-ṭālib (Ibn ʿInaba), 267
Umm al-kitāb, 38
unique copies, 436
Urdu, 276, 279, 280, 282, 283
ʿUthmān ibn ʿAffān, Caliph, 360
ʿUyūn al-akhbār (Idrīs, ʿImād al-Dīn), 50
ʿUyūn al-Anbāʾ (Ibn Abī Usaybiʿah), 436

Vajda, Georges, 415
varṇamālā, 282
Vine of the Tale of Truth (*Sataveṇī moṭī nī vel*) (Nūr Muḥammad Shāh, Sayyid), 284–5
virām, 279

Wajh-i dīn (Nāṣir-i Khusraw), 35
Wakhān, 347, 351, 361
walāya (spiritual authority), 359–60
walī (legatee; friend; authority; guardian), 358
waqf, 441
watermarks, 439

wilāya (authority; guardianship), 399–400, 401–2
Walker, Paul E., 41, 106, 108
Wiet, Gaston, 40
Words of the Lord (*Kalāme Maulā*), 283
writing *see* scripts
Wüstenfeld, Ferdinand, 32

al-Yaʿburī, Ghālib b. ʿAlī Ḥusayn Muḥsin al-Jabalī, 179 n.8
Yemen, 172, 174, 183, 434, 439, 440*t*, 442

Zāhid ʿAlī Collection, 37, 41, 145–8, 433, 445
Ẓahir al-Dīn Muhammad Bābur, 348
Zahr al-maʿānī (Idrīs, ʿImād al-Dīn), 48
zakat (alms), 406–7
Zanzibar, 281
Zarubin, Ivan I., 34
al-Ziriklī, Khayr al-Dīn, 82–4, 126
Zubdat al-tawārīkh (Kāshānī, Abū'l-Qāsim ʿAbd Allāh b. ʿAlī), 211, 263, 266

www.ingramcontent.com/pod-product-compliance
Lightning Source LLC
Chambersburg PA
CBHW051802230426
43672CB00012B/2600
* 9 7 8 0 7 5 5 6 4 5 3 8 1 *